How To Do Things With Rules

Law in Context

Editors: William Twining (University College London) and
Christopher Mc Crudden (Lincoln College, Oxford)

To our parents

Neither this book nor any other can say how a page *should* be read – if by that we mean that it can give a recipe for discovering what the page *really* says. All it could do – and that would be much – would be to help us to understand some of the difficulties in the way of such discoveries.

I A Richards, *How to Read a Page*

How To Do Things With Rules

A Primer of Interpretation

Fourth Edition

WILLIAM TWINING
Research Professor of Law, University College London

DAVID MIERS
Professor of Law, Cardiff Law School

CAMBRIDGE
UNIVERSITY PRESS

CAMBRIDGE UNIVERSITY PRESS
Cambridge, New York, Melbourne, Madrid, Cape Town, Singapore, São Paulo

Cambridge University Press
The Edinburgh Building, Cambridge CB2 8RU, UK

Published in the United States of America by Cambridge University Press, New York

www.cambridge.org
Information on this title: www.cambridge.org/9780521605939

First published by Butterworths 1976
Second edition 1982
Third edition 1991
Fourth edition 1999
Digitally reprinted (with corrections) by Cambridge University Press 2008

A catalogue record for this publication is available from the British Library

ISBN-13 978-0-521-60593-9 paperback

PREFACE TO THE FOURTH EDITION

All of us are confronted with rules every day of our lives. Most of us make, interpret and apply them, as well as rely on, submit to, avoid, evade and grouse about them; parents, umpires, teachers, members of committees, businessmen, accountants, trade unionists, administrators, logicians, and moralists are among those who through experience may develop some proficiency in handling rules. Lawyers and law students are specialists in rule-handling, but they do not have a monopoly of the art. A central theme of this book is that most of the basic skills of rule-handling are of very wide application and are not confined to law. There are certain specific techniques which have traditionally been viewed as 'legal', such as using a law library and handling cases and statutes. But these share the same foundations as rule-handling in general: they are only special in the sense that there are some additional considerations which apply to them and are either not found at all or are given less emphasis in other contexts.

The purpose of this book is to provide a relatively systematic introduction to one aspect of rule-handling: interpretation and application. It is written particularly for students of law and administration, but most of it is directly relevant to problems of rule-handling in non-legal contexts. Within legal education, the focus of attention is orthodox in that it concentrates on certain traditional skills and techniques which have commonly, though misleadingly, been referred to as 'legal method', 'juristic method' or 'thinking like a lawyer'. The approach is mildly unorthodox, in that it questions certain widely held assumptions about the nature of these techniques and about efficient ways of learning to master them. Accordingly, it may be useful to give an indication of some of the juristic and educational assumptions underlying our approach.

The juristic assumptions can be stated in simplified form as follows: specialists in law are characterised as much by their supposed mastery of certain kinds of skills as by their knowledge of what the law says. This is the core of the notion that law is essentially a practical art. Those who participate in legal processes and transactions, whether or not they are professionally qualified to practise law, are called upon to perform a variety of tasks. Legal practice encompasses such diverse activities as advising on the procedure of a particular course of action, collecting evidence, negotiating, advocacy, other kinds of spokesmanship, drafting statutes, regulations, contracts and other documents, predicting decisions of various types of courts, tribunals and officials, determining questions of fact, making and justifying decisions on questions of law, communicating information about legal rules, devising improvements in the law and so on. To perform these activities intelligently and efficiently requires a wide range of techniques, insights and abilities. Phrases like 'thinking like a lawyer' or 'legal method' or 'legal reasoning' are misleading in so far as they equate proficiency in handling legal rules and the raw materials of such rules with being a good lawyer. Rule-handling is only one aspect of the crafts of law. Furthermore, interpretation is only one aspect of rule-handling. But it is basic – firstly, because most rule-handling activities involve or presuppose it, and secondly, because a clear understanding of what is involved in interpretation inevitably throws light on a number of other matters as well.

Our approach is also based on a number of educational assumptions. Firstly, we think that it is more economical and more efficient to study certain aspects of rule handling directly than to leave the techniques to be picked up during the course of studying something else. This challenges the view, held by many teachers of law, that case-law techniques are best learned in the context of studying such subjects as Contract and Tort and that skill in handling statutory materials can incidentally be acquired in the course of studying such fields as Administrative, Revenue or Commercial Law. Outside legal contexts, the analogous view is that skill in rule-handling can only be acquired by experience. Such views are sometimes based on a confusion between laying a foundation for developing a skill and reinforcing that foundation through practice. This book proceeds from the premise that a direct approach is both a more economical and a more efficient way of starting off. Reinforcement through practice and experience is essential, but that should come later.

A second assumption is that the art of interpretation is best learned by a combination of theory and practice. Competent interpreters need to understand the nature of the raw material they are dealing with, in what contexts and under what conditions problems of interpretation arise, how interpretation relates to other activities and what is involved in arguing about competing interpretations; it is also useful for them to have a set of concepts for analysing and discussing these problems, and they need to be aware of some common fallacies and pitfalls to be avoided. Accordingly this book is a combination of text and exercises. Working through it involves active participation on the part of the reader. In this respect the book follows the sound pedagogical principle that underlies much of contemporary legal education: the value of learning by doing. If it achieves its objectives we hope that it will help to undermine two other fallacies – that emphasises on 'skills' is inevitably associated with philistine vocationalism and is necessarily illiberal, and that rigorous analysis is incompatible with a contextual approach.[1]

Thirdly, and most importantly, in this book we use 'legal method' to refer to some basic intellectual skills in reading and using materials of law study rather than professional competence. The basic skills of the law student and the skills and techniques of practising lawyers should not be conflated. The object of a law student is to learn: in this context the primary learning objective is to master certain skills of reading, analysis and reasoning. Such skills are not mechanical, for they involve understanding of some basic theory. In order to master the relevant skills a student needs to grasp the what, why and how of reading and using different materials for a wide variety of purposes. In order

---

1   William Twining, *Law in Context: Enlarging a Discipline* (1997), ch 9.

to read a reported case or a juristic text or a Community directive intelligently the student needs to know something about the nature of the material involved – how it is constructed, by whom, and for what purposes (the what). The same material may be studied by one person for quite different purposes: for example, a law student may read a group of cases on negligence or mistake in contract or bigamy in order to learn the substantive law or to prepare for a moot or to write an essay about the development of the subject or to consider the underlying policy critically, or, as in this book, as a vehicle for 'legal method', that is, to learn how to read and use precedents with different lenses for different purposes. Further, a student may be asked to read cases for some less orthodox purpose, such as comparing the styles of judicial opinions or digging out political biases, or setting a leading case in its historical context.[2] In these readings the nature of the material – the what – may remain the constant, but the appropriate skills and methods (the how) will vary according to the purpose of the reading (the why).

In this book, we focus mainly on materials involving rules: conventional sources of law (notably cases, legislation and international legal materials), texts embodying non-legal rules, and examples of rules which are unwritten, unspoken, or otherwise not in fixed verbal form. Appendix III, the 'Reading Law Cookbook', extends this approach briefly to other materials of law study. What is common to the general approach is that the essence of the method is asking questions in an orderly manner as a matter of routine. Reading law involves putting texts to the question; interpreting rules also involves disciplined questioning.

There is, of course, a close link between the intellectual skills that law students are expected to master and the practical skills and techniques of barristers, solicitors, judges and other participants in legal processes and transactions. This is because, even in legal education which is avowedly non-vocational, law is a participant-oriented discipline.[3] What this means in the present context is that studying law regularly, indeed inevitably, involves adopting the standpoints of notional participants in different legal contexts and operations. This goes far beyond simulated role-plays, such as moots, mock trials, and interviewing or negotiation exercises. Rather, almost all legal discourse assumes one or more participant perspectives: law students regularly talk *as if* they are legislators, policy makers, appellate judges, barristers, solicitors, defendants and so on. This is so imbricated in our legal culture that much of the time it is done unconsciously. One result is that it is easy to switch standpoints without realising it. In legal education perhaps the commonest form of stupidity is forgetting who one is pretending to be. This is one reason why, throughout this book, we emphasise the importance of consciously clarifying one's standpoint as a preliminary to reading, analysing, constructing arguments and so on.[4]

---

2   See Appendix III below, pp 427-429.
3   See William Twining, *Blackstone's Tower* (1994), pp 128-30; *Law in Context: Enlarging a Discipline*, op cit, pp 126-128.
4   See below, Chapter 1, section 11 and passim.

A simplified protocol for clarifying standpoint involves asking three questions: who am I? At what stage in what process am I? What am I trying to do? There is a fundamental difference between the standpoints of law students and actual participants in practical legal activities, for the primary purpose of a law student is to *learn*. Thus a beginning law student on reading chapter 1 of this book might clarify her standpoint as follows: who am I? A law student.[5] At what stage of what process am I? At an early stage of my general legal education. What am I trying to do? Learn. Learn what? How to read and use standard materials of law study for a variety of purposes. What purposes? Reading and using these materials from the standpoint of a law student *pretending to be* one or other of a range of standard participants in legal processes: social problem solver, rule-maker; official as implementer, good citizen, bad man, counsellor, advocate, judge, outside observer of various kinds.

The link is the pretence, but the purpose is to learn. And the learning objectives with which we are concerned relate to understanding as much as skill. For example, in chapter 9 we suggest that it is easier to understand the problems surrounding the *ratio decidendi* of a case if one adopts the standpoint of an advocate rather than that of a judge.[6] The student is advised to adopt this standpoint not in order to learn 'advocacy skills', but because from this point of view it is easier to differentiate puzzlements about role from puzzlements about precedent.

Changes in this edition

The first edition of this book was published in 1976 and the text was substantially revised and extended in 1982. The third edition which was published in 1991 took account of important developments that had made interpretation central to legal theory. We had, for example, to address critical legal theory, Ronald Dworkin's *Law's Empire*, the law and literature movement, and the so-called 'New Evidence Scholarship'.[7] We also dealt with important new developments such as *Davis v Johnson* and the increasing importance of Community Law and the European Convention on Human Rights and Fundamental Freedoms, as well as a greater emphasis on intellectual skills within legal education and the implications of the new technology. We tried to make the book more useful as an introduction to legal theory as well as legal method for a variety of types of reader, including beginning law students, non-law graduates taking conversion and professional courses and law students from civil law backgrounds coming to the common law for the first time. We have always hoped that much of this book would be of interest to non-lawyers who are concerned about problems of handling rules in their professional and personal lives.

In preparing this edition we have kept in mind the primary objective of providing an introduction to some fundamentals of rule-handling for a variety

---

5   One of either gender. In the text we variously refer to readers, users and interpreters of rules as he or she, unless the context specifically requires that it should be one or the other.
6   Chapter 9, section 6.
7   See William Twining, *Rethinking Evidence* (1990, 1994).

of audiences. In order to make this a flexible tool, we have further expanded the range of concrete illustrative material in Chapter 1, to include examples from human rights, environmental law, the laws of cricket, and rules within the home so that readers can choose issues and examples relevant to their interests and concerns.

During the past decade the theoretical literature has burgeoned, but we have decided that on the whole this does not require substantial changes to the theoretical foundations of an introductory work.[8] We have accordingly resisted the temptation to complicate the text by extensive reference to quite specialisied debates, some of which we have discussed in other contexts.[9] The basic arguments of the book have, therefore, not substantially changed, but we have taken the opportunity to refer to such significant legal developments as the Human Rights Act 1998, devolution, leading cases such as *Pepper v Hart*, *White v Jones* and *Kleinwort Ltd v Lincoln Council*, and to underline the constant presence in our legal system of Community law. More generally, we have taken account of the need for a cosmopolitan perspective as the processes of globalization and regionalization change the significance of national boundaries and increase the importance both of transnational and non-state law, and of normative pluralism – that is, the phenomenon of multiple normative orders, both legal and non-legal, co-existing and overlapping in shared historical spaces. Today no law student, or citizen concerned with law, can confine their attention to the domestic law of a single jurisdiction.[10] Knowledge too is being globalized: as the law student can now reach electronically beyond the physical confines of the paper law library, there is a greater need for disciplined intellectual procedures for reading and interpreting the mass of different kinds of material that are available.

To further these objectives, we have updated the illustrative material where it seems appropriate, but in some instances have kept older examples where we consider them to be particularly good illustrations of general points, even if the context or the details of the law have changed. For example, much has happened in the field of domestic violence since the Domestic Violence and

8 We have referred to directly relevant works such as Frederick Schauer's *Playing by the Rules* (1991), the major comparative works on precedent and statutory interpretation edited by Neil MacCormick and Robert Summers, and the writings on statutory interpretation by Francis Bennion, all of which are broadly in line with our own approach. We have given less attention to the literature on American constitutional interpretation and post-modern perspectives, not from lack of interest, but in order to avoid overloading the text. References to some of the specialised literature are given in Appendix IV.
9 See in particular, William Twining, *Rethinking Evidence* (1990, 1994), *Blackstone's Tower: the English Law School*, op cit; *Law in Context: Enlarging a Discipline*, op cit and a continuing series of essays on globalization and legal theory and general jurisprudence; David Miers, *The Deregulation Procedure: an Evaluation* (The Hansard Society for Parliamentary Government, 1999); 'Objectives and Systems in the Regulation of Commercial Gambling' in J McMillen (ed), *Gambling Cultures* (1996), and 'The Style of Legislation: Narrative norms and Constraining Norms' in J Bridge et al, (eds), *United Kingdom Law in the Mid-1990s* (1994).
10 William Twining, 'Globalization and Legal Theory; Some Local Implications' (1996) 49 *Current Legal Problems* II, 1.

Matrimonial Proceedings Act 1976 and its interpretation by the courts in 1976-80. However, the case study that is the culmination of Chapter 1 still brings together a wide range of themes and points that are an integral part of the book. Only minor changes have been made to Chapters 2 to 5, which comprise Part 2 of the book. However, we have reorganised the later chapters by making a sharper distinction between routine reading of materials of law study and problems of diagnosing conditions of doubt and constructing arguments about competing interpretations in disputed cases. Chapter 6, which commences Part 3 and in many ways we regard as the fulcrum of the book, makes explicit why we consider that most orthodox accounts radically oversimplify the sources of problems of interpretation, and why we think that standpoint is so important in determining whether or not there is a doubt about interpretation. (But the main message in this chapter is that the diagnostic model of conditions of doubt in interpretation can be routinely used as an analytical tool.) This reorganisation of Part 3 also gives a more prominent place to reading, using and interpreting statutory rules, reflecting both their constitutional significance and the impact of the law of the European Union and of the requirements of the Human Rights Act 1998. The discussion takes account of the 'better legislation' policy that is a powerful motif of the present arrangements and reform proposals for the modernization of law making within Parliament. Both this chapter (Chapter 7) and Chapters 8 and 9 (which concern respectively reading, using and interpreting legislation and cases) emphasise the importance of establishing clear reading routines as a sound basis for both the inexperienced and the experienced reader of legal material. From this problematic readings can be clarified and arguable interpretive strategies formulated. These points are further illustrated in a sophisticated analysis of the bigamy case, *Allen*, which raised a range of issues, among others, to do with the interpretation of statutory and case law rules. The discussion of lawyers' reasonings that is the central focus of Chapter 10 leads into a final section that both restates the main themes of the book and addresses some of the central theoretical issues concerning the relationship between reasoning and interpretation.

We have also made some changes to the content and sequence of the Appendices. As before, Appendix I contains supplementary material and exercises designed to reinforce the main messages of the book. They have been updated to reflect the significant legal developments to which we have referred above. Appendix II introduces some simple examples of algorithm design, a tool that we continue to regard as one of the most effective means for locating the source of many kinds of problematic readings of legislative and other rules. We have reversed the order of Appendices III and IV. Appendix III contains the 'Reading Law Cookbook', an introduction to a simple method for reading any legal material for differing educational purposes. It comprises an extension of the approach adopted in this book, particularly as advocated in Chapter 6. It might have been called *How to do Things with Texts*. We hope that it will reinforce some of the central messages of the book and encourage teachers and students in pre-law and first year courses to take the direct study of legal method seriously. Suggestions for further reading are contained in Appendix IV.

How to use the book

This book combines a general introduction to fundamental issues about interpretation with specific guidance on intellectual procedures and techniques of analysis supported by exercises designed to develop basic skills. It rejects sharp divisions between 'theory' and 'practice'. It has been designed to cater for the needs of several classes of reader, including various kinds of 'pre-law' students, those studying legal method in the first year of a law degree, those about to embark on the study of Jurisprudence in their second or third year, and anyone concerned with practical problems of rule-handling who is interested in underlying theory or the basic of the art of interpreting rules. Accordingly it may be useful to provide some guidance on different ways of approaching it.

A general introduction to the study of law

The non-lawyer and the beginning law student may find it useful to begin by doing the Newspaper Exercise in Chapter 1, section 1 and then to read the book as a general introduction to law and legal ways of thought. For this purpose it is sufficient to skim Chapter 1, pausing long enough to become familiar with the range of illustrative material and, in particular, *The Case of the Legalistic Child* (section 3.5), sections 7.1 to 7.3 on bigamy, the *Buckoke* case (section 8), Article 3 of the European Convention on Human Rights and Fundamental Freedoms (section 10.3.3) and the charts of the Bad Man in Boston (section 11.7). These are used as examples throughout the text. From time to time you may wish to refer back to the appropriate point in Chapter 1 to refresh your memory about details or to clarify an allusion, but it is not necessary to study all the materials or to try to answer all the questions in this chapter in order to understand the thrust of the analysis in the text. Depending on your background and your interests, some of Chapters 3, 7, 8, 9 and 10 may also be read lightly, if you find them too complicated or too detailed to start with.

An introduction to jurisprudence

Now that interpretation occupies such a central place in contemporary debates, a primer of interpretation is a particularly good vehicle for getting to grips for the first time with the ideas of Dworkin, Hart, Fuller, Llewellyn, critical legal scholars and other theorists. Because many of the issues and some of the examples will already be familiar to second or third year students, this should ease the transition from the study of particular fields of law to general theory. It should reinforce the message that Jurisprudence is not and should not be seen as an abstract subject only remotely connected with the study of substantive law. We subscribe to the view that interpretation and reasoning are central to all legal studies and legal practice.

Conversion and professional courses

Graduates in other disciplines who are about to embark on a 'conversion' course about law, such as the course leading to the Common Professional

Examination, may wish to treat this either as a general introduction to the subject which may point to some links with their earlier studies in, for example, philosophy, political or social science, literature or theology. They may also wish to use the book to lay a foundation for legal method, either as a preliminary to or at the start of their legal studies, in which case they should approach it in the same way as other beginning law students and treat it as a practical introduction to the art of interpretation. It can also be used by students pursing vocational courses leading to professional qualifications in law. Such students are expected to apply a range of skills to the task of giving effect to a client's instructions. This task typically involves the routine application of what become familiar laws and procedures but occasionally presents problematic issues about the location and interpretation of the applicable law. It is also typically the case that the student's standpoint is a given (adviser, advocate, etc); however it by no means follows that what is given will, in every set of circumstances, be unproblematic. The student 'adviser' or 'advocate' may well be presented with conflicting or difficult ethical matters that will influence the interpretation she will present to the client (or, possibly, the court).

An introduction to the common law method

Lawyers and law students with a background in the civil law or some other legal tradition may wish to read the text as an introduction to the supposedly peculiar ways of thought of common lawyers. One of the main themes of the book emphasises the continuities between problems of interpretation of legal and non-legal rules. There are, we believe, similar continuities between legal traditions. This is not to deny that there are distinctive characteristics of common law modes of thinking and reasoning. Rather, we suggest that such matters as the doctrine of precedent, the English 'rules' of statutory interpretation and the common law emphasis on reasoning by example are secondary rather than fundamental features of common law method. Moreover, disagreements about the importance of precedent, 'literal' and 'free' interpretation and reasoning by example are not unique to Anglo-American law. For civilians, Chapters 7-10 may be of special interest, but we suggest that earlier chapters be skimmed first in order to clarify the general perspective underlying the approach adopted in those later chapters.

A practical introduction to legal method

Our main purpose has been to aid the development of certain intellectual skills and habits of mind. Viewed thus this is a how-to-do-it book concerned with an important part of what is sometimes referred to as 'Legal Method', which is most commonly studied at the start of a law degree. While the text provides a general theoretical framework, reading it is no substitute for developing skills by doing exercises, answering questions and thinking critically about problems. For this purpose the recommended order is to do the exercises in Chapter 1 before moving on; to do some of the exercises in Appendix I immediately after reading the relevant chapter and finally to re-read the text as a whole and to follow up at least some of the suggestions for further reading.

The book is currently used (with additional introductory material) on some access courses which focus on legal method. We have kept their needs in mind, but in our experience the book works best if it is used in the latter part of an access course after a gradual build up which emphasises basic general skills of study and analysis that are taken for granted here.

For those who are looking for practical guidance for dealing with problems of rule-handling in their work, Chapters 2-6 and Appendix II are best treated as the core of the book. What is presented there is a fairly straightforward problem-solving approach to diagnosing and arguing about practical problems of interpreting rules of any kind. For this purpose the examples in Chapter 1, sections 3.5, 7.1-7.2, 8, 10.2 and 11.5, the diagnostic model in Chapter 6 and the short introduction to algorithms (Appendix II) may be sufficient to provide the necessary basic tools, without having to wander too far into the technicalities of the law and the mysteries of legal theory.

The subject is a complex one, involving many different levels of understanding: what we have tried to do is to provide a flexible starting point for developing some basic skills and for exploring a rich, but scattered literature in a number of disciplines. The exercises range from some quite elementary questions (some of which even have answers!) to problems which even advanced law students, using a law library, should find demanding.

We hope that law students will first be exposed to the book before they are swamped with masses of detailed information. We have taken our median audience to be beginning law students, but we have tried to make it a flexible tool which is accessible to those at the pre-law stage as well as to advanced students and experienced practitioners. We have used it in undergraduate, postgraduate, access and extra-mural courses in England, Wales, the United States and elsewhere. For obvious reasons different aspects have been emphasised depending on context. But nothing in our experiences suggests that the basic lessons are beyond the reach of the ordinary beginning law student or of interested readers of comparable intelligence, provided that they are willing to struggle with the detailed analysis. Anyone who is not prepared to do this cannot expect to become a competent interpreter.

W.L.T.
D.R.M.
Iffley and Cardiff, December 1998.

ACKNOWLEDGMENTS

In the first two editions we acknowledged the help and stimulus of a large number of people. We shall not list them by name again, but our gratitude is as great as ever.

The authors and publishers thank the following for their permission to reproduce copyright material: Aldine de Gruyter (Laurence Ross, *Settled Out of Court*); the American Sociological Association (Stewart Macaulay, *Non-contractual Relations in Business*); the Aristotelian Society (William Twining, *Torture and Philosophy* and Collingwood, *'On the So-called Idea of Causation'*); William Binchy; Butterworth & Co (P Cane, *Atiyah's Accidents, Compensation and the Law*); Jonathan Cape (I Shah, *Tales of the Dervishes*); Cassell PLC (Page, *Complete Etiquette for Ladies and Gentlemen*); Grove/Atlantic Inc (Boudin, *The Bust Book*); Headline Book Publishing Limited (Morgan, *Debrett's New Guide to Modern Manners*); the Controller of Her Majesty's Stationery Office (*CAS Occasional Paper No 13, The Judge Over Your Shoulder and Violence in Marriage*); Douglas Hay (*Albion's Fatal Tree*); Joseph Heller, Jonathan Cape and AM Heath (*Catch-22*); PH Gulliver, New York University Press and Routledge (*Social Control in an African Society*); HLA Hart, *The Concept of Law* (© Oxford University Press 1994, by permission of Oxford University Press); Hutchinson & Co (Joseph Raz, *Practical Reason and Norms*); the Incorporated Council for Law Reporting and Butterworth & Co (extracts from cases in Chapter 1 and Appendix I); Little, Brown & Co (Karl Llewellyn, *The Common Law Tradition* and N Mandela, *Long Walk to Freedom*); Maitland Publications (Julius Stone, *Legal System and Lawyers' Reasonings*); SFC Milsom and the Yale Law Journal (review of Grant Gilmore, *The Death of Contract*); Oxford University Press (Keith Hawkins, *Environment and Enforcement* and RM Hare, *Moral Thinking*); Penguin Books Ltd and Doubleday & Co (© 1961, Erving Goffman, *Asylums*); Plain English Campaign (*The Gobbledygook Test*); Routledge (Molly Brearly and Elizabeth Hutchfield, *A Teacher's Guide to Reading Piaget*; D Tattum, *Disruptive Pupils: System Rejects?* and Gulliver, *Social Control in an African Society*); Sydney University Law School (Fraser, *Cricket and the Law*); University of Valparaiso Law Review (*The Reading Law Cookbook*); Ward, Lock & Co (Ann Page, *Complete Etiquette for Ladies and Gentlemen*); Weidenfeld & Nicolson (Royston Lambert, *The Hothouse Society*) and the West Publishing Co (Roscoe Pound, *Jurisprudence*).

We also acknowledge our thanks to Richard Freeth and Penelope Twining for their assistance with the proofs and the index.

CONTENTS

Table of statutes

References in the right-hand column are to page numbers. Page references printed in **bold** type indicate where the statutory material is set out in part or in full.

Table of cases

Part One

Chapter 1

Some Food for Thought

In this chapter we have collected together some concrete examples that illustrate the main questions and themes that are explored in the book as a whole. The purpose of presenting them at this stage is partly to generate interest and puzzlement, and partly to encourage you to start to think actively about some basic issues.

The first two sections illustrate the pervasiveness of law and other forms of ordering in the world at large and in our daily lives. The Newspaper Exercise should make clear how law not only features on every page of the newspaper but also serves as a lens for both interpreting and constructing 'news'. Section 2 introduces the phenomenon of rule pluralism – the plain fact that each of us is subject to a multiplicity of legal and other orderings that co-exist, interact and sometimes conflict with each other at many different levels down to the very local, such as your neighbourhood, your club and your living room. Both sections reinforce the point that far from being an entirely new and strange subject, every beginning law student has had a wide experience of law as a party to contracts, as a family member, and as a student as well as a copyright-violator, debtor, trespasser, slanderer and almost certainly a criminal! Law and rules are everywhere and everyone has experienced them in many ways. What is new about studying law is not so much the subject-matter as the focus; for many of you this may be the first time you have consciously thought about legal and other rules in a sustained way.

The materials in Part One also indicate some of the varied contexts in which problems of interpretation of rules arise: relationships within the family, in everyday social life, in institutions such as schools, prisons and factories, in commercial relationships as well as in formal legal processes such as prosecutions for bigamy and claims for compensation, whether they are settled out of court or by litigation; one section deals with dispute settlement in a traditional African society, another with provisions protecting human rights under a written constitution and in International Law. This variety of contexts is intended to emphasise the thesis that nearly all the factors which give rise to difficulties of interpretation – what we shall refer to as the conditions of doubt – are present in a great variety of very different types of social situation, and can cause difficulty in almost any kind of case, whether it is trivial or momentous, simple or complex, legal or non-legal.

Each of the sections is designed to introduce one or more particular topics. The story of Solomon and the baby in section 3.1 illustrates the difference between questions of interpretation of rules and other aspects of adjudication and problem-solving, and, with the other extracts, introduces the notion of legalistic behaviour. The admittedly artificial example of the legalistic child (3.5) raises a variety of analytical issues about rules as responses to problems and the relations between rules, processes and roles. Sections 4 and 5 deal with questions about reasons for having rules and the relations between rules and results – especially gaps between what is prescribed by formal rules and the actual outcomes of particular processes. These materials also introduce another central theme of the book: that it is not only officials, adjudicators and judges who are faced with problems of interpretation of rules; any interpreter needs to clarify his situation by asking three preliminary questions: Who am I? At what stage in what process am I? What am I trying to do?

Next comes some specifically legal material. Section 6 contains examples of complex rules in fixed verbal form, taken from statutes and regulations. These seem to be difficult, if not impossible, to understand. Is this difficulty due to the complexity of the subject-matter, or of the rules, or to the way in which they are drafted? Is such complexity and obscurity inevitable? Are there ways of helping the bewildered interpreter to find his way around complex rules? Section 7 deals with the crime of bigamy, including the notoriously problematic section 57 of the Offences against the Person Act 1861 and *R v Allen*, which will be used throughout the book to illustrate many different points. There follows another bigamy case which highlights further difficulties connected with this section and illustrates the operation of the doctrine and techniques of precedent in a field where there have been recurrent disagreements among the judges. These materials, like some of the others, pose quite sharply the question: how and why do disagreements about interpretation of rules arise?

The case in the next section (8), *Buckoke v Greater London Council*, besides raising some further questions of interpretation, illustrates two classic dilemmas: that of someone who is faced with seemingly conflicting instructions, and that of judges when confronted with a statutory enactment which leads to an undesirable result. Can and should judges mitigate the rigours of the law where Parliament has been unwilling or unable to make an explicit exception covering apparently deserving cases? Underlying this is a more general issue: do officials (and others) ever have a discretion, or even a duty, to disobey the law?

Section 9 contains some extracts from what is perhaps the most famous single case in the common law, *Donoghue v Stevenson*. Though well known, not all the points that it illustrates are trite or obvious; and precisely because it is so frequently discussed, it provides a useful link with other writings, especially on case law and judicial law-making. We have included it primarily because it is a remarkably rich example of the operation of judicial techniques of reasoning.

Section 10 addresses the relationship between rules, principles and other norms. The major part of the material included here comprises provisions that are to be found in such documents as the Universal Declaration of Human Rights, the European Convention on Human Rights and Fundamental Freedoms, and domestic Bills of Rights, including the Human

Rights Act 1998. There are special considerations which affect the styles of drafting and approaches to interpretation of such provisions. The main examples selected here deal with extreme forms of treatment, notably 'torture, inhuman or degrading treatment or punishment' and 'cruel and unusual punishments'. These raise a number of issues: about the connections between moral principles and legal provisions, about the workability and the justification of 'absolute' prohibitions, especially in extreme cases, and about the relationship between ordinary municipal laws and rules which are claimed to be 'fundamental' or 'universal' or 'entrenched'. They also suggest some less obvious questions directly relevant to interpretation. Concepts like 'torture' and 'inhuman treatment' are rather more complex than they seem. It is worth asking questions about the use of highly emotive terms like 'torture' in drafting legal provisions and, as with most other examples in this chapter, about the interaction between appropriate modes of interpretation and the context of interpretation.

Section 11 brings out a theme which has been largely implicit in the earlier material: the crucial importance of differences of standpoint, role and objective in understanding problems of interpretation. We shall stress throughout the book that any particular problem of interpretation needs to be set in the context of some conception of a wider process – a series of events and decisions which have led up to the moment when the interpreter is faced with a choice and which will continue after that moment. Interpretation does not take place in a vacuum. The notion of a total process is just as important in non-legal contexts, where there may be few or no formal procedures, as in the typically formal context of legal processes. There is also a tendency in legal literature to assume, either explicitly or implicitly, 'top down' points of view – exemplified by the standpoint of a legislator, judge or other official making or applying law. There is accordingly a tendency to underplay or to ignore entirely the points of view of those who are subject to the rules – worm's-eye views or 'bottom up' perspectives. Yet typically (but not universally) the interpreter is someone who is confronted with a pre-existing rule, made by someone else, and which he has no authority to change. His standpoint may be neither that of the eagle nor the worm. The viewpoints of both eagles and worms, and of others, are directly relevant to problems of interpretation.

In the final section of this chapter we present an historical case study which links together in a vivid, and we hope interesting, way some of the main strands which have been illustrated separately by the preceding materials. The study is in essence the story of one phase of the law's response to the problem of domestic violence. This problem is probably as old as the institution of the family, but it was dramatised and brought into public attention in Britain during the 1970s and early 1980s. To put it in simple terms – the social and public reaction to the publicisation of the phenomenon of domestic violence prompted a political initiative which was partly translated into legislative action. This in turn produced a rather complex and unexpected response from the judiciary. Since the House of Lords' decision in *Davis v Johnson* the situation relating to domestic violence has continued to change, as has the law's response. It might be thought that this case study and the other materials in this chapter touch on issues which fall outside the scope of this book because they are not strictly speaking about interpretation. However, they are relevant to our purposes because problems of interpretation of rules need to be seen in the context of, and to be differentiated from, other questions relating to rules and social processes.

As was suggested in the Preface, it is not necessary to read the whole of Chapter 1 before proceeding to read the rest of the book. We do, however, recommend that you read the following sections at the outset: 3.5, 7.1-7.2, 8, 10.3 and 11. In reading Chapters 2-10, reference will be made from time to time to material in this Chapter which can be read in conjunction with the relevant passages. The material in Chapter 1 is usually followed by questions which we urge you to tackle, or at least to think about, as you come to them. They are supplemented by further material and questions in Appendix I.

1   The pervasiveness of norms

The Newspaper Exercise

Buy a copy of *The Times, The Independent, The Guardian, Financial Times* or *The Daily Telegraph.* Read through all of your chosen newspaper and mark the passages that have some 'legal' or 'law-related' content. Before starting this exercise, stipulate your working definition of 'legal' and 'law-related'. Then answer the questions below. You are advised to spend between four and six hours on this exercise.

QUESTIONS

1. Identify three passages in your newspaper that you would expect would be more easily understood by a person with a law degree.
2. What branches of law would you expect regularly to feature in, or be relevant to, understanding items in: the letters page; the sports pages; the arts section; the business section; and advertisements?
3. Identify the national legal systems and other bodies of law (eg public international law) that would be directly relevant to the items reported on one of the foreign/international pages in your newspaper.
4. Which features more prominently in your newspaper: legislation; case law; or 'non-legal' rules? Find examples of each.
5. Identify examples of social problems either created by law or to which law is expected to contribute to a solution.
6. Give examples from this newspaper of passages that caused you difficulty in deciding whether they fall within your working definition of 'legal' or 'law-related'.
7. What have you learnt from doing this exercise? For a suggested answer to this see W Twining, *Law in Context* (1997), pp 210-213.

2 Pluralism

2.1 Pluralism in law

Perhaps the most distinctive characteristic of the Western legal tradition is the coexistence and competition within the same community of diverse jurisdictions and diverse legal systems. It is the plurality of jurisdictions and legal systems that makes the supremacy of law both necessary and feasible.

(From H Berman, *Law and Revolution: the Formation of the Western Legal Tradition* (1983), p 10.)

2.2 Levels of law

Law is concerned with relations between agents or persons (human, legal, unincorporated and otherwise) at a variety of levels, not just relations within a single nation state or society. One way of characterising such levels is essentially geographical:

- global (as with some environmental issues, a possible *ius humanitatis* – eg mineral rights on the moon – and, by extension, intergalactic or space law);
- international (in the classic sense of relations between sovereign states and more broadly relations governed, for example, by human rights or refugee law);
- regional (for example, the European Union, the Council of Europe, and the Organisation of African Unity);
- transnational (for example, Islamic, Hindu, Jewish law, Gypsy law, transnational arbitration, a putative *lex mercatoria*, Internet law, and, more controversially, the internal governance of multi-national corporations, the Catholic Church, or institutions of organised crime);
- inter-communal (as in relations between religious communities, or Christian churches, or different ethnic groups);
- territorial state (including the legal systems of nation states, and sub-national jurisdictions, such as Northern Ireland or Quebec);
- sub-state (eg subordinate legislation, such as by-laws of the City of Cardiff) or religious law officially recognised for limited purposes in a plural legal system; and
- non-state (including laws of subordinated peoples, such as native North Americans, or Maoris) or illegal legal orders such as the Southern People's Liberation Army in Southern Sudan and the 'common law movement' of militias in the United States).

Which of these should be classified as 'law' or 'legal' is essentially contested within legal theory, and also depends on the context and purpose of the discourse.

(Adapted from W Twining, 'Mapping Law' NILQ, forthcoming, 1999.)

See further Appendix 1, sections A1 and A2.

2.3 Plural systems

'... it seems to me that the great mass of confusion and distress must arise from these less evident divergencies ... the moral law, the civil, military, common laws, the code of honour, custom, the rules of practical life, of amorous conversation, gallantry, to say nothing of Christianity, for those that practise it. All sometimes, indeed generally, at variance; none ever in entirely harmonious relationship to the rest; and a man is perpetually required to choose one rather than another, perhaps (in this particular case) its contrary. It is as though our strings were each tuned according to a completely separate system ... it is as though the poor ass were surrounded by four and twenty managers.'

'You are an anti-nomian,' said Jack.

'I am a pragmatist,' said Stephen.

(From Patrick O'Brian, *Master and Commander* (1971), p 319.)

2.4   A week in the life of a law student

Write down in chronological order the twenty main transactions and relations in which you were involved during the last week (for example, telephoned mother in Hong Kong; visited Registry re late payment of fees; played tennis with friend; received e-mail from suspected hacker; spent two hours with local family support centre; elected Treasurer of the Students' Law Society; attended tutorial on EU law). Identify the main legal and other normative orders substantially relevant to each of these transactions and relations.

2.5   Transnational and devolved systems

European Communities Act 1972, section 2(1): 'All such rights, powers, liabilities, obligations and restrictions from time to time created or arising by or under the Treaties, and all such remedies and procedures from time to time provided for by or under the Treaties, as in accordance with the Treaties are without further enactment to be given legal effect or used in the United Kingdom shall be recognised and available in law, and be enforced, allowed and followed accordingly; and the expression "enforceable Community right" and similar expressions shall be read as referring to one to which this section applies.'

Scotland Act 1998, section 1(1): 'There shall be a Scottish Parliament.'

Government of Wales Act 1998, section 1(1): 'There shall be an Assembly for Wales to be known as the National Assembly for Wales or Cynulliad Cenedlaethol Cymru (but referred to in this Act as the Assembly).'

3   Legalism

3.1   The judgment of Solomon

Then came there two women, that were harlots, unto the king, and stood before him. And the one woman said, O my lord, I and this woman dwell in one house; and I was delivered of a child with her in the house. And it came to pass the third day after that I was delivered, that this woman was delivered also: and we were together; there was no stranger with us in the house, save we two in the house. And this woman's child died in the night; because she overlaid it. And she arose at midnight, and took my son from beside me, while thine handmaid slept, and laid it in her bosom, and laid her dead child in my bosom. And when I rose in the morning to give my child suck, behold, it was dead: but when I had considered it in the morning, behold, it was not my son, which I did bear. And the other woman said, Nay; but the living is my son, and the dead is thy son. And this said, No; but the dead is thy son, and the living is my son. Thus they spake before the king.

Then said the king, The one saith, This is my son that liveth, and thy son is the dead: and the other saith, Nay; but thy son is the dead, and my son is the living. And the king said, Bring me a sword. And they brought a sword before the king. And the king said, Divide the living child in two, and give half to the one, and half to the other. Then spake the woman whose the living child was unto the king, for her bowels yearned upon her son, and she said, O my lord, give her the living child, and in no wise slay it. But the other said, Let it be neither mine or thine, but divide it. Then the king answered and said, Give her the living child, and in no wise slay it: she is the mother thereof. And all Israel heard of the judgment which the king had judged; and they feared the king: for they saw that the wisdom of God was in him, to do judgment.

(1 Kings iii, 16-28.)

QUESTIONS

1. Was the doubt in the case concerned with:
   1.1 the interpretation of a rule;
   1.2 a dispute about an issue of fact;
   1.3 solving a problem for the future in the best interests of the child;
   1.4 some other matter;
   or a combination of some or all of these?
2. Is it possible to formulate precisely the rule or rules, if any, which were applicable to this case?
3. For what reason(s) is this judgment thought to be wise?

3.2 An expensive cat

A man who was troubled in mind once swore that if his problems were solved he would sell his house and give all the money gained from it to the poor. The time came when he realised that he must redeem his oath. But he did not want to give away so much money. So he thought of a way out. He put the house on sale at one silver piece. Included with the house, however, was a cat. The price for this animal was ten thousand pieces of silver. Another man bought the house and cat. The first man gave the single piece of silver to the poor, and pocketed the ten thousand for himself.

Many people's minds work like this. They resolve to follow a teaching; but they interpret their relationship with it to their own advantage. Until they overcome this tendency by special training, they cannot learn at all.

(From I Shah, *Tales of the Dervishes* (1967), p 68.)

3.3 Portia's submission

Tarry a little; there is something else.
This bond doth give thee here no jot of blood;
The words expressly are 'a pound of flesh';
Take then thy bond, take thou thy pound of flesh;

But, in cutting it, if thou dost shed
One drop of Christian blood, thy lands and goods
Are, by the laws of Venice, confiscate
Unto the state of Venice.

(From *The Merchant of Venice*, Act IV, Scene I.)

QUESTIONS

1. Give examples of similar behaviour from legal and non-legal contexts.
2. Is there any significant difference between the behaviour of Portia and of the owner of the cat?
3. Does labelling behaviour as 'legalistic' necessarily involve passing a value judgment on it?

3.4 Catch-22

There was only one catch and that was Catch-22, which specified that a concern for one's own safety in the face of dangers that were real and immediate was the process of a rational mind. Orr was crazy and could be grounded. All he had to do was ask; and as soon as he did, he would no longer be crazy and would have to fly more missions. Orr would be crazy to fly more missions and sane if he didn't, but if he was sane he had to fly them. If he flew them he was crazy and didn't have to; but if he didn't want to he was sane and had to. Yossarian was moved very deeply by the absolute simplicity of this clause of Catch-22 and let out a respectful whistle.

'That's some catch, that Catch-22,' he observed.

'It's the best there is,' Doc Daneeka agreed.

Yossarian left money in the old woman's lap – it was odd how many wrongs leaving money seemed to right – and strode out of the apartment, cursing Catch-22 vehemently as he descended the stairs, even though he knew there was no such thing. Catch-22 did not exist, he was positive of that, but it made no difference. What did matter was that everyone thought it existed, and that was much worse, for there was no object or text to ridicule or refute, to accuse, criticize, attack, amend, hate, revile, spit at, rip to shreds, trample upon or burn up.

(From J Heller, *Catch-22* (1964), pp 54, 432.)

3.5 The Case of the Legalistic Child

Johnny, aged 7, is an only child. In recent months his mother has been mildly worried because he has developed a craving for sweet things and this has affected his appetite at meal times. She has commented to her husband, a practising lawyer, that Johnny 'seems to be developing a sweet tooth', and that 'he has been eating too much between meals', but until now she has done nothing about the problem. Then one afternoon she finds that Johnny has gone into the larder and helped himself to half a pot of strawberry jam. Bearing in mind her husband's insistence that discipline in the family should operate in accordance with 'the Rule of Law', she does not punish Johnny on this occasion. Instead she says: 'That's naughty. In future you are never to enter the larder without my permission.' 'What does enter mean, Mummy?' asks Johnny. 'To go into,' says his mother. 'OK,' says Johnny, relieved that he has got off so lightly.

Four incidents then follow in quick succession.

First, Johnny gets a broom and hooks out the pot of jam from the larder and helps himself. 'I didn't *enter* the larder,' he says.

Next, the cat enters the larder and attacks the salmon which mother has bought for a special meal to celebrate father's birthday. Mother, upstairs, hears Johnny hooting with laughter. She comes down to see him standing outside the larder door watching the cat eating the fish. 'I may not go into the larder,' he says.

The following day, at 5 pm, another pot of strawberry jam is found in the larder – empty. It was half-full at lunchtime. Johnny, who was playing on his own downstairs for much of the afternoon, denies all knowledge of the matter. There is no other evidence.

Finally, without any attempt at concealment, Johnny enters the larder, eats another pot of jam and deliberately knocks down a pile of cans. 'It's as if he were asking to be punished,' sighs Mother.

QUESTIONS

1. In *How Lawyers Think* (1937), Clarence Morris wrote: 'Problems occur in gross. The unit which appears to be a single problem at first glance is usually a complex of related difficulties, a confluence of more specific problems. Often the initial urge is to dismiss the whole difficulty with some easy, impulsive solution ...' (p 5). Explain how this quotation is relevant to the nature of Mother's 'problem' in the story.
2. Consider each of the incidents as an isolated case from the point of view of:
   2.1 Mother in her role as enforcement officer and prosecutor;
   2.2 Johnny, defending himself;
   2.3 Father as adjudicator;
   2.4 a family friend who has the reputation of being a good psychologist.
3. Construct an argument about the appropriate meaning to be attached to the word 'enter', from the point of view of:
   3.1 Mother prosecuting Johnny for a breach of her rule in the first instance;
   3.2 Johnny, defending himself.
   See further *R v Collins* [1973] QB 100.
4. State as many different interpretations as you can of 'That's naughty' in the context in which it was said. Is any one interpretation clearly right or better than the others?
5. Construct an account of the development of a solution to the problem through case-by-case decision, assuming that the sequence of events was (a) creation of the original rule, (b) the first incident, (c) adjudication of the first incident, (d) second incident, and so on. Would this be a more or less satisfactory way of solving this particular problem than by making a rule? Give reasons.
6. Draft a rule to fit Mother's diagnosis that Johnny is 'eating too much between meals'.
7. Do you think that a better approach would have been to give Johnny a clip on the ear immediately after the first incident? Would a hug have been

better? Give reasons for your answer. Under what circumstances is it appropriate to deal with problems *before*, rather than after they have arisen?

8. After the episodes concerning the larder, Father decides on a change of strategy. 'From now on,' he says, 'there will be only one rule that you must observe in this household: you must be reasonable at all times.'

   8.1 Is this a rule and, if so, is it a reasonable one?

   8.2 Give examples of practical problems of interpretation which might arise for (a) Johnny, and (b) his parents, under this provision.

   8.3 Does Father's 'rule' leave any outlet for Johnny's legalistic tendencies?

9. Johnny is watching his favourite television programme with Mother's agreement. Father, having just arrived home from work, walks into the room, and without a word to Johnny, switches over to another channel on which a current affairs programme is in progress. Johnny protests, 'You can't do that.'

   9.1 Is Johnny invoking a rule? If so, what rule?

   9.2 Are there any rules governing (a) watching television and (b) the distribution of housework where you live? If so, state them. *How* do you know whether there are rules about these activities and what they are?

10. What assumptions about family life and the role of rules within it are to be inferred from the behaviour of Johnny's parents? Is theirs, in your view, a satisfactory way of dealing with discipline in the family?

3.6 Rules, facts and values

In Anglo-American jurisprudence the game of baseball is often used to illustrate characteristic and often difficult issues concerning the application and interpretation of rules, issues that routinely figure in more complex legal contexts. Cricket, too, offers a familiar and accessible context analogous to law in which decision-making by umpires (judges) in response to players' (litigants) appeals (applications, submissions, appeals) can be used to introduce some basic notions about the inter-relationship between rules, facts, and values.

Law 27 of the game of cricket provides that the umpire's decision in response to an appeal by the fielding side is final, though he may alter his decision provided that he does so promptly. In *Cricket and the Law*, David Fraser comments that while instances where umpires have reversed their decisions because they decided that they were wrong are usually applauded, 'a more problematic scenario arises, especially in the days of televised instant and slow-motion action replays, when the umpire is seen to be wrong by other members of the cricket interpretive community, for example, by giving out a batsman who was not, "on the facts", out. The positivist position is, of course, that if the Umpire says the batsman is out and does not reverse his decision, then the batsman is indeed out. On the other hand, formalist or ethically-based critiques could be made in such a case. The batsman is not "out" unless his dismissal occurs in accordance with the Laws.'

Law 27 also provides that in exceptional circumstances 'the Captain of the fielding side may seek permission from the Umpire to withdraw an appeal providing the outgoing batsman has not left the playing area'. Usually such action would be appropriate simply because a player on the fielding side could confirm that the facts were not as the umpire believed them to be; for example, that the batsman did not in fact touch the ball with his bat and thus was not caught out. However, more complex instances may arise:

> ... it is sometimes true that an umpire has erred in law and the appeal should be withdrawn to avoid an injustice and a violation of the spirit of the game. Thus, in the second Test of the 1991 tour of the West Indies at the Bourda Ground in Georgetown, Dean Jones [an Australian batsman] was apparently bowled. As he left the crease to walk back to the pavilion, it became apparent that the umpire had signalled no-ball. With Jones still out of his crease, Carl Hooper of the West Indies removed a stump in a move which Peter Roebuck characterised as 'the sort of thing a Westpac lawyer might do', yet again demonstrating the parallels between the practices of Law and cricket. Jones was given out 'run out' by the square leg umpire. On these 'facts' the umpire erred in giving Jones out pursuant to Hooper's appeal. While a batsman may be run out from a no-ball (Law 24(10)), Law 27(5) governing appeals also indicates that,

> > 'The Umpires shall intervene if satisfied that a Batsman, not having been given out, has left his wicket under a misapprehension that he has been dismissed.'

> In this case, Jones left his crease without having been given out because the umpire with jurisdiction at the bowler's end had signalled no-ball. He was clearly not attempting a run, but was leaving his crease 'under a misapprehension'. Here, the umpire should have intervened and called Jones back. When he did not do so, he committed an error of Law by refusing or failing to exercise his jurisdiction. This error was compounded by giving Jones out on an appeal which had no basis in fact or Law. Because the umpire failed to act and then acted improperly, it could be argued that Viv Richards [the West Indies' captain] had a duty to the spirit of the game and to the letter of the Law, to withdraw his side's appeal.

(From D Fraser, *Cricket and the Law* (1993), pp 51, 53-54.)

QUESTIONS

1. List, in chronological order, the decisions as to matters of fact that were made by the umpires in the Dean Jones extract.
2. List, in chronological order, the decisions as to matters of law that were made by the umpires in the Dean Jones extract.
3. Formulate in your own words the error(s) of fact and of law made by the square-leg umpire when giving Jones 'run out'.
4. What values are relevant to the suggestion that Viv Richards had a duty to withdraw his team's appeal? In not withdrawing the appeal, was he being legalistic?

4 Rules and relationships

4.1 Interpersonal relationships

4.1.1 Social etiquette

Consider the following two passages, each of which contains suggested rules of etiquette governing a woman's social relationships with men.

> In her social relationships with men, the woman living alone must accept certain conventions.
> - She should not lunch or dine alone with a married man more than once or twice – unless their relationship is openly a business one that demands it.
> - She should never allow a man guest to stay on after a party at her flat or room after other guests have gone, or stay on herself at a man's party after the rest have left.
> - She should not entertain a man alone in her apartment, except for the few brief minutes when he calls for her before an evening out together; nor should she go alone to a man's bachelor flat or room. In most hostels and boarding houses, convention rules that if a man and woman are alone together, which may at times be perfectly permissible and necessary, the door must be left open.
> - The young woman living on her own will not accept an invitation from a man to visit his country home, unless she knows that his mother or other married relation will be there to act as hostess for him. Preferably, the invitation should come from his mother.
>
> But why bother with rules, if right feeling is the root of the matter? it may be asked. There are two answers to this. Firstly, as a matter of pure convenience, a rule of etiquette can save endless time-wasting decisions: in the absence of such a rule, one would have to think out afresh each day the problem of where to put the knives and forks on the table. Secondly, the acceptance by society as a whole of certain conventions of civilized behaviour does impose, even on the more selfish members of the community, some self-discipline, some need for consideration of others, some thought beyond mere self.

(From A Page, *Complete Etiquette for Ladies and Gentlemen* (1961), pp 7 and 3.)

> As there are, quite simply, the fewest hard and fast rules in the private domain, more effort and thought is expected of the individual. The first rule of the well-mannered private relationship is that it remains just that... At one time first dates were always instigated by men, and nice girls just had to wait until asked. This is no longer entirely the case. Traditionalists will always prefer the male initiative, but it is now often acceptable for women to invite men out for a date. However, what is easy for an assured woman may for a less confident or younger one seem an impossibility.

(From J Morgan, *Debrett's New Guide to Etiquette and Modern Manners* (1996), pp 189, 190.)

4.1.2 Rules of thumb

It may be of some help to examine the sort of reasons usually given for having rules. Our aim in doing this is not to survey comprehensively the possible ways of justifying rules. It is to look at some common ways of doing so in order to gain some insight into the nature of mandatory norms generally. Mill admirably summarises two very common reasons for having rules: 'By a wise practitioner, therefore, rules of conduct will only be considered as provisional. Being made for the most numerous cases, or for those of most ordinary occurrence, they point out the manner in which it will be least perilous to act, where time or means do not exist for analysing the actual circumstances of the case, or where we cannot trust our judgment in estimating them' (*A System of Logic*, 6, 12, 3). Rules are thus justified as time-saving devices and as devices to reduce the risk of error in deciding what ought to be done. We may add to these features the related justification of rules as labour-saving devices. A rule can be examined in tranquillity on the basis of the best information available concerning the factors likely to be present in the situations to which it applies. The rule states what is to be done in these situations on the balance of foreseeable reasons. When a situation to which it applies actually occurs the norm subjects can rely on the rule, thus saving much time and labour and reducing the risks of a mistaken calculation which is involved in examining afresh every situation on its merits.

(From J Raz, *Practical Reason and Norms* (1975; 1990), p 59. On rules of thumb see further F Schauer, *Playing by the Rules* (1991), pp 104-111.)

QUESTIONS

1. Many people would consider rules of etiquette old-fashioned and in some instances, absurd. Which of the rules, if any, in extract 4.1.1 would you regard as being absurd, and why?
2. Can you give a precise account of five important rules of etiquette which you accept?
3. Page and Raz mention a number of reasons for having rules. Can you think of any other general reasons?
4. On the face of it, the function of the rules in extract 4.1.1 is to tell various people what may or may not be done on certain occasions, but rules also have hidden functions. What do you think might be some of the hidden functions of these rules? See further L Davidoff, *The Best Circles* (1974).
5. What values govern the relationships mentioned in extract 4.1.1? Do you think it appropriate to embody them in a relatively specific code?

4.2 Domestic relationships

In *Home Rules* Denis Wood and Robert Beck analyse the spoken and unspoken rules that govern a particular family's use of their house and its contents. These rules govern such matters as protection of the house itself (make sure the porch door is always locked, to stop it banging on its hinges in the wind), of its contents (don't put hot coffee cups on the lacquered telephone table) and of the family members (don't leave sharp knives out on the kitchen table); control of the house and its contents (don't swing on the door; don't leave the bathroom towels on the floor); and appearance (don't smudge the windows; don't walk on the carpets in dirty shoes).

What is a home for a child but a field of rules? From the moment he rouses into consciousness each morning, it is a consciousness of what he must and must not do. If during the night his pillows have fallen on the floor, he must pick them up, *for pillows do not belong on the floor, they belong on the bed.* If he thinks of turning on the radio, he must keep it low, *for we do not play the radio loud before everyone is up ...* So many rules! No matter how you count them, the number is enormous. Is it one rule that the spoon must go to the right of the knife, and another that the knife must go to the right of the plate? Or is the way we set the table one rule altogether? Either way, the number of rules about no more than the way we eat, where we eat, when we eat, what we eat and who eats with us is alarmingly large. Hundreds of rules? If the meaning of rule is taken narrowly (*those spoons go in the drawer to the right of the stove*), there are more likely thousands. Yet without them the spoons might end up anywhere ... Without the rules the home is not a home, it is a house, it is a sculpture of wood and nails, of plumbing and wiring, of wallpaper and carpets.

(From D Wood and R Beck, *Home Rules* (1994), pp 1-2.)

Consider the main living area in your home. List twenty different norms (including rules of the law of the United Kingdom, social conventions, domestic decrees) governing the use, arrangement and disposition of the furniture and other physical objects that are in the room at present. Which of these rules relate to protection, control and appearance? How many are explicitly codified?

4.3 Institutional relationships

4.3.1 School rules

Rules are required by teachers to enable them to exercise authority over young persons, the kind of authority they would be denied outside of school. They are used to limit the freedom of action of others; and when teachers extend their authority to rules which question dress and personal appearance, and intrude beyond the school's boundaries of time and space, then youngsters become indignant and resentful. Rules are called upon to control and judge behaviour and performance, to arbitrate in areas of dispute, to give orders and expect compliance. But people in authority can make up rules as they go along, or, as so often happens in schools, invoke some personal rule which discharges the behaviour as a personal affront, as in 'Take that look off your face!' or 'Stand up straight and look at me when I talk to you!' For rules are not fixed and immutable but are open to interpretation, negotiation and modification in the process of rule-application. A consequence of which is that we not only experience between-teacher inconsistencies but inconsistencies of reaction from the same teacher to the same misbehaviour by a different pupil.

(From D Tattum, 'Disruptive Pupils: System Rejects?' in J Schostak and T Logan (eds), *Pupil Experience* (1984), p 99.)

Consider the following selection of rules concerning discipline in a school:

1. Paper must be put in dustbins or litter baskets in the playgrounds or into wastepaper baskets in School.
2. Children should not wear outdoor clothing in School. Jewellery may not be worn, this includes rings.
3. Chewing gum is unhygienic and is not allowed.
4. Biro pens spoil writing, use School pens or fountain pens.

5. Classes and individual children must walk in single file on stairs and corridors and always keep to the right.
6. After wash basins have been used, care must be taken to see that dirty water is emptied and the basin is left clean. Keep towels as clean as possible.
7. No bicycles to be ridden through the playground. Only bicycles which satisfy safety regulations will be allowed.
8. Except when staff request it, do not shift or re-arrange any furniture, do not tamper with window poles, windows, thermostats, curtain cords, etc.
9. Pupils may not enter the staff common rooms without hearing permission to do so given (after knocking) from within.

QUESTIONS

1. What can you learn about the school from the above rules?
2. Identify the main values which are promoted by these rules.
3. Rules may impose duties, distribute benefits, or confer power or discretion to act on certain persons; they may also be said to confer privileges, liberties, and to impose liabilities. What do the following rules do: nos 1, 4 and 7?
4. In what institutions other than schools might it be necessary to have rules regulating the discipline and hierarchy of its members? Does this suggest any general lessons about the use of rules as methods for regulating the behaviour of people in societies?
5. Devise a situation in which a legalistic child might avoid the intended effect of any one of the school rules above.
6. Comment on the drafting of the rules nos 2 and 9. Redraft each rule in the light of any criticisms you have thought of.

Consider the following examples of different attitudes to school rules:

- 'I ask myself *why* should I send this boy to his headmaster for being in town at 3.30; *why* should we put 16-year-olds to bed at 10 on Saturday nights; *why* should a boy be on time for every meal, every day; *why* should we force them to sing at compulsory house prayers? Why should we support this artificial state set up by the whims of old governors average age 93, whom you never see?' Prefect, eighteen, public school. (From R Lambert, *The Hothouse Society* (1968), p 174.)
- 'We must change the rules – they have become an entity in themselves divorced from their original intention. They allow for no original thinking – in their pride they assume themselves equal to any situation.' Boy, seventeen, public school (ibid, p 371).
- 'A study of children's ideas on punishment leads one to re-think the whole question of rules and regulations in schools. The planning of the schools and classroom must be such that the children's participation in it leads them to think in terms of the solution to problems rather than obedience or, more commonly perhaps, disobedience.' (From Molly Brearly and Elizabeth Hutchfield, *A Teacher's Guide to Reading Piaget* (1966), p 130.)
- 'While rules exist they will be broken. While rules exist the University is only encouraging students to start to break these rules on the basis of a principle. The principle being that students are capable and responsible enough to choose who their officers will be.' (Students protesting against university regulations governing elections of Student Union officers.)

QUESTIONS

1. Identify, as precisely as you can, the different attitudes to rules displayed in the quotations.
2. Do any of the quotations indicate that rules and their enforcement may have undesirable side-effects? If so, what might these be?
3. 'Rules are meant to be broken.' Do any of the quotations support this common attitude to rules? What are the implications of such an attitude?
4. Look carefully at the second quotation. Can you think of any rules which have become divorced from their original intention? What particular problems might this pose for an interpreter?
5. What assumptions about power, authority and discretion in the relevant institution are made in each of the quotations?

4.3.2 A university rule

A University rule of discipline reads: 'A student must not wilfully or persistently behave in a manner inconsistent with the proper functioning of the University or likely to bring the University into disrepute.'

QUESTIONS

1. Suppose you were the student member of the University's Discipline Committee:
   1.1 What kinds of behaviour do you think this rule is intended to cover?
   1.2 Do you think that the meaning of 'the proper functioning of the University' is likely to be the same in ten years' time?
2. Would a student be in breach of this rule who:
   2.1 cheated in an examination;
   2.2 used the University laboratories throughout her final year to synthesise cocaine;
   2.3 painted defamatory statements about a professor on the factory wall opposite the main entrance to the University;
   2.4 refused to wear a safety helmet in the engineering laboratories because to do so would be contrary to his religious beliefs;
   2.5 took drugs to improve her performance and accepted payments inconsistent with her amateur status while representing the University in an international student athletics meeting in France;
   2.6 disrupted a lecture being given by a visiting speaker whom he and many others thought held racist views; and
   2.7 wrote an article making serious allegations about the conduct and standard of examinations at the University, which was published in a national newspaper?

4.3.3 Total institutions

In institutions such as prisons and hospitals, the individual is submerged in sets of rules which govern and regulate almost every aspect of his life. Stripped of his individuality and treated in the same way as everyone else, the inmate of these 'total institutions' is faced with sets of rules which require constant attention and interpretation, and which can be invoked or waived by the institution's officials as punishments or rewards for his behaviour. These points are powerfully made in the following observations of the French philosopher Michel Foucault.

> In several respects, the prison must be an exhaustive disciplinary apparatus: it must assume responsibility for all aspects of the individual, his physical training, his aptitude to work, his everyday conduct, his moral attitude, his state of mind; the prison, much more than the school, the workshop or the army, which always involved a certain specialisation, is 'omni-disciplinary'. Moreover, the prison has neither exterior nor gap; it cannot be interrupted, except when its task is totally completed; its action on the individual must be uninterrupted: an unceasing discipline. Lastly, it gives almost total power over the prisoners; it has its internal mechanisms of expression and punishment: a despotic discipline. It carries to their greatest intensity all the procedures to be found in the other disciplinary mechanisms.
>
> And it must be admitted that the legal authorities can have no immediate control over all these procedures that rectify the penalty as it proceeds. It is a question, in effect, of measures that by definition can intervene only after the sentence and can bear only on something other than the offences. Those who administer detention must therefore have an indispensable autonomy, when it comes to the question of individualising and varying the application of the penalty: supervisors, a prison governor, a chaplain or an instructor are more capable of exercising this corrective function than those who hold the penal power. It is their judgment (understood as observation, diagnosis, characaterisation, information, differential classification) and not a verdict in the form of an attribution of guilt, that must serve as a support for this internal modulation of the penalty – for its mitigation or even its interruption.
>
> (From M Foucault, *Discipline and Punish* (1975, 1969 Penguin Books Ltd), pp 235-236, 246.)

Writing about patients in a mental hospital, the sociologist Erving Goffman draws attention to the way in which these rules provide 'a framework for personal reorganisation'.

> First, there are the 'house rules', a relatively explicit and formal set of prescriptions and proscriptions that lays out the main requirements of inmate conduct. These rules spell out the austere round of life of the inmate. Admission procedures, which strip the recruit of his past supports, can be seen as the institution's way of getting him ready to start living by house rules.
>
> Secondly, against this stark background, a small number of clearly defined rewards or privileges are held out in exchange for obedience to staff in action and spirit. It is important to see that many of these potential gratifications are carved out of the flow of support that the inmate had previously taken for granted. On the outside, for example, the inmate probably could unthinkingly decide how he wanted his coffee, whether to light a cigarette, or when to talk; on the inside, such rights may become problematic. Held up to the inmate as possibilities, these few recapturings seem to have a reintegrative effect, re-establishing relationships with the whole lost world and assuaging withdrawal symptoms from it and from one's lost self. The inmate's attention, especially at first, comes to be fixed on these supplies

and obsessed with them. He can spend the day, like a fanatic, in devoted thoughts about the possibility of acquiring these gratifications or in contemplation of the approaching hour at which they are scheduled to be granted. Melville's report on navy life contains a typical example: ... 'It is one of the most common punishments for very trivial offences in the Navy, to "stop" a seaman's grog for a day or a week. And as most seamen so cling to their grog, the loss of it is generally deemed by them a very serious penalty. You will sometimes hear them say, "I would rather have my wind *stopped* than my grog!"'

The building of a world around these minor privileges is perhaps the most important feature of inmate culture, and yet it is something that cannot easily be appreciated by an outsider, even one who has previously lived through the experience himself. This concern with privileges sometimes leads to generous sharing; it almost always leads to a willingness to beg for such things as cigarettes, candy, and newspapers. Understandably, inmate conversation often revolves around a 'release binge fantasy', namely, a recital of what one will do during leave or upon release from the institution. This fantasy is related to a feeling that civilians do not appreciate how wonderful their life is.

The third element in the privilege system is punishments; these are designated as the consequence of breaking the rules. One set of these punishments consists of the temporary or permanent withdrawal of privileges or the abrogation of the right to try to earn them. In general, the punishments meted out in total institutions are more severe than anything encountered by the inmate in his home world. In any case, conditions in which a few easily controlled privileges are so important are the same conditions in which their withdrawal has a terrible significance.

(From E Goffman, *Asylums* (1968), pp 51-3, reprinted by permission of Penguin Books Ltd.)

4.3.4 Prison rules

Rules 33 and 34 of the Prison Rules 1964, as amended (SI 1964/388; 1983/568) contain a number of provisions concerning prisoners' letters. They also refer to a prisoner's entitlement to visits. In the following extract we have edited the rules so as to deal only with the entitlement to letters.

33. Letters and visits generally.
(1) The Secretary of State may, with a view to securing discipline and good order or the prevention of crime or in the interests of any persons, impose restrictions, either generally or in a particular case, upon the communications to be permitted between a prisoner and other persons.
(2) Except as provided by statute or these Rules, a prisoner shall not be permitted to communicate with any outside person, or that person with him, without the leave of the Secretary of State.
(3) Except as provided by these Rules, every letter or communication to or from a prisoner may be read or examined by the governor or an officer deputed by him, and the governor may, at his discretion, stop any letter or communication on the ground that its contents are objectionable or that it is of inordinate length.
...

34. Personal letters and visits.
(1) An unconvicted prisoner may send and receive as many letters ... as he wishes within such limits and subject to such conditions as the Secretary of State may direct, either generally or in a particular case.
(2) A convicted prisoner shall be entitled -

(a) to send and to receive a letter on his reception into a prison and thereafter once a week ...

(3) The governor may allow a prisoner an additional letter ... where necessary for his welfare or that of his family.

(4) The governor may allow a prisoner entitled to a visit to send and to receive a letter instead.

...

(6) The board of visitors may allow a prisoner an additional letter ... in special circumstances ...

(7) The Secretary of State may allow additional letters ... in relation to any prisoner or class of prisoners.

(8) A prisoner shall not be entitled under this Rule to communicate with any person in connection with any legal or other business, or with any person other than a relative or friend, except with the leave of the Secretary of State.

(9) Any letter ... under the succeeding provisions of these Rules shall not be counted as a letter ... for the purposes of this Rule.

QUESTIONS

1. Are the rules mentioned by Goffman the only ones that apply to inmates of total institutions?
2. State as precisely as you can a convicted prisoner's entitlement to send and receive letters.
3. In what ways could the implementation and interpretation of rules 33 and 34 constitute rewards or punishments?

(Further exercises concerning the Prison Rules are set out in Appendix I, section A3.)

4.4 Public relationships

4.4.1   The will – no vehicles in the park

In his will made in 1868 a testator bequeathed a plot of land to the Mayor and Corporation of his home town to be converted into a public park, to be called 'Victoria Park' after Queen Victoria. One of the conditions of the bequest was that 'No carriages, broughams, or hansoms should be allowed in the Park, that the ladies and gentlemen of Belleville may the better enjoy the quietude of the scene'. The testator died in 1871 and his widow opened the Park in 1872. A by-law was passed in that year incorporating the rules governing the use of the park by the public. Regulation 1 reads: 'No carriage, coach, brougham, hansom or other vehicle shall be admitted to the park. The penalty for the infringement of this regulation shall be five shillings.' During the last decade of the century the Park was only patronised by members of the upper classes, but by 1899 this conventional barrier had long since disappeared. Today the Park is frequented by all sections of the local population. It is particularly popular with courting couples and with mothers, who bring their children to play there. The smaller boys of the town also kick footballs about and the place is not as quiet as it used to be.

During 1996 a group of teenagers took to riding their motorcycles up and down the access road that leads to the park-keeper's shed where he keeps the motor-mower. Some mothers complained to the park-keeper that their children were frightened and endangered by the motorcycles and he ordered the teenagers to leave. When they argued that they were doing nothing wrong, he informed them of the existence of regulation 1 of the by-law, but after expelling them, took no further action against them. On the following day he caused to be put up a notice saying: 'No vehicles allowed in the park; penalty £25.' Up to last week no action had been taken against anybody under the regulation.

Consider the following incidents which occurred last week in chronological order. After the determination of (1) it becomes a precedent for (2), and so on.

1. On Monday Miss Smith rides her pony along the paths of the Park.
2. On Tuesday afternoon a 12-year-old boy brings his rollerblades to the Park and starts to learn how to use them on the tarmac path. His parents have told him that it would be unsafe to learn in the street.
3. On Wednesday Councillor Jones, the Mayor and a practising lawyer, drives his car through the Park gates and parks it unobtrusively under a tree nearby. When asked by the park-keeper to remove the car, he says 'I am the Mayor. Anyway my car is not bothering anybody, it's not being driven in the park, it is not making a noise, it is not endangering anybody. Anyway I have been doing this for years and nobody stopped me. Anyway we have to consider the intention of the Council when it drafted the by-law and it cannot have intended to exclude cars, as cars had not been invented then. Anyway times have changed. Anyway the expression "any other vehicle" has to be read in its context and is limited to things of the same class. Since all the preceding things listed are horse-drawn vehicles, only such vehicles are prohibited by a strict interpretation of the regulation. Anyway I'm the Mayor and you had better mind your step.' Consider this argument (a) as a whole, (b) point by point. Advise the park-keeper.
4. Mrs Atkins lives at the top of a steep hill and has baby twins. To help her propel her perambulator up the hill she has ingeniously fitted to it a small petrol-driven motor, similar to that of a motor-mower. On Thursday she 'drives' her children round the park in the pram. Has she broken the regulation? If so, could it make any difference if she switches off the motor before entering the park?
5. On Friday a group of four teenagers bring their rollerblades in order to race each other around the perimeter road.
6. Mr Price, a retired postman aged 75, is disabled and can only move about by wheelchair. For the past five years he has been pushed around the park each morning by his daughter. Last month he acquired a motor for the chair; on Saturday he propels himself into the park, accompanied by his daughter. When he is in the middle of the park he suffers a heart attack. The daughter telephones for a taxi, which drives into the park, picks up Mr Price and takes him to hospital. This prompt action probably saved his life.
7. Does a penalty of 'five shillings' in the regulation mean 25p in 1999?
8. Draft a new regulation to replace regulation 1, bearing in mind particularly present-day social conditions in the town, the terms of the bequest, and

the events of the past week. Write a short note outlining the difficulties that have to be overcome and how you have tackled the problem.

4.4.2 A rule

The following by-laws used to be posted verbatim in Victoria Park, Leamington Spa:

> 'By-laws with respect to Pleasure Grounds made under section 164 of the Public Health Act 1875 for Victoria Park (1958):
>
> 5(i) A person shall not except in the exercise of any lawful right or privilege bring or cause to be brought into the pleasure ground any barrow, truck, machine or vehicle other than – (a) a wheeled bicycle, tricycle or other similar machine; (b) a wheelchair, perambulator or chaise drawn or propelled by hand and used solely for the conveyance of a child or children or an invalid.
>
> Provided that where the Council set apart a space in the pleasure ground for the use of any class of vehicle, this by-law shall not be deemed to prohibit the driving in or to that space by a direct route from the entrance to the pleasure ground of any vehicle of the class for which it is set apart.
>
> (ii) A person shall not except in the exercise of any lawful right or privilege ride any bicycle, tricycle or other similar machine in any part of the pleasure ground. Provided that this by-law shall not apply to any person riding a bicycle, tricycle or other similar machine (other than a mechanically propelled bicycle, tricycle or similar machine) along the perimeter road passing through the pleasure ground otherwise than to the obstruction or danger of any other person lawfully using the pleasure ground.'

QUESTIONS

1. In theoretical writings the standard example of this kind of prohibition is phrased in some such terms as: 'No vehicles allowed in the park.' Compare and contrast the style of drafting of the Leamington Spa by-law (a) from the point of view of an official called on to decide particular cases under the two provisions; (b) from the point of view of communication of the content of the provisions to those affected by them.
2. Using the Leamington Spa by-law as a model, draft amendments to meet the needs and conditions of Victoria Park, Belleville today.

5   Rules and results

> 'If rules were results there would be little need of lawyers.'
>
> (Karl Llewellyn)

In both legal and non-legal contexts it is commonly assumed that it is unusual for the results of particular cases to diverge significantly from what the applicable rules prescribe and that, where there is not an exact correspondence, something has gone wrong; for example, that the rules are being flouted or manipulated or ignored or that they are not working well. The following extracts suggest that the relationship between rules and results can be more complex than that.

5.1 Social control in an African society

Anthropologists have devoted a great deal of attention to modes of dealing with disputes in less-developed societies. The following account by Gulliver concerns the Arusha, a tribe in northern Tanzania, who traditionally had no officials, courts or judges, but who nevertheless had recognised procedures for handling disputes, mainly through negotiation and bargaining. Gulliver shows how a group can have generally accepted rules (norms), which play an important part in the processes of dispute settlement, yet the final outcome of the process more often than not involves some departure from the rules.

DISPUTE SETTLEMENT BETWEEN 'RELATED' PERSONS
The nature of negotiations between the two disputants, each with his supporters, is appreciably affected by the nature of relations existing between them, both in general terms and in respect of the particular matter in dispute. Where the disputants have been in some mutually valuable relationship, then they both have an interest in maintaining or restoring it. Each is inclined to accept compromise for the sake of the relationship; but at the same time each has a measure of bargaining power to use against the other. This is immediately obvious in the case of directly contractual situations, such as a dispute between father-in-law and son-in-law over bride-wealth ... or between a stock-owner and herdsman.... But a similar situation arises when a dispute lies between members of the same nuclear group – an inner lineage or age-group. Here again, each disputant has something to offer to induce the other to modify his claims or to acquiesce to a settlement. Thus in the first instance the considerations are the maintenance of the marriage and the affinal tie, or of the herding arrangements; and in the second instance, the maintenance of group unity, reciprocal assistance and mutual activity. In both kinds of situation, reconciliation between the disputants is most important, so that a successful resolution of the affair should go beyond the dispute itself.

On the other hand, disputants may have had little or even no significant relationship between them prior to the affair which precipitates their dispute, and they seek no particular relationship thereafter. In that event the bargaining power of each against the other is both weaker and of a different order. The process of reaching a settlement is different in those kinds of situation ...

Before beginning this examination, it is necessary to revert to the problem of the connection between pragmatic negotiation and the socially accepted norms of the Arusha. There has been, from time to time, a good deal of debate among anthropologists on the meaning of law in non-centralised, non-literate societies – including the proposition that such societies have no law, but only custom. It is not intended to engage in that argument here, for it is one which is too concerned with semantics and not sufficiently with social realities. Therefore I shall content myself by asserting that among the Arusha there are, as in any society, commonly enunciated and accepted norms of behaviour. Arusha speak of *embukunoto*, pl. *imbukunot*. These norms are well known, and each is similarly enunciated everywhere in the country. Not all transgressions of norms precipitate disputes, of course; only those which seem to a person to injure his interests or welfare are, or at his volition can be, made subject to regulatory procedures ...

Whilst it would be incorrect to say that an agreed settlement of a dispute never wholly conforms with the relevant, socially accepted norms, it is true to say that such precise conformity is the exception. Before I began to understand the general principles of the Arusha dispute process – but often having already recorded some of the norms from informants – I was frequently puzzled by the gap between the details of an agreed settlement and the declared norms. The norms themselves were invariably quoted during dispute discussions, and this confused me further. I noted that the Arusha themselves were not worried by this gap; indeed they seldom commented on it, although it was sometimes large. After beginning to appreciate Arusha concentration on compromise which would provide a mutually acceptable resolution of a dispute, I was almost inclined to describe them as cynical opportunists. If by that is meant 'unprincipled', it is a wrong description of the Arusha in these matters. Clearly they recognize norms, and they hold them in great respect: they are what make Arusha different from other peoples with whom they come into contact. In their modern opposition to outside influences, and their desire and attempt to preserve their distinct way of life, they have in fact come to emphasize these norms, rather than passively take them for granted. They are, then, guided by their principles of right behaviour, and they use them as the bases of claims to rights, but they accept an imperfect world in which an individual does not and should not expect to gain all the ideal rights prescribed by the approved norms. But equally, men hope to be able to avoid some of the obligations implicit in those norms. It is perhaps significant that the Arusha have no word that can be translated as 'justice', nor does any such concept appear in their ideology. It is an irrelevant consideration. They are prepared to agree to something which is as near to their claims as possible in the particular context of the strengths and weaknesses of the two parties to the negotiations. Further, they believe that undue insistence on one's 'rights' under these norms may well conflict with obtaining an effective settlement, and with establishing or maintaining otherwise satisfactory relations. Every dispute begins as the plaintiff contrasts, directly or by implication, the divergence between the defendant's behaviour and the relevant norm. The defendant's reply is usually to attempt to show that no real divergence exists; or, if it does, that some overriding and more general norm necessitates it. The process of negotiation continues from there ...

Thus the negotiating-strength of the disputants varies according to the circumstances of each particular case. Sometimes the 'letter of the law' is rigidly applied; sometimes a greater or lesser deviation from it is agreed to. Such variations from the norm of bride-wealth are not new in the ethnographic literature, and in themselves would scarcely have been worth comment, had not the Arusha often emphasized the specific constitution of a 'proper bride-wealth' containing explicitly described items. What is more important for present purposes is, that the possibility of departure from expressed and socially approved norms exists in reference to most, perhaps all norms, the transgression of which may precipitate a formal dispute. It can be said that in the process of discussions and negotiations towards a mutually acceptable resolution of a dispute, there is most usually a departure from the applicable norms in the end result. For the Arusha, one might say that it is what a plaintiff can obtain (after, if necessary, long negotiations) which is important, rather than what he ought to obtain.

(From P Gulliver, *Social Control in an African Society* (1963), pp 240-242, 252-253.)

5.2   Compensation for accidents

To understand the legal system and the nature of rights and duties, it is not sufficient to know the formal rules; one must know the law in action. The same principle holds for reasonable criticism and proposals for reforming the law. ... In this book

I wish to stress the sociological insight that rules are in part a function of the apparatus that applies them. [T]he term 'law' may have at least three distinct meanings, corresponding to three modes of application:

First, law can be understood as those rules that are enunciated by legislators and by appellate judges. These are the rules that appear in print, in newspapers and law books, and that are learned by rote, plus or minus some comprehension, by law students. This understanding is certainly that of most of my fellow students from law school days, and I dare say of many of my teachers as well.

Second, law can be understood as those rules that arise in the course of applying the first-level laws in the situation of a trial court.

The literature of jurisprudence has less often been concerned with a third meaning of law, which concerns those rules that arise in the course of applying the formal rules in private negotiated settlements. Holmes' revolutionary thought, that law is what the courts will do, did not go far enough. Quantitatively speaking, even trial courts are trivial mechanisms for determining legal relationships. The rules of the third level, the law in action, are not completely independent of the first and second levels, but, being further removed from the appellate courts in time, space, procedure, and personnel, they are more subject to distortions, modifications, and even negations of the formal rules than are the rules of the second level.

Students of trial court law have found it to be bent from the formal law in the direction of a sense of fairness brought to bear by the judge or jury in the individual case. The departure from formal law may be greater in cases decided by a jury, but it occurs as well in disputes decided by a judge. Where the unqualified formal rule strikes the decision-maker as unjust, his application of the rule bends it in the direction of his idea of justice, whether by distorting the facts of the situation so that the rule appears to give good results, or by overriding the rule and hiding behind a screen of rationalization or the silence of the jury room.

Law in action, as exemplified by the situation at hand – the adjustment of claims by representatives of insurance companies – involves additional sources of distortion of formal rules, virtually ignored by the students of courtroom law. These are the formally irrelevant situational pressures on the negotiators. The key role in this situation is that of the adjuster, who is typically a low-level employee of a large formal organization. (Sociologists customarily speak of such large, rule-oriented organizations as 'bureaucracies', following Max Weber; the term as used here in the technical sense is not pejorative.) In addition to his personal views of justice and equity, the adjuster brings to his work the pressure he feels in his role as an employee. Both intended and deliberate company policies on the one hand and unintended and 'accidental' pressures on the other affect the adjuster's performance and modify the outcomes of his negotiation of legal claims.

(Reprinted with permission from H Lawrence Ross, *Settled Out of Court: The Social Process of Insurance Claims Adjustment* (2nd edn, 1980), pp 6-8.)

The vast majority of tort claims are settled by negotiation and agreement between the claimant and the defendant's liability insurer, or, occasionally, the defendant personally, usually through the agency of solicitors on both sides. The Pearson Commission estimated from its various surveys that 86% of cases are settled without writ or summons being issued; 11% are settled after the issue of writ or summons but before the case is set down for trial, 2% are settled after setting down, and 1% are settled at the door of the court or during the trial, or are actually disposed of by trial. Many other surveys and studies confirm the general pattern of these figures. It seems that judges handle only about 4,500 cases per year, while about 300,000 others are settled without trial. On the basis of these facts, the tort system could be regarded as an administrative process handled by insurance adjusters and solicitors incorporating 'a right of appeal' to a court of law. Looked at from this point of view the system may be said to resemble the national insurance system more closely than might be thought at first sight. This latter system is run by an administrative process in which there is a right of appeal to various tribunals established under statute. But there are important differences apart from the obvious one that the 'appellate' tribunals for the tort system are the ordinary courts, while for the national insurance system they are statutory tribunals. In particular, national insurance administration is in the hands of the State and is handled by civil servants; on the other hand, the tort administrative machine is privately run. One consequence of this is that the object of the administrators who run the national insurance system is (or, at any rate, should be) to see that every claimant gets what he or she is legally entitled to receive; and the purpose of the appeal procedure is to put right mistakes. But in the tort system, the administrators are not concerned to see that the claimant gets what is legally due: the insurance adjusters who run the tort system are primarily concerned to settle cases for the lowest figure which they can induce the claimant to accept. The Winn Committee acknowledged that the parties do not really want a 'fair' settlement but a 'favourable' one.

In this light, the right of 'appeal' to the courts should be seen not so much as a mechanism to put right the mistakes of the adjudicators, but to be used as a weapon to induce the administrators to behave reasonably. This is why such a large proportion of cases in which proceedings are commenced, or even in which preparations are made for trial, never are tried, and this is why a former Chief Justice of Ontario has said that 'the judicial process is being used for other than judicial purposes. … It is being used as a threat to bring about an adjustment rather than as a means of adjudication'.

(From PS Atiyah, *Accidents, Compensation and the Law* (1993, 5th edn, by P Cane), pp 216-217.)

5.3 Non-contractual relations in business

Disputes are frequently settled without reference to the contract or potential or actual legal sanctions. There is a hesitancy to speak of legal rights or to threaten to sue in these negotiations. Even where the parties have a detailed and carefully planned agreement which indicates what is to happen if, say, the seller fails to deliver on time, often they will never refer to the agreement but will negotiate a solution when the problem arises apparently as if there had never been any original contract. One purchasing agent expressed a common business attitude when he said:

> 'If something comes up, you get the other man on the telephone and deal with the problem. You don't read legalistic contract clauses at each other if you ever want to do business again. One doesn't run to lawyers if he wants to stay in business because one must behave decently.'

Or as one businessman put it: 'You can settle any dispute if you keep the lawyers and accountants out of it. They just do not understand the give-and-take needed in business.' All of the house counsel interviewed indicated that they are called into the dispute settlement process only after the businessmen have failed to settle matters in their own way. Two indicated that after being called in house counsel at first will only advise the purchasing agent, sales manager or other official involved; not even the house counsel's letterhead is used on communications with the other side until all hope for a peaceful resolution is gone.

Law suits for breach of contract appear to be rare. Only five of the twelve purchasing agents had ever been involved in even a negotiation concerning a contract dispute where both sides were represented by lawyers; only two of ten sales managers had ever gone this far. None had been involved in a case that went through trial. A law firm with more than forty lawyers and a large commercial practice handles in a year only about six trials concerned with contract problems. Less than 10 per cent of the time of this office is devoted to any type of work related to contracts disputes. Corporations big enough to do business in more than one state tend to sue and be sued in the federal courts. Yet only 2,779 out of 58,293 civil actions filed in the United States District Courts in fiscal year 1961 involved private contracts. During the same period only 3,447 of the 61,138 civil cases filed in the principal trial courts of New York State involved private contracts. The same picture emerges from a review of appellate cases. [...]

At times relatively contractual methods are used to make adjustments in ongoing transactions and to settle disputes. Demands of one side which are deemed unreasonable by the other occasionally are blocked by reference to the terms of the agreement between the parties. The legal position of the parties can influence negotiations even though legal rights or litigation are never mentioned in their discussions; it makes a difference if one is demanding what both concede to be a right or begging for a favour. Now and then a firm may threaten to turn matters over to its attorneys, threaten to sue, commence a suit or even litigate and carry an appeal to the highest court which will hear the matter. Thus, legal sanctions, while not an everyday affair, are not unknown in business.

One can conclude that while detailed planning and legal sanctions play a significant role in some exchanges between businesses, in many business exchanges their role is small.

(From S Macaulay, 'Non-Contractual Relations in Business: A Preliminary Study' (1963) 28 *American Sociological Review* 55. See further, D Campbell and D Harris, 'Flexibility in Long-term Contractual Relationships: the Role of Co-operation' (1993) 20 *Journal of Law and Society* 166, discussing the ideas of Professor Ian MacNeill.)

QUESTIONS

1. Give examples of other situations in which the outcome of a dispute or other process does not conform precisely with the accepted substantive rules (a) in legal contexts, (b) in non-legal contexts.
2. Comment on the meaning and implications of Gulliver's statement that 'the Arusha have no word that can be translated as "justice", nor does any such concept appear in their ideology'.
3. What implications, if any, do the accounts by Ross, Atiyah and Macaulay have for an understanding of the notion of legal rights?
4. 'Another mode of termination is by what is called compromise: which, being interpreted is *denial of justice*' (J Bentham, *V Works* 35). Recently some scholars have written 'against settlement' (eg O Fiss (1989) 93 *Yale Law Journal* 1973). The great majority of civil claims are settled out of court,

many without formal proceedings ever being started (for figures, see M Zander, *Cases and Materials on the English Legal System* (7th edn, 1996), pp 34-36). Are all or most of these settlements 'denials of justice'?

5. 'The phrase "alternative dispute resolution" is revealing. The word "alternative" implies exceptional or secondary or even deviant in contrast with something that is normal or standard or ordinary. But alternative to what? To litigation? Hardly – for some of the standard alternatives such as negotiation, compromise, and mediation regularly feature as phases *within* litigation. To adjudication? If so, it is not just our theorists who are obsessed by the atypical: rather, court-centred thinking and discourse are deeply ingrained in our legal culture.' (From W Twining (1993) 56 *Modern Law Review* 380, 383.) What do you understand by alternative dispute resolution?

6. Who are the most important interpreters of rules in the contexts described in the extracts in sections 5.1-5.3? In each case would it be accurate to say that they were (a) applying; (b) manipulating; (c) bending; (d) waiving; (e) invoking; (f) ignoring, the relevant rules?

7. Compare the following two definitions of the phrase 'work to rule' taken from the case, *Secretary of State for Employment v ASLEF (No 2)* [1972] 2 All ER 949:

    7.1 '"Work to rule" has a perfectly well-known meaning, namely, "Give the rules a meaning which no reasonable man could give them and work to that".' (Sir John Donaldson, p 959)

    7.2 'Those rules are to be construed reasonably. They must be fitted in sensibly the one with the other. They must be construed according to the usual course of dealing and to the way they have been applied in practice. When the rules are so construed the railway system, as we all know, works efficiently and safely. But if some of those rules are construed unreasonably, as, for instance, the driver takes too long examining his engine or seeing that all is in order, the system may be in danger of being disrupted. It is only when they are construed unreasonably that the railway system grinds to a halt.' (Lord Denning MR, p 965)

    What do you think is meant by 'reasonable' in this context?

8. Does the fact that adherence to rules will often result in inconvenience to a great many people suggest that:

    8.1 there are too many rules?

    8.2 adherence to rules is a value that may be displaced for the sake of convenience?

    8.3 whoever first thought of the 'work to rule' was a shrewd interpreter of rules?

    Give reasons for whatever you think about these questions.

5.4 Regulation and compliance

Many areas of social and economic activity are nowadays regulated by agencies specifically created to ensure compliance with the standards imposed by law.

The following extracts describe one of the primary characteristics of the enforcement of these standards.

> Law may be enforced by compulsion and coercion, or by conciliation and compromise. In the enforcement of regulation, a distinct aversion is noticeable to sanctioning rule-breaking with punishment. Whether enforcement agents are concerned with air or water pollution control, consumer protection, health and safety at work, housing, discrimination, wage and price control, or the many other areas of social and economic life now considered to be the law's business, writers have observed a style of enforcement which seems to be predominantly conciliatory. ... the enforcement of regulation [may be] analysed in terms of two major systems or strategies of enforcement which I shall call *compliance* and *sanctioning.* ...
>
> Compliance is often treated as if it were an objectively-defined unproblematic state rather than a fluid, negotiable matter. Compliance, however, is an elaborate concept, one better seen as a process, rather than a condition. What will be understood as compliance depends upon the nature of the rulebreaking encountered, and upon the resources and responses of the regulated. The capacity to comply is ultimately evaluated in moral terms, and is of utmost importance in shaping enforcement behaviour. A greater degree of control is likely where a discharger is regarded as able to bear the expenditure for compliance; this issue is still a moral one, fundamentally, not one of economics.
>
> Compliance is negotiable and embraces action, time, and symbol. It addresses both standard and process. It may in some cases consist of present conformity. In others, present rule-breaking will be tolerated on an understanding that there will be conformity in future: compliance represents, in other words, some ideal state towards which an enforcement agent works. Since the enforcement of regulation is a continuing process, compliance is often attained by increments. Conformity to this process itself is another facet of compliance. And when a standard is attained, it must be maintained: compliance here is an unbounded, continuing state. It is not simply a matter of the installation of treatment plant, but how well that plant is made to work, and kept working. And an ideal, once reached, may be replaced or transformed by other changes – in consent, in water resource or land use, for example – which demand the achievement of a different ideal. Central to all of this is the symbolic aspect of compliance. A recognition of the legitimacy of the demands of an enforcement agent expressed in a willingness to conform in future will be taken as a display of compliance in itself. Here it is possible for a polluter to be thought of as 'compliant' even though he may continue to break the rules about the discharge of polluting effluent.
>
> A strategy of compliance is a means of sustaining the consent of the regulated where there is ambivalence about the enforcement agency's mandate. Enforcement in a compliance system is founded on reciprocity, for conformity is not simply a matter of the threat or the rare application of legal punishment, but rather a matter of bargaining. The familiar discrepancy between full enforcement and actual practice is 'more of a resource than an embarrassment'. Compliance strategy is a means of sustaining the consent of the regulated when there is ambivalence about an enforcement agency's legal mandate. The gap between legal word and legal deed is ironically employed as a way to attaining legislative objectives. Put another way, bargaining is not only adjudged a more efficient means to attain the ends of regulation than the formal enforcement of the rules, bargaining is, ultimately, morally compelled.

(From Keith Hawkins, *Environment and Enforcement* (1987), pp 1, 126-128, by permission of Oxford University Press.)

QUESTION

The research upon which these comments were made concerned water pollution control. For what reasons do you think that those whose job it is to enforce the law have adopted the compliance strategy described? See further A Ogus, *Regulation* (1994), pp 204-213.

6 Simple and complex rules

Though not true in all instances, one of the common characteristics of legal rules is structural and linguistic complexity. In this section we give examples of simple and complex rules. Some of these assume the detailed style that has been particularly associated with United Kingdom legislation, a style which has been often criticised for obscuring rather than illuminating what the rule-maker was trying to convey. It is, however, dangerous to assume that a rule is simple merely because it is short and apparently clear. When responding to his legalistic son Johnny, Father at one point says, 'there will be only one rule that you must observe in this household: you must be reasonable at all times.' (section 3.5, question 8). But is this a simple rule?

The examples in section 6.1 are drawn from a complex legislative regime, substantially the product of European Community initiatives, designed to protect the environment (see further S Elworthy and J Holder, *Environmental Protection*, 1997). They deal in particular with the protection of wild fauna. The legislative chronology is that in 1981 the United Kingdom Parliament enacted the Wildlife and Countryside Act whose broad purpose was to establish a legal framework for environmental protection. Sections 9-11 created offences of killing wild animals, together with some defences. In 1992 the European Community, building on an earlier initiative, adopted Directive 92/43/EEC on the conservation of the habitats of wild fauna and flora. Article 12 of the Habitats Directive imposes an obligation on Member States to establish a system of strict protection for specified animal species, to which Article 16 allows for some exceptions (called derogations). This Directive was transposed into United Kingdom law by statutory instrument – the Conservation (Natural Habitats, etc) Regulations 1994 (SI 1994/2716). Regulation 39 creates offences of harming wild animals, regulation 40 creates some exceptions to those offences, while regulation 41 prohibits particular methods of taking or killing wild animals. Further reference is made to these provisions in chapter 7, below p 225.

Section 6.2 contains an extract from the sentencing provisions contained in the Criminal Justice Act 1967. These provoked considerable difficulties in their application in the cases *R v Home Secretary, ex p Naughton* [1997] 1 All ER 426 and in *R v Governor of Brockhill Prison, ex p Evans* [1997] 1 All ER 439. The latter led to further difficulties in determining the consequences of the applicant's unlawful detention. In both cases, senior members of the judiciary, including Lord Bingham, the Lord Chief Justice, voiced their concerns about the complexity of the law. Sections 6.3 and 6.4 illustrate two ways in which rules may be simplified. The first is by the use of an alternative narrative form.

The second is by the use of an algorithm, which is a set of instructions for resolving a well-defined problem. A discussion of the structure of algorithms can be found in Appendix II, together with exercises and further examples of their use.

6.1 Protection of wildlife and the countryside

6.1.1 Sections 9-11 of the Wildlife and Countryside Act 1981

Protection of certain wild animals

9. (1) Subject to the provisions of this Part, if any person intentionally kills, injures or takes any wild animal included in Schedule 5, he shall be guilty of an offence.

(2) Subject to the provisions of this Part, if any person has in his possession or control any live or dead wild animal included in Schedule 5 or any part of, or anything derived from, such an animal, he shall be guilty of an offence.

(3) A person shall not be guilty of an offence under subsection (2) if he shows that -

(a) the animal had not been killed or taken, or had been killed or taken otherwise than in contravention of the relevant provisions; or

(b) the animal or other thing in his possession or control had been sold (whether to him or any other person) otherwise than in contravention of those provisions;

and in this subsection "the relevant provisions" means the provisions of this Part and the Conservation of Wild Creatures and Wild Plants Act 1975.

(4) Subject to the provisions of this Part, if any person intentionally-

(a) damages or destroys, or obstructs access to, any structure or place which any wild animal included in Schedule 5 uses for shelter or protection; or

(b) disturbs any such animal while it is occupying a structure or place which it uses for that purpose,

he shall be guilty of an offence.

(5) Subject to the provisions of this Part, if any person -

(a) sells, offers or exposes for sale, or has in his possession or transports for the purpose of sale, any live or dead wild animal included in Schedule 5, or any part of, or anything derived from, such an animal; or

(b) publishes or causes to be published any advertisement likely to be understood as conveying that he buys or sells, or intends to buy or sell, any of those things,

he shall be guilty of an offence.

(6) In any proceedings for an offence under subsection (1), (2) or (5)(a) the animal in question shall be presumed to have been a wild animal unless the contrary is shown.

Exceptions to s 9

10.(1) Nothing in section 9 shall make unlawful-

(a) anything done in pursuance of a requirement by the Minister of Agriculture, Fisheries and Food or the Secretary of State under section 98 of the Agriculture Act 1947, or by the Secretary of State under section 39 of the Agriculture (Scotland) Act 1948; or

(b) anything done under, or in pursuance of an order made under, the Animal Health Act 1981.

(2) Nothing in subsection (4) of section 9 shall make unlawful anything done within a dwelling-house.

(3) Notwithstanding anything in section 9, a person shall not be guilty of an offence by reason of -

(a) the taking of any such animal if he shows that the animal had been disabled otherwise than by his unlawful act and was taken solely for the purpose of tending it and releasing it when no longer disabled;

(b) the killing of any such animal if he shows that the animal had been so seriously disabled otherwise than by his unlawful act that there was no reasonable chance of its recovering; or

(c) any act made unlawful by that section if he shows that the act was the incidental result of a lawful operation and could not reasonably have been avoided.

(4) Not withstanding anything in section 9, an authorised person shall not be guilty of an offence by reason of the killing or injuring of a wild animal included in Schedule 5 if he shows that his action was necessary for the purpose of preventing serious damage to livestock, foodstuffs for livestock, crops, vegetables, fruit, growing timber or any other form of property or to fisheries.

(5) A person shall not be entitled to rely on the defence provided by subsection (2) or (3)(c) as respects anything done in relation to a bat otherwise than in the living area of a dwelling-house unless he had notified the Nature Conservancy Council of the proposed action or operation and allowed them a reasonable time to advise him as to whether it should be carried out and, if so, the method to be used.

(6) An authorised person shall not be entitled to rely on the defence provided by subsection (4) as respects any action taken at any time if it had become apparent, before that time, that that action would prove necessary for the purpose mentioned in that subsection and either -

(a) a licence under section 16 authorising that action had not been applied for as soon as reasonably practicable after that fact had become apparent; or

(b) an application for such a licence had been determined.

Prohibition of certain methods of killing or taking wild animals

11. (1) Subject to the provisions of this Part, if any person -

(a) sets in position any self-locking snare which is of such a nature and so placed as to be calculated to cause bodily injury to any wild animal coming into contact therewith;

(b) uses for the purpose of killing or taking any wild animal any self-locking snare, whether or not of such a nature or so placed as aforesaid, any bow or crossbow or any explosive other than ammunition for a firearm; or

(c) uses as a decoy, for the purpose of killing or taking any wild animal, any live mammal or bird whatever,

he shall be guilty of an offence.

(2) Subject to the provisions of this Part, if any person -

(a) sets in position any of the following articles, being an article which is of such a nature and so placed as to be calculated to cause bodily injury to any wild animal included in Schedule 6 which comes into contact therewith, that is to say, any trap or snare, any electrical device for killing or stunning or any poisonous, poisoned or stupefying substance;

(b) uses for the purpose of killing or taking any such wild animal any such article as aforesaid, whether or not of such a nature and so placed as aforesaid, or any net;

(c) uses for the purpose of killing or taking any such wild animal -

(i) any automatic or semi-automatic weapon;

(ii) any device for illuminating a target or sighting device for night shooting;

(iii) any form of artificial light or any mirror or other dazzling device; or

(iv) any gas or smoke not falling within paragraphs (a) and (b);

(d) uses as a decoy, for the purposes of killing or taking any such wild animal, any sound recording; or

(e) uses any mechanically propelled vehicle in immediate pursuit of any such wild animal for the purpose of driving, killing or taking that animal,

he shall be guilty of an offence.

(3) Subject to the provisions of this Part, if any person -

(a) sets in position any snare which is of such a nature and so placed as to be calculated to cause bodily injury to any wild animal coming into contact therewith; and

(b) while the snare remains in position fails, without reasonable excuse, to inspect it, or cause it to be inspected, at least once every day,

he shall be guilty of an offence.

(4) The Secretary of State may, for the purpose of complying with an international obligation, by order, either generally or in relation to any kind of wild animal specified in the order, amend subsection (1) or (2) by adding any method of killing or taking wild animals or by omitting any such method as is mentioned in that subsection.

(5) In any proceedings for an offence under subsection (1)(b) or (c) or (2)(b), (c), (d) or (e), the animal in question shall be presumed to have been a wild animal unless the contrary is shown.

(6) In any proceedings for an offence under subsection (2)(a) it shall be a defence to show that the article was set in position by the accused for the purpose of killing or taking, in the interests of public health, agriculture, forestry, fisheries or nature conservation, any wild animals which could be lawfully killed or taken by those means and that he took all reasonable precautions to prevent injury thereby to any wild animals included in Schedule 6.

6.1.2 *Articles 12 and 16 of the Habitats Directive 1992*

Protection of species

Article 12

(1) Member States shall take the requisite measures to establish a system of strict protection for the animal species listed in Annex IV(a) in their natural range, prohibiting:

(a) all forms of deliberate capture or killing of specimens of these species in the wild;

(b) deliberate disturbance of these species, particularly during the period of breeding, rearing, hibernation and migration;

(c) deliberate destruction or taking of eggs from the wild;

(d) deterioration or destruction of breeding sites or resting places.

(2) For these species, Member States shall prohibit the keeping, transport and sale or exchange, and offering for sale or exchange, of specimens taken from the wild, except for those taken legally before this directive is implemented.

(3) The prohibition referred to in paragraph 1(a) and (b) and paragraph 2 shall apply to all stages of life of the animals to which this Article applies.

(4) Member States shall establish a system to monitor the incidental capture and killing of the animal species listed in Annex IV(a). In the light of the information gathered, Member States shall take further research or conservation measures as required to ensure that incidental capture and killing does not have a significant negative impact on the species concerned.

Article 16

(1) Provided that there is no satisfactory alternative and the derogation is not detrimental to the maintenance of the populations of the species concerned at a

favourable conservation status in their natural range, Member States may derogate from the provisions of Articles 12, 13, 14 and 15(a) and (b):

(a) in the interest of protecting wild fauna and flora and conserving natural habitats;

(b) to prevent serious damage, in particular to crops, livestock, forests, fisheries and water and other types of property;

(c) in the interests of public health and public safety, or for other imperative reasons of overriding public interest, including those of a social or economic nature and beneficial consequences of primary importance for the environment;

(d) for the purpose of research and education, of repopulating and re-introducing these species and for the breedings operations necessary for these purposes, including the artificial propagation of plants;

(e) to allow, under strictly supervised conditions, on a selective basis and to a limited extent, the taking or keeping of certain specimens of the species listed in Annex IV in limited numbers specified by the competent national authorities.

6.1.3 *Regulations 39-41 of the Conservation (Natural Habitats, etc) Regulations*

Protection of wild animals of European protected species

39.(1) It is an offence-

(a) deliberately to capture or kill a wild animal of a European protected species;

(b) deliberately to disturb any such animal;

(c) deliberately to take or destroy the eggs of such an animal; or

(d) to damage or destroy a breeding site or resting place of such an animal.

(2) It is an offence to keep, transport, sell or exchange, or offer for sale or exchange, any live or dead wild animal of a European protected species, or any part of, or anything derived from, such an animal.

(3) Paragraphs (1) and (2) apply to all stages of the life of the animals to which they apply.

(4) A person shall not be guilty of an offence under paragraph (2) if he shows -

(a) that the animal had not been taken or killed, or had been lawfully taken or killed; or

(b) that the animal or other thing in question had been lawfully sold (whether to him or any other person).

For this purpose 'lawfully' means without any contravention of these Regulations or Part I of the Wildlife and Countryside Act 1981.

(5) In any proceedings for an offence under this regulation, the animal in question shall be presumed to have been a wild animal unless the contrary is shown.

(6) A person guilty of an offence under this regulation is liable on summary conviction to a fine not exceeding level 5 on the standard scale.

Exceptions from regulation 39

40.(1) Nothing in regulation 39 shall make unlawful -

(a) anything done in pursuance of a requirement by the agriculture Minister under section 98 of the Agriculture Act 1947 or section 39 of the Agriculture (Scotland) Act 1948 (prevention of damage by pests); or

(b) anything done under, or in pursuance of an order made under, the Animal Health Act 1981.

(2) Nothing in regulation 39(1)(b) or (d) shall make unlawful anything done within a dwelling-house.

(3) Notwithstanding anything in regulation 39, a person shall not be guilty of an offence by reason of -

(a) the taking of a wild animal of a European protected species if he shows that the animal had been disabled otherwise than by his unlawful act and was taken solely for the purpose of tending it and releasing it when no longer disabled;

(b) the killing of such an animal if he shows that the animal has been so seriously disabled otherwise than by his unlawful act that there was no reasonable chance of its recovering; or

(c) any act made unlawful by that regulation if he shows that the act was the incidental result of a lawful operation and could not reasonably have been avoided.

(4) A person shall not be entitled to rely on the defence provided by paragraph (2) or (3)(c) as respects anything done in relation to a bat otherwise than in the living areas of a dwelling-house unless he had notified the appropriate nature conservation body of the proposed action or operation and allowed them a reasonable time to advise him as to whether it should be carried out and, if so, the method to be used.

(5) Notwithstanding anything in regulation 39 a person -

(a) being the owner or occupier, or any person authorised by the owner or occupier, of the land on which the action authorised is taken, or

(b) authorised by the local authority for the area within which the action authorised is taken,

shall not be guilty of an offence by reason of the killing or disturbing of an animal of a European protected species if he shows that his action was necessary for the purpose of preventing serious damage to livestock, foodstuffs, crops, vegetables, fruit, growing timber or any other form of property or fisheries.

(6) A person may not rely on the defence provided by paragraph (5) as respects action taken at any time if it had become apparent before that time that the action would prove necessary for the purpose mentioned in that paragraph and either -

(a) a licence under regulation 44 authorising that action had not been applied for as soon as reasonably practicable after that fact had become apparent, or

(b) an application for such a licence had been determined.

(7) In paragraph (5) 'local authority' means -

(a) in relation to England and Wales, a county, district or London borough council and includes the Common Council of the City of London, and

(b) in Scotland, a regional, islands or district council.

Prohibition of certain methods of taking or killing wild animals

41.(1) This regulation applies in relation to the taking or killing of a wild animal-

(a) of any of the species listed in Schedule 3 to these Regulations (which shows the species listed in Annex V(a) to the Habitats Directive, and to which Article 15 applies, whose natural range includes any areas of Great Britain), or

(b) of a European protected species, where the taking or killing of such animals is permitted in accordance with these Regulations.

(2) It is an offence to use for the purpose of taking or killing any such wild animal -

(a) any of the means listed in paragraph (3) or (4) below; or

(b) any form of taking or killing from the modes of transport listed in paragraph (5) below.

(3) The prohibited means of taking or killing of mammals are -

(a) blind or mutilated animals used as live decoys;

(b) tape recorders;

(c) electrical and electronic devices capable of killing or stunning;

(d) artificial light sources;

(e) mirrors and other dazzling devices;

(f) devices for illuminating targets;

(g) sighting devices for night shooting comprising an electronic image magnifier or image converter;

(h) explosives;

(i) nets which are non-selective according to their principle or their conditions of use;

(j) traps which are non-selective according to their principle or their conditions of use;

(k) crossbows;

(l) poisons and poisoned or anaesthetic bait;

(m) gassing or smoking out;

(n) semi-automatic or automatic weapons with a magazine capable of holding more than two rounds of ammunition.

(4) The prohibited means of taking or killing fish are -

(a) poison;

(b) explosives.

(5) The prohibited modes of transport are -

(a) aircraft;

(b) moving motor vehicles.

(6) A person guilty of an offence under this regulation is liable on summary conviction to a fine not exceeding level 5 on the standard scale.

QUESTIONS

1. Compare reg 40 of the statutory instrument with section 10 of the 1981 Act. Do they have the same legal content? In what ways do their structures differ?

2. Compare reg 41 of the statutory instrument with section 11 of the 1981 Act. Which is easier to read, and why?

Additional exercises on these provisions are contained in Appendix I, section B, question 5, p 395 and Appendix III, p 417.

6.2   Section 67 of the Criminal Justice Act 1967

By section 33(1) of the Criminal Justice Act 1991, a 'short-term' prisoner who has served half of his sentence must be released on licence. A short-term prisoner is defined in section 33(5) as a person serving a sentence of imprisonment of less than four years. For the purpose of this subsection, consecutive and concurrent sentences are treated as a single term of imprisonment. Section 41 provides that the amount of time that a prisoner must serve may be reduced by any 'relevant period' of detention. Section 67 defines what is meant by that phrase:

> (1) The length of any sentence of imprisonment imposed on an offender by a court shall be treated as reduced by any relevant period, but where he was previously sentenced to a probation order, a community service order, an order for conditional discharge or a suspended sentence in respect of that offence, any such period falling before the order was made or suspended sentence passed shall be disregarded for the purposes of this section.

(1A) In subsection (1) above 'relevant period' means - (a) any period during which the offender was in police detention in connection with the offence for which the sentence was passed; or (b) any period during which he was in custody - (i) by reason only of having been committed to custody by an order of a court made in connection with any proceedings relating to that sentence or the offence for which it was passed or any proceedings from which those proceedings arose; or (ii) by reason of his having been so committed and having been concurrently detained otherwise by an order of a court ...'

QUESTIONS

1. Can you think of a way to present section 67 so that it is easier to read?
2. Suppose a prisoner, P, is arrested and charged with an offence, O1. P is remanded in custody in respect of O1 for 81 days and is then released on bail. While on bail P is arrested and charged with a second offence, O2, and is then remanded in custody for both O1 and O2 for 239 days. On the following (240th day), having been tried and convicted of both offences, P is sentenced to 18 months' imprisonment in respect of each offence, to run consecutively. These 36 months are treated as a total of 1,094 days' imprisonment. However, P is entitled to a reduction in that total, based on the periods of time already spent on remand in custody. The question arises, how is 'the relevant period' to be calculated? Is it:
   (a) 81 days (for O1) plus 239 days (for O1 and O2 together) = 320 days, thus reducing the total (before any other reductions or additions) to 774 days; or
   (b) 81 days (for O1) plus 239 days (for O1) and 239 days (for O2) = 559 days, thus reducing the total (before any other reductions or additions) to 535 days?
3. Suppose a prisoner, P, is arrested and charged with an offence, O1. P is remanded in custody in respect of O1 for 62 days and is then released on bail. While on bail P is arrested and charged with a second offence, O2, and is remanded in custody for that offence (but not for O1) for 73 days. On the following (74th) day, having been tried and convicted of both offences, P is sentenced to one year's imprisonment for O1 and two years' imprisonment for O2, to run concurrently. The total term is therefore two years, which is treated as 731 days' imprisonment. However, P is entitled to a reduction in that total, based on the periods of time already spent on remand in custody. The question arises, how is 'the relevant period' to be calculated? Is it:
   (a) 73 days (for O2 only, because O2 is the dominant sentence), thus reducing the total (before any other reductions or additions) to 658 days; or
   (b) 73 days (for O2) plus 62 days (for O1) = 135 days, thus reducing the total (before any other reductions or additions) to 546 days?

For discussion of the further difficulties to which this second instance gave rise, see below, pp 324-325. Further exercises are set out in Appendix I, section A4.2 and in Appendix II.

6.3   Safety at zebra crossings

Two of the rules which motorists must observe when approaching a zebra crossing are (a) to give precedence to pedestrians, and (b) not to overtake any other vehicles.

Regulation 8 of the 'Zebra' Pedestrian Crossing Regulations 1971 (SI 1971/1524) as amended by SI 1990/1828 reads:

> Every foot passenger on the carriageway within the limits of an uncontrolled zebra crossing shall have precedence within those limits over any vehicle and the driver of the vehicle shall accord such precedence to the foot passenger, if the foot passenger is on the carriageway within those limits before the vehicle or any part thereof has come on to the carriageway within those limits.
>
> For the purpose of this Regulation, in the case of such a crossing on which there is a street refuge or central reservation the parts of the crossing which are situated on each side of the street refuge or central reservation as the case may be shall each be treated as a separate crossing.

Paragraph 71 of *The Highway Code* (1996) (which is accompanied by a picture of a zebra crossing not reproduced here) puts the obligation this way:

> As you approach a Zebra crossing, look out for pedestrians waiting to cross (especially children, elderly people and people with disabilities). Be ready to slow down or stop to let them cross. When someone has stepped on to a crossing, you MUST give way. Allow more time for stopping on wet or icy roads. Do not wave people across; this could be dangerous if another vehicle is approaching.

So far as overtaking is concerned, paragraph 10 of the 1971 Regulations reads:

> The driver of a vehicle while it or any part of it is in a zebra controlled area and it is proceeding towards the limits of an uncontrolled zebra crossing in relation to which that area is indicated (which vehicle is in this and the next succeeding Regulation referred to as 'the approaching vehicle') shall not cause the vehicle, or any part of it -
> (a) to pass ahead of the foremost part of another moving motor vehicle, being a vehicle proceeding in the same direction wholly or partly within that area, or
> (b) subject to the next succeeding Regulation, to pass ahead of the foremost part of a stationary vehicle on the same side of the crossing as the approaching vehicle, which stationary vehicle is stopped for the purpose of complying with Regulation 8.
>
> For the purposes of this Regulation -
> (i) the reference to another moving motor vehicle is, in a case where only one other motor vehicle is proceeding in the same direction in a zebra controlled area, a reference to that vehicle, and, in a case where more than one other motor vehicle is so proceeding, a reference to such one of those vehicles as is nearest to the limits of the crossing;
> (ii) the reference to a stationary vehicle is, in a case where only one other vehicle is stopped for the purpose of complying with Regulation 8, a reference to that vehicle and, in a case where more than one other vehicle is stopped for the purpose of complying with that Regulation, a reference to such one of those vehicles as is nearest to the limits of the crossing.

This is supplemented by 'the next succeeding Regulation':

> **11.**(1) For the purposes of this Regulation, in the case of an uncontrolled zebra crossing, which is on a road, being a one-way street, and on which there is a street refuge or central reservation, the parts of the crossing which are situated on each side of the street refuge or central reservation as the case may be shall each be treated as a separate crossing.

Algorithm designed to show eligibility for a married woman's retirement pension

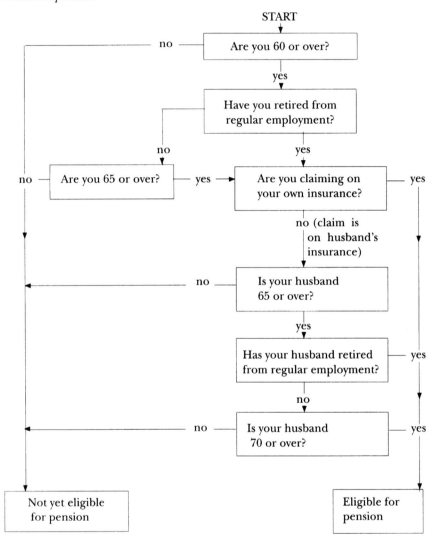

(2) Nothing in paragraph (b) of the last preceding Regulation shall apply so as to prevent the approaching vehicle from passing ahead of the foremost part of a stationary vehicle within the meaning of that paragraph, if the stationary vehicle is stopped for the purpose of complying with Regulation 8 in relation to an uncontrolled zebra crossing which by virtue of this Regulation is treated as a separate crossing from the uncontrolled zebra crossing towards the limits of which the approaching vehicle is proceeding.

The Highway Code says (paragraph 72):

You MUST NOT overtake or park on a Zebra, Puffin or Pelican crossing, including the area marked by zig-zag lines. Even when there are no zig-zags, do not overtake just before the crossing.

QUESTIONS

1. What are the main differences in style and scope between the formulations in *The Highway Code* and the regulations?
2. For what purposes were the different formulations intended, and do you think that they succeed?
3. What has been lost and what has been gained as a result of the simplification in *The Highway Code?*
4. Which formulation do you think is most likely to lead to practical difficulties in interpretation?
5. Can you think of any other ways in which the rules contained in the regulations could be set out so as to help drivers and pedestrians understand how to behave at zebra crossings?

6.4 Diagrammatic presentations

The following is drawn from DHSS leaflet NI1, reprinted with permission from W Ryan et al, *The Increasing Use of Logical Trees in the Civil Service* (1970), CAS Occasional Paper No 13 (HMSO), pp 4-5. Superseded as a matter of law, it remains an object lesson in value of the algorithm as a means of simplifying a text.

The earliest age at which a woman can draw a retirement pension is 60. On her own insurance she can get a pension when she reaches that age, if she has then retired from regular employment. Otherwise she has to wait until she retires or reaches age 65. At age 65 a pension can be paid irrespective of retirement. To get a pension on her husband's insurance, however, she must be 60 or over and retired, and her husband must be 65 or over and retired from regular employment, or 70 if he does not retire before reaching that age.

A man over 70 or a woman over 65 is treated as retired whether working or not, and regardless of the amount of work done.

QUESTIONS

1. Read the passage set out above once carefully; and then look carefully at the algorithm and work your way around it for a few moments.
(a) Now keep a record of the time it takes you to determine whether MW is eligible for a pension under this section, by using only the algorithm, in the following case.

MW is a married woman who lives at 31 Cedar Street, Piltdown. Although she is 67, she is in good health and has a part-time job with AmCo. Her husband, who is 68, is still working full-time as a watch-repairer. MW is claiming on his insurance.

(b) Now keep a record of the time it takes you to determine whether MW is eligible for a pension under this section, by using only the narrative, without looking at the algorithm.

MW is a married woman who lives at 67 Beech Grove, Piltdown. She retired two years ago from her job as a part-time secretary for AmCo. Her husband (aged 71) is in part-time employment (six hours per week) as a gardener. MW is not claiming on her own insurance. MW is 64 and is in poor health.

7 Bigamy

In this section we include the statutory provision which makes bigamy an offence and the judgment in *R v Allen* which concerned the interpretation of the first words of that provision, 'Whosoever, being married, shall marry ...'. *Allen* raised a number of different issues to which reference will be made later, in particular in chapter 10, and you are encouraged to read it closely. Look especially at Cockburn CJ's view of the policy behind section 57 and the use which he makes of it in his interpretation of the section. Also consider his reaction to the different interpretations of the words 'shall marry' and to the kinds of argument which were presented to him.

The following case, *Taylor*, shows how decisions in prior cases become established and interpreted to meet the circumstances of subsequent cases, and how the doctrine of precedent, which is discussed in chapter 9, applies to decisions concerning the criminal law.

Further cases and exercises on bigamy are included in Appendix 1, section A5. We have used bigamy as one of the main examples throughout this book because section 57 has given rise to many judicial doubts and disagreements and because the cases illustrate a number of significant points about precedent, interpretation of statutes, and legal reasoning. Although there are relatively few prosecutions, bigamy turns out to be rather interesting in itself. So it is particularly important to bear in mind that the point of including these materials is not to teach you about the law of bigamy.

7.1 Offences against the Person Act 1861, section 57

Whosoever, being married, shall marry any other person during the life of the former husband or wife, whether the second marriage shall have taken place in England or Ireland or elsewhere, shall be guilty of felony, and being convicted thereof shall be liable to be kept in penal servitude for any term not exceeding seven years; and any such offence may be dealt with, inquired of, tried, determined, and punished in any county or place in *England or Ireland* where the Offender shall be apprehended or be in custody, in the same manner in all respects as if the offence had been actually committed in that county or place: Provided, that nothing in this section contained shall extend to any second marriage, contracted elsewhere than in England and Ireland by any other than a subject of Her Majesty, or to any person marrying a second time whose husband or wife shall have been continually absent from such person for the space of seven years then last past, and shall not have been known by such person to be living within that time, or shall extend to any person who, at the time of such second marriage, shall have been divorced from the bond of the first marriage, or to any person whose former marriage shall have been declared void by the sentence of any court of competent jurisdiction.

7.2   *R v Henry Allen* (1872) LR 1 CCR 367 (Court for Crown Cases Reserved)

The judgment of the Court was delivered by Cockburn CJ:

This case came before us on a point reserved by Martin B. at the last assizes for the county of Hants. The prisoner was indicted for having married one Harriet Crouch, his first wife being still alive. The indictment was framed upon the statute 24 & 25 Vict. c. 100, s.57, which enacts that 'whosoever being married shall marry any other person during the life of the former husband or wife shall be guilty of felony'. The facts of the case were clear. The prisoner had first married one Sarah Cunningham, and on her death he had married his present wife, Ann Pearson Gutteridge. The second wife being still living, he on the 2nd of December, 1871, married one Harriet Crouch. So far the case would appear to be clearly one of bigamy within the statute, but, it appearing that Harriet Crouch was a niece of the prisoner's first wife, it was objected, on his behalf, that since the passing of 5 & 6 Wm. 4 c. 54, s.2, such a marriage was in itself void, and that to constitute an offence, within 24 & 25 Vict. c. 100, s.57, the second marriage must be one which, independently of its bigamous character, would be valid, and, consequently, that the indictment could not be sustained. For the proposition that, to support an indictment for bigamy, the second marriage must be one which would have been otherwise valid, the case of *R v Fanning* ((1866) 10 Cox C.C. 411), decided in the Court of Criminal Appeal in Ireland, was cited, and in deference to the authority of the majority of the judges in that Court, Martin B. has stated this case for our decision.

It is clear that, but for the statutory inability of the parties to marry one another if free, the marriage of the prisoner with Harriet Crouch would have been within the 57th section of the Act. The question is, whether that circumstance alters the effect of the prisoner's conduct in going through the ceremony of marriage with Harriet Crouch while his former wife was still living. The same question arose in the case of *R v Brawn* ((1843) 1 C. & K. 144), which was tried before Lord Denman on the earlier statute of 9 Geo. 4, c. 31, s.22, the language of which was precisely the same as that of the present. In that case the prisoner, a married woman, had, during her husband's lifetime, married a man who had been the husband of her deceased sister. The same point as is now raised being taken on behalf of the prisoner, Lord Denman overruled the objection. 'I am of opinion,' said his Lordship, 'that the validity of the second marriage does not affect the question. It is the appearing to contract a second marriage, and the going through the ceremony, which constitutes the crime of bigamy, otherwise it could never exist in the ordinary cases, as a previous marriage always renders null and void a marriage that is celebrated afterwards by either of the parties during the lifetime of the other. Whether, therefore, the marriage of the two prisoners' – the male prisoner had been included in the indictment as an accessory – 'was or was not in itself prohibited, and therefore null and void, does not signify; for the woman, having a husband then alive, has committed the crime of bigamy by doing all that in her lay by entering into marriage with another man.' In the earlier and analogous case of *R v Penson* ((1832 5 C. & P. 412) a similar objection had been taken, on the ground that the second marriage was invalid, by reason that the woman whom the prisoner was charged with having married whilst his first wife was alive, had for the purpose of concealing her identity been described as Eliza Thick, her true name being Eliza Brown. But Gurney B., who tried the case, overruled the objection, being of opinion 'that the parties could not be allowed to evade the punishment for such an offence by contracting a concertedly invalid marriage'.

We should have acted without hesitation on these authorities had it not been for the case, already referred to, of *R v Fanning*, decided in the Court of Criminal Appeal in Ireland, a case which, if not on all fours with the present is still closely analogous to it, and which, from the high authority of the Court by which it was decided, was entitled to our most attentive consideration. We therefore took time to consider our judgment.

The facts in *R v Fanning* were shortly these. The prisoner, being a Protestant, and having within twelve months been a professing Protestant, was married, having a wife then living, to another woman, who was a Roman Catholic, the marriage being solemnized by a Roman Catholic priest.

Independently of the second marriage being bad as bigamous, it would have been void under the unrepealed statute of the 19 Geo. 2, c. 13, which prohibits the solemnization of marriage by a Roman Catholic priest where either of the parties is a Protestant, and declares a marriage so solemnized null and void to all intents and purposes.

On an indictment against the prisoner for bigamy, the invalidity of the second marriage was insisted on as fatal to the prosecution. The point having been reserved, seven judges against four in the Court of Criminal Appeal held the objection to be fatal, and quashed the conviction. After giving our best consideration to the reasoning of the learned judges who constituted the majority of that Court, we find ourselves unable to concur with them, being unanimously of opinion that the view taken by the four dissentient judges was the right one.

The reasoning of the majority of the Court in *R v Fanning* is founded mainly on the verbal criticism of the language of the 24 & 25 Vict c. 100, s.57; and the words being that 'if any person, being married, shall marry any other person', it was insisted that whatever sense is to be given to the term 'being married', the same must be given to the term 'marry' in the subsequent part of the sentence, and that consequently, it being admitted that the term 'being married' implies a perfect and binding marriage, the second marriage must also be one which, but for the prohibition of the statute, would be – whether as regards capacity to contract marriage or the manner in which the marriage is solemnized – binding on the parties.

Two authorities were relied on in support of this reading of the statute, namely, the language of Tindal C.J., in delivering the opinion of the judges in the House of Lords in the well-known case of *R v Millis* ((1844) 10 Cl. & F. 534) and the decision of the Judge Ordinary of the Divorce Court in the case of *Burt v Burt* ((1860) 2 Sw. & Tr. 88). In the first of these cases Tindal C.J. undoubtedly says that the words 'being married' in the first part of the sentence, and the words 'marry any other person', in the second, must of necessity point at and denote 'marriage of the same kind and obligation'. But it must be borne in mind that the question before the House of Lords was, whether the first marriage, not the second, was valid, the invalidity of the second not being in question at all. In order to show that the first marriage, which had been solemnized by a Presbyterian minister, at his own house, between a member of the Established Church in Ireland and a Presbyterian, amounted to no more than a contract *per verba de praesenti*, and had failed to constitute a valid marriage, the Chief Justice of the Common Pleas insists that, if such a marriage had occurred in the second instance instead of the first, it would not have been held sufficient to support an indictment for bigamy. The case put by the Chief Justice was not the point to be decided, it was only used for the purpose of argument and illustration. Whether the incapacity of the parties to contract a binding marriage independently of the bigamy would take a case like that of *R v Fanning* out of the statute, was not present to his mind or involved in the decision of the case before the House. And the Chief Justice expressly states that, though the conclusion he had arrived at was concurred in by the rest of the judges, his reasoning was entirely his own. The language of the learned Chief Justice must therefore be taken as extra-judicial, and cannot bind us in expounding the statute now under consideration. The case of *Burt v Burt*, in like manner, falls altogether short of the question we have now to decide. It was a suit for a divorce instituted by a married woman against her husband on the ground of bigamy, adultery and desertion. To establish the bigamy, evidence was given that the husband had married a woman in Australia according to the form of the Kirk of Scotland, but there was no proof that the form in question was recognized as legal by the local law. Upon this latter ground the Judge Ordinary held that a second marriage was not proved so as to make good the allegation of bigamy. All, therefore, that this case shows is, that a second marriage by a form not recognized by law will not amount to bigamy under the Divorce Act. Admitting, as we are disposed to do, that the construction of the two statutes should be the same, the decision in *Burt v Burt* will not, as will presently appear, be found to conflict with our judgment in the present case, the second marriage having been celebrated according to a form fully recognized by the law.

We may, therefore, proceed to consider what is the proper construction of the statutory enactment in question, unfettered by these authorities. Before doing so it should, however, be observed, that there is this difference between the case of *R v Fanning* and the present, that the form of marriage there resorted to was one which, independently of the bigamous character of the marriage, was, by reason of the statutory prohibition, inapplicable to the special circumstances of the parties, and ineffectual to create a valid marriage, whereas, in the case before us, independently of the incapacity, the form would have been good and binding in law. This distinction is expressly adverted to by Christian J., in his judgment as distinguishing the case before the Irish judges from that of *R v Brawn*, and it may be doubted whether, but for this distinction, the learned judge would not have come to a different conclusion. The other judges, constituting the majority, do not, however, rest their judgment on this distinction, but plainly go the length of overruling the decision of Lord Denman in *R v Brawn*. Their judgments proceed on the broad intelligible ground, that to come within the statutes against bigamy the second marriage must be such as that, but for its bigamous character, it would have been in all respects, both as to the capacity of the parties and the ceremonial adopted, as binding as the first. Differing altogether from this view, and being prepared to hold that, so long as a form of marriage has been used which the law recognizes as binding, whether applicable to the particular parties or not – and further than this is not necessary to go – the offence of bigamy is committed, we have only adverted to the distinction referred to in order to point out that our decision in no degree turns upon it, but rests on the broader ground taken by the dissentient judges in the Irish court.

When it is said that, in construing the statute in question, the same effect must be given to the term 'marry' in both parts of the sentence, and that, consequently, as the first marriage must necessarily be a perfect and binding one, the second must be of equal efficacy in order to constitute bigamy, it is at once self-evident that the proposition as thus stated cannot possibly hold good; for if the first marriage be good, the second, entered into while the first is subsisting, must of necessity be bad. It becomes necessary, therefore, to engraft a qualification on the proposition just stated, and to read the words 'shall marry' in the latter part of the sentence, as meaning 'shall marry' under such circumstances as that the second marriage would be good but for the existence of the first. But it is plain that those who so read the statute are introducing into it words which are not to be found in it, and are obviously departing from the sense in which the term 'being married' must be construed in the earlier part of the sentence. But when once it becomes necessary to seek the meaning of a term occurring in a statute, the true rule of construction appears to us to be, not to limit the latitude of departure so as to adhere to the nearest possible approximation to the ordinary meaning of the term, or to the sense in which it may have been used before, but to look to the purpose of the enactment, the mischief to be prevented, and the remedy which the legislature intended to apply. Now, we cannot agree either with Fitzgerald B., in his judgment in *R v Fanning*, that the purpose of the statutes against bigamy was simply to make polygamous marriages penal, and that, consequently, it was only intended to constitute the offence of bigamy where the second marriage would, but for the existence of the first, be a valid one; or with those judges who, in *R v Fanning* found their judgments on the assumption that, in applying the statute against bigamy, the second marriage must be one which, but for the first, would be binding. Polygamy, in the sense of having two wives or two husbands, at one and the same time, for the purpose of cohabitation, is a thing altogether foreign to our ideas, and which may be said to be practically unknown; while bigamy, in the modern acceptation of the term, namely, that of a second marriage consequent on an abandonment of the first while the latter still subsists, is unfortunately of too frequent occurrence. It takes place, as we all know, more frequently where one of the married parties has deserted the other; sometimes where both have voluntarily separated. It is always resorted to by one of the parties in fraud of the law; sometimes by both in order to give the colour and pretence of marriage where the reality does not exist. Too often it is resorted to for the purpose of villanous fraud. The ground on which such a marriage is very properly made penal, is that it involves an outrage on public decency and morals, and creates a public scandal by the prostitution of a solemn ceremony, which the law allows to be applied only to a legitimate union, to a marriage at best but colourable and fictitious, and which may be made, and too often is made, the means of the most cruel and wicked deception. It is obvious that the outrage and scandal involved in such a proceeding will not be less, because the parties to the second marriage may be under some special incapacity to contract marriage. The deception will not be the less atrocious, because the one party may have induced the other to go through a form of marriage known to be generally binding, but inapplicable to their particular case. Is the scandal or the villainy the less because the man, having represented to the woman, who is his dupe, and to the priest, that he is a Roman Catholic, turn out afterwards to be a Protestant? Such instances as those we have referred to, thus involving public scandal or deception, being plainly within the mischief which we may reasonably assume it must have been the purpose of the legislature to prevent, we are of opinion that we ought not to frustrate the operation of a very salutary statute, by putting so narrow a construction on it as would exclude such a case as the present, if the words are legitimately capable of such a construction as would embrace it. Now the words 'shall marry another person' may well be taken to mean shall 'go through the form and ceremony of marriage with another person'. The words are fully capable of being so construed, without being forced or strained; and as a narrower construction would have the effect of leaving a portion of the mischief untouched, which it must have been the intention of the legislature to provide against, and thereby, as is fully admitted by those who contend for it, of bringing a grave reproach on the law, we think we are warranted in inferring that the words were used in the sense we have referred to, and that we shall best give effect to the legislative intention by holding such a case as the present to be within their meaning. To assume that the words must have such a construction as would exclude it, because the second marriage must be one which, but for the bigamy, would have been as binding as the first, appears to us to be begging the entire question, and to be running directly counter to the wholesome canon of construction, which prescribes that, where the language will admit of it, a statutory enactment shall be so construed as to make the remedy co-extensive with the mischief it is intended to prevent.

In thus holding it is not at all necessary to say that forms of marriage unknown to the law, as was the case in *Burt v Burt*, would suffice to bring a case within the operation of the statute. We must not be understood to mean that every fantastic form of marriage to which parties might think proper to resort, or that a marriage ceremony performed by an unauthorized person, or in an unauthorized place, would be a marrying within the meaning of the 57th section of 24 & 25 Vict. c. 100. It will be time enough to deal with a case of this description when it arises. It is sufficient for the present purpose to hold, as we do, that where a person already bound by an existing marriage goes through a form of marriage known to and recognized by the law as capable of producing a valid marriage, for the purpose of a pretended and fictitious marriage, the case is not the less within the statute by reason of any special circumstances, which, independently of the bigamous character of the marriage, may constitute a legal disability in the particular parties, or make the form of marriage resorted to specially inapplicable to their individual case.

After giving the case of *R v Fanning* our best consideration we are unanimous in holding that the conviction in the case before us was right, and that the verdict must stand good.

Conviction affirmed.

QUESTIONS

1. State the facts of *Allen* in chronological order. Was there any question of fact in issue before the Court for Crown Cases Reserved in the case?
2. Formulate as precisely as you can the main question of interpretation (the question of law) that was at issue in this case.
3. Imagine that you were counsel for the defence. What proposition(s) of law would you have had to persuade the court to accept in order to win the case? What reasons might you have advanced in support of the proposition(s)?
4. 'The essence of the offence of bigamy lies in the previous marriage and its continuance. It is only because of the wrong done by the wickedness of going through a form of marriage with the knowledge of the impediment of a prior marriage that the subsequent marriage merits punishment.' Per Dixon J, *Thomas v R* (1937) 59 CLR 279, 311.

   Why *should* bigamy be an offence? Is the reason that it involves the 'prostitution of a solemn ceremony' the only or the main reason? If so, should it make a difference whether the ceremony took place in a church or a register office? Should those whose religion permits polygamy, such as Muslims, be subject to the law of bigamy?
5. Do you think, from the point of view of a layman, that it was right that Allen should have been convicted? Give reasons for your answer. What was

the source of doubt about interpretation in this case – bad drafting, doubt about policy, doubt about the facts in this case, or what?
6. Redraft the section in words that would leave no doubt as to the application of the law in *Allen*.

7.3 *R v Taylor* [1950] 2 All ER 170 (Court of Criminal Appeal)

Lord Goddard CJ delivered the following judgment of the court:

The appellant pleaded Guilty before the recorder at the Central Criminal Court to an indictment containing two counts. In the first count he was charged that on Dec. 18, 1946, he married Lilian Smithers during the lifetime of his wife, Alice Julie Taylor, and in the second count it was alleged that on Dec. 24, 1948, he married Olive Briggs during the lifetime of his said wife.

The appellant was lawfully married to his wife, who is still alive, in 1925. In April, 1927, he went through a form of marriage with another woman. In November, 1942, having left the second woman, he went through another form of marriage. In respect of that marriage he was charged at Maidstone Assizes in November, 1944, with bigamy, but the indictment charged him with committing bigamy during the lifetime of the woman with whom he had gone through the first bigamous marriage, who was then believed to be his lawful wife. When it was shown that she was not, a verdict of Not Guilty was returned. In 1945 he was charged at the Central Criminal Court in respect of the bigamy he had committed in April, 1927, but that charge failed because there was no evidence given by the prosecution that when he went through the second ceremony of marriage in 1927 his first wife was alive. He was, however, convicted on a count in the indictment of making a false declaration for the purpose of the marriage register, and for that offence he was bound over. His habit of contracting marriages continued because he went through another ceremony in 1946 and a fourth ceremony in 1948, and it was in respect of those two marriages that he was charged at the Central Criminal Court last March and pleaded Guilty.

He appealed against his sentence, and he would not have got leave to appeal against it if he had been properly convicted, but when this court saw the papers with a view to considering whether leave to appeal against sentence should be given, it at once appeared that at the time when he went through the bigamous ceremonies in 1946 and 1948 he had not seen his wife for very many years. The wife had said that the last time she saw him was in 1925, and it was either in 1925 or 1927 that these spouses had last seen each other. We, therefore, inquired how it was that the appellant pleaded Guilty, and his counsel (who had appeared for him at the trial) told us that he felt unable to advise him to take any other course because of the decision of this court in *R v Treanor (or McAvoy)*. In that case, in somewhat similar circumstances, the court held that, where more than one bigamous ceremony was shown, in respect of any second or subsequent bigamous ceremony, the prisoner was deprived of the defence that he had not seen his wife for seven years and not known that she was alive. That case seemed to the court to need further consideration, and, accordingly, we gave leave to the appellant to appeal against his conviction so that a full court might assemble to consider the decision in that case.

I should like to say one word about the re-consideration of a case by this court. A court of appeal usually considers itself bound by its own decisions or decisions of a court of co-ordinate jurisdiction. For instance, the Court of Appeal in civil matters considers itself bound by its own decisions or by the decisions of the Exchequer

Chamber, and, as is well known, the House of Lords always considers itself bound by its own decisions. In civil matters it is essential in order to preserve the rule of *stare decisis* that that should be so, but this court had to deal with the liberty of the subject and if, on re-consideration, in the opinion of a full court the law had been either mis-applied or misunderstood and a man has been sentenced for an offence, it will be the duty of the court to consider whether he has been properly convicted. The practice observed in civil cases ought not to be applied in such a case, and in the present case the full court of seven judges is unanimously of opinion that *R v Treanor (or McAvoy)* was wrongly decided.

The offence of bigamy, so far as it is a temporal offence, was created in the first place by the statute 1 James 1, c. 11, where it is provided by s. 1:

'... if any person or persons within his Majesty's Dominions of England and Wales, being married, or which hereafter shall marry, do at any time after the end of the session of this present Parliament, marry any person or persons, the former husband or wife being alive ... then every such offence shall be felony ...'

It is clear that what is aimed at there is not merely bigamy, a second illegal ceremony, but what I may call polygamy – any number of marriages, because the words are: 'shall marry any person or persons'. There is a proviso:

'Provided always, that neither this Act, nor any thing therein contained, shall extend to any person or persons whose husband or wife shall be continually remaining beyond the seas by the space of seven years together, or whose husband or wife shall absent him or herself the one from the other by the space of seven years together, in any parts within his Majesty's Dominions, the one of them not knowing the other to be living within that time.'

It is clear that under that statute the defence of absence for seven years without knowledge of the spouse being alive was a defence however many times the ceremony of marriage had taken place. I need not take up time by reading the next statute, the Offences against the Person Act, 1828, because s. 57 of the Offences against the Person Act, 1861, with which we are immediately concerned, is in substance in the same form. [Lord Goddard CJ then read section 57.]

It is obvious that the words 'second marriage' in the enacting part of the section must be given the same construction as must be given to those words when they appear in the proviso. It is clear that by limiting the words in the enacting part of the section which constitutes the felony to the second ceremony and not a third and subsequent ceremonies, a man could be convicted only if he had married twice and not if he had gone through a third, fourth, or fifth subsequent ceremony. In *R v Treanor (or McAvoy)*, however, it was held that ([1939] 1 All E.R. 332):

'This proviso means precisely what it says, nothing more or less – any second marriage, and not any second or subsequent marriage.'

The court went on to say that the proviso was not to be artificially expanded into applying to a second or subsequent marriage.

The short point on which this court can decide this case, and it seems to me to be the true way of deciding it, is this. A charge of bigamy is an allegation that on a particular day the person charged went through a ceremony of marriage when his lawful wife was alive. The court, therefore, is dealing with two ceremonies of marriage only and no more – the lawful marriage and the polygamous marriage. When the polygamous marriage is proved, it is open to the defendant to show that at the time of that polygamous marriage he had not heard of his wife for seven years, and it does not seem to this court that it is then open to the prosecution to say: 'You cannot avail yourself of that defence because there have been other ceremonies of marriage between the lawful marriage and the ceremony in respect of which you are charged.' The offence committed which is charged is the offence of going through the ceremony alleged at a time when the lawful wife was alive. Therefore, a defendant has a defence if it is shown that at the time he went through the marriage which is charged against him as a felony he had not seen his wife for seven years and had not known her to be living within that time. Any other construction would lead to very astonishing results. If a man went through a form of marriage when he had not seen his wife for seven years and had not known her to be living – in which case he would have a good defence under the proviso – and the woman who he had married secondly died and he went through a third form of marriage, still not having known that his first wife was alive, could it be said that he could not plead absence of knowledge? It is enough to say that, while we do not differ from the opinion the court expressed in *R v Treanor (or McAvoy)* that 'second marriage' must be strictly construed, the second marriage which has to be considered is the second marriage charged in the indictment and no other. Therefore, for those reasons, although we do not differ from the construction put on the section in *R v Treanor (or McAvoy)*, we do differ from the result that the court there held followed from that construction. Accordingly, we hold in the present case that, although the appellant might have been charged with other offences, he should not have been convicted of the offence of bigamy, and, therefore, these convictions must be quashed.

Appeal allowed.

QUESTIONS

1. What were the facts in *Taylor*? Were any of them more important than any others? By what criteria could you decide whether a fact is important in a case?
2. What issue(s) arose in this case?
3. Restate the arguments (a) for, and (b) against, Taylor. Which of them did the Court of Criminal Appeal find convincing?
4. For what proposition(s) of law is *Taylor* an authority?

7.4   The American Model Penal Code, Article 230.1 (1985)

(1) *Bigamy.* A married person is guilty of bigamy, a misdemeanor, if he contracts or purports to contract another marriage, unless at the time of the subsequent marriage:
(a) the actor believes that the prior spouse is dead; or
(b) the actor and the prior spouse have been living apart for five consecutive years throughout which the prior spouse was not known by the actor to be alive; or
(c) a Court has entered a judgment purporting to terminate or annul any prior disqualifying marriage, and the actor does not know that judgment to be invalid; or
(d) the actor reasonably believes that he is legally eligible to remarry.

QUESTION

If this article had been the law in England, would it have made any difference to the two cases?

8   Discretion to disobey

Buckoke v Greater London Council [1971] 2 All ER 254 (Court of Appeal, Civil Division)

Lord Denning MR:

The controversy

For many years there has been a controversy in the fire service. It is this: what is the duty of the driver of a fire engine when he comes to traffic lights which are at red? The Fire Brigades' Union say that he must obey the law. No matter how urgent the call, he must wait till the lights turn green. Even if it means losing precious seconds, he must wait all the same. The chief officer of the London Fire Brigade says No; he is not going to order the driver to wait. If the road is clear and the driver stops for a second and makes sure that it is safe to cross, he can shoot the lights so as to get to the fire as soon as possible. But, if he thinks it better to wait until the lights go green, he is at perfect liberty to do so. The decision is his, and his alone. The controversy has been considered by the Central Fire Brigade Advisory Council. It has been before the Home Secretary and the Secretary of State for Scotland. They have declined to interfere either by legislation, or otherwise. So the rival views have been brought before us to decide between them.

In accordance with his view, the chief officer of the London Fire Brigade, with the support of the Greater London Council has issued an instruction. Its formal description is brigade order 144/8, dated 3 February 1967. It states:

> '*Traffic light signals* – Drivers of fire brigade vehicles are under the same obligation at law to obey traffic light signals as the drivers of other vehicles. If however, a Brigade driver responding to an emergency call decides to proceed against the red light, he is (unless signalled to proceed by a police constable in uniform) to stop his appliance, car, or other vehicle at the red light, observe carefully the traffic conditions around him, and to proceed only when he is reasonably sure that there is no risk of a collision; the bell is to be rung vigorously and/or the two-tone horn sounded and the blue flashing light(s) operated. Extreme caution is to be used and the driver is not to cross until it is clear that the drivers of other vehicles appear aware that he is proceeding. The onus of avoiding an accident in such circumstances rests entirely on the Brigade driver, who is to remember that a collision might well prevent his vehicle from reaching its destination and might also block the road for other essential services; no call is so urgent as to justify this risk.'

The Fire Brigades' Union takes exception to that order. They say that it is unlawful because it is an encouragement to the drivers to break the law. They determined to test the legal position. They told some 20 of their members, the plaintiffs, to refuse to travel with a driver unless he gave them an assurance that he would observe the law and would never cross the lights when they were at red. The drivers refused to give that assurance. Whereupon the plaintiffs refused to travel with the drivers. The chief officer took disciplinary proceedings against the plaintiffs. They were charged under the Fire Services (Discipline) Regulations 1948 (SI 1948/545, reg 1 and Schedule) with:

> 'Disobedience to orders, that is to say, if he disobeys, or without sufficient cause fails to carry out, any lawful order, whether in writing or not.'

The plaintiffs thereupon brought this action against the Greater London Council, the defendants. They claimed a declaration that order 144/8 of 3 February 1967 was an unlawful one; and an injunction restraining the defendants from continuing with the disciplinary proceedings.

The issue in the action depends, I think, on this: was the order of the chief fire officer 144/8 lawful or unlawful? If it was lawful, the plaintiffs had no possible justification for refusing to travel with the driver. If it was unlawful, they could justifiably say that they had sufficient cause for their refusal; because they were not bound to travel with a driver who was under unlawful orders.

The statutory provisions

There is no doubt that, on a strict reading of the statute, a fireman is bound to obey the traffic lights just as much as anyone else. If he does not do so, he may be prosecuted to conviction; his licence may be endorsed; and if it is endorsed three times he may be disqualified from driving and thus lose his job – and the fire service would lose a man.

The statutory provisions are as follows. By s. 14 of the Road Traffic Act 1960, as amended (by the Road Traffic Act 1962, s.8, Sch. I, Part 2):

'... where a traffic sign ... has been lawfully placed on or near a road, a person driving or propelling a vehicle who ... (b) fails to comply with the indication given by the sign, shall be liable on summary conviction to a fine not exceeding fifty pounds.'

By the Traffic Signs Regulations and General Direction 1964, (S.I. 1964 No. 1857) regs 7 and 34:

'7. Section 14 of the Road Traffic Act 1960 shall apply ... to the red signal when shown by the light signals ...

34. (1) ... (a) the red signal shall convey the prohibition that vehicular traffic shall not proceed beyond the stop line ...'

as to which see *Ryan v Smith* ([1967] 2 Q.B. 893). By s. 7 (1) of the Road Traffic Act 1962, when a person is convicted of disobeying a traffic light signal:

'... the court shall order that particulars of the conviction, and, if the court orders him to be disqualified, particulars of the disqualification, shall be endorsed on any licence held by him. ...'

By s.7 (2):

'If the court does not order the said person to be disqualified, the court need not order particulars of the conviction to be endorsed as aforesaid if for special reasons it thinks fit not to do so.'

By s. 5(3) of the 1962 Act, where a person has already two previous convictions which have been endorsed:

'... the court shall order him to be disqualified for ... not less than six months ... unless the court is satisfied, having regard to all the circumstances, that there are grounds for mitigating the normal consequences of the conviction. ...'

Those provisions, taken in all their strictness, apply to fire engines, ambulances and police cars as much as to anyone else. None of them is exempt from obeying the red lights. But by special permission they are exempt from obeying the speed limit: see s. 79 of the Road Traffic Regulations Act 1967.

The defence of necessity

During the argument I raised the question: might not the driver of a fire engine be able to raise the defence of necessity? I put this illustration. A driver of a fire engine with ladders approaches the traffic lights. He sees 200 yards down the road a blazing house with a man at an upstairs window in extreme peril. The road is clear in all directions. At that moment the lights turn red. Is the driver to wait for 60 seconds, or more, for the lights to turn green? If the driver waits for that time, the man's life will be lost. I suggested to both counsel that the driver might be excused in crossing the lights to save the man. He might have the defence of necessity. Both counsel denied it. They would not allow him any defence in law. The circumstances went to mitigation, they said, and did not take away his guilt. If counsel are correct – and I accept that they are – nevertheless such a man should not be prosecuted. He should be congratulated.

Mitigating the rigour of the law

Accepting that the law, according to the strict letter of it, does compel every driver to stop at the red light, no matter how great the emergency, even when there is no danger, then the question arises: can the chief officer of the fire brigade issue an order authorising his men to depart from the letter of the law?

This raises an important question. It is a fundamental principle of our constitution, enshrined in the Bill of Rights (1688), that no one, not even the Crown itself has the 'power of dispensing with laws or the execution of laws'. But this is subject to some qualification. When a law has become a dead letter, the police need not prosecute. Nor need the justices punish. They can give an absolute discharge. So also when there is a technical breach of the law in which it would be unjust to inflict any punishment whatever. The commissioner of police may properly in such a case make a policy decision directing his men not to proceed: *R v Metropolitan Police, ex parte Blackburn* ([1968] 2 Q.B. 118, at 136) where it was said that a chief officer of police can 'make policy decisions and give effect to them, as for instance, was often done when prosecutions were not brought for attempted suicide'. So in this case, I have no doubt that the commissioner of police could give directions to his men – he may indeed have done so, for aught I know – that they need not prosecute when the driver of a fire engine crosses the lights, so long as he uses all care and there is no danger to others. This would be a justifiable policy decision so as to mitigate the strict rigour of the law. If any police officer, notwithstanding this direction should prosecute for this technical offence, I would expect the justices to give the driver an absolute discharge under s.7 of the Criminal Justice Act 1948. Thus by administrative action, backed by judicial decision, an exemption is grafted on to the law.

We were told that in practice the police do not prosecute the driver of a fire engine for crossing the lights at red except when there has been an accident and they think that he has not taken proper care. They then prosecute him both for crossing the lights at red and also for careless driving. The driver has no defence to crossing the lights and pleads guilty to that charge. He disputes the careless driving, and may or may not be found guilty of it. I would hope that, if he is acquitted of careless driving he would be given an absolute discharge on the charge of crossing the lights.

I take it, therefore, that the commissioner of police can give a policy direction to his men saying that they need not prosecute a fireman for crossing the lights at red when there is no danger. If the commissioner of police can do this, I see no reason why the chief officer of the fire brigade should not do likewise. He can say to his men: 'So long as you stop and see that all is clear before crossing the lights, no disciplinary action will be taken against you.' That is a justifiable administrative step taken by him in the public interest. We should, I think, back it by our judicial decision today. I hold therefore, that order 144/8 of 3 February 1967 was a perfectly lawful order.

The disciplinary proceedings

Seeing that order 144/8 was a lawful order, I think that the disciplinary proceedings must go on.

Suppose that a driver were to say to a crewman: 'I am going to break the law and crash the red lights, even when it is dangerous to do so,' I think that the crewman could justifiably refuse to travel with that driver. He would not be bound to submit himself to danger in that way: see *Ottoman Bank v Chakarian* ([1930] A.C. 277). But it is altogether different when the driver says: 'I am not going to crash the lights except when there is no risk of collision, and then only after taking the precautions laid down in brigade-order 144/8.' If the officer orders the crewman to travel with such a driver, it is a lawful order, and the crewman has no sufficient cause for failing to carry it out.

Plowman J., ([1970] 2 All E.R. 193, at 195 et seq.) devoted a considerable part of his judgment to *Ex parte Fry* ([1954] 2 All E.R. 118) but that case was not canvassed before us. It does not warrant the proposition that the rules of natural justice do not apply to disciplinary bodies. They must act fairly just the same as anyone else; and are just as subject to control by the courts. If the firemen's disciplinary tribunal were to hold an order to be a lawful order, when it was not, I am sure that the courts could interfere; or, if it proceeded contrary to the rules of natural justice in a matter of serious import, so also the courts could interfere. But, as in this case, the order was lawful and the tribunal will, I have no doubt, do what is just, there is no ground whatever for interfering.

Conclusion

We have considered here the fireman. Like principles apply to ambulance men and police officers. The law, if taken by the letter of it, says that they are not to shoot the lights when they are at red. But the public interest may demand that, when all is clear, they should follow the precedent set by Lord Nelson. If they should do so, no man should condemn them. Their chief officer says that he will not punish them. Nor should the justices. Now that we in this court support what the chief officer has done, it means that, in point of practice, we have grafted an exception on to the strictness of the law so as to mitigate the rigour of it. It may now truly be said that firemen, ambulance men and police officers are to be excused if they shoot the lights when there is no risk of a collision and the urgency of the case so demands. The courts of the United States have done somewhat similar, but on rather special grounds: *Lilly v State of West Virginia* ((1928) 29 Fed. Rep. (2nd Ser.) 61). We do it on practical grounds but none the worse for that.

Should the law be amended so that there is not even a technical breach? I think that it should. By making it an offence without exception, Parliament has opened the way to endless discussion in fire stations which should be brought to a close. I hope that our judgment today will do something to end them. But Parliament can do it better.

I would dismiss this appeal.

QUESTIONS

1. What question(s) of law arose in this case?
2. Is a court the most appropriate body to determine questions of this sort? What other persons or bodies could have taken action which would have

had the result that the issue was not left to be settled by a court? Which in your opinion was the most appropriate body for solving the problem? Give reasons for your answers.

3. What did the case decide? Is it authority for the proposition that it is lawful for a fire-engine driver answering an emergency call to shoot the lights?
4. What reasons does Lord Denning MR give for his decision?
5. Write a comment on the judgment from the point of view of the Fire Brigade Union.
6. Lord Denning says: 'Thus by administrative action, backed by judicial decision, an exemption is grafted on to the law'; later, he refers to Parliament 'making it an offence without exception'. What, if anything, is the difference between an exception and an exemption in this context?
7. In 1975 the following exception to the normal rule that traffic must stop at a red light was introduced (see the Traffic Signs Regulations and General Directions 1994 (SI 1994/1519), reg 34(1)(b)):

> '(a) ... the red signal shall convey the prohibition that vehicular traffic shall not proceed beyond the stop line ...
> (b) on an occasion when a vehicle is being used for fire brigade, ambulance or police purposes and the observance of the prohibition conveyed by the red signal as provided by the last preceding sub-paragraph would be likely to hinder the use of that vehicle for the purpose for which it is being used on that occasion, then the said sub-paragraph shall not apply to that vehicle; but instead the prohibition conveyed to that vehicle by the red signal shall be that that vehicle shall not proceed beyond the stop line, or as the case may be as provided by the said sub-paragraph, beyond the signals in such a manner or at such a time –
>> (i) as is likely to cause danger to the driver of any other vehicle proceeding on or from another road or on or from another part of the same road in accordance with the indication of the light signals operating there in association with the said red signal or as to necessitate the driver of any other such vehicle to change its speed or course in order to avoid an accident, or
>> (ii) in the case of any traffic which is not vehicular, as is likely to cause danger to that traffic proceeding on or from another road or on or from another part of the same road.'

7.1 What considerations do you think were relevant to the decision to allow this exception?
7.2 Do the terms of the exception meet the Union's difficulty as expressed in *Buckoke v Greater London Council?*
7.3 Can you think of any devices other than creating this exception which would achieve the same objectives?
8. Is it paradoxical to talk of lawful departures from legal rules? See *IRC v National Federation of Self-Employed and Small Businessmen Ltd* [1982] AC 617, and MR Kadish and SH Kadish, *Discretion to Disobey* (1973).
9. *Buckoke v Greater London Council* addresses the question of necessity as a defence to a criminal prosecution. Does the decision offer any defence to a person who, though uninsured, (a) takes over the wheel when the driver suffers a heart attack, (b) is hijacked by criminals and threatened that if she

does not drive the car, her child who is also in the car will be injured by them? (See further N Lacey and C Wells, *Reconstructing Criminal Law* (2nd edn,1998), pp 313-325.)

9   *Donoghue v Stevenson* [1932] AC 562 (House of Lords)

Donoghue v Stevenson is one of the most famous cases in the common law. It is frequently used to illustrate points about matters that fall within the compass of this book. It is thus a useful link with the existing literature on a number of topics. It also provides a good illustration of many other relevant points to which less attention has been paid in the past. Because of pressure of space, we have not been able to reproduce the two speeches of Lord Buckmaster and Lord Atkin in their entirety. We have selected certain passages from the report, which are extensively referred to, especially in chapter 9, in order to illustrate at this stage some of the fundamental aspects of rules extracted from judicial decisions, notably the notion of a 'ladder of abstraction' and techniques for handling precedents. It is important that you study the extracts below closely; in particular, compare the level of generality at which the facts, the issue and the decision of the case are stated in the different extracts. Law students are recommended to study the two speeches intact in the law reports.

> By an action brought in the Court of Session the appellant, who was a shop assistant, sought to recover damages from the respondent, who was a manufacturer of aerated waters, for injuries she suffered as a result of consuming part of the contents of a bottle of ginger-beer which had been manufactured by the respondent, and which contained the decomposed remains of a snail. The appellant by her condescendence averred that the bottle of ginger-beer was purchased for the appellant by a friend in a café at Paisley, which was occupied by one Minchella, that the bottle was made of dark opaque glass and that the appellant had no reason to suspect that it contained anything but pure ginger-beer; that the said Minchella poured some of the ginger-beer out into a tumbler, and that the appellant drank some of the contents of the tumbler; that her friend was then proceeding to pour the remainder of the contents of the bottle into the tumbler when a snail, which was in a state of decomposition, floated out of the bottle; that as a result of the nauseating sight of the snail in such circumstances, and in consequence of the impurities in the ginger-beer which she had already consumed the appellant suffered from shock and severe gastro-enteritis. The appellant further averred that the ginger-beer was manufactured by the respondent to be sold as a drink to the public (including the appellant); that it was bottled by the respondent and labelled by him with a label bearing his name; and that the bottles were thereafter sealed with a metal cap by the respondent. She further averred that it was the duty of the respondent to provide a system of working his business which would not allow snails to get into his ginger-beer bottles and that it was also his duty to provide an efficient system of inspection of the bottles before the ginger-beer was filled into them, and that he had failed in both these duties and had so caused the accident. ...

> 1932. May 26, *Lord Buckmaster* (dissenting). My Lords, the facts of this case are simple. On August 26, 1928, the appellant drank a bottle of ginger-beer, manufactured by the respondent which a friend had bought from a retailer and

given to her. The bottle contained the decomposed remains of a snail which were not, and could not be, detected until the greater part of the contents of the bottle had been consumed. As a result she alleged, and at this stage her allegations must be accepted as true, that she suffered from shock and severe gastro-enteritis. She accordingly instituted the proceedings against the manufacturer which have given rise to this appeal.

The foundation of her case is that the respondent, as the manufacturer of an article intended for consumption and contained in a receptacle which prevented inspection, owed a duty to her as consumer of the article to take care that there was no noxious element in the goods, that he neglected such duty and is consequently liable for any damage caused by such neglect. After certain amendments, which are now immaterial, the case came before the Lord Ordinary, who rejected the plea in law of the respondent and allowed a proof. His interlocutor was recalled by the Second Division of the Court of Session, from whose judgment this appeal has been brought. ... [1932] A.C. 566.

Now the common law must be sought in law books by writers of authority and in judgments of the judges entrusted with its administration. The law books give no assistance, because the work of living authors however deservedly eminent, cannot be used as authority, though the opinions they express may demand attention; and the ancient books do not assist. I turn, therefore to the decided cases to see if they can be construed so as to support the appellant's case. One of the earliest is the case of *Langridge v Levy* ((1837) 2 M. & W. 519). It is a case often quoted and variously explained. There a man sold a gun which he knew was dangerous for the use of the purchaser's son. The gun exploded in the son's hands, and he was held to have a right of action in tort against the gunmaker. How far it is from the present case can be seen from the judgment of Parke B., who, in delivering the judgment of the Court, used these words: 'We shall pause before we make a precedent by our decision which would be an authority for an action against the vendors, even of such instruments and articles as are dangerous in themselves at the suit of any person whomsoever into whose hands they might happen to pass, and who should be injured thereby'. ... [Ibid, p 567.]

The case of *Langridge v Levy* therefore, can be dismissed from consideration with the comment that it is rather surprising it has so often been cited for a proposition it cannot support. [Ibid.]

The case of *Winterbottom v Wright* ((1842) 10 M. & W. 109) is on the other hand, an authority that is closely applicable. Owing to negligence in the construction of a carriage it broke down, and a stranger to the manufacture and sale sought to recover damages for injuries which he alleged were due to negligence in the work, and it was held that he had no cause of action either in tort or arising out of contract. This case seems to me to show that the manufacturer of any article is not liable to a third party injured by negligent construction, for there can be nothing in the character of a coach to place it in a special category. It may be noted, also, that in this case Alderson B. said: 'The only safe rule is to confine the right to recover to those who enter into the contract, if we go one step beyond that, there is no reason why we should not go fifty. ... [Ibid., p 568.]

Of the remaining cases, *George v Skivington* ((1869) L.R. 5 Ex. 1) is the one nearest to the present, and without that case, and the statement of Cleasby B. in *Francis v Cockrell* ((1870) L.R. 5 Q.B. 501), and the dicta of Brett M.R., in *Heaven v Pender* ((1883) 11 Q.B.D. 503), the appellant would be destitute of authority. *George v Skivington* related to the sale of a noxious hairwash, and a claim made by a person who had not bought it but who had suffered from its use, based on its having been negligently compounded, was allowed. It is remarkable that *Langridge v Levy* was used in support of the claim and influenced the judgment of all the parties to the decision. Both Kelly C.B. and Pigott B. stressed the fact that the article had been purchased to the knowledge of the defendant for the use of the plaintiff, as in *Langridge v Levy*, and Cleasby B., who, realizing that *Langridge v Levy* was decided on the ground of fraud, said: 'Substitute the word "negligence" for "fraud" and the analogy between *Langridge v Levy* and this case is complete.' It is unnecessary to point out too emphatically that such a substitution cannot possibly be made. No action based on fraud can be supported by mere proof of negligence.

I do not propose to follow the fortunes of *George v Skivington*; few cases can have lived so dangerously and lived so long. Lord Sumner, in the case of *Blacker v Lake & Elliot Ltd* ((1912) 106 L.T. 533) closely examines its history, and I agree with his analysis. He said that he could not presume to say that it was wrong, but he declined to follow it on the ground which is, I think, firm that it was in conflict with *Winterbottom v Wright*. [Ibid, p 570.]

Lord Atkin. My Lords, the sole question for determination in this case is legal: Do the averments made by the pursuer in her pleading, if true, disclose a cause of action? I need not restate the particular facts. The question is whether the manufacturer of an article of drink sold by him to a distributor, in circumstances which prevent the distributor or the ultimate purchaser or consumer from discovering by inspection any defect, is under any legal duty to the ultimate purchaser or consumer to take reasonable care that the article is free from defect likely to cause injury to health. I do not think a more important problem has occupied your Lordships in your judicial capacity: important both because of its bearing on public health and because of the practical test which it applies to the system under which it arises. ... [Ibid, p 579.]

At present I content myself with pointing out that in English law there must be, and is, some general conception of relations giving rise to a duty of care, of which the particular cases found in the books are but instances. The liability for negligence, whether you style it such or treat it as in other systems as a species of 'culpa', is no doubt based upon a general public sentiment of moral wrongdoing for which the offender must pay. But acts or omissions which any moral code would censure cannot in a practical world be treated so as to give a right to every person injured by them to demand relief. In this way rules of law arise which limit the range of complainants and the extent of their remedy. The rule that you are to love your neighbour becomes in law, you must not injure your neighbour; and the lawyer's question, Who is my neighbour? receives a restricted reply. You must take reasonable care to avoid acts or omissions which you can reasonably foresee would be likely to injure your neighbour. Who, then in law is my neighbour? The answer seems to be – persons who are so closely and directly affected by my act that I ought reasonably to have them in contemplation as being so affected when I am directing my mind to the acts or omissions which are called in question. ... [Ibid, p 580.]

There will no doubt arise cases where it will be difficult to determine whether the contemplated relationship is so close that the duty arises. But in the class of case now before the Court I cannot conceive any difficulty to arise. A manufacturer puts up an article of food in a container which he knows will be opened by the actual consumer. There can be no inspection by any purchaser and no reasonable preliminary inspection by the consumer. Negligently, in the course of preparation, he allows the contents to be mixed with poison. It is said that the Law of England and Scotland is that the poisoned consumer has no remedy against the negligent manufacturer. If this were the result of the authorities, I should consider the result a grave defect in the law. ... [Ibid, p 582.]

There are other instances than of articles of food and drink where goods are sold intended to be used immediately by the consumer, such as many forms of goods sold for cleaning purposes, where the same liability must exist. The doctrine supported by the decision below would not only deny a remedy to the consumer who was injured by consuming bottled beer or chocolates poisoned by the negligence of the manufacturer, but also to the user of what should be a harmless proprietary medicine, an ointment, a soap, a cleaning fluid or cleaning powder. I confine myself to articles of common household use, where every one, including the manufacturer knows that the articles will be used by other persons than the actual ultimate purchaser – namely, by members of his family and his servants, and in some cases his guests. I do not think so ill of our jurisprudence as to suppose that its principles are so remote from the ordinary needs of civilized society and the ordinary claims it makes upon its members as to deny a legal remedy where there is so obviously a social wrong. [Ibid, p 583.]

It now becomes necessary to consider the cases which have been referred to in the Courts below as laying down the proposition that no duty to take care is owed to the consumer in such a case as this.

In *Winterbottom v Wright* it is to be observed that no negligence apart from breach of contract was alleged – in other words, no duty was alleged other than the duty arising out of the contract; it is not stated that the defendant knew, or ought to have known, of the latent defect. The argument of the defendant was that, on the face of the declaration, the wrong arose merely out of the breach of a contract, and that only a party to the contract could sue. The Court of Exchequer adopted that view, as clearly appears from the judgments of Alderson and Rolfe BB. There are dicta by Lord Abinger which are too wide as to an action of negligence being confined to cases of breach of a public duty. The actual decision appears to have been manifestly right; no duty to the plaintiff arose out of the contract; and the duty of the defendant under the contract with the Postmaster-General to put the coach in good repair could not have involved such direct relations with the servant of the persons whom the Postmaster-General employed to drive the coach as would give rise to a duty of care owed to such servant. ... [Ibid, pp 587-589.]

My Lords, if your Lordships accept the view that this pleading discloses a relevant cause of action you will be affirming the proposition that by Scots and English law alike a manufacturer of products, which he sells in such a form as to show that he intends them to reach the ultimate consumer in the form in which they left him with no reasonable possibility of intermediate examination, and with the knowledge that the absence of reasonable care in the preparation or putting up of the products will result in an injury to the consumer's life or property, owes a duty to the consumer to take that reasonable care.

It is a proposition which I venture to say no one in Scotland or England who was not a lawyer would for one moment doubt. It will be an advantage to make it clear that the law in this matter, as in most others, is in accordance with sound common sense. I think that this appeal should be allowed. [Ibid, p 599.]

Appeal allowed.

QUESTIONS

1. From a non-legal point of view, do you think that the plaintiff should have been able to recover in this case if her allegations were true? Why?
2. Which judge was more 'legalistic' – Lord Atkin or Lord Buckmaster?
3. Which is the most appropriate way of describing the respondent (original defendant) in this case:
   3.1 a Scottish manufacturer of ginger-beer in opaque bottles;
   3.2 a manufacturer of aerated water;

3.3 a manufacturer of consumable products (food or drink);

3.4 a manufacturer of products;

3.5 a person who, in the course of trade, puts goods into circulation;

3.6 a person who puts into circulation a potentially harmful item;

3.7 a neighbour, that is to say a person who could reasonably have foreseen that persons in the position of the plaintiff could have been directly affected by any act or omission on his (the defendant's) part which was likely to cause injury?

Are any of the above descriptions inaccurate or untrue?

4. The questions in question 3 contain an example of 'a ladder of abstraction', that is to say a continuous sequence of categorisations from a low level of generality up to a high level of generality. Construct a ladder of abstraction in respect of the object that caused the harm in *Donoghue v Stevenson*.

5. Do we know from the report of the case whether the facts alleged by the appellant (pursuer) were historically true?

6. What were the material facts of *Donoghue v Stevenson*? What are the differences between the following formulations? What differences are *material*?

6.1 There were two neighbours and one injured the other by negligent conduct.

6.2 A Scottish shop assistant (in Paisley) received as a gift from a male friend an opaque glass bottle, which was closed by a metal cap, and which contained ginger-beer and a decomposing snail. The bottle was manufactured in a factory of a Scottish manufacturer of aerated water. The presence of the snail was attributed to carelessness on the part of the manufacturer or his employees. There was no contractual relationship between the Scottish manufacturer and the shop assistant.

6.3 An article of drink was sold by the manufacturer to a distributor in circumstances which prevented the distributor and the ultimate purchaser and consumer from discovering by inspection, a defect which was likely to and did in fact cause injury to the health of the ultimate consumer. The manufacturer had failed to take reasonable care to prevent the defect.

6.4 A manufacturer of products sold a product in such a form as to show that he intended it to reach the ultimate consumer in the form in which it left him, with the knowledge that the absence of reasonable care in the preparation or putting up of the products would result in injury to the consumer's life or property. The manufacturer failed to take reasonable care, and injury resulted to the ultimate consumer.

7. Which, if any, of the formulations in 6.1-6.4 did Lord Atkin consider to be the most precise statement of the material facts? Give reasons for your answer.

10 Rules, principles and other norms

As part of their efforts to give an adequate account of what makes legal decision-making authoritative, modern legal theorists have sought answers to two questions concerning rules and such other forms of normative prescription as principles. The first concerns the differences between the two, while the second concerns the implications that these differences have for such an account. The views of one influential writer, Ronald Dworkin, are discussed in more detail in chapter 3, pp 125-127 below. As a way of introducing some of the issues which these questions raise, we give in this section first some examples of what might be regarded as propositions on the borderline between rules and principles. This is followed by a series of extracts concerning human rights and fundamental freedoms, classically one of the areas of legal and moral discourse where discussion of the relationship between rules and principles is of the first importance.

10.1 Principles and maxims

In the Preface to the First Edition of *A Selection of Legal Maxims* (1845), Herbert Broom wrote (at p v):

> In the Legal Science, perhaps more frequently than in any other, reference must be made to first principles. Indeed, a very limited acquaintance with the earlier Reports will show the importance which was attached to the acknowledged Maxims of the Law, in periods when civilization and refinement had made comparatively little progress. In the ruder ages, without doubt, the great majority of questions respecting the rights, remedies, and liabilities of private individuals were determined by an immediate reference to such Maxims, many of which obtained in the Roman Law, and are so manifestly founded in reason, public convenience, and necessity, as to find a place in the code of every civilized nation. In more modern times, the increase of commerce, and of national and social intercourse, has occasioned a corresponding increase in the sources of litigation, and has introduced many subtleties and nice distinctions, both in legal reasoning and in the application of legal principles, which were formerly unknown. This change, however, so far from diminishing the value of simple fundamental rules, has rendered an accurate acquaintance with them the more necessary, in order that they may be either directly applied, or qualified, or limited, according to the exigencies of the particular case, and the novelty of the circumstances which present themselves. If, then, it be true, that a knowledge of first principles is at least as essential in Law as in other sciences, certainly in none is a knowledge of those principles, unaccompanied by a sufficient investigation of their bearing and practical application, more likely to lead into grievous error. In the present Work I have endeavoured, not only to point out the most important Legal Maxims, but also to explain and illustrate their meaning; to show the various exceptions to the rules which they enunciate, and the qualifications which must be borne in mind when they are applied.

One of the maxims Broom included in this work was '*cessante ratione, cessat ipsa lex*' (below, pp 190-194). Another set of maxims are those known as 'the maxims of equity'. These are set out as follows in *Snell's Principles of Equity* (28th edn by P Baker and P Langan, 1982):

1. Equity will not suffer a wrong to be without a remedy.
2. Equity follows the law.
3. Where there is equal equity, the law shall prevail.
4. Where the equities are equal, the first in time shall prevail.
5. He who seeks equity must do equity.
6. He who comes into equity must come with clean hands.
7. Delay defeats equities.
8. Equality is equity.
9. Equity looks to the intent rather than to the form.
10. Equity looks on that as done which ought to be done.
11. Equity imputes an intention to fulfil an obligation.
12. Equity acts *in personam.*

To these we might add such other propositions as, 'no man shall profit from his own wrong', 'the neighbour principle', 'promises should be kept' and so-called 'principles' of statutory interpretation.

10.2   Family Law Act 1996, section 1

Section 1 of the Family Law Act 1996 provides:

> The court and any person, in exercising functions under or in consequence of Parts II and III, shall have regard to the following general principles-
> (a) that the institution of marriage is to be supported;
> (b) that the parties to a marriage which may have broken down are to be encouraged to take all practicable steps, whether by marriage counselling or otherwise, to save the marriage;
> (c) that a marriage which has irretrievably broken down and is being brought to an end should be brought to an end-
> > (i) with the minimum distress to the parties and to the children affected;
> > (ii) with questions dealt with in a manner designed to promote a good continuing relationship between the parties and any children affected as is possible in the circumstances; and
> > (iii) without costs being unreasonably incurred in connection with the procedures to be followed in bringing the marriage to an end; and
> (d) that any risk to one of the parties to a marriage, and to any children, of violence from the other party should, so far as reasonably practicable, be removed or diminished.

QUESTIONS

1. What is the difference, if any, between a rule, a maxim and a principle?
2. Give examples of:
    2.1 a maxim that is not a principle;
    2.2 a rule that is not a maxim;
    2.3 a principle that is not a rule.
3. What is the significance of the phrase 'general principles' in section 1 of the Family Law Act 1996? Could the same effect be achieved by the use of different words?

10.3   Human rights and freedoms

10.3.1   Universal Declaration of Human Rights

Article 3: Everyone has the right to life, liberty and security of person.

Article 5: No one shall be subjected to torture or to cruel, inhuman or degrading treatment or punishment.

Article 9: No one shall be subjected to arbitrary arrest, detention or exile.

Article 10: Everyone is entitled in full equality to a fair and public hearing by an independent and impartial tribunal, in the determination of his rights and obligations and of any criminal charge against him.

Article 11:
1. Everyone charged with a penal offence has the right to be presumed innocent until proved guilty according to law in a public trial at which he has had all the guarantees necessary for his defence.
2. No one shall be held guilty of any penal offence on account of any act or omission which did not constitute a penal offence, under national or international law, at the time when it was committed. Nor shall a heavier penalty be imposed than the one that was applicable at the time the penal offence was committed.

10.3.2   Constitution of the United States, 8th Amendment

Excessive bail shall not be required, nor excessive fines imposed, nor cruel and unusual punishments inflicted.

10.3.3   European Convention on Human Rights and Fundamental Freedoms (1950)

Article 3: No one shall be subjected to torture or to inhuman or degrading treatment or punishment.

Article 5:
(1) Everyone has the right to liberty and security of person. No one shall be deprived of his liberty save in the following cases and in accordance with a procedure prescribed by law:
(a) the lawful detention of a person after conviction by a competent court;
(b) the lawful arrest or detention of a person for non-compliance with the lawful order of a court or in order to secure the fulfilment of any obligation prescribed by law;
(c) the lawful arrest or detention of a person effected for the purpose of bringing him before the competent legal authority on reasonable suspicion of having committed an offence or when it is reasonably considered necessary to prevent his committing an offence or fleeing after having done so;
(d) the detention of a minor by lawful order for the purpose of bringing him before the competent legal authority;
(e) the lawful detention of persons for the prevention of the spreading of infectious disease, of persons of unsound mind, alcoholics or drug addicts or vagrants;
(f) the lawful arrest or detention of a person to prevent his effecting an unauthorized entry into the country or of a person against whom action is being taken with a view to deportation or extradition.
(2) Everyone who is arrested shall be informed promptly, in a language which he understands, of the reasons for his arrest and of any charge against him.

(3) Everyone arrested or detained in accordance with the provisions of paragraph 1(c) of this Article shall be brought promptly before a judge or other officer authorized by law to exercise judicial power and shall be entitled to trial within a reasonable time or to release pending trial. Release may be conditioned by guarantees to appear for trial.

(4) Everyone who is deprived of his liberty by arrest or detention shall be entitled to take proceedings by which the lawfulness of his detention shall be decided speedily by a court and his release ordered if the detention is not lawful.

(5) Everyone who has been the victim of arrest or detention in contravention of the provisions of this Article shall have an enforceable right to compensation.

Article 15

(1) In time of war or other public emergency threatening the life of the nation any High Contracting Party may take measures derogating from its obligations under this Convention to the extent strictly required by the exigencies of the situation, provided that such measures are not inconsistent with its other obligations under international law.

(2) No derogation from Article 2, except in respect of deaths resulting from lawful acts of war, or from Articles 3, 4 (paragraph 1) and 7 shall be made under this provision.

10.3.4   *The Human Rights Act 1998*

This Act incorporates into the law of the United Kingdom certain of the rights contained in the European Convention on Human Rights: Articles 2 to 12 and 14 of the Convention; Articles 1 to 3 of the First Protocol, and Articles 1 and 2 of the Sixth Protocol, as read with Articles 16 to 18 of the Convention. Amongst other matters, it imposes obligations on those interpreting legislation to do so in a way which is compatible with these Convention rights, and creates a procedure whereby legislation may be amended by order in the event that it is found to be incompatible with such rights. These matters will be discussed in Chapters 7 and 8.

QUESTIONS

1. Article 3 of the European Convention is said to be an 'absolute prohibition' in that it makes no provision for exceptions and it is not subject to derogation 'in time of war or other public emergency threatening the life of the nation' (Article 15). In what sense is it 'absolute'?
2. Would the *scope* of Article 3 be different if it were amended to read:
   (a) 'No one shall be subjected to inhuman or degrading treatment or punishment';
   (b) 'No one shall be subjected to inhuman treatment or punishment';
   (c) 'No one shall be subjected to inhuman treatment'.
3. Would these amendments alter the *meaning* or the *substance* of Article 3? If so, in what respect(s)?
4. Is it possible to distinguish between what counts as 'torture' under Article 3 and what morally counts as 'torture'?
5. Could Article 3 be expressed without resort to emotive terms?
6. Which of the following do you consider are violations of Article 3:
   6.1 In a small jail on an otherwise desert island in the tropics, a prisoner, guarded by a single jailer, is found to have died of thirst. A committee of

enquiry established to investigate the reason for the death set out to test four alternative hypotheses (there could, of course, be many others):
   (a) that the jailer deliberately withheld water from the prisoner for sadistic reasons;
   (b) that the jailer deliberately withheld water in order to coerce the prisoner to do or say something, for example to reveal the whereabouts of a cache of buried treasure;
   (c) that the jailer was either reckless or negligent in failing to provide the prisoner with water, for example he went on a binge for three days and forgot all about him;
   (d) that the jailer died and no one else was available to bring water to the prisoner.
6.2 As a part of certain kinds of military training, 'volunteers' are subjected to severe and realistic 'interrogation in depth', allegedly in order to teach them how to resist torture if they are captured by the enemy.
6.3 A prisoner or mental patient was so violent that the only feasible means of controlling him was to manhandle him, strip him and keep him in a straitjacket for a substantial period. It was found as a matter of fact that the means used were not disproportionate to the risks of not controlling him and that no other means was available. Is this (a) 'degrading'; (b) 'inhuman' treatment? If (b), does it follow from this that no means is 'inhuman' provided that it is proportionate to the end in question?
6.4 An adult mental patient is subjected to electric-shock treatment by doctors who believe that this will be for his own good. What arguments can be advanced for holding that this is not a violation of Article 3, if:
   (a) he has freely consented to the treatment?
   (b) his mental condition is such that it is certified by two psychiatrists that he is incapable of making a rational choice about his treatment?
   (c) the patient is a mentally retarded 7-year-old child?
   (d) the patient has refused consent?
   (e) the patient has been certified to be insane because of his deviant political beliefs?
7. The President of Xanadu, a benevolent despot dedicated to rule on utilitarian principles, decides to sign an international convention which contains an absolute prohibition against torture, etc. He signs, on the grounds that (a) the document will generally promote utility; (b) it is very unlikely that the conditions that he would consider justifying the use of torture will arise in practice; (c) any express exception incorporating these conditions would probably be abused by other signatories. Shortly after signing he is confronted with the following situation. The police capture a terrorist who informs them that unless some prisoners are released from jail within twelve hours, his colleagues will cause the explosion of a number of very powerful bombs situated so that the deaths of hundreds of people are virtually guaranteed. The terrorist indicates that he will tell the police of the whereabouts of the bombs, and how they may be defused, once he has a guarantee that the prisoners have been released. Considering this to be an extreme case, the President authorises the police to torture the terrorist so as to extract the information concerning the bombs. Later, terrorism becomes endemic and

the President is persuaded 'in the public interest' to set up a torture squad. Nevertheless, five years later he renews his support for the Convention. Has the President acted consistently as a utilitarian?

8. 'Torture is the systematic and deliberate infliction of acute pain in any form by one person on another, or on a third person, in order to accomplish the purpose of the first against the will or interest of the second.' (B Paskins, 'Torture and Philosophy', *Proceedings of the Aristotelian Society* (1978), p 169.) Is this definition entirely adequate as an elucidation of 'torture' in Article 3?

9. Consider the Eighth Amendment of the US Constitution and Article 3 of the European Convention, with regard to the following:
   9.1 capital punishment;
   9.2 corporal punishment of males (a) in prison, (b) in schools, (c) in the home;
   9.3 corporal punishment of females, as above;
   9.4 solitary confinement;
   9.5 castration of rapists after conviction for a second offence;
   9.6 imprisonment for life;
   9.7 imprisonment in an overcrowded and insanitary jail.

10. To what extent is it appropriate that such factors as local public opinion, religious tradition or political instability should be taken into account in determining the scope of Article 3 of the European Convention?

10.3.5   *The influence of a Constitution on private law*

Why has Irish negligence law placed so much emphasis on broad principle and so little on overt policy analysis? The explanation can surely be traced to the influence of the Constitution. The creative energies of the judges have been channeled into the development of constitutional jurisprudence.

The articulation of previously unenumerated personal rights and the attempt to harmonise these rights with each other and with the personal rights specified in the Constitution have encouraged the judiciary to resort to a rhetoric of general principle rather than to speak frankly of the underlying policy issues. The precedential force of decisions from the common law treasury has been grossly compromised. The Irish courts have sifted through the leading negligence cases from other jurisdictions and abstracted only the broad statements of principle, disdaining the adjectival clauses.

(From William Binchy, *Negligence in Ireland: The Unlikely Brew of Principle, Policy and Constitutional Torts*, unpublished paper, cited with permission of the author.)

10.3.6   *Conflicting claims to rights*

Let us take any typical conflict between claims to rights. A racist organization seeks to reserve a public hall for a meeting, and it is obvious that, if the meeting is held, there will be incitement to racial hatred and a danger of violence (we need not ask who will start it). The public authority which controls the hall, urged perhaps by the police, refuses to make the hall available. The racist organization then protests that it is being denied its right to free speech. The public authority counters that it has an obligation to preserve the right of minorities not to have hatred preached against them, and that the public has a right to be protected against outbreaks of violence. Here we have a very typical case of conflict between rights, comparable in all respects to the conflicts of duties discussed earlier ... Another instance is the well canvassed conflict between the right of a woman to dispose of her own body and the right of the foetus (or of the person whom the foetus would become) to life. In such conflicts both rights may be important *in general;* the problem is, which should be overridden in a particular case. Certainly, in the public meeting case, the right to freedom of speech is of great importance; but so are the other rights which conflict with it.

(From RM Hare, *Moral Thinking* (1981), p. 155, by permission of Oxford University Press.)

QUESTION

Does this passage suggest that there are no universal moral principles?

10.3.7   Medical treatment

Hare refers to the conflict between a woman's right to dispose of her own body and that of the foetus she is carrying to life. In *Re T (adult: refusal of medical treatment)* [1992] 4 All ER 649, a case in which a very seriously ill patient who claimed to be a Jehovah's Witness refused to give her consent to a blood transfusion considered clinically necessary to her survival, Lord Donaldson MR said (pp 652-653), 'An adult patient who, like Miss T suffers from no mental incapacity has an absolute right to choose whether to consent to medical treatment, to refuse it or to choose one rather than another of the treatments being offered. The only possible qualification is a case in which the choice might lead to the death of a viable foetus. That is not this case and, if and when it arises, the courts will be faced with a novel problem of considerable legal and ethical complexity. This right of choice is not limited to decisions which others might be regard as sensible. It exists notwithstanding that the reasons for making the choice are rational, irrational, unknown or even non-existent.'

Later that same year the question concerning the 'possible qualification' arose in an application by a health authority for a declaration to authorise a Caesarian section on a woman patient whose unborn child would undoubtedly die if such operation were not carried out. The mother had refused the operation on the ground that it conflicted with her religious beliefs. How would you decide as between the competing rights of the mother that she cannot lawfully be forced to undergo medical treatment to which she does not consent, and those of the unborn child to life? Does saying that the unborn child has a 'right' to life beg the question? See *Re F (in utero)* [1988] Fam 122; *Re S (adult: refusal of medical treatment)* [1992] 4 All ER 671 and *St George's Healthcare NHS Trust v S* [1998] 3 All ER 673.

11 Standpoint and role

11.1 A limerick

There was a young student from Ealing
Who got on a bus to Darjeeling
The sign on the door
Said 'Don't spit on the floor'
So he lay back and spat on the ceiling.

QUESTIONS

1. Write down in order of priority which three of the following propositions
   are closest to your initial reaction to this limerick:
   1.1 An above/below average limerick.
   1.2 There are no buses from Ealing to Darjeeling.
   1.3 What immature behaviour/clever boy!
   1.4 Why not spit out of the window?
   1.5 The wisest course is to ignore such behaviour.
   1.6 He has/has not violated the rule.
   1.7 An example of poor drafting.
   1.8 Why 'lay back'?
   1.9 What has this to do with law?
2. In respect of each proposition, who is the most likely person to make such
   a statement? In what context? See further W Twining 25 *Journal of Law and
   Society* (1998) 603, 613-615.

11.2 General

A car skids while cornering at a certain point, turns turtle, and bursts into flame.
From the car-driver's point of view, the cause of the accident was cornering too fast,
and the lesson is that one must drive more carefully. From the county surveyor's
point of view, the cause was a defective road surface, and the lesson is that one must
make skid-proof roads. From the motor-manufacturer's point of view, the cause was
defective design, and the lesson is that one must place the centre of gravity lower.

(From RG Collingwood, 'On the So-called Idea of Causation' (1937-8), *Proceedings
of the Aristotelian Society*, pp 85, 96.)

But the different meanings of the term 'law' are not the only source of difficulty in
discussions of the 'nature of law'. If we restrict the term to the body of authoritative
materials for guidance of judicial and administrative determination, it is possible
to look at those materials from more than one standpoint, and the answer to the
question, what is law? will depend much upon the standpoint from which it is asked.

There are at least six standpoints from which law in the sense of the body of
authoritative precepts may be looked at.

First is the standpoint of the lawmaker. He thinks of something that ought to be
done or ought not to be done and so of a command to do it or not to do it. ...

Second is the standpoint of the individual subject to the legal precept, who would
walk in the straight path of social conduct and wishes it charted for him. If, instead

he is the bad man of whom Mr Justice Holmes speaks, who has no care for the straight path but wishes to know what path he may take with impunity, he will no doubt think of a legal precept as a threat. But the ordinary man who does not 'wash the idea in cynical acid' has more commonly thought of it as a rule of conduct, a guide telling him what he ought to do at the crisis of action. This is the oldest idea of a law. It goes back to the codified ethical custom of the earlier stages of legal development.

Another standpoint is that of a judge who has a case before him for decision or a ruling to make in the course of a trial; or that of an administrative official called upon to make some determination. Here the significant thing seems to be a body of authoritative grounds or models or patterns of decisions or of administrative determination.

Fourth, there is the standpoint of the counsellor at law or legal adviser, who would advise a client as to what he may do or may not do safely, or how he may act with assurance that courts and administrative officials will back him and further his quest of desired results. From this standpoint law may seem to be a body of threats of official action upon given states of fact, or it may seem to be a body of bases of prediction of official action. Even looked at in this way, however, it must be insisted that a law or a legal precept is not a prediction, as some realists deem it. It is the adviser not the law that does the predicting. As Mr Justice Cardozo pointed out a law or a legal precept is a basis of prediction.

Fifth, there is the standpoint of the jurist or teacher who is called on to put in the order of reason the materials recognized or established as the basis of decision or at hand for the counsellor, or provided for the guidance of the citizen or individual. He may find it hard to say that one of the foregoing aspects, as things are today, is more significant than another, or to find the more inclusive order which will enable him to fit a theory to all of these points of view. From his own special point of view he is likely to regard a law or a legal precept as a basis of development of doctrine.

Finally, there is the standpoint of the entrepreneur or man of business, which was taken at one time by writers on the nature of law but is less heard of today. From this standpoint legal precepts have been thought of as charts and legal conceptions as devices for the carrying out of business plans or carrying on of business enterprises.

It is submitted that the different ideas of a law, reached from these several standpoints, can be unified in terms of the idea from the standpoint of the judge. Judges and benches are expected to and for most practical purposes will follow and decide in accordance with the established precept or established starting point for legal reasoning developed by an authoritative technique. Hence, the precept or developed starting point may serve as a command or threat, or as a rule of conduct, or as a basis of prediction, and the legal conception may serve as a business device.

(Reprinted from R Pound, *II Jurisprudence* (1959), pp 129-132, with permission of the West Publishing Company.)

11.3   On punishment: utilitarians v retributionists

On the other hand we have the institution of punishment itself and recommend and accept various changes in it because it is thought by the (ideal) legislator and by those to whom the law applies that, as a part of a system of law impartially applied from case to case arising under it, it will have the consequence, in the long run, of furthering the interests of society.

One can say, then, that the judge and the legislator stand in different positions and look in different directions; one to the past, the other to the future. The justification of what the judge does, qua judge, sounds like the retributive view; the justification of what the (ideal) legislator does, qua legislator, sounds like the utilitarian view. Thus both views have a point (this is as it should be since intelligent and sensitive persons have been on both sides of the argument); and one's initial confusion disappears once one sees that these views apply to persons holding different offices with different duties, and situated differently with respect to the system of rules that make up the criminal law. ...

The answer, then, to the confusion engendered by the two views of punishment is quite simple: one distinguishes two offices, that of the judge and that of the legislator, and one distinguishes their different stations with respect to the system of rules which make up the law; and then one notes that the different sorts of considerations which would usually be offered as reasons for what is done under the cover of these offices can be paired off with the competing justifications of punishment. One reconciles the two views by the time-honoured device of making them apply to different situations.

But can it really be this simple? Well, this answer allows for the apparent intent of each side. Does a person who advocates the retributive view necessarily advocate, as an institution, legal machinery whose essential purpose is to set up and preserve a correspondence between moral turpitude and suffering? Surely not. What retributionists have rightly insisted upon is that no man can be punished unless he is guilty, that is, unless he has broken the law. Their fundamental criticism of the utilitarian account is that, as they interpret it, it sanctions an innocent person's being punished (if one may call it that) for the benefit of society.

(From J Rawls, 'Two Concepts of Rules' (1955), 64 *Philosophical Review*, 3, pp 6-7.)

11.4   The counsellor

He is not like the person pressing for legislation, who must often push out to the limit of the feasible and risk pushing beyond; in that area you get what you can get while the legislative getting is good. In sharp contrast, office-counsel can in all but rare circumstances play well inside any penumbra of doubt; he can work, like an engineer, with a substantial margin of safety; he can chart a course which leaves to others the shoal waters and the treacherous channels. For unlike the ordinary advocate, the counsellor need not take the situation as it comes, but can shape and shore it in advance; he can draft documents and set up lasting records against the accidents of memory, death or disappearance of witnesses, even to some extent against the hazard of bad faith – doubly so if he keeps his protective drafting within those bounds of reason which make a court want to give effect to manifest intent; trebly so if he sets a picture of situation and purpose which can appeal even to an outsider as sensible, reasonable, and inherently probable - and it is comforting how much of this last can be gotten by careful counsel into documentary form. Besides (or perhaps first), office-counsel are in a peculiarly good position to study and discriminate among rules and rulings with reference to how strong and solid any of them is, how much weight it will carry, how far the relevant type-situation is already at home in judicial understanding, or is of a character to find a ready welcome. After such discrimination, it is on the rocklike law-stuff that the sane counsellor does his building. Finally, wherever advising counsel can rely on being able to control any relevant litigation, another vital contingency is set to dwindling.

(From K Llewellyn, *The Common Law Tradition* (1960), p 383.)

11.5   The civil servant

1.   You are sitting at your desk granting licences on behalf of your Minister. Your enabling statutory powers are in the widest possible terms: 'The Secretary of State may grant licences upon such conditions as he thinks fit'. With power like that you might think that there could be no possible ground for legal challenge in the courts whatever you do. But you would be wrong.

2.   Scarcely a day passes without the *Times Law Reports* containing one or more cases where someone is challenging the decisions, or actions, of central or local government or a public body. There has been a considerable rise in the number of such challenges in recent years. The procedure by which such challenges are normally made is known as 'judicial review' and the law which the courts apply in such cases is known as administrative law. In 1974 there were only 160 applications for leave to seek judicial review. By 1985 the figure had grown to more than 1,230 and in the same year a similar procedure was introduced in Scotland. The increase is probably due in the main to the following factors:
*   The simplification of the judicial review procedure coupled with a requirement by the courts that this procedure rather than any other court procedure should be used.
*   'Nothing succeeds like success.' A few well publicised cases have alerted individuals and pressure groups to the possibilities of judicial review as a means of achieving their objective.
*   An increasing willingness on the part of the judiciary to intervene in the day-to-day business of government, coupled with a move towards an imaginative interpretation of statutes. ...

Who makes the decisions?

23.   In this pamphlet we have referred to 'the decision-maker' to cover as appropriate both the Minister or other person formally charged with making the decision and the official who will in fact have the conduct of the matter. The courts accept that Ministers cannot personally make every decision which bears their name. This is known as the *Carltona* principle from the leading case of that name. Thus the courts have held that where the relevant legislation provided that breathalysing apparatus had to be approved by the Secretary of State it was perfectly lawful for an Assistant Secretary in the Home Office to approve the apparatus on behalf of the Secretary of State. Whilst such 'vertical' delegation is perfectly lawful you must be careful to avoid delegating the decision-making to an outside body (and merely rubber-stamping that decision) or delegating the decision-making power to another department if yours is the department which ought to be making the decision.

Questions to ask yourself
*   Have you got the powers to do what you want to do? Are you merely adopting a particular statutory interpretation which happens to suit what you want to do?
*   Are you exercising the power for the purpose for which it was given?
*   Are you acting for the right reasons? Have you taken into account all relevant information and excluded irrelevant considerations?
*   You may not need to spell out the reasons for your decision but if you do are the reasons which you give the correct ones?
*   Will you hear and consider the point of view of people likely to be affected by the decision? Have they been put in the picture sufficiently so that they have a fair opportunity to make representations?

- Have you allowed in your timetable sufficient time for consultation and representation?
- Have you made up your mind in advance or given that impression, eg have you merely blindly followed departmental policy without considering the circumstances of the particular case? If you propose to follow a general policy in a particular case should you make it clear when communicating your decision that you have carefully considered the individual application to see whether it merited an exception being made?
- Have you or anyone involved in making the decision any conflicting interest which might lead someone to suppose that there is bias?
- Are there any grounds for thinking you might not be acting fairly? Have you led anyone to suppose that you will be acting differently from what is now intended?
- Has the decision-making been wrongly delegated?
- Do you propose to act in a way which a court may regard as abusing your power or generally so unreasonable that it is likely to find against you?

(From *The Judge Over Your Shoulder* (Treasury Solicitor's Department, 1987))

11.6   The Bad Man

Take the fundamental question, What constitutes the law? You will find some text writers telling you that it is something different from what is decided by the courts of Massachusetts or England, that it is a system of reason, that it is a deduction from principles of ethics or admitted axioms or what not, which may not coincide with the decisions. But if we take the view of our friend the Bad Man we shall find that he does not care two straws for the axioms or deductions, but that he does want to know what the Massachusetts or English courts are likely to do in fact. I am much of his mind. The prophecies of what the courts will do in fact, and nothing more pretentious, are what I mean by the law.

(From OW Holmes Jr, 'The Path of the Law', 10 *Harvard Law Review* (1897), pp 457, 460-461.)

11.7   The Bad Man and legal theory

Who is the bad man?

In the present context, the Bad Man is not a revolutionary nor even a reformer out to change 'the system'. The Bad Man's concern is to secure his personal objectives within the existing order as painlessly as possible; he is not so much alienated from the law as he is indifferent to all aspects which do not affect him personally. Unlike Sartre's Saint Genet, he is not one who has a problem of identity – who defines his being in terms of the system and who is driven to do acts *because* they are criminal or antisocial. Nor is he a subscriber to some perverse ethic which turns conventional morality upon its head. The Bad Man is amoral rather than immoral. He is, like Economic Man and Bentham's 'civilized' actors, a rational calculating creature. In this and in other respects he does not necessarily reflect in a realistic manner the characteristics of actual deviants. Like Dahrendorf's *homo sociologicus*, he 'can neither love nor hate, laugh nor cry. He remains a pale, incomplete, strange, artificial man.' Indeed, there appears to be no reason why the Bad Man should not be an artificial person, such as a corporation. In short, he is a theoretical construct with as yet unexplored potential as a tool of analysis.

A simple flow-chart: the Bad Man in Boston

Decision to seek professional advice before acting	Decision on what advice to give	Decision whether or not to act	Action; investigation; detection; apprehension	Decision to prosecute; decision on choice of charge (possible plea-bargaining)	Decision to plead guilty or not guilty	Miscellaneous decisions on tactics and procedure and on conduct of trial	Decisions on facts and law	Decision on sentence	Decision to appeal by losing party	Decision of appellate court	Miscellaneous post-conviction decisions
Bad Man (or Good Citizen)	'Counsellor'	Bad Man (or Good Citizen)	Miscellaneous participants	Prosecutor	Bad Man and professional adviser	Miscellaneous participants	Court (judge and possibly jury)	Court	Losing party and professional advisers	Appellate court	Miscellaneous participants

Note in regard to predictions: differences as to the base line for prediction, the range of events to be predicted, the part played by prediction in the various decisions.

Perhaps we can go a little further and suggest that the Bad Man can be defined in terms of prediction. He is the person whose only task is to predict what will happen to him if he embarks on some particular course of action. Here we may anticipate a possible objection. Although it may be granted that prediction is central to the role of the Bad Man, it is admitted that there are others who are similarly concerned – for example, the lawyer who has to decide whether it is worth appealing an adverse decision, the advocate who needs to predict how the personnel of a particular court will react to some line of argument or to the testimony of some witness, the judge who may wish to predict the likelihood of reversal on appeal or the possible effects of sending an offender to jail, the legislator who is concerned with the likely effects of a legal provision on patterns of behaviour. And the scientist – is he not also concerned with prediction?

A simple response is that, although these may all be valid observations, they are not objections to defining the Bad Man in terms of prediction. A comprehensive prediction theory would need to give a comprehensive answer to a question such as 'Who is concerned with predicting what events at what point in time for what purposes using what means?' With the exception of the scientist, whose standpoint raises special difficulties, all the other characters are predicting as part of some other task; for example, the advocate predicts in order to perform the task of persuasion. For some purposes it may be useful to isolate the task of predicting *simpliciter*, for other purposes prediction is more usefully seen as part of a cluster of tasks. In other words, the Bad Man is a device for isolating for special consideration the task of predicting certain kinds of events.

An alternative presentation

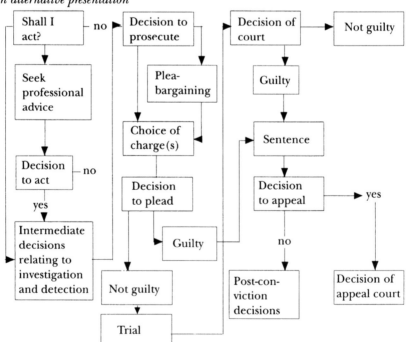

The idea of prediction provides no basis for distinguishing between the standpoints of the Good Citizen and of the Bad Man. It is not incompatible with good citizenship to be concerned with predicting the likely consequences of one's actions. The Bad Man, however, is affected by guidance as to his actions *only* insofar as such guidance predicts the ultimate consequences of those actions. Take, for example, the situation of a law-abiding individual seeking advice on his liability to pay income tax. If his conscience permits him to make a clear distinction between tax avoidance and tax evasion (as far as the law recognizes such a distinction), he may ask what lawful course of action will leave him with the most money. If he has a tender social conscience, he may reject certain kinds of lawful avoidance devices as immoral; nevertheless, he may wish to predict what his net income is likely to be. There may also be occasions when the Good Citizen can be said to have a moral duty to predict the likely consequences of his actions. The difference between the Bad Man and the Good Citizen does not rest on the latter's indifference to prediction, but on the former's indifference to morality. ...

Thus, the Bad Man has two characteristics: his badness and his citizenship. The distinction between law and morality is related to the former characteristic, the idea of prediction to the latter. When Holmes advised his audience to adopt the standpoint of the Bad Man, he was not seriously urging them to use the Bad Man as an ethical model; rather, he was suggesting that they look at law from the perspective of a citizen who is concerned with predicting the consequences of his actions. He was in effect saying that as intending private practitioners of law they should put themselves in the shoes of the legal adviser of citizens, good or bad. From that standpoint their main concern should be with prediction.

According to Holmes, the Bad Man is anxious to predict what the 'courts will do in fact'. Even if we allow that by 'do', Holmes refers not only to judicial decisions on questions of fact and law, but also to the sanctions courts are likely to impose, this still seems to be an unduly restrictive answer. Such a response reflects, perhaps, a court-centeredness on Holmes' part, with possible overtones of 'appellate court-itis'.

Suppose, for example, that our friend the Bad Man is in Boston (or Cambridge) wondering whether or not to do some specific act. He may ask, 'What are the chances that a Massachusetts court would hold this type of act to be criminal?' But this is only one of a series of questions pertinent to the decision whether or not to do the act. He needs to estimate the likelihood of the authorities discovering the commission of the act; how energetically, if at all, they are likely to investigate it and other matters related to detection and apprehension; if apprehended, whether there will be a decision to prosecute and, if so, the likelihood of conviction; the likely effect of pleading guilty or not guilty; and the probable nature of the sanction if he is convicted. If he wants to follow the total process through, the Bad Man may also need to consider a whole range of possible post-conviction decisions. The decisions of courts are merely a single phase in what Lasswell terms a 'flow of determinative activities' which go to make up the total process which may affect the Bad Man. And, of course, if one is talking about actual people who are in danger of being 'busted', not only do they need to predict a wider range of possible events, but they also need to perform tasks other than prediction. A comprehensive picture of legal process on the Holmesian model would take all of these considerations into account.

(From W Twining, 'The Bad Man Revisited', 58 *Cornell Law Review* (1973), pp 275, 280-283. See further, Twining, 'Other People's Power: the Bad Man and English Positivism.' 63 *Brooklyn Law Review* (1997), p 189.)

11.8 Users

In Esmeralda, city of water, a network of canals and a network of streets span and intersect each other. To go from one place to another you have always the choice between land and boat: and since the shortest distance between two points in Esmeralda is not a straight line but a zigzag that ramifies in tortuous optional routes, the ways that open to each passerby are never two, but many, and they increase further for those who alternate a stretch by boat with one on dry land.

And so Esmeralda's inhabitants are spared the boredom of following the same streets every day. And that is not all: the network of routes is not arranged at one level, but follows instead an up-and-down course of steps, landings, cambered bridges, hanging streets. Combining segments of the various routes, elevated or on ground level, each inhabitant can enjoy every day the pleasure of a new itinerary to reach the same places. The most fixed and calm lives in Esmeralda are spent without any repetition.

Secret and adventurous lives, here as elsewhere, are subject to greater restrictions. Esmeralda's cats, thieves, illicit lovers move along higher, discontinuous ways, dropping from a rooftop to a balcony, following gutterings with acrobats' steps. Below, the rats run in the darkness of the sewers, one behind the other's tail, along with conspirators and smugglers: they peep out of manholes and drainpipes, they slip through double bottoms and ditches, from one hiding place to another they drag crusts of cheese, contraband goods, kegs of gunpowder, crossing the city's compactness pierced by the spokes of underground passages.

A map of Esmeralda should include, marked in different coloured inks, all these routes, solid and liquid, evident and hidden. It is more difficult to fix on the map the routes of swallows, who cut the air over the roofs, dropping long invisible parabolas with their still wings, darting to gulp a mosquito, spiraling upward, grazing a pinnacle, dominating from every point of their airy paths all the points of the city.

(From I Calvino, *Invisible Cities* (1974), pp 88-89.)

11.9 The revolutionary

From a revolutionary's standpoint, there are a variety of strategies that could be adopted to achieve change, ranging from principled passivity in the face of state action through selective (tactical) use of non-violence, to the determined and regular use of violence. Another choice is whether to use the law which, as a representation of the state the revolutionary is committed to overthrow, whenever it offers opportunities to assist individuals to escape punishment for their revolutionary conduct.

Using law as a conventional legal defence

A conventional legal defense means using the facts and the law – technicalities, rules of evidence, Constitutional rights – to win a case. It can be used alone, or combined with a political defense. This approach is useful when a good plea bargain has not been offered or when you think you have a very good chance of winning. Legal technicalities have also been used to delay final judgment on a case until the political situation changed to the defendant's benefit. After the Columbia University busts, the defense lawyers stalled until the new University administration was appointed, which dropped the complaints against five hundred of the students. Using existing laws does tend to legitimate a legal system which we oppose. Asking the judge to enforce those laws on our behalf reinforces the myth that courts are neutral, and compliance with conventional courtroom procedures may add to the sanctity of the law. Nevertheless, at the present time, conventional legal defense does keep activists out of jail and free to organize.

(From K Boudin et al, *The Bust Book: What To Do Till The Lawyer Comes* (1969), pp 92-93.)

Violence or non-violence?

We also discussed whether the campaign should follow the Ghandian principles of non-violence or what the Mahatma called *satyagraha,* a non-violence that seeks to conquer through conversion. Some argued for non-violence on purely ethical grounds, saying it was morally superior to any other method.... Others said that we should approach this issue not from the point of view of principles but of tactics, and that we should employ the method demanded by the conditions. If a particular method or tactic enabled us to defeat the enemy, then it should be used. In this case, the state was more powerful than we, and any attempts at violence by us would be devastatingly crushed. This made non-violence a practical necessity rather than an option.

(From N Mandela, *Long Walk to Freedom* (1994, 1995) Abacus edn, pp 146-147.)

QUESTIONS

1. The word 'standpoint' is ambiguous. It is sometimes used to mean the same as 'role' or 'vantage point' or a special way of looking at things – 'from the standpoint of an economist or an historian'. How is the term used:
   1.1 in relation to the Bad Man?
   1.2 in the quotation from Pound?
   1.3 in the phrase 'from the standpoint of Father as Judge'?
2. In the passages from Collingwood and Rawls, are the various persons (eg the county surveyor and the manufacturer, the legislator and the judge) *disagreeing?* What do you think of the claim that clarification of standpoint is a useful device for disposing of unnecessary or imagined disagreements?
3. Analyse and differentiate the respective standpoints and roles of Mother, Johnny and Father in the *Case of the Legalistic Child.* Which role is the easiest, and which the hardest, to define?
4. One way of unpacking 'standpoint' is through a series of questions:
   'Who am I?'
   'At what stage in what process am I?'
   'What am I trying to do?'
   Comment on the following responses to the limerick in section 11.1, as an attempt to illustrate the meaning and significance of these questions for the purpose of legal theory:
   Q: Who am I?   A: A student from Ealing.
   Q: At what stage in what process am I?   A: Half way to Darjeeling.
   Q: What am I trying to do?   A: Spit!
5. Is the picture of the city of Esmeralda in section 11.8 analogous to a picture of a legal order from the standpoint of a tax consultant, Holmes' Bad Man, or other users?

12   Domestic violence: a case study

12.1   Introduction

The outline of the story is quite simple: largely because of the activities of and controversy surrounding Mrs Erin Pizzey and her associates in Chiswick during the early seventies, problems of domestic violence became a focus of public attention; consequently in 1974-75 a Select Committee on 'Violence in Marriage' was set up by the House of Commons. After only five months it submitted a Report (on violence in marriage), which was followed shortly afterwards by a private Member's Bill on Domestic Violence. During its passage through Parliament, the Bill was supported by the government, sections 1 and 2 being redrafted by the government draftsmen and introduced during the Committee stage. It was enacted in 1976 as the Domestic Violence and Matrimonial Proceedings Act 1976. Section 1, one of its important provisions, gave rise to problems of interpretation; it gave county courts jurisdiction, on the application of a spouse or cohabitee, to grant injunctions with respect to molestation and, most significantly, occupation of the matrimonial home. For a time many injunctions were granted to applicants to exclude the spouse or partner from the matrimonial home, notwithstanding that he or she was the owner or tenant.

Then in *B v B* the Court of Appeal held that this jurisdiction did not affect rights of property, with the result that this new remedy was only available in the rare case where the complainant, typically the woman, was the sole owner or occupier of the home, ie an injunction was not available to prevent the man from exercising his lawful rights to occupy the home. *B v B*, in the view of many, including the original supporters of the Bill, defeated the purpose of the Act. The decision in *B v B* was followed in *Cantliff v Jenkins* but challenged in *Davis v Johnson*. In this case a majority of the full Court of Appeal (five judges, an unusual occurrence in itself) refused to follow *B v B*, citing *inter alia* the report of the Select Committee and Hansard in support of their interpretation of the section. On appeal by the man, the House of Lords upheld the decision of the Court of Appeal on the specific issue but unanimously condemned both its interpretation of the doctrine of precedent and the use of Hansard and the Select Committee Report as aids to interpretation.

The story is relevant to our purposes for many reasons, the most important of which are as follows: first, this is a striking example of a split of opinion (8-8) by senior judges on the interpretation of a recent statute when the mischief that it was intended to remedy seemed clearly to indicate only one interpretation. The factors giving rise to this disagreement and the arguments which were advanced on each side are of interest, both at the level of technical detail and in respect of more general attitudes to statutory interpretation. Secondly, the Select Committee's Report is a particularly interesting example of some of the difficulties involved in defining, diagnosing and responding to social problems; it also illustrates some uses and limits of law-making in these processes. The particular legal provision which attracted so much attention was, at best, a very modest contribution to the partial alleviation of one aspect of 'the problem'. Yet this narrow remedy illustrates rather neatly how the relationship between narrowly defined 'social problems' and broader social conditions and issues is echoed, but not paralleled, by the relationship between a new piece of legislation and the existing fabric of the law. The problem of 'battered partners' is bound up with alcoholism, poor housing, and various kinds of social deprivation – among other things. The provision of even short-term relief for victims of domestic violence was thought by lawyers to have undesirable implications for the law of property. Thirdly, *Davis v Johnson* is a leading case on the doctrine of precedent and the use of extrinsic aids to interpretation; it is also a dramatic and historically important example of what was at the time a continuing conflict between the House of Lords and Lord Denning and some of his brethren in the Court of Appeal.

Since the House of Lords' decision in *Davis v Johnson* there have been a number of further judicial and statutory responses to the problems associated with domestic violence and the occupation of the matrimonial or shared home. The law at the time of writing is contained in Part IV of the Family Law Act 1996. Professor Michael Freeman's commentary in Current Law Statutes Annotated is a helpful summary of the social context of and legal background to the present remedies. Thus while there continue to be important developments concerning this issue, the utility of this case study as illustrative of some detailed points concerning the interpretation of cases and statutes and, more broadly, of judicial and legislative responses to social problems, remains compelling. Indeed, current discussions of the nature of domestic violence and of what constitute appropriate legal remedies display very similar features to those which characterised the discussions that preceded the Domestic Violence and Matrimonial Proceedings Act 1976.

12.2   Extracts from the Select Committee's Report

First Special Report from the Select Committee on Violence in Marriage, 1974-75 HC 533

The Select Committee appointed to consider the extent, nature and causes of the problems of families where there is violence between the partners or where children suffer non-accidental injury and to make recommendations have made progress in the matter to them referred, and have agreed to the following Report:-

...

4. Violence in marriage is a wide and difficult subject. It involves a whole range of issues: the general attitudes of men to women and vice versa, the attitudes of spouses to one another, basic causes of violence in general, alcohol, housing problems, the law and legal services, social services and facilities, psychiatric problems, emergency services, police and other attitudes and facilities, and many more. In five months of work we have not been able to find any easy solutions. They do not exist. We have therefore decided to make a short interim report, referring only to a few of the many aspects of the problems, and leaving the bulk of the evidence which we have received to speak for itself. We have done this simply because shortage of time and resources available to us prevented us from doing otherwise.

5. A general impression must be recorded at the outset. We have been disappointed and alarmed by the ignorance and apparent apathy of some Government Departments and individual Ministers towards the extent of marital violence. Hardly any worthwhile research into either causes or remedies has been financed by the Government. Responsibility is diversified between many Government Departments. No fewer than seven are concerned: the Home Office,

the Department of Health and Social Security, the Department of Education and Science, the Department of the Environment, the Lord Chancellor's Office, the Scottish Office and the Welsh Office. Only in a very few of these Departments does the problem of marital violence receive anything other than a very low priority either in terms of manpower or financial resources.

Definition

6. No two cases of violence between the partners in a marriage are the same. We recognize therefore that we are reporting on women in a wide variety of situations but with no single identifiable complaint with a known cure. If a definition is required, that proposed by a Committee of the Royal College of Psychiatrists is probably better than most: 'a battered wife is a woman who has suffered serious or repeated physical injury from the man with whom she lives' (Evidence, p. 100). The definition thus includes women who are cohabiting with men to whom they are not married (see para. 52). In using the word 'battered' in this Report we realize that physical violence is not necessarily any less tolerable than verbal or emotional assault, and that - particularly in the wider sense - men are 'battered' by women as well as vice versa. We will therefore be publishing as an example (as Appendix 5 to our evidence) one short letter from a husband who alleges that he has been battered. We believe, however, that we should concentrate on the problems of women, who form the vast majority of those physically battered. They are often with inadequate means and with dependent children, and in need of shelter or help or advice for themselves and their families.

The scale of the problem

7. Little indeed is known about how much violence in marriage there is, and whether or not it is increasing. What is clear is that the number of battered wives is large – much larger than may be thought – and that the demand for places in the refuges which have been opened reflects the pent up need. Several estimates, all on small samples, with inadequate information and using different definitions, have been made. For what it is worth, the Parliamentary Under-Secretary of State, Welsh Office, using the limited Colchester Study (Evidence, p. 101, para. 15) and other information, thought that there might be perhaps 5,000 battered wives in Wales each year, out of a figure of 680,000 married women (1971 census). Despite our efforts, we are unable to give any estimates of what the likely numbers are; several witnesses talked in terms of the tip of an iceberg, and this seems to us to be correct. Most witnesses agreed (and this is almost certainly correct) that all strata of society are involved, although the better-off are perhaps less likely to seek outside help in solving their problems (though they may be more ready to seek advice from solicitors). All witnesses were agreed, however, on the need for research on the scale of the problem as well as on causation and remedies (see para. 58).

The nature of the problem

8. Some people, including some in high places, still scorn the thought of a battered wife. Is it not a husband's right to beat her? Is it not her fault? Should she not just leave? Might she even enjoy being beaten? Such people should not forget that a large percentage of all known murders take place within the family setting: home is for many a very violent place. At least some of those murdered were maltreated wives who did not or could not leave in time.

9. We were presented with horrifying evidence of particular cases, and have no doubt that the physical injuries, often inflicted regularly over a period of many years, are very severe in many cases.

10. For example, a Mrs X gave oral evidence anonymously on 12th March. She was beaten frequently over a period of sixteen years before she left her husband. In her own words 'I have had ten stitches, three stitches, five stitches, seven stitches, where he has cut me'. 'I have had a knife stuck through my stomach; I have had a poker put through my face; I have no teeth where he knocked them all out; I have been burnt with red hot pokers; I have had red hot coals slung all over me; I have been sprayed with petrol and stood there while he has flicked lighted matches at me'. These assaults did not just take place when he was drunk, but 'at any time; early in the morning; late at night; in the middle of the night he would drag me out of bed and start hitting me, he would do it in front of the children. He never bothered if the children were there'. 'I have been to the police. I nicked my husband. He gave me ten stitches, and they held him in the nick over the weekend and he came out on Monday. He was bound over to keep the peace, that was all. On the Tuesday he gave me the hiding of my life'...

12. Perhaps as bad or even worse for the women than the physical violence are the loss of self confidence and self respect that are involved, the inability to understand what is happening, and the moral, emotional and economic problems inherent in a decision to do what appears best for their children, their menfolk and themselves. The evidence of Dr Gayford, a psychiatrist who is making a special study of the subject, and of those battered women who agreed to appear before us, was particularly moving and persuasive.

13. The practical problems of such women are never identical. Very often they include problems of homelessness, of finance, of the need for support from outside agencies and of protection by the law. What immediate steps can a woman take when she finds herself homeless and perhaps nearly penniless, with young children and perhaps in the middle of the night, as a result of domestic violence? What help and advice should be offered by the police, the local authorities and other agencies to her, to her children, to her husband? How much liaison should there be between those offering help and advice? What should be done to assist her in legal proceedings, if necessary, and in providing for her longer-term future, either back with her husband or alone in a one parent family? And what, if anything, can be done to reduce the likelihood of violence in the first place? We now attempt to deal with some aspects of these questions.

Causation

14. We have had no evidence that the husband alone is responsible for this violence. The behaviour of the wife is relevant. So, too, is the family's environment, their housing and employment conditions, their physical and mental health, their sexual relationship and many other factors. Very little research has been done and much more is certainly necessary. What has been done has been confined to small samples and usually without the husband's co-operation; it suggests however very clearly that those women who marry (and become pregnant) very young and after short or non-existent periods of courtship are particularly at risk, that drinking of alcohol may well trigger off or accentuate violence, and that children living in an environment of domestic violence may be predisposed to violence in their own adult lives. It is hard to distinguish between cause and effect, and to discover the causal relationship between psychiatric problems, heavy drinking, sexual difficulties, violence, inability to communicate, etc.

Prevention

15. The prevention of violence within marriage is as difficult as the prevention of violence in any other situation. Only when the causes of violence are better known and

understood will society be in a position to prevent it. Until that Utopia is reached not a great deal can be done to prevent a man from maltreating his wife initially. The law, however it is enforced, is unlikely to stop him, at least the first time (see paras. 42-53). Most violence has a complex origin and therefore attention to only one or two problems is unlikely to be sufficient to make very much impact on the overall problem. Even so we are prepared to recommend a 3-point plan for urgent consideration.

[16-18. The Committee recommends that formal instruction be given in school about the legal aspects of family life, that the Government pursue a vigorous publicity campaign against excessive consumption of alcohol, and that steps be taken to help identify children at risk.]

Alleviation

19. The programme for prevention is inevitably a long term one. However we are convinced that some immediate action can be taken to alleviate the problem. Before turning to the Finer Committee Report and to legal aspects (including police services), we make suggestions and recommendations under the following headings: 24-hour Advisory Services, Refuges, Housing, needs of the children, needs of the husbands, financial and other supporting services, and Medical Services.

24-hour advisory services

20. The crisis centres should have three primary roles. Firstly, they should provide an emergency service, hence the 24-hour requirement. This means they will need to develop very close liaison with the local medical, social, legal and police services. A very important link will be with the refuges which we are proposing below, to which they will refer women who need a place of safety. Secondly, they should be specially responsible for the coordination of the local arrangements already available to women and children in distress. We have been impressed by the fact that one of the prime problems for the family in stress is the need to consult with several different professionals, in different places, employed by different agencies, very often not relating together very effectively. A battered wife needs the advice and help of a police officer, a doctor, a health visitor, a lawyer, a housing department officer, a social security officer, a clergyman, a probation officer, a marriage guidance counsellor, a citizens advice bureau worker and a social worker, just to name the most obvious. The third and non-emergency role we see for the family crisis centres is the development of specialist advisory services, education and publicity programmes, group support and meetings for women with similar problems.

...

The law in England and Wales

42. We have already referred in para. 41 to the recommendations of the Finer Report on law reform. No laws, however well enforced, can prevent marital assaults. We consider however that improvement of the law can be of material assistance to the problem. If the criminal law of assault could be more uniformly applied to domestic assaults there seems little doubt that it would give some protection to the battered wife. If the enforcement of the civil law could be made more satisfactory a man who had beaten his wife once might well be prevented from repeating his crime. We consider this further in the following paragraphs together with the legal problems associated with the homelessness of one or other partner that often follows assault between them.

...

Injunctions

45. We accepted the evidence from women and lawyers that civil injunctions restraining husbands from assaulting their wives, or ordering husbands to leave and keep away from the matrimonial home, were on occasions 'not worth the paper they were written on', as the present enforcement procedure of applying for the man to be committed to prison was too slow adequately to protect the woman concerned. We therefore recommend that where a Judge grants an injunction either restraining the husband from assaulting his wife or ordering him to keep away from the matrimonial home, he should have power to grant a power of arrest if, from the evidence before him, he is satisfied that there has been an assault occasioning actual bodily harm and that there seems to be a likelihood that the wife is in continuing danger of assault. When serving the injunction on the man the solicitor would also serve a copy on the Superintendent of the local police station. This would confer power on the police to arrest the man should it appear that he has either entered (or attempted to enter) the matrimonial home when he has been ordered to keep away, or (where the injunction restrains the husband from assault) that he has committed an assault upon his wife or that there is immediate danger of assault. There would be a duty on the police to notify the solicitor of the arrest and the solicitor would be under a duty to find a Judge to deal with the alleged breach as soon as possible, with a specified time limit. Should the injunction be discharged the solicitor would notify the police concerned. We recognize the arguments against involving the police in civil law but consider this is the only way to make enforcement effective and that the problem of battered women is exceptional enough to require an exceptional remedy.

46. It would also be helpful if there were a general practice whereby solicitors should send copies of injunctions to the local police station so that the police would be aware of the position and more ready to assist should there be further trouble. When solicitors serve any injunction, if it is feared there may be a breach of the peace, it would assist if the police were ready to accompany solicitors and/or process servers.

47. It is not satisfactory that at present women have either to start divorce proceedings or judicial separation proceedings, or undertake to the court to do so, before they may obtain an injunction in the Family Division of the High Court or Divorce County Court. The only other present means of obtaining an injunction is by claiming one in the High Court in an action founded on assault: in the County Court damages must also be claimed for injury or loss occasioned by an assault. This is, to some extent, used by cohabitees who do not have access to the Divorce Courts, but is not used, according to the President of the Family Division, Sir George Baker, by married women (Evidence, 2nd July).

48. We were grateful for the information from Sir George Baker that consideration is being given to the Rules of the Supreme Court being amended to permit a woman, married or unmarried, to apply for an injunction by means of an Originating Summons setting out that she has suffered an assault occasioning actual bodily harm, without having first to start proceedings for divorce or judicial separation. We trust that there will be no delay in making this amendment, since no legislation is involved. We also note that present powers under the Matrimonial Homes Act 1967 to regulate occupation by the spouse do not permit the husband to be even temporarily excluded from the matrimonial home, and we consider it would partly solve this problem if the Act were amended to allow such exclusion.

Magistrates' courts

49. We would also wish to see better protection given to married women who apply in matrimonial proceedings to the Magistrates' Court. Whereas Divorce County Courts are often up to 20 or 30 miles from the towns which they serve and

in many areas Divorce Judges do not sit daily, Magistrates' Courts exist in most small towns and there are relatively few houses which are not within 5 miles of a Magistrates' Court. Most of these Courts sit frequently, 2 or 3 days weekly at least. Another factor which makes Magistrates' Courts more convenient than the County Court is that the procedure in the latter is rather cumbersome usually requiring Affidavits, and documentation in the Court Offices, all of which take some time. Generally it is only in cases where the solicitor is very familiar with this type of proceeding, and the danger has already been marked by actual injury, that injunctions will be made by the Higher Courts, when they can be made within 48 hours. We would wish to see the necessary procedure simplified, and we understand that this is already under consideration. In contrast no such documentation is required in the Magistrates' Court and where the wife is not seeking to end the marriage an immediate remedy, if immediate hearings could be made available, would often be provided more conveniently at the Magistrates' Court than in the Divorce County Court or High Court. We therefore also recommend that, as suggested by the Law Commission in its Working Paper No. 53, Magistrates are given power in matrimonial proceedings to make an injunction restraining the husband from assaulting the wife and, when necessary, temporarily excluding him from the matrimonial home. In addition, we recommend bringing the grounds for obtaining a matrimonial order in the Magistrates' Court into line with grounds for obtaining a divorce. Such a reform may well save public funds as some legal aid certificates for abortive divorce and solicitors' costs in preparing for divorce proceedings would be prevented if adequate relief of this nature was available in the Magistrates' Courts where costs are lower.

Cohabitees

52. We have not yet taken evidence relating particularly to the problem of cohabitees or common law wives, but we are aware that such women and their children are in a weaker position when they seek protection and financial relief. If the suggestion of Sir George Baker to amend the Rules of the Supreme Court to permit such women to claim an injunction in the Court is adopted their position would be somewhat improved. In addition we recommend that consideration is given to amending the Guardianship of Minors Act 1971 and 1973 so that when paternity is proved there is power, on application to the County Court or High Court, to settle any property occupied as a home. This power would enable the court to permit the parent caring for the children to have sole occupation of the property during their minority, so that a woman who is caring for the children could continue living with them in their former home, even if she had no legal interest in the property, after the breakdown of the relationship.

Access to the law

53. We consider that if the law as it stands was fully implemented, if police practice was improved as we recommend, if all lawyers advised their clients on all remedies available to matrimonial proceedings and took all necessary steps to obtain injunctions and were on hand to enforce any breach of such injunctions, and if in addition there was liaison between all the different agencies involved, the practical problems facing battered wives would be vastly decreased. We therefore recommend that serious attention be paid by all these agencies to instructing their personnel in the remedies available to battered women, and that in addition a referral list of solicitors willing to deal with such cases in each locality be held by the police and other agencies so that women can be referred to suitable solicitors to help them at an early stage. Women should also be informed of any refuge in their areas. If the system of having a solicitor

on hand at Magistrates' Courts to help defendants spreads, such a solicitor would be a suitable person to be able to tell women who came to the Court how to obtain the help they need. Many solicitors' offices are both intimidating to most women and inaccessible, not being in the areas in which they live, and usually only receiving clients on appointments days and sometimes weeks ahead. We consider that law centres are potentially admirably suited to deal with the emergency situation caused by domestic violence, being situated in the community with links with other agencies and flexible working hours, and we recommend that more law centres take on this type of work, if thought advisable transferring cases once the immediate emergency has been dealt with to local solicitors.

Summary of recommendations

Our recommendations are, in brief, as follows -
1. The Committee should be re-established very promptly in the next Session (para. 2);
2. Much more serious attention should be given within our school (and further education) system to the problems of domestic conflict (para. 16);
3. The Government should now introduce a vigorous publicity campaign against the excessive use of alcohol, and should formulate a positive policy on the advertisement of alcohol (para. 17);
4. As much as possible must be done to break the cycle of violence by attention to the welfare and special needs of vulnerable children (para. 18);
5. Each large urban area should have a well publicised family crisis centre open continuously (para. 20);
6. Specialized refuge facilities should be available very readily and rapidly (para. 21);
7. The application for grant from the National Women's Aid Federation should be sympathetically and urgently considered (para. 25);
8. Payments to Chiswick Women's Aid should continue temporarily (para. 25);
9. Legislation, if it is necessary, should be introduced as soon as possible to clarify the duty of local authorities to provide temporary accommodation for battered women who leave home (para. 26);
10. The Finer Report proposals on local authority and private tenancies of homes should be implemented at an early date (para. 28);
11. The Department of the Environment must ensure that more refuges are provided by local authorities and/or voluntary organisations (para. 29);
12. One family place per 10,000 of the population should be the initial target (para. 29);
13. Medical schools and nursing colleges should give special attention to the social dynamics of family life, and to the medical (both physical and psychiatric) correlates of marital disharmony (para. 40);
14. Consultations should continue between the Government and the local authorities to ascertain how far the Finer Committee recommendations can be implemented in the short term without an unacceptably high demand on financial resources (para. 41);
15. Chief Constables should review their policies about the police approach to domestic violence (para. 44);
16. Each police force should keep statistics about incidents of domestic violence, and these should be recorded separately in the National Statistics supplied by the Home Office (para. 44);
17. Where a Judge grants an injunction either restraining the husband from assaulting his wife or ordering him to keep away from the matrimonial home, he should have power to grant a power of arrest if he is satisfied that there has been an assault occasioning actual bodily harm and that there seems to be a likelihood that the wife is in continuing danger of assault (para. 45);

18. Magistrates should be given power in matrimonial proceedings to make an injunction restraining the husband from assaulting the wife and, when necessary, temporarily excluding him from the matrimonial home (para. 49);
19. The grounds for obtaining a matrimonial order in the Magistrates' Court should be brought into line with grounds for obtaining a divorce (para. 49);
20. The principle laid down in the case of *Bassett v Bassett* should be uniformly applied where wives apply for an order that their husbands be ordered to leave, and, when the wife is in danger, decisions should be reached swiftly to avoid her being homeless (para. 50);
21. Serious attention should be paid by all the agencies involved in instructing their personnel in the remedies available to battered women, and a referral list of solicitors willing to deal with such cases in each locality should be held by the police and other agencies (para. 53);
22. More law centres should deal with the emergency situation caused by domestic violence (para. 53);
23. The Scottish law of evidence should be amended in respect of assaults taking place between husband and wife in the matrimonial home (para. 55);
24. A Scottish divorce bill should be introduced in the next Session by the Government as a Government Bill (para. 57);
25. One or two crisis centres should be set up as action research projects (para. 58);
26. The Government should expedite a decision of principle as to whether to provide the finance recommended in this Report.
27. Conferences should be held up and down the country within the next nine months to consider this Report (and the Evidence to be published as soon as possible after it) and to decide for each area what the best local response to its recommendations should be (para. 64);
28. Shortly after this period of nine months the Government should report to Parliament on the action taken and the further action planned, both at national and at local level (para. 64).

12.3   The Private Member's Bill

BILL to amend the law relating to matrimonial injunction; to provide the police with powers of arrest for the breach of injunction in cases of domestic violence; to provide for the obtaining of such injunction in the absence of a claim for damages; and to make further provision for the protection of the rights of victims of domestic violence.

BE IT ENACTED by the Queen's most Excellent Majesty, by and with the advice and consent of the Lords Spiritual and Temporal, and Commons, in this present Parliament assembled, and by the authority of the same, as follows:-

Matrimonial injunction.

1. Notwithstanding anything to the contrary in any enactment or rule of law relating to the jurisdiction of county courts, a county court may, on the application of a party to a marriage, grant an injunction restraining the use of violence by the other party to the applicant or excluding the other party from the whole or part of the premises occupied by the parties as their home, if satisfied that such an order is necessary for the protection of the applicant.

Powers of arrest.

2 (1) Where a judge makes an order:
(a) restraining a spouse or co-habitee from using violence towards the other spouse or co-habitee; or

(b) to vacate or not to come within a specified distance of a dwelling house; or both, he may attach a power of arrest thereto if he is satisfied -
  (i) that the Respondent has assaulted the Applicant occasioning actual bodily harm; and
  (ii) there is a likelihood of further assaults.
(2) A power of arrest attached to an order under subsection (1) above shall authorize any constable to arrest a person whom he reasonably suspects to have disobeyed the order by having committed an assault, or by having entered the area or place specified in the order, as the case may be.
(3) Where a constable arrests a person under subsection (2) above he shall forthwith seek the direction of a judge regarding the time at which and the place to which the arrested person is to be brought before the judge, but shall in any event release the arrested person if he is not brought before a judge within 24 hours of the direction being sought.
(4) Rules of court shall be made for the purposes of this section and to provide for service of the said order duly endorsed as to service on the person to whom it is addressed and on the senior officer of a Police Station in the district where the person who applied for the said injunction resides.

Amendment of Matrimonial Homes Act 1967, c. 75.

3. In section 1(2) of the Matrimonial Homes Act 1967 (which provides for applications for orders of the court declaring, enforcing, restricting or terminating rights of occupation under the Act or regulating the exercise by either spouse of the right to occupy the dwelling-house):-
(a) for the word 'regulating' there shall be substituted the words 'prohibiting, suspending or restricting'; and
(b) at the end of the subsection there shall be added the words 'or requiring either spouse to permit the exercise by the other of that right'.

Order restricting occupation of matrimonial home.

4(1) Where each of two spouses is entitled, by virtue of a legal estate vested in them jointly, to occupy a dwelling-house in which they have or at any time have had a matrimonial home, either of them may apply to the court, with respect to the exercise during the subsistence of the marriage of the right to occupy the dwelling-house, for an order prohibiting, suspending or restricting its exercise by the other or requiring the other to permit its exercise by the applicant.
(2) In relation to orders under this section, section 1(3), (4) and (6) of the Matrimonial Homes Act 1967 (which relate to the considerations relevant to and the contents of, and to the jurisdiction to make, orders under that section) shall apply as they apply in relation to orders under that section; and in this section 'dwelling-house' has the same meaning as in that Act.
(3) Where each of two spouses is entitled to occupy a dwelling-house by virtue of a contract, or by virtue of any enactment giving them the right to remain in occupation, this section shall apply as it applies where they are entitled by virtue of a legal estate vested in them jointly.
(4) The occupation of a dwelling-house by one spouse shall for purposes of the Rent Act 1968 (other than Part IV thereof) be treated as possession by both spouses, notwithstanding that the other spouse is excluded from occupation by an order under this section.

Short title and extent.

5(1) This Act may be cited as the Domestic Violence Act 1976.
(2) This Act shall not extend to Northern Ireland or Scotland.

12.4 Domestic Violence and Matrimonial Proceedings Act 1976

1976 CHAPTER 50

An Act to amend the law relating to matrimonial injunction; to provide the police with powers of arrest for the breach of injunction in cases of domestic violence; to amend section 1(2) of the Matrimonial Homes Act 1967; to make provision for varying rights of occupation where both spouses have the same rights in the matrimonial home; and for purposes connected therewith. [26th October 1976]

BE IT ENACTED by the Queen's most Excellent Majesty, by and with the advice and consent of the Lords Spiritual and Temporal, and Commons, in this present Parliament assembled, and by the authority of the same, as follows:-

Matrimonial injunctions in the county court.

1(1) Without prejudice to the jurisdiction of the High Court, on an application by a party to a marriage a county court shall have jurisdiction to grant an injunction containing one or more of the following provisions, namely:-
(a) a provision restraining the other party to the marriage from molesting the applicant;
(b) a provision restraining the other party from molesting a child living with the applicant;
(c) a provision excluding the other party from the matrimonial home or a part of the matrimonial home or from a specified area in which the matrimonial home is included;
(d) a provision requiring the other party to permit the applicant to enter and remain in the matrimonial home or a part of the matrimonial home;
whether or not any other relief is sought in the proceedings.
(2) Subsection (1) above shall apply to a man and a woman who are living with each other in the same household as husband and wife as it applies to the parties to a marriage and any reference to the matrimonial home shall be construed accordingly.

Arrest for breach of injunction.

2(1) Where, on an application by a party to a marriage, a judge grants an injunction containing a provision (in whatever terms)-
(a) restraining the other party to the marriage from using violence against the applicant, or
(b) restraining the other party from using violence against a child living with the applicant, or
(c) excluding the other party from the matrimonial home or from a specified area in which the matrimonial home is included,
the judge may, if he is satisfied that the other party has caused actual bodily harm to the applicant or, as the case may be, to the child concerned and considers that he is likely to do so again, attach a power of arrest to the injunction.
(2) References in subsection (1) above to the parties to a marriage include references to a man and a woman who are living with each other in the same household as husband and wife and any reference in that subsection to the matrimonial home shall be construed accordingly.'
(3) If, by virtue of subsection (1) above, a power of arrest is attached to an injunction, a constable may arrest without warrant a person whom he has reasonable cause for suspecting of being in breach of such a provision of that injunction as falls within paragraphs (a) to (c) of subsection (1) above by reason of that person's use of violence or, as the case may be, of his entry into any premises or area.

(4) Where a power of arrest is attached to an injunction and a person to whom the injunction is addressed is arrested under the subsection (3) above:-

(a) he shall be brought before a judge within that period of 24 hours beginning at the time of his arrest, and

(b) he shall not be released within that period except on the direction of the judge, but nothing in this section shall authorize his detention at any time after the expiry of that period.

(5) Where, by virtue of a power of arrest attached to an injunction, a constable arrests any person under subsection (3) above, the constable shall forthwith seek the directions-

(a) in a case where the injunction was granted by the High Court, of that court, and

(b) in any other case, of a county court,

as to the time and place at which that person is to be brought before a judge.

Amendment of Matrimonial Homes Act 1967. 1967 c. 75.

3. In section 1(2) of the Matrimonial Homes Act 1967 (which provides for applications for orders of the court declaring, enforcing, restricting or terminating rights of occupation under the Act or regulating the exercise by either spouse of the right to occupy the dwelling-house),

(a) for the word 'regulating' there shall be substituted the words 'prohibiting, suspending or restricting'; and

(b) at the end of the subsection there shall be added the words 'or requiring either spouse to permit the exercise by the other of that right'.

Order restricting occupation of matrimonial home.

4(1) Where each of two spouses is entitled, by virtue of a legal estate vested in them jointly, to occupy a dwelling-house in which they have or at any time have had a matrimonial home, either of them may apply to the court, with respect to the exercise during the subsistence of the marriage of the right to occupy the dwelling-house, for an order prohibiting, suspending or restricting its exercise by the other or requiring the other to permit its exercise by the applicant.

(2) In relation to orders under this section, section 1(3), (4) and (6) of the Matrimonial Homes Act 1967 (which relate to the considerations relevant to and the contents of, and to the jurisdiction to make, orders under that section) shall apply as they apply in relation to orders under that section; and in this section 'dwelling-house' has the same meaning as in that Act.

(3) Where each of two spouses is entitled to occupy a dwelling-house by virtue of a contract, or by virtue of any enactment giving them the right to remain in occupation, this section shall apply as it applies where they are entitled by virtue of a legal estate vested in them jointly.

Short title, commencement and extent.

5 (1) This Act may be cited as the Domestic Violence and Matrimonial Proceedings Act 1976.

(2) This Act shall come into force on such day as the Lord Chancellor may appoint by order made by statutory instrument and different days may be so appointed for different provisions of this Act:

 Provided that if any provisions of this Act are not in force on 1st April 1977, the Lord Chancellor shall then make an order by statutory instrument bringing such provisions into force.

(3) This Act shall not extend to Northern Ireland or Scotland.

12.5 *Davis v Johnson* [1979] AC 264 at 272

12.5.1 The facts

Jennifer Davis had been living with Nehemiah Johnson for three years, and they had a 2-year-old daughter. Davis applied for and was granted the tenancy of a council flat in Hackney, but at Johnson's request, the tenancy was put in their joint names. While they lived there, Johnson beat Davis frequently, often very violently. In September 1977 she left the flat, taking their daughter, and went to Erin Pizzey's refuge for battered wives. The refuge was very overcrowded, and in October, Davis applied for an injunction under the 1976 Act to exclude Johnson from the flat, so that she could return to it. The county court judge granted the injunction, but following the Court of Appeal's decision in *Cantliff v Jenkins* shortly afterwards, it was withdrawn by a county court judge upon application by Johnson.

12.5.2 Lord Denning MR's judgment in the Court of Appeal [1979] AC 272–283

The Act of 1976

To my mind the Act is perfectly clear. Rejecting words that do not apply, section 1(1) says that

> 'on an application by a party to a marriage a county court shall have jurisdiction to grant an injunction containing ... (c) a provision excluding the other party from the matrimonial home ...'

Subsection (2) deals with our very case. It says:

> 'Subsection (1) above shall apply to a man and a woman who are living with each other in the same household as husband and wife as it applies to the parties to a marriage...'

No one, I would have thought, could possibly dispute that those plain words by themselves cover this very case. They authorized the judge in the county court to grant an injunction excluding the man from this flat. So I turn to the reasoning of the two decisions of this court which have said the contrary. I must take each of their reasons in order, although it will take longer than I would have wished.

The comparison with the High Court jurisdiction

The judges in *B v B* [1978] Fam. 26 were much influenced by the opening and concluding words of section 1(1). For myself I think they add nothing and subtract nothing. But this is what they say: 'Without prejudice to the jurisdiction of the High Court, ... whether or not any other relief is sought in the proceedings.'

In *B v B* the judges seem to have thought that the High Court had little or no jurisdiction to exclude a husband from the matrimonial home. They said, at p. 34C-D, that if section 1(1) gave such jurisdiction to a county court,

> 'then it produces the quite astonishing result that the substantive law in the county court is different from the substantive law to be applied in the High Court.'

[Lord Denning then gave a series of examples of the broad jurisdiction of the Family Division of the High Court to grant injunctions to a wife in need of protection from her husband.]

Interference with rights of property

The second reason given by the judges in *B v B* [1978] Fam. 26 was that section 1 should be so construed as not to interfere with rights of property. It said that there was 'an elaborate legislative code upholding the rights inter se of spouses in relation to the occupation of the matrimonial home' contained in the Matrimonial Homes Act 1967 as now amended by sections 3 and 4 of the Act of 1976; and that, in view of that code, section 1 of the Act of 1976 should be regarded as procedural only and not as interfering with the substantive rights of the parties. It did not, therefore, enable the court to exclude Mr B. since he had 'an indefeasible right as against Mrs B. to continue in occupation in virtue of his tenancy.' Nor did it enable the court in the second case [*Cantliff v Jenkins* [1978] Fam. 47] to oust Mr Jenkins because he, as joint tenant with Miss Cantliff, had a legal right as a joint tenant to be in possession.

Mr Joseph Jackson before us placed reliance on that second reason. He urged that there should be no interference with rights of property. But when pressed as to its consequences, it soon became clear that, if this view were correct, it would deprive section 1 of any effect at all. Mr Jackson said that, as between husband and wife, section 1(1) did not give the court any power to make an order excluding the husband from the matrimonial home so long as he was the owner or joint owner of the matrimonial home or the tenant or joint tenant. It could only make an order when the wife was the sole owner. But so limited, section 1(1) was not needed at all; for a wife who is the sole owner can rely on her legal right to exclude him. Then, as between a man and woman living together unmarried, Mr Jackson said that the woman could never invoke section 1(2) so long as the man was the owner or joint owner of the home, or the tenant or joint tenant of it: but only when the woman was the sole owner or tenant of it. But in practice the woman never is the sole owner or tenant.

So it seems to me that that second reason must be bad too. In order to give section 1 any effect at all, the court must be allowed to override the property rights of the man: and to exclude him from the matrimonial home, whatever his property rights may be.

The authority of the House of Lords

The third reason given by the court in *B v B* [1978] Fam. 26 was that on the authority of the House of Lords in *Tarr v Tarr* [1973] A.C. 254 there was a general principle of construction that an enactment should not be construed so as to affect the rights of property: and that, if 'battered wives' were to be enabled to turn out the men, it would mean 'a very drastic inroad into the common law rights of the property-owning spouse.' Similarly, said Mr Jackson before us, the personal rights of the deserted wife were not allowed to override the property rights of the husband: and he cited the decision of the House of Lords in *National Provincial Bank Ltd v Hastings Car Mart Ltd* [1965] A.C. 1175. I venture to suggest that that concept about rights of property is quite out of date. It is true that in the 19th century the law paid quite high regard to rights of property. But this gave rise to such misgivings that in modern times the law has changed course. Social justice requires that personal rights should, in a proper case, be given priority over rights of property. In this court at least, ever since the war we have acted on that principle. Whenever we have found a husband deserting his wife or being cruel to her, we have not allowed him to turn out his wife and his children and put them on the street. Even though he may have, in point of law, the absolute title to the property as owner, no matter whether it be the freehold of a fine residence or the tenancy of a council house, his property rights have been made in this court to take second place. I know that in those two cases the House of Lords reversed the decisions of this court and gave priority to property rights. But Parliament in each case afterwards passed laws so as to restore the decisions of this court. I prefer to go by the principles underlying the legislative enactments rather than the out-dated notions of the past. In my opinion, therefore, we should reject the suggestion that in this Act of 1976 Parliament intended to give priority to the property rights of the husband or the man. So the third reason, to my mind, fails.

Joint tenancies

I am afraid that I cannot see any possible justification for the decision in *Cantliff v Jenkins* [1978] Fam. 47. The woman there was joint tenant with the man. No joint tenant is entitled to oust the other from the property which they own jointly: see *Jacobs v Seward* (1872) L.R. 5 H.L. 464 and *Bull v Bull* [1955] 1 Q.B. 234. If he does so, the court will not only restore her, but will also order him out. If he were allowed to remain, it would be useless simply to allow her to return: because, as soon as she got in, he would turn her out again. So the court must be able to order him out. That was the very decision of this court in *Gurasz v Gurasz* [1970] P. 11.

The fifth reason - for how long?

In *Cantliff v Jenkins* [1978] Fam. 47 the Court of Appeal were influenced by the thought that an injunction under section 1 would be unlimited in point of time. They asked, at p. 51F-G, the rhetorical question 'For how long?' and answered it by saying that

> 'As a practical matter, such an injunction, unlimited in point of time, would be equivalent to a transfer of property order, continuing as long as the other party was living.'

That does not frighten me in the least. But in point of practice, I cannot imagine that, in these cases, under section 1 any injunction would last very long. It is essentially a short-term remedy to meet an urgent need. Under the guidance of their legal advisers, the parties will be able to come to a solution between themselves. Thus the council may transfer the tenancy into the woman's name. So may a private landlord. Or there may be divorce proceedings in which the court may make an order transferring the title. Or the parties may come together again. Or one or the other may form a new relationship. And so far as rent and rates are concerned, the judge can easily see to those. If the wife is on social security, she will get an allowance with which to pay these.

The phrase 'are living' in subsection (3)

The judges in *B v B* [1978] Fam. 26 felt difficulty with the words 'are living with each other in the same household.' They felt that on the literal meaning of the words they must be living with each other at the time when the woman applies to the court. They realized that in most cases the woman would have already left the house at the time when she makes her application. So the literal meaning would deprive the subsection of much of its effect.

   To my mind these words do not present any difficulty. They are used to denote the relationship between the parties before the incident which gives rise to the application. If they were then living together in the same household as husband and wife, that is enough.

The proceedings in Parliament

So, in my opinion, the reasons given by the judges in those two cases were erroneous. But I wish to go further. I notice that in neither case were the judges referred to the Report of the Select Committee, nor to the proceedings in Parliament. If the judges had been referred to those, they would have discovered the intention of Parliament in passing this Act: and they would, I am sure, have given effect to that intention.

This shows how important it is that a court should, in a proper case, have power to refer to the report of a select committee or other *travaux préparatoires*. It will enable the court to avoid an erroneous construction of the Act: and that will be for the good of all. So I will proceed to consider them in this case.

First, the House of Commons appointed a Select Committee on Violence in Marriage. They heard much evidence and presented a very informative report on July 30, 1975. It formed the basis of the Act of 1976. There is clear authority that the court can read it so as to ascertain the 'mischief which the Act was intending to remedy. Such is plain from the decision of the House of Lords in *Black-Clawson International Ltd v Papierwerke Waldhof-Aschaffenburg AG* [1975] A.C. 591. The House there overruled this court [1974] Q.B. 660. The decisive factor was that they were referred to the report of a committee under the chairmanship of Greer L.J. and we had not been. If we had seen it, we should not have fallen into error. While all the law lords agreed that judges could read the report so as to ascertain the 'mischief' there was a difference of opinion as to whether they could read the 'recommendations' that it contained. I must say that it seems to me the whole of such a report should be open to be read. It is absurd to suggest that the judges are to be selective in their reading of it. As Lord Dilhorne observed: 'Have they to stop reading when they come to a recommendation?'; see [1975] A.C. 591, 622. And as Lord Simon of Glaisdale said, at p. 646:

> Where Parliament is legislating in the light of a public report I can see no reason why a court of construction should deny itself any part of that light and insist on groping for a meaning in darkness or half-light.'

Second, the Parliamentary debates on the Domestic Violence Bill. Some may say – and indeed have said – that judges should not pay any attention to what is said in Parliament. They should grope about in the dark for the meaning of an Act without switching on the light. I do not accede to this view. In some cases Parliament is assured in the most explicit terms what the effect of a statute will be. It is on that footing that members assent to the clause being agreed to. It is on that understanding that an amendment is not pressed. In such cases I think the court should be able to look at the proceedings. And, as I read the observations of Lord Simon of Glaisdale in *Race Relations Board v Dockers' Labour Club and Institute Ltd* [1976] A.C. 285, 299, he thought so too. I would give an instance. In the debate on the Race Relations Act 1968 there was, I believe, a ministerial assurance given in Parliament about its application to clubs: and I have a feeling that some of their Lordships looked at it privately and were influenced by it: see *Race Relations Board v Charter* [1973] A.C. 868, 899-901. I could wish that in those club cases we had been referred to it. It might have saved us from the error which the House afterwards held we had fallen into. And it is obvious that there is nothing to prevent a judge looking at these debates himself privately and getting some guidance from them. Although it may shock the purists, I may as well confess that I have sometimes done it. I have done it in this very case. It has thrown a flood of light on the position. The statements made in committee disposed completely of Mr Jackson's argument before us. It is just as well that you should know of them as well as me. So I will give them.

The statements in Parliament

So far as section 1(1) was concerned, the clause was inserted in the Standing Committee on June 30, 1976. In introducing it, the Member of Parliament in charge (Miss Richardson) proposed a new clause and said:

'The position has recently been considered by the Court of Appeal and restated in *Bassett v Bassett* ... The new clause would result in a uniform practice being applied in domestic proceedings of this kind, whether or not matrimonial proceedings were in progress.'

So far as subsection (2) was concerned (dealing with unmarried women), she said:

'In these cases, under existing law, an injunction can be obtained only by means of an action of assault which in county courts must include, I understand, a claim for damages. Even an injunction obtained in this way would not extend to the question of the occupation of the home when the applicant is not the sole owner or the official tenant ... the law should be extended to cover these cases. This is what we are seeking to do here.'

She went on to say: 'The words "living with each other in the same household" are intended to avoid a casual relationship, but to indicate a continuing state of affairs.'

It may interest you all to know that she went on to express her gratitude to those who had given her so much assistance in the drafting of the new clause, including the Lord Chancellor and his staff and the parliamentary counsel, and for the Law Commission's suggestions which had been taken into the Bill. 'I hope that now,' she said, 'we really have got it right.' This hope was completely frustrated by *B v B*. It is surely permissible for us now to get it right.

So it seems to me that on the true construction of this statute, with all the aids that we have at hand, it is plain that the deputy judge in the county court in this case was entitled to make the original order which he made, ordering the man to vacate the house and allowing the woman and her child to return to it: and, in my view, the cases in this court of *B v B* and *Cantliff v Jenkins* were wrongly decided.

Departure from previous decisions

I turn to the second important point: Can we depart from those two cases? Although convinced that they are wrong, are we at liberty to depart from them? What is the correct practice for this court to follow?

On principle, it seems to me that, while this court should regard itself as normally bound by a previous decision of the court, nevertheless it should be at liberty to depart from it if it is convinced that the previous decision was wrong. What is the argument to the contrary? It is said that if an error has been made, this court has no option but to continue the error and leave it to be corrected by the House of Lords. The answer is this: the House of Lords may never have an opportunity to correct the error: and thus it may be perpetuated indefinitely, perhaps for ever. That often happened in the old days when there was no legal aid. A poor person had to accept the decision of this court because he had not the means to take it to the House of Lords. It took 60 years before the erroneous decision in *Carlisle and Cumberland Banking Co v Bragg* [1911] 1 K.B. 489 was overruled by the House of Lords in *Gallie v Lee* [1971] A.C. 1004. Even today a person of moderate means may be outside the legal aid scheme, and not be able to take his case higher: especially with the risk of failure attaching to it. That looked as if it would have been the fate of Mrs Farrell when the case was decided in this court; see *Farrell v Alexander* [1976] Q.B. 345, 359. But she afterwards did manage to collect enough money together and by means of it to get the decision of this court reversed by the House of Lords: see *Farrell v Alexander* [1977] A.C. 59. Apart from monetary considerations, there have been many instances where cases have been settled pending an appeal to the House of Lords: or, for one reason or another, not taken there, especially with claims against insurance companies or big employers. When such a body has obtained a decision of this court in its favour, it will buy off an appeal to the House of Lords by paying ample compensation to the appellant. By so doing, it will have a legal precedent on its side which it can use with effect in later cases. I fancy that such may have happened in cases following *Oliver v Ashman* [1962] 2 Q.B. 210. By such means an erroneous decision on a point of law can again be perpetuated for ever. Even if all those objections are put on one side and there is an appeal to the House of Lords, it usually takes 12 months or more for the House of Lords to reach its decision. What then is the position of the lower courts meanwhile? They are in a dilemma. Either they have to apply the erroneous decision of the Court of Appeal, or they have to adjourn all fresh cases to await the decision of the House of Lords. That has often happened. So justice is delayed – and often denied – by the lapse of time before the error is corrected. The present case is a crying instance. ...

So much for principle. But what about our precedents? What about *Young v Bristol Aeroplane Co Ltd* [1944] K.B. 718?

The position before 1944

I will first state the position as it was before the year 1944. The Court of Appeal in its present form was established in 1873. It was then the final court of appeal. Appeals to the House of Lords were abolished by that Act and only restored a year or two later. The Court of Appeal inherited the jurisdiction of the previous courts of appeal such as the Exchequer Chamber and the Court of Appeal in Chancery. Those earlier courts had always had power to reconsider and review the law as laid down in previous decisions: and, if that law was found to be wrong, to correct it: but without disturbing the actual decision. I take this from the statements of eminent judges of those days who knew the position. In particular in 1852 Lord St. Leonards L.C. in *Bright v Hutton* (1852) 3 H.L. Cas. 341, 388, said in the House of Lords:

'... You are not bound by any rule of law you may lay down, if upon a subsequent occasion, you should find reason to differ from that rule; that is, that this House, *like every court of justice*, possesses an inherent power to correct an error into which it may have fallen.'

Likewise in 1877 Lord Cairns L.C. in *Ridsdale v Clifton* (1877) 2 P.D. 276, 306-307. Then in 1880 the new Court of Appeal on two occasions departed from the earlier decisions of the Court of Appeal in Chancery. It was in the important cases of *In re Hallett's Estate* (1880) 13 Ch.D. 696 and *Mills v Jennings* (1880) 13 Ch.D. 639, given on February 11 and 14, 1880, within four days of one another. In the latter case the Court of Appeal declared in a single reserved judgment (and among their members was James L.J. who had an unrivalled experience of 40 years of the practice of the court) that:

'As a rule, this court ought to treat the decisions of the Court of Appeal in Chancery as binding authorities, but we are at liberty not to do so when there is a sufficient reason for overruling them. As the decision in *Tassell v Smith* (1858) 2 De G. & J. 713 may lead to consequences so serious, we think that we are at liberty to reconsider and review the decision in that case as if it were being re-heard in the old Court of Appeal in Chancery, as was not uncommon (see *Mills v Jennings*, 13 Ch.D. 639, 648-649).'

Four years later in *The Vera Cruz (No 2)* (1884) 9 P.D. 96, Brett M.R. with 27 years' experience of the previous practice, said, at p. 98:

'... there is no statute or common law rule by which one court is bound to abide by the decision of another of equal rank, it does so simply from what may be called the comity among judges. In the same way there is no common law or statutory rule to oblige a court to bow to its own decisions, it does so again on the grounds of judicial comity.'

And Fry L.J. said, at p. 101:

> Bearing in mind the observations of Lord St. Leonards (he by a slip said Lord Truro) in *Bright v Hutton* (1852) 3 H.L. Cas. 341 and Lord Cairns in *Ridsdale v Clifton* (1877) 2 P.D. 276, I think that we are not concluded from entertaining this case;...'

Two years later in 1886 in *Ex parte Stanford* (1886) 17 Q.B.D. 259, 269 Lord Esher M.R. [formerly Sir William Brett] called together the full court of six so as to disregard an earlier decision of a court of three. He explained his action quite clearly in *Kelly Co v Kellond* (1888) 20 Q.B.D. 569, 572 in a passage very apposite today:

> 'This court is one composed of six members, and if at any time a decision of a lesser number is called in question, and a difficulty arises about the accuracy of it, I think this court is entitled, sitting as a full court, to decide whether we will follow or not the decision arrived at by the smaller number.'

Those were all judges who knew the old practice: and the principles stated by them were accepted without question throughout the next 50 years. In *Wynne-Finch v Chaytor* [1903] 2 Ch. 475 the full court overruled a previous decision of the court. Afterwards Greer L.J. repeatedly said that this court could depart from a previous decision if it thought it right to do so: see *Newsholme Bros v Road Transport and General Insurance Co Ltd* [1929] 2 K.B. 356, 384 and *In re Shoesmith* [1938] 2 K.B. 637, 644. In another case in 1941, *Lancaster Motor Co (London) Ltd v Bremith Ltd* [1941] 1 K.B. 675, the Court of Appeal again did not follow a previous decision. So much for the practice until 1944.

Young v Bristol Aeroplane Co Ltd

The change came about in 1944. In *Young v Bristol Aeroplane Co Ltd* [1944] K.B. 718 the court overruled the practice of a century. Lord Greene M.R., sitting with a court of five, laid down that this court is bound to follow its previous decision as well as those of courts of coordinate jurisdiction: subject to only three exceptions: (i) where there are two conflicting decisions, (ii) where a previous decision cannot stand with a decision of the House of Lords, (iii) if a previous decision was given per incuriam.

It is to be noticed that the court laid down that proposition as a rule of law. That was quite the contrary of what Lord Esher had declared in *The Vera Cruz* in 1884. He said it arose only as a matter of judicial comity.

Events have proved that in this respect Lord Esher was right and Lord Greene was wrong. I say this because the House of Lords in 1898 had held itself bound by its own previous decisions as a rule of law: see *London Street Tramways Co. Ltd v London County Council* [1898] A.C. 375. But yet in 1966 it discarded that rule. In a statement headed Practice Statement (Judicial Precedent) it was said:

> 'Their Lordships nevertheless recognize that too rigid adherence to precedent may lead to injustice in a particular case and also unduly restrict the proper development of the law. They propose, therefore, to modify their present practice, and, while treating former decisions of this House as normally binding, to depart from a previous decision when it appears right to do so (see [1966] 1 W.L.R. 1234).'

That shows conclusively that a rule as to precedent (which any court lays down for itself) is not a rule of law at all. It is simply a practice or usage laid down by the court itself for its own guidance: and, as such, the successors of that court can alter that practice or amend it or set up other guide lines, just as the House of Lords did in 1966. Even as the judges in *Young v Bristol Aeroplane Co Ltd* [1944] K.B. 718, thought fit to discard the practice of a century and declare a new practice or usage, so we in 1977 can discard the guide lines of 1944 and set up new guide lines of our own or revert to the old practice laid down by Lord Esher. Nothing said in the House of Lords, before or since, can stop us from doing so. Anything said about it there must needs be obiter dicta. This was emphasized by Salmon L.J. in this court in *Gallie v Lee* [1969] 2 Ch. 17, 49:

> 'The point about the authority of this court has never been decided by the House of Lords. In the nature of things it is not a point that could even come before the House for decision. Nor does it depend upon any statutory or common law rule. This practice of ours apparently rests solely upon a concept of judicial comity laid down many years ago and automatically followed ever since ... Surely today judicial comity would be amply satisfied if we were to adopt the same principle in relation to our decisions as the House of Lords has recently laid down for itself by pronouncement of the whole House.'

The new guide lines

So I suggest that we are entitled to lay down new guide lines. To my mind, this court should apply similar guide lines to those adopted by the House of Lords in 1966. Whenever it appears to this court that a previous decision was wrong, we should be at liberty to depart from it if we think it right to do so. Normally – in nearly every case of course – we would adhere to it. But in an exceptional case we are at liberty to depart from it.

Alternatively, in my opinion, we should extend the exceptions in *Young v Bristol Aeroplane Co Ltd* [1944] K.B. 718 when it appears to be a proper case to do so. I realize that this comes virtually to the same thing, but such new exceptions have been created since *Young v Bristol Aeroplane Co Ltd*. For instance, this court can depart from a previous decision of its own when sitting on a criminal cause or matter: see the recent cases of *R v Gould* [1968] 2 Q.B. 65 and *R v Newsome* [1970] 2 Q.B. 711. Likewise by analogy it can depart from a previous decision in regard to contempt of court. Similarly in the numerous cases when this court is sitting as a court of last resort. There are many statutes which make this court the final court of appeal. In every jurisdiction throughout the world a court of last resort has, and always has had, jurisdiction to correct the errors of a previous decision: see *Hadfield's case* (1873) L.R. 8 C.P. 306, 313 and Pollock's *First Book of Jurisprudence* (1896), pp. 333-334. In the recent case of *Tiverton Estates Ltd v Wearwell Ltd* [1975] Ch. 146, we extended the exceptions by holding that we could depart from a previous decision where there were conflicting principles-as distinct from conflicting decisions – of this court. Likewise we extended the notion of per incuriam in *Industrial Properties. (Barton Hill) Ltd v Associated Electrical Industries Ltd* [1977] Q.B. 580. In the more recent cases of *In re K. (Minors) (Children: Care and Control)* [1977] Fam. 179 and *S (BD) v S (DJ) (Children: Care and Control)* [1977] Fam. 109, this court in its jurisdiction over children did not follow the earlier decision of *In re L (Infants)* [1962] 1 W.L.R. 886. I would add also that, when the words of the statute are plain, then it is not open to any decision of any court to contradict the statute: because the statute is the final authority on what the law is. No court can depart from the plain words of a statute. On this ground may be rested the decisions in *W & JB Eastwood v Herrod* [1968] 2 Q.B. 923 and *Hanning v Maitland (No 2)* [1970] 1 Q.B. 580, where this court departed from previous interpretations of a statute. In *Schorsch Meier GmbH v Hennin* [1975] Q.B. 416 we introduced another exception on the principle 'cessante ratione legis cessat ipsa lex.' This step of ours was criticized by the House of Lords in *Miliangos v George Frank (Textiles) Ltd* [1976] A.C. 443: but I venture to suggest that, unless we had done so, the House of Lords would never have had the opportunity to reform the law. Every court would have held that judgments could only be given in sterling. No one would have taken the point to the Lords, believing that it was covered by *In re United Railways of Havana and Regla Warehouses Ltd* [1961] A.C. 1007. In this present case the appellant, Miss Davis, was at first refused legal aid for an appeal, because the point was covered by the two previous decisions. She was only granted it afterwards when it was realized by the legal aid committee that this court of five had been specially convened to reconsider and review those decisions. So, except for this action of ours, the law would have been regarded as settled by *B v B* [1978] Fam. 26 and *Cantliff v Jenkins* [1978] Fam. 47: and the House of Lords would not have had the opportunity of pronouncing on it. So instead of rebuking us, the House of Lords should be grateful to us for giving them the opportunity of considering these decisions.

The truth is that the list of exceptions from *Young v Bristol Aeroplane Co Ltd* [1944] K.B. 718 is now getting so large that they are in process of eating up the rule itself: and we would do well simply to follow the same practice as the House of Lords.

Conclusion

Here we have to consider a jurisdiction newly conferred on the county courts of England for the protection of battered wives. It is most important that all the county courts up and down the country should know at once what their powers are to protect these women: and, if the jurisdiction exists, it is most important that the county courts should exercise it at once so that the law should give these women the protection which Parliament intended they should have. This is a very recent Act: it has only been in force 4½ months. It is almost inevitable in the early stages, with all the urgency attaching to the applications, that some errors may be made. If they are made, and it appears to the Court of Appeal, on further consideration, that a previous decision was clearly wrong, in my opinion we can depart from it. I would prefer to put it on the ground that this court should take for itself guide lines similar to those taken by the House of Lords; but, if this be not acceptable, I am of the opinion that we should regard it as an additional exception to those stated in *Young v Bristol Aeroplane Co Ltd* [1944] K.B. 718, especially as by so doing we can better protect the weak and do what Parliament intended.

I would therefore allow the appeal and restore the decision of the original deputy circuit judge who ordered the man to vacate the council flat.

12.5.3 Extracts from the speeches of Lords Diplock and Scarman, and Viscount Dilhorne in the House of Lords

Lord Diplock: 'My Lords, this appeal is from a judgment of the Court of Appeal which, by a majority of three out of five members who sat (Lord Denning M.R., Sir George Baker P. and Shaw L.J.; Goff and Cumming-Bruce L.JJ. dissenting), purported to overrule two recent previous decisions of its own as to the meaning of a statute.

Put in a nutshell, the basic question of statutory construction that has given rise to so acute a conflict of judicial opinion is whether section 1 of the Domestic Violence and Matrimonial Proceedings Act 1976 does no more than provide additional, expeditious and more easily available remedies to prevent threatened invasions of existing legal rights originating from other sources, whether statutory or at common law, or whether it also, of itself, creates new legal rights as well as new remedies for threatened invasion of them. The former I will call the 'narrower,' the latter the 'broader' meaning. In *B v B (Domestic Violence: Jurisdiction)* [1978] Fam. 26 on 13 October 1977, the Court of Appeal consisting of Megaw, Bridge, and Waller L.JJ. decided unanimously that it bore the narrower meaning: it gave additional remedies but created no new legal rights. In *Cantliff v Jenkins (Note)* [1978] Fam. 47 on 20 October 1977, the Court of Appeal then consisting of Stamp, Orr, and Ormrod L.JJ., while holding itself to be bound by the decision in *B v B* since it regarded that case as indistinguishable, took occasion, again unanimously, to express its concurrence with the reasoning of Bridge L.J. in *B v B* and added, for good measure, an additional reason in support of the narrower meaning placed upon the section in that previous judgment. For my part, I think that *Cantliff v Jenkins* was distinguishable from *B v B* but it is conceded that the facts in the instant case are indistinguishable from those held by the Court of Appeal in *Cantliff v Jenkins* to be relevant to its decision in that case. So, when the instant case came before the Court of Appeal, there was a preliminary question which fell to be determined; and that was whether the court was bound by its previous decisions in *B v B* and *Cantliff v Jenkins*. The view of a majority of three was that it was not so bound, though their individual reasons for so holding were not identical. This opened the way to a fresh consideration of the meaning of the statute by all five members. On this question they were divided four to one. Cumming Bruce L.J. sided with the six Lords Justices who in the two previous cases had adopted the narrower meaning of section 1; the remainder were of opinion that it bore the wider meaning and did create new legal rights as well as new remedies for threatened violation of them. So, of the members of the Court of Appeal who sit regularly in civil matters (of whom there are now 17) there were seven who had adopted the narrower meaning of the section, three who, together with the President of the Family Division, had preferred the wider meaning, and a silent minority of seven regular members of the Court of Appeal whose views had not been expressed by the conclusion of the hearing of the instant case in the Court of Appeal.

I draw attention to this arithmetic because if the view expressed by Lord Denning M.R., Sir George Baker P. and Shaw L.J. that the Court of Appeal was not bound by its own previous decisions is correct, this would apply to its decision in the instant case; and had there been no appeal to your Lordships' House to cut the Gordian knot, it would have been open to the Court of Appeal in any subsequent cases to give effect to the wider or the narrower construction of section 1 of the Domestic Violence and Matrimonial Proceedings Act 1976 according to the preference of the majority of the members who happened to be selected to sit on that particular appeal.

My Lords, the difference of judicial opinion as to the true construction of the section has spilled over into this House; for although I agree that on the facts of this case it may be that the order of the Court of Appeal could be upheld, and that the actual decision of *Cantliff v Jenkins* was wrong, I nevertheless find myself regretfully compelled to part company with the rest of your Lordships and to align myself with the seven Lords Justices who have expressed their preference for the narrower meaning. This cannot affect the disposition of the instant appeal nor will it affect the application of the Act in subsequent cases; for the section means what a majority of this House declares it means. But it does make the score of appellate opinions in favour of the broader and the narrower meanings eight all.

Although on the question of the construction of section 1 of the Domestic Violence and Matrimonial Proceedings Act 1976 this House has not been able to reach unanimity, nevertheless on what in the instant case was the first question for the Court of Appeal, viz. whether it was bound by its own previous decisions, I understand us to be unanimous, so I too will deal with it first.

So far as civil matters are concerned the law upon this question is now clear and unassailable. It has been so for more than 30 years. I do not find it necessary to trace the origin and development of the doctrine of stare decisis before the present structure of the courts was created in 1875. In that structure the Court of Appeal in civil actions has always played, save in a few exceptional matters, an intermediate and not a final appellate role. The application of the doctrine of stare decisis to decisions of the Court of Appeal was the subject of close examination by a Court of Appeal composed of six of its eight regular members in *Young v Bristol Aeroplane Co Ltd* [1944] K.B. 718. The judgment of the court was delivered by Lord Greene M.R. Its effect is summarized accurately in the headnote as being that:

> 'The Court of Appeal is bound to follow its own decisions and those of courts of co-ordinate jurisdiction, and the 'full' court is in the same position in this respect as a division of the court consisting of three members. The only exceptions to this rule are: - (1) The court is entitled and bound to decide which of two conflicting decisions of its own it will follow; (2) the court is bound to refuse to follow a decision of its own which, though not expressly overruled, cannot, in its opinion, stand with a decision of the House of Lords; (3) the court is not bound to follow a decision of its own if it is satisfied that the decision was given per incuriam, e.g., where a statute or a rule having statutory effect which would have affected the decision was not brought to the attention of the earlier court.'

The rule as expounded in the *Bristol Aeroplane case* was not new in 1944. It had been acted upon on numerous occasions and had, as recently as the previous year, received the express confirmation of this House of Viscount Simon L.C. with whose speech Lord Atkin agreed: see *Perrin v Morgan* [1943] A.C. 399, 405. Although prior to 1944 there had been an occasional deviation from the rule, which was why a court of six was brought together to consider it, there has been none since. It has been uniformly acted upon by the Court of Appeal and re-affirmed, notably in a judgment of a Court of Appeal of five, of which Lord Denning as Denning L.J. was a member, in *Morelle Ltd v Wakeling* [1955] 2 Q.B. 379. This judgment emphasized the limited scope of the per incuriam exception to the general rule that the Court of Appeal is bound by its own previous decisions. The rule has also been uniformly accepted by this House as being correct. Because until recently it has never been questioned, the acceptance of the rule has generally been tacit in the course of recounting the circumstances which have rendered necessary an appeal to your Lordships' House; but occasionally the rule has been expressly referred to, as by Viscount Simon L.C. in the *Bristol Aeroplane case* itself [1944] A.C. 163, 169, and by Lord Morton of Henryton and Lord Porter in B*onsor v Musicians' Union* [1956] A.C. 104, 120, 128.

Furthermore, the provisions of the Administration of Justice Act 1969 which authorize 'leap-frog' appeals in civil cases direct from the High Court to this House are based on the tacit assumption that the rule as stated in the *Bristol Aeroplane case* is correct. One of the two grounds on which a High Court judge may authorize a 'leap-frog' appeal is if he is satisfied that a point of law of general importance involved in his decision:

> 'is one in respect of which the judge is bound by a decision of the Court of Appeal or of the House of Lords in previous proceedings, and was fully considered in the judgments given by the Court of Appeal or the House of Lords (as the case may be) in those previous proceedings (section 12(3)(b)).'

The justification for by-passing the Court of Appeal when the decision by which the judge is bound is one given by the Court of Appeal itself in previous proceedings is because that court also is bound by the decision, if the point of law was fully considered and not passed over per incuriam.

So the rule as it had been laid down in the *Bristol Aeroplane case* [1944] K.B. 718 had never been questioned thereafter until, following upon the announcement by Lord Gardiner L.C. in 1966 [*Practice Statement (Judicial Precedent)* [1966] 1 W.L.R. 1234] that the House of Lords would feel free in exceptional cases to depart from a previous decision of its own, Lord Denning M.R. conducted what may be described, I hope without offence, as a one-man crusade with the object of freeing the Court of Appeal from the shackles which the doctrine of stare decisis imposed upon its liberty of decision by the application of the rule laid down in the *Bristol Aeroplane case* to its own previous decisions; or, for that matter, by any decisions of this House itself of which the Court of Appeal disapproved: see *Broome v Cassell & Co Ltd* [1971] 2 Q.B. 354 and *Schorsch Meier GmbH v Hennin* [1975] Q.B. 416. In his judgment in the instant appeal, Lord Denning M.R. refers to a number of cases after 1966 in which he suggests that the Court of Appeal has either refused to apply the rule as laid down in the Bristol Aeroplane case or has added so many other exceptions to the three that were stated by Lord Greene M.R. that it no longer operates as a curb on the power of the Court of Appeal to disregard any previous decision of its own which the majority of those members who happen to be selected to sit on a particular appeal think is wrong. Such, however, has not been the view of the other two members of the Court of Appeal who were sitting with the Master of the Rolls in any of those cases to which he refers. Where they felt able to disregard a previous decision of the Court of Appeal this was only because, in their opinion, it fell within the first or second exception stated in the *Bristol Aeroplane* case.

When *Miliangos v George Frank (Textiles) Ltd* [1975] Q.B. 487 was before the Court of Appeal Lord Denning M.R. appears to have reluctantly recanted. That was a case in which Bristow J. had held that he was bound by a decision of this House in *In re United Railways of Havana and Regla Warehouses Ltd* [1961] A.C. 1007, despite the fact that the Court of Appeal had purported to overrule it in the *Schorsch Meier case*. On appeal from his decision Lord Denning M.R. disposed of the case by holding that the Court of Appeal was bound by its own previous decision in the *Schorsch Meier case*. He added, at p. 503:

> 'I have myself often said that this court is not absolutely bound by its own decisions and may depart from them just as the House of Lords from theirs: but my colleagues have not gone so far. So that I am duty bound to defer to their view.'

The reasons why his colleagues had not agreed to follow him are plain enough. In an appellate court of last resort a balance must be struck between the need on the one side for the legal certainty resulting from the binding effect of previous decisions, and, on the other side the avoidance of undue restriction on the proper development of the law. In the case of an intermediate appellate court, however, the second desideratum can be taken care of by appeal to a superior appellate court, if reasonable means of access to it are available; while the risk of the first desideratum, legal certainty, if the court is not bound by its own previous decisions grows even greater with increasing membership and the number of three-judge divisions in which it sits – as the arithmetic which I have earlier mentioned shows. So the balance does not lie in the same place as in the case of a court of last resort. That is why the Lord Chancellor's announcement about the future attitude towards precedent of the House of Lords in its judicial capacity concluded with the words:

'This announcement is not intended to affect the use of precedent elsewhere than in this House.'

Much has been said in the instant case about the delay and expense which would have been involved if the Court of Appeal had treated itself as bound by its previous decision in *B v B* [1978] Fam. 26 and *Cantliff v Jenkins* [1978] Fam. 47, so as to make it necessary for the respondent to come to this House to argue that those decisions should be overruled. But a similar reasoning could also be used to justify any High Court or county court judge in refusing to follow a decision of the Court of Appeal which he thought was wrong. It is true that since the appeal in the instant case was from the county court, not the High Court, the 'leap-frog' procedure was not available, but since it was conceded that the instant case was indistinguishable from *Cantliff v Jenkins*, there was no need for anything but the briefest of hearings in the Court of Appeal. The appeal to this House could in that event have been heard before Christmas instead of in January: and at less cost. The decision could have been announced at once and the reasons given later.

Of the various ways in which Lord Denning M.R.'s colleagues had expressed the reasons for continuing to regard the rule laid down in the *Bristol Aeroplane case* [1944] K.B. 718 as salutary in the interest of the administration of justice, I select those given by Scarman L.J. in *Tiverton Estates Ltd v Wearwell Ltd* [1975] Ch. 146, 172-173, in the Court of Appeal.

> 'The Court of Appeal occupies a central, but, save for a few exceptions, an intermediate position in our legal system. To a large extent, the consistency and certainty of the law depend upon it. It sits almost always in divisions of three: more judges can sit to hear a case, but their decision enjoys no greater authority than a court composed of three. If, therefore, throwing aside the restraints of *Young v Bristol Aeroplane Co. Ltd.*, one division of the court should refuse to follow another because it believed the other's decision to be wrong, there would be a risk of confusion and doubt arising where there should be consistency and certainty. The appropriate forum for the correction of the Court of Appeal's errors is the House of Lords, where the decision will at least have the merit of being final and binding – subject only to the House's power to review its own decisions. The House of Lords, as the court of last resort, needs this power of review: it does not follow that an intermediate appellate court needs it and, for the reasons I have given, I believe the Court of Appeal is better without it, save in the exceptional circumstances specified in *Young v Bristol Aeroplane Co Ltd*.'

My own reason for selecting this passage out of many is because in the following year in *Farrell v Alexander* [1976] Q.B. 345 Scarman L.J. again referred to it in dissociating himself from the view, to which Lord Denning M.R. had by then once again reverted, that the Court of Appeal was not bound by any previous decision of its own that it was satisfied was wrong. What Scarman L.J. there said, at p. 371, was:

> '...I have immense sympathy with the approach of Lord Denning M.R. I decline to accept his lead only because I think it damaging to the law in the long term – though it would undoubtedly do justice in the present case. To some it will appear that justice is being denied by a timid, conservative, adherence to judicial precedent. They would be wrong. Consistency is necessary to certainty – one of the great objectives of law. The Court of Appeal – at the very centre of our legal system – is responsible for its stability, its consistency, and its predictability: see my comments in *Tiverton Estates Ltd v Wearwell Ltd* [1975] Ch. 146, 172. The task of law reform, which calls for

wide-ranging techniques of consultation and discussion that cannot be compressed into the forensic medium, is for others. The courts are not to be blamed in a case such as this. If there be blame, it rests elsewhere.'

When *Farrell v Alexander* ([1977] A.C. 59) reached this House Scarman L.J.'s way of putting it was expressly approved by my noble and learned friends Viscount Dilhorne, at p. 81, and Lord Simon of Glaisdale at p. 92, while the other member of this House who adverted to the question of stare decisis, Lord Russell of Killowen, at p. 105, expressed his 'unreserved disapproval' of that part of Lord Denning M.R.'s judgment in which he persisted in his heterodox views on the subject.

In the instant case Lord Denning M.R. in effect reiterated his opinion that the Court of Appeal in relation to its own previous decisions should adopt the same rule as that which the House of Lords since the announcement in 1966 has applied in relation to its previous decisions. Sir George Baker P., on the other hand, preferred to deal with the problem of stare decisis by adding a new exception to the rule in the *Bristol Aeroplane case* ([1944] K.B. 718), which he formulated as follows:

> 'The court is not bound to follow a previous decision of its own if satisfied that that decision was clearly wrong and cannot stand in the face of the will and intention of Parliament expressed in simple language in a recent statute passed to remedy a serious mischief or abuse, and further adherence to the previous decision must lead to injustice in the particular case and unduly restrict proper development of the law with injustice to others.'

Shaw L.J. phrased the exception rather differently. He said:

> 'It would be in some such terms as that the principle of stare decisis should be relaxed where its application would have the effect of depriving actual and potential victims of violence of a vital protection which an Act of Parliament was plainly designed to afford to them, especially where, as in the context of domestic violence, that deprivation must inevitably give rise to an irremediable detriment to such victims and create in regard to them an injustice irreversible by a later decision of the House of Lords.'

My Lords, the exception as stated by Sir George Baker P. would seem wide enough to cover any previous decision on the construction of a statute which the majority of the court thought was wrong and would have consequences that were regrettable, at any rate if they felt sufficiently strongly about it. As stated by Shaw L.J. the exception would appear to be what might be termed a 'one-off' exception. It is difficult to think of any other statute to which it would apply.

In my opinion, this House should take this occasion to re-affirm expressly, unequivocally and unanimously that the rule laid down in the *Bristol Aeroplane case* [1944] K.B. 718 as to stare decisis is still binding on the Court of Appeal.

I come now to the construction of section 1 of the Domestic Violence and Matrimonial Proceedings Act 1976 under which the applicant, Miss Davis, sought an injunction against the respondent, Mr Johnson, to exclude him from the council flat in Hackney of which they were joint tenants.

I am in agreement with your Lordships that upon the facts that I have summarized the county court judge had jurisdiction to grant an injunction excluding Mr Johnson temporarily from the flat of which he and Miss Davis were joint tenants. I reach this conclusion notwithstanding that, in disagreement with your Lordships, I remain unpersuaded that section 1(2) bears the broader meaning rather than the narrower one. As my opinion that the narrower meaning is to be preferred will not prevail I shall resist the temptation to add to or elaborate upon the reasons given by Bridge

L.J. in *B v B* [1978] Fam. 26 for that preference. There are, however, two initial matters of more general application to the interpretation of statutes that arise out of the judgment of the Court of Appeal. Upon these I wish to comment.

I have had the advantage of reading what my noble and learned friends Viscount Dilhorne and Lord Scarman have to say about the use of Hansard as an aid to the construction of a statute. I agree with them entirely and would add a word of warning against drawing too facile an analogy between proceedings in the Parliament of the United Kingdom and those *travaux préparatoires* which may be looked at by the courts of some of our fellow member states of the European Economic Community to resolve doubts as to the interpretation of national legislation or by the European Court of Justice, and consequently by English courts themselves, to resolve doubts as to the interpretation of Community legislation. Community legislation viz. Regulations and Directives, are required by the Treaty of Rome to state reasons on which they are based, and when submitted to the Council in the form of a proposal by the Commission the practice is for them to be accompanied by an explanatory memorandum by the Commission expanding the reasons which appear in more summary form in the draft Regulation or Directive itself. The explanatory memoranda are published in the Official Journal together with the proposed Regulations or Directives to which they relate. These are true *travaux préparatoires*; they are of a very different character from what is said in the passion or lethargy of parliamentary debate; yet a survey of the judgments of the European Court of Justice will show how rarely that court refers even to these explanatory memoranda for the purpose of interpreting Community legislation.

A closer analogy with *travaux préparatoires* is to be found in reports of such bodies as the Law Commissions and committees or commissions appointed by government or by either House of Parliament to consider reforming particular branches of the law. Where legislation follows upon a published report of this kind the report may be used as an aid to identify the mischief which the legislation is intended to remedy; but not for the purpose of construing the enacting words in such a way as to conform with recommendations made in the report as to the form the remedy should take: *Black-Clawson International Ltd v Papierwerke Waldhof- Aschaffenburg AG* [1975] A.C. 591. This does not mean, of course, that one must shut one's eyes to the recommendations, for a suggestion as to a remedy may throw light on what the mischief itself is thought to be; but it does not follow that Parliament when it legislates to remedy the mischief has adopted in their entirety, or, indeed, at all, the remedies recommended in the report.

This is well illustrated in the instant case. The report on which the Domestic Violence and Matrimonial Proceedings Act 1976 was undoubtedly based is the Report of the Select Committee of the House of Commons on Violence in Marriage published in July 1975 (H.C. 553/1). It deals almost exclusively with the plight of married women exposed to violence by their husbands and resulting homelessness for themselves and their children. In the single paragraph referring to unmarried couples described (regrettably I think) as 'cohabitees,' the members of the committee disclaim any particular knowledge of the problem, on which they had not taken evidence. Nevertheless they recommended that so far as the grant of injunctions against violence by their paramours was concerned mistresses should have the same procedural rights as married women. As regards homelessness of mistresses, however, all the committee recommended was that the Guardianship of Minors Acts should be amended to provide that where there was a child of the illicit union of which paternity could be proved, the court should have power to make orders giving the mistress while she was caring for the children during their minority sole right of occupation of the premises which had been occupied by the unmarried couple as their home. Whatever section 1(2) of the Act may do it does not do that ([1979] A.C. 322-331).

Lord Scarman: My Lords, the central question in this appeal is as to the construction of s. 1 of the Domestic Violence and Matrimonial Proceedings Act 1976. ... A layman could be forgiven for thinking that the section was tailor-made to enable a county court judge to make the order that was made in this case. But in three cases reaching the Court of Appeal in the last few months Lords Justices have taken a different view. They found the section difficult and obscure. In *B v B* [1978] Fam. 26 the court (Megaw, Bridge and Waller L.JJ.) accepted the submission that the provisions of section 1 of the Act do not alter in any way the substantive law affecting parties' rights to occupy premises and that, in considering the question whether relief can be granted under the section, the court must consider the respective rights and obligations of the parties unaffected by the provisions of the section. In the result, the court in *B v B* held that an unmarried woman could not obtain under the section an order excluding from the home the man with whom she was living, unless she could show that she had a right by the law of property to exclusive possession of the premises. In other words, while she could get relief against molestation, as specified in subsection (1)(a) and (b), she could not get an order enabling her to occupy the home under (c) or (d) of the subsection.

In *Cantliff v Jenkins* [1978] Fam. 47 another division in the Court of Appeal followed this decision.

In the present case a specially constituted five-judge bench of the Court of Appeal has by a majority (4 to 1) rejected the interpretation put upon the section by the court of *B v B* and has held that the full range of relief set out in subsection (1), i.e., orders containing all or any of the relief set out in (a), (b), (c) and (d) of the subsection, is available to an unmarried woman, who can bring herself within subsection (2).

For reasons which I shall briefly outline, I have reached the conclusion that the case of *B v B* was wrongly decided. In my view the relief specified in (a), (b), (c) and (d) of the subsection is available to an unmarried family partner. I would, therefore, dismiss the appeal.

The Act is a short one, its substance being contained in four sections. Section 1 enables the county court to grant the injunctive relief specified in subsection (1), irrespective of whether the applicant is married or unmarried. Section 2 enables a court which grants an injunction in matrimonial proceedings or under section 1 to add to it in certain circumstances a power of arrest. Sections 3 and 4 amend the Matrimonial Homes Act 1967 so as to eliminate two weaknesses in that Act revealed by recent judicial decisions. Section 5 declares the short title, commencement and extent of the Act. That is all there is to it.

Section 1 consists of two subsections. Subsection (1) enables a party to a marriage to make application to a county court. It is without prejudice to the jurisdiction of the High Court and it empowers a county court (any county court, whether or not invested with divorce jurisdiction) to grant an injunction 'whether or not any other relief is sought'. Clearly the subsection provides a new remedy additional to, but not in substitution for, what already exists in the law.

Subsection (2) enables an unmarried woman (or man) who is living with a man (or woman) in the same household as husband and wife to apply to the county court under subsection (1) and expressly provides that reference in subsection (1) to the matrimonial home shall be construed as a reference to the household in which they are living together. This reference indicates to my mind that those provisions of subsection (1), which make available to married people an injunction excluding the other party from the matrimonial home and an injunction requiring the other party to permit the applicant to enter and remain in the matrimonial home, are intended to be available also to unmarried partners.

The availability of paragraphs (c) and (d) of subsection (1) to unmarried partners without any express restriction to those who have a property right in the house had an important bearing on the answer to the question which I consider to be crucial to a correct understanding of the scope of the section; i.e., what is the mischief for which Parliament has provided the remedies specified in subsection (1)? It suggests strongly that the remedies are intended to protect people, not property: for it is highly unlikely that Parliament could have intended by the sidewind of subsection (2) to have introduced radical changes into the law of property. Nor is it necessary so to construe the section. The personal rights of an unmarried woman living with a man in the same household are very real. She has his licence to be in the home, a right which in appropriate cases the courts can and will protect: see *Winter Garden Theatre (London) Ltd v Millennium Productions Ltd* [1948] A.C. 173, per Viscount Simon at pp. 188-191; *Binions v Evans* [1972] Ch. 359, per Lord Denning M.R. at p. 367 and *Tanner v Tanner* [1975] 1 W.L.R. 1346. She has also her fundamental right to the integrity and safety of her person. And the children living in the same household enjoy the same rights.

Bearing in mind the existence of these rights and the extent to which they are endangered in the event of family breakdown, I conclude that the mischief against which Parliament has legislated by section 1 of the Act may be described in these terms: – conduct by a family partner which puts at risk the security, or sense of security, of the other partner in the home. Physical violence, or the threat of it, is clearly within the mischief. But there is more to it than that. Homelessness can be as great a threat as physical violence to the security of a woman (or man) and her children. Eviction – actual, attempted or threatened – is, therefore, within the mischief: likewise, conduct which makes it impossible or intolerable, as in the present case, for the other partner, or the children, to remain at home.

Where, in my opinion, the seven Lords Justices fell into error, is in their inference that because the section is not intended to give unmarried family partners rights which they do not already enjoy under existing property law it cannot be construed as conferring upon the county court the power to restrict or suspend the right of possession of the partner who does have that right under the property law or to confer for a period a right of occupancy which overrides his right of occupancy which overrides his right of possession. I find nothing illogical or surprising in Parliament legislating to over-ride a property right, if it be thought to be socially necessary. If in the result a partner with no property right who obtains an injunction under paragraph (c) or (d) thereby obtains for the period of the injunction a right of occupation, so be it. It is no more than the continuance by court order of a right which previously she had by consent: and it will endure only for so long as the county court thinks necessary. Moreover, the restriction or suspension for a time of property rights is a familiar aspect of much of our social legislation: the Rent Acts are a striking example. So far from being surprised, I would expect Parliament, when dealing with the mischief of domestic violence, to legislate in such a way that property rights would not be allowed to undermine or diminish the protection being afforded. Accordingly I am unmoved by the arguments which influenced the Court of Appeal in *B v B* [1978] Fam. 26 and *Cantliff v Jenkins* [1978] Fam. 47. Nor do I find it surprising that this jurisdiction was given to the county court but not the High Court. The relief has to be available immediately and cheaply from a local and easily accessible court. Nor am I dismayed by the point that the section, while doing no more for married women than strengthen remedies for existing rights, confers upon an unmarried woman protection in her home including a right of occupation which can for a period over-ride the property rights of her family partner.

For these reasons, my conclusion is that section 1 of the Act is concerned to protect not property but human life and limb. But, while the section is not intended to confer, and does not confer upon an unmarried woman property rights in the home, it does enable the county court to suspend or restrict her family partner's property right to possession and to preserve to her a right of occupancy (which owes its origin to her being in the home as his consort and with his consent) for as long as may be thought by the court to be necessary to secure the protection of herself and the children.

How, then does the section fit into the law? First, the purpose of the section is not to create rights but to strengthen remedies. Subsection (2) does, however, confer upon the unmarried woman with no property in the home a new right. Though enjoying no property right to possession of the family home, she can apply to the county court for an order restricting or suspending for a time her family partner's right to possession of the premises and conferring upon her a limited right to occupancy. In most cases the period of suspension or restriction of his right and of her occupancy will prove, I expect, to be brief. But in some cases this period may be a lengthy one. The continuance of the order will, however, be a matter for the discretion of the county court judge to be decided in the light of the circumstances of the particular case.

Secondly, the section is concerned to regulate relations between the two family partners. It does not, for instance, prevent the property owner from disposing of his property. It does not confer upon an unmarried woman any right of occupation of the family home comparable with that which a married woman has and can protect against all the world under the Matrimonial Homes Act 1967.

Thirdly, and most importantly, the grant of the order is in the discretion of the country court judge. It is for him to decide whether, and for how long, it is necessary for the protection of the applicant or her child. Normally he will make the order 'until further order,' each party having the right to apply to the court for its discharge or modification. The remedy is available to deal with an emergency; it is, as my noble and learned friend, Lord Salmon has said, a species of first aid. The order must be discontinued as soon as it is clear, upon the application of either or both family partners, that it is no longer needed.

For these reasons I would dismiss the appeal. I have had the advantage of reading in draft the speeches of my noble and learned friends. Lord Diplock and Viscount Dilhorne. I agree with what my Lord, Lord Diplock, has said on the principle of *stare decisis* in the Court of Appeal. I also agree with what my Lord, Viscount Dilhorne, has said on the use of Parliamentary material in the interpretation of statutes, and would wish to add only a few observations of my own.

There are two good reasons why the courts should refuse to have regard to what is said in Parliament or by Ministers as aids to the interpretation of a statute. First, such material is an unreliable guide to the meaning of what is enacted. It promotes confusion, not clarity. The cut and thrust of debate and the pressures of executive responsibility, essential features of open and responsible government, are not always conducive to a clear and unbiased explanation of the meaning of statutory language. And the volume of Parliamentary and ministerial utterances can confuse by its very size. Secondly, counsel are not permitted to refer to Hansard in argument. So long as this rule is maintained by Parliament (it is not the creation of the judges), it must be wrong for the judge to make any judicial use of proceedings in Parliament for the purposes of interpreting statutes.

In *Black-Clawson International Ltd v Papierwerke Waldhof-Aschaffenburg AG* [1975] A.C. 591 this House clarified the law on the use by the courts of *travaux préparatoires*. Reports such as are prepared by the Law Commission, by Royal Commissions, by law reform bodies and Select Committees of either House which lead to legislation may be read by the courts to identify the mischief, including the weaknesses in the law, which the legislation is intended to remedy or reduce. The difficulty, however, remains that one cannot always be sure, without reference to proceedings in Parliament which is prohibited, that Parliament has assessed the mischief or understood the law in the same way as the reporting body. It maybe that, since membership of the European Communities has introduced into our law a style of legislation (regulations having direct effect) which by means of the lengthy recital (or preamble) identifies material to which resort may be had in construing its provisions, Parliament will consider doing likewise in statutes where it would be appropriate, e.g., those based on a report by the Law Commission, a Royal Commission, a departmental committee, or other law reform body. ([1979] A.C. 345-50.)

Viscount Dilhorne: 'There is one other matter to which I must refer. It is a well and long established rule that counsel cannot refer to Hansard as a aid to the construction of a statute. What is said by a Minister or by a member sponsoring a Bill is not a legitimate aid to the interpretation of an Act: see *Craies on Statute Law*, 7th ed. (1971), pp. 128-129. As Lord Reid said in *Beswick v Beswick* [1968] A.C. 58, 73-74:

> 'In construing any Act of Parliament we are seeking the intention of Parliament and it is quite true that we must deduce that intention from the words of the Act ... For purely practical reasons we do not permit debates in either House to be cited: it would add greatly to the time and expense involved in preparing cases involving the construction of a statute if counsel were expected to read all the debates in Hansard, and it would often be impracticable for counsel to get access to at least the older reports of debates in Select Committees of the House of Commons; moreover, in a very large proportion of cases such a search, even if practicable, would throw no light on the question before the court.'

If it was permissible to refer to Hansard, in every case concerning the construction of a statute counsel might regard it as necessary to search through the Hansards of all the proceedings in each House to see if in the course of them anything relevant to the construction had been said. If it was thought that a particular Hansard had anything relevant in it and the attention of the court was drawn to it, the court might also think it desirable to look at the other Hansards. The result might be that attention was devoted to the interpretation of ministerial and other statements in Parliament at the expense of consideration of the language in which Parliament had thought to express its intention.

While, of course, anyone can look at Hansard, I venture to think that it would be improper for a judge to do so before arriving at his decision and before this case I have never known that done. It cannot be right that a judicial decision should be affected by matter which a judge has seen but to which counsel could not refer and on which counsel had no opportunity to comment. ([1979] A.C. 337.)

12.5.4 *Postscript on the use of Hansard*

In the case *Pepper (Inspector of Taxes) v Hart* [1993] AC 593 the Appellate Committee of the House of Lords agreed by a majority to 'permit reference to Parliamentary materials where (a) legislation is ambiguous or obscure, or leads to an absurdity; (b) the material relied upon consists of one or more statements by a Minister or other promoter of the Bill together if necessary with such other Parliamentary material as is necessary to understand such statements and their effect; (c) the statements relied upon are clear.' (Lord Browne-Wilkinson at p 640).

We discuss in chapter 8 the implications of this important decision.

Part Two

Reading, using and interpreting rules in general

Chapter 2

Problems and Mischiefs

In recent years academic law has been dominated by friendly rivalry between two main types of approach. The more traditional one, sometimes known as the 'black letter' or 'expository' approach, treats the systematic exposition and analysis of legal rules ('doctrine') both as the starting point and the almost exclusive focus of the study of law. In this view, sociological, historical, critical and other perspectives are at best ancillary and should only be introduced *after* the student has gained an extensive basic knowledge of the law-as-it-is.

The expository approach has been challenged by those who favour broader approaches to the study of law. A variety of concerns has stimulated this movement, some educational, some scientific, some philosophical and some frankly political or ideological. These differing concerns have stimulated a correspondingly rich, but sometimes confusing, variety of perspectives, ranging from those who maintain that no aspect of law can be understood unless it is seen within the perspective of a grand social theory, such as that of Max Weber or a variant of Marxism, to those who would merely supplement the traditional diet of cases, textbooks, lectures and 'nut-shells' with some extracts from policy documents and writings by social scientists – and perhaps an occasional statute.

The approach adopted in this book is sometimes referred to as 'contextual'. We accept this label if it is taken to mean that law is our primary discipline; that legal rules, institutions, processes, personnel and techniques are the primary subject of study but that, for purposes of understanding, rational criticism or developing basic skills, legal ideas and phenomena are nearly always best viewed in some broader context rather than studied in isolation as if they were things in themselves.[1] Furthermore, we believe that legal concepts, rules and institutions often do not themselves provide the best starting point for study. 'Context first' is a good working rule of thumb, provided that it is not interpreted and applied too rigidly.

One feature of the traditional approach is the way it treats problems of interpreting cases and statutes. The *rules* of statutory interpretation and the *doctrine* of precedent are the main focus of attention. There is a tendency to treat both the rules *of* interpretation and the rules *to be* interpreted as things in themselves; when analysis goes beyond the rules to the study of their purposes or rationales or the processes by which they came into existence, there is a tendency to work back from the rules to these 'contextual' aspects.

---

1 On 'context' see W Twining (1974) 1 *Brit Journal of Law and Society* 64–68.

The approach adopted here diverges from the traditional treatments in three main ways. Firstly, we consider the rules of statutory interpretation and the doctrine of precedent to be relatively minor dimensions of the problems and processes of legal interpretation. They have a place, but it is secondary, and it comes near the end of this study. Secondly, as has already been indicated, we believe that problems of interpretation of legal rules share many characteristics of problems of interpreting other kinds of rules: thus this book tries to set legal interpretation in the context of problems of interpreting rules generally. Thirdly, applying the 'context first' maxim, we begin by looking at the nature of problems before considering the nature of rules in general and the use of rules as responses to problems. Diagnosis before prescription is another good rule of thumb.

A problem arises for an individual when she is faced with a puzzling question to answer, or a difficult choice to make, or some obstacle in the way of achieving a particular objective. A person is faced with a *theoretical* problem when she is confronted by a question calling for an answer that dissolves the puzzlement or solves the problem, without necessarily calling for action. A person is faced with a *practical* problem when there is some doubt about what to do. It is unwise to draw too sharp a line between theoretical and practical problems.

Confronting and solving practical problems is part of everyday living for individuals. When we are confronted with lighting a new gas cooker, driving an unfamiliar car or moving through a crowd we may have to pause to try to work out, perhaps through trial and error, how to cope with the difficulties and obstacles in the way of achieving the objective. Our responses to this kind of situation often become automatic or semi-automatic, so that we can spot, diagnose and solve the problem without having to pause to analyse the situation and work out a solution. We may proceed by intuition or unreflective imitation, by hunch based on experience or by following precedents. Many of our patterns of behaviour can be interpreted as learned or conditioned responses to problem situations. When our response is to some extent automatic, it seems inappropriate to call the process of reasoning and co-ordinating behaviour towards a specific goal 'solving a problem'; for we usually restrict that term to situations in which there is some unresolved difficulty or obstacle that the actor wishes to change, avoid, eliminate or overcome by conscious effort.

Problems arise not only for individuals, but also for groups or classes of people or for whole societies. For example, the *Buckoke* case stemmed from a problem that affected the fire service directly, and indirectly affected society as a whole.[2] Juvenile delinquency, family violence or poverty are examples of what are often referred to as 'social problems'. This term was defined in a leading sociology textbook as 'some piece of social behaviour that causes public friction and/or private misery and calls for collective action to solve it'. As later editions of that book show, as one moves away from the unique problems of the individual actor to more general problems, analysis tends to become more complex.[3]

2 Chapter 1, section 8.
3 P Worsley et al, *The New Introducing Sociology* (revised 3rd edn, 1992), pp 23-34. The definition is in the 2nd edn (*Introducing Sociology*), p 51.

One reason for this centres round *who* defines the problem: the problematic aspects of relations between the police and adolescent blacks in England may look very different from the relative perspectives and values of a senior police officer and an unemployed black youth; they may be perceived in a different light again by a Cabinet Minister or a member of an international committee on race relations. It is a widely held view that the 'problem' of abuse of soft drugs represents the imposition of the value of dominant interests on the less powerful, the main 'victims' being young people. Whether or not this is an acceptable interpretation, it is incontrovertible that one could expect a radically different definition of 'the drug problem' from those who support the criminalisation of drug abuse and from many young people for whom the attitudes of 'middle-aged, middle class busy-bodies' may constitute 'the problem'.[4]

Furthermore, collective decision-making and action tend to be more complex than individual decision and action. So the question arises: who participates with what resources and opportunities through what procedures in producing a 'solution'? Where many persons or several problems are involved it may be unrealistic to expect a pattern of response that will neatly fit a simple rationalistic model of diagnosis, prescription and action. Nevertheless, such a model is a useful starting point for our purposes. In this chapter we shall first explore in an elementary fashion the main ingredients in a rationalistic approach to problem-solving by individuals, in order to identify some of the different points at which things may have happened in a sequence of events with the result that doubts or puzzlements arise for interpreters of rules at a later stage in the process. We shall also examine some of the limitations of this model when applied to individual and to more general problems.

In talking about problems here we shall for the most part be referring to situations in which the actor has to pause to *diagnose* the problem and work out consciously some method of resolving it. However, it is important to recognise from the outset that the process of problem-solving can range from laborious and lengthy rationalistic analysis, perhaps coupled with a process of trial and error, to instantaneous intuitive or semi-automatic response. Similarly, the process preceding the creation of a particular rule could have involved lengthy analysis, debate and deliberation by a large number of people, or it could equally well have involved an intuitive response by a single person or something in between.

A simplified model of problem-solving behaviour by individuals can be characterised in a number of stages as follows:

(a) *clarification* of the actor's *standpoint* – especially, *role, objectives* and *general position*;
(b) *perception* by the actor of certain 'facts' constituting a particular situation;
(c) *evaluation* of one or more elements in the situation as mischievous or undesirable or as presenting an obstacle to the attainment of some objective(s);[5]

---

4   See D Farrier, *Drugs and Intoxication* (1980); Worsley, op cit (1992), chapter 11.
5   Of course, some 'problems' may be both enjoyable and self-imposed, such as climbing a difficult mountain peak or solving a crossword puzzle.

(d) *identification* of relevant moral considerations and a range of possible courses of action that might be taken in order to *solve* the problem;

(e) *prediction* of likely obstacles and costs associated with each possible course of action;

(f) *prescription*, that is to say choice of a general policy and means of effecting that policy for dealing with the problem;

(g) *implementation* of the prescription.[6]

The first five steps can all be subsumed under the notion of diagnosis, but the fourth step also marks the start of a search for solutions: diagnosis sometimes overlaps with prescription.

There are many ways of analysing problem-solving processes. This characterisation is useful for present purposes, because it can form the basis for identifying a number of points at which disagreements may arise or wrong turnings be taken which may create difficulties at a later stage in the process.

Let us apply the model to Mother's behaviour in dealing with Johnny.[7] The story began when Mother saw Johnny eating jam in the kitchen at 3 pm. In the account presented in Chapter 1, the accuracy of Mother's observation was not challenged. But, of course, she might have misperceived the situation. For instance, Johnny may have only been pretending to eat jam; it may have been someone other than Johnny whom she saw; it might in fact have been tea-time, and so on. To put this in general terms, things can go wrong at the very start of a process of problem-solving if facts are misperceived or incompletely perceived or some relevant information was not available.

Secondly, Mother did not like what she saw. In other words, she made a judgment that Johnny's behaviour was *mischievous*. But it could well be the case that Johnny saw nothing wrong with his behaviour. And it is not impossible that Father, on hearing about this, might have agreed with Johnny rather than with Mother about the rightness or wrongness of his action. In other words, when someone says that there is a problem, this involves a value judgment that something is wrong or undesirable or needs to be dealt with, but others might disagree with this evaluation.

Thirdly, in her response Mother made certain implicit assumptions about her standpoint, her role and her objectives. The exact nature of these assumptions could be the subject of elaborate analysis. It is enough to observe here that she took her standpoint as being that of Johnny's mother; that she conceived of her role as including the promotion of Johnny's health, well-being and moral education; and that in her approach to the problem she took into account such factors as her relationship with Father and the latter's views on how discipline should be administered in the household. Such factors are relevant not only to her response to the situation, but also to her original perception and evaluation of it. For, although it is analytically useful to distinguish between perception of the facts in a situation, evaluation of them, and clarification of standpoint, as a matter of psychological fact these elements

---

6 Compare the advice given to government departments that are considering introducing regulations: Cabinet Office, *The Better Regulation Guide* (1998).

7 Chapter 1, section 3.5.

may be so closely interrelated as to be indistinguishable in practice. For fact, value, role and vantage-point are all intimately bound up in the process of perception.

Mother's *diagnosis* of the mischief was that Johnny was 'eating between meals'. This was by no means the only way of characterising the problem, even by someone who agreed with Mother's view of the facts and her judgment that something was wrong. The mischief could have been characterised as stealing, eating things that are bad for his teeth or disobedience. It might even be the case that, although Mother characterised the situation as eating between meals, what really concerned her was the implicit criticism of her cooking. In short, at the stage of diagnosis the principal actors may *misdiagnose*, even by their own standards, by picking on an element other than the one that has disturbed them; or they may produce an incomplete or inappropriate diagnosis, by identifying only one of a number of such elements. Furthermore, other people may disagree about which elements in the situation are mischievous and why. To give a slightly less obvious example: a child psychiatrist might agree with Mother and Father that there was something wrong about Johnny helping himself to half a pot of strawberry jam, but suggest that this was symptomatic of a craving for affection or of some other emotional problem. Similarly, people may confuse symptoms with diseases as well as disagree about the precise nature of a disease. Where people disagree on diagnosis, they are likely also to disagree about the appropriateness of particular prescriptions. A rule prohibiting Johnny from going into the larder is not likely to go far in solving problems arising from lack of affection; it may even make matters worse.

In a rationalistic approach to problems it is not very sensible to talk about solutions until one has agreed on a diagnosis. It is, of course, common in actual life for people to proceed directly to choosing solutions, before they have tried to diagnose the problem. Even where attempts are made to diagnose problems, it may not be possible to introduce appropriate remedies to alleviate their causes; people may agree about the one without agreeing about the other. In addition, the appropriate remedies may be too expensive, long term or difficult to introduce; they may require substantial changes in the behaviour and attitudes of individuals, in the practices of groups and institutions or even in the political and economic ordering of society. Disagreement about both the causes and the nature of the remedies which would be appropriate to deal with such social problems as 'road rage' in Britain in 1999, family violence or drug abuse, are ample evidence of these considerations. Such problems often involve conflicting factors which in turn often serve to make some possible remedies inappropriate or unacceptable. Inexpensive, short-term and easily implemented remedies which relieve the symptoms may in many cases be the only practicable options.

Similarly in legal contexts it is hardly surprising to find responses to problems that do not fit a simple rationalistic model of problem-solving. Inertia, delay, diverting attention, buying time by setting up a committee, cosmetic or token measures, placebos, 'knee jerk' calls for new offences or increased penalties, are all familiar features of political and legal life. *Cognoscenti* are also quick to spot somewhat less obvious spectacles such as 'moral panics', the Micawber Response ('It will all come right in the end'), the Way of the Baffled Medic

(Prescribe first, Diagnose later – if at all), the Nelson Touch ('I see no problem') and Success ('The problem is now officially solved' or, simply, 'It works').

Let us for the sake of argument accept Mother's characterisation of the problem as one of preventing Johnny from eating between meals. Let us also accept her judgement that the problem, so diagnosed, is capable of solution. If she had paused to ponder about the range of possible ways of achieving this object, a number of alternatives might have occurred to her: she could produce such nice meals that he would not be tempted to eat at other times; she could bribe Johnny by offering him rewards or inducements if he disciplined himself; she could reason with him by pointing out the consequences to his health or his character or his relations with his parents if he indulged in this kind of behaviour; she could reduce the opportunities by restricting Johnny's movements, by keeping very little food in the house or by locking the larder door; she could give him a clip on the ear; or she could make a rule or series of rules. To solve her 'problem' it is not necessary for her to restrict herself to a single device. In the event, she decided to make a rule rather than to tackle the problem by other means.

The next stage was for Mother to design a rule aimed at preventing Johnny eating between meals. It was open to her to formulate a rule co-extensive with the policy – for example, 'Johnny may never eat between meals without Mother's permission'. However, she devised an instrument that was not co-extensive with the mischief – on the one hand, Johnny had opportunities for eating between meals without entering the larder; on the other hand, Johnny interpreted the rule to mean that he was prohibited from entering the larder even to protect his parents' interests. To make matters worse, Mother's formulation of the rule gave Johnny the opportunity to exploit a possible doubt about the meaning of the word 'enter' to secure some jam from the larder.

It is arguable that in her role as rule-maker Mother took not merely one wrong turning, but several. Even if no issue were taken with her original perception of the facts of the first incident, or with her feeling that something was wrong, it could be argued that she inappropriately or incompletely diagnosed the original problem; that her values or her priorities were questionable; that she failed to consider the range of possibilities open to her to solve it; that, having chosen a possibly inappropriate means for solving it, she made matters even worse by establishing a rule that was by no means co-extensive with the mischief,[8] and by leaving a further loophole through her use of the word 'enter' – although in fairness to her, some sacrifice in succinctness would probably have been entailed to cover the broom case.

Up to this point in the story Mother has been the main actor. After the original creation of the rule, some new, complicating factors arise: in particular, Mother acquires other roles, for instance those of prosecutor and advocate, as well as retaining some rule-making power, in that she still has an opportunity to change the rule, at least for the future. Secondly, the fact that a rule has been created has changed her position: from now on the situation will be defined, at least in part, in terms of the rule, which will have created

8 See below, pp 191–192.

expectations about her future behaviour as well as Johnny's and Father's. And Johnny's response has added some new elements; for instance, it may now be interpreted as a more general challenge to her authority. Mother's 'problem' is no longer a simple one of preventing Johnny from eating between meals; Johnny's attitude to authority, his relations with his parents and possibly other aspects of Mother's relations with Father are all now relevant. As the story develops, the situation changes, and Mother is confronted with further choices: whether to tell Father about each incident immediately after it has arisen and, if so, how to present it to him; whether to revoke or change the rule and so on. In short, 'Mother's problem' is neither simple nor static; it contains a number of complex elements and changes over time. Moreover, at no stage in this story is Mother's problem identical with Johnny's problem or with Father's problem. Whether it is appropriate to refer to this situation as containing one problem or a series of closely related problems is largely a matter of semantics.

It is worth making two further points at this stage. Firstly, unlike some theoretical problems, practical problems do not typically admit of one single correct solution. A well-defined theoretical problem such as a crossword puzzle or a chess problem may admit of only one correct answer, although this is not necessarily the case. Practical problems tend to be less neat. As we have seen, the relatively specific objective of preventing Johnny eating between meals could be furthered by a number of devices, which could be used as alternatives or in combination. There was not a single correct solution to the problem so defined, but rather a range of possible alternatives of varying degrees of appropriateness to the task in hand. Similarly, 'success' in solving a practical problem is typically a relative matter. Mother's rule, despite its shortcomings, may have been partially successful in reducing the amount Johnny ate between meals, even if it did not entirely eliminate it. Rulemakers usually have to be satisfied with less than 100% success.

Secondly, the story of Johnny illustrates some of the limitations, as well as the uses, of a simple rationalistic model of problem-solving behaviour. There are dangers in seeing problems and solutions as neatly packaged, isolated events. Even a seemingly simple situation can be shown to involve an indefinitely large number of intricately related ingredients in a complex continuing process, in which problems are not necessarily static or well-defined, or perceived or evaluated in identical terms by different actors; similarly 'solutions' may be more or less well-defined, they may be more or less successful in securing particular objectives, and they may also contribute in turn to the generation of new problems. The *Case of the Legalistic Child* reminds us that rules can create problems as well as contribute to their solution and that problems tend to cumulate.

If an apparently simple situation turns out on analysis to be so intricate, we should not be surprised to find the task of analysing more general situations, such as those that confront law-makers in society, to be correspondingly more complex. In the nursery there was initially only one actor who was seeking to diagnose and resolve in a relatively short space of time a situation perceived as problematic; in society as a whole, or in intermediate contexts, a number of complicating factors may be expected: for example, capacity to influence events may be distributed among a variety of people with different vantage points, roles, values, interests and concerns; procedures for decision and action may be slow, arcane, complicated; a policy or rule, once instituted, may be difficult to change or revoke and may, in a sense, take on a life of its own – and so on. Such factors can be used to point to further limitations of the model of problem-solving behaviour outlined above. But this should not be taken as a counsel of despair. For although the model does not claim to be in any sense complete, this does not mean to say that it is useless. Provided its limitations are recognised, the simplicity of the model is an advantage for present purposes, that is to give a broad overview of some of the most common kinds of condition that give rise to puzzlements about interpretation of rules. All the points made about rules as problem-solving devices in relation to the *Case of the Legalistic Child* can be made about laws as problem-solving devices in more complex contexts.

Let us illustrate this briefly by applying the model to the problem that arose in *Buckoke*, taking the standpoint of the Home Secretary. One of the tasks he (and the Secretary of State for Scotland) is called upon to perform is to make recommendations to Parliament for legislation concerning road traffic. As the Court of Appeal emphasised, it was largely due to Parliament's failure to deal with the situation that the various parties in the case, including the Court, were confronted with certain difficulties. The general factual background of the problem, as set out in the report of the case, does not appear to have been disputed. However, the Home Secretary might wish for some more detailed information, such as estimates of the likely consequences to property-owners, fire-crews and other road-users of directives that a driver could, or could not, jump the lights; his basic problem could be stated in such terms as: how to ensure the objective of the speedy arrival of fire engines at fires while minimising the risk of harm to road-users (including firemen). A range of theoretically possible solutions might be considered: eg the provision of police escorts on all fire engines; redirection of traffic by policemen; a change in fire-engine design so that traffic lights can be remotely controlled by the driver; the provision of more fire engines and stations so as to cut down the number of traffic lights to be jumped, particularly in areas of high fire risk; the enactment of an exception, in favour of fire engines, to the general rule; the enactment of an exception in all emergencies; and so on. No doubt some of these ideas are not feasible, or are even ridiculous. Within the fire service, the penultimate was the preferred solution and was introduced by statutory instrument. The grounds for the prior refusal to adopt this expedient are a matter for speculation. There may be a natural reluctance to make special exceptions to the rules governing road traffic; difficult policy choices arise as to what the scope of the exception should be; and in what circumstances it ought to operate. Moreover, the drafting of an exception might possibly be troublesome, for example, in the need for a definition of 'emergency'.[9]

Much of the interest prompted by this case stems from the differences of standpoint of the various actors. To put it simply: Parliament's problem was

9 Chapter 1, section 8, question 7.

whether to make a special exception to a generally beneficial rule, while the Chief Fire Officer was concerned to promote the objective of getting to the fires as quickly as possible despite Parliament's refusal to assist. The problem from the Fire Brigade Union's point of view was how to rescue its members from the dilemma of disobeying orders or breaking the law. The Court of Appeal saw its role not only as determining certain technical issues of law, but also in supporting the Chief Fire Officer, criticising Parliament and the plaintiffs and going as far as it could to mitigate the rigour of the law without purporting to change an Act of Parliament.

The *Buckoke* case is an example of a situation in which there was a high degree of consensus about the basic facts, the social values, the diagnosis of the original problem and the most desirable way of solving it; but many social problems are not as straightforward as this. Somewhat more complex is the case study of domestic violence.[10] This illustrates changes in the social facts underlying a problem (for example the scale, the forms and the distribution of violence in the home), changes in public awareness of, concern for and categorisation of the problem, and changes in official and other responses to it. These range from inertia through merely symbolic or cosmetic reforms, to more determined efforts to tackle it, such as more vigorous enforcement of existing laws, creation of new laws, education (eg of health visitors to recognise signs of violence or of the public about alcoholism) and through better co-ordination of the efforts of different kinds of functionaries and specialists. It also illustrates some of the complexities and limits of trying to use law to combat what is almost universally and unquestioningly regarded as a social evil in the way that the 'abuse' of certain soft drugs is not.

The Report of the Select Committee on Violence in Marriage illustrates some further points.[11] In many respects this quite modest policy document is a model of what an official report should be: the committee openly acknowledged that neither the scale nor the causes of domestic violence were fully known or understood, and they were sensitive to the difficulties of defining the scope of the problem for their immediate purposes. Should they for example deal only with physical violence to wives, or extend their enquiry to include all women or spouses or partners or children? Should they include threats of physical violence and what might be termed emotional or psychological violence? They recognised the close connections between domestic violence and other social problems such as alcoholism, poor housing, adolescent marriage and pregnancy. They were sensitive to the dangers of over-generalisation about many key aspects of the subject. They talked in terms of 'alleviating' rather than 'solving' the problem, and they made reasonably clear distinctions between long term strategies and short- and medium-term responses. In considering possible uses of law they emphasised that as much might be achieved by more effective implementation of existing laws as by making new ones, that laws are not self-executing, and that in this case there

10 Chapter 1, section 12.1.
11 Chapter 1, section 12.2.

were financial and other obstacles to effective law enforcement – for example, the police had traditionally been reluctant to intervene in domestic disputes.

The report makes clear that several different areas of both substantive and procedural law were potentially relevant, but they probably underestimated the difficulty of harmonising the new remedy (an injunction to protect the battered partner) with traditional property concepts, especially where the partners were not married. Account is taken both of the importance and of the practical difficulties of making available speedy, cheap and effective remedies which would in practice be accessible to and used by the victims. There is in particular an unusual sensitivity to the limits of effective legal action, and a clear recognition that, at the most, law is only one of a range of social resources available for mitigating this kind of problem and that it is often best used in connection with other strategies such as education, preventive action by social workers and the provision of more crisis centres and refuges. The difficulties of maintaining liaison between different agencies and specialists are emphasised. Finally, the committee, well aware that part of the problem was that the recommendations of two previous reports had not been implemented, went out of their way to emphasise that the report was only a modest contribution to diagnosing and confronting an intractable problem which was not yet fully understood. All in all this provides a far better model of a measured and rational official response to a social problem than many more pretentious and expensive reports. It contrasts even more sharply with the crude simplicities to which we are daily exposed in the media and elsewhere – symbolised by the standard gut reaction to each new alleged crisis: 'There ought to be a law against it'. All of these factors form part of the context of the particular problems of interpretation that arose in *B v B* and *Davis v Johnson* which will be considered in Chapter 8.

Many social problems involve wider ramifications and greater potential for disagreement about facts, values, categorisation and priorities than do either the *Buckoke* case or domestic violence. As problems aggregate, so do attempted solutions and responses. Also there is a widely held view that holistic solutions tend to be more satisfactory, but less easy to achieve, than fragmented or piecemeal ones. Some of the most acute difficulties in making and interpreting rules concern how they fit in with other rules; similarly there is always potential friction between new reforms and existing institutions, rules, policies and practices. It is beyond the scope of this book to attempt to provide a full treatment of what is involved in analysing social problems.[12] The intellectual procedure outlined in this chapter merely represents the first stage in a relatively systematic approach to diagnosing conditions of doubt in interpretation.[13]

12 See generally C Wright Mills, *The Sociological Imagination* (1959, 1970).
13 For exercises on chapter 2, see Appendix 1, section A5, questions 6 and 7, and section B, questions 1 and 2, pp 395 and 395.

Chapter 3

Of Rules in General

In this chapter we introduce some of the more important general considerations relevant to understanding the nature of rules. After examining the concept of 'rule' and its relation to such notions as principles, policies and values, we consider briefly some standard distinctions concerning the form and structure of rules, and the difference between general exceptions and exemptions in particular cases. We then deal in turn with the variety of rules and the relations between rules within a single aggregation or 'system', between different systems of rules, and between systems of rules and external factors. Next we consider in an elementary way some general theories about the functions of rules, rules as techniques of social management and differences between instrumentalist, formalist and other perspectives on rules, with particular reference to the notion of rules as instruments of power. The purpose of this chapter, then, is to provide a fairly simple theoretical basis from which to proceed to explore what is involved in the interpretation of rules.

1 What is a rule?

In ordinary talk the word 'rule' has many usages. In the present context we are not concerned with 'rule' in the sense of reign, eg the rule of Queen Victoria, or in the sense of a habit or empirical generality, as in 'as a rule he catches the 9.55 train to London', or in the sense of a calculating instrument, such as a slide-rule.[1] 'Rule' is used here to mean a general norm mandating or guiding conduct or action in a given type of situation. A typical rule in this sense prescribes that in circumstances X, behaviour of type Y ought, or ought not to be, or may be, engaged in by persons of class Z. Particular attention needs to be paid to four aspects of this formulation:

(a) A rule is normative or *prescriptive*, that is to say it is concerned with ought (not), may (not) or can (not), in relation to behaviour, rather than with factual *description* of behaviour.
(b) A rule is *general* in that it is concerned with *types* of behaviour in *types* of situation or circumstances; a prescription governing a unique event is not a rule.

---

1   Newton Garver, 'Rules', in P Edwards (ed), *Encylopaedia of Philosophy* (1967), pp 230-233.

(c) Rules both guide and serve as standards for *behaviour*, that is to say activities, acts or omissions. In the present context we are concerned solely with *human* behaviour.

(d) Rules provide one kind of *justifying* reason for decision or action. When asked, 'Why did you do this?', the actor may justify the action by reference to a rule, for example, 'Because I was required/permitted/empowered to do so under Regulation...'

The definition of 'rule' adopted here is deliberately broad. As one writer puts it, there are many sorts of action, there are many kinds of guidance, and there are many different ways of prescribing.[2] Some rules impose duties to act or prohibit certain types of behaviour; some confer discretionary powers; others provide for distribution of benefits; yet others specify conditions that need to be satisfied for certain consequences to follow, such as the rules prescribing the method of scoring in Association Football or the rules laying down the requirements of a valid will.[3] Some prescriptions are categorical and specific ('Under no circumstances whatsoever is behaviour of type X permitted'), but others are provisional, or are merely guides, or are subject to numerous unstated exceptions. In this broad sense, 'rule' is a term for the genus of which precepts, regulations, conventions, principles, and guiding standards are species. It is not difficult to produce examples of borderline cases over which people might reasonably disagree, for one reason or another, as to whether or not they deserve to be called 'rules', eg (i) 'the neighbour principle'; (ii) 'an advocate should never press an absurd distinction'; (iii) 'promises should be kept'; (iv) 'guidelines'.[4]

Some of the complexities at the borderlines are illustrated by two examples. First, a distinction is sometimes drawn between prudential and normative prescriptions. A prudential prescription, such as a working rule of thumb, provides guidance as to how to achieve a certain objective.[5] For example, the cricketers' maxim 'never drive against the spin' advises batsmen how to avoid a particular consequence, in this case hitting the ball in the air. Prudential prescriptions may be directed to immoral or illegal ends, such as how to deceive one's spouse or how to evade tax. The relation is solely one of means to ends. A normative prescription, on the other hand, is not merely a recommendation about efficient means or methods of achieving a given end. It involves a judgment about what constitutes good or lawful or valid conduct. Questions about the basis of such judgments are perennial questions of philosophy which form an important part of the background of any study of rules, but are beyond the scope of our immediate enquiry. Here it is pertinent to note that while what is purely prudential or expedient often conflicts with what is considered to be moral or lawful or otherwise right, many examples of actual rules combine

---

2 Ibid.
3 Raz points out that rules of this type are neither mandatory nor permissive nor power-conferring; because they only guide behaviour indirectly, he maintains that they are not norms. J Raz, *Practical Reason and Norms* (1975), pp 117, 186.
4 Chapter 1, section 10.1.
5 On rules of thumb see F Schauer, *Playing by The Rules* (1991), pp 3-5, 104-111.

both prudential and normative elements: for example, driving under the influence of drink is imprudent, unlawful and immoral, and a particular prescription against such behaviour may reflect all three kinds of concern. This book deals with problems of determining the scope and meaning of normative prescriptions, but much of what we have to say may incidentally be relevant to interpreting purely prudential prescriptions, whether or not they deserve to be called rules.

Another distinction, given prominence by Professor Ronald Dworkin, is between rules, principles and policies.[6] According to Dworkin, 'rules are applicable in an all-or-nothing fashion'; if the rule is valid it dictates the result; for example, the rule in baseball that provides that if a batter has had three strikes he is out. Dworkin uses 'principle' generically to refer to those standards which guide, but do not *ipso facto* determine, the result, such as the legal maxim that 'no man shall profit from his own wrong'. Legal principles have 'the dimension of weight' and can conflict without being invalid – in a given context the result has to be determined by weighing competing principles. A 'policy' is that kind of standard 'that sets out a goal to be reached, generally an improvement in some economic, political, or social feature of the community', such as the policy of decreasing road accidents. The distinction between principles and policies sometimes collapses, in much the same way as the distinction between prudential and normative prescriptions, but for some purposes it is important to distinguish between standards that are to be observed because they advance some goal deemed to be desirable, and standards that are a requirement 'of justice or fairness or some other dimension of morality'.[7]

Dworkin was by no means the first jurist to emphasise distinctions between rules, principles and policies. His account of these notions has been very prominent in recent juristic debate because it is one starting point of his critique of legal positivism, exemplified by HLA Hart's *The Concept of Law*. It may be useful, in clarifying some preliminary issues, to explore some differences between Dworkin's approach and that adopted in this book.

The first is mainly a matter of terminology, but also has a direct bearing on some issues of substance. We have deliberately adopted a definition of 'rule' which is broad enough to include Dworkin's notion of 'principles', preferring to use such terms as categorical precepts to cover his rather narrow conception of a rule. But for its rather technical, and perhaps abstruse, associations, the term 'norm' could have been substituted throughout for 'rule' without affecting the substance of the analysis.

We have deliberately adopted a broad, and admittedly vague, definition of rule which emphasises neither the 'all-or-nothing' nor the 'hard-and-fast' qualities sometimes associated with the notion. One reason for rejecting Dworkin's 'all-or-nothingness' as a necessary element in the notion of 'a rule' is that this obscures three separate ideas: the level of generality or particularity of a prescription; its precision or vagueness; and its status or force in dictating,

---

6   R Dworkin, *Taking Rights Seriously* (1977), especially pp 22ff.
7   Ibid.

guiding or influencing a result. In ordinary usage it is quite common to differentiate between rules and principles on the basis that to qualify as a rule a prescription has to be 'precise' or 'specific' – two different ideas. For example, the term 'male persons' is more precise (ie less vague), but less specific (ie more general) than 'student'. One might say of the maxim 'no man should profit from his own wrong' that it is a principle because it is too general and too vague to count as a 'hard-and-fast' rule. Dworkin's distinction between rules and principles rests on a third ground: for him, a rule *dictates* a particular result; a principle merely points in a particular direction, as a factor to be weighed by the decision-maker. This is an illuminating distinction and a crucial one for Dworkin's purposes. However, as we shall see, levels of generality and the status of a prescription in influencing a result are both matters of degree, subject to innumerable gradations. Moreover, there is often a correlation in practice between level of generality, precision and prescriptive status: 'no man should profit from his own wrong' is general, vague, subject to numerous exceptions and can at best serve as a guide. But some very general prescriptions – such as the moral principle that no one should be tortured under any circumstances whatsoever – have the status of a categorical precept: for those who accept it, it dictates the result in all situations where a decision whether or not to torture arises – the concept of torture, as we shall see, is neither very precise nor very vague:[8] it is more precise than 'inhuman treatment', but nevertheless there are many borderline cases. Thus an absolute moral prohibition against torture is fairly general, only moderately precise, but quite categorical. For our purposes, it is a matter of indifference whether such a prescription is categorised as a moral principle or a moral rule.

Thus we have stipulated for present purposes a definition of 'a rule' which is somewhat broader than the term is sometimes used in ordinary discussion and much broader than the usage popularised by Dworkin in the context of recent jurisprudential debates. We have deliberately not made any degree of specificity or precision or prescriptive status a necessary condition for the usage of the term. From time to time, it may be useful to differentiate between general and specific rules, between vague and precise rules, between categorical precepts and mere guides or other standards which do not dictate results. Such distinctions have a bearing on problems of interpretation, but to insist on them at the start would introduce an artificial and premature rigidity into the discussion. Levels of generality, precision and prescriptive force are all matters of degree.

This leads on to a second point: in our view Dworkin's distinction between rules and principles is artificially sharp, for there are relatively few clear examples, in law or elsewhere, of norms that have the 'all-or-nothing' characteristic that he ascribes to rules. No prominent legal positivist who has elucidated law in terms of rules, such as Hart, or of norms, such as Kelsen, has been committed to the view that law is made up solely of categorical precepts.[9]

---

8   See below, pp 195-196.
9   HLA Hart, *Postscript to The Concept of Law* (1994), pp 259ff.

To attribute such a view to 'positivism' is to set up an artificial target for attack. The principles of statutory interpretation, the neighbour principle, and perhaps even the maxims of Equity[10] can, in our view, all be accommodated in a positivist conception of law. They are 'posited',[11] ie man-made.

It is not necessary for present purposes to nail our flag firmly to the mast of some particular legal theory, but we acknowledge that we are more persuaded to some mild version of positivism (exemplified, perhaps, by Hart's sympathetic critic Neil MacCormick) than to the views of Dworkin. In our view, an adequate account of a legal system in terms of rules or norms would need to include and to differentiate between many different kinds of rules, including precepts, principles, guiding standards, accepted practices, customs, conventions and several types of maxims. The material of law is so rich, so complex and so shot through with fine gradations that we are sceptical of the value of attempting a comprehensive taxonomy of types of rules. It is beyond the scope of this book to attempt a rounded theory of and about law. For the more modest objective of exploring some of the main recurrent problems of interpreting all kinds of rules, some working distinctions between different kinds of rules are especially important and useful, and will be introduced as we proceed. Some of these are fairly standard within the jurisprudence of legal positivism; some of them are suggested by its critics, such as Fuller and Dworkin. For present purposes a comprehensive classification of different kinds of rules is unnecessary, even if it were feasible, but Dworkin's distinction between rules and principles is too rigid and too simple to provide an adequate starting point for an exploration of problems of interpretation.

Thirdly, Dworkin distinguishes between *legal* rules and *legal* principles as part of his critique of *legal* positivism. In this respect our focus is broader, for, as has already been emphasised, one of the central themes of this book is that many of the factors giving rise to difficulties in interpretation of legal rules are not unique to legal contexts. We are more concerned here to present legal interpretation and reasoning as an example of interpretation of rules and practical reasoning generally, than to explore what, if anything, is unique or peculiar about legal ways of thought. In the later chapters on legislation, case law and legal reasoning in interpretation, some special features of interpretation in legal contexts will be identified, for example the existence of developed rules about precedent and the interpretation of statutes, but even there the thrust of our analysis will be that these are rather less important than they are sometimes thought to be when compared to other factors that regularly bear on problems of interpretation.

Most of the examples in this book will be categorical precepts – that is relatively specific and unqualified prescriptions which fall squarely within the definition of 'rule' stipulated above. But it is not necessary to concern ourselves unduly with the borderlines of this definition, because most of what we have to say about interpretation applies, to a greater or lesser extent, to borderline cases as well as to clear examples of rules.

10 Chapter 1, section 10.1.
11 N Simmonds, *Central Issues in Jurisprudence* (1986), pp 99-100.

Much attention has been devoted in the literature to elucidating the notion of a rule and disentangling it from other notions such as 'habit', 'prediction', 'practice', 'command' and 'value'.[12] To put the matter very briefly, whereas predictions and statements of habits and practices are capable of verification or falsification, that is to say they are (logically) capable of being tested as to whether they are empirically true or false, statements of rules and commands are propositions of a different logical kind, which are not directly either verifiable or falsifiable. 'Johnny always brushes his teeth' or 'Johnny will probably brush his teeth on Friday next' are potentially capable of being shown to be empirically true or false. But this is not *prima facie* the case with statements of the kind 'Johnny, brush your teeth!' or 'Johnny must always brush his teeth', although such statements are based on assumptions which can be shown to be true or false, such as the assumption that Johnny has teeth.

Rules resemble habits and practices in that all three notions relate to behaviour and are general. Moreover, some kinds of rules, such as customs and conventions, grow out of habits or practices – for instance, what is at first merely habitual may become customary as it gains approval or forms the basis of other people's expectations. Statements of habits or practices are species of *factual generalisations*; statements of rules are expressed in the *normative* language of 'ought', 'must', 'may' and 'can'.

The relationship between rule and prediction is of a different kind. Rules are by definition general; predictions may be general or particular. Unlike rules, predictions can turn out to be true or false. Rules have sometimes been confused with predictions because rule-statements are sometimes used as an aid to prediction. For example, a solicitor may look up a statute or other legal provision in order to predict how a court is likely to treat a client in certain circumstances. If the legal provision is clear, the solicitor will be able to make a reasonably confident prediction of how a court will decide, if certain facts are established before it. But the legal provision is not a prediction; it is used as an aid to prediction – and it is a foolish solicitor who always relies on legal rules alone in trying to predict for clients the likely consequences of a course of action, just as the Bad Man in Boston would need to take many factors into account in predicting what would be likely to happen to him if he decided to do some specific act.[13] To confuse rules with predictions is to confuse rules with one of the uses of rules.

Similarly, rules and commands are separate but related notions. Both *prescribe* behaviour; but there are important differences. Firstly, some commands are not rules, because they lack the element of *generality* ('Come here immediately'). Secondly, by no means all rules take the form of commands – the notion of command suggests that certain behaviour is *required* ('must') or *prohibited* ('do not'), whereas many rules *permit* or *authorise* behaviour or *confer powers* or *establish* institutions or procedures. They also serve as standards for criticising or evaluating behaviour. Thirdly, the notion of a command suggests that it is the expression of the *will* of a specific source,

---

12 See especially HLA Hart, *The Concept of Law* (2nd edn, 1994), passim; F Waismann, *The Principles of Linguistic Philosophy* (1965), chapter 7.
13 Chapter 1, section 11.6.

a *commander*, who is typically human, but who may be divine. While some rules are direct expressions of the will of a person or body that issues them, other rules have different sources. For instance, the rules of English grammar were not laid down by any specific person or body of persons; we are tempted to say they 'just growed', as a way of indicating a much more complicated process of evolution which could not be said to have been willed by anyone in particular. However, some rules can be appropriately expressed in the form of general commands, for example 'Never go into the larder without my permission.' Perhaps because some rules of substantive law, especially in areas such as criminal law, can be fitted more or less into this form, theorists such as John Austin have depicted laws as species of commands (viz general commands made by authority and backed by threats). While the analogy is quite close in some respects, the theory is now generally discredited; one reason is that, whereas legal rules that impose duties can be made to fit the model fairly easily, the command theory does not give an adequate account of legal rules that confer powers or grant licences or constitute certain activities, such as the making of a valid will.

2   Rules and values

The precise nature of the relationship between rules and values is complex. We may say of a rule that it furthers, embodies or conflicts with some value such as human happiness or the right to life.[14] For example, section 57 of the Offences against the Person Act 1861 may be said to promote such values as the sanctity of monogamous marriage, the solemnity and dignity of a religious ceremony, and the protection of potential victims of bigamous unions. On the other hand, some school rules may be considered to conflict with the values of a liberal education, and the rule requiring vehicles to stop at a red traffic light, to conflict with the desirability of fire engines reaching their destination as quickly as possible. Many rules represent a compromise between conflicting values: in the case of those governing road traffic, the safety of road-users on the one hand, convenience and traffic progress on the other.

In these instances it is relatively easy to distinguish between the rule and the values it represents. In its simplest form, the relationship is one of means (the rule) and ends (the value(s)). However, the distinction is not always so clear-cut. For example, Article 3 of the European Convention on Human Rights could be said directly to embody absolute moral principles against torture, inhuman and degrading treatment.[15] In this instance we can see that the rule and the values it embodies are co-extensive but distinct, because the rule was

---

14 'The term "values" may refer to interests, pleasures, likes, preferences, duties, moral obligations, desires, wants, needs, aversions and attractions, and many other modalities of selective orientation' (International Encyclopaedia of Social Sciences). A theory of value is concerned with what features of these modalities are good or desirable or right. Anthony Giddens defines "values" as "Ideas held by human individuals or groups about what is desirable, proper, good, or bad" *Sociology* (1st edn, 1991), p 733.
15 Chapter 1, section 10.3.3.

created by formal procedures, is expressed in fixed verbal form and is subject to interpretation which may be somewhat narrower than some might like to see, and which may take into account factors other than these moral principles.

In some contexts the distinction between rules and values may collapse. For example, it would be artificial to maintain that in protesting against Father's behaviour in peremptorily switching television channels, Johnny was invoking a 'rule' rather than a 'value', or vice versa.[16] Such situations may be too indeterminate for the distinction between rules and values to be meaningful. However, even where a relatively well-defined rule exists and can be differentiated from the values which it promotes, it does not follow that there will never be any doubt as to the absolute or relative preference to be given to that rule: it may conflict with other rules promoting different values, or with values promoted by the system of which it is part, or it may simply be an inappropriate or inadequate vehicle for promoting those values.

Another important distinction is between values which are held to be intrinsically good, such as the right to life, concern for others, telling the truth, or freedom from racial, sexual, or physical abuse, and values which are good because they promote desirable consequences (extrinsic values) such as brushing one's teeth and keeping fit (health) or doing homework (educational advancement). Some values may be good both intrinsically and extrinsically: for example moral philosophers often argue that keeping one's promises is desirable as a good in itself and because it promotes good consequences such as mutual reliability, credibility and the fulfilment of legitimate expectations (all important for successful commercial practice). In addition, the very fact that a proposition is formulated *as a rule* is thought, particularly in legal contexts, to entail the promotion of values intrinsic to the 'enterprise of subjecting human conduct to the governance of rules', such as predictability, consistency, non-retroactivity and order. These intrinsic values have been collectively called 'fidelity to law',[17] and as we shall see in later chapters, conflict may arise between them and the particular values promoted by the rule at hand.

The distinction between intrinsic and extrinsic values is important in another context, namely the justification of action and of rules prescribing action. The appeal to values in support of actions is a subject which has provoked disagreement among moral philosophers. To put the issue very simply, there are three main views as to the criteria which may be adopted to determine the claim of any action (or rule) to be right. The first formulates these criteria in terms of abstract principles such as justice, fairness, equality, liberty, or respect for human life and dignity; values which are held to be intrinsically or self-evidently good. Such a view is technically called deontological, although moralist will do for short. If a moralist were attempting to justify the use of torture in an extreme case, she would have to argue that in this context the values of the right to life of many innocent people and the right of the state to take action to protect its citizens outweigh the individual terrorist's right to

16 Chapter 1, section 3.5, question 9.
17 See L Fuller, *The Morality of Law* (1969).

freedom from inhuman or degrading treatment. Typically such a moral dilemma provokes disagreement both as to the values which are appropriate in the context and the weight that is to be attached to them; and this feature is to be found in other paradigm cases of moral choice such as abortion, capital punishment and the control of pornography.

The second view looks exclusively to the effects or consequences of the action in issue; if it maximises human happiness or general welfare, or some other consequences deemed to be good, it is justifiable. This view is known as utilitarian or, more broadly, consequentialist, which is how we shall refer to it.[18] In the torture example a consequentialist would ask not what moral principles are at stake but what would have the more beneficial effect for everyone? This may yield a different answer than for moralists, some of whom may take the view that torture is *always* wrong. Consequentialists admit no such absolutes – whether it is ever right to torture a person in extreme cases depends on the actual or potential effects. Often, as with torture, consequentialists and moralists may agree as to the wrongness or rightness of a particular action, but the possibility that a consequentialist can come up with a different answer in such a case has been the subject of perennial disagreement among philosophers.

The third view, sometimes known as ethical pluralism, employs a mixture of consequentialist and moralist arguments; and this is indeed how many people typically argue. When asked why, for example, she is opposed to the easy availability of pornographic books and films, a person might reply that they exploit and degrade women and encourage the commission of sexual offences. In legal contexts, too, it is commonplace to appeal to both types of criteria as supplying tests to determine the rightness of rules and of their interpretation.

3 The form and structure of a rule

It is important to distinguish between rules and *verbal formulations* of rules. Many rules are expressed in words – for instance, the rules of table tennis as adopted by the Table Tennis Federation, the principles of contract as set out in standard textbooks and practitioners' works, and the rule about the larder prescribed for Johnny by his mother. But we are all familiar with unspoken rules. In your family, or within a social circle in which you move, there may be a number of rules which are regularly followed and invoked although they have never been articulated. Similarly, many rules of English grammar and usage had existed for a long time before anyone tried to put them into words, and there are still languages governed by rules that have never been expressed in words. Unspoken rules are not necessarily simple. As Wittgenstein observed: 'The tacit conventions on which the understanding of everyday language depends are enormously complicated.'[19]

18 Utilitarianism (maximization of general welfare) is one form of consequentialism.
19 L Wittgenstein, *Tractatus Logico-Philosophicus* (1971 edn), p 37.

Often we can treat the expression or formulation of a rule as being for practical purposes the rule itself; but it is sometimes crucial to distinguish between the notion of a rule and the notion of a formulation of a rule. One reason why this distinction can be important is because some difficulties about interpreting rules arise from the fact that they have no agreed or official verbal formulation or that the rule has only been partly expressed in words. Disagreements may then arise as to what is precisely the 'correct' or 'true' wording of the rule. This particular kind of doubt is absent where there is an agreed official text in which the rule is expressed in a specific form of words.

There is a second, less obvious, reason for distinguishing between the notion of a rule and the notion of the verbal formulation of a rule. The same rule may be expressed in a number of different grammatical forms without any significant change in its substance. For example: 'Johnny, never go into the larder unless I say you may'; 'Johnny may go into the larder only with his mother's permission'; 'Under no circumstances whatsoever may Johnny enter the larder at any time of night or day unless express permission has been given by his mother'; 'You may go into the larder if, and only if, I say that you may'.

The substance of the rule in all the above examples may be identical for most practical purposes; but the grammar and syntax of the sentences and the grammatical forms (nouns and verbs) used to express the rules are quite varied.[20] In handling rules it can be important to realise that the substance of the rule and the syntax of its formulation are different matters.

One further point needs to be made about the logical structure of rules. For our purposes any rule, however expressed, or even if it has not been expressed, can be analysed and restated as a compound conditional statement of the form 'If X, then Y'. The first part, 'if X', which is known as the *protasis*, describes a type of situation – it indicates the scope of the rule by designating the conditions under which the rule applies. The second part, 'then Y', known as the *apodosis*, is prescriptive – it states whether the type of behaviour governed by the rule is prohibited ('may not', 'ought not'), required ('ought' or 'must'), permitted ('may') and so on. Gottlieb puts the matter thus:

> Any utterance which is designed to function as a rule must have the potential of being reduced, expanded, analysed or translated into a standard form such as 'in circumstances X, Y is required/permitted.' ... Normative utterances need not... be completely formulated. The crucial question about such an utterance, from a functional viewpoint, is whether it lends itself to a restatement in normative form.[21]

Thus the rule about the larder can be restated as follows:

Protasis	*Apodosis*
If Johnny enters the larder without permission from Mother...	...then Johnny is in breach of a duty (not to enter).

---

20 'Syntax' is used here in the sense of 'the arrangement of words (in their proper form) by which their connexion and relation in a sentence are shown' (Oxford English Dictionary, Shorter Edition, 2a).

21 G Gottlieb, *The Logic of Choice* (1968), p 40.

This formulation of the rule involves an element of repetition. The agent (Johnny) and the activity prohibited by the rule (entering the larder) appear in both the protasis and the apodosis. It might be more elegant, and certainly would be more succinct, to break the statement up in a different way, for example:

Protasis	*Apodosis*
If and only if Mother gives permission,	may Johnny enter the larder

or

Unless Mother gives permission,	Johnny must not enter the larder.

But for our purposes it is convenient to include in the protasis all the ingredients of the rule that could give rise to a question of fact in a particular case governed by the rule: the person or persons whose behaviour is governed by the rule (the agent), the type of behaviour involved (acts, omissions, activities) and the conditions under which the rule applies (eg the absence of permission). To put the matter another way: for our purposes, *all ingredients that have a bearing on the scope of the rule should be included in the protasis.*[22]

The reason for this recommendation is that, for purposes of analysis and interpretation, it is often important to distinguish between the *scope* of a rule (what fact-situations does it govern?) and its *character* (what kind of prescription?). This will become apparent when we deal with the distinction between questions of fact and questions of interpretation, the problem of the *ratio decidendi* and other topics.

Two problematic aspects of analysing the protasis and apodosis of rules have attracted attention in traditional jurisprudence. First, the elucidation and analysis of the standard normative concepts that typically occur in the apodoses of rules, such as duty ('ought'), privilege/licence ('may'), power ('can') and disability ('cannot'), have been the subject of much discussion and controversy. In order to keep the exposition simple, nearly all of the examples in the text will relate to duties and privileges. But if you are puzzled by any of these concepts or the relationships between them, you might find it helpful to refer to one of the standard discussions cited in the suggestions for further reading.[23]

Another puzzling question is the relationship between rules and sanctions, such as punishments or damages. In our view, some rules are backed by

---

22 G von Wright, *Norm and Action* (1963), chapter 2, distinguishes six ingredients of norms that are prescriptions: the character, the content, the condition of application, the authority, the subject(s) or agent(s) and the occasion. Our recommendation is that the condition, the subject and the occasion should all be included in the protasis, even if some are repeated in the apodosis for clarity. The apodosis is then confined to specifying the *character* of the norm (prohibition, permission, requirement etc). Compare the analysis of the legislative sentence in George Coode, 'On Legislative Expression', reprinted in E Driedger, *The Composition of Legislation* (2nd edn, 1976), discussed in A Watson-Brown, 'The Classification and Arrangement of the Elements of Legislation' (1997) 18 *Statute Law Review* 32.

23 Below, pp 437-438.

sanctions and others are not. When a rule is backed by a sanction, the question arises whether the sanction is prescribed by the rule, ie is prescribed in the apodosis, or whether the sanction for the breach of that rule is prescribed by another, independent, but connected, rule.[24] For present purposes it is more satisfactory to treat the prescription of the sanction as a separate rule, for example:

Protasis	*Apodosis*
Rule 1. If Johnny enters the larder without Mother's permission...	...he is in breach of a duty.
Rule 2. If Johnny is in breach of a duty not to enter the larder...	...he is liable to be made to stand in the corner for not less than 20 minutes.

Note that the apodosis of rule 1 becomes the protasis of rule 2. Complex bodies of rules may on analysis reveal quite long chains of rules connected to each other in this way. However, in ordinary discourse two such connected rules may be run together in a compound proposition which looks like the statement of a single rule:

Protasis	*Apodosis*
If Johnny enters the larder without Mother's permission...	...he is liable...

Provided this is recognised as a convenient form of shorthand there is no harm in using it. But for the purposes of analysis, for example in constructing algorithms, it may sometimes be necessary to differentiate between a substantive rule and the sanction(s) prescribed for its non-observance.

4   Rules, exceptions and exemptions

When Mother said 'in future you are never to enter the larder *without my permission*', she made one *explicit exception* ('without my permission') to a general prohibition against entry. Similarly, the proviso to section 57 of the Offences against the Person Act 1861 sets out a number of situations in which the general prohibition against bigamy does not apply.[25] These are straightforward examples of explicit exceptions that accompany the general prescription and are generally considered to form part of the rule.

In law explicit exceptions to a statutory provision may be found in a different place, such as a separate section of the same statute, or in a prior or subsequent

---

24 On the question, 'What is one rule?' – the problem of individuation – see M James, 'Bentham on the Individuation of Laws' in M James (ed), *Bentham and Legal Theory* (1973), pp 91ff.
25 Chapter 1, section 7.1.

statute. Whether or not we choose to say that such provisions are part of the original rule, or that rule B provides an exception to rule A, analytically the function of such explicit exceptions is clear: it is to delimit the scope of the rule.

Even the most detailed and carefully drafted statutory provision does not contain a *complete formulation* of the rule.[26] For there is the possibility that further exceptions may be implied. For instance, some of the general principles of criminal liability may provide the basis for a defence to a charge of bigamy even though they are not explicitly mentioned in the Offences against the Person Act 1861. Thus a person is not guilty of bigamy in the absence of *mens rea* or if he went through the second ceremony under duress.[27] Thus implied exceptions also delimit the scope of the rule, by indicating conditions under which it does not apply.

If Johnny had entered the larder to rescue the salmon from the cat, the situation is less clear-cut. It would be open to Father to hold that Johnny was not in breach of the rule, because entry in this kind of situation was impliedly permitted; he might hold that Johnny was technically in breach of the rule, but refuse to punish him (on an analogy with an absolute discharge); he might decide to waive the rule in this particular case, thereby granting Johnny an *exemption* on this occasion, but not implying a general *exception* to the rule in this kind of case.[28]

Such distinctions might have no practical consequences for Johnny – for him they might be distinctions without a difference. But it would be wrong to infer from this that such distinctions are unimportant in all contexts. Thus in law there may be practical consequences for a person who has been convicted, but given an absolute discharge rather than acquitted; and the *Buckoke* case is an example of practical consequences of the distinction between an exemption and an exception.[29] If they had been able to graft a general exception on to the road traffic legislation, the Court of Appeal could have put firemen and their superiors in a much more satisfactory position than they were when it was left to the discretion of the police, magistrates and others 'to follow the precedent set by Lord Nelson' when drivers of fire engines were technically in breach of the law. As it turned out, the Court of Appeal was only able to recommend that individual drivers be exempted from criminal proceedings and exhort Parliament to change the law.

More important for our purposes is the point that such distinctions are analytically important in considering puzzlements about interpretation. Philosophers have debated for a long time whether, as Kant suggested, it is always wrong to make exceptions to a moral rule.[30] The distinction between a

---

26 On incomplete formulations, see HLA Hart, 'The Ascription of Responsibility and Rights' in A Flew (ed), *Logic and Language* (First Series) (1951), chapter 8; F Waismann, 'Verifiability', ibid, pp 119-124.
27 See N Lacey and C Wells, *Reconstructing Criminal Law* (2nd edn, 1998), pp 49-53, 313-325, and *R v Gould*, Appendix 1, section A5, p 385.
28 K Baier, The Moral Point of View (1965), pp 96-100; cf the 'absolute' prohibition on torture in the European Convention, chapter 1, section 10.3.3.
29 Chapter 1, section 8.
30 See Baier, op cit, p 100.

general exception and an exemption in a particular case is a useful starting point from which to tackle some of the most common sources of doubt about interpretation of rules. But, as we shall see in due course, this distinction is in need of refinement, because it takes for granted a sharp distinction between 'the general' and 'the particular'; whereas generality and particularity are matters of degree and some of the most difficult choices in interpretation relate to choosing an appropriate level of generality.[31]

5 The variety of rules

One reason why the notion of 'rule' is such an important one not only in law, but in fields as varied as linguistics, sociology, anthropology, education, psychology and philosophy, is that there is hardly any aspect of human behaviour that is not in some way governed or at least guided by rules; indeed, there are some kinds of acts, such as pawning in chess, that can be said to be *constituted* by rules, in the sense that the act could not even be conceived of without the rules. Using language, playing games, courting, getting married, reasoning in mathematics, making decisions in committee, buying and selling a house, passing sentence on a person convicted of crime, and even fighting a war are all to a large extent rule-governed activities.[32] These are sometimes contrasted with activities such as going for a walk or kissing, but even they are circumscribed by rules, for example legal rules as to where you may walk, or tacit conventions as to when you may kiss, after what preliminaries, in what manner. The generality, and attendant vagueness, of the notion of a rule reflects the pervasiveness and importance of rules as social phenomena. Sociologists have emphasised the point that rules are one of the main devices used by people to 'define situations' and 'construct reality'. Understanding the nature of rules is important not only for the actors, but also for those who wish to describe or explain social behaviour.

There are, of course, very many different kinds of rules, or to put the matter more precisely, many different ways of classifying rules into types. Rules can be categorised by the kind of activity they govern, eg the rules of mathematics, the rules of football, or the rules governing road traffic; by their source, eg statutory rules, judge-made rules, rules made by mother, rules laid down by God, or customary rules; rules can be categorised by the character of the prescription – permissions, requirements, prohibitions, power-conferring rules, rules that define and constitute behaviour, such as the rules for moving a queen in chess or the rules for making a valid will, and so on; rules may be classified by the form in which they appear, such as in officially approved fixed verbal form, informally stated rules (for instance some judicial formulations of rules) or unspoken rules; and rules may be classified by the kinds of people who are subject to them: for example, rules for officials, rules for ordinary people, rules for members of a club or other limited group. Some modes of

31 See chapter 1, section 9, questions 3 and 4, and below, pp 165-166, 332-333.
32 See Baier, op cit, pp 68-72; cf Waismann, *The Principles of Linguistic Philosophy*, op cit, chapter 8.

classifying rules have been the subject of deep philosophical puzzlements and disagreements; for instance the differences and relations between legal and moral rules, social rules and conventions, rules and standards, rules of etiquette and rules of thumb.[33]

It is obviously not possible here to attempt to provide a comprehensive account of all these distinctions and classifications. Nor is it necessary to do so. But it is important for us to be aware of the pervasiveness of rules and of the many variations that are to be found between them. Also, in order to understand what is involved in interpreting rules in legal and non-legal contexts, it may be helpful to grasp a number of distinctions. We have already distinguished between rules and formulations of rules, between rules and uses of rules and between the notion of a rule and other notions such as values, habits, commands, practices and predictions. Later we shall distinguish between rules and reasons for rules (chapter 9), and between problems of interpretation of rules and other problems connected with rules (such as finding facts under a rule or getting rid of a rule (chapter 4)). At this point it may be useful to introduce briefly two further distinctions.

Firstly, there are rules expressed in fixed verbal form and rules not expressed in fixed verbal form. Some, such as statutory rules, are expressed in a particular form of words which has official status, so that it is not open to interpreters to change the wording. Thus, one of the cardinal maxims of statutory interpretation is 'Never paraphrase a statute'. Other rules, as we have seen, may have been expressed differently at different times, may have been only partly articulated or may never have been expressed in words at all. From the point of view of the interpreter, each type to some extent presents different problems. Rules in fixed verbal form provide a definite text as a starting point and this removes a lot of potential uncertainty. *Prima facie*, the task of the interpreter is to attach a meaning to a particular word or words.[34] To do this she can be helped by an understanding of the nature of language and meaning, and by certain techniques of linguistic analysis. Very often the words help to reduce the scope of possible doubt. But occasionally the wording may be an obstacle to the interpreter or the source of a doubt which would not have occurred if the rule had not been frozen into a form of words.

Conversely, the absence of a definite and clear formulation of the rule opens the gate to many disagreements about its scope, sometimes about its very existence. Problems of interpretation flood in through that gate. Yet it is a mistake to assume that all rules not expressed in fixed verbal form are, by reason of their form, necessarily vague or perplexing. Many unspoken rules are treated as sufficiently precise and sufficiently well understood to serve their functions adequately in most situations. Some of the problems of interpreting rules apply equally to those that are expressed in fixed verbal form and to those that are not. The form of words is an important factor both in limiting and creating problems of interpretation, but it is by no means the only factor that occasions doubt, as we shall see.

---

33 Chapter 1, section 4.1.2; Schauer, op cit, passim.
34 Chapter 5, section 4.

Another distinction, which has been given prominence in jurisprudence by Professor HLA Hart, is that between *primary* and *secondary* rules. Hart summed up the difference as follows:

> Under rules of the one type, which may well be considered the basic or primary type, human beings are required to do or abstain from certain actions, whether they wish to or not. Rules of the other type are in a sense parasitic upon or secondary to the first; for they provide that human beings may by doing or saying certain things introduce new rules of the primary type, extinguish or modify old ones, or in various ways determine their incidence or control their operations. Rules of the first type impose duties; rules of the second type confer powers, public or private. Rules of the first type concern actions involving physical movement or changes; rules of the second type provide for operations which lead not merely to physical movement or change, but to the creation or variation of duties or obligations.[35]

The distinction between primary and secondary rules is not uncontroversial, but it is a useful one. Professor Hart claims that it provides the key to understanding some of the most perplexing features of the notions of 'law' and 'legal system'.[36] For our purposes, it is useful for a number of reasons. In this book most of our examples relate to problems of interpretation of primary rules, but it is important to bear in mind that secondary rules are also frequently the subject of interpretation. Furthermore, where a rule is part of a complex system of rules, it may be necessary to look not only at the rule itself, but also at its relationship to a network of other primary and secondary rules. In practice many problems of rule-handling arise from the complexity of the interrelationships within a body of rules and between bodies of rules. An introductory work should concentrate on the elementary components of its subject; for most of the time we shall concentrate on analysing problems and puzzlements relating to the interpretation of single primary rules. But from time to time it will be necessary to remind ourselves that legal systems and other systems of rules are not simply like bundles of sticks, or even as simple and straightforward as the traditional symbol of legal complexity – a seamless web – they are even more complicated than that, and one key to unravelling the complexities is the distinction between primary and secondary rules. This leads us on to the notion of a 'system' of rules and to problems arising from the coexistence of separate or loosely related 'systems'.

6 Rules and systems

It is usually artificial, but convenient, to talk of single rules, for most rules belong to some agglomeration. Like problems, rules cumulate and aggregate: unlike problems there are often cogent reasons for treating rules as an integral part of some larger system. However, this may be artificial in that it suggests a greater degree of integration and internal consistency than is warranted by the facts. How systematic, for example, is that complex congeries of rules,

35 Hart, op cit, p 81.
36 Ibid, chapter 3.

institutions, ideas and traditions which has evolved over centuries and which we glibly call 'the English legal system'?[37]

How far it is feasible, sensible or desirable to think and talk in terms of systems of rules is one of the perennial problems of legal theory. On one view, a legal system is an internally consistent, 'gapless' body of rules within which it is theoretically impossible for two rules to be in conflict. At its extreme, the notion of 'system' is taken literally; logical consistency is a prime value and rigorous logical analysis is the main, perhaps the only, tool for resolving doubts in interpretation. It is the role of the 'legal scientist' to create and maintain this consistent, systemic quality. Few jurists have subscribed unreservedly to the extreme version of this view. Even Hans Kelsen, who is sometimes depicted as the leading protagonist of a systemic conception of law, allowed for the possibility of inconsistent norms coexisting within the same system, and for dynamic processes of interpretation which could take account of changing conditions and values.

This systemic view of law has traditionally exerted a powerful influence on legal thinking, and continues to do so.[38] One of the most articulate and sophisticated of its modern statements is contained in the writings of Ronald Dworkin, in particular in his book *Law's Empire*. Dworkin bases his argument for the proposition that there is one right answer to every disputed question of law, even in the hardest case, on the idea of 'the integrity' of law. The best justification for any judicial decision is the one that reconciles the decision, first, with the existing authorities (fit), and then, insofar as any doubts remain, on the basis of a coherent view of the principles of political morality underlying the institutions of the system (justification). The task of Dworkin's ideal judge, Hercules, is to dig out and interpret these principles to form a coherent whole:

> Law as integrity asks judges to assume, so far as this is possible, that the law is structured by a coherent set of principles about justice and fairness and procedural due process, and it asks them to enforce these in the fresh cases that come before them, so that each person's situation is fair and just according to the same standards. That style of adjudication respects the ambition integrity assumes, the ambition to be a community of principle.[39]

It is not possible to do justice here to the subtleties and refinements of Dworkin's thesis that the system (which includes its operatives) should be true to itself, nor to the many critical assessments that it has prompted. There is an undoubted attraction in an aspirational model that requires judges and related interpreters to try to construct 'the best interpretation' they can by digging deeper, drawing on arguments and analogies throughout the system and seeking to interpret that system as a unity based on a coherent underlying philosophy. This is a powerful way to construct cogent arguments and one

---

37 For example, in their introductory book, *English Legal System in Context* (1996), Cownie and Bradney reflect this uncertainty both by the omission of the definite article before the phrase, English legal system, and, throughout the book, by apostrophising it.
38 On the application of systems theory to law under the rubric of autopoiesis, see G Teubner, *Law as an Autopoeitic System* (1993). For a thorough discussion see H Baxter, 'Autopoiesis and the "relative autonomy" of law' (1998) 19 *Cardozo Law Review* 1987.
39 R Dworkin, *Law's Empire* (1986), p 243.

that is not necessarily conservative in tendency, for Hercules may well challenge authorities and settled ideas by considering them in relation to other parts of the system and to its political morality; it is one way of being radical.

By contrast, many have taken the view that the notion of law as a system of rules is at best a hopelessly optimistic fiction, and at worst, misguided and dangerous. Misguided because it induces unrealisable expectations of order and certainty and obscures the messy reality of life; and dangerous because it encourages an approach to interpretation and exposition that is insensitive to the complexities and nuances of social facts, social change and conflicting values. Brian Simpson, for example, has forcefully argued that it is historically and sociologically unrealistic to depict the development and methods of the common law in the kind of terms which Dworkin employs. It is clear for all to see that most common law doctrine has evolved through *ad hoc*, piecemeal, case-by-case resolution of narrowly defined issues. Both in method and substance the common law is far too untidy to fit the model of a comprehensive, gapless code. To present the common law as a system of rules is to confuse idealism with reality:

> Put simply, life might be simpler if the common law consisted of a code of rules, identifiable by reference to source rules, but the reality of the matter is that it is all much more chaotic than that, and the only way to make the common law conform to the ideal would be to codify the system, which would then cease to be common law at all.[40]

He continues:

> We must start by recognising what common sense suggests, which is that the common law is more of a muddle than a system, and that it would be difficult to conceive of a less systematic body of law.[41]

Charles Sampford takes Simpson's realism a step further. He argues that nowhere does law have the quality of a 'system' attributed to it by most jurists, including Kelsen, Hart and Dworkin. Rather, 'like society, law is partially organised into institutions but it does not have an overall structure, the shifting paths of the many chains of relations defying attempts to define one. These institutions are part of the social mêlée.'[42] Nevertheless few have subscribed to a wholly anarchic view of law; even the so-called extreme realists did not see law as a wilderness of single decisions, totally unpatterned and with no concern for internal coherence or consistency.

It is tempting to try to reconcile these seemingly contradictory views of the systemic nature of law by suggesting that those who espouse them are in fact pursuing different intellectual ambitions. Thus, whereas Dworkin's theory is a prescriptive one, which sets a noble, if unattainable, aspiration for individual judges, a realist standpoint seeks to describe what is, not what ought to be.[43]

---

40 AWB Simpson, 'Common Law and Legal Theory' in W Twining (ed), *Common Law and Legal Theory* (1986), chapter 2, at p 15.
41 Ibid, p 24.
42 C Sampford, *The Disorder of Law* (1989), p 261.
43 Ibid, pp 84–85. However, Sampford also criticizes Dworkin's prescriptive/aspirational theory.

As we have seen, an understanding of different standpoints can be helpful when disentangling competing theories,[44] but in this instance the temptation to treat this as a complete answer should be resisted. This is so first because the leading 'system' theorists, including Hart and Dworkin, claim to be advancing theories that have the merit of stating not only what ought to be, but what is. Hart asserts that the *Concept of Law* is 'an essay in descriptive sociology',[45] while Dworkin, more cautiously, claims to give an interpretive account of actual legal practices, especially best practice.[46] Conversely, many of those writing in the common law tradition claim to be advancing theories that have the merit of stating not only what is, but what ought to be. 'Muddling through' may appear to be an incoherent approach to problem-solving, but in reality, they argue, it produces the best results.[47] This view justifies the pragmatism of the common law by an appeal to such factors as the manner in which decisions come to be made by judges, that is, on the basis of discrete and unique sets of facts whose material similarity to other sets of facts has yet to be determined and may prove controversial, and on the difficulty of translating this single decision into a rule to govern all future similar sets of facts.

In essence, the pragmatic approach makes a virtue, firstly of the notorious reluctance of English judges to go very far beyond the facts of the case at hand and, secondly, of the traditional antipathy to codification that has been displayed by most English lawyers and politicians since the last century. Thus by no means everyone accepts the idea that a principled, systematic approach to adjudication or to government is best, and there are profound differences in attitude and perception at both the descriptive and the prescriptive levels.

We need not pursue this fundamental debate very far here, but it is important to note the continuing tension in interpretation between arguments based on consistency and other kinds of arguments. To put the matter very simply: one context is the other rules within the system; another context is factors outside the system – ranging from society at large to the context and objectives of the particular rule and the circumstances of the case under consideration. Every interpreter needs to be aware of the potential for tension between the systemic context and the social context. The relationships between the rule to be interpreted and other rules is almost always a relevant factor in interpretation; but whether it is sufficient to be satisfied with weak terms like 'fit', 'compatibility', 'coherence', and 'gravitational pull', or whether one should be reaching for strict logical consistency, is a regular source of doubt and disagreement.

Another potential source of tension is between alternative, coexisting or competing bodies of rules. Conflicts between legal and moral rules or principles are familiar enough; the relationship between legal and moral rule-systems is

---

44 Chapter 1, section 11.2.
45 HLA Hart, op cit, preface.
46 R Dworkin, *Law's Empire* (1986), introduction. See S Guest, *Ronald Dworkin* (2nd edn, 1997).
47 The strengths and weaknesses of the English 'pragmatic' tradition are usefully discussed by PS Atiyah, *Pragmatism and Theory in English Law* (1987), chapters 2 and 3. He concludes that a good deal of alleged pragmatism is based on implicit theory and may not be as unsystematic as it claims.

a standard battleground of jurisprudence; and for the first 25 years of the United Kingdom's membership of the European Community the question whether the laws of the Community could override those enacted at Westminster was a matter of continuing, often sharp debate.[48] In ordinary life most of us have to cope with a variety of sets of rules which may impinge simultaneously – the law of the land, social conventions, institutional regulations, and our own moral and perhaps religious values. Some of these may be treated as sub-systems of a single system; others may be seen as more or less independent rule-systems; the extent of their mutual compatibility may vary tremendously.[49]

In some social contexts 'rule density' may take extreme forms: the 'total institutions' depicted by Erving Goffman, such as prisons, hospitals, barracks and boarding schools. The short passage quoted in chapter 1, section 4.2.3 deals with only part of the matter: the relatively formal house-rules and the less formal systems of rewards, privileges and punishments imposed by the staff.[50] In a prison, for example, the inmate is typically subject to other bodies of rules, ranging from international and municipal law (in theory at least, a prisoner can claim rights under the European Convention or sue a prison officer for assault, for example), to the codes of conduct imposed by his fellow inmates or small groups of them. Similarly, the proprietor or manager of a small business, such as a garage or a factory employing forty or fifty people, will find that his relations with his employees, with manufacturers and suppliers, with consumers and other clients, with different departments of local and central government, with his insurers, landlord and others, are all governed by a bewildering, often frightening, number of rules. He may find that rules of contract, tort, company law, employment law, landlord and tenant law, planning, public health, trading standards, consumer protection, VAT, weights and measures, health and safety at work, and many other branches of municipal law impinge on his daily activities. Even finding out about the existence of such rules, let alone interpreting and applying them may be a continuous source of worry, expense and effort. This may be only part of the story. He may also be governed by local authority by-laws, EC regulations, trade association rules, codes of practice, business usage, accounting procedures, custom and practice on the shopfloor and other informal norms within his own organisation, local social conventions and the ways of local officials. The extent to which all of these are or seem to be compatible with each other will naturally vary considerably; even when he can break through the Kafkaesque uncertainty to discern what is governed by rule and what by discretion, he may find himself facing acute dilemmas, posed by competing or conflicting rules from different 'systems'.

Rule density is a familiar feature of modern industrial societies. It often leads to complaints that there is 'too much law'. It is often thought to be closely

---

48 Finally resolved in *R v Secretary of State for Transport, ex p Factortame (No 2)* [1991] 1 AC 603. See chapter 7, section 2.1.

49 On legal pluralism, see chapter 1, section 2.

50 'Rule density' applies both to the phenomenon of co-existing rule systems and to the existence of a multiplicity of rules within a single alleged 'system'.

associated with interventionist or paternalistic government. However, as we shall see in Chapter 7, the relationship between prevailing ideology and the amount of legislation is more complex than that. In the present context our concern is not to arouse sympathy for the poor inmate or businessman, beset by a multitude of demanding and potentially conflicting rule-systems. It is rather to make the point that when confronted with a particular rule an interpreter may not merely be concerned to interpret it in the light of other rules in the same system; he may also be concerned to reconcile it with rules which form part of other systems as well as with factors other than rules. A single-system model of interpretation may prove to be too simple in some contexts.

7 Reifying rules: a note of warning

When we talk of a situation, an event or an act we are normally not tempted to think of them as 'things' even though we use the grammatical form of a noun and often qualify them with adjectives, attach predicates to them or make them the subjects or objects of transitive verbs. Similarly when we talk of reasons having 'weight' or 'strength', of breaking 'the chain' of causation, or of links in 'a chain' of reasoning, we may not need to be reminded that we are talking metaphorically. Words like 'rule', 'norm' and 'standard' are also abstract nouns, but there seems to be a greater temptation in ordinary discourse to 'thingify' (or 'reify' or 'hypostatise') them, that is to talk about them *as if* they are objects in the real world which we can see or touch or measure or examine for their characteristics. This is partly due to the fact that rules are sometimes expressed in a form which does have a physical embodiment: the laws of Moses were engraved on tablets of stone; legislative rules enacted by the United Kingdom Parliament can be found in the statute book; school or university rules may be posted on a physical or electronic notice board. We talk quite naturally of reading, drafting, breaking or writing down rules. Normally it is clear that it is not the tablet of stone or the notice or the book which is the actual object of such actions, but sometimes we may fall into the trap of confusing the rule with its physical expression. Often this is quite harmless, but there are hidden dangers, not least that we may be tempted to speak more confidently about the existence or the identity of a rule than is warranted by the context. Accordingly it is important to recognise that talking about the 'scope' of rules involves a spatial concept that is no less metaphorical than talking about the weight of reasons, just as talking in terms of making, waiving, evading, manipulating, handling or doing 'things' with rules or words is a convenient, but metaphorical, way of talking.

Let us illustrate the point by considering some of the difficulties of determining the existence and identity of an alleged rule in a fairly indeterminate situation. When Father entered the room where Johnny was watching television and peremptorily switched to another channel without saying a word, [51] suppose that the following exchange ensued:

51 Chapter 1, section 3.5, question 9.

J (outraged): 'Hey, you can't do that!'

F: 'Why not?'

J: 'There is a rule against it.'

F: 'We don't have any rules for watching TV.'

J: 'Mum says we do. Anyway there are rules of good manners against this sort of thing.'

F: 'Show me!'

Johnny's protest is couched in terms of appealing to a rule and is likely to win more sympathy from readers than some of his other claims. At a commonsense level, it does seem that Father has violated some standard, but how can it be shown that such a standard exists, and what is it exactly – a rule concerning television-watching, some principle of justice, or some convention of polite or civilised behaviour? If the latter, what precisely is the convention involved? How can Johnny demonstrate the existence of a particular rule that Father has violated? To put the matter in more general terms: under what circumstances is it true to say that a rule exists? and on what grounds can one identify a particular rule as *the* one that has been broken?

These general questions raise important and difficult philosophical issues. In this relatively straightforward case, it is not difficult to suggest some ways in which Johnny might take up Father's challenge. He might hoist Father with his own petard by pointing out that he had reprimanded Johnny for exactly the same behaviour on some previous occasion; or he might claim that Mother had told him that he should always ask permission before switching channels; or he might invoke an analogy: 'It's like not interrupting when other people are talking.' Given his precociousness and lawyer-like qualities, he might boldly assert a general principle: 'It is unreasonable to change channels in the middle of a programme without at least obtaining the consent of those who are watching.' Father might or might not accept any or all of these as satisfying his demand for a demonstration that there was some rule that he had violated on this occasion. But even in this rather clear case, in which nearly everyone would agree that some standard has been violated by a more powerful party, there is considerable indeterminacy about how precisely the situation is to be interpreted. If the reasonableness or appropriateness or unacceptability of Father's behaviour, when in conflict with Johnny, were less clear-cut, the interpretation of the situation would be even more problematic.

Consider now a variation on this episode: Father enters the room and switches channels without saying a word. Johnny is very angry and glares at him, but says nothing. Father, noticing Johnny's reaction, switches back to the original channel and smiles apologetically. We might be able to give a plausible account of this interaction without invoking notions such as rules or standards. It might lead us to reassess the balance of power between father and son. Or one could say that Johnny tacitly invoked a rule, which Father recognised and acknowledged that he had violated. In interpreting a situation in this way we typically use words like 'rule' and 'standard' as a shorthand for describing what are essentially very complex processes and interactions, which may be fraught with ambiguities.

Many of the standard examples with which we are concerned in this book posit a situation in which an interpreter is confronted with a pre-existing rule. The rule is taken as given, it is a datum: the problem for the interpreter is to explore and determine the scope (and possibly the meaning and rationale) of the rule. In many contexts it is quite reasonable to assert or to assume that a rule exists and can be identified. In the larder episode, Johnny's ploys for dealing with his parents did not include doubting the existence or identity of the rule prohibiting entry to the larder or Mother's capacity, in the sense of authority and power, to make such a rule. The disagreement was about the scope of a particular rule which was acknowledged by both sides to exist, to be identified and to be valid. Similarly, in the convoluted history of disagreements about the scope of the English offence of bigamy, no one has seriously questioned the existence of a law against bigamy, the identity of the primary rule (section 57 of the Offences against the Person Act 1861) or its validity.

However, such doubts can and do arise in both legal and non-legal contexts. In non-legal contexts it is often far from clear whether a particular situation can appropriately be interpreted in terms of rules at all and, if so, how to identify what the rules are. Doubts about the very existence of a legal rule may be relatively rare; but disputes about the validity of a rule are more frequent, for example in respect of delegated legislation under the *ultra vires* doctrine, or in determining the constitutionality of acts of state legislatures in the United States and like jurisdictions. Likewise, the Human Rights Act 1998 raises, for the first time in a United Kingdom context, the possibility that legislative provisions enacted by Parliament may be challenged and declared incompatible with the European Convention on Human Rights. Doubts about the identity of an alleged rule or principle are, as we shall see, commonplace in the context of case law.

For the purpose of examining what is involved in interpreting rules, it is often necessary to take for granted the existence, the identity and the validity of a given rule – to treat the rule to be interpreted as a given. If doubts of this kind arise, they are often best viewed as preliminaries to interpretation rather than as problems of interpretation. It is, however, important to recognise that in some contexts there is considerable indeterminacy about such matters and that they are a frequent source of puzzlement, confusion and disagreement. In order to discuss interpretation of rules we have to postulate the existence of particular rules to interpret, but we should always be on our guard against being more confident about such assumptions than the situation may warrant. And one useful precept is always to bear in mind that rules are not things, we merely talk *as if* they are.

In the preceding analysis we have by implication introduced a distinction between interpreting a situation and interpreting a rule; it has also been suggested that it is useful to distinguish between doubts arising prior to interpretation and doubts arising in the process of interpretation. These can be useful working distinctions, but we must be careful not to place much weight on them, for in some contexts they collapse.

In dealing with rules in fixed verbal form, whether written or unwritten, we can generally use these distinctions with some confidence. Once the rule is identified, and its validity confirmed, we have a reasonably clear starting point from which to proceed to the task of determining its scope. Moreover, as we shall suggest later, interpreting rules is a rather more straightforward matter than interpreting situations. A rule in fixed verbal form is much more like a thing than a rule not in fixed verbal form, and it is correspondingly easier to take its existence and its identity for granted and to proceed from there.

This is not the case with rules not in fixed verbal form, such as rules derived from cases. For here we are concerned with a much more elusive kind of subject-matter, and to talk of 'determining the existence' of such rules or of 'identifying' or 'finding' them is much closer to the language of metaphor. There is no firm text or foundation on which to anchor. The raw materials from which to extract, formulate and interpret such rules can be more elusive than shifting sands. Moreover, like problems, rules and situations are rarely static. As Fuller argues, many rules are in a continual state of development. In order to interpret the rules we will often have to interpret the situation. In order to proceed we need concepts such as rules and standards, and even codes, but we need to be aware of the artificiality of talking in such terms – it is as if we are forced to talk with more confidence and more precision than the situation warrants. How, for example, can we be *sure* that the silent exchange between Father and Johnny involved the tacit invocation and acknowledgement of a rule? Or was it that Father was frightened of his son? If so, was this because he feared a moral sanction, such as the disapproval of other members of the family?

In particular contexts, of course, there may be factors to bolster our confidence: settled ways of thought, accepted conventions of communication, even manuals of interpretation. Thus in interpreting any particular area of legal doctrine based on case law there are many institutionalised and relatively settled 'steadying factors', as Karl Llewellyn called them,[52] to assist in the process of determining the scope of particular rules. On many points of common law we *can* talk with confidence and the same is true of many rules not in fixed verbal form in non-legal contexts. Nevertheless, in such contexts, a very great strain may be put on artificially precise distinctions. To take but one example: in the context of case law interpretation, the main focus for the interpreter is nothing so concrete as particular rules nor so elusive as a total situation, rather it is judicial opinions or judgments, the raw material from which formulations of doctrine are extracted. It is only in a loose, metaphorical sense that common law rules 'exist' and are interpreted; it is more exact to say that formulations of common law doctrine are extracted or constructed from judicial opinions. The ways in which cases – the raw material of common law rules – are transformed into settled 'doctrine' are complex, varied and elusive; this is a topic about which there is little consensus among jurists.[53]

52 KN Llewellyn, *The Common Law Tradition* (1960), pp 19ff.
53 Simpson, op cit.

8 The functions of rules[54]

Why have rules? What are they for? In view of the enormous variety of kinds of rules, and the many different contexts in which they operate, it is difficult to give very general answers to questions like this. It is sometimes said that the main function of rules is to guide behaviour. But this is not very informative. For instance, it does not tell us when it is helpful or necessary to have general guides to behaviour and when attempts to provide general guidance are useless or even counter-productive. Nor is guidance the only function of rules. Rules may be introduced, for example, in order to communicate information or values, in order to make a public declaration of support for a moral principle or a particular policy, in order to economise effort, or as a form of window-dressing – perhaps as a lazy or cheap way of avoiding coming to grips with an intractable problem. The functions of rules are almost as varied as the types of rules. The functions of rules of grammar are not identical with the functions of rules in social relations. And in addition to the obvious functions of a rule in a particular context, there may be secondary or hidden functions, which can easily be overlooked.

We can be a little more specific, although still operating at a very general level, if we examine some of the functions of rules in human groups. And this may also help to bring out a point that many functions performed by rules could also be performed without them. For instance, Mother might have been more successful in keeping Johnny out of the larder by locking the door instead of making a rule.

The American jurist, Karl Llewellyn, developed a theory about the functions of rules in social groups, popularly known as the 'Law Jobs Theory'.[55] This can be briefly restated as follows: All of us are members of groups, such as a family, a club, a teenage gang, a school or commercial organisation, a trade union, a political party, a nation state, the world community. In order to survive and to achieve its aims, in so far as it has aims, *any* human group has to meet certain needs or ensure that certain jobs are done. The first, perhaps the most important, of these jobs is to channel behaviour and expectations of members of the group in order to avoid conflicts or disputes within it. Secondly, when disputes arise, they have to be resolved or, at least, be kept at a tolerably low level, or else the group will disintegrate or its objectives will be frustrated or impaired. Thirdly, as the circumstances of the group change, so the behaviour and expectations of members of the group have to be adjusted to such changes in order to avoid conflicts and disappointments. Fourthly, decision-making in the group needs to be regulated both in respect of who has power and authority to participate in decisions and in respect of the procedures by which decisions are arrived at. This allocation of authority and power is typically the primary function of a 'constitution' of, for example, a club or a nation state. Fifthly, in

---

54 Waismann, 'Verifiability', op cit, pp 132ff; on 'function', see R Merton, *Social Theory and Social Structure* (1967).
55 KN Llewellyn, *Jurisprudence* (1962), chapter 15, and references below at pp 437-438.

any group, but especially in complex groups, techniques, skills and devices need to be developed for satisfactorily meeting the first four needs. Channelling behaviour, settling disputes, making smooth adjustments to change and providing for acceptable ways of reaching decisions can often be difficult tasks, involving high levels of skill or quite refined or sophisticated devices. Rules are one type of device for doing the law jobs. Skill in making rules suited to their purposes, and skill in interpreting rules or handling them in other ways, are part of the general job that Llewellyn called 'The Job of Juristic Method'.[56] Some of these skills are highly specialised and may become the province of a few individuals with narrowly defined roles such as legislative draftsmen; but others are basic to many aspects of rule-handling.

It is important to grasp two points about this theory. Firstly, although it is called the 'Law Jobs Theory', it is not restricted to the role of official law in a national legal system. It is very much wider than that. It concerns the regulation and operation of *all* human groups and it emphasises problems that are common to them. It is accordingly very useful for our purposes, in that, just as we emphasise problems concerning the interpretation of rules in many different types of social context, so Llewellyn emphasises the universality of the conditions that give rise to the need for rules.

Secondly, Llewellyn stresses the point that rules are one of the main devices for performing the law jobs, but they are not the only ones. For example, within the family perfectly satisfactory patterns of behaviour regarding the watching of television may develop without any resort either to consciously created rules or even to the development of tacit conventions (although it would be an unusual situation in a family of several people in which there were absolutely *no* rules or conventions relating to such matters as how to determine which television programme to watch when different members of the family want to watch different programmes). Or, to take an example from a legal context, let us look at the problem of promoting harmonious race relations in a plural society. Among those who desire to promote harmonious relations, some people believe that legislation, such as that embodied in race relations laws, is useless or worse than useless. 'You cannot legislate harmony', they might argue. On the other hand, many people believe that race relations legislation is important, perhaps even necessary, for controlling and reducing racial conflict. Some would argue that the existing race relations legislation in Britain is too narrow and too timid and should be greatly extended. But few people would argue that all the problems of racial harmony could be resolved by law alone. These are just two examples of situations in which questions arise about the value of resorting to rules at all in order to resolve problems.

Llewellyn's theory is useful as a starting point for our analysis. But it needs elaboration in a number of ways. In particular it is important to emphasise that the functions he lists are not the only tasks that rules may perform. Llewellyn's account is concerned mainly with direct regulation of behaviour and expectations by rules and other devices. In this view, an ineffective rule is useless or worse than useless. But rules are sometimes introduced in order to

---

56 W Twining, 'The Idea of Juristic Method: a Tribute to Karl Llewellyn' (1993) 48 *Miami Law Review* 119.

educate or to communicate approval or disapproval, even if there is very little chance of getting the bulk of those who are subject to them to conform immediately. For example, during the Prohibition era in the United States there came a time when it was clear to many people that the Prohibition laws were not effective in reducing the consumption of alcohol; and it was even arguable that, by driving the distribution of spirits into the hands of the criminal world, the net result may have been to increase rather than decrease the total consumption of alcohol by certain classes of people.[57] It is generally acknowledged that Prohibition gave a boost to organised crime, by giving it a profitable economic base. Some supporters of Prohibition would have no doubt accepted these as good reasons for giving up trying to control this form of social behaviour by means of law; but others could argue that, whether or not Prohibition legislation was effective, it performed a valuable function by expressing *disapproval* of a particular form of social behaviour, even though the state was not in practice able to enforce conformity.[58]

It is sometimes said that the main function of some school rules and certain kinds of safety regulation is to inculcate people into acceptance of certain values or standards. Similarly, in Soviet Russia one of the primary functions of law was seen to be *educative*.[59] And this is seen by some as a secondary function of legislation on race relations and equal opportunities.[60]

An approach to rules, in both legal and other contexts, that presents them as deliberate instruments designed to further in a direct fashion clear policies is really too simple. Indeed, if 'function' were equated with 'purpose', the picture painted by the 'Law Jobs Theory' would be misleading. For not every group, or every rule, has clear 'purposes'. Some rules may have been created unthinkingly, as an instinctive response without any clear purpose or policy behind them; some may have evolved in some obscure and complex way; and some may have survived to be dysfunctional, even if originally they had some useful purpose. Similarly, some rules that developed in response to one kind of need may have survived to perform some quite different kind of function. Many legislative rules represent a compromise between competing interests or values. Moreover, a single rule or set of rules may have a complex set of functions, not all of which are concerned with directly influencing the behaviour they purport to regulate. A good example again is to be found in the following classic statement on the purposes of race relations legislation:[61]

(a) A law is an unequivocal declaration of public policy.
(b) A law gives support to those who do not wish to discriminate, but who feel compelled to do so by social pressure.
(c) A law gives protection and redress to minority groups.

57 A Sinclair, *Prohibition: The Era of Excess* (1962).
58 Similar and even more complex considerations arise in relation to drug control at a global level today; see United Nations International Drug Control Programme, World Drug Report 1997.
59 See R Cotterrell, Sociology of Law (2nd edn, 1992), chapter 4.
60 See A Lester and G Bindman, *Race and Law* (1972), pp 85-89, and J Gregory, *Sex, Race and the Law: Legislating for Equality* (1988).
61 Race Relations Board, First Annual Report (1967), para 65.

(d) A law thus provides for the peaceful and orderly adjustment of grievances and the release of tensions.

(e) A law reduces prejudice by discouraging the behaviour in which prejudice finds expression.

Not everyone will agree with this statement, but it clearly illustrates the variety of claims that can be made about the purposes of a law.

In interpreting rules it is of paramount importance to try to ascribe clear and coherent purposes, policies or principles behind them; but it is equally important to realise that such efforts may be wholly or partly unsuccessful. A model of a legal rule as an instrument of policy is very useful. But in using this model, we need to be aware that the problem may be rather more complex and subtle than appears on the surface. In particular, we need to be aware that rules may have *latent* as well as *manifest* functions,[62] that they often have unforeseen consequences, that a rule may be serving a different function from that which was originally intended when it was created, and that some rules are, as judged by the standards of the moment, pointless or positively dysfunctional or counter-productive. Moreover, there may be no clear consensus about one or more of these matters and this too may be a source of perplexity.

9   Rules as techniques of social management

Some of the main examples of rules used so far have been 'primary' rules, which impose duties directly on those who are subject to them, such as the rule about the larder or the prohibition against bigamy in section 57 of the Offences against the Person Act 1861. But it is important that such penal rules should not be regarded as providing a simple prototype to be used on all, or even a majority of, occasions on which rules are to be introduced to deal with a given problem. A useful corrective is contained in Robert Summers's account of what he terms the basic techniques of law.[63] Adopting the standpoint of the legislator or other 'social manager', Summers distinguishes five basic techniques that are available to be used, as alternatives or in combination, to give effect to given policies:

(a) law as a grievance-remedial instrument (recognition of claims to enforceable remedies for grievances, actual or threatened);
(b) law as a penal instrument (prohibition, prosecution and punishment of bad conduct);
(c) law as an administrative-regulatory instrument (regulation of generally wholesome activity, business or otherwise);

62 Merton, op cit. For example, the manifest function of an identification parade is to produce evidence for use in court; however, it may have the latent function of stimulating a confession or guilty plea ('see, the game is up') or persuading the police that the case should be dropped for lack of evidence. On 'functionalism' see R Cotterrell, op cit, chapter 3.
63 R Summers and C Howard, *Law, its Nature, Function and Limits* (2nd edn, 1972), pp 21ff; R Summers, 'The Technique Element in Law' (1971) 59 *California Law Review* 733.

(d) law as an instrument for ordering governmental (or other authoritative) conferral of public benefits (governmental conferral of substantive benefits such as education, welfare and highways);

(e) law as an instrument for facilitating and effectuating private arrangements (facilitation and protection of private voluntary arrangements, economic and otherwise).

Each of these techniques may be illustrated by reference to two general areas of social policy which we encountered in Chapter 1 – the protection of individuals from the production of unwholesome food and drink, and the facilitation and preservation of monogamous family life. Thus, in the former case, manufacturers, sellers and others may be liable to pay compensation by way of damages in contract or tort for loss or injury suffered by an individual customer or consumer (grievance-remedial); in addition, they may be subject to criminal sanctions under food and drugs legislation (penal); the method of manufacturing, processing and distribution may be regulated by a system of licensing and inspection (administrative-regulatory); positive steps towards the provision of a healthy diet may be taken through such devices as the provision of free or cheap milk in schools or dietary counselling of pregnant mothers (benefit-conferring); and some aspects of relations between manufacturers, consumers and others may be left to be determined by the parties concerned, by contract or otherwise, with the law playing a facilitative role, for example by giving recognition to agreements for the servicing of food-processing equipment (private arrangements).

Similarly, all five techniques are used in many societies to support the institution of monogamous marriage. The choice of partner is left largely to private arrangement; the formation and regulation of marriage is primarily dealt with by administrative-regulatory provisions, some of which are backed by penal laws; the grievance-remedial technique can be used to protect monogamous marriages, for example by providing remedies for adultery or loss of consortium (but in England and America, at least, this technique is much less frequently employed). Various kinds of tax relief, children's allowances (if confined to legitimate children) and widows' pensions are examples of benefit-conferral devices that can be used, among other things, to encourage or discourage certain patterns of family arrangement.

Summers's analysis is useful for our purposes for three main reasons. Firstly, it underlines the variety of ways in which rules can be employed by the rule maker; in particular, it warns against overemphasis on the *pathological* aspects of law, that is the prosecution and punishment of acts considered to be antisocial and the provision of remedies when things have gone wrong. Law is also introduced to regulate, to facilitate and to confer and distribute benefits. Broken contracts and broken marriages represent only a proportion of all contracts and marriages, and the law has at least as important a role to play in the creation, definition and facilitation of these relationships as in the clearing up of the mess after things have gone wrong.

When a troublesome problem arises in society, such as hijacking or urban terrorism, one instinctive response, typified by the phrase 'there ought to be a law', is to think in terms of creating new offences or imposing harsher sanctions.

Summers's theory is a salutary corrective to this tendency to think solely or mainly in terms of the penal, and to a lesser extent grievance-remedial, techniques. For example, recent experience suggests that hijacking can be combated effectively only by deploying a wide range of methods and devices, with regulatory techniques (through such means as efficient systems of surveillance at airports) having a potentially much greater role to play than penal sanctions (such as capital punishment), the main function of which may be more symbolic than deterrent.

Secondly, by drawing attention to law as an administrative-regulatory instrument in addition to its penal and remedial uses, Summers's analysis underlines the development in recent years of two important and fruitful areas of legal scholarship in this country. One has been concerned with the expansion of administrative law and its remedies, the other has focused upon the nature and the parameters of legal regulation. This latter area of study is especially associated with the socio-legal studies movement.[64]

Thirdly, Summers's analysis is concerned specifically with the basic techniques of *law*; but, as with Llewellyn's 'Law Jobs Theory', it can be applied with little or no modification in non-legal contexts, and can be used to illustrate certain basic lessons about rules as problem-solving devices.[65] Thus, had Mother employed a similar analysis when deciding how to prevent Johnny eating between meals, she would have been in a position to consider more systematically the range of techniques open to her in securing this objective. By requiring Johnny to seek permission before entering the larder, and implicitly threatening punishment if he did not, she resorted to a combination of the regulatory and penal techniques; but she might equally have considered such devices as requiring Johnny to pay for any food he takes (grievance-remedial), or providing him with more satisfying and attractive meals, possibly as part of a bargain with him (benefit conferring). Because Mother is in a position of authority over him, a bargain between her and Johnny does not fit neatly into the 'private-arranging' category. But it is not difficult to envisage situations within the nuclear family that fit the category; for example, in a family with several children competing for various scarce commodities, a parent may lay down explicit rules for distribution, or may make *ad hoc* distributions as occasions arise, or may leave it to the children to sort out such conflicts by private arrangement between themselves.[66]

10 Two views of rules

Implicit in the 'Law Jobs Theory' and in Summers's analysis is a view of rules as instruments of policies aimed at solving problems, that is to say as means to

---

64 PA Thomas, (ed), *Socio-Legal Studies* (1997) and R Cotterrell, *Law as Community* (1995), chapter 4. See also Appendix IV, suggestions for further reading.
65 What Summers includes under 'law' encompasses much more than legal rules.
66 One way of looking at Summers's theory is as an extension and elaboration of Llewellyn's 'Job of Juristic Method'.

ends in problem situations. One of the most famous statements of this view is to be found in the 'Mischief Rule' for the interpretation of statutes, as expounded by the Barons of the Exchequer in *Heydon's Case* in 1584:[67]

> That for the sure and true interpretation of all statutes in general (be they penal or beneficial, restrictive or enlarging of the common law) four things are to be discerned and considered: 1st. What was the common law before the making of the Act. 2nd. What was the mischief and defect for which the common law did not provide. 3rd. What remedy the parliament hath resolved and appointed to cure the disease of the commonwealth. And 4th. The true reason of the remedy. And then the office of all the Judges is always to make such construction as shall suppress the mischief, and advance the remedy, and to suppress subtle inventions and evasions for continuance of the mischief and *pro privato commodo*, and to add force and life to the cure and remedy, according to the true intent of the makers of the Act *pro bono publico*.

A similar view of rules as instruments directed against problems and mischiefs underlies the seductive common law maxim, '*cessante ratione, cessat ipsa lex*', which, freely translated, means: 'Reason is the soul of the law, and when the reason of any particular law ceases, so does the law itself'. Both *Heydon's Case* and the *cessante* maxim concern interpretation; they both assume that the role of the interpreter is to further the intention of the legislator, either in respect of furthering particular policies or to promote certain ideals or principles.[68] Where there is an element of discretion or choice in interpretation, the role of the judge may be seen as that of a junior partner in the enterprise of law-making; translated to the context of rule-making in general this involves a view of rules as problem-solving devices, as attempted remedies for mischiefs or as embodiments of general moral principles.

There are, of course, ways of looking at rules other than as means to ends. It is also common for rules to be seen as things in themselves, which have an existence independent of any motive, reason, purpose or policy that may have originally inspired them. This view implies that, for the person subject to it, the rule is there to be followed; for the interpreter the task is to ascertain the true meaning of the rule and apply it without regard to the original purposes or the consequences. Consider the following statements:

> That is the rule and we must stick to it.

> Their's not to reason why.

67 (1584) 3 Co Rep 7a. *Heydon's Case* can be interpreted as taking mischiefs of the law, rather than social problems, as the starting point and, as Lord Scarman observed: 'The Barons by their resolution illustrate neatly the relationship in English eyes, between the common law and statute law. The common law is a seamless fabric covering all the activities of man; the statute is the tailor's stitch in time, to patch the fabric where gaps or other defects appear in the course of wear' (*Law Reform: the New Pattern* (1968), p 46). Whether this is an appropriate conception of statute law at the close of the twentieth century is debatable; see below, pp 280-281.
68 On the relationship between instrumentalist/consequentialist and deontological reasons for rules see above p 129 and below pp 185-186.

If the precise words used are plain and unambiguous, in our judgment we are bound to construe them in their ordinary sense, even though it do lead, in our view of the case, to an absurdity or manifest injustice.[69]

These two views of rules are commonly found opposed to each other in a variety of contexts. The attitude exemplified by *Heydon's Case* is commonly referred to by such terms as 'liberal', 'functional', 'the Grand Style of judging'.[70] Where it is appropriate to generalise about this attitude, we shall refer to it as 'instrumentalism'. The contrasting view is commonly associated with such epithets as 'legalistic', 'literal', 'formalistic' and 'conformist'. We shall use 'formalism' as a general term to refer to the second view.

It is necessary to enter two caveats at this point: first, although instrumentalist and formalist approaches are regularly found opposed to each other, there is need for caution in generalising about them, especially without reference to some particular context. Not only are there different versions of instrumentalism and formalism, but also the appropriateness of one or other kind of attitude varies considerably from context to context. For example, it is difficult to conceive of a rational approach to rule-making in which rules are viewed as things in themselves rather than as means to ends; from a rule-maker's point of view, making purposeless rules is a pointless activity. On the other hand, there are circumstances in which unquestioning adherence to rules by a person subject to them or by an official charged with administering them is considered a duty to be carried out however unpleasant the consequences, and powerful reasons can sometimes be advanced for such a posture.[71]

Secondly, it is easy to be seduced, by emotive associations of some words commonly used in connection with each of the two views, into prejudging the appropriateness of a particular posture in a particular context. Statements like 'he interprets the law in accordance with the letter rather than the spirit' leave little doubt about the speaker's sympathies; a value judgement is implied. Terms like 'Grand Style', 'creative' and 'liberal' on the one hand, and 'literal', 'legalistic', 'strict' and 'formalistic' on the other, may suggest that the instrumentalist is always to be supported and formalism is always to be opposed. In particular, there is a natural tendency in the literature to assume that an instrumentalist approach is always more 'rational' than a formalistic one. This tendency is endemic in the academic discussions of 'judicial law-making' in which 'creative', 'liberal', 'bold' judges are regularly cast as heroes and 'timorous', 'literal-minded', 'blinkered' strict constructionists are presented, if not as villains, at least as obstructionists. We are anxious to avoid this kind of naive romanticism which oversimplifies and obfuscates a number of complex questions.[72]

69 Per Jervis CJ, *Abley v Dale* (1851) 11 CB 378, 391.
70 K Llewellyn, The Common Law Tradition, op cit, passim.
71 F Schauer (op cit, pp 105-107), has an interesting discussion of Captain Prescott's famous prescription, 'Don't fire until you see the whites of their eyes'. This he suggests may have originated as a generalisation based on Prescott's experience as a rifleman, may have been transformed into a prudential rule of thumb, but may have been converted into a rule embodied in an order which would be punished for its violation. There are occasions when 'blind obedience' is expected of those subject to rules; in such circumstances there may be good reasons for treating rules as 'things in themselves' on the part of both rulers and subjects.
72 On 'legalism' in interpretation, see below, Chapter 4, section 5.

In this book we shall try to steer a course between naive instrumentalism and dogmatic formalism, but we acknowledge a bias in favour of a view of rules as instruments for solving problems. However, in later chapters we shall develop a number of themes that will serve to bring out both the limitations of a simple model of rules as means to ends, and some of the main reasons that may be advanced to justify a formalist posture in some contexts. In particular we shall at least touch on the following general topics:

(a) adherence to rules as a value, especially when the scope of the rule is clear;
(b) the distinction between a rule and reasons for a rule, and the variety of relationships between rules and reasons for rules;
(c) the relationship between rule-makers and rule-interpreters and the fallacy involved in assuming that interpreters will necessarily view their role as partner, agent or subject of the rule maker;
(d) the error of assuming that a word can have only one meaning attached to it – the 'proper meaning fallacy' – and the core of sense in literal approaches to interpretation of rules in fixed verbal form;
(e) the relationship between 'lawyer-like' and 'legalistic' approaches to interpretation.

To conclude: instrumentalist and formalist views of rules are regularly found in opposition to each other. Whether an individual in a particular situation is likely to adopt an instrumentalist or a formalist posture or something in between may depend on a variety of factors, such as his or her personality, conception of role, immediate purposes, other variables in the immediate situation and so on. The same person adopts one attitude to rules in one situation and a quite different one in another, without necessarily being inconsistent. It is accordingly dangerous to generalise about attitudes to rules, but it does not follow from this that no patterns are to be discerned – for example, some judges have marked formalistic tendencies, while others do not.

11 Other perspectives on rules

A comprehensive theory of rules would have to give an account of such matters as the validity of rules, the value of adherence to rules, the relationship between rules and the exercise of power and authority, and variations in attitudes to rules; all of these ultimately affect interpretation, but they are generally separable from an analysis of it, and are beyond the scope of this book.

Thus questions of interpretation may be part of a process of determining the validity of a rule, for example in deciding whether a regulation is inconsistent with an Act of Parliament, or even in resolving the very profound issues raised when an interpreter is confronted with a rule that is apparently formally valid but which he regards as fundamentally immoral; but doubts about interpretation normally arise in respect of rules that are assumed to be valid. Similarly, not all interpreters feel themselves under an obligation to adhere to rules: the Bad Man, a revolutionary or a tax consultant may not like the result indicated by a seemingly clear rule, and one way of avoiding the result may be through 'interpretation'; in this situation the value of adherence to rules is directly relevant to an analysis of interpretation and it would be misleading to ignore it. However, wider issues which are of central concern to, among others, political and moral philosophers, such as what is the basis of an obligation to obey or observe laws or other rules, or the circumstances under which disobedience (or other forms of non-observance) is morally justifiable, are too complex to be pursued here.

Many rules are instruments for the exercise of power. A friend with mild anarchist sympathies suggested that this book should have been called *How To Do Things to People*. His point was that problems are usually defined and rules are often used as weapons, sometimes as instruments of repression, by those who have power, and that we had too readily accepted official or other 'top-down' definitions of problems and perspectives on rules and had taken inadequate account of those who are subject to them. We do not accept this as fair criticism, for several reasons. Firstly, not all rules are instruments of control or repression; they can also serve to guide, to facilitate, to constitute activities, to confer benefits, to ensure fair procedures and even to protect those subject to them.[73] Secondly, Johnny, the Bad Man, the Unhappy Interpreter and others represent 'bottom-up' perspectives that feature prominently in our analysis.[74] So too are those who use a legal order for their own private ends. Thirdly, in so far as rules are made, interpreted and enforced by governments and other powerful agencies, it is their definitions of the problems and their responses or 'solutions' which are typically the subject of interpretation; they are aspects of the situation confronting the interpreter. Even those who are fundamentally opposed to the structure of power in a given system may still need to become proficient at handling rules within it, like the authors of the passage from *The Bust Book*, quoted in chapter 1, section 11.9. Nevertheless our friend's criticism may serve as a reminder of the significance of power as a dimension of rule-handling and of the danger of unthinkingly accepting 'official' definitions of problems and situations.[75] Analysis of power relations may sometimes have a direct bearing on diagnosis of particular instances of doubt in interpretation as in the conflict between Father and Johnny over watching television.[76] However, in our view, questions about power relations are to some extent severable from questions about interpretation, and should be treated as conceptually distinct.[77]

---

73 cf W Twining, 'Other People's Power' (1997) 63 *Brooklyn Law Review* 189.
74 See chapter 1, section 11.8.
75 For a criticism of the tendency of lawyers to transform and to define unduly narrowly many problems that are presented to them, see Z Bankowski and G Mungham, *Images of Law* (1976), pp 32ff.
76 Above, pp 143-144.
77 For exercises on chapter 3, see Appendix I, section B, below, pp 395-396.

Chapter 4

Interpretation and Application

'[T]he interpretive function may be said to be the central function of a legal system.'
(Talcott Parsons)

In Chapter 1 we illustrated some points about Holmes's Bad Man by presenting a simplified model of Anglo-American criminal process in the form of a 'flowchart' entitled 'The Bad Man in Boston'.[1] This chart depicted the criminal process as a series of decisions and events, involving a variety of participants with different roles to perform at different stages in the process. When the Bad Man is viewed in the context of this process, it is easy to see that he is only one of a number of participants, and that his concern with predicting future events is only one aspect of a complex cluster of tasks that occur at different points in the process, in which other tasks are involved, such as detection, determining what has happened in the past, and sentencing.

In Chapter 2 we focused mainly, but not entirely, on the standpoint of the rule-maker, that is to say on actors who are in a position to introduce, change or adjust a rule in the process of tackling a problem. From now on our attention will shift to a different standpoint, to that of a person confronted with a pre-existing rule who is in one way or another puzzled about how to interpret or to apply it. We shall call this the standpoint of the puzzled interpreter;[2] the central question addressed in this and the next three chapters is, what are the main conditions that give rise to puzzlements about interpreting rules?

To answer this question, we shall first explore what might be meant by terms such as 'interpretation' and 'application' of rules, how interpretation relates to other rule-handling activities and *who* is typically called on to interpret rules, in what contexts and for what purposes. In the next chapter we shall consider some standard imperfections of rules and rule-statements that tend to give rise to difficulties. Then, in Chapter 6, we propose to adapt and broaden the flowchart in order to present some of the main conditions of doubt in the context of a more general model of typical processes involving the creation and handling of rules. We argue that this model is a useful tool for clarifying the nature of the doubts that an interpreter may experience when called on to read, use and interpret a pre-existing rule, in particular, doubts about the interpretation of statutory and case law rules.

---

1   Chapter 1, section 11.7.
2   The puzzled interpreter includes both those people who have power and authority to change the rule in the course of interpretation and those who do not. See below, section 3.

1 Interpretation: what?

Theologians interpret the Bible; producers, actors and critics interpret plays; musicians interpret Beethoven's symphonies; historians interpret past events; and lawyers, as part of their professional work, are regularly called on to interpret statutes, regulations, cases, contracts, wills and other types of document.

The word 'interpretation' has various shades of meaning; in respect of rules, 'to interpret' is generally used in the sense of 'to clarify, the scope of' or 'to attribute a meaning to' a rule or part thereof. In some contexts it can be treated as being synonymous with such words as 'elucidate', 'expound', 'explain' or 'construe', all of which suggest that the subject-matter has an established or settled meaning which it is the role of the interpreter to search for, discover and bring to light, as in a hunt for buried treasure. But often the word 'interpret' is used to suggest a wider role for the interpreter, one that involves an element of elaboration or choice or even of creation. Typically it calls for exercise of the elusive quality of 'judgement'. Thus the buried treasure analogy is inappropriate in the context of Olivier's interpretation of Hamlet, or Brendel's 'free' interpretation of a Beethoven sonata, or a Muslim theologian's 'free' interpretation of the Koran (*ijtihad*).[3] In such contexts it would seem odd to treat interpretation as solely a matter of explanation or discovery; the interpreter is working with material that offers a greater or lesser degree of scope for choice and intervention on his part.

The scope for choice and creativity in interpretation depends in part on the malleability of the raw material to be interpreted, in part on the interpreter's situation and conception of his role, and in part on a variety of other factors. In this book we are concerned with the interpretation of rules, of formulations of rules, and in later chapters of sources of law, that is to say the raw materials of rules of law, such as cases and statutes. In rule-handling contexts it is common to contrast approaches to interpretation by such terms as 'strict', 'literal', 'liberal' and 'free'; such adjectives can be taken to represent various points along a continuum, which ranges from simple search and discovery of a clear settled meaning, to activity that is nearer to relatively unfettered creation of something new.

In theology a distinction is drawn between exegesis (the strict linguistic interpretation of biblical texts) and hermeneutics (the search for the spiritual truth behind the texts). The term 'hermeneutics' was introduced into social science by Dilthey and others, and has become established in that context as characterising the view that human actions are to be explained through the internal meanings they have for the actors themselves. It has been suggested that Hart, with his emphasis on the internal view of rules, adopts a hermeneutic approach to law.[4]

---

3 This term refers to the right of individual interpretation on points on which no general agreement has yet been reached; see H Gibb, *Mohammedanism* (2nd edn, 1953), p 66. See further J Schacht, *An Introduction to Islamic Law* (1964) and K Masud, B Messick and D Powers (eds), *Islamic Legal Interpretation* (1996).
4 DN MacCormick, *HLA Hart* (1981), p 29.

There is an affinity between hermeneutics in theology and social science and liberal approaches to interpretation in law, in that they all emphasise intention and purpose as central features of the search for 'meanings'. In the present context we shall from time to time extend the term 'interpretation' to include both determining 'the scope' of rules – the precise circumstances which they cover – and their 'meaning'. These are two separate, but closely related, ideas: a soldier or bureaucrat, for example, may have a precise conception of the scope of a rule or regulation and apply it 'woodenly' without understanding its rationale or 'point'; in doubtful cases, the meaning of a rule (perhaps explicated in terms of intention, purpose and context) may be a valuable aid to determining its scope; but one may be interested in 'the meaning' of a relatively clear rule for other reasons, for example in order to criticise it or merely out of interest.

We are now sailing near some very deep waters. What is involved in 'understanding' a situation, a rule, or the law is a central, and extremely problematic, question of social theory. Recently, interpretation in law has attracted the attention of scholars from other disciplines, including linguistics, semiotics (the study of signs), rhetoric, literary theory and the history of ideas. There has been a particularly lively series of debates about analogies between the interpretation of legal, literary and theological texts. In writing an introduction to the interpretation of rules we have been faced with a dilemma: we cannot reasonably be expected to deal in detail with this wide range of complex issues and diverse perspectives, but neither can we treat them as irrelevant. Our strategy will be to concentrate on the difficulties of determining the scope of particular rules – the narrow aspect of interpretation – for these are sufficiently complex to warrant special attention; but we shall suggest that it is nearly always useful, and often necessary, to search for, probe, ascribe or construct the meaning of a rule (the nature of the enterprise is another matter of contention) in order to determine its scope, and that this is an inherently problematic task. In Chapter 10 we shall comment briefly on some recent contributions of the Law and Literature movement, critical legal studies and the writings of Ronald Dworkin in the hope that this will at least open the way to exploring a rich, varied and rapidly expanding literature. As we shall see, we are sceptical of the suggestion that 'interpretation' always means making the text the best it can be. That depends on the standpoint and the context of the interpreter.[5]

This leads on to a second warning: it is tempting to treat exegesis and literal interpretation as superficial, and liberal and hermeneutic approaches as profound. After all, the words and the text look like the surface, while exploring meaning, purpose and context involves plunging into those murky depths; 'the letter killeth, but the spirit giveth life'. This is an attractive view, but it involves assumptions that are both superficial and dangerous. It assumes, for example, that textual analysis is *easier* than ascribing or constructing purposes;[6] it assumes that liberal interpretation is always to be preferred to literal; it makes

---

5 Chapter 10, section 7, and Appendix IV.
6 Chapter 5, section 2.

no allowance for purposeless, irrational or meaningless rules; and, most dangerous of all, it sets up rigorous analysis of texts *in opposition* to the exploration of meaning, intention, purpose and context.[7] As we proceed we shall challenge each of these assumptions, without concealing our general preference for a liberal and contextual approach. The skilful interpreter pays attention to standpoint, text and context.

1.1 Law and fact

Interpretation of rules must initially be distinguished from fact-finding under a rule. In legal contexts, this distinction is typically characterised in terms of 'questions of fact', 'questions of law' and 'questions of mixed fact and law'. While these exact terms are perhaps not commonly used in non-legal contexts, the distinction is a familiar one. For example, 'did Johnny use a broom to get the jam?' is a question of fact, while the question whether his use of the broom constituted an 'entry' is a question involving the scope of the word 'entry' and is a question of interpretation. If the issue were to be posed in the form of a single question, 'Did Johnny enter the larder?', it would be a question of mixed fact and interpretation.

However, there are special implications of the distinction in legal contexts. In English law these are, firstly, that decisions on questions of fact generally do not constitute precedents for later interpreters, whereas decisions on questions of law often do; secondly, that in jury trials questions of fact are in general reserved for the jurors, whereas questions of law are exclusively for the judge to answer (the judge may however withdraw some questions of fact or give directions to the jurors concerning how they should decide a question); thirdly, that decisions on questions of law are generally required to be supported by public justifications, whereas there is no such general requirement in our system for determinations of fact;[8] fourthly, that in the case of appeals against findings of criminal liability, both the grounds of appeal and the conditions under which it may be allowed tend to be more favourable to the convicted person where the appeal involves a question of law than where it involves a question of fact alone or a question of mixed fact and law;[9] and fifthly, that appeal courts will not reverse a finding of fact (because they will neither have seen nor heard the witnesses give evidence under examination) unless the finding reached by the lower court could not be supported by the evidence presented to it, or was so unreasonable as to suggest that it did not really understand what the rule's requirements are.

In short, important practical consequences flow from the distinction between questions of fact and questions of law. However, determining the

---

7 By contrast, see the approach to the interpretation of Community Law followed by the European Court, which combines these different approaches: Chapter 8, section 5.

8 This is not true in some civil law systems, such as the Netherlands, which does not have juries and where judges at first instance are required to give reasons for their findings of fact.

9 For details of the rules governing criminal appeals see, eg, P Murphy (ed), *Blackstone's Criminal Practice* (1998), section D22.

conceptual basis upon which the distinction rests is by no means easy.[10] There are two main reasons for this. The first is that the law treats as questions of fact, questions which in non-legal contexts might not obviously be thought of in this way. There are two aspects to this point: the first concerns questions relating to the quality of a person's act or omission, or of some state of affairs, which can, to the level of probability required by the court, be shown to have occurred, while the second concerns the interpretation of 'ordinary' words in statutes.

In order to explore the first of these, it is initially helpful to distinguish two kinds of factual conclusion that a court may be invited to reach after the parties have presented their evidence about the truth of a given proposition of fact: either that it is true or, because no direct evidence is available on the matter, that it is more probable than not that it is true. For example, in a simple civil case of negligent driving, evidence will be led by the plaintiff about such observable matters as the road's environment (was it in a built up area or near a school?) and its condition (was it a narrow lane or a dual carriageway?), the weather conditions (was it day or night, overcast or sunny?) and the presence of other cars or pedestrians. These are matters on which direct evidence can be led; that is, the evidence of witnesses present at the scene of the accident. Having heard that evidence a court would be able to say that the road was, as a matter of fact, a single lane carriageway and, as a matter of inference, that it was more probable than not that at the time in question, a driver driving in a westerly direction on that road would, given that he was driving into the setting sun, have experienced difficulty in seeing clearly what was in front of him. All of these are conclusions of fact; but the court has not yet concluded that in driving in the way that he did in the circumstances it has found to be factually true or more probable than not, the driver was driving 'negligently'. This, too, is 'a question of fact', but is clearly not a question that can be answered merely by looking at the 'facts' surrounding the driving. To say that the driver was driving 'negligently' is to make a *judgement* about the quality of his driving measured against the driving qualities of some notional non-negligent (careful) driver, and this judgement is, for legal purposes, as much a finding of fact as is the finding that the road was a single carriageway, or that it was a sunny day. Similarly, the question whether a surgeon conducted a medical procedure 'negligently' is a question of fact, in which the surgeon's actions are measured against the court's notion of what is the appropriate standard to expect from a non-negligent surgeon in that particular field of medicine.

At this point the picture becomes a little more complicated. While the question, was *this* driver or *this* surgeon negligent is (on the facts found to be true or more probable than not) a question of fact, the question of what *is* the appropriate standard of care for drivers or surgeons is a question of law. In the case of surgeons, this is established in a famous case, *Bolam v Friern Hospital*

---

10 T Endicott, 'Questions of Law' (1998) 114 *Law Quarterly Review* 292. For a vivid account of the way in which lawyers from different legal cultures interpret problems as involving a question of law or question of fact, see Yves Dezalay and Bryant Garth, *Dealing with Virtue* (1996).

Management Committee.[11] Sometimes, therefore, these are called 'questions of mixed fact and law', and they are a staple feature of both civil and criminal law. A classic example from the criminal law is the question in a murder trial whether the defendant 'intentionally' killed the victim. This combines in one, two quite separate questions: firstly, what is the defintion of 'intention' in the common law crime of murder (a question of law) and, secondly, given the definition, does the evidence show (directly or by inference) that he did 'intend' to kill (a question of fact).

Whether the facts as shown to be true or more probable than not meet some specified statutory attribute or quality is likewise a commonplace question. Adapting the circumstances of the possibly negligent driver, we could also ask whether he was guilty of 'careless' (without due care and attention)driving, contrary to section 3 of the Road Traffic Act 1988. Other examples are contained in sections 8-14 of and Schedule 1 to the Police and Criminal Evidence Act 1984: whether the material on the premises specified in the application is likely to be of 'substantial' value to the investigation and whether it was 'practicable' to communicate with any person entitled to grant entry to the premises.[12] But as with the question, what do we mean when we ask, in a common law context, did the defendant 'intentionally' kill, we might also wish to ask, what do we mean by 'careless' driving, or 'substantial' value or whether communication was 'practicable'? In other words, before we can answer the factual question, we need clarification on a definitional question. This leads us to a consideration of the second aspect mentioned above: the interpretation of ordinary words in statutes.

Starting from the basic proposition that the interpretation of legislation must, because it states the law, ultimately be a question of law, the courts recognise two approaches to the interpretation of legislative words. Firstly, where a word has been given a technical or a specifically legal meaning either by statutory or judicial decision, an interpreter should attribute that meaning to it. If she attributes to it some other meaning, then she is wrong as a matter of law. If this erroneous interpretation is appealed it will (and must, because it cannot represent the law) be reversed. Of course, there may be some doubt about the scope of the word, but whatever it is, it is a question of law. On the other hand, where the word is an ordinary word of the English language, it is for the interpreter to attribute to it a meaning that it ordinarily bears in the context in which it appears; this is a question of fact: 'when the court is faced with an ordinary word which could be used in a variety of shades of meaning, it [is] not for the court to try to conjure out of thin air some precise definition such as might be found in a statute'.[13] For example, suppose that during the apartheid era a protestor ran onto the Centre Court at Wimbledon distributing leaflets condemning apartheid in South Africa while two white South African players were in the middle of a game. Whether that action

---

11 [1957] 2 All ER 118.
12 Appendix 1, section A4.1.
13 Per Walker LJ, *Sussex Investments Ltd v Secretary of State for the Environment* [1998] PLCR 172 (as a matter of law, a 'houseboat' need not be boat-shaped).

constituted 'insulting behaviour' within the meaning of section 5 of the Public Order Act 1936 was a question to be answered by what the trial court understood by the word 'insulting'. So long as it gives the word a meaning that it ordinarily bears in that context, an appeal court will not reverse a trial court's decision even though it disagrees with it; but it will do so if the decision 'was unreasonable in the sense that no tribunal acquainted with the ordinary use of language could reasonably reach that decision'.[14] It will also do this where the word has a well-established meaning in the context of the particular statutory provision.[15]

The second main reason why it is difficult to give a definitive account of the conceptual basis for the distinction between questions of law and questions of fact is because the courts have no settled criteria for determining whether a question is one of law or fact. For example, while the consequences of the two approaches to the interpretation of statutory words outlined in the preceding paragraph are clear, what is not clear is the basis upon which an interpreter should make the initial judgment of a word as being one which is 'ordinary' or which bears a technical or specialised meaning.[16] In general the courts have treated a question variously over the years as one of fact and as one of law.[17] As it has traditionally proved difficult to predict how the courts will classify any given question, some writers regard the *purpose* of the classification as the determining factor. For example, those issues that are thought suitable for a jury to decide or are, on the other hand, thought unsuited to be the subject of an appeal or to give rise to precedents, will be treated as questions of fact. Determining what is suitable entails an assessment of the advantages and disadvantages of such treatment.[18] Treating a question as one of fact allows the law to reflect cultural standards as they vary across time and place, to be applied relatively easily by lay magistrates or juries (who will receive less complex directions from the trial judge), and to be compatible with everyday understanding. To counter the criticism that the law will be uncertainly and

14 Per Lord Reid, *Brutus v Cozens* [1973] AC 854, 861. In *Cutter v Eagle Star Insurance Co Ltd* [1998] 4 All ER 417, the House of Lords held that for the purposes of the Road Traffic Act 1988, the question whether the place at which the accident occurred was a 'road' was 'always one of fact'.
15 *Shah v Barnet London Borough Council* [1983] 2 AC 309.
16 For example, whether the words 'offer' and 'consideration' appearing in penal statutes should be given their technical legal meanings as derived from the law of contract, or an ordinary meaning that might be closer to the legislation's purpose: *Fisher v Bell* [1961] 1 QB 394 and *R v Braithwaite and Girdham* [1983] 2 All ER 87.
17 For example, on the meaning of the word 'dishonestly' in the Theft Act 1968 see *R v Feely* [1973] QB 530 and *R v Ghosh* [1982] QB 1053; and on whether a contract to perform services is a contract *for* service or a contract *of* service see *Midland Sinfonia Concert Society v Secretary of State for Social Services* [1981] ICR 454 and *O'Kelly v Trusthouse Forte* [1983] ICR 728. Sometimes, the court will simply assert that the matter is a a question of mixed fact and law which it is entitled to review: *Smith v Abbott* [1994] 1 All ER 673.
18 See for example Wien J on the meaning of the word 'antique' in s 58(2) of the Firearms Act 1968 (*Richards v Curwen* [1977] 3 All ER 426) and Lord Woolf on the application of the phrase 'frequent attention ... in connection with his bodily functions' in s 35(1)(a) of the Social Security Act 1975 to the assistance given to a blind person to bathe and feed himself, and to walk in unfamiliar surroundings: *Mallinson v Secretary of State for Social Security* [1994] 2 All ER 295. See further, J Bell and G Engle QC, *Cross on Statutory Interpretation* (3rd edn, 1995), pp 59-60.

inconsistently applied, a question may instead be treated as one of law. This increases appellate control over the decisions of lower courts and tribunals and so ensures a greater degree of uniformity in adjudication.[19]

Despite these difficulties of classification, some questions are clearly ones of law or fact. Questions whose answers depend upon the existence of evidence showing that a fact is true or more likely than not to be true are always questions of fact. Sometimes this evidence assumes material form, such as a photograph, a document or fingerprints on a weapon; often it comprises the evidence of a witness, perhaps an expert, who can testify as to what they have experienced. In either case the evidence may be open to challenge on the ground that it cannot tell the truth about that which is in issue (for example, the document is a forgery or the eyewitness was not in line of sight at the material time), that it is inconclusive (for example, the fingerprints are smudged or the eyewitness was viewing a dimly-lit event) and thus the probability of the alleged fact being true is low, or that, even if the evidence is true, it should not (with or without qualification) be allowed in (for example, if the eyewitness is an accomplice). We should be careful, however, not to speak of these apparently simple cases involving the identification of objects and persons as though, once identified, the 'facts' require no further elaboration. Against the notion that facts may be thought of as 'speaking for themselves' White argues 'the lawyer knows that to prove his (or her) case he must not only demonstrate the truth or probability of certain propositions of fact; he must present to the judge or juror a way of looking at the case as a whole that will make sense; and it must "make sense" not merely as a matter of factual likelihood, but as a predicate to action'.[20]

To revert to our example of a possibly negligent driver, questions of this kind seek to answer who was driving what car on what day in what town (which may be answerable only by a process of inference, because no one actually saw the defendant but his car was seen and he has no alibi for the material time), other questions of fact seek to answer such questions as how the driver (whoever he was) was driving, or what the manner of his driving suggested about his degree of concentration on the task in hand. For example, a photograph may show heavy tyre marks on a road surface starting 20 metres from and stopping half-way across a zebra crossing. The question is whether we should describe the driving evidenced by these facts as normal, fast or excessive in the circumstances, and the braking as controlled, sudden or late. (The Highway Code gives 23 metres as the stopping distance travelling at 30 mph in normal conditions.[21]) However it does not follow that because we can conclude, as a matter of fact, that the tyre marks indicate that the driver was driving fast, that we can also conclude that he

---

19 See *R v Spens* [1991] 4 All ER 421 where the Court of Appeal held that the need for consistency in the interpretation of contractual or legislative documents was so important that in deciding whether the defendant's conduct fell within the requirements of the City Code on Takeovers and Mergers, the court would approach its interpretation of the Code as a question of law rather than, as would normally be the case with the construction of documents, a matter of fact.

20 J White, *Heracles' Bow* (1985), p 160. See further, W Twining, *Rethinking Evidence* (1994), pp 238-249 and A Zuckerman, 'Law, Fact or Justice?' (1986) 66 *Boston University Law Review* 487.

21 *The Highway Code* (1996).

was in breach of a given rule of law governing driving; we have yet to determine whether this driving amounts to 'careless' or possibly 'dangerous' driving contrary to the Road Traffic Act 1988. As we have seen, this question too, is a question of fact, and thus where magistrates or juries have to determine whether a defendant drove 'carelessly' or 'dangerously', an appeal court will only interfere with their decision if no one acquainted with the ordinary use of these words could possibly have reached a similar judgment.

Similarly, some questions are always questions of law: questions concerning procedure, jurisdiction, the admissibility of evidence or the applicable law; so too, the question whether a question is one of fact or law is itself a question of law.[22] In almost all of the examples used in this book, actual and hypothetical, the facts are not in dispute. This eliminates one difficulty which is central both to legal practice and to many problems in real life involving rules in non-legal contexts. For in many problem situations there is a doubt or dispute about what actually happened. Such questions fall outside the scope of this work, but that is not to suggest that they are unimportant.[23]

1.2 Interpretation and application

It is useful to distinguish between the notions of interpreting and applying a rule, although in practice this distinction is often blurred. Strictly construed, 'interpretation' refers to clarification of the general scope or meaning of a rule. Sometimes interpretation of a rule may be called for without reference to any particular situation or event, in much the same way as a compiler of a dictionary sets out to elucidate the meanings of a word without necessarily referring to any particular occasion on which it has been used. Similarly, a statute may have an interpretation section which provides definitions or elucidations of the words that it uses. These give general guidance for future applications of the rule. However, doubts about interpretation most commonly arise with reference to some particular event or case that may allegedly have occurred or may be hypothetical. In such contexts it is not always easy to distinguish between interpreting a rule (general) and applying it to the facts of the case (particular).

It is important to realise why the distinction often breaks down: whenever a rule is applied to a particular case to produce a particular result, interpretation of the rule is involved; but how the rule was interpreted may be left unstated or implicit. If there was some doubt about what the result in a given case should be, it does not follow that it will be clear whether the doubt was one of interpretation or application or both; nor will it necessarily be the case that the doubt was resolved either by moving from the general to the particular or by moving from the particular to the general; moreover, terms like 'general' and 'particular' are relative matters, and some of the most difficult choices to be made in interpretation relate to choosing appropriate levels of generality.[24]

---

22 *Edwards v Bairstow* [1956] AC 14.
23 See T Anderson and W Twining, *Analysis of Evidence* (1991).
24 See chapters 9 and 10.

One of the characteristics of the common law tradition is a preference for proceeding by case-by-case decision rather than by the formulation of clear general rules or principles in advance. The common law often moves from particular to general, or even from particular to particular, rather than from general to particular. When a court, or other authoritative interpreter, decides that a particular case falls within the scope of a general doctrine, it may expressly or impliedly leave open questions about the scope of the relevant rule or principle to be determined in future cases. This can be restated analytically as follows: 'If X, then Y'. To state of a particular example, 'This is a case of X', involves *interpreting* the rule or principle because it says something about its scope, even though it leaves open questions about its outer limits. There is a difference between saying 'This is a clear case of X' and providing a general definition of X, but both are examples of the interpretation of X.[25]

2 Rule-handling

Consider the following sets of verbs, all of which are commonly used with 'rule' or 'rules' as their object:

(a) draft, make, amend, adapt, adopt;
(b) promulgate, announce, communicate;
(c) find, identify;
(d) state, expound, elucidate, analyse, explain, restate, paraphrase;
(e) interpret, apply, distinguish, invoke;
(f) obey, conform to, observe, work to, stick to, act on;
(g) disobey, break, flout, ignore, avoid, evade;
(h) twist, stretch, manipulate, restrict, bend, emasculate, waive, make an exception to;
(i) enforce, uphold, defend, criticise, attack, disapprove;
(j) repeal, nullify, render nugatory, abrogate.

This list, which is far from exhaustive, gives some indication of the range of activities involved in 'handling rules'. The groupings suggest a rough and ready way of differentiating various types of rule-handling activities. A whole book could be devoted to elucidating and exploring the relationships between these and other connected activities. A comprehensive theory of rule-handling in general would need an elaborate apparatus of concepts and distinctions – consider, for example, some of the nuances involved in differentiating between 'disapproving' and 'criticising' a rule, or between 'obeying' rules and 'working to rule'. For the purpose of indicating in a very general way the relationship between interpretation and other rule-handling activities, such refinements

---

25 See chapter 9, section 7, and also W Twining, *Rethinking Evidence* (1994), chapter 7. A classic account of case-by-case reasoning is by John Wisdom, on which see DC Yaldon-Thomson, 'The Virginia Lectures', in R Bambrough (ed), *Wisdom: Twelve Essays* (1974), chapter III.

are unnecessary, although they may be illuminating. We shall confine ourselves to emphasising three points at this stage.

Firstly, some of the verbs in the list are clear instances of activity that is commonly understood as 'interpretation', while others, such as 'to bend', 'to twist' or 'to emasculate', are arguably on the borderline; in the context of rule-handling, in so far as such words imply some determination of the scope of a rule, they are justifiably treated as examples of interpreting. Secondly, some of the activities are a precondition of interpretation, though independent of it. Generally speaking, interpreting a rule presupposes that it is in existence and has been identified and is probably accepted as valid.[26] One can find, announce or promulgate a rule without interpreting it, but it would usually be odd to say that one can interpret a rule that has yet to come into existence, or be discovered. It is not inconceivable that such a statement could make sense in some contexts; for example, there is an intimate relationship between interpreting a rule and drafting a rule in fixed verbal form. A draftsman will typically try to anticipate possible meanings that might be attached to his formulation and will try to use words in such a way as to exclude interpretations that will defeat the rule's objective(s). Of the draftsman, it may be said that he interprets in anticipation of the existence of the rule. And in respect of a rule not in fixed verbal form, stating the rule in a particular way may be a way of interpreting it, or of disguising the fact that creative interpretation is taking place. For formulation of a rule typically involves an element of choice.

Thirdly, some of the verbs *presuppose* interpretation. Thus, 'to obey', 'to disobey', 'to flout', 'to work to', 'to evade' and 'to criticise' typically presuppose that some meaning has been attached to the rule by the actor, whether implicitly or explicitly. It is possible also to use terms like 'disobey' or 'comply with' to describe the behaviour of an actor who is unaware of the rule in question; but such a description itself presupposes some interpretation of the rule.

The point that interpretation may be presupposed by, or may form part of, some other activity deserves emphasis for two reasons: firstly, it is because so many rule-handling activities presuppose or involve interpretation that we are justified in calling skill in interpretation a basic skill; and secondly, whenever interpretation forms part of another activity, that activity is part of the overall context that provides standards for judging the appropriateness of a particular interpretation. For example, an advocate may advance a particular interpretation of a statute as part of the task of trying to persuade a court to decide the outcome in favour of her client; this role and this objective provide a basis for evaluating the appropriateness of her interpretation. Interpretation is typically an element in some more complex activity or task involving rule-handling; some rule-handling activities do not necessarily involve interpretation, for example promulgating or repealing a statute; but many rule-handling activities involve or presuppose interpretation and in such circumstances the task of interpretation needs to be viewed in the context of the activity as a whole.

---

26 See above, p 145. Of course, questions concerning the validity of a rule may involve issues of interpretation: for example, determining whether a particular regulation is *intra vires* a statute or, in the United States, whether a legislative provision is constitutional may involve interpretation of several provisions.

3 Who interprets?

In considering the functions of rules and problem-solving by rules we were concerned mainly, but not exclusively, with questions about what difference it makes to have or not to have rules. These questions are particularly important for one kind of participant, the actor who is in a position to influence events by introducing, abolishing or otherwise changing a rule – in other words the legislator or rule-maker, whether this be Parliament, a local authority, a university senate, the officers of a club drafting a constitution, a judge interpreting a statute, a parent or Grandad making up or 'remembering' 'house-rules' to suit his convenience during a tense game of croquet.[27]

But this kind of option is not open to all participants. Many problems concerning rules arise in a situation where the rule exists; it is a datum confronting the actor. To her it may be an obstacle or a threat or a guide or an aid or a support or a tool or a puzzle or many other things. Depending on who she is and what she is trying to do, she may wish to conform with, obey, invoke, apply, rely on, wield, manipulate, avoid, evade, twist, flout or ignore it. She may use it as a guide to decision or to action, as an aid to prediction, as a reason justifying a particular course of action or in persuading someone else to come to a particular decision, as a bargaining counter and so on. In the almost infinite number of social processes and social transactions in which rules are an element, there is a corresponding variety of uses of rules. As we have seen, many of these activities presuppose or involve interpretation. If I am a citizen trying to avoid paying unnecessary taxes, yet keeping within the confines of the law, I need to have some conception of what the relevant rules mean. Similarly, if I am setting out to disobey some law as a protest, I need to have a reasonably clear idea of the scope and meaning of the law in question, if only because I shall look rather foolish if it turns out that my purported act of 'disobedience' involved no infraction of any rule.

The distinction between persons in a position to change rules and persons confronted by a pre-existing rule is neither simple nor clear-cut. It is a truism that rules often change in the process of interpretation by official interpreters, such as judges. The most obvious example is of rules not in fixed verbal form, such as case law based rules in the common law; but one could also say that the scope of the 'due process' clause in the Fifth Amendment to the Constitution of the United States has expanded over the years, even though the text has remained unchanged. In formal contexts, customary and other rules not in fixed verbal form emerge, evolve, change, fade away and die, often through the acts and choices of unidentified people who have no clearly recognised authority or power. But the distinction is none the less worth preserving, for there are many cases where a person confronted with a rule is

---

27 Typically such a person has both authority and power to introduce, modify, change or abrogate the rule. But it is worth remembering that the effectiveness of a rule may be influenced by people who have no authority to change it – for instance, where the police turn a blind eye to breaches of traffic regulations committed by the drivers of emergency vehicles, such as fire engines; cf *Buckoke v Greater London Council*, discussed in chapter 1, section 8.

not in a position to change it for the future. There is a difference, for example, between a judge who in coming up with an unlikely interpretation of a statute is said to have 'stretched' or 'extended' it, thereby creating a precedent for the future, and someone, perhaps a junior official, who may purport to 'bend a rule', but whose interpretation none the less leaves the rule unchanged afterwards.

It is not possible here to give a comprehensive account of all the different types of actor who need to interpret rules as part of performing some role or task. But it is useful to look at some of the standard situations in which questions of interpretation arise and to see the relationship of various kinds of actor to each other within the context of a single process. To start with a legal example: the sequence of decisions and other events that constitute what we call 'criminal process' falls into a fairly standard pattern, as illustrated by the flowchart of 'the Bad Man in Boston'.[28] As that chart shows, in legal processes there are a great many types of participant, but the main ones apart from the parties themselves are usually taken to be the legislator (rule-maker), the counsellor (adviser), the advocate, the judge (or other decider) and the law-enforcer (who features at various points in the process from investigation and detection to execution of the decisions of the court). Each of these categories of participant can be defined in terms of notional roles: rule-making, advising, persuading, fact-finding, rule-interpreting and applying, justifying decisions, enforcing and so on.

These roles overlap; for instance, persuading a judge (advocacy) and justifying a decision on a point of law (as in a reported judgment in a case) both involve giving *valid reasons* of an almost identical kind. An advocate in persuading a judge often seeks to promote a result in a case by 'selling' a good justification. Similarly, the judge in particular may sometimes be involved in legislating, in the sense of making or changing rules. Not only do the roles of participants in legal processes overlap, sometimes in quite complex ways, but often a single participant may have more than one role – for instance, the same person may be involved in fact-finding, rule interpretation and application and determining the sanction, if any, to be imposed on the losing party.

This analysis of some of the basic tasks of rule-handling applies in non-legal as well as in legal contexts. Of course, in practice there will often be less differentiation between roles of participants in simpler kinds of social processes than there are in typical legal processes. This is one reason why there is an element of artificiality in talking of Mother as the 'legislator', law enforcer and prosecutor, and of Father as the judge. But the tasks of rule-making, advocacy, fact-finding, rule-applying and so on are identifiable in the family situation, even if they are not clearly differentiated in the minds of the participants or if they are all allocated to only one or two persons.

This differentiation of different roles and standpoints is a key element in the method of diagnosis of puzzlements about rules which is developed below. The model of criminal process illustrates some of the main roles involved in

28 Chapter 1, section 11.7.

rule-handling in a highly structured process in which some of the participants have authority to change or modify the rules and some do not. But it does not give a comprehensive account of all the conceivable roles involved in rule-handling and all the possible uses of rules that may be encountered in different kinds of social interaction. For example, rules may be invoked in bargaining as arguments, as we saw in the Arusha examples,[29] or as threats, for instance in crude blackmail or more subtle kinds of pressuring; they are often invoked as justifications for past or future behaviour; similarly, we shall come across situations where the rule-maker may be embarrassed or frustrated or defeated in an argument by having his own rule quoted against him, an example of being 'hoist with one's own petard'. To analyse such examples it is often useful to identify the standpoint and role of the relevant participants, and to explain their use of one or more rules in the particular context in terms of who they are, what their situation is, and what they are trying to do.

Some of these points can be illustrated briefly by returning to the *Case of the Legalistic Child.* Assume that Mother has reported the broom-handle episode to Father and he has decided to hold a hearing with Mother as the prosecutor, Johnny conducting his own defence, and himself in the role of impartial adjudicator.

From Johnny's standpoint, his perception and evaluation of the situation may be different from Mother's, but the situation is defined to some extent by the existence of the rule, which provides an important criterion for determining what facts or allegations are relevant or irrelevant. Johnny's role is also dictated largely by the context; if his primary object is to avoid punishment (there might of course be others), he has a number of tactical choices open to him. Thus, he may dispute the facts, advance one or more interpretations of 'enter' consistent with his having committed no offence, or admit that an offence has been committed but plead in mitigation. These are the obvious lawyer-like moves.[30] But if he is a good advocate, he will try to anticipate the likely response of the 'court' to any particular argument and this may lead him to choose to adopt some quite different tactic, such as persuading his Father to treat the whole episode as a joke. Johnny in the role of advocate may have a problem with regard to what tactics to adopt, but his role and aims are clear: to try to persuade Father to reach an acceptable result.

Father's position on the other hand is quite different. One reason for this is that the standpoint of the 'impartial adjudicator' is less well defined. There are a number of elements in the situation that might be relevant to diagnosis of Father's problem: for example, his loyalty to Mother and his concern to uphold her authority; his own decree, which might be viewed as eccentric, that discipline in the family should operate in accordance with the Rule of Law; his concern to be fair to Johnny; perhaps a feeling that Johnny's behaviour

---

29 Chapter 1, section 5.1.

30 Cf the familiar tale in Punch of the lawyer's son who was charged with having broken the schoolroom window: 'In the first place, sir, the schoolroom has no window; in the second place, the schoolroom window is not broken; in the third place, if it is broken, I did not do it; in the fourth place it was an accident'. Cited by Glanville Williams in *Learning the Law* (11th edn, 1982), p 20.

is reprehensible but that Mother has mishandled the situation by inept rule-making and possibly also by deciding to 'prosecute' in an inappropriate case; and he may wish to take into account the likely effect on Johnny and on relations within the family of any action that he decides on in this situation.

In diagnosing his problem and deciding how to act, Father may place considerable emphasis on some of the above factors and may give little or no weight to others, and his choices are likely to be influenced, among other things, by his conception of his role. To take two extreme examples: if he considers his role to be essentially that of the 'impartial judge', he might define the problem very narrowly as being concerned solely with the interpretation of Mother's rule, and he might deliver judgment along the following lines: 'The only question for determination in this case is: did Johnny enter the larder? Since neither Johnny's body, nor any part of it, crossed the threshold of the larder, he is not guilty under the rule. I leave open the question whether, if only part of his person, such as a hand, had crossed the threshold, this would have constituted an entry.'

On the other hand, if Father chooses to cast himself in the role of 'the wise Father', he might well see this as an opportunity for trying to change Johnny's relationship with his Mother or for teaching him some general lessons about relationships within the family or about rule-handling and advocacy. Here Father would have to emphasise a number of elements in this situation in addition to the rule and would define the problem much more broadly than he would if he considered his role to be that of impartial adjudicator. Thus, what is an appropriate method of approach for a puzzled interpreter depends to a large extent upon his standpoint and his conception of his role; and in the archetypal situation of judge or impartial adjudicator, there is typically a lack of precise definition of that role, which creates a corresponding lack of precision about what constitutes the best way to proceed. Thus, as with problem-solving, clarification of standpoint and role is an important preliminary to interpretation.

One of the weaknesses of many traditional accounts of legal interpretation is that they concentrate, explicitly or implicitly, on a single standpoint – typically that of the impartial judge or of a neutral expositor. This is inadequate for two main reasons. Firstly, such allegedly 'neutral' or 'impartial' roles are notoriously problematic. An extraordinary amount of attention has been paid in jurisprudence to questions about the proper role of judges. Do they and should they make law or only apply it? Do they make policy? How far can a judge be impartial in doubtful cases? All too often doubts about the proper role of judges have been conflated with puzzlements about interpretation. We shall suggest later that discussions of one of the central problems of interpreting cases – the traditional problem of determining the *ratio decidendi* – have been made unnecessarily complicated because puzzlements about role have been confused with puzzlements about interpreting precedents.[31] If one looks at what is involved in interpreting a prior case from a standpoint in which the role is relatively clear, for example that of an advocate, it is very much easier to

---

31 Chapter 9, section 6.

give an account of the matter because doubts about role and doubts about interpretation are then clearly differentiated.

An even more important objection to the traditional concentration on the standpoints of judges and expositors is that little or nothing is said about what constitutes appropriate interpretation by other actors and what difficulties confront them. This leads to a radical impoverishment of most discussions of legal interpretation, sometimes to the point that they are seriously misleading. Sir Rupert Cross laid great stress on the fact that 'the vast majority of statutes never come before the courts for interpretation';[32] but he then proceeded to an analysis which is seemingly based on the assumption that those who interpret such statutes all behave as if they anticipate that they will be interpreted judicially. This is, at best, a tremendous oversimplification. Civil servants, the police, businessmen, accountants, insurance claim adjusters, practising lawyers and ordinary citizens may all be concerned to predict or to speculate about likely judicial interpretations of particular rules – and past or potential future, authoritative rulings have special significance from the internal point of view of anyone who wishes to adhere to a rule – but in the course of conducting their affairs such people inevitably take many other factors into account, some of which are intimately tied up with their respective standpoints and roles.

In order to hammer this point home, let us postulate three characters: a cautious solicitor, an adventurous barrister, and an unhappy interpreter. When a client, whether good citizen or Bad Man, consults a solicitor (or other professional adviser) he may pose the question: 'If I do X, what will happen to me?' He is in effect asking his adviser to predict some of the consequences of his proposed course of action. Suppose that the solicitor feels that there is some doubt about the scope of some potentially relevant rule, which will form part of the basis for her advice. What would be an appropriate interpretation in the circumstances? She may, of course, explain her doubts to her client, but if pressed for a definite answer the cautious solicitor will probably place a *pessimistic* interpretation on the rule – she will in a sense interpret against her client in order to allow a margin of error.[33] When drafting documents most solicitors typically indulge in such pessimistic or cautious interpretations, for sound reasons – it is part of their job to anticipate contingencies, including adverse interpretations. In our hypothetical situation it would be a rather narrow and unhelpful solicitor who would base her advice solely on a prediction of how the applicable substantive law would be interpreted in the courts, especially if the rule is part of one of Cross's 'vast majority' which are rarely if ever litigated in practice.

Suppose then that the client, in spite of the cautious solicitor's advice, does X, and is unfortunate enough to be sued or prosecuted as a result. Suppose that he decides to contest the case on a point of law and the adventurous barrister is briefed to represent him: how will the latter interpret the applicable rule(s)? Clearly it would be inappropriate in preparing his argument to adopt

---

32 J Bell and G Engle QC, *Cross on Statutory Interpretation* (3rd edn, 1995), p 1.
33 Cf Appendix 1, section G1, question 3.

the solicitor's interpretation. Instead he may behave as if he is optimistic and consider possible interpretations that would produce a result in his client's interests and, if this is a test case, in the interests of other persons in similar situations. In actually arguing the point in court he may concentrate on the most plausible of several possible interpretations, any one of which would be consistent with winning. Thus in respect of the same act a client's legal representatives may give different interpretations of a doubtful rule – one pessimistic, the other optimistic – and *they will both be right* given their respective roles and situations. This, in simplified form, is part of the daily experience of legal practice. It is obvious, but it is forgotten or glossed over by nearly all traditional accounts of legal interpretation.

Finally, let us consider another fictitious character whom we shall call the unhappy interpreter. This is a person who is confronted by a rule which, at least at first sight, seems to be in conflict with what he wants to do or what he believes to be right. If we revert for a moment to the mechanistic model of decision-making, then to say that an interpreter has a doubt in the particular case would be to say that he was in doubt about the scope of the rule, or its application to the facts, or both, so that the result was in doubt. However, such a model is too simple as a description of most decision-making processes, and it is not uncommon for interpreters to be in doubt about the result for some reason unconnected with either of the premises. The paradigm case of the puzzled interpreter who, though he wishes to conform to the rule, is genuinely puzzled about its scope or application may be usefully contrasted with that of the interpreter who is confronted with a rule about whose scope he has little or no doubt, but who, *for that reason*, is faced with a problem. There are various reasons why an interpreter in this situation may be dissatisfied: he may be in general disagreement with the policy behind the rule;[34] he may sympathise with the policy but dislike the particular rule as an instrument for furthering it; he may be in general sympathy with both rule and policy, but for some other reason wish to avoid the result that would be produced by a straightforward application of the rule in this class of case; or there may be some feature of the particular case that leads him to desire a result other than that suggested by the most obvious interpretation of the rule. Put simply, he wants something despite the rule.

The unhappy interpreter's problem then is that, although the scope of the rule may be clear, at least on the surface, it is an obstacle to his securing the result he desires. Faced with this type of situation, an interpreter may be in a position to secure the desired result by some means other than interpretation, for example by flouting, waiving or avoiding the rule; but where he is not, the temptation to interpret the rule by bending, stretching or straining it frequently arises. We should not be lured by the emotive associations of such terms as 'manipulative' or 'legalistic' into thinking that such activities are indulged in only by villains. Portia's interpretation of Shylock's contract with Antonio was a classic example of legalistic interpretation; Portia is generally considered to be a heroine, and her

---

34 Cf chapter 1, section 11.9.

objectives honourable; yet the means she used is generally regarded as a clear example of 'legalism'.[35]

In these situations a conflict may arise between the wish to manipulate a clear rule in order to achieve the desired result, and the value of adherence to rules; faced with this conflict the unhappy interpreter may choose to uphold a straightforward interpretation of the rule. This is often the case where the unhappy interpreter is a judge. The law reports abound with judicial regrets that testify to the acute nature of this conflict; though the value of adherence to the rule and the ultimate obtaining of a change may both be secured by perverse interpretation, as Coleridge J pointed out, 'Perhaps the most efficacious mode of procuring good laws, certainly the only one allowable to a Court of Justice, is to act fully up to the spirit and language of bad ones, and to let their inconvenience be fully felt by giving them full effect'.[36]

The possible manipulation of the rule does not exhaust the unhappy interpreter's alternatives in dealing with his problem. Words like 'bend', 'stretch' and 'strain' suggest some settled or established meaning that is being altered or departed from in the course of interpretation. But it is important to emphasise that doubt is a relative matter. It is not uncommon in both legal and non-legal contexts for some participants to express doubts about the interpretation or application of a rule, while others maintain that it is clear. Accordingly, the unhappy interpreter may be able to pave the way for a less obvious interpretation, by creating or establishing a doubt which then needs to be resolved. It may be the job of an advocate or other interpreter to engineer doubts in order to achieve his objective. Indeed, some, like the fictional judge in Fuller's *The Case of the Speluncean Explorers*, may positively relish doing so:

> My brother Foster's penchant for finding holes in statutes reminds one of the story told by an ancient author about the man who ate a pair of shoes. Asked how he liked them, he replied that the part he liked best was the holes. That is the way my brother feels about statutes; the more holes they have in them the better he likes them. In short he doesn't like statutes.[37]

Doubt and unhappiness are both relative matters. There is no sharp line to be drawn between genuine puzzlement about the scope and meaning of a rule, exploiting possible ambiguities or uncertainties and setting out deliberately to sow the seeds of doubt about what previously was assumed to be clear. In this context we need not take the notion of unhappiness too seriously: the trade unionist working to rule, Johnny sparring with his parents and the advocate involved in the cut and thrust of the adversarial process may or may not be enjoying themselves in pursuing their objectives through exploiting available leeways. What is clear is that some kind of conflict is involved, and the unhappy interpreter at least seems to be fighting against the spirit, the

---

35 Chapter 1, section 3.3.
36 Per Coleridge J in *Pocock v Pickering* (1852) 18 QB 789, 798. For some more complex examples, see Douglas Hay's account of eighteenth-century judges administering the death penalty, in D Hay et al, *Albion's Fatal Tree* (1975), especially pp 29 and 33.
37 L Fuller, 'The Case of the Speluncean Explorers' (1949) 62 *Harvard Law Review* 616, 634.

purpose or the intention, or what has hitherto been assumed to be the settled meaning of the rule. This leads on to questions about the relationship between rule-makers and rule-interpreters.

4 Rule-makers and rule-interpreters

> With all its subtleties, the problem of interpretation occupies a sensitive central position in the internal morality of the law. It reveals as no other problem can, the co-operative nature of the task of maintaining legality. If the interpreting agent is to preserve a sense of useful mission, the legislature must not impose on him senseless tasks. If the legislative draftsman is to discharge his responsibilities he, in turn, must be able to anticipate rational and relatively stable modes of interpretation. This reciprocal dependence permeates in less immediately obvious ways the whole legal order. No single concentration of intelligence, insight and good will, however strategically located, can insure the success of the enterprise of subjecting human conduct to the governance of rules.[38]

This passage is a relatively sophisticated example of the view that the relationship between rule-maker and interpreter is essentially one of *co-operation*. Thus judges are spoken of as agents or junior partners of rule-makers; the role of officials is to carry out, enforce, apply or uphold the will of the legislator. While this represents a conception of the interpreter's role that would, for example, be subscribed to by many official interpreters, it is important to recognise that co-operation is not the only possible relationship between rule-makers and interpreters. When the interpreter is not an official, the relationship can range from complete co-operation to outright hostility. Antonio in *The Merchant of Venice* reminds us that the 'devil can cite Scripture for his purpose';[39] Johnny is hardly in a co-operative relationship with Mother, nor is this a realistic way of describing the attitude of the Bad Man, a revolutionary or a tax consultant.

The attitudes of potential interpreters may have important implications for the style of drafting of rules in fixed verbal form. Karl Llewellyn, who was prepared to rely on the good faith of most businessmen and the good sense of most judges, justified the 'open' style of drafting of the Uniform Commercial Code in the following terms: 'Technical language and complex statement cannot be wholly avoided. But they can be reduced to a minimum. The essential presupposition of so reducing them is faith in the courts to give reasonable effect to reasonable intention of language'.[40] Contrast this statement with the following conception of the task of the draftsman of a revenue statute: '[I]t is not enough to attain to a degree of precision which a person reading [the statute] in good faith can understand; but it is necessary to attain if possible to a degree of precision which a person reading in bad

---

38 L Fuller, *The Morality of Law* (1969), p 91.
39 W Shakespeare, *The Merchant of Venice*, Act 1, scene 3.
40 Memorandum on the Uniform Commercial Code (1940), quoted in W Twining, *Karl Llewellyn and the Realist Movement* (1973), p 526.

faith cannot misunderstand. It is all the better if he cannot pretend to misunderstand it.'[41]

Co-operation between rule-makers and officials is no doubt a more natural relationship, but it cannot be taken for granted. At the general level of political theory the relationship between the legislature and other branches of government is not necessarily to be viewed as that of partnership in a single joint enterprise. The notion of checks and balances, the doctrine of judicial review, the concept of judges as watchdogs are all reminders that such a monolithic view of a polity is too simple. Legal history can provide many examples of judges acting in ways which suggested that their role was to frustrate rather than to further the will of the legislature. Fuller's statement of the ideal is not one that is universally accepted even as an ideal, still less as a realistic description.

Moreover, even where an official interpreter sees his role to be essentially one of co-operation, he may in particular instances be faced with difficult choices as to how to perform that role. A rule may have proved to have been an imperfect instrument of its policy; it may have been overtaken by social change, technological innovation or a shift in public opinion; the way in which the rule-maker actually behaved at the time of the making of the instrument and the way he might have been expected to behave in the circumstances actually confronting a court at a later date are not necessarily identical. Judges placed in this kind of situation do not respond in a uniform fashion: some try to mitigate the situation, as in *Buckoke*, some see their role as being to interpret and apply the statute without regard for the supervening events; others may go even further and seek to provoke legislative action by underlining the absurdity of the existing provision, as did Darling J when confronted with section 3 of the Sunday Observance Act 1679: 'In my opinion the best way to attain that object is to construe it strictly, in the way the Puritans who procured it would have construed it; if that is done it will very soon be repealed.'[42]

These examples should be sufficient to show that the relationship of rule-makers and interpreters is a complex one and that the co-operative model, however attractive, is an over-simplification.

5   Legalism

We have already encountered several examples of interpretation or other behaviour that might be labelled 'legalistic' and we shall come across more in later chapters. In the nursery example, Johnny is called 'the legalistic child', but it might also be said that Father's notion of ordering the family according

---

41 Per Stephen J in *Re Castioni* [1891] 1 QB 149, 167. And see Brooke LJ, formerly Chairman of the Law Commission, exasperated by Parliament's unwillingness to enact the Commission's Draft Criminal Code, indicating that the courts should take the initiative on a particular matter, implying that if Parliament didn't like the outcome, then it should respond accordingly; *B v DPP* [1998] 4 All ER 265.

42 Per Darling J in *Slater v Evans* [1916] 2 KB 403, 405.

to 'the Rule of Law' or of holding formal hearings, and Mother's insistence on trying to enforce her rules in trivial or doubtful cases are also 'legalistic'. Portia, tax consultants, the unhappy interpreter, working to rule and 'Catch 22' provide further standard instances. 'Literal' interpretation by judges and others is also sometimes referred to in such terms as 'literalistic', 'legalistic' or 'formalistic'.

Such concepts are elusive and require quite elaborate elucidation. Here we shall merely make a few elementary observations on different kinds of legalism, on the emotive associations of the term, and on some motives and functions of legalistic behaviour.

The adjective 'legalistic' is variously applied to behaviour, to attitudes, to persons, to judicial styles, and even to whole legal systems and cultures. In respect of behaviour and attitudes, it is important to distinguish between at least three primary uses, which reflect different standpoints: liking to have lots of rules or complex formal procedures; insisting on adhering closely to existing rules, for instance by enforcing clear, but petty, infractions; and interpreting rules in a literal, strict or rigid way. Each of these is closely associated with a different standpoint or role: thus the first relates to *rule-making*, the second to *enforcement* or *observance*, and the third to *interpretation*. There is no necessary correlation between 'legalistic' behaviour in respect of each standpoint. The same person may favour having a lot of rules, but be prepared to waive or ignore existing rules in certain circumstances and she may generally favour either liberal or literal interpretation, without being inconsistent. Similarly a rule-maker may oppose the creation of formal rules and procedures *because* she believes that, once created, they should or will be rigorously enforced or strictly interpreted. For example, a university teacher may quite consistently oppose the drawing-up of very detailed regulations governing marking and classifying examination scripts, because if such regulations exist she will feel bound to apply them strictly or to interpret them in a literal or rigid fashion. Similarly a trade unionist may increase the impact of a work-to-rule by interpreting some rules very broadly or liberally and then insisting on adhering rigidly to them as interpreted, even though she may dislike or disapprove of their content. Thus, the prolific rule-maker, the stickler for rules and the strict or literal interpreter have different characteristics, which may or may not coincide in the same person.

In regard to interpretation of existing rules, some further differentiations are required. Whereas the unhappy interpreter may see some rule (if interpreted in a particular way) as an *obstacle* to achieving his particular ends, a judge or administrator may adopt a literal or strict interpretation for different reasons, for example in order to avoid being seen to be 'making rules' or to advance (or frustrate) the intention of the rule-maker. As we shall see later, it is sometimes the case that 'creative' or 'liberal' judges, such as Lord Denning or Lord Atkin, are driven to resort to 'legalistic' interpretation in order to get rid of prior adverse precedents, for it is the bold or innovative judge rather than his more cautious colleague who tends to be troubled by such precedents.[43]

---

43 Chapter 9, section 5.

These elementary observations should at least be enough to expose two common assumptions as being at best dubious and possibly fallacious: viz the idea that 'legalism' is necessarily bad and the idea that legalistic behaviour is to be explained solely or even mainly in terms of individual psychology.

In many contexts terms like 'legalism' and 'formalism' are emotive, carrying with them the suggestion of disapproval. For example, lawyers sometimes contrast 'lawyerlike' and 'legalistic' behaviour, perhaps implying that the former is 'professional' and involves good judgement, and that the latter is dishonest, narrow-minded or immature. However, choosing to have few or many rules, to stick closely to existing rules or to ignore, waive or only partially enforce them, to interpret them broadly or narrowly, strictly or liberally, are not choices which can sensibly be evaluated generally, and outside some specific context. To put the matter very briefly: the functions and dysfunctions of formalism (including legalism as one of its manifestations) are very varied, especially if one includes making, enforcing, observing and interpreting rules within its ambit. Literal interpretation may be prompted by a desire to do justice in a particular case or to reveal the absurdity of a particular rule, or by a policy of judicial restraint or in order to give effect to some presumption – for example, the presumption of innocence or a presumption in favour of preserving existing property rights. Legalistic interpretation, in this sense, is not in itself either good or bad.

A second doubtful assumption is that legalistic behaviour is primarily a function of individual psychology, to be explained in terms of the personality and attitudes of people as individuals. We have ourselves talked of 'the legalistic child', of formal-style judges, of literalists and rigorists and sticklers for rules. No doubt individuals do exhibit tendencies or patterns of behaviour which can be explained, at least partly, in terms of psychological variables. It should, however, be clear from what has been said that such behaviour might also plausibly be explained in terms of a variety of other factors, such as context, role and immediate purpose. Thus the same judge may adopt a literal approach to one statute and a liberal approach to another for reasons which have little or nothing to do with his personality or general attitudes. Many judges do just this. The moral is that one should be wary of over-generalising about the behaviour of individual interpreters from a limited number of examples.

It is not possible here to explore in detail or in depth the nature, forms and functions of formalism and legalism. It is an important and neglected subject.[44] It may help to give an intimation of one aspect of its wider significance by ending with a quotation from Douglas Hay's interpretation of one example of legalism:

(M)ost penal statutes were interpreted by the judges in an extremely narrow and formalistic fashion. In part this was based on seventeenth-century practice, but as more capital statutes were passed in the eighteenth century the bench reacted with an increasingly narrow interpretation. Many prosecutions founded on excellent evidence and conducted at considerable expense failed on minor errors of form in the indictment ... If a name or date was incorrect, or if the accused was described as

44 See further R Summers, 'How Law is Formal and Why it Matters' (1997) 82 *Cornell Law Review* 1165.

a 'farmer' rather than the approved term 'yeoman', the prosecution could fail. The courts held that such defects were conclusive, and gentlemen attending trials as spectators sometimes stood up in court and brought errors to the attention of the judge. These formalisms in the criminal law seemed ridiculous to contemporary critics, and to many later historians. Their argument was (and is) that the criminal law, to be effective, must be known and determinate, instead of capricious and obscure. Prosecutors resented the waste of their time and money lost on a technicality; thieves were said to mock courts which allowed them to escape through so many verbal loopholes. But it seems likely that the mass of Englishmen drew other conclusions from the practice. The punctilious attention to forms, the dispassionate and legalistic exchanges between counsel and the judge, argued that those administering and using the laws submitted to its rules. The law thereby became something more than the creature of a ruling class – it became a power with its own claims, higher than those of prosecutor, lawyers, and even the great scarlet-robed assize judge himself. To them, too, of course, the law was the Law. The fact that they reified it, that they shut their eyes to its daily enactment in Parliament by men of their own class, heightened the illusion. When the ruling class acquitted men on technicalities they helped instil a belief in the disembodied justice of the law in the minds of all who watched. In short, its very inefficiency, its absurd formalism, was part of its strength as ideology.[45]

6   Leeways for interpretation and application

In a mechanistic model of decision-making the relationship between rule, facts and results can be expressed in the form of a syllogism. The adjudicator discovers and states the rule as the major premise, he discovers and states the material facts as the minor premise, and the result follows as a necessary conclusion. A question of interpretation arises when the interpreter has a *choice* either as to the scope of the major premise or as to how it is to be applied to the facts (which are given). How is it possible for such questions to arise? A brief answer, which will be elaborated in due course, is as follows.

Firstly, rule-makers often deliberately confer a discretion on rule interpreters, such as judges or civil servants, to determine borderline or otherwise difficult cases; or they may establish a general policy, but make a deliberately vague instrument of the policy and leave the working out of detail to the point of application.

Secondly, rule-makers may fail to foresee all possible contingencies, with the result that doubts may arise as to whether the rule was intended to apply in circumstances that the rule-maker seems not to have anticipated; and, closely related to this, rule-makers' aims are prone to vagueness and questions may arise about the precise effect that might have been intended in a particular case.

Thirdly, in respect of rules in fixed verbal form, even if the draftsman wishes to anticipate every contingency, language is too imprecise and malleable an instrument to foreclose every possibility.

---

45 D Hay et al, op cit, p 33.

Fourthly, in the case of rules not in fixed verbal form, additional uncertainties may arise at the stage of formulation of the rule (if that stage is ever reached) and because there may be no generally agreed starting point for discussion about its scope and application.

Fifthly, there is the factor of consistency. A major task of interpretation is reconciling rules (and sources of rules, such as cases), for typically a single rule belongs to some larger agglomeration or system. How far internal logical consistency within a body of rules should be treated as one, or even *the*, cardinal value for interpreters is, as we have seen, one of the perennial questions of jurisprudence.[46] The relevant point is that, in so far as consistency is a value, it forms a basis both for creating problems for interpreters and for helping to resolve them. A doubt about interpretation may be resolved by looking to other rules, but doubts about interpretation of a seemingly straightforward and clear rule can be *raised* by pointing to another rule that is arguably inconsistent with it.

Deliberate delegation of discretion, ignorance of fact, indeterminacy of aim, the limitations of language, the fluidity of rules not in fixed verbal form, conflicts between the value of internal consistency within a system and other values, and divergencies of aim or role or situation between the rule-maker and the interpreter, are merely some of the most common conditions that give rise to problems of interpretation and application of rules. Later we shall elaborate and expand this list of conditions of doubt. At this point it is worth emphasising that while factors such as these create leeways for interpretation, the leeways are not limitless. The puzzled or unhappy interpreter is presented with some choice, but the range of possible or plausible or otherwise appropriate interpretations is in practice subject to constraints. The nature and force of such constraints will vary from context to context. For example in discussing the leeways open to advocates and judges in American state appellate courts, Karl Llewellyn identified fourteen 'major steadying factors' which tended to reduce doubts and limit the range of choice in practice, such as the mental conditioning of lawyers, the prior identification and sharpening of the issues, accepted ways of handling authoritative sources of law and of presenting arguments in court, and the constraints of group decision-making and of publicity.[47] His list could no doubt be greatly extended. Such 'steadying factors' vary according to the context and the participants involved. Typically they operate as a counterweight to conditions which occasion or give opportunities for doubts and disagreement. In a given context it is often a matter of delicate judgement to determine the extent and the limits of choice in interpretation.[48]

---

46 Chapter 3, section 6 and Chapter 10.
47 KN Llewellyn, *The Common Law Tradition* (1960), esp pp 19ff, and *The Case Law System in America* (1989).
48 For exercises on chapter 4, see Appendix I, section C, pp 396-397. For references to the extensive literature on discretion, see Appendix IV.

Chapter 5

Imperfect Rules

Someone asked to describe her model of a technically perfect rule might reply: A rule is perfect if (*a*) it has a single clear and acceptable aim; (*b*) it is so clearly and precisely expressed that it leaves no room for doubt about its application in any possible case, and no loopholes for those who might wish to escape its effects; (*c*) its scope is co-extensive with its purpose; and (*d*) it is certain to achieve its purpose without undesirable side-effects.

In a famous passage in *The Concept of Law*, Hart outlined some of the reasons why this is not only unattainable, but also undesirable as a model for all legal rules:

> Whichever device, precedent or legislation, is chosen for the communication of standards of behaviour, these, however smoothly they work over the great mass of ordinary cases, will, at some point where their application is in question, prove indeterminate; they will have what has been termed an *open texture*. So far we have presented this, in the case of legislation, as a general feature of human language; uncertainty at the borderline is the price to be paid for the use of general classifying terms in any form of communication concerning matters of fact. Natural languages like English are when so used irreducibly open textured. It is, however, important to appreciate why, apart from this dependence on language as it actually is, with its characteristics of open texture, we should not cherish, even as an ideal, the conception of a rule so detailed that the question whether it applied or not to a particular case was always settled in advance, and never involved, at the point of actual application, a fresh choice between open alternatives. Put shortly, the reason is that the necessity for such choice is thrust upon us because we are men, not gods. It is a feature of the human predicament (and so of the legislative one) that we labour under two connected handicaps whenever we seek to regulate, unambiguously and in advance, some sphere of conduct by means of general standards to be used without further official direction on particular occasions. The first handicap is our relative ignorance of fact: the second is our relative indeterminacy of aim. If the world in which we live were characterised only by a finite number of features, and these together with all the modes in which they combine were known to us, then provision could be made in advance for every possibility. We could make rules, the application of which to particular cases never called for a further choice. Everything could be known, and for everything, since it could be known, something could be done and specified in advance by rule. This would be a world fit for 'mechanical' jurisprudence.[1]

In the last chapter we set out to give an account of what is meant by interpreting, how it is related to other rule-handling activities and who are typically the

---

1   HLA Hart, *The Concept of Law* (2nd edn, 1994), pp 127-128.

actors involved in the process of interpretation. We now propose to look a little more closely at some of the most important conditions of doubt, in the form of a commentary on, and elaboration of, this quotation. We are in general agreement with Hart's view that a system of rules that left no room for choice in interpretation is neither feasible nor desirable, but in the course of the argument we shall suggest that the reasons for this are rather more complex than this passage suggests. We shall consider the argument under five heads:

(a) the factual context of rules;
(b) intentions, reasons and purposes;
(c) the role of purposes and other reasons in interpretation;
(d) rules and language;
(e) the open texture of rules.

1   The factual context of rules

Hart suggests that the first handicap of a human rule-maker who wishes to regulate conduct 'unambiguously and in advance' is 'our relative ignorance of fact'. Except in regard to closed systems, such as noughts and crosses, few rule-makers can anticipate all the possible combinations of circumstance to which their rules might be applicable, and so they cannot anticipate all the contingencies that might arise to be determined. For example, the law maker in 1861 probably did not think of Muslim marriages, let alone same sex marriages and changed sex marriages. But the relationship of good rule-making to the world of fact is very much more complicated than that. The omniscient rule-maker would need to know not merely all the possible permutations and combinations of fact-situations that might fall within the scope of the rule; if his purpose in introducing the rule is to influence certain kinds of behaviour in a particular way, he needs to have knowledge of the situation he is trying to influence, the likely effects any particular rule or group of rules will have on the situation and how the situation is likely to develop. Rule-makers in the role of problem-solvers are not merely concerned with anticipating possibilities, they are also concerned to influence events in changing situations. Actual rule-makers are more or less well informed about the situation confronting them, more or less well placed to foretell how the overall situation will change over time, and more or less well placed to predict the likely consequences of introducing a particular measure.

There is a further dimension to the factual context of rule-making. Every event in life is unique and infinitely complex. Rules are blunt instruments which lump together fact-situations into classes to be treated alike; they generalise and they simplify. Every decision to resort to rules involves a decision to treat certain differences as immaterial and to treat complex events as if they were simple. Perhaps the most difficult problems facing rule-makers concern choices as to the level of generality at which to frame the rule, with what degree of precision and with what provision for exceptions: at one extreme is the very precisely worded, very general, purportedly absolute rule which makes few or no concessions to the complexity and particularity of actual events; at the other extreme is the instrument that is so vague and so open-ended as to raise doubts as to whether it can be appropriately referred to as a 'rule' at all.

Thus the perfect rule-maker needs more than omniscience, in the sense of a complete knowledge of existing circumstances and of all possible combinations of factual circumstances; he also needs a capacity accurately to predict consequences and future, causally unconnected, developments, and an infallible judgment about what constitutes an appropriate level of generality in a given context. While the development of an empirical social science of law may help understanding of the present and the past and, to some extent, prediction of future likelihoods, judgements about levels of generality inevitably involve other considerations, to which we now turn.

2   Intentions, reasons and purposes

In the passage quoted above, Hart refers to 'our relative indeterminacy of aim' as one of the features of the human predicament that handicaps attempts to regulate conduct in advance by means of rules. This brings us to the important topic of the role of intentions, aims, purposes and other reasons in the interpretation of rules. A good deal of confusion attends these notions both in the literature and in practice, perhaps for two main reasons: firstly, terms like 'legislative intent', 'the aim of the rule', 'the purpose of the statute' and 'the reason of/for the rule' (*ratio legis*) are commonly used to cover a wide range of situations and factors that need to be differentiated. There is a tendency to use such terms too simply or too confidently or in ways which take too much for granted. In this area a precise and discriminating vocabulary is especially important. Secondly, the subject is complex. The mental processes of rule-makers are varied and often complicated; they may be difficult to discover or fathom; there is room for disagreement about how much weight should be given to the intentions, purposes and reasons of the original rule-makers, when these are clear, as against other factors;[2] and, as we shall see, terms like intention and aim are often *attributed* or *ascribed* to rules even when there is no determinate or ascertainable rule-maker.

In order to pick our way through some of these complexities we shall postulate a seemingly simple model of rationalistic rule-making and interpretation, and explore first some potential complications within it and then further difficulties arising through deviations from the model. Let us, therefore, start with the following situation: some years ago a single rule-maker, Lionel (L), made a rule. L was an almost ideal candidate for the job: he was intelligent, well-informed, honest, rational and a skilled draftsman. Furthermore, he gave his full attention to the task and he consistently sought to promote values which were generally accepted in the relevant community.

---

2   For references to recent debates between Dworkin, Bork and others about the 'original intent' of the US Constitution, see below, pp 375ff.

He made rules only after he had been through a careful and rational procedure for problem-solving. Suppose that we adopt the standpoint of a co-operative interpreter (C) confronted, shortly after L's death, by one of L's rules made five years previously. C is puzzled by a point of interpretation of this rule and he wishes to interpret it in accordance with L's intentions, purposes and reasons. In order to do this, C sets out to ascertain what these were or, failing that, to try to reconstruct as best he can what they would have been had L addressed himself to the problem.

Even in this very simple situation, some questions need to be clarified. Firstly, *what* precisely is being referred to by L's 'intention', 'purpose' and 'other reasons'? Secondly, *how* should C set about trying to discover or ascribe L's intentions and purposes? Thirdly, what *weight* should C give to them, once they have been clarified, in comparison with other considerations? For example, the social context or the community's values may have changed, some other relevant event may have occurred since the original rule was made or there may be some special features in the particular case under consideration.[3]

The first question can be approached by differentiating several matters which might be encompassed by the term L's 'intent'. Adapting a useful analysis by Gerald MacCallum, we can distinguish several cases and possible deviations from them:[4]

Object of intent	*Some possible deviations*	*Term*
1. L intended to make *a* rule.	L did not intend to make a rule; eg he merely ventured an opinion.	(un)intended rule (A).
2. L intended to make *this* rule Y.	L intended to make rule Z rather than rule Y.	(un)intended rule (B).
3. L intended to make this rule as an instrument for dealing with a specific problem.	L only made this rule in order to further some ulterior purpose unconnected with the substance or scope of the rule (eg because he was bribed or for political gain).	(irrelevant) motive.
4. L intended to use the words that were in fact used in the text of the rule.	The rule was not in fixed verbal form or L intended to use some word(s) other than those that were in fact used.	(un)intended words.
5. L intended that the words should be understood according to some settled convention or technical usage.	The words to be interpreted had no settled meaning or L did not know what the words meant or had no clear intent as to meaning.	intended meaning of words.

3 See below, chapter 6.
4 G MacCallum, 'Legislative Intent' (1966) 75 *Yale Law Journal* 754. For a more recent discussion, see A Marmor, *Interpretation and Legal Theory* (1992).

Object of intent	*Some possible deviations*	*Term*
6. (*a*) L intended that the rule should cover situations of type O but not situations of type P.	L had no clear intention as to scope.	intended scope.
6. (*b*) L intended that this rule should/should not repeal, make an exception to or otherwise change other rule(s).	L had no clear intention as to possible effects on other rules; the rule had affected other rules in ways not contemplated by the rulemaker.	(un)intended effects.
7. L intended that this rule should have a particular (direct or indirect) impact on behaviour or attitudes or have other consequences.	L had no clear intent as to consequences of the rule or the rule did not have the consequences intended or it had other unintended consequences.	purpose/(un)intended consequences.
8. L made this rule for some clear reason(s) other than or in addition to its consequences, eg to embody a moral principle.	L had no clear reasons for making the rule; the rule represented a compromise between several conflicting reasons.	reasons for a rule.

It should not be necessary to explain and illustrate all of these categories. However, it is worth making a few points about them. Firstly, it should be clear that phrases like 'legislative intent' or 'the intention of the rule-maker' are systematically ambiguous. In this context confusion is more likely to arise from uncertainty about the object (intention as to what?) than from doubts about the meaning of 'intention', which is a notoriously elusive concept in other contexts. We are not much concerned here with reckless, negligent or accidental rule-making, although we may be concerned with inadvertence on the part of the rule-maker.

Secondly, when confronted by a rule made by a determinate rule-maker we normally take it for granted that L (1) intended to make a rule, (2) intended to make *this* rule, (3) had some conception of its scope and meaning, and (4) at least in the case of rules in fixed verbal form, intended to use the words that were in fact used in the text. Usually these are fairly safe assumptions although unintended rules and unintended words are not unknown.[5] Similarly, even where L had some purely incidental motive for making the rule (eg he was bribed), he may nonetheless have had some conceptions about its scope, the meaning of the words used and its likely consequences. Clear deviations from any of these assumptions can be treated as special cases which share the characteristic that the interpreter is not likely to gain much help from trying to ascertain L's actual 'intention' as an aid to interpretation, for L had no relevant intentions.

---

5 It is presumed that Acts are drafted without error. See F Bennion, *Statutory Interpretation* (3rd edn, 1997), p 320, and *Statute Law* (3rd edn, 1990), chapter 18.

Thirdly, the relationship between 'intention', 'purpose' and 'reasons' needs to be clarified. As used here, L's 'intention' refers to his intention as to *making a* rule and *this* rule; his intention as to the *words* used to express the rule and as to the *meanings* to be attached to the words; his intention as to the *scope* of the rule and its relationship to other rules (its *effects*). In ordinary usage, L's 'intention' may also be extended to cover intended consequences (purpose), his motives and possibly his reasons for making this rule in the way he did. But such extensions give too much work to the concept of 'intention' and may cause confusion. Rather we would suggest that so far as is feasible, distinctions should be made between *intention*, incidental *motives, purposes* and other *reasons*.

In this context clarity is served by confining 'purpose' to intended consequences – the hoped-for impact of the rule on external matters such as conduct, attitudes and events, but excluding its 'effects' on other rules within the same system.[6] Of course, consequences may be direct or indirect; so may purposes. For example, the direct purpose of a rule making rape or hijacking an offence may be to reduce the incidence of such conduct. However, many rules have *ulterior* purposes: for example, regulations requiring searches of passengers before boarding have as a *direct* purpose, reducing the number of weapons taken aboard the aircraft; the main *ulterior* purpose is to reduce the incidence of hijacking. There can be a progression of means to ends in which the intermediate stages are both means and ends – a person does A in order to secure B, which is a means to secure C in order to secure D, and so on.

We refer to 'purposes and other reasons', for under the notion of 'reasons for rules' are included both intended consequences and non-consequential reasons, such as principles embodying values which are not directed towards the future. For example, an important reason for a rule entitling a person to be represented in disciplinary proceedings is that this represents a principle of natural justice. The rule may or may not have good consequences in practice, but the reason is independent of the consequences, for such principles of justice are non-consequentialist, as exemplified in extreme form by the maxim: 'Let justice prevail though the heavens fall' (*fiat justitia, ruat caelum*). Similarly much of the European Convention on Human Rights and many statutory provisions are based on non-consequentialist or on mixed reasons.

Finally, it is worth noting that intentions, purposes and other reasons may be more or less precise and may operate at different levels of generality.[7] For example, L may have had a clear intention as to scope but only rather vague purposes; again, he may have had a clear idea as to the general purpose of the relevant measure, but have been relatively unconcerned with the details. Most rule-makers pay more attention to some aspects of their task than to others. As with other aspects of rule-making, inadvertence is a relative matter.

So far we have concentrated on a simple model of a single rule-maker and a co-operative interpreter. In the chart some possible complications were noted

---

6 It is often important to distinguish between the impact of a rule on other rules (effects) and on actual situations – the 'real world' (consequences). See further below, pp 210-211.

7 In some contexts it is quite common to distinguish different levels of purposes, between general goals, and at lower levels of generality, more specific aims and yet more specific objectives. Unfortunately there is no standardised terminology for these various categories.

when L's performance fell below some ideal standard of good and rational rule-making. It is not difficult to imagine other deviations: for example, L may be under very heavy pressure of work; he may be corrupt or incompetent; there may be no consensus in the community about the relevant values; the interpreter may be unhappy rather than co-operative, and so on. Some of these have already been considered, others will be discussed later. At this stage we need to pause to consider the situation where L is not a single identified person but is either indeterminate or collegiate.

2.1 Indeterminate and collegiate rule-makers

A sharp contrast to the model of a single actor consciously setting out to diagnose a problem and designing a rule as a means of solving or mitigating it, is provided by William Graham Sumner's account of the growth of 'folkways':

> ... from the first acts by which men try to satisfy needs, each act stands by itself, and looks no further than the immediate satisfaction. From recurrent needs arise habits for the individual and customs for the group, but these results are consequences which were never conscious, and never foreseen or intended. They are not noticed until they have long existed ... [and a] long time must pass ... before they can be used as a basis from which to deduce rules for meeting, in the future, problems whose pressure can be foreseen. The folkways, therefore, are not creations of human purpose and wit. They are like products of natural forces which men unconsciously set in operation ... which reach a final form of maximum adaptation to an interest, which are handed down by tradition and admit of no exception or variation, yet change to meet new conditions, still within the same limited methods, and without rational reflection or purpose.[8]

This account of how folkways come into existence contains elements of exaggeration and over-simplification. It serves as a useful reminder that rules not in fixed verbal form tend not to be the intentional and conscious creations of a single person at an identifiable point in time. But the ways such rules come into existence are many and various: conscious factors may have a greater role to play in many cases than Sumner suggests; new rules and adaptations of old ones may arise in response to particular dramatic crises or events rather than to recurrent needs,[9] or they may develop through a series of conscious *ad hoc* decisions, as in case law. Thus notions such as intention and purpose may not apply to many rules not in fixed verbal form, yet the situation out of which they grew, the needs or mischiefs to which they were a response and the values or policies underlying them may all be of concern to the interpreter. If the relevant information is not available to him, he may nevertheless have to *attribute* some mischief and values to the rule in order to make sense of it; and the speculative nature of such attribution may be another condition of indeterminacy and hence of doubt.

The topic of the intention of collegiate rule-makers has attracted much attention, especially in the specific context of judicial interpretation of statutes.

---

8 WG Sumner, Folkways (1906, 1960), pp 19-20.
9 See, for example, K Llewellyn and E Hoebel, *The Cheyenne Way* (1941), pp 29-30.

This is an extremely difficult and controversial area, with an extensive and sophisticated literature. Some of the difficulties can be illustrated by postulating a simple case. A committee of twelve persons has voted by a majority of 9-3 to introduce a new rule, which had been drafted and introduced by two of the majority. A doubt later arises as to the intended meaning of one of the words in the rule. Several questions need to be differentiated:

(a) Can two or more people have shared or common intentions?
(b) If so, is it meaningful to talk of a group of two or more people having 'an intention'?
(c) If so, does a group have 'an intention' in the same sense as an individual?
(d) In the case of collegiate rule-making and, in particular, in the case of the committee, with whose intentions are we concerned: the whole committee; the majority; the proponents; or someone else?
(e) In interpreting rules made by collegiate rule-makers, are we concerned with *ascertaining* or merely with *imputing* or *ascribing* the relevant intention?
(f) What procedures and resources are typically available to the interpreter in ascertaining or imputing intention in this kind of context?

There seems to be no consensus in the literature, or in practice, in respect of *any* of these questions.[10] This can be shown by considering two of many possible reactions – one sceptical, the other claiming to represent common sense. The general attitude of the sceptic is that talk of 'the intention' of a collegiate rule-maker is at best a crude fiction and is potentially highly misleading. He might deal with the example of the committee along the following lines: 'No two persons have identical intentions; even where two persons might have similar intentions, it will in practice be impossible to ascertain with precision how similar they were in fact; accordingly, to talk of a group of two or more people having "an intention" is to employ a simplifying fiction, which will at best be a rough and speculative approximation of the actual intentions of the individuals involved; but whose intentions are in issue? It was the committee, not the proponents, who made the rule; but could those members who voted against it be said to have had an intention about the meaning of the relevant words? Perhaps one or more of them voted against it because they felt that these words were ambiguous or because their meaning was all too clear and was objectionable. Are their intentions irrelevant? Those who voted for the rule may have each interpreted the words differently, if they had considered the matter at all. Suppose one of those who voted for the rule had not even read the draft and had no intention about the disputed point? Suppose one or more of the majority had voted for the rule because they interpreted the rule differently from the proponents? Suppose the draft was a *verbatim* copy of a rule made by some other body – are we seriously expected to try to ascertain the intention of the draftsmen of the original rule, even if that were feasible?

10 R Dworkin in *Law's Empire* (1986), chapter 6, purports to give a coherent answer to most of them.

Surely such considerations (and I could add many more) indicate that there is no possibility of *discovering* the intention of the rule-maker. Accordingly all we can do is *impute* an intention to the committee by way of fiction. But *how* are we to set about this? There is no agreed method of doing so; therefore, the interpreter is free to impute whatever intention he pleases. But why bother, if the purpose of ascertaining or imputing intention is to help the interpreter to resolve genuine puzzlements? Talk of "intention" in this kind of context is purely figurative or fictitious, and conceals the true nature of what is involved in interpretation.'

To which an upholder of a common-sense view, let us call her Earthy, might reply: 'Sceptic has identified some genuine and some spurious difficulties, but he has greatly exaggerated the extent and significance of the genuine ones. The plain fact is that we all regularly talk of "the intention" of groups of people without any danger of being misunderstood; even some alleged sceptics, such as Gray and Payne,[11] have acknowledged that the intention of the legislature is often perfectly clear and obvious; and legislatures are much more complex bodies than committees. It may be the case that no two people have absolutely identical intentions about anything, but we do not need such a high degree of conformity for talk of collective intentions to be meaningful and helpful in interpretation. If I say "my team intends to score a goal", you know perfectly well what I mean. So with committees and legislatures. Of course, what is meant by "the intention" of a group is not exactly the same as what is meant by "the intention" of an individual but, as all lawyers know and ordinary usage acknowledges, they are similar enough for most practical purposes. There may be occasions when it is difficult to decide exactly whose intentions to take into account, but these difficulties can be greatly exaggerated. In the present example we may be able to infer the intended meaning from the text by careful reading and, if there is any doubt, we can consider other evidence such as what was said in committee or in an explanatory memorandum drafted by the proponents. Because what the text of the rule and what they said about it are *evidence* of their intent, it is appropriate to talk of trying to discover or ascertain intention. Of course, the evidence may be meagre and the inferences that we can draw from it may be weak and we may have to rely to some extent on guesswork, but this is true in other factual enquiries. Sometimes, too, sifting and enquiring about the evidence may be more trouble than it is worth – which is one of the reasons traditionally given for excluding policy documents and Hansard from formal legal arguments about statutory interpretation.[12] Whether we talk of ascertaining or more weakly of imputing or ascribing intentions, this is not a purely subjective matter, as Sceptic suggests. It can involve research, careful exegesis and rigorous argument. "Interpret according to intent" may not resolve all problems, but is a cardinal principle of sound interpretation.'

The arguments of Sceptic and Earthy are only samples of the many differing views to be found in the literature. We cannot pursue the matter further here; nor

11 JC Gray, *The Nature and Sources of the Law* (2nd edn, 1921), pp 170-189; DJ Payne, 'The Intention of the Legislature in the Interpretation of Statutes' (1956) 9 *Current Legal Problems* 96.
12 See now *Pepper v Hart* [1993] AC 593, below, pp 288ff.

do we intend to take sides on these complex issues. Suffice to say that sceptical arguments should be taken as a warning against glib or over-confident use of terms like 'legislative intent', but the common-sense view at least suggests that as a practical matter some of the difficulties have been exaggerated in the literature.[13]

The arguments of Sceptic and Earthy at least raise some relevant considerations bearing on questions about what constitute appropriate methods and resources for ascertaining or ascribing intentions and purposes to rule-makers and to rules. In non-legal contexts there is no agreed or proper method but, as Earthy suggested, insofar as evidence of intention is available, the problem of drawing inferences from that evidence is not in principle different from the problem of trying to ascertain or ascribe intention in other factual enquiries. In the context of statutory interpretation, however, some special policy considerations have given rise to controversy about the range of material that should be allowed to be explicitly referred to in legal arguments in court when there is doubt about the intention (or purposes or other reasons) behind a particular legislative provision. This issue, which was debated in *Davis v Johnson*, will be considered in Chapter 8. We turn now to the uses and limits of purposes, and other reasons for rules, as aids to interpretation.

3 The role of purposes and other reasons in interpretation

We have already seen that a simple view of rules as means to ends is at once dangerous and necessary.[14] From the standpoint of a rule-maker the concept of purpose is indispensable: it is pointless to make purposeless rules. We have also seen that people are often called on to interpret rules that appear to them to have no discernible purpose or to have outlived their original purpose or to be purposeless for some other reason; and that there is an approach that favours treating rules as things in themselves, without regard to, perhaps even in spite of, their purposes, however clear and attractive these may be. Thus, notions such as purpose and goal are not an absolutely essential precondition for interpreting a given rule. Yet it is also a widely held view, which we share, that careful examination of the purpose(s) of a rule is a vital aid to resolving doubts in interpretation.

At this point it is useful to look more closely at relations between rules and purposes (and other reasons for rules) in order to identify some further aspects of the conditions that give rise to doubts in interpretation.

The classic statement of the Mischief Rule in *Heydon's Case* is echoed in the Latin maxim, '*cessante ratione, cessat ipsa lex*'.[15] The literal translation of this maxim suggests a potential ambiguity: 'The reason of the law ceasing, the law itself ceases'. Normally this is interpreted to refer to the *scope* of a law – the gist of the maxim being that as far as possible common law rules should be

---

13 Appendix IV, p 439.
14 Chapter 3, secton 10.
15 See above, p 153. See also *Miliangos v George Frank* [1976] AC 443.

interpreted to be co-extensive with their purposes or policies; it could be taken to mean that the scope of a rule extends up to the limits of its reason, but no further. But the maxim is sometimes invoked to justify ignoring or refusing to follow a rule on the ground that the original reason for it no longer exists. Sometimes the claim is that the rule no longer exists: in this latter view the maxim means *when* the reason ceases, the law ceases. This is a proposition that has clearly not been generally accepted by English law.[16]

Even when the maxim is interpreted as referring to the *scope* of a law rather than to its continued existence, it is best taken as an example of a general maxim that is subject to an indefinite number of exceptions. It is relevant here to spell out some of the reasons for treating with caution such a simple rationalistic view of law and of rules in general. Firstly, it is important not to confuse the notion of a rule with the notion of the reason(s) for a rule, for there are many clear examples where they are not co-extensive. When a relatively precise rule is introduced to deal with a clearly defined mischief, there are at least five possible relations between them:

(a) the rule may be co-extensive with the mischief:

    . . . .   mischief
    ————————   rule

(b) the rule may be wider than the mischief:

    . . . . . .   mischief
    ————————   rule

(c) the rule may be narrower than the mischief:

    . . . .   mischief
    ————   rule

or

    . . . .   mischief
    ————   rule

(d) the rule and the mischief may overlap, but cover different areas:

    . . . . . .   mischief
    ————   rule

(e) the rule and the mischief may not even overlap at all:

    . . . . .   mischief
    ————   rule

This can be simply seen from the *Case of the Legalistic Child.* Assuming that any consumption of food or drink by Johnny between meals would indeed be a mischief, the following examples illustrate the first four relationships.

(a) Johnny may not consume any food or drink between meals.
(b) Only if he has Mother's express permission may Johnny consume food or drink, or enter the larder.
(c) Johnny may not eat food from the larder between meals.
(d) Johnny may not enter the larder without Mother's permission.

---

16 On desuetude see CK Allen, *Law in the Making* (7th edn, 1964), pp 478-482; AL Diamond, 'Repeal and Desuetude of Statutes' (1975) 28 *Current Legal Problems* 107; G Calabresi, *A Common Law for the Age of Statutes* (1982).

The rather less likely example (e) is illustrated by the example of the child psychiatrist who diagnosed the mischief as being a craving for affection; from this point of view the larder rule is at best irrelevant and has virtually nothing to do with the mischief.

Only in (a) is the rule co-extensive with the mischief, but even there the rule should not be confused with its purpose – for instance, if the household has a written set of rules, formally promulgated, the rule may officially survive long after the reason for it has disappeared. As a child grows older some rules will fit less and less well unless they are adjusted or abrogated. In some contexts rules often outlive their original purposes, but sometimes they acquire new rationales.

Many doubts and dissatisfactions on the part of interpreters relate to situations where the rule and the mischief are not co-extensive. If the interpreter favours the policy behind the rule, she may be distressed because there is a 'loophole' or 'gap' by means of which the policy has been frustrated. Or the situation may be that the rule blocks harmless or socially desirable behaviour that does not offend against the policy, for instance Johnny entering the larder not to help himself to food, but to save his father's dinner. In so far as the interpreter is concerned to further the policy, she may wish to interpret the rule so that its scope is as close as possible to the scope of the mischief. But how far it will be possible for her to do this will depend on a number of factors, some of which may be quite outside her control. Thus it cannot be taken for granted that a rule can always be interpreted so as to be co-extensive with its purpose.[17]

Secondly, the *cessante* maxim, literally interpreted, assumes that every law has a single clear reason. But a rule may have no reasons, or may have outlived its original reasons, it may have been the result of a compromise, or it may have several reasons which could conflict with each other in certain contexts. There is anyway an element of artificiality in treating single rules in isolation. Moreover, reasons for rule-making are not all of one type and the relationship between them can be quite complex.[18]

Thirdly, the maxim encourages, though it does not compel, a dangerous assumption that the purpose(s) of a rule, once identified, will be precise enough to determine its scope. But purposes and reasons are at least as subject to indeterminacy as rules. Indeed, 'the policy of a statute' often shares many of the characteristics of rules not in fixed verbal form, and there is a widely held view among legislative draftsmen that precise statements of purpose may create more problems than they resolve.[19] It is often the case that a rule is more precise than its purpose – for instance, the overall purpose of a taxing statute may be to raise revenue, but the instruments for achieving this often are extremely complex, technical and precise. Reasons and purposes may be helpful in giving a general sense of direction, but they are often not very helpful in drawing precise boundaries and determining borderline cases.

Finally, the *cessante* maxim assumes that the role of the interpreter is to further the reasons for the rule. But, as we have seen, it cannot always be

---

17 On over-inclusive and under-inclusive rules, see Schauer (1991), op cit, passim, esp 31-44.
18 Chapter 3, section 2.
19 See below, pp 251-252.

taken for granted that the relationship between rule-maker and interpreter is simply one of partners in a shared enterprise. A consensus about values cannot be taken for granted; the situation may have changed since the creation of the rule, and the role and objectives of the interpreter may differ to a greater or lesser extent from that of the rule-maker.

The *cessante* maxim, literally interpreted, illustrates a simple model of rules as instruments of policies, purposes or other reasons. This model assumes that every law (and, in the present context, every rule) has a single, precise, ascertainable and acceptable reason which is co-extensive with its rule and which can determine its scope. None of these is a necessary attribute of reasons for rules; indeed, the interpreter for whom all five conditions are satisfied is fortunate. Thus indeterminacy of aim is only one aspect of why reasons for rules may give rise to conditions of doubt or may be of limited utility in resolving such doubts.

So far the analysis of the *cessante* maxim has been largely negative. It is important to restore the balance, for emphasis on some of the limitations of naive instrumentalism might give the impression that there is no merit in viewing rules as instruments of policies, as means to ends or as remedies for mischiefs. Two points may serve as correctives at this stage.

Firstly, our analysis of the various possible relations between a mischief and a rule designed to remedy it postulated a relatively precise rule designed to deal with a clearly defined mischief. But, in so far as the rule is incomplete or its scope is unclear in some other way, the distinction between a rule and the reason(s) for it begins to break down. Yet, generally speaking, the incomplete rule provides the standard case of doubt in interpretation.

It is picturesque to depict the relationship between a rule and the reason(s) for it in such terms as these: 'reason seeps in to fill the gaps'; 'reason is a compass which points the general direction of the rule'; 'rule and reason are fused at the point of indeterminacy'; 'the reason is part of the rule'. Such metaphors if not overused can be illuminating, but we should not let them tempt us into confusing rules with their reasons. We have seen that in some contexts rules and reasons can be differentiated and are not necessarily co-extensive. There are examples, for instance in the Uniform Commercial Code, where the reasons are expressly stated in the legislative text and could be said to be *part of the rule*.[20] There are examples of vague and otherwise incomplete rules. But in the context of interpretation the distinction is important because, in the process of determining the scope of a rule, the reason(s) for the rule may be only one of a number of aids to interpretation, although often one of the most important. To talk of the reason for a rule as being *part* of the rule obscures this.

A second corrective to the sceptical view of the *cessante* maxim is that, because purposes or other reasons are often vague or indeterminate, it does not follow that they are unhelpful or useless. As aids to interpretation they may not on their own resolve all of an interpreter's problems (for example in drawing a precise line on a continuously varying continuum),[21] but where

---

20 See, for example, Uniform Commercial Code, s 4-107 (1) and, more generally, s 1-102. Preambles are a regular feature of European Union legislation; see below, p 223.
21 See below, section 5.1.

elucidation of purpose can provide a general sense of direction it provides a broad context or framework within which detailed consideration of other kinds of factor may be fitted. Purposes and reasons can still be an interpreter's best aid.

Thus the exploration and attribution of purposes and of other reasons to rules, is, in our view, a vital ingredient in a rational approach to interpretation. Even the unhappy interpreter, confronted with what seems to him to be an obstacle, may benefit from a clear understanding of how and why that obstacle came into existence. To abandon purposes and reasons as aids is to give up the best hope of achieving an acceptable degree of rationality in approaching problems of interpretation. Such defeatism leads to the Way of the Baffled Medic – prescription without diagnosis, concentration on cures without any understanding of diseases.[22]

4   Rules and language

Suppose that a park in your home town has a sign at its entrance gate that reads 'No vehicles allowed in the park',[23] it would be obvious in the context that motorcars, buses and motorcycles are clear examples of prohibited 'vehicles'. Similarly, if someone suggested that handbags or trouser pockets or shopping baskets were excluded, you could confidently dismiss the idea as absurd. But would you be so sure about an ice-cream van, an invalid carriage, a child's tricycle, a donkey-cart, a skateboard or a pair of rollerblades? It is said that the word 'vehicle', like all general classifying words, has both a core of settled meaning and a surrounding area in which its meaning is not clear, sometimes called 'a penumbra of uncertainty'. Typically, those cases that fall within the penumbra share some attributes with the standard instances but will lack some others, and may be accompanied by further attributes not to be found in the core cases. Thus a child's tricycle shares attributes with a standard instance of a 'vehicle', the motorcycle, but obviously lacks others, and this discrepancy or divergence from the standard instance creates doubt as to whether the tricycle should be designated 'a vehicle'. Vague words like 'vehicle' provide a standard example of what Hart refers to as an irreducible feature of language – its open texture.[24]

Even talking in terms of a single core of meaning may be too simple; as Ludwig Wittgenstein shows with the word 'game',[25] its ordinary usage cannot be adequately elucidated either in terms of a core and a penumbra or in terms of a set of necessary conditions for its use, or even in terms of a jointly sufficient set of conditions. Rather 'game' seems to cover a range of interconnected activities which are related to one another in that they all share some

---

22 See W Twining, 'The Way of the Baffled Medic', (1992) 12 *Legal Studies* 348, 353-354; *Rethinking Evidence* (1994), chapter 10.
23 This is a standard example used in juristic discussions of open texture; eg Hart, op cit, pp 128ff; G Gottlieb, *The Logic of Choice* (1968) chapter 8; and chapter 1, section 4.3.
24 And what is a 'road': *Cutter v Eagle Star Insurance Co Ltd* [1998] 4 All ER 417; see below, p 285.
25 See Appendix 1, section D, question 2, p 398.

characteristics with some other activities, some of which are typically thought of as games and some not, but they do not all share all of the same characteristics. Thus patience is like bridge because it involves equipment and is governed by rules; but it is unlike it because there are no teams; bridge is like football because there are teams and a system of scoring, but unlike it because no special clothing is worn; football is like war because there is typically special clothing, sides, equipment, physical exertion and rules governing its conduct, but war is not usually thought of as a game, except ironically or metaphorically.

The complexities on the borderline of a concept are further illustrated by the following analysis of a paradigm case of torture and some variations upon it:[26]

Paradigm	*Some Variations*
1. The intentional	1. Reckless, careless, accidental etc.
2. application	2. threats, hints, pretences
3. of 'acute' (ie, (a) intense and (b) of short duration)	3. 'temporal': gradations of duration and intensity
4. corporal (ie directly affect in active or passive capacities including deprivation of sleep, stress, anxiety, mental anguish)	4. privative (eg sensory or social isolation; deprivation of liberty or privileges etc)
5. pain	5. 'painless', or even pleasurable, conditioning or treatment; hallucination; trickery, manipulation of unconscious or unaware victim; education?
6. by officials	6. by others (eg freedom fighters, kidnappers, school bullies, individuals)
7. acting under express authority	7. acting without authority; (gradations of tolerance or condonation by superiors)
8. on a captive	8. unconfined
9. and non-consenting	9. consenting – eg human experimentation, military training, electric shock treatment, aversion therapy, masochist. Degrees of voluntariness
10. person	10. other sentient beings (eg dogs, lobsters, trees?)
11. against his/her interest	11. for the good of the victim (eg to save his/her soul; to cure or educate)
12. for the purpose	12. for no clear or rational purpose; gradations of clarity of purpose; unconscious motives

26 From WL Twining, 'Torture and Philosophy', *Proceedings of the Aristotelian Society*, vol LII (1978), at pp 151-152 (reprinted by courtesy of the Editor of the Aristotelian Society, © 1978 The Aristotelian Society).

Paradigm	*Some Variations*
13. of coercing	13. some other purpose (eg disabling, breaking the will, terrorising)
14. that person	14. other person(s)
15. to do an act (typically to give truthful information or to make a true confession)	15. to desist or refrain from other types of act (eg political activity; statement irrespective of its truth)
16. which it is (probably) in his/her power to do	16. which is not in his/her power to do
17. immediately	17. at some future time (eg to broadcast for the enemy); revenge or punishment for past acts
18. in the public interest (ie preponderant utility)	18. for some sectional interest; counter-productively

How many of the elements in the paradigm case are necessary conditions for the usage of the word 'torture'? What combinations of them would be *jointly sufficient* for its use?

The use of the word 'torture' in the European Convention on Human Rights is interesting in a number of respects. At first sight it is superfluous, for are not all examples of torture also examples of 'inhuman treatment'?[27] It has been suggested that 'torture' is an aggravated form of inhuman treatment and to find that a particular activity is torture is considered to involve a more serious violation of Article 3, although the main sanctions are the strength of condemnation and the adverse publicity. However, it is probably the case that some of the most objectionable features of particular instances of torture – for example sexual humiliation, long-term psychological damage or the purely sadistic infliction of pain – are themselves aggravating features rather than necessary conditions for the use of the word 'torture'. Similarly, we might say that some of the worst incidents of bigamy (eg cruel deception) are not defining conditions of 'bigamy'.[28]

Words like 'game' and 'torture' illustrate the point that what is involved in clarifying the scope and meaning of a term – in interpreting rules as in other contexts – can be a rather more complex matter than merely seeking for, or stipulating, a *definition*; rather, modern conceptual analysis stresses the value of *elucidating* words in the context of their ordinary usage, by such techniques as considering standard or paradigm cases and deviations from them and by considering words and phrases in the context of standard sentences in which they occur.[29]

It is not news to lawyers that language is an imperfect instrument which is often imperfectly used. Advances in analytical philosophy, semantics and linguistics have greatly increased general understanding of the nature and uses of language and its inherent limitations as a precise and efficient instrument of communication. Clearly, one of the most important conditions

27 *Ireland v United Kingdom* (1978) 2 EHRR 25.
28 Chapter 1, section 7.2, question 4, and Appendix 1, section A5, questions 3 and 4, pp 393-394.
29 HLA Hart, 'Definition and Theory in Jurisprudence' (1953) 70 *Law Quarterly Review* 37.

of doubt in interpretation arises either from the faulty use of language in formulating rules, such as inappropriate vagueness or inadvertent ambiguity, or from the inescapable indeterminacy of language, especially of general classifying terms like 'vehicle', which are commonly used in formulations of rules. 'No definition of an empirical term will cover all possibilities', wrote Waismann;[30] nor will any formulation of a rule.

It is also a truism that a good command of language is one of the most important of lawyer-like qualities. Language is the main medium of legal discourse; words and concepts are basic tools in the performance of such common tasks as drafting, interpreting, analysing, arguing and communicating; similarly, the acquisition of linguistic skills and awareness is central to the development of skill in interpreting rules. At the risk of belabouring the obvious, it is worth spelling out what is involved in a good command of language, why it is important for interpreters of rules, and how to set about achieving it.

Language is important as it is the main, but not the only, medium for communication of rules. The choice of apposite words is crucial for the draftsman of rules in fixed verbal form, while from the interpreter's point of view problems of language are often the most important single condition of doubt. But rules not in fixed verbal form are also often expressed in words, although they may be communicated in other ways, commonly by examples.[31] The process of arriving at a formulation of such a rule is closely analogous to drafting a rule in fixed verbal form, but with two important differences. Whereas opportunity for the formulation of rules in fixed verbal form is virtually monopolised by one type of actor, the draftsman, this is not so for the other kind of rule. Here other actors may participate, as for example in an English appellate case concerned with a non-statutory rule, where it is possible for counsel for each side to suggest competing formulations of the rule, and for each of the judges to formulate perhaps more than once, a statement of the rule. Each relevant participant has the opportunity to perform a role similar to that of a draftsman; but, and this is the other point of difference between the two types of rule, while one of the formulations may subsequently become authoritative, no participant's formulation of a rule not in fixed verbal form has the status of a frozen, binding text.

From the point of view of the addressee of a formulation of a rule, its language and syntax are of critical importance. Linguistic skills such as ability to spot ambiguities, to recognise vagueness, to identify the emotive pull of a word and to make appropriate allowances for it, and to analyse and elucidate class words and abstractions, are basic to the task of interpretation. Moreover, as different addressees may offer competing interpretations in certain situations, so linguistic skills become important in the process of justifying a particular interpretation. The relationship between interpretation and reasoning will be discussed later, but it is worth noting here that other linguistic

---

30 F Waismann, 'Verifiability' in A Flew (ed), *Logic and Language* (First series, 1951), pp 117, 123; see further F Waismann, *The Principles of Linguistic Philosophy* (1965), pp 221-225.
31 Hart, op cit, pp 124-127; on case-by-case decisions, see Chapter 4, section 1.2.

skills, such as the abilities to spot (and avoid) the proper meaning fallacy and other false assumptions about language,[32] and to identify various types of ambiguity, are crucial to the development of skill in both interpretation and reasoning.

One aspect of language, namely the special part played by class words and other abstractions in communicating formulations of rules, deserves special mention. Hart puts the matter as follows:

> If it were not possible to communicate general standards of conduct, which multitudes of individuals could understand, without further direction, as requiring from them certain conduct when occasion arose, nothing that we now recognise as law could exist. Hence the law must predominantly, but by no means exclusively, refer to *classes* of person, and to *classes* of acts, things and circumstances; and its successful operation over vast areas of social life depends on a widely diffused capacity to recognise particular acts, things and circumstances as instances of the general classifications which the law makes.[33]

Thus practising lawyers and others who regularly handle general rules need to be skilled in handling class words and other abstract concepts.

Some of the more puzzling questions of legal theory also involve the elucidation of highly abstract concepts such as 'law', 'right', 'duty', 'justice', 'causation', 'fact', 'rule', 'decision' and so on. This kind of analysis is notoriously demanding. In Britain the dominance of analytical jurisprudence within legal theory, and the relatively significant emphasis placed on analytical jurisprudence within legal education, have had as one of their main grounds of justification that the development of this kind of analytical skill is important for legal practice as well as for legal theorising.[34] It is not relevant here to debate the respective claims of this and other approaches to the study of jurisprudence; but one of the consequences of the dominance of analytical jurisprudence in Britain, and its close associations with analytical philosophy, has been that there is a rich and sophisticated literature readily accessible to those who wish to take advantage of it. The path to mastery of the relevant linguistic skills is not by any means an easy one; but rather than try to duplicate existing introductory works on semantics and clear thinking, we propose merely to give some elementary suggestions about where to begin.

It is worth emphasising that an important precondition to the kind of command of language required for interpretation is an understanding of the medium. Some people may have a natural facility for handling language in certain kinds of way, but there are too many false assumptions and misconceptions about language in general currency for it to be safe to rely on native wit alone.

The literature on the nature of language is vast, controversial and often confusing. Fortunately, some of the most important points can be made quite simply. In a valuable corrective to misguided attempts prematurely to immerse students in the theoretical literature, Hart wrote as follows:

---

32 See below, p 199.
33 Op cit, p 124.
34 See, for example, HLA Hart in (1957) 105 *U Pennsylvania Law Review* 953.

It is indeed important in jurisprudence to notice certain cardinal features of language, neglect of which has often led to sterile and misleading controversy. Yet it is of the first importance, if these things are to be communicated to lawyers, that they should not be encumbered by any obscure or questionable philosophical theory. This can be done with the use of simple examples, perhaps in the following way.

First: Words are vague; they have only a core of settled meaning, but beyond that a penumbra of borderline cases which is not regimented by any conventions, so that although a motor-car is certainly a 'vehicle' for the purpose of a rule excluding vehicles from a park, there is no conclusive answer as far as linguistic conventions go to the question whether a toy motor-car or a sledge or a bicycle is included in this general term.

Secondly: Words are ambiguous, ie have more than one relatively well settled use. A testator leaves his vessels to his son. If the question is whether this includes his flying-boat, it is the *vagueness* of 'vessel' which is the source of the trouble; but if the question is whether the bequest refers to the testator's boats or his drinking-cups, *ambiguity* is responsible.

Thirdly: We are tempted, when we are faced with words, to look round for just one thing or quality for which the word is supposed to stand. It is often wise to resist this temptation. Perhaps the words stand not merely for one kind of thing but for a range of diverse, though related things. We should not assume whenever we use the expression 'possession' that this must on all occasions refer to the same state of affairs, and the same is true of words like 'crime' and 'law' itself. Moreover, words like 'right' and 'duty' do not directly stand for any states of affairs.

Fourthly: For any account descriptive of any thing or event or state of affairs, it is always possible to substitute either a more specific or a more general description. What we refer to as a Rolls Royce may also be referred to as a vehicle, a motor-car, someone's property, etc. So, too, in answer to the question, 'What did he do?', we may say 'He killed her', or 'He struck her', or 'He moved his arm', or 'He contracted the muscle of his arm'. All of these may be true, but only one of them may be appropriate. What controls the selection of the appropriate description depends on the context and purpose of the inquiry. If we are physiologists we may describe what happened in terms of muscular movements; if we are conducting a criminal investigation when killing is a crime we shall choose the language made appropriate by the legal rule and say he killed her. Plainly the constant possibility of more or less specific description is important to bear in mind when considering the notion of the 'material' facts of the case or in any account of the components of a criminal act.

Fifthly: Obsession with the notion that words must always stand for the same 'qualities' or the same set of qualities whenever they are used has stimulated two contrapuntal tendencies. The first is to insist that words like 'possession' or 'law' *must*, in spite of appearance, stand always for the same common qualities and the diversity is only apparent: this leads to the imposition on the diversity of the facts of a spurious 'constructive' or fictitious unity. The second tendency is to insist that only some one of the range of cases in which a word is used is the proper or 'real' meaning of the word: so that international law is not 'really' law. As against both these tendencies, it is a good thing to repeat that words do not have one true or proper meaning.[35]

A sixth matter, which particularly concerns rules in fixed verbal form, is the fact that communication of the effect of the rule may be obscured by poor

---

35 HLA Hart, 'Dias and Hughes on Jurisprudence', (year?) 4 *Journal of Society of Public Teachers of Law* (NS 1953) 144-145.

grammatical construction. An example of this is syntactic ambiguity; that is to say, within the framework of the sentence, a particular word or expression is capable of affecting two, or possibly more, other parts of the sentence, and this raises inconsistent or incompatible interpretations as to the effect of the rule as a whole.

Syntactic ambiguity is not restricted to the world of rule-communication. There is a generally accepted meaning of the phrase 'standard brown eggs', but there is an ambiguity here which permits two alternative interpretations, that it means eggs of any shape or size, but of a standard brown colour, or eggs of a standard shape and size, which are also brown in colour. This particular example has been resolved for most purposes in favour of the second interpretation. Where such ambiguity is present, resort is generally had to the context in which the phrase is used; this was the approach the court took which had to decide whether the word 'grave' in the phrase 'grave financial or other hardship' modified not only 'financial' but also 'other hardship'.[36] This type of problem is not uncommon in law, but unlike the use of vague terms (which can be deliberate and sensible), syntactic ambiguity is almost always a defect that can and should be avoided at the formulatory/drafting stage.

Apart from these elementary points, there are of course many other aspects of language that bear upon interpretation. Even at this elementary level, an interpreter requires an understanding of such subjects as definition and other techniques of elucidation, emotive meaning, language functions and common fallacies about language. We were tempted to devote a whole chapter to an elementary exposition of these topics, but given the ready accessibility of a number of excellent introductory works we have decided not to try to cover the same ground and have confined ourselves to making a number of suggestions for further reading.[37]

5 The open texture of rules

To conclude, we propose to deal briefly with two further topics: continuous variation and implied exceptions.

5.1 Continuous variation

There is a story of an engineer who was engaged in designing an instrument that could measure length within a margin of error of one-millionth of a centimetre. Shortly after he had solved his problem he stopped to talk to some workmen who were drilling a hole in a pavement to find a gas main; he told

---

36 *Rukat v Rukat* [1975] 1 All ER 343. See W Wilson, 'Questions of Interpretation (1987) *Statute Law Review* 142, 144-147.
37 See p 438 below. Language is not the only factor that can give rise to conditions of doubt; see chapter 6 below and D Miers, review of J Evans, *Statutory Interpretation* (1990) *Cambridge Law Journal* 350.

them of his achievement. 'You theoreticians can afford your margins of error,' was the response, 'but in our work we have to be *absolutely* accurate.'

Precision and vagueness are relative matters. They are characteristics of rules as well as of formulations of rules. One of the most difficult problems facing both rule-makers and interpreters is where exactly to draw the line at some point along a continuum. Wherever the line is drawn there is a possibility of almost identical cases falling on different sides of it. The problem is a familiar feature of everyday decision-making: fixing a closing date for applications; deciding borderline cases in an examination or a competition; setting a selling price; deciding where to stop bidding in an auction, and so on. It is, of course, a familiar one to lawyers. It is one kind of question of degree and it is a truism that some of the most difficult questions are questions of degree.

There is a natural tendency to treat the problem of continuous variation as one that necessarily involves *arbitrary* choices. Holmes J, in a famous dissent, put the matter this way:

> When a legal distinction is determined, as no one doubts that it may be, between night and day, childhood and maturity, or any other extremes, a point has to be fixed or a line has to be drawn, or gradually picked out by successive decisions, to mark where the change takes place. Looked at by itself without regard to the necessity behind it, the line or point seems arbitrary. It might as well or might nearly as well be a little more to the one side or the other. But when it is seen that a line or point there must be, and that there is no mathematical or logical way of fixing it precisely, the decision of the legislature must be accepted unless we can say that it is very wide of any reasonable mark.[38]

The context of this and other similar statements by Holmes J was that of American constitutional litigation in which the Supreme Court was called upon to decide upon the constitutionality of sharp lines drawn by the legislature. Holmes J, in pursuance of a policy of judicial restraint in constitutional cases, argued that such statutory provisions should be allowed to stand, provided that the line was drawn within an area where reasonable men might disagree; from this standpoint there is a penumbra of certainty (clearly unreasonable points) and a core of doubt, thus:

clearly		clearly
unreasonable	reasonable	unreasonable

The fact of drawing the line is not arbitrary, argued Holmes, because a line has to be drawn; but, this passage implies, the exact choice of a point where the line is drawn may be arbitrary. This is not very helpful to the person who has to draw the line (the rulemaker, in a broad sense). For him the difficulty is not *whether*, but *where*, a line should be drawn. The root of the difficulty is to settle on a point at which a reasoned answer can be given to the question:

---

38 *Louisville Gas Co v Coleman* 277 US 32, 41 (1928) Holmes J (dissenting). For two further related dissents by Holmes J, see *Schlesinger v Wisconsin* 270 US 230 (1925) and *Weaver v Palmer Bros Co* 270 US 402 (1926); extracts from these cases are reprinted and discussed in M Lerner, *The Mind and Faith of Justice Holmes* (1943), pp 249-251, 257-261. See also pp 205-206.

'Why here?' It may be that the best answer in given circumstances is 'A line has to be drawn somewhere and no reason can be advanced for suggesting why any other point is to be preferred.' But detailed examination of the particular problem may suggest reasons, which may be good without being compelling, for preferring one or two points to all others, or, at least, for narrowing the field of choice. Common examples of such reasons would include: 'for the sake of simplicity', 'it's a round number', 'it splits the difference', 'to go beyond this point would open the floodgates',[39] 'it is better to err on the side of leniency than of toughness' (or vice versa), 'there are likely to be fewer borderline cases at point X than at point Y', 'it is better to have a few who feel lucky to be included, than a few who feel unlucky to be excluded'.

In Appendix I there is an exercise concerning a situation in which a committee has to settle on criteria for eligibility for joining a club for bearded men. The notion of a beard had been selected not so much for its entertainment value as for the more serious reason that in this case more than one continuum is involved: days of growth, number of hairs, length of hairs and so on.[40] If tackled properly the problem should provide examples of the following general points.

(a) Many different kinds of *reason* can be advanced for preferring one point to others in a situation in which a point has to be selected somewhere along a continuously varying line; in so far as good reasons can be advanced for preferring one point to another, the choice is not *arbitrary*, even though the reasons are not compelling.
(b) Many of the reasons depend on *relevant information* being available about the situation, for example the purposes of the club, the likely number of applications, constraints on accommodation, and other inhibitions on unlimited membership.

---

39 See, for example, the famous dictum of Alderson B in *Winterbottom v Wright* (p 57 above); 'The only safe rule is to confine the right to recover to those who enter into the contract; if we go one step beyond that, there is no reason why we should not go fifty'. This was quoted with approval by Lord Buckmaster in *Donoghue v Stevenson*, but the subsequent history of the tort of negligence suggests that the difficulty of settling the limits of liability is not necessarily a sufficient reason for not taking the first step and that reasons can be advanced for imposing some limits. When Lord Nottingham asked: 'Where will you stop if you do not stop here?' he received a robust reply: 'Where any visible inconvenience doth appear'. The 'floodgates' argument invoked by Baron Alderson and Lord Nottingham tends to be conservative and is often overstated, but it is not necessarily a bad argument in all contexts. See the House of Lords decision in *White v Chief Constable of the South Yorkshire Police* [1999] 1 All ER 1 concerning the extent of liability in negligence for psychiatric injury, in particular Lord Steyn ('Thus far and no further') at 38-39, and Lord Hoffmann at 48. In a different context, see the rejection of the argument that diplomatic relations between the United Kingdom and Chile would be harmed if the House of Lords were to rule that its former head of state, General Pinochet, was not immune to extradition to Spain; *R v Bow Street Metropolitan Stipendiary Magistrate, ex p Pincohet Ugarte* [1998] 4 All ER 897; decision set aside, *R v Bow Street Metropolitan Stipendiary Magistrate, ex p Pinochet Ugate (No 3)* [1999] NLJR 497. On other kinds of consequentialist argument, see below, pp 358ff.
40 Appendix 1, section E, question 5. Compare: when is a tea break 'too long' (*R v Industrial Injuries Commission, ex p AEU* [1966] 2 QB 31); and, how many prostitutes constitute a brothel (*Donovan v Gavin* [1965] 2 QB 648)?

(c) Depending on the context, the rule-maker may be well advised to consider re-posing the issue in such a way that a problem of continuous variation is not involved; multiple criteria may be more satisfactory than a single criterion; it may be unnecessary or unwise to lay down any precise criteria in advance of considering particular cases. In general, there is a range of alternative strategies for tackling this kind of problem; reasonably satisfactory solutions to such problems are not necessarily impossible or arbitrary.

5.2 Implied exceptions

One aspect of the incompleteness of rules is the possibility that an exception to the rule may be implied by the interpreter. While this may not always be the case, the scope for implying exceptions is often much greater than may appear on the surface; in this respect rules are often less complete than they seem. As we have seen in Chapter 3, it is a familiar feature of English criminal law that certain defences and other exceptions to a statutory provision for a criminal offence may be implied on the basis of general principles of liability in criminal law.[41] Thus even legal rules in fixed verbal form may be subject to exceptions based on rules or principles that may not themselves be in fixed verbal form, or that did not exist at the time of the creation of the rule in question.

It is useful here to distinguish two types of situation. To revert to the familiar example used in relation to vagueness, 'No vehicles allowed in the park'. This example is phrased in the form of an absolute prohibition. It has often been used to illustrate the point that many class words have a core of settled meaning and a penumbra of doubtful cases. The point is also commonly made that cases that fall within the penumbra may be decided on the basis of non-linguistic considerations: thus it would be reasonable to interpret the rule so as to allow invalid chairs into the park, not on the basis of the physical characteristics of such chairs as phenomena, nor on whether an invalid chair would be treated as a 'vehicle' in ordinary usage, but because to admit such chairs could reasonably be interpreted as furthering rather than defeating the purposes of the rule (for example, a policy of providing facilities for quiet recreation). Whether or not it would be accurate to say of such a decision that 'an exception has been made in the case of invalid chairs' is not a question of much moment.

The situation might be different, however, if there were a fire in the pavilion in the centre of the park. The park-keeper, a policeman at the scene and, conceivably at a later date, a court, might be called on to decide whether an exception to the rule could be implied in the case of a fire engine or an ambulance entering in the circumstances. The *Buckoke* case shows that such questions arise in practice and that they can cause difficulty.[42]

It would surely be 'stretching' language to say that a fire engine is not a vehicle, but it would not necessarily be considered unreasonable for

---

41 Section 4; see also *R v Gould*, Appendix I, section A5, p 385.
42 Chapter 1, section 8.

authoritative interpreters to imply an *exception* in this kind of case or, alternatively, to waive the rule on this particular occasion without changing it for the future. This example brings together and illustrates three points that have all been made earlier: (a) that a rule can be open-textured independently of the language of its formulation; (b) that a distinction needs to be drawn between 'making an exception' to a rule and 'granting an exemption' under it; (c) that the open texture of rules is not necessarily to be considered a defect; or, to put the matter differently, incompleteness is not the same as imperfection.[43]

43 For exercises on chapter 5, see Appendix I, section D, pp 397-398.

Part Three

Reading law: reading, using and interpreting legislation and cases

Chapter 6

Routine and Problematic Readings

1 Routine readings

In this Part of the book we apply the lessons about rules in general that were explored in Part Two to the task of reading, interpreting and using the two principal sources of law in the United Kingdom. They are the decisions of the superior courts and the legislative rules enacted in the Westminster Parliament and by the European Union. A central theme is that those who seek to use or rely on rules of law derived from these sources are able to do so, as a matter of routine, without difficulty. Much of the activity of using law is unproblematic in the sense that only exceptionally are issues raised concerning its scope or application. This is, for example, true for those employed in the regulated industries such as gas, water, electricity, transport and financial services, in executive agencies, local government or other public sector bodies or in private commerce, whose job it is to advise on the application of the law to their activities. It is also so for the solicitor advising private individuals about the buying and selling of their houses, the making or interpretation of their wills, or the myriad of other transactions or events affecting their lives which have a legal dimension.

In saying that in the vast majority of instances the reader of these sources of law is unlikely to be in doubt about the scope or application of a rule of law, we are not saying that the reading of that rule of law is necessarily easily accomplished. The rule may be appear to be clear in this case, but has to be found within a complex statutory context (possibly also involving secondary legislation) and to be checked against other criteria (such as decisions of the superior courts or secondary rules of interpretation contained in codes of practice, administrative circulars and the like). These readings may be routine readings, but they are best accomplished by the adoption of a procedure which ensures that the reader is alerted to these and other requirements, and, where there may be doubts about its application or scope, assists in the identification of the source or nature of that doubt. Nor are we saying that the interpretation or application of case law or statutory rules can in particular instances be differentiated in the abstract as between 'easy' or 'hard' cases. Whether an interpreter's reading of a rule is routine or problematic depends on who she is and the purposes for which she is reading it.

In the Preface and in the materials on standpoint in chapter 1, section 11,[1] we set out a procedure to be used by readers of cases and statutes (and other

---

1   See above, pp 67ff. See further Appendix III, the *Reading Law Cookbook*.

sources of law) who are coming to those texts for the first time. It involves asking three questions: who am I? At what stage in what process am I? What am I trying to do? Answering these simple but essential questions in turn provides the basis upon which problematic readings can be pursued; that is, readings that assist in the identification of the conditions contributing to a doubt about the rule's scope or application, and in the construction of arguments designed to address those doubts in a particular way. In our view, there is no essential difference between routine and problematic readings: the latter is an extension of the former. Section 2 of this chapter outlines a model for diagnosing common conditions of doubt which can be used to assist the reader of a rule who is puzzled about its scope or application. Chapters 7 and 8 illustrate the application of these procedures to the routine and problematic reading of legislation; Chapter 9 deals with case law rules.

2 · Problematic readings: conditions of doubt

It is useful at this point to draw together some threads by attempting to answer in general terms the question: under what conditions do doubts arise concerning interpretation of rules? The purpose of this section is to outline a diagnostic model in the form of a checklist of common conditions of doubt that arise where an interpreter is confronted with a pre-existing rule in fixed verbal form, and is puzzled about the general scope of the rule or about its application to a particular set of circumstances. We shall explore the uses and limitations of this model in this kind of situation and the extent to which it can be applied in other contexts, especially where the rule to be interpreted is not in fixed verbal form.

To say that a person is in the position of a puzzled interpreter typically presupposes four conditions:

(a) that the interpreter has a clear conception of his or her standpoint, situation and role – in other words, who can give reasonably clear answers to the questions: Who am I? At what stage in what process am I? What am I trying to do?

(b) that the potentially relevant rules have been identified, but not necessarily formulated in words;

(c) that there is a doubt either about the scope of one (or more) rule(s) or its (their) application to a given fact-situation, or both, or else a doubt about what to do, given that the interpreter is dissatisfied, for one reason or another, with the conclusion suggested by the most obvious interpretation or application of the rule(s);

(d) that the interpreter's puzzlement does not relate to his or her standpoint or role or aims, nor to the validity of the rules in question unless a question of validity is raised by reference to one or more other rules.

For purposes of analysis it is convenient to characterise the tasks of clarifying standpoint, role and objective, and of identifying the potentially relevant rules and determining their validity, as preliminaries to interpretation, but some or all of them may in practice be intimately bound up with and difficult to distinguish sharply from the process of interpretation itself.

Assuming that the preliminaries to interpretation are at least provisionally settled, as with an orderly approach to problem-solving the next step is diagnosis, that is the attempt to identify as clearly as possible the nature and source(s) of the difficulty. One way to approach diagnosis is to establish at what point(s) in the process some event occurred that may have contributed to the interpreter's doubt. Let us begin with a standard case involving the following elements: a single consciously made rule in fixed verbal form; a process analogous to those involved in the Bad Man in Boston or the *Case of the Legalistic Child*;[2] and an interpreter who is called upon to perform the role of impartial adjudicator and who is puzzled about the interpretation or application of the rule in a particular case. The question is: what exactly is puzzling about this case?

Given the variety of types of rule, and the multiplicity of contexts in which they are to be found, it is unlikely that a single model can be devised to fit all rule-processes. However, it is possible to present a relatively simple picture of typical processes, which would apply to a wide variety of contexts, non-legal as well as legal. Such a model can be of particular use, first to illustrate some of the more common sources of doubt which arise in interpretation, and secondly as a starting point for diagnosing puzzlements and doubts about interpretation and application in particular cases. In commenting on this model we shall indicate some of its limitations and ways in which it can be adjusted to take account of peculiar or special features in particular contexts.

2.1   Some common conditions of doubt: a diagnostic model

The process can be broken down into four stages as follows:

STAGE I	*STAGE II*	*STAGE III*	*STAGE IV*
Conditions arising before the rule came into existence	Difficulties and errors arising at the rule-making stage	Conditions occurring after the creation of the rule	Special features of the particular case

Stage I   Conditions arising prior to the creation of the rule

1. Erroneous, incomplete or inadequate apprehension of the factual context of the original situation giving rise to the problem.
2. Incomplete or otherwise unacceptable evaluation of the original situation by the rule-maker.
3. Inappropriate or unacceptable categorisation of the original problem.
4. Lack of clear policy objectives, or competing or inconsistent or otherwise inadequate policy objectives.
5. Sheer complexity of the original situation.

2   Chapter 1, sections 11.6 and 3.5 above, respectively.

6. The problem was not suitable for dealing with by means of rules.
7. The existing system of rules, institutions and arrangements made a solution difficult or impossible for this particular problem.

This stage covers events that arise during the process of perceiving and diagnosing problems to the point at which a decision has been taken to use rules as the, or as one, means for resolving the problem. This was discussed at length in Chapter 2, and further examples will be found in later chapters.

Stage II   The rule-making stage: incomplete, indeterminate or imperfect rules

8. Doubts about intention; for example:[3]
   (a) Rule made inadvertently, or doubtful whether it was intended to make a rule (unintended rule A).
   (b) Doubtful whether it was intended to make *this* rule (unintended rule B).
   (c) Doubtful whether it was intended to use these words (unintended words).
   (d) Doubt as to what meaning, if any, was intended in respect of these words (meaning).
   (e) Doubt whether the rule was intended to cover this situation (scope).
   (f) Doubt as to intended effect of this rule on other rules (effects).
   (g) Doubt whether these (social, economic, other factual) consequences were intended (purposes).
   (h) Doubt as to which were the reasons, if any, for making the rule (reasons for rule).
9. Imperfect or doubtful relationship of the rule(s) to other rules within the same 'system', for example:
   (a) Uncertain whether this rule repeals, makes an exception to, or has other effects on prior rules.
   (b) Uncertain whether this rule is *ultra vires* or unconstitutional or otherwise invalid because of prior rules.
   (c) Uncertain whether some general principle (eg *mens rea*) applies to this rule.
   (d) Uncertain whether this rule was *new* or whether it is to be interpreted in the light of its predecessors and of interpretations of them.
   (e) Uncertain whether past interpretations of other related or analogous rules are applicable to this one.
   (f) Potentially related rules difficult to locate or identify.
10. Imperfect or doubtful relationship of this rule (or body of rules) to rules of some other 'system'.

---

3   See above, Chapter 5, section 2. Note that there is some overlap between doubts relating to intention and some of the other conditions listed.

11. The instrument or other means adopted for implementing or furthering the objectives not co-extensive with those objectives (narrower, broader, overlapping, unconnected).[4]

12. Policy objectives not likely to be furthered in fact by this policy or by this rule as an instrument of the policy.

13. Poor drafting, for example:
   (a) Poor organisation.
   (b) Style of drafting inappropriate to the instrument.
   (c) Inappropriate choice of words (eg ambiguity; inappropriate vagueness; superfluous words used; undue prolixity; same word used in different sense elsewhere; word used in different sense from ordinary or technical usage).
   (d) Obscure because of complexity.
   (e) Rule is silent about, or does not provide for, certain contingencies ('gaps').
   (f) Intentional obscurity.
   (g) Scope for implying exceptions unclear.
   (h) Internal inconsistency or other logical flaws; seemingly contradictory provisions (eg Catch 22).
   (i) Other faults in drafting (eg error of law by draftsman; inappropriate rigidity; potentially related rules overlooked by draftsman).

14. Deliberate delegation of discretion by use of broad or vague terms or by other means.

15. The draftsman was presented with an insoluble or almost insoluble drafting problem ('undraftability').

16. Difficulties occasioned during post-drafting stage (eg last-minute amendments, inadequate or misleading or otherwise defective promulgation or communication of contents of the rule to those affected).

Stage II, the rule-making stage, deals both with the process of rulemaking and with the product, the rule itself. Some rules are defective because of avoidable error on the part of the draftsman: for example, an unintentional ambiguity or loophole; an unnecessarily labyrinthine statute; a formulation of a rule unnecessarily broader or narrower than its purposes. On the other hand, some rules give rise to choices of interpretation because they are incomplete or imperfect, not because of incompetence on the draftsman's part but for some other reason; for example, there may have been a deliberate delegation of discretion to official interpreters by the rule-maker; or it may have been impracticable for the draftsman to construct a rule co-extensive with its policy; doubts may have arisen because of the limitations of language as a medium of communication or just because there are a great many other rules in the system, or because of a lack of clear or consistent policies behind the rule(s).

Other factors that may result in conditions of doubt arising at this stage are connected with the legislative or rule-making process as such. A small number of draftsmen working to an overcrowded schedule is a condition of the British

4   See above, p 191.

legislative process that does not help good law-making. Political factors in this process may also operate as an obstacle to sound law-making, as for example where a statute or other instrument is drafted obscurely in order that its full import may not be apparent to those who might oppose it, if they understood it. Similar, but not identical, factors operate in administrative rulemaking and in the ways that rules are created or established in complex organisations such as universities, large commercial organisations or trade unions.

Stage III Events after the creation of the rule

17. Change in factual context since creation of the rule (eg social, economic or technological change).
18. Change in mores or prevailing values since creation of the rule, resulting in conflict between the rule and newer values.
19. Change in some values resulting in conflict of values relating to the rule.
20. Change in meanings of words since creation of the rule.
21. Past enforcement pattern of this rule (eg this rule normally not enforced in this type of case).
22. Uncertainty as to weight to be given to the conventions, policies and practices adopted by those charged with implementing the rule.
23. This rule has been seen to have bad or absurd consequences or effects.
24. Past authoritative interpretations of this rule in conflict or unsatisfactory; for example because they failed to deal appropriately with other authoritative interpretations (precedents).
25. Subsequent creation of other rules affecting this rule.

This stage covers those events that occur after the original creation of the rule and that give rise to conditions of doubt about its interpretation at a general level, as contrasted with any special features of the particular case. In considering the relationship between rule-makers and interpreters, we suggested that a simple model of interpretation as a part of a process of communication and co-operation failed to take into account not only the point that an interpreter may have different values or objectives from the rule-maker, but also that his overall situation may be different by virtue of events that have taken place since the creation of the rule. Such events can be of various kinds: the original social situation giving rise to the mischief may have changed in one or more respects; advances in technology may have caught the rule-maker unawares; public opinion (or the values of a group concerned with the rule) may have shifted; some defects in the rule may have become apparent; new rules may have been made which are difficult to reconcile with the rule to be interpreted; decisions may have been taken which now function as precedents,[5] or otherwise bear on interpretation (as in the policy not to prosecute drivers of fire engines mentioned in *Buckoke*[6]); and such precedents may themselves be difficult to interpret or to reconcile with each other. It is not intended to

5   See Chapter 9.
6   See chapter 1, section 8.

deal at length with the relationships between law and change, and the ways in which particular rules and institutions adapt (or survive without adaptation) to changing social conditions. The essential point is that many kinds of event may occur after the creation of a rule, and that these can give rise to doubts in interpretation; the task of diagnosis is to identify how the situation has changed and what difficulties this poses for the interpreter.

Stage IV   Special features of the present case

26. Disagreement or uncertainty about what the facts were, or how they should be categorised.

27. Decision to invoke the rule dubious (eg the decision to prosecute in this case dubious or claimant 'standing on rights' or invoking a forgotten rule or the claim is frivolous or vexatious).

28. Issues framed inappropriately (eg choice of inappropriate charge or cause of action, defective pleadings or inadequate wording of appeal).

29. Unfair or inappropriate procedures followed.

30. Doubts as to role of this decision-maker or whether this is the right arena for this case.

31. Doubts about the decision of an inferior court or tribunal; for example:

   (a) Controversial or eccentric ruling or reasoning by decision-maker at first instance.

   (b) Doubt as to whether decision at first instance should be interfered with in this case or this type of case (eg appeal court uncertain whether or not to substitute its own judgment as to 'reasonableness' in this kind of case).

   (c) Doubt as to the legality, rationality or procedural propriety of a decision taken by an inferior court, tribunal or public official.

32. This case an example of an extraordinary contingency not provided for by the rule-maker.

33. This case on the borderline of the rule.

34. Special features of this case which give rise to feelings of sympathy or antipathy (fireside equities).[7]

35. Embarrassing result in this case (eg relations with a foreign government,[8] popular/unpopular accused) or uncertainty as to the consequences of a particular result in this case.

36. Difference of views between interpreter(s) and others as to one or more of the above.

Stage IV concerns those doubts that may be wholly or partly attributable to special features of the particular case under consideration, such as a judgment by the interpreter that the decision to initiate proceedings was ill-advised, that

---

7   For an explanation and elaboration of this term, see K Llewellyn, *The Common Law Tradition* (1960), pp 268-270.

8   See *R v Bow Street Metropolitan Stipendiary Magistrate, ex p Pinochet Ugarte* [1998] 4 All ER 897, Lord Nicholls at p 941 and Lord Steyn at p 946; decision set aside [1999] NLJR 497.

there was some defect in the procedures that have been adopted, or that there is some extraordinary feature of the facts that gave rise to the present case. This kind of condition may be a troublesome matter for all kinds of interpreters, but it is especially characteristic of the situation of the unhappy interpreter confronted with a rule that more or less clearly indicates a result that he or she considers undesirable for one reason or another. While it may be open to an authoritative decision-maker to try to mitigate the consequences by such devices as derisory damages or an absolute discharge (or their extra-legal analogues), such problems may be viewed by the unhappy interpreter as sufficiently troublesome to justify attempting to interpret or apply the rule in a way that avoids the unwelcome outcome.

Some of the conditions of doubt listed under Stage IV illustrate the fuzziness of the distinctions between interpretation and application, and 'the general' and 'the particular'. For example, condition 32 (extraordinary contingency not provided for by the rule-maker) or 34 (features of the instant case that give rise to feelings of sympathy or antipathy) do not belong clearly to the general or the particular. Each is *potentially* capable of being of wider significance than the particular case, but not necessarily to be treated as such. Indeed, whether or not to treat such features of a case as unique (for practical purposes) or as particular examples of a class, may be one of the choices confronting the interpreter. Thus the distinction between Stage IV and the other stages should not be treated as a rigid one.[9]

2.2   Uses and limitations of the diagnostic model

Most of the conditions of doubt included in the diagnostic model have been discussed, or at least touched on, in earlier chapters; some will be further elaborated or illustrated in the chapters on cases and legislation. Accordingly, it can be treated as a summary of the main points that are made in this book about the conditions of doubt in interpretation. However, it is also designed to be used as an aid to pinpointing, with a fair degree of precision, what is giving rise to puzzlement or difficulty in a particular case. In brief it is a practical tool for diagnosing doubt in interpretation. It may be helpful at this point to give some guidance on the uses and limitations of this tool, even though this involves some repetition.

The purpose of this kind of diagnosis is to tease out the factors which are giving rise to difficulty, in order to arrive at a better understanding of what problems of interpretation are involved and to identify the main starting points for arguments about possible competing interpretations. For identifying the conditions of doubt not only helps to clarify the issues, but also indicates some of the main factors that are relevant to reasoning about them. In this respect, our analysis differs substantially from the majority of the standard legal texts.[10]

---

9 For example, condition 32 may be indistinguishable from condition 12(e) in some cases.

10 The closest to our conception of the conditions of doubt in interpretation is F Bennion, *Statute Law* (3rd edn, 1990), chapters 15-19. See also 'Court technique' in his *Statutory Interpretation* (3rd edn, 1997), Appendix A.

A number tend either to concentrate on identifying remedies for problems of interpretation without first identifying their causes,[11] or, where they do pursue this task, to present such problems as being primarily attributable to the structural characteristics of the English language.[12] Moreover, these accounts are conducted principally in the context of the interpretation of statutory rules. Texts which also deal with the problems that arise in the interpretation of case law rules typically present these as having little in common with the interpretation of rules in fixed verbal form and as being in the main constituted by the need to reconcile the apparent rigours of the doctrine of precedent with its practice. The limitations of an approach that fails to recognise first that some doubts are common to the interpretation of both case law and statutory rules, and second that the range of doubts that interpreters may have frequently goes beyond problems of language and of precedent, can readily be seen in reported cases such as those contained in this book. In short, such an approach does not reflect the complexities of interpretive practice.

The first step, as we have suggested, is to differentiate doubts about interpretation and other doubts which we have referred to as preliminaries to interpretation. This is particularly important in situations in which it is not clear whether there are any rules or what the potentially applicable rules are. For the tasks of identifying and finding rules are not the same as interpreting them. It is even more important to try to separate doubts about the role and objectives of the interpreter, and doubts about what constitutes a correct or appropriate interpretation of a rule in a given context. Because this distinction sometimes breaks down or is difficult to apply in practice, we have included in the model a few factors (especially in Stage IV) which, strictly speaking, bear on preliminaries to interpretation. For example, condition 30 (doubts as to the role of the decision-maker or whether this is the right arena for the case) or 31(b) (doubt as to whether the interpretation by a decision-maker at first instance should be upheld on appeal) involve questions about role; in practice – and they frequently cause difficulty in legal contexts – they are quite difficult to disentangle from questions about interpretation in a strict sense. The same is true of condition 26 (disagreement or uncertainty about the facts), for it is often the case that the main problem facing an advocate or adjudicator is how to characterise 'the facts' so that they fit the protasis of a pre-existing rule. As a practical matter, the objective is not so much to classify the sources of difficulty as to clarify their nature as best one can.

This leads on to a second point. The model provides a rough checklist rather than a set of mutually exclusive categories. There is, for example, an intimate connection between conditions 33 (this case is on the borderline of

---

11 For example, J Holland and J Webb, *Learning Legal Rules* (3rd edn, 1996) and S Lee and M Fox, *Learning Legal Skills* (2nd edn, 1994).

12 For example, J Farrar and A Dugdale, *Introduction to Legal Method* (3rd edn, 1990), pp 141-144. More detailed are J Bell and G Engle QC, *Cross on Statutory Interpretation* (3rd edn, 1995) and F Bennion's magisterial *Statutory Interpretation*, op cit. A particularly sophisticated analysis of the relationship between language and interpretation difficulties is J Evans, *Statutory Interpretation* (1988).

the rule) and 12(c) (vagueness), and between 12(e) (gaps) and 32 (extraordinary contingency not provided for). Often it will not be easy to decide which of two or more conditions fit the particular case most closely or whether it is more appropriate to treat both as being present. This is an area so full of complexities and nuances that rigid distinctions and mutually exclusive categories would introduce a suggestion of precision that is likely to be both artificial and misleading.

In using the model a number of other points should be borne in mind. Often in a single case several conditions may operate in combination. For example, in the *Case of the Legalistic Child*, Father has first to clarify his role as a preliminary to interpretation;[13] in diagnosing the problem of interpretation he might decide that in addition to making a dubious diagnosis of the original problem (conditions 2, 3 and 4) and making a rule which was both vague (12(c)) and not co-extensive with its objective (9), Mother had been foolish in trying to enforce the rule on this occasion (27), with the result that he has a dilemma as to whether to uphold Mother's authority (30, 35) or to acknowledge that Johnny has found a loophole (12(e), 32); underlying this may be a tension between his desire to uphold the 'Rule of Law' and the antipathy aroused by Johnny's obnoxious behaviour (34). Similarly, as we shall see, cases like *Allen* and *Davis v Johnson* involve the combination of several different conditions of doubt in quite complex ways, with no single factor predominating. Thus in *Allen* the ambiguity of 'shall marry' (12(c)) was a necessary condition for disagreement – for if the words had not been ambiguous, there would have been no dispute – but the main argument centred round other factors, notably the interpretation of cases interpreting section 57 (24) and the basic rationale for bigamy (4, 17, 18, 25). Some of these factors, notably the original policy and the relevant authorities, were given particular weight, but all of these factors played a part in the arguments.[14]

The model follows the chronological order of a normal sequence of events, but it is worth noting that this is not the only, or necessarily the best, order in which to approach the task of diagnosis. For example, it may well be appropriate for the unhappy interpreter to identify at an early stage any features of the case that may be contributing to his dissatisfaction, such as that unfair procedures have been followed. One reason for this is that in such cases there may be other strategies for resolving the problem without resort to interpretation, for strained or innovative interpretation is only one of the methods open to an unhappy interpreter in order to achieve the result he desires.

The diagnostic model, then, should be looked at as a flexible aid to sharpening one's awareness of the points causing difficulty in a problem of interpretation. It is important to bear in mind that the list does not claim to be comprehensive, that the categories are not mutually exclusive and that several conditions may co-exist in quite complex ways. The best way to get to grips with the list is to try to apply it to concrete cases. One can do this either by considering examples of problem situations or by analysing the reasoning

13 See above, pp 170-171.
14 Chapters 1, sections 7.2 and 12.5 respectively; see also Appendix. I, section F, question 6.

used by others in disputed cases. The Law Reports provide an excellent source both for learning how to use the model and for testing and refining it; for one of its uses is as a tool for careful analysis of decided cases.[15] Whatever purpose it is being used for, it is important to bear in mind that its primary value is to help answer the question: 'What precisely is or was puzzling about this case?'

In answering this question it has become commonplace for many writers to distinguish between hard and clear cases in law.[16] If this implies that cases are inherently more or less problematic, the diagnostic model reminds us that doubt is relative to standpoint: the question is, hard for whom, clear for whom? The sight of judges and other interpreters disagreeing over whether or not there is a doubt about a case, and if so, what is its nature, is by no means uncommon.[17] But this does not mean that one of them is right in some objectively provable way about whether a doubt exists and that the other is by that measure wrong. Although there are conditions external to the interpreter which make it more or less easy to sustain or to deny a doubt (for example, the preponderance of judicial authority or the clarity of the language of the rule in its context), whether or not the doubt exists is relative to the interpreter's standpoint. Thus there will be some interpreters who are simply too inexpert or unfamiliar with the context to be in doubt; the more expert interpreters who wish to convince others that *they* can see a doubt will first have to explain it before showing how it may be resolved. In other words, experts may entertain doubts simply by virtue of their expertise.

Sometimes, of course, it serves the interpreter's purpose to argue that a matter is in doubt. Many leading cases, such as *Donoghue v Stevenson*,[18] have become authoritative precisely because a proposition of law that legal opinion had treated as being clear was challenged in a path-breaking way. Similarly, it took persistence and imaginative lawyering to argue and eventually to establish the proposition that, under Article 6 of the European Convention for the Protection of Human Rights and Fundamental Freedoms, prisoners have a right of access to a court of law.[19]

Conversely, it may serve the interpreter's purpose to suppress or limit doubts. For example, because of the cost of re-opening or reconsidering their decisions, bureaucracies may *treat* cases about which others have raised doubts as clear. From a civil servant's standpoint, a 'routine' case is often so, not because it is clear, but because there are good systemic reasons against allowing the argument that it is a hard case to prevail.[20] Legal systems often grade the seriousness of doubts that litigants may raise as a means both of minimising

15 See Appendix 1, section E, questions 3 and 4.
16 R Dworkin, 'Hard Cases' (1975) 87 *Harvard Law Review* 1057.
17 See, for example, the disagreements between Lords Denning, Diplock and Scarman as to the nature of the doubts to be resolved in *David v Johnson*; chapter 1, section 12.5 and below, pp 267-268.
18 Chapter 1, section 9.
19 *Golder v United Kingdom* [1975] 1 EHRR 524. Cf The Human Rights Act 1998. See also *Gideon v Wainwright* 372 US 335 (1963) in which persistence and the creative use of doubt finally established that due process under the United States' Constitution included a prisoner's right to counsel; A Lewis, *Gideon's Trumpet* (1966).
20 See C Sampford, *The Disorder of Law* (1989), pp 42-43.

and of regulating the flow of appeals to the higher courts. One example of this is the dual requirement that for an appeal on a matter of criminal law to be heard by the House of Lords, the lower court must certify that a point of law of general public importance is involved, and secondly, that it must appear to that court or to the House of Lords that the point is one which ought to be considered by the final court of appeal. For the litigants, it will be a matter of which of them will convince the court that the doubt meets or fails to meet these standards.

Accordingly, it is misleading to think of hard and clear cases as if the doubt lies in the case. Of course some conditions of doubt may be a feature of the case or its surrounding context, but the doubting is done by its interpreters. As Bankowski and MacCormick observe:

> Problems of operative interpretation arise then because, in the adversarial system, litigants can find or contrive differences over the 'obvious' meaning of a statutory text; or, where one seems to have the advantage on that point, because the other can press other arguments as to the right way of solving a dispute once the statutory text is viewed in its whole legal and social context.[21]

Sometimes, in argument, the presence or absence of a doubt is flatly asserted,[22] but in legal contexts at least, interpreters usually (and sometimes are required to) set down their analysis of any doubt they assert (or deny) is present in the case. It was with this in mind that the diagnostic model presented above was formulated. It was specifically designed to fit most easily a situation involving:

(a) a single, consciously made rule in fixed verbal form;
(b) a relatively simple process which can be roughly depicted in terms of a sequence of events beginning with the perception of a general problem situation and ending with a particular case, in which certain preliminaries to interpreting (such as determining 'the facts') had been completed; and
(c) an interpreter in the situation of an impartial adjudicator called on to interpret and apply the rule in the present case.

Given the diversity of rules, of contexts of interpretation, and of interpreters, it would be unreasonable to expect a single model to fit all conceivable situations. However, we think that this one is sufficiently flexible to be of some help in reasonably straightforward cases even where one or more of the conditions in (a), (b) and (c) above are not present. Provided that it is recognised for what it is, viz a rough illustrative checklist of some common conditions of doubt in interpretation, it can be useful at least as a starting point in a wide variety of contexts.

It would not be appropriate to attempt to present here an elaborate series of alternative models for use in different contexts.[23] But it may help to illustrate

---

21 Z Bankowski and DN MacCormick, in MacCormick and Summers (eds), *Interpreting Statutes: A Comparative Study* (1991), chapter 10.
22 For example, Lord Denning in *Davis v Johnson*; see chapter 1, section12.5.2.
23 For a very elaborate model for the interpretation of treaties, see M McDougal, H Lasswell and J Miller, *The Interpretation of Agreements and World Public Order* (1967).

some of the uses and limitations of this one, by considering briefly how it might apply to standard cases of rules not in fixed verbal form.

Stages I and II postulated a single actor consciously setting out to diagnose a problem and designing a rule as a means of resolving it. A contrasting picture of the ways some rules come into being is given in William Graham Sumner's account of the growth of folkways, which was discussed in Chapter 5.[24] This emphasised the absence of a determinate rule-maker; to talk of intention, policy, purpose or reason in relation to such rules is problematic, yet it is difficult to make sense of them or to attribute meaning or significance to them without resort to such terms. Thus there may be an added dimension of indeterminacy and obscurity about the contexts out of which some rules not in fixed verbal form have emerged. Similarly, in the formulation of such rules, typically no one participant has the status of a draftsman whose formulation is accepted as *the* text of the rule. Accordingly, doubts arising from poor draftsmanship are less likely to occur, but the identity, the level of generality and what constitutes an acceptable formulation of the rule, are correspondingly more likely to be indeterminate.

All of the conditions in Stage III are potentially applicable to rules not in fixed verbal form, but the distinction between events prior and subsequent to the making of the rule breaks down in respect of such rules. Typically, there is not an identifiable moment of time when the rule came into existence; and, in the absence of a frozen text, there is a greater flexibility, and thus more scope for evolution and adaptation. Here again, generalisations need to be treated with caution: texts can evolve and change over time, as well as be subjected to varying interpretations; conversely, some rules not in fixed verbal form can be as rigid and petrified as rules written down on tablets of stone. Nevertheless, the adaptive capacity of flexible rules is worth stressing, for it is important to remember that difficulties for interpreters may have been eliminated as well as created earlier in the process.

All the conditions listed in Stage IV are potentially relevant to interpretation of rules not in fixed verbal form, but it is worth reiterating that the distinction between interpretation and application is particularly inclined to break down in this context.

So far we have concentrated on situations in which problems have been defined fairly narrowly and a limited number of rules has been treated as relevant. But problems and rules cumulate. It is often artificial to the point of being misleading to treat a problem or a rule as an isolated phenomenon. Where rules are themselves part of a large and complex agglomeration or system (which may or may not be 'systematic' in the sense of being orderly), other rules may both generate problems and provide some or all of the means for resolving them.[25] As we have seen, an additional source of doubt in some contexts is how far a particular agglomeration of rules is to be treated as a closed and internally consistent system which is theoretically capable of resolving all its problems internally, and how far co-existing systems of rules

24 See above, p 187.
25 See above, Chapter 3, section 6.

are capable of being harmonised. In other contexts involving rules, similar questions may also arise about the weight to be given to claims to logical consistency when these claims conflict, or appear to conflict, with other considerations.

The difficulties and dangers of treating problems and rules in isolation from their broader context, the fact that problems tend to accumulate and that each attempted solution can contribute to the creation of further problems, and the practical constraints which often bar the way to a solution which is direct, simple and neat are all factors which need to be taken into account in a realistic approach to diagnosis of doubt in interpretation. Much of the history of English private law can be read as a story of complex interstitial adjustments within a relatively complex and outwardly static system of rules and remedies. Professor Milsom has neatly summarised the nature of this process, a summary which provides a useful warning against naive rationalism in diagnosis.

> From time to time, pretending that he belongs in a law school, the medievalist puts on a course with some such title as 'mechanics of legal development'. Part of it goes like this. The law is a reiterated failure to classify life. There have always been categories like tort and contract (the medieval words were trespass and covenant); each cycle begins with fact situations being pinned up under the one or the other without much need for thought. Under each heading, the preoccupations of the formative period dictate more or less clear rules; and the system as a whole acquires mathematical force. But as soon as the force is compelling, the system is out of date. Both the classification itself and the rules within each category formed around yesterday's situations; when today's are pinned up on the same principle, they are subjected to rules and yield results no longer appropriate. The individual lawyer cannot hope to get the rules changed for his client, but he can often try to have his case reclassified. No doubt a promise is a promise: but it may also be or imply a statement, and if the rules of contract do not effectively enforce the promise, the statement may still trigger essentially tortious rules about reliance. This is how assumpsit began, not, of course, as the conscious device of a profession suddenly aware that its rules of contract were out of date, but as a back door to justice in a few hard cases. For the front door, the law of contract governing at the time, you needed a document under seal; this once sensible requirement of proof for large transactions was being forced upon small ones by economic and jurisdictional changes, hitting first and worst those who themselves acted on their agreements but had no document with which to attack the other side. It was for such victims that lawyers first sought out a backdoor 'tort theory'. But the inappropriateness of sealing wax for daily business turned it into the main entrance: most agreements were made on the footing that any litigation would be in *assumpsit*, and the document under seal came to be used only for special transactions. And so our first law of contract died its death, and there was conceived that which was to flourish in the late 19th and early 20th centuries ...[26]

---

[26] S Milsom, review of Grant Gilmore, 'The Death of Contract' (1975) 84 *Yale Law Journal* 1585. For exercises on Chapter 6, see Appendix I, section E, pp 398–400.

Chapter 7

Legislation

1 Introduction

In this and the following chapter we apply the lessons of chapter 6 to reading, using and interpreting legislation. We shall, for the most part, be concerned with the principal form of legislation enacted by the United Kingdom Parliament, the public general Act. The discussion is set against the background of profound and exciting changes to the constitution: devolution, the introduction into our law by means of the Human Rights Act 1998 of the European Convention on Human Rights, and the continuing expansion of the European Union's competence over policy and law-making within the United Kingdom. Devolution means that the legislation enacted at Westminster will not be the only source of statutory law in Scotland, Wales or Northern Ireland.[1] Statutory instruments will be the means by which the Welsh Assembly will exercise its legislative competence, while both the Scottish Parliament and the Northern Ireland Assembly may enact both primary and secondary legislation. The users of legislative rules on every side of the internal borders of the United Kingdom will need to develop routines for reading these laws, which may in time acquire their own national characteristics. We begin this chapter with a short account of the principal characteristics of Community legislation and of the Human Rights Act 1998.[2] We deal with the interpretation of these two sources of law in chapter 8.[3]

2 The European Dimension

2.1 Community legislation

Throughout the period of the United Kingdom's membership of the European Community (now Union), Community law has assumed an increasingly significant part in our legal system. From its original conception of a common

---

1 Until direct rule was established in 1972 the Northern Ireland Parliament had power to enact primary and secondary legislation on matters not 'excepted' or 'reserved' from it. Both the Scottish Office and the Welsh Office have had power to enact secondary legislation, but the devolution powers are in a different league.
2 See Appendix IV for details of standard works on Community law and the European Convention on Human Rights.
3 Chapter 8, section 5.

market in goods, services, capital and labour, Community law deals regularly with such domestic matters as agriculture and fisheries, the environment, employment, competition and company law, and consumer protection.[4]

Three important consequences flow from our membership of the European Union. Firstly, it may make laws that form part of our legal system without any intervening action on the part of the Westminster Parliament being either necessary, or indeed permissible.[5] Such laws are called regulations and they are directly applicable as the law of the United Kingdom. Community law may also require national governments to alter their law where necessary (and usually within a time scale) so that it conforms to a prescribed pattern. These are called directives. We deal with them in greater detail below.

Secondly, in certain circumstances Community law confers rights upon individuals which national courts are obliged to uphold. This is called 'direct effect'. These rights may be enforceable against the governments and the institutions of Member States (vertical effect) or against non-governmental bodies and natural persons (horizontal effect). Being directly applicable in domestic law, regulations have direct vertical and horizontal effect.[6] Because a directive imposes obligations on national governments and not on private individuals, it cannot have horizontal effect. Also, because it requires implementation by the Member State, a directive has direct vertical effect only when its provisions are clear, precise, unconditional, and do not depend on any further action being taken either by the Community or national authorities.[7]

Finally, national courts have an overriding obligation to comply with the duties placed on them by the Court of Justice of the European Communities. Bates identifies these as falling into three broad categories:

> (i) a duty to disapply domestic law inconsistent with directly effective Community law; (ii) a duty to interpret national law, whether or not it is implementing Community law, in the light of the wording and purpose of that law, as far as it is possible for them to do so; and (iii) a duty to award damages to an individual against a Member State for loss caused by the failure of the State to implement Community law properly.[8]

(a) The structure of Community legislation

At the apex of the hierarchy of legal texts comprising Community legislation are the Treaties which established the Community (Paris 1951 and Rome 1957) and subsequently the European Union (Maastricht 1992). Comparable to a

4 See D Miers, 'The Development of the European Community 1973-1995' in P Giddings and G Drewry (eds), *Westminster and Europe* (1995), ch 1.
5 European Communities Act 1972, s 2; chapter 1, section 2.5.
6 On direct vertical effect, see *Marshall v Southampton and South West Hampshire Area Health Authority* [1986] QB 401.
7 *Van Gend en Loos v Nederlandse Administratie der Belastingen*: C-26/62 [1963] ECR 1; T Hartley, *The Foundations of European Community Law* (3rd edn, 1994), p 200.
8 T StJ Bates, 'United Kingdom Implementation of Directives' (1996) 17 *Statute Law Review* 27. See *R v Secretary of State for Transport, ex p Factortame (No 2)* [1991] 1 AC 603. See also F Bennion, *Statutory Interpretation* (3rd edn, 1997), pp 1004-1010; *Marleasing SA v La Comercial Internacional de Alimentacion SA*: C-106/89 [1990] ECR I-4135; *Francovich v Italy*: C-6, 9/90 [1992] IRLR 84.

written constitution, these and the other treaties agreed by Member States provide the authority (the 'Treaty base') for the Acts that are adopted by the Community's law-making institutions: the Commission, the Council of Ministers and the European Parliament. Acts of the European Union are of three types: regulations, directives, and decisions. By Article 189 of the Treaty of Rome:

> A regulation shall have general application. It shall be binding in its entirety and directly applicable in all Member States.
>
> A directive shall be binding, as to the result to be achieved, upon each Member State to which it is addressed, but shall leave to the national authorities the choice of form and methods.
>
> A decision shall be binding in its entirety on those to whom it is addressed.

Being lower in rank than the Treaties these must be interpreted so as to conform to them, and can be annulled if they are incompatible with the Treaty provisions on which they are based. Of the three forms of secondary Community legislation, regulations are the most numerous, followed by decisions and directives. The choice of Act depends on a variety of factors. The Community's Principal Legal Adviser notes that regulations are used where the Community has a management function, such as in customs and agriculture; directives to harmonise national laws 'with a view, for example, to removing barriers to trade'. Decisions, which are addressed to particular Member States or sectors within the Community, may be designed to promote specific programme objectives set by the Council.[9]

Article 190 of the Treaty of Rome requires that legislative Acts 'shall state the reasons on which they are based and shall refer to any proposals or opinions which were required to be obtained pursuant to this Treaty'. In giving effect to this Article all Community legislation commences (unlike Acts of Parliament) with a preamble, comprising 'citations' (the authorising Treaty provision(s), and any proposals from, opinions of, or consultations with Community institutions which prefaced the adoption of the Act), which commence 'having regard to', and 'recitals', being statements of the Act's purpose(s) or motivation; these commence 'whereas'.[10] For example, the preamble to the Habitats Directive begins:[11]

> Having regard to the Treaty establishing the European Economic Community, and in particular Article 130s thereof,
>
> Having regard to the proposal from the Commission,
>
> Having regard to the opinion of the European Parliament,
>
> Having regard to the opinion of the Economic and Social Committee,

---

9 R Wainwright, 'Techniques of Drafting European Community Legislation: Problems of Interpretation' (1996) 17 *Statute Law Rev* 7. The Treaty on European Union 1992 (the Maastricht Treaty) introduced the principle of 'subsidiarity'. This means that Community decisions should be taken 'as closely as possible to the citizen'. Easy to state, the principle is more difficult to put into practice; see Miers (1995), op cit, pp 26-27.

10 The procedural background is summarised in R Wainwright, 'The Future of European Community Legislation in the Light of the Recommendations of the Sutherland Committee and the Principle of Subsidiarity' (1994) 15 *Statute Law Rev* 98; K Collins et al, 'Policy Entrepreneurs: the Role of European Parliament Committees in the Making of EU Policy' (1998) 19 *Statute Law Review* 1.

11 See Chapter 1, section 6.1.2 for Articles 12 and 16.

Whereas the preservation, protection and improvement of the quality of the environment, including the conservation of natural habitats and of wild fauna and flora, are an essential objective of general interest identified by the Community, as stated in Article 130r of the Treaty; [there follow 20 further recitals]

Community legislation is the product of a complex, lengthy and sometimes acrimonious process of negotiation. The Commission first consults those to be affected by its proposed legislation. The proposal itself then takes the form of a complete draft text which must state its Treaty base, its motivation and the operating part – the law. Besides providing the legal authority for the Act, the Treaty base also determines the procedures to be followed in the other law-making institutions. In the case of particularly controversial proposals, such matters as the voting procedure in the Council of Ministers (qualified majority or unanimity) and the nature of the involvement of the European Parliament assume considerable political as well as legal significance. The final step is the adoption of the law which, in the case of directives, requires further action on the part of Member States. The Acts are published in the Official Journal of the Community in the eleven official languages, each having equal authenticity.[12] This places a premium on the use of a clear drafting style. In 1993 the European Council adopted a resolution designed to make Community law as 'clear, simple, concise and understandable as possible'. We return to this later in this chapter in the context of the debate about drafting style within the United Kingdom.[13]

(b)   Implementing directives

Article 12 of the Habitats Directive requires Member States to 'take the requisite measures to establish a system of strict protection for the animal species listed in Annex IV(a) in their natural range, prohibiting ....'.[14] As with other directives, there is a variety of ways in which the United Kingdom government could comply with this obligation.[15] It may be that existing primary or secondary legislation meets the standards imposed by the directive, in which case nothing more needs to be done. Whether or not it does is a matter of interpretation for the civil servants in the relevant government department, such as the Department of Trade and Industry (eg for company law) or the Ministry of Agriculture, Fisheries and Food (eg for food safety). Or it may be that the power to require compliance exists in primary legislation, but has yet to be implemented. In that case, the making of appropriate secondary legislation may suffice. An alternative is to make regulations under section 2(2) of the European Communities Act 1972.

12 The existence of legislative texts in plural linguistic forms is common in Europe and Canada. Under the Government of Wales Act 1998 there will for the first time in the United Kingdom be bilingual (secondary) legislation; see s 122.
13 Below, pp 245ff.
14 Chapter 1, section 6.1.2.
15 See T StJ Bates, 'United Kingdom Implementation of EU Directives' (1996) 17 *Statute Law Rev* 27; A Samuels, 'Incorporating, Translating or Implementing European Union Law into UK Law' (1998) 19 *Statute Law Rev* 80. Compare the position in Ireland, E Donelan, 'The Role of the Office of Parliamentary Draftsman in the Implementation of European Directives in Ireland' (1997) 18 *Statute Law Rev* 1.

The final method entails the transposition of the directive's language into primary or secondary legislation. This is known as the 'copy-out' technique. It has been adopted in response to the concern that the inappropriate use of any of the other three methods might leave the United Kingdom open to legal action by the Commission, or, possibly, by individuals, on the ground that the method chosen has resulted in either under- or over-implementation of the directive.[16] An example of this technique can be seen in the definition of offences in regulation 39 of the Conservation (Natural Habitats etc) Regulations 1994 reproduced in chapter 1, section 6.1.3, which is taken (with some minor linguistic variation) from Article 12 of the directive.[17] Of itself, however, this does not complete the implementation, as regulation 39 must be read subject to the exceptions in regulation 40, which are taken from section 10 of the parent legislation, the Wildlife and Countryside Act 1981. Where the copy-out technique is used in conjunction with existing legislation, the danger remains that any variation in the implementing legislation may fail to meet the directive's requirements. In the present case, regulation 40(3)(c) provides for exceptions in the case of an 'act which was the incidental result of a lawful operation': 'It is possible that the European Court of Justice may not consider this meets the 'overriding public interest' standard identified in Article 16(1)(c).'[18] Apart from questions concerning the United Kingdom's compliance with its Community obligations, the adoption of differing drafting techniques can imply, as the Law Commission noted in its 1969 Report on the Interpretation of Statutes, differing interpretive techniques.[19]

2.2   The Human Rights Act 1998

This section describes briefly the two principal implications of the Human Rights Act 1998 for the status of existing and future legislation enacted in the United Kingdom.

(a)   Existing primary and secondary legislation

So far as existing legislation is concerned, section 4 of the Act gives power to the higher courts to make a 'declaration of incompatibility'. Where the court is to determine whether a provision of primary legislation is compatible with a 'Convention right' it may make such a declaration if it is satisfied that the provision is incompatible. In the case of subordinate legislation, the court may make the same declaration where it is additionally satisfied that the primary legislation prevents removal of the incompatibility.[20] Rectification of such incompatibility may be made in the usual manner by the revocation of the subordinate legislation or by the enactment of amending primary legislation.

---

16 See L Ramsey, 'The Copy-out Technique: More of a 'Cop-out' than a solution?' (1996) 17 *Statute Law Review* 218.
17 Above, p 34.
18 Ramsey, op cit, p 226.
19 Law Commission, *The Interpretation of Statutes* (1969, Law Com No 21), para 5. Below, p 297.
20 Subordinate legislation includes Acts of the Scottish Parliament (s 21(1)).

However, where the case for rectification is 'compelling', section 10 provides that the Minister may by order amend the primary legislation, either to remove the incompatibility directly, or, where the incompatibility lay in the subordinate legislation, indirectly, by amending the parent Act. These 'remedial orders' may also be used where it appears to the Minister that a legislative provision has become incompatible as a consequence of a decision taken by the European Court of Human Rights in proceedings against the United Kingdom.

It should be noted, firstly, that section 10 permits the amendment of primary legislation by means of statutory instrument. This is itself an unusual power, though one which has, since the enactment of the Deregulation and Contracting Out Act 1994, become a regular feature of parliamentary procedure.[21] Orders made under section 10 will be subject to parliamentary scrutiny. Secondly, it is the government's intention that remedial orders shall not become the routine response to declarations of incompatibility; there must be 'compelling reasons' for proceeding under section 10. In debate the government resisted efforts to categorise such reasons, preferring to respond to particular instances which might be regarded as compelling.[22] It should also be noted that the Act imposes no obligation on the United Kingdom government to respond in any way to declarations of incompatibility.

(b) Future primary legislation

So far as the future is concerned, section 19 of the Act requires the Minister in charge of the Bill, before its Second Reading, to 'make a statement to the effect that in his view the provisions of the Bill are compatible with the Convention rights'. These 'statements of compatibility' will, the government hopes, be a strong spur to the courts to find in particular cases that the section with which they are dealing, should the question arise, is indeed compatible with the Convention. For this the courts will look to the Official Report of Parliamentary Debates (Hansard) to see what the Minister said. The ministerial statement cannot be dispositive, but it will undoubtedly be highly persuasive. Much will depend on its clarity.[23]

3 Reading legislation: What? Why? How?

3.1 Legislation: meaning

The term 'legislation' can be used to encompass a wide variety of rules in fixed verbal form, including Acts of Parliament, the rules of European Community law, and subordinate legislation such as statutory instruments and the by-laws of local authorities. It can also include rules issued by statutory bodies and executive agencies which, though not enacted by a formal legislative

---

21 See D Miers, *The Deregulation Procedure: An Evaluation* (The Hansard Society for Parliamentary Government, 1999). See further below, pp 243-244.
22 See Vol 317, HC Debates, cols 1330-31 (21 October 1998).
23 See below, p 295.

process, are nevertheless usually regarded as binding by those to whom they are addressed.[24] They have become of increasing importance in our society. We shall concentrate on statutes, being the primary legislation with which law students are most familiar. Our aim is to identify those features of the legislative process that contribute to some of the difficulties which may be encountered when reading, using and interpreting statutory rules. Chapter 8 deals specifically with their interpretation. Although what we shall say directly concerns statutes, many of the features discussed apply to a greater or a lesser extent to the preparation and publication of other forms of legislation, and of other rules in fixed verbal form.

The process by which legislation is prepared and enacted has, for many years, been the object of criticism. In 1969 the Law Commissions published a Report on the interpretation of statutes which drew attention to the links between the methods by which legislation is drafted and the ways in which it is interpreted.[25] A few years later the Renton Report provided a detailed and influential critique of the preparation of legislation,[26] and as the Hansard Society's Report published in 1992 clearly shows, much of this criticism continues to be valid.[27] A central weakness of the system is that the institutional arrangements concerning the preparation and enactment of legislation have been inadequate to the task; in particular, the practices that constitute the legislative process have not encouraged the reasoned improvement of the Bills which are debated in Parliament. Accordingly, many of the reforms that have been proposed involve change to the rules of parliamentary procedure.[28]

3.2 Legislation: scope

The public general Act is one of the primary instruments by which a government can implement its policies;[29] it remains the single most important source of law in our legal system:

---

24 See D Miers and A Page, *Legislation* (2nd edn, 1990), pp 1-17 and D Miers, 'The Style of Legislation: Narrative Norms and Constraining Norms' in J Bridge (ed), *United Kingdom Law in the Mid 1990s* (1994), pp 407-439.

25 Law Commission, *The Interpretation of Statutes*, op cit.

26 *The Preparation of Legislation* (1975, Cmnd 6053; Chairman: Sir David Renton); hereafter cited as *Renton*.

27 'Making the Law', the Report of the Hansard Society Commission on the Legislative Process (1992; Chairman: Lord Howe); hereafter cited as *Hansard Society Report*.

28 See the four Reports published by the House of Commons and two by the House of Lords during the 1980s and early 1990s: Second Report of the Select Committee on Procedure, Public Bill Procedure (1984-85, HC 49), Second Report of the Select Committee on Procedure, Allocation of Government Time to Bills in Standing Committee (1985-86, HC 324), Second Report of the Select Committee on Procedure (1989-90, HC 19-I), Select Committee on Sittings of the House, (1991-92, HC 21-I; the 'Jopling' Report); and in the House of Lords, the Select Committee on the Committee Work of the House (1991-92 HL 35-I; the 'Jellicoe' Report) and the Select Committee on Sittings in the House (1994-95, HL 9; the 'Rippon' Committee).

29 In 'Making Better Law: A Review of the Hansard Commission on the Legislative Process' (1993) 14 *Statute Law Rev* 75, M Rush noted: 'as Harold Lasswell succinctly defined it in the title of one of his books, politics is about *Who Gets What, When, How* and the law is one of the major ways of deciding that question'.

There is hardly any part of our national life or of our personal lives that is not affected by one statute or another. The affairs of local authorities, nationalized industries, public corporations and private commerce are regulated by legislation. The life of the ordinary citizen is affected by various provisions of the statute book from cradle to grave. His birth is registered, his infant welfare protected, his education provided, his employment governed, his income and capital taxed, much of his conduct controlled and his old age sustained according to the terms of one statute or another. Many might think that as a nation we groan under this overpowering burden of legislation and ardently desire to have fewer rather than more laws. Yet the pressure for ever more legislation on behalf of different interests increases as society becomes more complex and people more demanding of each other. With each change in society there comes a demand for further legislation to overcome the tensions which that change creates, even though the change itself may have been caused by legislation, which thus becomes self-proliferating.[30]

So far as its legislative competence has not been superseded by that of the European Union, the United Kingdom Parliament is, according to the fundamental tenets of the doctrine of the sovereignty of Parliament, free to legislate on any matter it chooses. So far as the selection of subject matter is concerned, it is nevertheless the case that there are some legislative initiatives which governments must pursue if they are in any meaningful sense to govern: the annual financial legislation (including at least one Finance Act, which gives legislative effect to the government's Budget proposals, together with Appropriation and Consolidated Fund Acts) is the principal example.

Beyond this, public general Acts are used to regulate a vast range of activities. For example, statutes were enacted between 1993 and 1997 to amend the law of education; to establish the National Lottery; to establish the General Osteopathic Council and to regulate the profession of osteopathy; to abolish the presumption that a boy under 14 years of age is incapable of having sexual intercourse; to make provision consequential on the signing of the Treaty on the European Union signed at Maastricht on 7 February 1992; to privatise the railways; to place the Secret Intelligence Service (MI 6) and the Government Communications Headquarters (GCHQ) on a statutory basis; to make further provision for the protection of Antarctica; to permit trading on a Sunday; to give effect to a variety of conventions governing maritime salvage and pollution; to make changes to the law governing the sale and supply of goods; to consolidate the law on value added tax; to readmit South Africa as a member of the Commonwealth; to abolish unemployment benefit and replace it with a new means tested jobseekers' allowance; to establish the Child Support Agency; to permit hearsay evidence to be routinely admitted in civil proceedings; to regulate activity centres used by young persons; to protect the Olympic sign from commercial exploitation; to provide for student loans made by the Student Loan Company to be subsidised by the private financial sector; to introduce mediation into the law of divorce; to rectify a gap in the law of theft as identified by a decision of the House of Lords; to abolish the distinction between a trust for sale and a strict settlement and replace them with a new

30 *Renton*, para 7.3.

concept, the trust of land; to provide for the construction, management and operation of the Channel Tunnel; to abolish treasure trove; to give effect to an international convention protecting United Nations workers; to introduce new restrictions on gun ownership; to pave the way for the introduction of new rules governing civil proceedings; to provide for the acquisition of British citizenship by some British nationals resident in Hong Kong at the date of its return to the Republic of China; to amend the law concerning the deduction from an award of damages of money received by the plaintiff from sources funded by the taxpayer; and to provide for the holding of referendums on a Scottish Parliament and a Welsh Assembly.

These are but thirty of the 273 public general Acts enacted during these five years. Their political origins are diverse, as is their intended impact. Some were enacted in response to the recommendations of the Law Commission (Sale and Supply of Goods Act 1994, Trusts of Land and Appointment of Trustees Act 1996, Family Law Act 1996) or a specially-appointed committee (Civil Procedure Act 1997), some to give effect to the United Kingdom's international obligations (Antarctic Act 1994, Merchant Shipping (Salvage and Pollution) Act 1994, United Nations Personnel Act 1997) and some to fulfill our obligations as members of the European Union (European Communities (Amendment) Act 1993). Some were intended to consolidate existing legislation (Value Added Tax Act 1994), some to amend existing law (Social Security (Recovery of Benefits) Act 1997), and some to replace old law with wholly new legislation (Treasure Act 1996). Some were instances of governmental responses to unforeseen events (Activity Centres (Young Persons' Safety) Act 1995 (which followed the canoeing fatalities in Lyme Regis Bay in 1994), Firearms (Amendment) Act 1997 (which followed the killing of 16 schoolchildren in Dunblane in 1996)), and some were instances of the then government's planned ideological commitments (Railways Act 1993, Sunday Trading Act 1994, Referendums (Scotland and Wales) Act 1997). Some are very short – the Sexual Offences Act 1993 comprises two sections – others very long – the Education Act 1993 comprises 308 sections and 21 Schedules.

Despite their diversity, these examples are only a small part of the total legislative output during this five-year period; their significance is that, with a few exceptions, they all represent the direct implementation of the government's policy on the matter in question. The exceptions are those measures (for example, the British Nationality (Hong Kong) Act 1997) which were promoted by backbench MPs or Peers, but as their enactment is entirely dependent on the government's approval, they too can be regarded as aspects of government policy.[31]

---

31 Most private Member's Bills are government Bills in all but name. Many are in fact measures which the department has been unable to place in the legislative programme and for which it wishes to seek a sponsor. Since no other private Member's Bill will succeed about which the government is, at worst, neutral, it is fair to say that all private Member's Bills give effect to government policy. Where the government favours a Bill that has genuinely originated with a private Member, it may make the services of a parliamentary draftsman available to its sponsors, as was done with the Domestic Violence and Matrimonial Proceedings Bill, or allow some of its own time for debate, or even adopt it as a government measure. Conversely, government opposition will almost inevitably mean that the Bill will be defeated.

3.3 Legislation: consultation, policy-making and programming

The legislation that finally appears on the statute book each year can only be understood in the context of the management of legislative business within modern government. This is the subject of a rich and varied literature, three key features of which will be briefly discussed here: consultation, policy-making and the programming of legislation.[32]

(a) Consultation

Within government, those primarily responsible for a given proposal, that is, the Minister and the civil servants who, if it goes ahead, will comprise the 'Bill team', are expected to engage in routine consultation with other departments. These include the territorial departments, the Treasury, if, as most proposals do, there are public expenditure or fiscal implications, and any other affected department. Outside the government there are hundreds of groups representing a vast range of interests who seek to influence policy in their favour. When a measure is proposed they will lobby Ministers and other officials to drop, amend, delay or expedite its proposals according to whether they see them as prejudicial or advantageous to their interests. In addition to these groups, many statutes are implemented by the existing personnel of such branches of the executive as the Customs and Excise, the Inland Revenue, the police, local authorities and the executive agencies. When representatives of these bodies are consulted about legislative proposals, they too assume the role of pressure groups; they have their own aspirations, values, programmes and priorities and can promote these in concert with or at the expense of other groups (including other governmental departments), with as much vigour, if less publicity, as non-governmental organisations.

Despite the routine publication of Green and White papers, and of other consultative documents, many remain critical of the government's commitment to the value of public consultation. The Hansard Society Commission received substantial evidence from a wide range of groups and individuals complaining about the limited opportunities for pre-legislative consultation. It noted: 'the overwhelming impression from the evidence is that many of those most directly affected are deeply dissatisfied with the extent, nature, timing and conduct of consultation on bills as at present practised.'[33] The Commission made a number of suggestions to improve the position, which we consider further below.[34]

(b) Policy-making

A second important feature of the system concerns the way in which policy is made. A diagnostic model of problem-solving may suggest that policy-making and law-making are rational processes involving the identification of goals and values, the selection of policies available for achieving those goals, the

---

32 For a fuller discussion of these matters, see D Miers and A Page, op cit.
33 *Hansard Society Report*, para 113.
34 See pp 237-238.

prediction of the consequences, good and bad, which may flow from the adoption of each policy and, finally, the choice of the policy with consequences which most closely match the goals to be secured and which accords with the preferred values.[35] Such a high degree of rationality is rarely achieved in practice. What happens may fit more closely a pattern which has been called incrementalism. Ends and means are often difficult to separate for the purpose of evaluation, and so analysis tends to be confined to a series of well-rehearsed options familiar to all the participants. Often the resulting choice will in practice be close to the existing position; it is as if the test of a good policy is the one upon which all interested parties have least disagreement. A colloquial description of this process is 'muddling through'.[36]

It is also a mistake to regard all statutory rules, even those which are expressly intended to further some policy, purely in instrumental terms. Many statutory rules have significant symbolic dimensions which may be just as important to the rule-makers (and to potential interpreters) as their intended instrumental effects, for example, legislation penalising the possession of certain drugs or making some types of racial or sexual discrimination unlawful.[37]

(c)   Programming Bills

Notwithstanding that a great number of interests may need to be consulted, and typically their consent secured, before a given aspect of government policy is translated into a legislative proposal and thence into a Bill, the decision whether to proceed is the government's alone. We saw earlier how wide is the scope of legislative activity. The constraints on the parliamentary timetable mean that there is a limit on the number of measures that can be enacted in any one session. It is difficult to generalise about numbers, nor is there any particular reason why one normal session should differ from any other (though 1997 was an election year), but taking the five years from 1993 to 1997, the highest number of measures enacted in any one year was 63 (1996 and 1997), the lowest 41 (1994). Of these, some 10 or 12 each year are private Member's Bills.

The vast proportion of the annual statutory output represents either major commitments made by the party now in government or when it was in opposition, or more routine requests from government departments to extend or modify their powers when these are found to be inadequate for their administrative tasks. Some, for example, the Department for Education and Employment, the Department of Social Security and the Home Office, routinely promote two or three major Bills every year; others, such as the Ministry of Defence, very few. But for at least the past fifty years, there have always been more proposals emanating from departments than the parliamentary timetable can accommodate. The question for government is how to manage, within the time available, each of its department's demands

---

35 See the advice given by the Cabinet Office's Better Regulation Unit to government departments which are considering regulating a matter falling within their area of responsibility, Better Regulation Guide (1998), Part One, section 2; and ch 2, pp 115-116.
36 See J Richardson and A Jordan, *Governing Under Pressure* (2nd edn, 1985), D Butler, A Adonis and T Travers, *Failure in British Government: the Politics of the Poll Tax* (1994).
37 See, eg J Gregory, *Sex, Race and the Law: Legislating for Equality* (1988) and above pp 140-141.

to initiate legislation, and then, having introduced the measure, how to secure its enactment in a manner that makes the most effective use of the parliamentary timetable.

There are, therefore, two aspects to the programming of legislative business in Parliament. The first relates to the government's decision as to what Bills to introduce, when and in which House. Successive governments have responded to this by authorising a Cabinet committee 'to prepare and submit to the Cabinet drafts of the Queen's Speeches to Parliament and proposals for the Government's legislative programme'.[38] This Committee chooses between the competing demands of departments according to such criteria as the necessity or urgency of the proposed measure, its length and place within the government's own political agenda, its suitability for introduction in the House of Lords, and its degree of political controversy (of special importance in an election year).[39]

The Commons' exclusive initiative in relation to taxation and expenditure means that the Finance Bill must be introduced there; likewise measures of 'first class' constitutional importance. While less compelling, there is a strong expectation that Bills which are politically controversial or which are substantial features of the government's political agenda (typically those signalled in the Queen's Speech at the opening of the session) should be introduced in the Commons. Conversely, Consolidation Bills are invariably introduced in the House of Lords. Beyond these, it is a matter of choice for the government, though there is a tendency to introduce in the Lords 'law reform' measures, that is, measures that particularly deal with procedural law or with technical areas of law.[40]

Similarly, there are only a few constraints on the government's choice about when to introduce a Bill. It is generally accepted that major items will be introduced early in the session; indeed one or two will almost certainly be published within a few days of the debate on the Queen's Speech. An early start does not, however, signal either that the Bill is complete, or that an early completion of its parliamentary stages can be expected. While departments may make the effort to ensure that when published, the Bill represents their settled policy, it is by no means uncommon for Bills to be introduced upon which the sponsoring department has yet to agree key issues. One result is that, late in the day, the government tables amendments introducing wholly new material. This tendency to 'legislate as you go' has been criticised as being an abuse of the legislature, in particular in the House of Lords, where the

---

38 Ministerial Committee QFL; see www.cabinet-office.gov.uk/cabsec/1998/cabcom/qfl.htm.
39 A brief account of this process is given in the *Hansard Society Report*, paras 27-31. See D Miers, 'Legislation and the Legislative Process' (1998) 29 *The Law Librarian* 87. The government's legislative programme is defined in s 31 of the Government of Wales Act 1998 as consisting of 'the bills which (at the beginning of the session) are intended to be introduced in either House of Parliament by a Minister of the Crown'. The section requires the Secretary of State for Wales to consult the Welsh Assembly, as appears to him to be appropriate, about the programme's content.
40 These may be based on proposals of the Law Commission. Also introduced in the Lords are Statute Law Revision and Statute Law (Repeal) Bills which are prepared by the Law Commission for the purpose of rationalising the statute book. See below, p 258.

legislative stage often appears to be no more than an extension of the drafting process.[41]

The second aspect of the programming of legislative business relates to the management of Bills once introduced in Parliament. This, too, is the responsibility of a Cabinet Committee, whose tasks include consideration of 'the parliamentary handling of Government Bills'.[42] A key factor is timetabling. This is crucial in the Commons, where the parliamentary year is heavily over-committed not only to the debate of public Bills but also to the scrutiny of expenditure and of executive actions. But, as the Commons Modernisation Committee noted, however important the passing of legislation may be, proposals for reform must be placed in the context of the proper balance between these various functions.[43] The choice of length of debate is informed by a normative framework mediated through what are called 'the usual channels', that is, the Whips' offices of the government and the official opposition. This choice is no simple procedural matter.[44] An important consideration is the generally acknowledged expectation that the government will give sufficient time for the opposition to debate Bills, especially those that are complex or politically controversial. Apart from their political side-effects, invocation of the procedures by which debate may be curtailed, typically the use of 'guillotine' motions at the Commons Committee stage, means that there will be a number of sections approved by Parliament as law but which have never been debated. Attempts to scrutinise the quality of the legislation that is proposed may thus be entirely thwarted as the opposition concentrates its effort on those clauses it perceives as politically important. Moreover, the old notion that delaying the government's programme by lengthy and time wasting debate is an effective means of opposition has become almost entirely redundant; the government will 'get its business'.

3.4 The preparation of a Bill

A striking feature of the system for the preparation of the Bills themselves is that it is both highly centralised and conducted by a very small group of civil servants (the number has remained around 30 for a number of years), all of whom are lawyers. Established in 1869 within the Treasury Department, the principal task of the Parliamentary Counsel Office is to draft Bills for the government's legislative programme. Until recently the Office had a monopoly

---

41 See D Miers and J Brock, 'Government Legislation: Case Studies', in D Shell and D Beamish, (eds), *The House of Lords at Work* (1993), p 134. The *Hansard Society Report* was also critical of this practice; paras 115 and 484-5, and Appendix 5.

42 The full terms of reference of the Ministerial Commitee on Legislation (LEG) are 'to examine all draft Bills, to consider the parliamentary handling of Government Bills, European Community documents and Private members' business, and such other related matters as may be necessary, and to keep under review the Government's policy in relation to issues of Parliamentary procedures'. See www.cabinet-office.gov.uk/cabsec/1998/cabcom/qfl.htm.

43 Scrutiny of legislation accounts for perhaps a third of the time used on the floor of the House of Commons. Select Committee on Procedure, *The Modernisation of the House* (1996-97, HC 190), para 18 (hereafter, the *Modernisation Committee*). See Miers (1998), op cit.

44 *Modernisation Committee*, para 58.

over this key aspect of the implementation of government policy, but a limited experiment in privatisation produced neither the cost savings nor the increase in productivity that were sought.[45] In fulfilling its primary role, the Parliamentary Counsel Office appears, at least to outsiders, to have developed a rigorous, arcane and, until recently, somewhat inflexible craft-tradition, although the draftsmen themselves continue to have an enviable reputation for technical proficiency. Whereas in the past their rare public pronouncements suggested an uncomfortable level of hubris, the Office now enjoys a less distant and more open relationship with its critics. This has largely come about as a result, firstly, of its willingness to engage in public debate about its responsibilities for the production of statutes which are both legally accurate and clearly written. Secondly, its critics have accepted that the problem of complexity in legislation is as much the inevitable consequence of inadequate departmental preparation conducted to an unrealistic time-scale as it is of any shortcomings in the draftsmen's competence.[46]

The nature of the draftsmen's task and their position in the legislative process combine to make their work extraordinarily difficult and demanding. Firstly, the draftsmen typically act in response to written instructions; in theory they are meant to act as a channel through which the policy passes to emerge in rule form, but in practice they may exercise considerable influence on the way the policy is to be implemented: 'common law draftsmen are more than mere mechanics.'[47] Even where, as in the United Kingdom, the draftsmen's instructions tend to be detailed and are usually carefully prepared, their role as interpreter of the potential effect of the proposed law on existing and other contemplated legislation, and on the practices and procedures of legal officials and institutions, may bring them into conflict with the policy-maker's needs, for example, for speed in the preparation of the Bill.

Draftsmen typically work at a high level of generality and complexity; yet they are expected to express complicated concepts in simple language and to fit each clause into a tangled undergrowth of existing law. Moreover, what is required by the policy-maker may not easily be translated into legal provision; some of the factors that constrain the choice of drafting options stem from the interaction between political objectives and the legal possibilities. On occasion they may be expected to redesign the Bill as the instructing department modifies its policy, sometimes in a wholly opposite direction.[48] Although debates seldom have an impact on the content of a Bill unless the government assents to the proposed changes, it does not follow that a Bill once drafted and published remains in that form as it progresses through Parliament. On the contrary, the draftsman may have to redraft particular

---

45 'Contracting out drafting: a British experience' (1996) 17 *Statute Law Rev* 152.
46 G Engle QC, 'Bills are Made to Pass as Razors are Made to Sell: Practical Constraints in the Preparation of Legislation' (1983) *Statute Law Review* 7, and 'The Legislative Process Today', (1987) *Statute Law Review* 71; *Hansard Society Report*, paras 115-120.
47 N Jamieson, 'Getting in on the Act – Antipodean Style' (1994) 15 *Statute Law Review* 192, 198, referring to the memoirs of Sir Harold Kent (*In On the Act* (1979)), a former parliamentary draftsman.
48 See Engle (1983), op cit, on the Broadcasting Bill 1980.

clauses more than once as the instructing department seeks to resolve issues which are raised during debate.

Secondly, the draftsman has a number of different audiences whose expectations will not necessarily all point in the same direction. The sponsoring Minister needs to consider how to present both to Parliament and to the public the contents of the Bill, how she proposes to defend it (the more so if it is controversial); how it will be approached in Committee and at the Report stage, and so on. She will know that parliamentary procedure requires that each clause must be separately put in Committee, and will thus be tempted to prefer a few long clauses to many short ones. Apart from those MPs or peers who may have assisted in the formulation of its policy, faced with a new measure, the parliamentarian wants to know what it is intended to do, and how it may affect those whose interests he represents. These needs may be catered for by one type of arrangement of the clauses of the Bill, but the draftsman must also consider the needs of those who are to implement its substance, for example, the police, trading standards officers or the Health and Safety Executive. The needs of judges may be different again.

Political compromise and short-term expediency are also natural obstacles to neat, rationalistic law-making. Although it may overstate the position, the following somewhat cynical observation does catch the flavour of some of the pressures exerted on a draftsman:

> [He] ... is the servant and victim of all sorts of external forces beyond his own control – idealistic reformers in a hurry to build Utopia the day after tomorrow, pragmatic politicians who want to catch the tide of popularity with the showy amendment of some much publicised quirk of the law, wrangling parliamentarians lacerating a Bill with amendments for party purposes.[49]

3.5   The legislative process

(a)   Shortcomings of the traditional position

It is relatively easy to describe the essence of the parliamentary process through which public Bills pass before they become law.[50] It is less easy to say that the attention which Parliament gives to them will be sufficiently close as to identify and resolve potential doubts about their interpretation.

Following its First Reading, an entirely formal stage involving no debate or vote, a Bill is ordered to be printed and a date is agreed for its Second Reading. Here its sponsor (in the case of a government Bill this will be a Minister or the Secretary of State of the lead department) sets out its main principles, and at the conclusion of the debate there is a vote. If the Bill receives a Second

---

49 Comment, (1968) 118 *New Law Journal* 360. Thus Mustill LJ was right when he commented that 'in all the flurry of legislation, evasive action and counter-legislation' surrounding s 35 of the Government Finance Act 1985, the conclusion that he reached in *R v Lambeth London Borough Council, ex p Secretary of State for the Environment* [1991] COD 132 might well 'not have corresponded with the general intention of those who caused it to be enacted'. The decision was overruled by the Community Charges (Substitutes Setting) Act 1991.

50 See Miers and Page, op cit, and the *Modernisation Committee* for a fuller account.

Reading (which in the case of a government Bill is, unless something is seriously amiss, a foregone conclusion), it is then committed to the Committee stage. Here the details of the Bill are considered and amendments to its clauses debated.[51] Some changes may be made (in the case of a government Bill, only if the government is prepared to accept them) and the Bill, with any changes, is reported back to the House. It is then at its Report stage, which will often involve further debate on amendments unsuccessfully moved in Committee and which are moved again. This stage is followed by Third Reading, usually a quiet debate in which the principles of the Bill are reiterated by its sponsor; it is then sent to the other House where it follows essentially the same sequence. The Bill then finally returns to the House in which it was first introduced, and any amendments that have been made in the meantime by the other House are debated and voted upon. That concluded, the Bill is sent for the Royal Assent, an entirely formal stage.

This simplified picture is complicated by other factors concerning parliamentary procedure and the management of public Bills.[52] What cannot be ignored is the powerfully voiced criticism that Parliament's traditional mode of operation, in particular in the Commons, means that it is seriously failing to discharge one of its primary functions, namely, the effective scrutiny of government legislation. One informed critic has, if somewhat colourfully, observed:

> The system has been geared entirely to getting bills through, regardless of whether they are properly scrutinised. During the standing-committee stage of line by line scrutiny, government backbenchers are actively discouraged from participating lest their speeches delay progress on a bill, so they can be seen doing their constituency correspondence and, depending on the season, their Christmas cards. If a formal guillotine is imposed, this stage is even worse since large parts of a bill may not be properly considered at all. Attempts by the opposition to put forward amendments are almost invariably rebuffed on partisan grounds. Moreover, the more important and controversial the bill, the less likely is Parliament to play a creative part in its scrutiny. The result is a mass of hastily considered and badly drafted bills, which often later have to be revised.[53]

A primary reason for this state of affairs is that the procedures for enacting Bills were largely devised at the end of the nineteenth century with the object of limiting debate in order to expedite the government's business. Since then both the quantity and complexity of legislation have greatly increased, but with relatively minor changes to the procedural context. The extended sessions, long sittings, the frequent use of timetable motions and the brief intervals between a Bill's stages which characterise an overcrowded timetable inevitably mean that it is difficult for Parliament to perform its claimed role in reviewing both the principle and the detail of government legislation. These points have

---

51 Some, called 'probing' amendments, are designed only to find out more about the policy behind or implementation of a clause, and are not seriously intended to change the Bill. Nevertheless, using *Pepper v Hart*, the Minister's replies could well be of value in supporting a contested interpretation; see below, pp 289ff.
52 See Miers (1998), op cit.
53 P Riddell, *Parliament under Pressure* (1998), pp 28-29.

been accepted by Parliament, which has, in recent years, introduced a number of procedural changes, both in the Commons and in the Lords.[54] Even so, as the Commons Modernisation Committee accepted in 1997, much remains to be done:

> From the evidence we have received and our own impressions, we have concluded that both Houses fail to fulfill their legislative functions as effectively as they could do. In particular, the House of Commons as a whole should consider more deliberately for each individual bill how its scrutiny could be as effective as possible in the time available.[55]

What would doing better entail? The Modernisation Committee set out the following criteria as essential in its view to successful reform:

(a) The Government of the day must be assured of getting its legislation through in reasonable time (provided that it obtains the approval of the House).

(b) The Opposition in particular and Members in general must have a full opportunity to discuss and seek to change provisions to which they attach importance.

(c) All parts of a Bill must be properly considered.

(d) The time and expertise of Members must be used to better effect.

(e) The House as a whole, and its legislative Committees in particular, must be given full and direct information on the meaning and effect of the proposed legislation from those most directly concerned, and full published explanations from the Government on the detailed provisions of its Bill.

(f) Throughout the legislative process there must be greater accessibility to the public, and legislation should, so far as possible, be readily understandable and in plain English.

(g) The legislative programme needs to be spread as evenly as possible throughout the session in both Houses.

(h) There must be sufficient flexibility in any procedures to cope with, for example, emergency legislation.

(i) Monitoring and, if necessary, amending legislation which has come into force should become a vital part of the role of Parliament.[56]

(b) The 'better legislation' agenda

The proposals that have been suggested aim to make legislation more workable in practice and more accessible to its users. One means of accomplishing this would be to increase the opportunities for consultation about the Bill as drafted. As we saw earlier, consultation on the proposed contents of a Bill is routine at the pre-parliamentary stage, but once introduced, the First Reading has never offered any opportunity for debate. Following the Hansard Society Report,[57] the Modernisation Committee recommended that some Bills could be committed *ad hoc* to a First Reading Select Committee, whose purpose would be to scrutinise the Bill before its Second Reading. The Committee's view was

---

54 In the Commons, see the Jopling Report, op cit; and in the Lords, the Jellicoe and the Rippon Reports, op cit.
55 *Hansard Society Report*, para 314; *Modernisation Committee*, paras 2, 4 and 13.
56 *Modernisation Committee*, para 14.
57 *Hansard Society Report*, para 343.

that this would provide an opportunity for the House as a whole, for individual backbenchers, and for the opposition to have an early and real input into the form of the legislation which subsequently emerges. Above all, the Committee argued, such a procedure should 'lead to better legislation and less likelihood of subsequent amending legislation'.[58]

A connected proposal, and one which also addresses the criticism that those who are particularly likely to be affected by them should be given more information about their proposed contents, is that Bills should be accompanied by more user-friendly explanatory material. Currently, a Bill is, when published, prefaced by an Explanatory Memorandum which gives a broad statement of its purpose followed by more detailed resumés of the content of each of its clauses. There has never been a 'simple non-technical explanation' published contemporaneously with the Bill which is designed to assist its potential users, nor has the production of such an explanation been a task which could reasonably be expected of Parliamentary Counsel. However, it has been agreed that a single document entitled 'Explanatory Notes', written in plain English and politically neutral, should accompany the Bill on publication.[59]

Once given its First Reading, there is within each House a variety of routes that a Bill could take. In the Commons one normally thinks of the progression as being: Second Reading held in the Commons' chamber ('on the floor of the House'), Committee stage held there or in a Standing Committee, and Report, Third Reading and consideration of Lords' amendments all on the floor of the House. But as the Modernisation Committee observed, there are a number of other options, unswerving adherence to what it calls 'the principal route' being one of the reasons why public Bills are not as effectively scrutinised as they might be. Thus it proposed that greater use could be made of Second Reading Committees, and of Special Standing Committees or of Select Committees at the Committee stage, and that aspects of the later stages, at least for uncontroversial Bills, could be taken off the floor of the House. It also made some proposals concerning the management of business, and for the carry-over of a Bills from one session of Parliament to the next. The parliamentary session has always been the ultimate timetable for public Bills, and for some time it has been argued that where a non-controversial Bill has virtually completed its parliamentary stages, its loss upon prorogation represents a waste of time and effort.[60]

---

58 *Modernisation Committee*, paras 20, 32-33 and 93.
59 It would be based on the Notes on Clauses prepared by departmental civil servants for Ministers' use at Second Reading and the subsequent stages, Second Report from the Select Committee on the Modernisation of the House of Commons (1997-98; HC 389). In the House of Lords, see the Second Report from the Select Committee on Procedure of the House (1997-98, HL 38) and House of Lords Debates, Vol 583, cols 1485-1495 (4 December 1997). Notes on Clauses, which have not usually been made available to the public, were, in the case of the Scotland Bill, published on the Internet and sold through the Stationery Office; see R. Brazier, 'The Scotland Bill as Constitutional Legislation' (1998) 19 *Statute Law Rev* 12, 19.
60 *Modernisation Committee*, paras 15-16, 38-40, 50-51, 67-70, 94, 99 and 102. The proposal concerning carry over was agreed in the Lords later in 1997: Second Report from the Select Committee on Procedure of the House (1997-98; HL 38); House of Lords Debates, Vol 583, cols 1485-1495, op cit. See generally, Miers (1998), op cit.

Whereas Commons procedures routinely seek to take legislative business off the floor of the House, the Lords tradition has been to keep it there. There are no standing commitees, and while Bills have occasionally been committed to a public Bill committee, the Committee stage (along with all the other stages) of public Bills has always taken place on the floor of the House. Other differences are that the Lords do not use allocation of time orders, and that all amendments are debated. In addition, amendments may be made at Third Reading. The House has only recently introduced a number of changes increasing the options for the appointment of committees to examine public Bills. It is not yet possible yet to say whether these reforms' various purposes, which include improvement to the quality of legislation, are being realised. The new alternatives are by no means routinely used, and the evidence of their success in other areas is, to date, mixed.[61]

Put at its simplest, the legislative task, as conceived by the Hansard Society Report and others, is to create laws that are clear and accessible to those affected by them. The reforms to the way in which the Commons scrutinises public Bills stand in a long tradition of self-examination followed by exhortation that the House must do better. Where these reforms have been implemented (and the occasions are few enough), they have done so because their effect will coincide with the government's wish to 'get its business' as effectively as possible and with the opposition's wish to maximise its opportunity to test the government. In general, radical restructuring of the manner in which legislative business is conducted in the Commons, however rational, is less likely to appeal to what has traditionally been its conservative attitude to reform than incremental change that accepts political reality as a starting point.[62] In this respect the Modernisation Committee's proposals offer a much greater prospect of realisation than do the systemic changes proposed by the Hansard Society Report.

3.6   The intelligibility of legislation

Modern statutes are concerned primarily to determine the structure and powers of public authorities, the privatised utilities and executive agencies, and to a lesser extent to regulate the conduct of citizens and private organisations. The achievement of these objectives frequently involves a delegation of powers to those responsible for the statute's implementation, for example, to act 'reasonably' or as the body in question 'thinks fit'. This reliance upon discretionary power, which has become a prominent feature of government law-making over the past fifty years continues to provoke concern.[63] This concern is reflected in the substantial expansion by the courts

---

61 See the First Report from the Select Committee on Procedure of the House (1996-97, HL 20) and the Second Report from the Select Committee on Procedure of the House (1997-98, HL 38).

62 Recognition of these realities lies at the heart of the proposals made by the *Modernisation Committee*, paras 57 and 59.

63 C Harlow and R Rawlings, *Law and Adminstration* (2nd edn, 1997), pp 111ff; D Galligan, *Discretionary Powers* (1986).

of the scope of judicial review, which has in turn prompted civil servants to pay increased attention to the manner in which they reach their decisions.[64]

Whatever the extent of the discretion conferred by statutory rules, those which are addressed to civil servants or public bodies are frequently supplemented by a wide range of handbooks, circulars, pamphlets, codes of practice, directives and other documents mostly prepared by the responsible government department. Where the statute confers benefits or imposes liabilities upon citizens and private organisations, some of these documents may be made publicly available. Their function is to indicate how an Act's provisions are to be interpreted and implemented in particular cases - to give guidance on what is 'reasonable' or 'fit'. One example is the set of four statutory Codes of Practice elaborating the conditions under which the police shall exercise the powers conferred on them by the Police and Criminal Evidence Act 1984, which relies extensively on the use of the word 'reasonable' as a condition of their exercise.

A statutory rule both states the law and communicates it to those affected by it, and since no rule can foreclose all possibilities – not even one that is clearly and precisely drafted – the object is to reduce cases of doubtful application to a minimum. However, it is generally agreed that statutory rules are not always especially intelligible, and that in some instances they defy the efforts of even the most sympathetic interpreters to make sense of them. Thus, to the inevitable uncertainties of application generated by unforeseen cases, difficulties may arise because of the unintelligibility of the legislation. The criticisms that have been made in recent years are that there are too many statutes enacted in too much detail, that the traditional methods of amendment are unhelpful to the reader, and that they are drafted in a style that obscures rather than makes clear their meaning.

(a) 'Too much' and 'too detailed' legislation

Three issues are implicit in this complaint. The first is concerned with what should be the proper role of the state in the regulation of behaviour. At one extreme is the conception of a minimal state, one which is limited to the narrow functions of protection against force, theft and fraud, and the enforcement of contracts;[65] at the other is a state which actively seeks to promote the general welfare, for example, by requiring people to do things for their own (or others') good. Some who complain that there is too much legislation mean that the government is too ready to intervene or to meddle in people's affairs when their conduct should be a matter of individual choice, but the relationship between a government's political ideology and the rules which emanate from it is certainly not a simple one. As we saw in chapter 3, rule density is a familiar feature of our bureaucratic society,[66] and the quantity and complexity of government-inspired rules have been increasing irrespective of the ideological

---

64 *Council of Civil Service Unions v Minister for the Civil Service* [1985] AC 374, and chapter 1, section 11.5.
65 This is the conception argued by R Nozick in *Anarchy, State and Utopia* (1975).
66 See above, pp 142-143.

convictions of the governing party. The reasons for this are themselves complex. Put very simply, as the modern world becomes more complicated, so do its techniques of control, and bureaucracy itself conduces to the creation of rules. One of the primary purposes of many rules is to control the behaviour of officials by limiting the discretion they exercise, for example, in the conferral of benefits or the imposition of burdens upon the citizen. Moreover, while the particular content of rules affecting such matters as town and country planning and land use, housing, the renting of accommodation, immigration, weights and measures, food and drugs, education and so on may vary, there will, in a society such as ours, always be rules on these matters. Even where a Conservative government is committed to a policy of dismantling some of the state's apparatus through privatisation and deregulation, such activity still requires the enactment of rules. Indeed, it may be observed that some of the most substantial Acts of Parliament enacted in recent years have precisely been those that have privatised the former public utilities; for example, the Electricity Act 1989 (113 sections, 18 Schedules, 192 pages) and the Water Act 1989 (194 sections, 27 Schedules, 419 pages). It may be that under Nozick's minimal state, there would be 'less law' than exists under the kind of regime prevailing in the United Kingdom; but it should not be forgotten that one version of the Socialist utopia also postulated the withering away of law.

The second issue centres on the appropriateness of statutory intervention in particular contexts. In some instances it may be virtually impossible to devise specific legal provisions to give effect to more general rules or to policies; for example to control the objectionable aspects of cheque book journalism, to define and protect privacy, or to control what is available on the Internet.[67] On the other hand, it may be argued, for example, that existing statutory controls are adequate and simply require regular or systematic enforcement, or that an Act of Parliament is not suitable to the problem which may be better dealt with by the allocation of financial resources, changes in institutional practices, the introduction of voluntary codes of self-regulation, or other remedies. Whether a government is regarded as unduly interventionist in its use of statutory control is a complex question involving the critic's political ideology, value preferences and priorities. At one level, a government may legislate because it wishes to be seen to be 'doing something' in response to a loud public outcry about a particular matter,[68] while at another, the legislation may reflect its more deeply held view that the matter in question is, in terms of its own political philosophy, amenable to statutory control.

The third issue is primarily concerned with the amount of detail included in modern legislation. The argument here is that much of what is contained in the 2000 or so pages of primary legislation enacted annually would be better placed in secondary legislation, thus relieving Parliament of the pressure implicit in trying (unsuccessfully) to debate the whole Bill on the floor of

---

67 See the Report of the Committee on Privacy (Cmnd 5012, 1972), ch 4: 'What is Privacy?'; s 1(3)(c) of the Defamation Act 1996 dealing with innocent defamation published on the Internet.
68 See above, pp 117-118.

each House, in favour of concentrating on its main principles and the main strategies proposed to implement them. Allowing that detail is inevitable in some form, it is further argued that as matters stand, the obvious fact that governments seek to enact more statutes than the parliamentary session can comfortably accommodate means that the draftsman is placed under increasing pressure to meet the government's timetable, to the detriment of well crafted statutes.

It is already the case that governments enact 'framework' or 'skeleton' Bills, that is, Bills which state the basic parameters of the matter specified in the long title and provide for subordinate powers which 'are so important that the real operation of the legislation is entirely by the orders and regulations made under it'.[69] Two examples, to which reference was made earlier,[70] are the Jobseekers' Act 1995 and the Activity Centres (Young Persons' Safety) Act 1995. This latter short Act stemmed from a canoeing accident in Lyme Regis bay. It makes provision for the regulation and safety of activity centres used by people under 18 years of age:

> The Secretary of State is given power by order to designate a licensing authority for adventure centres, and power by regulations to set conditions as to who may hold licences, what requirements are placed on licence holders, what fees can be charged and how licences may be revoked or varied. Regulations may also create criminal offences concerned with licensed activities, though the Act itself provides for the maximum penalties. Without the order and the regulations, there would be no licensing regime for leisure centres, and the primary legislation would have been passed to no effect. It was therefore only when the 12 pages of secondary legislation were made, some nine months after the four-page Act was passed, that the licensing regime of activity centers was able to begin.[71]

A central issue for Bills of this kind concerns the opportunities for Parliament to scrutinise the all-important detail. Here, too, there are serious deficiencies. Though each can be subject to scrutiny, very few of the 1,500-2,000 statutory instruments made each year are. The procedural issues concerning the enactment of secondary legislation are themselves a substantial and difficult matter; it is sufficient to say that here, too, there has been constant dissatisfaction with the way in which Parliament deals with them, and equally little consensus as to the way forward.[72]

One suggestion that would certainly subject some instruments to parliamentary scrutiny (certainly those major instruments implementing framework Bills) is based on the experience of the deregulation procedure. Under section 1 of the Deregulation and Contracting Out Act 1994, Parliament may approve proposals to amend primary legislation by means of secondary legislation where the section to be amended or repealed imposes a burden on business which may be varied or removed without compromising any necessary protection for the consumer or others affected by that section. The procedures

69 P Silk, *The Assembly as a Legislature in the National Assembly Agenda* (1998), p 73.
70 Above, pp 228-229.
71 Silk, op cit, p 72.
72 See *Hansard Society Report*, paras 364-387 and the Report from the Procedure Committee, Delegated Legislation (1995-96, HC 152).

with which such proposals must comply are complex, but in essence require the sponsoring department to engage in mandatory consultation with affected groups prior to the presentation of its proposed deregulation order under section 1 of the Act. This must be accompanied by the department's assurances concerning the extent of consultation, and its analysis of the relevant cost and protection issues. The proposal is considered by committees of both the Commons and the Lords; in the latter case, the Select Committee on Deregulated Powers and Deregulation, a committee which pre-dated the 1994 Act, and in the former, the Deregulation Committee, established solely for this purpose.

The parliamentary consensus is that the experiment has been a success.[73] With its structured opportunity for the taking and consideration of evidence, regarded by the Hansard Society Report as the model for effective parliamentary scrutiny of Bills, the deregulation procedure offers a useful model for other contexts. Michael Ryle, a former Clerk of Committees in the House of Commons and the Hansard Society Report's secretary has asked:[74]

> If such improved consultation arrangements and improved parliamentary scrutiny can be introduced for deregulation orders, why cannot such practices be adopted, with adaptations, for other parts of the legislative process ... ?

What Ryle envisages is a shift in the balance of detail between primary and secondary legislation: Bills would in essence set the framework of the principles and main provisions of the policy for which legislative approval is sought; there would then be three levels of 'secondary' legislation. The first of these would deal with 'the more important provisions for the implementation of Acts' and:

> ... should be set out in major orders which should be prepared on the basis of consultation carried out on the same lines as for deregulation orders. These orders should also be subject to much the same procedures for parliamentary scrutiny and approval as have been agreed for deregulation orders, except that more than one Committee would clearly be needed and membership of the Committees would have to be made more subject-specialised, perhaps by the use of added members.[75]

The second, addressing less important details, would be subject to the existing affirmative and negative resolution procedure, while the third level of secondary legislation would embrace very minor or purely administrative details that could be dealt with by instruments not subject to parliamentary procedure.

Clearly, this is an ambitious agenda. So far as it recommends the *routine* use of framework Bills, all sides would have to be satisfied that the procedures set for their consideration permit adequate scrutiny of their principles and main provisions. By contrast, even the *occasional* use of framework Bills has been the subject of criticism.[76] One of the main complaints is precisely that when

---

73 See Miers (1999), op cit; Special Report from the Select Committee on Delegated Powers and Deregulation (1996-97, HL 72), Part 2, paras 36 and 39.

74 M Ryle, 'The Deregulation and Contracting Out Bill 1994 – A Blueprint for the Reform of the Legislative Process?' (1994) 15 *Statute Law Rev* 170, 179.

75 Ibid, p 180.

76 For example, the Criminal Injuries Compensation Act 1995, which imposes a statutory duty on the Secretary of State to establish a criminal injuries compensation scheme, but provides no guidance whatsoever about the scope of the scheme.

approved, such Bills say nothing of the law's content – as the example of the Activity Centres (Young Persons) Act 1995 demonstrates – and those with doubts can only be assured (if they are) that the government will act upon the commitments it gave when moving the Bill. These reservations might well be alleviated if it were the case that Members and peers knew that the main orders implementing the Act, and passed as secondary legislation, would be subject to a process of examination similar to that which applies to deregulation proposals. Accordingly, some cautionary notes should be sounded. The measures considered by the deregulation Committees are self-contained, discrete proposals which seldom generate wider policy issues; typically they address matters that are technical (though this is not to gainsay that consumers may need protection) and are sometimes of very limited compass. As Ryle indicates, any significant extension of this model to deal routinely with the major implementing orders (and who would judge these to be?) would require an equally significant extension in this new committee structure. If the detail were debated in committees based on the deregulation model, time would of course be saved in standing committee, but over their four-year life the two committees have reported on less than fifty deregulation proposals, a small fraction of the total of clauses dealt with at the Committee stage of public Bills.

(b) Methods of amendment

It is a rare occurrence if a Bill does not amend existing statutory provisions in some way, and some statutes are enacted for the specific purpose of amending the existing law.[77] Whichever is the case, it is clear that the method of amendment employed is of considerable importance to potential users.

Two main methods have been used in United Kingdom Acts, textual and non-textual amendment. Non-textual amendment takes the form of a narrative statement which seeks to explain the effect of the amendment on the original provision. For example, section 4(1) of the Civic Amenities Act 1967 provides:

> The power conferred by subsection (1) of section 4 of the Historic Buildings and Ancient Monuments Act 1953 to make grants for the purposes mentioned in that subsection shall include power to make loans for those purposes, and references to grants in subsections (3) and (4) of that section shall be construed accordingly.

The amendment is therefore indirect; it adds matters to the earlier legislation by a process of reference. Even a modest statute can become quite difficult to read as more and more referential amendments are made.[78] Textual amendment on the other hand directly amends the original provision by expressly providing for the addition, deletion or substitution of words or phrases. This permits the reader physically to correct his own text as directed,

---

77 For many years it has also been possible to amend Acts of Parliament by means of secondary legislation, where the Act itself contains what is colloquially known as a 'Henry VIII clause'. The use of this device has not always been viewed favourably. By comparison, the amendment or repeal of primary legislation by deregulation orders made under s 1 of the Deregulation and Contracting Out Act 1994 has received widespread approval; see Miers (1999), op cit.
78 The example is used by G Thornton QC, *Legislative Drafting* (3rd edn, 1987), p 338 to illustrate his criticism of referential amendment.

and is ideally suited to the requirements of information technology. An important difference between the two is that with the non-textual method it is possible for someone reading the amendment to obtain a rough idea of its effect on the original provision without actually referring to it; whereas with textual amendment, the clause is meaningless without simultaneous reference to the provision it is amending; all that the amending section does is to say that some new words are being added to or taken away from the original, but without any further reference to what is being altered.[79]

The non-textual method was the subject of considerable criticism by statute law users, and by some draftsmen.[80] The Renton Committee recommended that textual amendment should be used wherever possible,[81] and it is now accepted as the usual practice.[82] Some obstacles remain. Those statutes which have already been amended non-textually are not suitable for the textual method, and in some instances the textual method would greatly increase the length of Bills. Thirdly, although the textual method enables the user to make the appropriate changes on a copy of the amended Act so as to achieve an authoritative statement of the law in one place, such direct substitution can be laborious and, where the affected Act is heavily amended, physically impossible to achieve on the printed page. One statutory device that accomplishes this task is the Keeling Schedule, which restates the statutory text in its amended form as a Schedule to the amending Act.[83]

(c)   The complexity of statutory rules: drafting style

United Kingdom statutes have traditionally been very detailed in their formulation of the factual circumstances to which they apply and of the legal consequences which those circumstances attract. One consequence of this drafting style is the enactment of statutory rules which are so complicated that they can only with the greatest difficulty (if at all) be understood by those implementing them.[84] But where, because of its complexity, a user who is familiar with the subject-matter of a provision cannot, after a reasonable

---

79 See, for example, s 8 of the Knives Act 1997. The reason why the non-textual method was adopted in this country was because Sir Henry Thring, the first holder of the position of First Parliamentary Counsel to the Treasury in 1869, saw it as the draftsman's duty, when preparing amending clauses, to provide MPs with a draft which allowed them to get an idea of the legal effect of the amendment for the purpose of debate, without having to look up the original provision. This was called the 'four corners doctrine'. As this method became entrenched, so further amendment of a previously amended provision had to be effected in the same way.

80 'The traditional United Kingdom style, therefore, produced a pottage comprising direct amendments, indirect amendments and provisions incorporating both techniques. The effect at least to one not nurtured from his early years on English statutes, is confusing, particularly so as it rests on a stream of invidious but inevitably inconsistent decisions as to which amendments should properly be effected by one method, which by the other, and which by both.' Thornton, op cit, p 339.

81 *Renton*, recommendation 41. For an example, see s 3 of the Domestic Violence and Matrimonial Proceedings Act 1976; above, p 89.

82 F Bennion, op cit, p 211.

83 An example is Schedule 2 to the Criminal Evidence (Amendment) Act 1997.

84 See the comments of the Court of Appeal in the two cases concerning the interpretation of s 67 of the Criminal Justice Act 1967; chapter 1, section 6.2.

expenditure of intellectual effort and within a reasonable time, make sense of it in relation to a given set of circumstances, it is appropriate to inquire whether it could not have been more clearly drafted.

In recent years the debate about drafting style has focused on the advantages of a 'plain English' approach.[85] This is an important debate which has attracted considerable attention. While its central thesis commands widespread support, draftsmen in English-speaking jurisdictions have embraced its implications for their practice with varying degrees of enthusiasm; the reservations are least in New Zealand and Australia.[86] As in other contexts in which what appear to be self-evidently desirable practices are ranged against those that have traditionally been the object of criticism,[87] it is easy to over-simplify the issues. It is tempting, but misleading, to assume that the primary legislative audience is the general public, or at least, that sector to whom it most closely relates – employees, pensioners, consumers of financial services, landowners, publicans, the holders of driving licences and so on. The draftsman does not set out to draft Bills so that those affected cannot understand them; to the contrary, if they can, so much the better. But as we have seen, Bills have a variety of audiences, and it would be unusual for the linguistic interests of the general public to take priority over those of the officials or others responsible for their implementation. What is for a group of civil servants an entirely satisfactory exercise in plain English may indeed be found wanting by those affected by their decisions; but the lessons to be derived from this conclusion do not necessarily include rewriting the Act so that those affected can understand it. The main lessons are that 'plain English' is context dependent; secondly, that the primary function of an Act is to state the law as precisely as its sponsors wished and only secondarily to make that statement as intelligible as possible to its various audiences; and thirdly, that if it is apt to provide the general public with such assistance as will enable them to understand the Acts that apply to them, there are likely to be many more effective methods than the limited opportunities provided by the confines of the statute.[88]

Care should also be taken not to polarise the claimed virtues of different drafting styles: on the one hand those associated with the traditional style – legal accuracy and certainty – and on the other, those of a plain English

---

85 The plain English movement has been carried forward by such groups as the Plain English Campaign and the Plain Language Commission. On the former, see Appendix I, section F, question 5, pp 400-402. On the latter, see M Cutts, *Lucid Law* (1994), *Plain English Guide* (1995). The campaign also extends to the language of insurance policies, tenancy agreements and other private legal documents.

86 See New Zealand Law Commission, The Format of Legislation (1993, NZLC R27); the Law Reform Commission of Victoria, *Plain English and the Law* (1987, Report No 9); I Turnbull QC, 'Clear Legislative Drafting: New Approaches in Australia' (1990) 11 *Statute Law Review* 161.

87 For example, where literalism is presented as inevitably less intellectually respectable an approach to interpretation than liberalism; Chapter 4, section 5.

88 For example, the explanatory leaflets and other notes routinely provided by the body implementing the statute, which may use flow charts or other diagrammatic presentations to assist the reader to the outcome relevant in her case; see chapter 1, section 6.3 and Appendix II. See also F Bennion, 'If It's Not Broke Don't Fix It: A Review of the New Zealand Law Commission's Proposals on the Format of Legislation' (1994) 15 *Statute Law Review* 164. An everyday example of such explanatory material is the Highway Code (chapter 1, section 6.3).

approach – clarity and simplicity. Each of these dimensions is itself a continuum, as a leading Commonwealth draftsman and advocate of a plain language approach to drafting has observed:

> If we regard only the readability of the language used (and not the legal effect), these styles are segments of a continuous spectrum of readability. At one end of the spectrum is the worst form of the traditional style, with long, convoluted sentences, long words and archaic legal expressions. In the middle is plain language, with shorter sentences and more familiar words, and at the other end is general principles drafting, with very simple sentences and very little detail. These styles can be given distinctive names because each is recognisable in its typical form; but in practice they can merge into one another, and a law may fall anywhere within this spectrum.
>
> On the other hand, if we regard the legal effect of these styles, the precision (also called 'certainty'), also differs, but not in strict relationship to the position on the spectrum of readability. For some distance along the spectrum, the traditional and plain language styles are equally precise. Further along the spectrum, plain language drafting becomes less precise if simplicity is over-emphasised. Finally, general principles drafting is the least precise, in the sense that it speaks only in general terms.[89]

In short, there is nothing inherent in the traditional style that necessitates a use of language which hinders rather than helps understanding; it is often possible to state propositions of law both precisely and simply. The task for the draftsman is, so far as his instructions and the existing state of the law permit, to find that point on the spectrum where 'the traditional and the plain language styles are equally precise'. Difficulties arise where the concepts on which the law is based are particularly complex, or additional detail should be included to avoid ambiguity. Where the goals of precision and simplicity conflict, precision must be given priority. This follows from the draftsman's primary duty, which is to give legal effect to the policy being advanced by the government (or other sponsor). The relationship between precision (certainty, legal accuracy) and readability (simplicity, clarity) can be presented diagrammatically:

Readability

		Achieved	Not achieved[90]
Precision	Achieved	1	2
	Not achieved	3	4

Recognising that both precision and readability are matters of degree, of these possible outcomes, cell 1 is the ideal state, cell 4 a total failure. The conflict between precision and readability is captured in cell 2 (precise, readable only

89 I Turnbull QC (formerly First Parliamentary Counsel, Commonwealth of Australia), 'Plain Language and General Principle' (1998) 18 *Statute Law Review* 21.
90 This is not to be taken literally, in the sense of 'unreadable'. If the text were so it would be impossible simultaneously to say whether it displayed any degree of precision.

with difficulty), while cell 3 represents a dangerous failure: that a provision may be readable but imprecise. 'If [the draftsmen] write a statute that is rapidly comprehensible and does not fulfil the [legislator's] intent, they have failed. In fact, the rapid comprehension, by lulling readers into believing that the statute is properly drafted and inducing them not to spend much time analysing it, may delay the discovery of the failure until it is too late to remedy it.'[91] The dangerous failure has been the object of some attention, as exponents of the plain English school have sought to redraft particular Acts or individual sections, while draftsmen have responded by pointing to the errors thereby committed: 'there is a price to pay for ... clarification. It consists in sacrificing the policy, or certainty or aptness to simplicity of expression.'[92] What this demonstrates is not the failure of a plain language approach, but a failure on the part of the person undertaking the re-drafting. 'In the hands of experienced legislative drafters, plain language can be sufficiently precise, although it might not always be quite as plain as some enthusiasts would like.'[93]

With its emphasis on the interests of the reader, the plain English debate also offers opportunities to move beyond the anecdotal nature of the case against the traditional approach. This often amounts to a simple catalogue of individual difficulties which users have encountered when reading, applying, using or referring to the legislation in question.[94] Even where these difficulties genuinely flowed from complexities inherent in the statute itself, rather than from an external context, they do not serve to give a systematic account of the prevalence of drafting deficiencies. We have no way of knowing, nor has any attempt been made to analyse, what proportion of the statute book might be judged stylistically deficient.[95] More promising are the variety of 'usability' tests which sample typical users' experience with the legislation with which they are familiar.[96] These provide focused responses which can be used both to identify the cause of particular interpretational difficulties, and to suggest appropriate remedies. For example, the introduction of a variety of section headings was found in a local empirical study to save time and to increase the accuracy of the users' understanding of the legislation.[97]

Before examining further the practical response of the government and of Parliamentary Counsel to this debate, it is useful to consider briefly the historical context within which the traditional style of drafting developed. Long before the Parliamentary Counsel Office was created in 1869, a detailed drafting style had become established in the eighteenth and early nineteenth centuries.

---

91 J Stark, 'Should the Main Goal of Statutory Drafting be Accuracy or Clarity?' (1994) 15 *Statute Law Rev* 207, 209.
92 E Sutherland, 'Clearer Drafting and the Timeshare Act 1992: A Response from Parliamentary Counsel to Mr Cutts' (1993) 14 *Statute Law Review* 163, 170. This article was written in response to the alternative version set out in M Cutts, *Unspeakable Acts: the Language and Typography of an Act of Parliament* (Words at Work, 1993). Cutts' own response was published as 'Plain English in the Law' (1996) 17 *Statute Law Review* 50.
93 Turnbull (1997), op cit, p 26.
94 For examples of these complaints see Miers (1994), op cit, p 425.
95 D Miers, 'Legislation, Linguistic Adequacy and Public Policy' [1986] *Statute Law Review* 90; J Stark, 'Reader Expectation Theory and Legislative Drafting' (1996) 17 *Statute Law Review* 210.
96 See Appendix 1, section F, question 5, p 401; Cutts (1996), op cit.
97 G Stewart, 'Drafting and the Marginal Note' (1995) 16 *Statute Law Review* 21, 49ff.

One reason for this was that the draftsmen were usually Chancery practitioners who simply adopted the detailed style commonly used for drafting private legal texts. Also significant was the judiciary's response to the increasing use of legislation by nineteenth century governments to effect social change. Because statutes were seen as an addition to the common law, the courts took the view that they should be interpreted strictly, with each word being given effect. If a set of circumstances did not fall squarely within the words of a section, it was held not to apply to them. Draftsmen came to anticipate this reaction, and assumed a drafting style which sought to ensure that the courts took account of every situation contemplated by the policy. This style involved very detailed specification of the factual circumstances and their legal consequences. While at common law there was authority permitting free expression in drafting, with the result that there was an absence of common form in textual expression, ever since legislative drafting became the responsibility of lawyers specifically appointed to the task, draftsmen have sought to identify good drafting technique and to recommend, though not prescribe, standard practice. One of the earliest of these was George Coode, who in 1843 notably formulated the following conception of the legislative sentence:

> ... the expression of every law essentially consists of, first, the description of the legal Subject; secondly, the enunciation of the legal Action. To these, when the law is not of universal application, are to be added, thirdly, the description of the Case to which the legal action is confined; and, fourthly, the Conditions on performance of which the legal action operates.[98]

This articulation of the protasis and apodosis of a legal rule,[99] which may further be analysed into discrete statements of the classes of persons, things and events to which the rule applies, arose from the perceived need to ensure the completeness of any legislative act. Its 'excessive individuality' was one of the prime complaints made of statutes during the nineteenth century, but when the Parliamentary Counsel Office was established, among other reasons, with a view to improving the standard of drafting, the result was that this style became institutionalised in what became known as 'the Thring technique': 'the single-sentence subsection festooned with exceptions, conditions and provisos'.[1] The judiciary's reaction was to develop further the presumption against statutory changes in the common law and to interpret statutes in a very pedantic way.[2] Nowadays they are as likely to be critical of the constant

---

98 G Coode, 'On Legislative Expression' (reproduced in E Driedger, *The Composition of Legislation: Legislative Forms and Precedents* (2nd edn, 1976), Appendix A). For modern analysis see S Fung and A Watson-Brown, 'Traditional Drafting in Common Law Jurisdictions' (1995) 16 *Statute Law Rev* 167; J Stark, 'Legislative Sentences' (1995) 16 *Statute Law Review* 187; A Watson-Brown, 'The Classification and Arrangement of the Elements of Legislation' (1997) 18 *Statute Law Rev* 32.

99 Above, p 132.

1   Kent, op cit, p 106.

2   This reaction has been explained in terms of the judiciary's earlier 'predilection for common law doctrines' and a consequent hostility to statutes as a source of law; Law Commission, *The Interpretation of Statutes*, op cit, para 10. Not surprisingly, governmental reaction to the resulting interpretation included both frustration that its policies had been rendered ineffective, and distrust of the judiciary's motives, in particular where public law and taxation

addition of new legislation coupled with the government's failure to modernise the statute book as they are to blame the traditional drafting style for the interpretational difficulties that they encounter.[3]

One of the primary recommendations of the Renton Report was that 'in principle the interests of the ultimate users should always have priority over those of the legislators'.[4] When made, this constituted a significant departure from the customary view of the relationship between the draftsman and the user. Attractive as it sounds, it disguises the point that a statute typically has a number of users whose level of comprehension of its legal effects will vary considerably, and thus the draftsman has to exercise a choice as to the level of comprehension at which to aim. Some years ago Sir William Dale suggested that Acts of Parliament should confine themselves to broad and simple statements of principle, leaving the elaboration of the details of policy to the courts. He argued that United Kingdom legislation would be greatly improved by the adoption of such a system, which is commonly associated with the drafting styles to be found in the civil law tradition.[5] This suggestion is also attractive, but it is too simple. Firstly, not all civil law drafting employs general principles unsupported by detailed provisions,[6] and the European Council's 1993 resolution for drafting clear Community legislation suggests that the

were involved. See R Stevens, *Law and Politics* (1979), discussing the interpretation of taxing statutes by the House of Lords in *IRC v Duke of Westminster* [1936] AC 1: 'The actual conscious or subconscious motives of the Law Lords in the *Westminster* case provided a fertile field for speculation, but its effects were clear. The case finally gave the balance of advantage to those with resources sufficient to hire the best legal talent, who might then camouflage the substance of their transaction under some formal disguise. It did not, of course, mean that the taxpayer always won in litigation. It did, however, signal that tax litigation had become an arid, semantic (and often antisocial) vicious circle, and frequently the result of this was a windfall for the taxpayer. Worse still, the attitude that led the judges to examine form rather than substance proved remarkably difficult to undo even when the legislature did intervene' (pp 207-208). A radically different approach to tax avoidance is to be found in cases decided by the House of Lords during the 1980s and 1990s: *Ramsay v IRC* [1982] AC 300; *Furniss v Dawson* [1984] AC 474; *Craven v White* [1989] AC 398; *IRC v McGuckian* [1997] 3 All ER 817; see below, p 286.

3 See for example, Lord Bridge in a debate on the English language, 416 HL Debates, cols 777-778 (28 January 1981) and Lord Bingham LCJ's comments in *R v Governor of Brockhill Prison, ex p Evans*, discussed in ch 1, section 6.2.

4 *Renton*, recommendations 8 and 19.

5 Sir W Dale, *Legislative Drafting: A New Approach* (1977), pp 6-7. By way of example, Dale compared extracts from copyright laws then in force in Great Britain, France and West Germany. He argued that the differences in style meant that the West German and French versions gave a 'perhaps general, but firm and intelligible, statement of what copyright is [and] the nature and extent of the right'; whereas the British statute was 'so weakened by qualifications and conditions, so diluted by the introduction of extraneous and particular matters' that its provisions were 'neither brief, nor general, nor firm, not even intelligible'. The Copyright Act 1956 was repealed and replaced by the Copyright, Designs and Patents Act 1988.

6 For example, French law displays the same characteristics as are complained of in this country – lack of codification, complexity and an absence of express repeals; F Bennion, 'How They Do Things in France' (1995) 16 *Statute Law Rev* 90; J Bell and G Engle QC, *Cross on Statutory Interpretation* (3rd edn, 1997), p 302. See generally U Karpen (ed), *Legislation in European Countries* (1996).

'European' style was itself in need of reform.[7] Secondly, there are limitations on the value of comparisons of this kind. Styles of drafting depend upon the historic and prevailing conceptions of the role of and the relationship between the constituent elements of the state, in particular those of the legislature and the judiciary, and the ways in which these roles and relationships are institutionalised and regulated. It is also unrealistic to expect the draftsmen to engage in radical change in the absence of government approval. The bulk of modern legislation concerns the powers of officials and of regulatory bodies, for whose exercise the government requires certainty of definition and scope, preferably without constant recourse to the courts by way of judicial review.[8] This demand is shared by the judiciary who, by virtue of the Human Rights Act 1998, may be required to consider the certainty and the clarity with which the relationship between the state and the individual is in particular cases expressed. In their wish for commercial, fiscal and regulatory certainty, statute law users, too, can be equally conservative.[9]

Two associated recommendations made by the Renton Report which would in a particular way give effect to the spirit of Dale's suggestion, were that statutes should contain 'statements of principle' and, 'when they are the most convenient method of clarifying the scope and effect of legislation', statements of purpose.[10] Proponents argue that such statements will assist the interpreter either by making the Act's objectives clearer or by giving clear guidance as to the manner in which it should be interpreted. Section 1 of the Family Law Act 1996 is an example of a statement of principle;[11] section 1(1) of the Children Act 1989: 'when a court determines any question with respect to the upbringing of a child ... the child's welfare shall be the court's paramount consideration', Lord Renton's example of a statement of purpose.[12]

Such statements may, in particular cases, assist the interpreter. But there are dangers. 'If the statement has legal effect and covers the same ground as later detailed provisions, there is a risk of real or apparent inconsistency. If the statement is not intended to have legal effect, the courts may give it some effect

---

7   See Wainwright (1996), op cit, p 17. J O'Reilly 'Coping with Community Legislation – a Practitioner's Reaction' (1996) 17 *Statute Law Review* 15, 17: 'Very often the legislation itself is so diffuse and dense that it takes a considerable effort to understand it. Often it is a question of fully comprehending the commercial or agricultural concept concerned and trying to understand its application. A good example of the change that has occurred is in agriculture. The complications surrounding dairy farming are now not unlike tax planning.' The Council's guidelines are set out below, pp 252-253.

8   'Most people think that it is more important for legislation to be precise and for Parliament rather than the courts to have the last word, so to speak.' Lord McIntosh of Haringey answering for the government on a question concerning the use of purpose clauses; House of Lords Debates, Vol 583, col 87 (11 November 1997).

9   J Smith, 'Legislative Drafting: English and Continental' [1980] *Statute Law Review* 14, 22; *Hansard Society Report*, op cit, para 219.

10 Renton, recommendations 13 and 15.

11 Chapter 1, section 10.2.

12 It is not immediately apparent how this section, which requires a particular approach to the interpretation of the Act, can be distinguished from a statement of principle. Clearer examples are s 1 of the Legal Aid Act 1988, s 1 of the Arbitration Act 1996 and s 28 of the Crime and Disorder Act 1998.

with unintended results.'[13] Nor does it follow that the court will be able to achieve the statutory objective. The Matrimonial Proceedings and Property Act 1970 specified in section 5 the judge's purpose in matrimonial proceedings. This was to 'place the parties, so far as it is practicable and, having regard to their conduct, so far as it was just to do so, in the financial position in which they would have been if the marriage had not broken down and each had properly discharged his or her financial obligations and responsibilities towards the other'. In practice this became impossible to achieve and was deleted by the Matrimonial and Family Proceedings Act 1984. Here, 'Parliament deliberately declined to define any alternative statutory objective'.[14] For these reasons the Hansard Society Report reached the pragmatic conclusion that where they can be helpful, purpose clauses could be used, but that they should not be adopted as a general practice. This, too, is the conclusion that has been reached by successive governments.[15]

There is, on the other hand, clear evidence that Parliamentary Counsel are increasingly employing a more accessible drafting style; as in other areas of British political life, radicalism generally proceeds incrementally.[16] The Arbitration Act 1996, for example, is widely regarded as a model of clarity, both in language and in layout.[17] Likewise the Children Act 1989, whose enactment was prefaced by extensive and intensive consultation between all those involved in child welfare.[18] Other Acts display many of the features commonly associated with clear writing: short sentences; where appropriate, colloquial, rather than technical language; and self-contained sections dealing with a particular matter without cross-referencing to other sections. One of the best examples of this accessibility is the Human Rights Act 1998, which is written in a style that is surely intended to make it as easy as possible for the lay user to understand.[19] In these particular respects, Parliamentary Counsel would have little difficulty in recognising the general value of the European Council's drafting guidelines (allowing for differences between the two systems) as a statement of good drafting practice:[20]

- the wording of the Act should be clear, simple, concise and unambiguous; unnecessary abbreviations, 'community jargon' and excessively long sentences should be avoided;
- imprecise references to other texts should be avoided as should too many cross-references which make the text difficult to understand;

---

13 Lord McIntosh of Haringey, op cit, col 88. For an example of the point concerning inconsistency, see *Page v Lowther* [1983] STC 799; F Bennion, *Statutory Interpretation*, op cit, p 564.
14 *White v White* [1998] 4 All ER 659, 666, per Thorpe LJ.
15 *Hansard Society Report*, pp 223-224; Lord McIntosh, op cit. Twenty years ago the government was saying the same; Vol 412 HL Debates, col 1588 (7 August 1980).
16 Of the Renton Report's recommendations, about half are regularly implemented; Lord Renton, House of Lords Debates, Vol 584, col 1584 (21 January 1998).
17 A Samuels, 'How To Do It Properly: the Arbitration Act 1996' (1997) 18 *Statute Law Rev* 58. For a critical analysis of the layout of the Scotland Act 1998 see R Brazier, op cit, p 19.
18 Dame Margaret Justice Booth, 'The Children Act 1989 – the Proof of the Pudding' (1995) 16 *Statute Law Rev* 13.
19 For example, using the word 'must' rather than 'shall' to denote an obligation; and, in a break with tradition, this and the Government of Wales Act 1998 contain sentences which begin with the word 'But'.
20 Resolution (OJ 1993 C166/1).

- the various provisions of the Acts should be consistent with each other; the same term should be used throughout to express a given concept;
- the rights and obligations of those to whom the Act is to apply should be clearly defined;
- the Act should be laid out according to the standard structure; (chapters, sections, articles, paragraphs);
- the preamble should justify the enacting provisions in simple terms;
- provisions without legislative character should be avoided (eg wishes, political statements);
- inconsistency with existing legislation should be avoided as should pointless repetition of existing provisions. Any amendment, extension or repeal of an act should be clearly set out;
- an Act amending an earlier Act should not contain autonomous substantive provisions but only provisions to be directly incorporated into the Act to be amended;
- the date of entry into force of the Act and any transitional provisions which might be necessary should be clearly stated.

The ambitious Tax Law Rewrite also holds out the prospect of more 'user-friendly' drafting techniques. The immediate origins of this project stem from 1995, when the then Chancellor of the Exchequer instructed the Inland Revenue to examine the feasibility of tax simplification. The subsequent reports stressed the need both for a high degree of user involvement in the project, and for the adoption of a clearer and more comprehensible drafting style.[21] One of the ways in which this could be accomplished is the *selective* use of general principles provisions. Parliamentary draftsmen are not about to abandon their existing practices wholesale in favour of an untested and, arguably, untestable preference for drafting solely in terms of general principles, as advocated by Dale and others, but may be persuaded of their usefulness as one drafting technique to be used when apt. Commending their use, Turnbull was keen to avoid the dogmatism that alienates the pragmatic draftsman:[22] 'the question is not simply whether a Bill should be a "general principles" Bill or not. A Bill may contain as many, or as few, general principles provisions as the policy-makers decide.'[23] In this respect Turnbull's advice reflects the permissiveness to be found in the preface to the first edition of one of the leading works on drafting.[24]

21 Useful summaries are D Slater, 'Towards a Parliamentary Procedure for the Tax Law Rewrite' (1998) 19 *Statute Law Rev* 65; J Dyson, 'Interpreting Tax Statutes' in M Freeman (ed), *Legislation and the Courts* (1997), p 45. See www.open.gov.uk/inrev/rewrite.htm

22 See Engle (1983), op cit.

23 Turnbull (1997), op cit, p 30.

24 'This text aims to serve as a guide, but most certainly does not claim to set forth dogmatically those practices which are right and condemn contrary practices as wrong. There is usually no clear cut right and wrong way to deal with a particular problem, though there may be ways that are clearly wrong', Thornton, op cit, p viii.

3.7 Rationalising the statute book

The term 'statute book' refers to the surviving body of enacted legislation published by authority, not in a single volume but in a number of publications which even the most experienced professional can find difficult to handle. The most important developments in recent years have been the application of information technology to the retrieval of statutory material coupled with the publication of statutes and statutory instruments on the Internet.[25] Less well established in this context are expert systems. These are computer programs which have been constructed 'in such a way that they are capable of functioning at the standard of (and sometimes even at a higher standard than) experts in given fields.'[26] They are an application of computer technology to artificial intelligence systems, in legal contexts designed to facilitate problem-solving and reasoning with rules. They generally exhibit three characteristics: they display to the user the lines of reasoning that lead to particular conclusions, they rely on the kinds of knowledge and opinion that their (expert) users would be likely to employ, and they are flexible, allowing modifications to their databases to be made without great difficulty. While expert systems in law are in their infancy, they offer considerable promise to parliamentary draftsmen, who already have routine access to developments in IT applications. They can be used diagnostically, to elicit specific solutions to problems, or conversely, for planning purposes: the system can be presented with a preferred solution and asked to identify the legal steps required to achieve it. Thirdly, they can be used as a guide through especially complex legal procedures, such as, for example, can be encountered in tax law. Last, and by no means least, they can be used to assist in drafting both individual provisions and whole Bills.

For the user of legislation, the retrieval of relevant provisions can be a relatively straightforward task. This consists, firstly, in identifying and locating the relevant primary legislation, and secondly, in checking whether any secondary legislation has been made under the powers conferred by the Act. This legislation typically takes the form of one or more statutory instruments.[27] They are as much a part of the law as their parent Act, and any user of statute law must be familiar with their publication and indexing arrangements. Indeed, they will, for a number of reasons, become more important. Firstly, as 'remedial orders', they are the means by which primary legislation may be amended in compelling cases for the purpose of ensuring its conformity to the European Convention on Human Rights.[28] Secondly, they will routinely be used by the

25 From 1996 and 1997 respectively. See www.hmso.gov.uk/acts.htm. Parliamentary debates and the progress of Bills can also be followed. Commercially available CD-ROM applications permit the user to assemble in one place statutory provisions on a particular area. On Community law, see www.europa.eu.int/eur-lex. It is also possible to access via the Internet statutes enacted in other jurisdictions; see Editorial, 'Surfing the Statutes' (1998) 19 *Statute Law Review* v.
26 R Susskind, *The Future of Law* (1996). An example of their application is P Capper and R Susskind, *Latent Damage Law – The Expert System* (1988).
27 There are other forms of secondary legislation; see F Bennion, *Statutory Interpretation*, op cit, pp 192-197.
28 Above, section 2.2.

Welsh Assembly, the Scottish Parliament and the Northern Ireland Assembly. They will, finally, become the vehicle for what would otherwise have been contained in primary legislation if the government should extend the scope of the deregulation procedure or find that framework Bills offer increasingly effective opportunities to legislate.

It is not our objective to describe the best ways of completing the task of locating the statutory law relevant to the reader's purposes.[29] There are, however, some general points we wish to make relating to its completion and to wider issues associated with the classifications used by publishing systems.

Firstly, there are many enactments dealing with some subject areas, for example taxation, road traffic, criminal law and procedure, public health and housing. Finding one's way around the statute book in areas such as these can be a time-consuming and frustrating experience. This may be aggravated by the fact that the relevant legislation on any particular topic is to be found scattered among a number of different statutes, often having nothing in common with one another or with the topic. A primary reason for this is that statutes in this country have never been systematically classified and enacted as part of a comprehensive scheme dealing with each subject area. The standard classification followed in the official annual volumes, *Public General Acts and Measures*, is chronological, that is, based upon the order in which statutes receive the Royal Assent.

There are alternatives which employ subject based systems: *Statutes in Force, Halsbury's Statutes* and *Halsbury's Laws*.[30] Of these, *Statutes in Force* is an official publication launched in 1972. Legislation which is considered to belong to a common category is assembled under a single title, such as agency, agriculture, ancient monuments and memorials, animals, etc, and within each title it is further arranged chronologically. The advantage of this system for the user is that she knows that all provisions relating to a given matter, such as theft or divorce, will be found under one heading. The disadvantage for the draftsman and the legislature is that it will result in a large number of statutes, as amendments have to be separately enacted where they concern separate

---

29 See generally P Clinch, *Using a Law Library* (1992). See Appendix IV, pp 439-440.
30 Some Commonwealth countries to whom the traditional British method of preparing Bills was exported during the nineteenth century maintain statute books which are very much easier to use than our own. One of their key features is the publication every ten years or so (or possibly more frequently in the case of statutes subject to constant amendment) of a set of revised statutes which incorporate all amendments into one authoritative statement of the law contained in a single statute for each subject. This means that the user often only has to refer to the most recent edition of statutes revised, and only look in one place for the governing legislation on any one subject; any amendments to the provisions with which he is concerned should not be more than ten years old. The ability to produce such regular series of revised statutes (available also on CD-ROM and the Internet) in such countries as Canada, Australia, New Zealand and in many American state jurisdictions is based upon a number of considerations which do not obtain in this country, apart from being less affected by entrenched attitudes and inertia: a smaller quantity of legislation, due in part to a shorter legal history and, in some cases, a separation of responsibility for legislation between state and federal government; the use of textual methods of amendments; and, for the most part, the adoption of the principle of one subject, one Act. For Australia, see www.austlii.edu.au

subjects. An initial difficulty which also had to be tackled by the editors of *Statutes in Force* lies in the choice of categories which are to be used as the basis for organisation. Although there are many well-established legal categories, they are neither uncontroversial nor immutable. Individual statutory provisions do not present themselves as members of readily defined groupings, and there may be genuine disagreement as to the appropriateness of choosing one category in preference to another. Thus the categories currently employed by the three main subject-based indexing systems vary both in total number (*Statutes in Force* 131, *Halsbury's Statutes* 140 and *Halsbury's Laws* 166) and in the criteria upon which their individual subject groupings are based. These include abstract legal categories (eg tort), the control of public services (eg gas) and activities (eg town and country planning), the control of private services (eg carriers) and activities (eg factories), and institutional arrangements (eg local government). Arguably unsatisfactory, these variations may simply reflect the absence of any one classificatory basis to English law.[31]

Designed as a self-renewing, self-expanding and permanent edition, it took a decade to publish all the titles in *Statutes in Force*. When the project was conceived it was the most ambitious move for many years to improve the organisation of the statute book, but with advances in information technology it is already technically dated and in arrears. It relies for its currency, and thus for its authority, on the regular publication of Cumulative Supplements, but it has suffered from two connected limitations. The first is the lapse of time between the date of publication (the cover date) and the date on which it becomes available to libraries (the receipt date). This is a measure of delay between the compilation and the issue of authoritative information. The second is the lapse of time between the cover date and the time when the Supplement is consulted (the present time). This is a measure of decay in the authority of the information contained in that Supplement. The former is a fixed unit of time, the latter increases daily until a new Supplement is published. In a survey conducted in 1994, Clinch found the median period of delay to be 9.5 months, and that of decay, 26 months.[32] It is likely that *Statutes in Force* will in due course be superseded by the Statute Law Database, currently being developed by the Lord Chancellor's Department.

In the absence of a comprehensive statutory code agreed upon by the government to which all new enactments can be systematically assimilated, the primary technique adopted in this country to meet the complaint that statutes are scattered, is consolidation. A consolidating statute is one that re-enacts in one place a number of provisions, previously to be found in a number of statutes, which relate to one subject. Responsibility for preparing consolidation programmes in England has since 1965 been the statutory duty of the Law Commission. In Scotland, the Scottish Law Commission and the Lord Advocate's department have been jointly responsible for the preparation of Consolidation Bills. In its 1997 Report, the Law Commission described its responsibilities for consolidation as follows:

31 F Lawson, 'Analysing a Legal System', [1982] *Juridical Review* 161; J Jolowicz (ed), *Division and Classification of Law* (1969).
32 P Clinch, 'Statutes Probably Not in Force' (1994) 15 *Statute Law Rev* 64.

The need for [consolidation] arises if over a period of time several statutes are enacted on the same subject, making it difficult to find out what the law is. The process of consolidation involves different enactments on the same subject being drawn together to form a rational structure in a single statute. This makes the law more comprehensible, both to those who apply it and to those affected by it. If anomalies are revealed in the process of consolidation, various devices (such as amendments recommended by the Law Commission) are available to rectify them. But, if a change needed to rectify an anomaly is of such a nature that it ought to be made by Parliament in the normal way, a paving Bill is required or else the anomaly is reproduced. The process of consolidation requires the support and participation of the Government department within whose responsibility the subject matter falls.[33]

The record of the English Law Commission is impressive, but a number of factors inhibit the speed at which consolidation can proceed. Firstly, there is a limited number of draftsmen available for secondment to the Law Commission to prepare Consolidation Bills. Secondly, as the quotation above indicates, consolidation is not always a simple matter of taking sections from existing statutes and re-enacting them verbatim in one Bill. Where the sections have been amended according to the non-textual method, work must initially be done to establish the precise effect of such amendments. It may be, as with the current work on the consolidation of the sentencing powers of the courts, that the law is both unusually difficult and complex.[34] Unravelling the law requires the assistance of the lead department, but as a Chairman of the Law Commission noted, 'one of the major stumbling blocks often turns out to be the decision by the department to devote its resources to something else'.[35] Where amending legislation is required prior to the consolidation, the Commission will require the government's agreement to include a paving Bill in the legislative programme, or to effect the amendments in one of the agreed programme Bills. Although such amendments are usually non-contentious, they may offer procedural opportunities to the opposition to delay the Bill, and Ministers are consequently not always inclined to agree to their inclusion. Alternatively, the pressure on the legislative programme may be such that the government will not agree to the inclusion of an additional Bill.[36] Thirdly, the enactment of a consolidation Act does not mean that the department has

---

33 The Law Commission, *Thirty-second Annual Report 1997, Modern Law for Modern Needs* (Law Com No 250), para 6.1. Law Commission reports are available on the Internet.
34 Ibid, para 6.4. See also chapter 1, section 6.2.
35 The Hon Mrs Justice Arden DBE, 'Improving the Statute Book: A Law Reformer's Viewpoint' (1997) 18 *Statute Law Rev* 169.
36 Consolidation Bills are subject to special parliamentary procedures. There are three main types of Consolidation Bill: those which simply re-enact existing provisions *verbatim*; those which re-enact existing provisions with corrections and minor improvements under the Consolidation of Enactments (Procedure) Act 1949; and those which include amendments to give effect to recommendations of the Law Commissions. Following their Second Reading in the House of Lords, where they are invariably introduced, all Consolidation Bills are committed to the Joint Select Committee on Consolidation Bills, whose task is to ensure that the Bill, of whatever type, is properly prepared. One of the reasons why Consolidation Bills are dealt with in this way is to save debating time; but as presently constituted, the Committee could probably not cope with an increased output from the draftsman without adding to its membership or altering its procedures, both of which changes would have to be approved by Parliament.

thereby precluded itself from further new legislation in that area. The Companies Act 1985, the product of a painstaking consolidating process, was, within a year, radically amended by the Insolvency Act 1986, itself a consolidating Act. 'Since then there has been a steady stream of amendments which added dozens of new sections in the Act, often by statutory instrument and often for the purpose of implementing the requirements of EC directives.'[37] In short, legislative life goes on and consolidation often does little more than mark a particular stage in that life.

The Law Commission's role with regard to the rationalisation of the statute book should not be seen as being merely a technical exercise. As part of its mission to make the law 'simpler, fairer and easier to use',[38] it is also responsible for the preparation of Statute Law Revision and Statute Law (Repeals) Bills, each of which requires a judgment to be made about the substantive value of the measure to be repealed. The former repeals statutes which are 'obsolete, spent, unnecessary or superseded', while Statute Law (Repeal) Bills repeal those which are 'no longer of practical utility'. The Commission's judgments about these kinds of statutes may attract little political concern, but the same would not be true of the suggestion that there should be a permanent legislative committee in Parliament whose function would be to 'bring forward proposals for updating, consolidating and developing the law in relation to relatively uncontentious matters', and which would be obliged to consult the Law Commission about such proposals.[39] What such a committee might perceive as the uncontentious updating or development of the law is no guarantee that it will be similarly regarded by the government, even if such perception is shared by the Law Commission. This is the lesson repeatedly seen in the political response to some of the Law Commission's proposed changes to family law and, most strikingly, in the government's unwillingness to enact the Commission's Draft Criminal Code.

Published in 1989, the Law Commission's Criminal Code has for the past decade been awaiting legislative implementation. The Home Office's refusal to find time for its enactment is substantially attributable to the greater political priority that it attached to the many other measures amending the criminal law or affecting the operation of the criminal justice system which it promoted, during the 1990s; for example, confiscating the proceeds of drug trafficking and of terrorism, defence disclosure, criminal appeals, serious fraud, extradition, the relaxation of formerly complex and restricting rules governing the admissibility of evidence, and the sentencing powers of criminal courts.[40] Critics point not only to the wasted efforts of those who drafted the Code, but

---

37 Arden, op cit, pp 170-171.
38 Mr Justice Brooke (then Chairman of the Law Commission), 'The Role of the Law Commission in Simplifying Statute Law' (1995) 16 *Statute Law Review* 1.
39 Op cit, para 1.20.
40 Nor is the acceptability of the Commission's law reform proposals any longer dependent on the availability of time for debate on the floor of the House. As a result of the changes to parliamentary procedure made during the 1990s, a public Bill will, in the Commons, normally be referred to a Second Reading Committee if its main purpose is to give effect to proposals contained in a Law Commission Report. In the Lords, such Bills are referred to the Special Public Bill Committee procedure.

also to the continuing waste of the taxpayer's money implicit in the pursuit of criminal appeals which, had the Code been enacted, would have been unnecessary and unjustified.[41]

What may finally persuade the government to enact the Code (in whole or in parts) are the requirements of the Human Rights Act 1998. Article 7 of the Convention on Human Rights provides that a person shall not be held guilty of any criminal offence on account of any act or omission which did not constitute an offence when committed. The Article has been interpreted by the European Court of Human Rights to require offences to be defined with reasonable precision.[42] The courts will be required by section 2 to take the jurisprudence of the European Court into account where Convention rights issues arise. They are in general enjoined by section 3 to read primary legislation so as to give effect to it in a way which is compatible with such rights.[43] This requirement applies whenever the legislation was enacted and will therefore extend to the Offences against the Person Act 1861, one of many Acts to be replaced by the Code. Moreover, any future legislation creating new criminal offences will require the Minister to state its compatibility with the Convention. The present lack of clarity in key areas of the criminal law might make such a statement difficult to formulate.[44]

What this history underlines is the irreducibly political nature of law reform. The enactment of the Criminal Code, as with the implementation of any other Law Commission proposal, or indeed any proposal more widely designed to improve the preparation of legislation,[45] requires the political will of the government of the day. Recognition of the political reality should not, however, be equated with pessimism: since the last edition of this book was published there has undoubtedly been change for the better.[46]

---

41 See H Brooke, 'The Law Commission and Criminal Law Reform' [1995] *Criminal Law Review* 911; J Smith, 'The Law Commission's Criminal Law Bill: A Good Start for the Criminal Code' (1995) 16 *Statute Law Review* 105; Rt Hon Lord Bingham of Cornhill, 'A Criminal Code: Must we Wait for Ever?' [1998] *Criminal Law Review* 694. On the Law Commission generally, and on the government's record in implementing its proposals, see S Cretney, 'The Law Commission: True Dawns and False Dawns' (1996) 59 *Modern Law Review* 631.

42 *Welch v United Kingdom* (1995) 20 EHRR 247.

43 Chapter 8, section 5.2.

44 See the Law Commission's comments, op cit, para 1.25.

45 For reviews of these proposals, see Miers, (1986), op cit; Arden, op cit.

46 For exercises on chapter 7, see Appendix I, section F, questions 1-5, pp 400-401.

Chapter 8

Interpreting Legislation

> I still think that the interpretation of legislation is just part of the process of being a good lawyer; a multi-faceted thing, calling for many varied talents; not a subject which can be confined in rules.[1]

Statutory provisions are read, used and interpreted by a wide variety of people: judges, magistrates and their clerks, members of tribunals, civil servants, officials in local authorities and other public corporations, employees in the privatised industries, trade union officials, architects, chartered surveyors, accountants, barristers, solicitors, shopkeepers, employers, students and others. For many of these the application of a statutory provision in a given instance will usually be a routine matter. Where doubts do arise about its scope or meaning, or about its relationship with other provisions, they may often be easily resolved, for example by reference to an authoritative ruling or text, or to some technique of interpretation supplied by the context. However, not all doubts are so easily resolved. This chapter builds on the procedures presented in chapter 6 for identifying conditions of doubt in the interpretation of statutes and for constructing arguments for and against alternative answers.[2] Where appropriate, points will be illustrated by reference to *Davis v Johnson*.[3] We have also drawn extensively on the cases reported in the All England Law Reports for 1998. In section 5 of this chapter we consider briefly some particular features of the interpretation of Community law and of the Human Rights Act 1998.

1   Clarification of standpoint and role

The first stage, as always, is to ask, Who am I? At what stage in what process am I? What am I trying to do? The draftsman of taxing statutes, for example, has the opportunity to formulate the clauses in a Bill so as to forestall interpretations by those who wish to minimise the tax to be paid. At the same time he is working to the instructions of a government department such as the Inland Revenue or Customs and Excise, and is under pressure to complete the Bill on time. Both factors limit what the draftsman can do. As we have seen, his duty is to prepare a Bill which gives legal effect to the department's

---

1   Lord Wilberforce, HL Debates, Vol 418, col 73 (9 March 1981).
2   The conditions which are presupposed are set out in chapter 6 above, pp 209-213.
3   Note the wide range of potential interpreters identified in para 20 of the Select Committee's Report; Chapter 1, section 12.2.

policy and which complies with the parliamentary rules of public Bill procedure. We saw in Chapter 7 that ensuring legal effectiveness may entail the subordination of clarity to precision of formulation; this has frequently been the case with anti-avoidance provisions. That this priority may prove troublesome subsequently is not the draftsman's prime consideration. Nevertheless he must be sensitive to the responses of tax-collecting agencies, tax avoiders and the judiciary, and try to formulate the Bill's clauses in such a way that the government's desired interpretation is clear.

For the tax consultant the sections of the Act are a datum, the starting point from which interpretation proceeds, but unlike the draftsman he may regard the government's objectives as a challenge to his ingenuity in achieving the lawful minimisation of his client's liability to pay tax. The interpretive techniques he employs are constrained by the attitudes and behaviour of others, notably the Inland Revenue, which has its own policies and practices – for example the selective enforcement of taxing provisions as formulated in its extra-statutory concessions – which may go beyond what the government intended or the judiciary regard as justifiable.[4] Although subject to judicial control, the Revenue is, from the tax consultant's standpoint, often more significant by virtue of its power to accelerate or delay the assessment process to suit the inspector, to institute proceedings based on its own interpretations or with the benefit of unpublished special commissioners' decisions, and to settle claims by negotiation. This is true also for the taxpayer who seeks to challenge an assessment.[5]

2   Checking the currency of the statutory material

Normally the tasks of finding and assembling the statutory text can be carried out by using *Statutes in Force, Halsbury's Statutes,* an electronic information retrieval system such as LEXIS-NEXIS, CELEX or Lawtel, or possibly an expert system. The effect of amendments may be less easy to determine; where non-textual amendment is used, the reader must be able to reformulate the original rule in such a way as to give precise legal effect to the amendments to it (a process known as conflation). In some cases this may be the source of doubt.[6]

Identifying and, where appropriate, restating the statutory text are tasks which are normally straightforward, but sometimes occasion difficulty. Apart from the use of the standard referencing services, completing them may involve some ingenuity, such as spotting or establishing connections between separate

---

4   *Vestey v IRC* [1980] AC 1148. See the discussion of 'legitimated interposition' in M Kadish and S Kadish, *Discretion to Disobey* (1973), pp 66-72.

5   See the comments made by Professor Peter Willoughby who personally pursued his own appeal in *IRC v Willoughby* [1997] 4 All ER 65; *Amicus Curiae* (1998), p 8.

6   Section 3 of the Domestic Violence and Matrimonial Proceedings Act 1976 textually amended the Matrimonial Homes Act 1967 and s 4 incorporated provisions of that Act by reference; chapter 1, section 12.4 above. The 1976 Act was itself textually amended by s 89(2)(a) of and Schedule 2, para 53 to the Domestic Proceedings and Magistrates' Courts Act 1978, and was repealed by the Family Law Act 1996.

statutory provisions (both primary and secondary), conflating lengthy and technical non-textual amendments to an earlier text, using algorithms and other visual devices to help understanding,[7] or creating a doubt which requires resolution through the adoption of a less obvious interpretation. This last alternative may be attractive to the unhappy interpreter, but he may be hard put to it to convince others of its plausibility.

The next important steps are to discover when the statute came (or comes) into force, to what period of time it applies, its duration and its geographical extent.

2.1 Commencement

Section 4 of the Interpretation Act 1978 provides:

> An Act or provision of an Act comes into force-
> (a) where provision is made for it to come into force on a particular day, at the beginning of that day;
> (b) where no provision is made for its coming into force, at the beginning of the day on which the Act receives the Royal Assent.

Sometimes an Act will contain a section specifying the day on which it is to come into force. For example, the Interpretation Act 1978, which received the Royal Assent on 20 July 1978, provides in section 26 that 'This Act shall come into force on 1 January 1979'. Where the government intends to postpone its commencement, perhaps because administrative arrangements need to be made for its implementation, the Act will give power to a named authority to specify the commencement day. Sometimes it will provide that parts of it shall come into force on a particular day or event, while the other parts await a commencement order. Modern legislation displays a wide variety of commencement provisions.[8] The Human Rights Act 1998, for example, provides by section 22 that some of its sections 'come into force on the passing of this Act', and that 'the other provisions shall come into force on such day as the Secretary of State may by order appoint'. Section 22(3) goes on to provide, again in a typical formulation, that 'different days may be appointed for different purposes'. The Act may go further, requiring the Secretary of State to consult certain groups, or publish codes of practice or guidelines concerning its implementation, before he makes the order.

Commencement Orders take the form of statutory instruments. The postponement of the commencement of Acts is commonplace;[9] for example,

---

7   Appendix II.
8   F Bennion, *Statutory Interpretation* (3rd edn, 1997), p 202.
9   Entire parts or particular sections may remain inoperative for many years (or not be brought into force at all: *R v Secretary of State for the Home Department, ex p Fire Brigades' Union* [1995] 2 AC 513). In *Bringing Acts of Parliament into Force* (1997, Cmnd 3695) government departments identified provisions in 69 Acts enacted between 1979 and 1992 which had not been brought into force. That substantial parts of recently enacted statutes are cast into this 'legislative limbo' (Editorial, (1997) 18 *Statute Law Rev* v) may be a matter of judicial criticism; see Buxton LJ, *R v Manning* [1998] 4 All ER 876, 895.

it was provided for in the Domestic Violence and Matrimonial Proceedings Act 1976.[10] Although the implementation of this new remedy was a matter of some urgency, substantial changes in the administration of county court business had to be made first. Accordingly, section 5 of the Act, which received the Royal Assent on 26 October 1976, gave powers to the Lord Chancellor to bring it, or parts of it, into force on such days as he chose; but it went on to specify that if any of the Act's provisions were not in force by 1 April 1977, he should make an order bringing them into force.

2.2 Time of application

In the absence of a contrary intention, a statute applies only to circumstances falling within its scope which arise following its commencement. Two occasions when a statute operates with respect to a time prior to its enactment may be distinguished: *retrospective* and *retroactive*.[11] A statute is retrospective in effect when it attaches new consequences to an event which occurred prior to its enactment; for example to indemnify a particular action or to give compensation in respect of a particular injury. A statute is retroactive in effect when it is deemed to have come into force at a time prior to its enactment. Both types are relatively rare; a statute requires express language to have such effect. In addition there is a presumption against making previously lawful acts illegal by either device.[12]

2.3 Duration

Once enacted, a statutory provision remains in force until it is repealed by another Act of Parliament.[13] Sections 15-16 of the Interpretation Act 1978 provide, essentially, that the legal quality of any action taken or status enjoyed under the repealed Act shall not be affected by the repeal, unless the contrary intention appears. A statute may also expire by virtue of a time limit specified

---

10 Chapter 1, section 12.4 above. The Commencement Order was made on 25 March 1977, bringing the Act into force on 1 June 1977; Domestic Violence and Matrimonial Proceedings (Commencement) Order 1977, SI 1977/559.

11 This follows E Driedger, 'Statutes, Retroactive Retrospective Reflections' (1978) 56 *Canadian Bar Review* 264. An example of retrospective effect is s 22(4) of the Human Rights Act 1998.

12 Sometimes designated, *nullum crimen sine lege.* See Article 7 of the European Convention on Human Rights, and, in the case of Community law, *R v Kirk* 63/83 [1985] 1 All ER 453. An example of a highly controversial statute having retrospective effect is the War Crimes Act 1991.

13 The Justices of the Peace Act 1361 gives magistrates the useful and often used power to bind over the parties who appear before them to keep the peace; *R v Clerkenwell Metropolitan Stipendiary Magistrate, ex p Hooper* [1998] 4 All ER 193. On repeal by statutory instrument, see above, pp 242-243. On rare occasions, a court may hold that an earlier statutory provision has been impliedly repealed by a later one. Of much greater importance is the compatibility that the courts must seek between domestic law on the one hand, and Community law and 'Convention rights' under the Human Rights Act 1998 on the other; below, section 5.

in the Act,[14] but the principle of desuetude (disuse) is inapplicable to United Kingdom legislation.[15]

2.4 Geographical extent

The traditional presumption is that a statute will apply to the whole of the United Kingdom unless it provides otherwise. For example, section 5(3) of the Domestic Violence and Matrimonial Proceedings Act 1976 states that it 'shall not extend to Northern Ireland or Scotland'.[16] Where it is intended that it should apply to Northern Ireland, the Act may, for the avoidance of doubt, specifically so provide, as does section 22(6) of the Human Rights Act 1998. Great Britain consists of England, Wales and Scotland. There are regular instances of statutes enacted at Westminster which apply only in Scotland, or which, like the 1976 Act, are stated not to apply there. With the creation of the Scottish Parliament, Westminster will no longer have primary legislative competence over matters devolved to Edinburgh by the Scotland Act 1998. Westminster will, however, retain its legislative competence over 'reserved matters'. By contrast, there are very few examples of statutes applying only to Wales. As Wales, unlike Scotland, has no separate legal system, statutes enacted at Westminster which apply to England apply equally to Wales. This will remain the case following the establishment of the Welsh Assembly. It will, however, be for the Assembly in Cardiff to give Welsh effect to that primary legislation by means of its own statutory instruments. These may, depending on the scope for variation permitted by the Act and the Assembly's own priorities in respect of the matters covered by it, differ in detail from their English equivalents. As with devolution to Scotland, the Government of Wales Act 1998 reserves a number of matters from the Assembly's competence.

It is also usually the case that statutes apply only to events occurring within the jurisdiction to which they extend. To this there are some exceptions. These are provisions which have extra-territorial effect. This does not mean that Parliament has sought to enact law to be applied in other states. Extra-territorial legislation brings within the jurisdiction of the courts events occurring outside the United Kingdom. Firstly, a statute may provide that conduct which amounts

14 Where a statute is intended to be of temporary effect, provision will be made for it to expire on a specific day, after a specific period of time, or on the occurrence of a specific event. During the 1970s and 1980s a number of statutes were enacted which gave the police extraordinary powers to deal with terrorism, removing many of the traditional rights and liberties of a person suspected of having committed a 'terrorist' offence. These Acts were of a 'temporary' nature. For example, s 27 of the Prevention of Terrorism (Temporary Provisions) Act 1989 provided that the substance of the Act 'shall remain in force until 22 March 1990'. The section went on to provide that the Act shall then expire unless it was continued in force by an order made under s 27(6) for a further twelve-month period.
15 On desuetude, see above, p 191 and *R v East Sussex Quarter Sessions, ex p Hew Hove Albion Club Ltd* (1970) 69 LGR 259. Acts of the old Scots Parliament and old treaties in international law may be held to have fallen into desuetude, if long disregarded in practice.
16 See above, p 89, and generally, Bennion, op cit, pp 245-299.

to a crime in Great Britain will be so also where committed by a British subject abroad. Accordingly, that person may be prosecuted once he comes within the jurisdiction. An example is bigamy, which applies to second marriages which have taken place 'in England or Ireland or elsewhere'.[17] Secondly, a statute may apply to acts committed abroad by non-British subjects, so that they too are amenable to the jurisdiction of the British courts once they enter Great Britain. An example is section 134 of the Criminal Justice Act 1988, which made torture, wherever committed in the world, criminal under UK law and triable here.[18]

3 Identification of the conditions of doubt

The next stage is the identification of the exact word or phrase causing difficulties and of the conditions of doubt which give rise to them. The statutory words provide a natural and convenient starting point, and it is usually best to incorporate them into a question indicating the issue which they raise. For example, in *Allen* a single question of law can be formulated in neutral terms as follows: 'What is the meaning of "shall marry" in section 57 of the Offences Against the Person Act 1861?'[19]

Sometimes one may be puzzled by a rule because its style defeats or obscures its substance. This may occur where the rule is unusually long, is subject to a number of qualifications, contains a large number of subordinate clauses, employs negatives or the passive voice, has an unusually complicated syntactical structure, employs words which are archaic, ambiguous, vague, technical, obscure or unfamiliar, or any combination of these.[20]

There are other conditions, too, which may occasion puzzlement. For example, the rule may be comprehensible in the sense that an interpreter thinks he understands its language, but it somehow appears incongruous when set against the object which it is supposed to secure; or the rule may be comprehensible but rendered puzzling by subsequent judicial or other interpretive action; or again the rule may be comprehensible but appear harsh when applied to the facts of the case at hand.[21] Counsel for Johnson presented the argument in favour of his client largely on the basis that the interpretation sought by Davis would be in conflict with the statutory words and the purposes for which the legislation was enacted. If Davis were granted an injunction, he argued, a mistress would be given the same rights as a married woman, yet there was nothing in the 1976 Act to suggest that so substantial a change in matrimonial law was intended. The 1976 Act was enacted to ease the procedural limitations on the grant of injunctions by county courts, and thus could not be envisaged as also giving an unmarried person the right to exclude from the 'matrimonial home' his or her 'spouse'

---

17 Chapter 1, section 7.1.
18 See *R v Bow Street Metropolitan Stipendiary Magistrate, ex p Pinochet Ugarte (No 3)* [1999] 2 All ER 97, HL.
19 See below, p 309.
20 Chapter 6 above, pp 210-211, conditions of doubt nos 13(c), (d) and (i).
21 Ibid, conditions of doubt nos 11, 12, 21, 24 and 34.

when in law the 'spouse', like Johnson, had a right to be there by virtue of being a joint tenant, with Davis, of the council flat.

The condition of doubt to which counsel is referring may be described as the imperfect relationship between the rule at hand and the existing system of rules; more particularly, it may be said that the interpretation favoured by opposing counsel would be in conflict with a well-established set of rules governing husband and wife.[22] In addition, counsel for Johnson has to cope with the decision of the Court of Appeal granting the injunction and seemingly approving this interpretation, and with other obstacles which will be considered below.

A striking feature of *Davis v Johnson* is the variation in the views of the different judges as to the conditions of doubt. It is probably the case that none of them considered the style of section 1 to be problematic; although subsection (1) is a lengthy sentence, it can be readily broken down into a number of reasonably clearly defined occasions on which an injunction may be granted. There was agreement between some of the judges that the difficulty lay in determining the scope of the section, but within this agreement there were different diagnoses of the exact difficulty. Lord Denning would admit to no doubt about the scope of section 1. He says near the beginning of his judgment, 'To my mind the Act is perfectly clear', and after quoting from the section continues, 'No-one I would have thought could possibly dispute that those plain words by themselves cover this very case'.[23] For him, the doubts were created by what he regarded as the perverse interpretation of the section in the earlier decisions of the Court of Appeal, *B v B* and *Cantliff v Jenkins*, whose effect was aggravated by the inhibiting rules of the doctrine of precedent. Past authoritative decisions were the difficulty. In addition, his Lordship took the view that doubts about the mischief which the Act was intended to remedy could have been easily discovered were it not for the rules precluding explicit reliance on parliamentary proceedings in a court of law. Difficulties were thus created, in Lord Denning's view, by the institutional practices concerning precedent and the interpretation of statutes.[24]

Lords Diplock and Scarman both thought that there were doubts about the scope of section 1, but disagreed as to their exact nature. For Lord Diplock, as for counsel for Johnson, the doubt lay in the seeming conflict between the procedural provisions of section 1 and the existing substantive law relating to the protection of married women and of proprietary interests. In his opinion, the question concerning the scope of section 1 was whether it merely provided a more expeditious remedy in cases where the unmarried partner already held a proprietary interest, as in *Cantliff v Jenkins* and *Davis v Johnson* (the narrow view), or whether it extended to provide a remedy even to an unmarried partner who held no proprietary rights in the premises named in the injunction, as in *B v B* (the wider view).

Lord Scarman approached the issue somewhat differently. He agreed that it was 'highly unlikely that Parliament could have intended by the sidewind of

---

22 Chapter 6 above, p 210, conditions of doubt nos 8(f) and 9(a).
23 Chapter 1, section 12.5.2.
24 Chapter 6 above, p 212, conditions of doubt nos 22 and 24.

subsection (2) to have introduced radical changes into the law of property', but took the view that as the Act was concerned with personal rights (injunctions are personal remedies), it was not necessary to construe the section so as to imply such an effect upon property law. The difficulty arose not because the section was obscure or because it conflicted with existing property rights but because the Lords Justices in the earlier appeals *B v B* and *Cantliff v Jenkins* has misperceived the nature of the remedies being provided in the Act. Had they recognised that it was to do with personal rights they would, like Lord Scarman, have found 'nothing illogical or surprising in Parliament legislating to override a property right, if it be thought to be socially necessary'.[25]

Their Lordships were agreed that Lord Denning's creation of a fourth exception to the rule that the Court of Appeal is bound by its own decisions and his explicit references to Hansard added to the difficulties in the case;[26] and Lord Diplock and Viscount Dilhorne in particular disapproved in unequivocal terms these novel techniques of interpretation.

4   The construction of arguments

In the interpretation of statutes, as for rules in fixed verbal form generally, the text of the rule(s), is a natural starting point. The question arises: how far is it helpful and permissible to look beyond the text to other material as aids to interpretation?

In many areas of public administration such as education, immigration, employment, social security, taxation, housing and the environment, there exists what may be called a specialist subculture of rules, practices, conventions and procedures concerning the interpretation of the governing statutory provisions.[27] Familiarity with this kind of context will almost always be of help to an official, either directly or by analogy, and will also form an essential part of the context for other interpreters. These examples of 'soft law' will often answer questions about the interpretation or application of statutory rules, but their authority depends ultimately upon the courts. In this respect statutes tend to differ from non-legal rules in three ways: there are rules which govern the interpretation of statutes; there is a wide range of types of material which is potentially relevant to interpretation of a statutory text; and there are some rules which govern the use of such material by requiring, permitting or prohibiting consideration of it by certain interpreters and, in some instances, by giving authoritative status to arguments based upon it. In non-legal contexts there tend to be few or no rules in fixed verbal form; there is usually little or no legislative 'furniture' which can be used as an aid to interpretation, and it is even less likely that there will be rules regulating the use of such aids.

25 Chapter 1, section 12.5.3.
26 See now *Pepper v Hart* [1993] AC 593, below, pp 288ff.
27 R Baldwin, *Rules and Government* (1995); C Harlow and R Rawlings, *Law and Administration* (2nd edn, 1997), pp 152-158.

But, and as we shall find with the doctrine of precedent,[28] the rules governing the interpretation of statutes and the use of aids tend, for the most part, to be permissive and vague. For example, Bankowski and MacCormick distinguish between material which, though not compelling upon a court (such as the statutory language itself), appears strongly relevant to the issue in hand (such as another part of the same statute), and material that is admissible and upon which a court could rely if it chose but which does not obviously call for attention (such as a commentary in a textbook). But as they immediately caution:

> The degree of persuasiveness being context-dependent, there is no clear cut-off point between the persuasive (the 'should-material') and the simply admissible (the 'may-material'). The court's use of such material in its justification of the interpretation finally given is at its discretion, the value of the material being to indicate the weight or relative weight of the arguments for the favoured interpretation.[29]

Thus the difference between the interpretation of legal and non-legal rules in fixed verbal form is not as great as it might seem.

The first step at this stage is for the interpreter to identify and assemble the raw material from which he will draw arguments to support or undermine alternative interpretations. Beyond such factors as the time at his disposal, the availability of the material and the optimal use of his resources, there are no limits on the kinds of raw material which he might identify as being useful. The fact that some of it cannot be explicitly referred to in judicial settings is for these purposes irrelevant; they may still help to suggest good arguments. Of course the kinds of material which are admissible in courtrooms, and which may be authoritative there – such as prior judicial decisions on the words in issue – are very likely to be treated as authoritative in other contexts, such as in communications between solicitors who have no intention of going to court. But it would be quite wrong to infer from the standard treatments of statutory interpretation, which deal with the explicit authoritative status of particular kinds of argument and the sources from which they are drawn, that material which is not admissible in a courtroom is without value in preparing arguments to be presented there or in some other context. The following discussion describes briefly three sources from which arguments for and against alternative interpretations may be drawn; statutory material, judicial decisions, and other extrinsic material, and indicates the acceptability of these in a courtroom.

4.1 Statutory material

(a) Internal

Frequently the scope or meaning of a rule is qualified by other rules in the same statute. Such qualifications may extend or limit the rule, provide for

---

28 Below, Chapter 9, section 4.2.
29 Z Bankowski and D N MacCormick in DN MacCormick and R Summers, *Interpreting Statutes: A Comparative Study* (1991), p 376.

specific applications of an otherwise general rule, specify how a particular rule is to be implemented, state exceptions, or attach a specific meaning to a word or phrase. Qualifications of the last sort are generally contained in an interpretation or definition section, while some of these others may appear in Schedules at the end of the statute, or be promulgated separately by means of a statutory instrument. In addition, all statutes contain a long title which indicates the object of the enactment, while older statutes contain lengthier preambles explaining not only what the Act is intended to do, but also why. Such statements of institutionalised intent are rare now, but arguably could be profitably revived.[30] Other non-enacting parts of the statute, such as the short title, side (or marginal) notes, and cross headings may also provide some guidance.[31]

Draftsmen use express words where they intend one provision to be qualified by another, but its interpretation may nevertheless be affected by other rules not specifically referred to. Many doubts about interpretation have arisen because of the uncertain relationship between one provision and another in the same statute,[32] but it is also a common kind of reasoning to compare the wording of particular sections so as to advance or support a preferred interpretation. For example, in *Davis v Johnson*, counsel for Johnson argued as follows: at the time of Davis's application for an injunction restraining Johnson from occupying the council flat, she was in fact living in the Chiswick Women's Refuge; thus she and Johnson were not, as section 1 requires, 'living with each other in the same household' and accordingly, on a literal construction of the section, she was not entitled to an injunction. This interpretation is supported by a comparison of the words in section 4 of the Act which deals with injunctions restricting occupation of the matrimonial home by a husband or wife. Here the Act speaks of a person who is 'entitled ... to occupy a dwelling house ...' This section does not require the party applying for an injunction to be at that time in occupation; it is necessary only that he or she had a right to occupy.

30 See, for example, *Effort Shipping v Linden SA* [1998] 1 All ER 495, 503. See further chapter 5, section 2; and the Report of the Committee on the Preparation of Legislation (1975, Cmnd 6053; Chairman: Sir David Renton; hereafter *Renton*), paras 11.6-11.8. Preambles are routine in Community law; above, p 223. The long title may offer some guidance as to the interpretation of words or phrases; see *R v Crown Court at Southwark, ex p Bowles* [1998] 2 All ER 193, where the long title of the Proceeds of Crime Act 1995 was used in conjunction with sub-headings in the statute to justify giving different meanings to similar words used in different contexts.

31 There is, as Cross observes, a 'bewildering mass of conflicting dicta' on the admissibility of and weight to be attached to these items as aids to interpretation; J Bell and G Engle QC, *Cross on Statutory Interpretation* (3rd edn, 1995), p 124. They cannot displace words that are clear in their context, but may be helpful if they are not. See for example *Cutter v Eagle Star Insurance* [1998] 4 All ER 417, 425, in which Lord Clyde referred to the long title and to the heading of Part II of the Road Traffic Act 1930 (from which the Road Traffic Act 1988 was in part drawn) as providing 'some support' for his conclusion, and *Dawson v Wearmouth* [1998] 1 All ER 271, 274 in which a sidenote is used as part of the court's reasoning. On the utility of marginal notes to the interpreter, see G Stewart, 'Legislative Drafting and the Marginal Note' (1995) 16 *Statute Law Review* 21, 39ff.

32 Or because of the uncertain usage of the same word in the same or different sections; so, in its opening words, s 57 of the Offences against the Person Act 1861 uses the word 'marry' in different senses (see chapter 10 below, p 347).

The comparison therefore suggests that had Parliament intended an applicant such as Davis to succeed if she could show that she was 'entitled to occupy' the flat, then the draftsman could have so provided. Instead, section 1 requires her to be living with Johnson. For Lord Denning, this literal approach to section 1 would 'deprive the subsection of much of its effect'. In order not to produce that result, he took the view that the words were used to denote their relationship before the incident, rather than as laying down a factual condition to be met.[33]

(b) External

To a limited extent the interpretation of statutes is regulated by statute, the most important being the Interpretation Act 1978.[34] However, the traditional approach to judicial interpretation, which has repeatedly been endorsed by the Law Commission, the Renton Committee and by the government, is that it is the function of the judiciary to interpret with the minimum of direction from Parliament how they should set about their task.[35]

The question of the extent to which statutory interpretation should be the subject of precise and general rules is raised in a quite specific way in relation to what can and cannot be achieved by an Interpretation Act. The enactment in a single place of a number of standardised definitions and conventions can, it is felt, help the draftsmen and those users who are familiar with the provisions. It can also reduce the length of some statutes and other instruments. Thus even the relatively modest provisions of the Northern Ireland Interpretation Act 1954 had the effect, according to one authority, that without it, 'the annual volumes of the Northern Ireland Statutes would, upon a conservative estimate, be approximately one-third larger than they are'.[36] But

---

33 Chapter 1, section 12.5.2, pp 92-94.
34 The Act has been amended in a number of respects to take account of new definitions introduced in later legislation. See Bennion, op cit, Appendix C. On occasion it falls to be interpreted, see *R v Thames Magistrates' Court, ex p Horgan* [1998] 1 All ER 559.
35 A noteworthy but unsuccessful attempt to change the traditional relationship between Parliament and the judiciary was Lord Scarman's sponsorship of Interpretation of Legislation Bills in the 1979-80 and 1980-81 sessions of Parliament. Both were based on the Law Commissions' draft Bill published in 1969, and would have authorized explicit reliance for the purpose of ascertaining the meaning of a word or phrase on a variety of sources then excluded by the courts, notably policy documents prepared by official agencies upon which Acts are based. The principal objections were that they confused the constitutional division of function between the courts and Parliament; that they would create further difficulties for the government draftsmen who would be drafting Bills knowing that other texts not prepared by them would be construed with the statutory text to produce an interpretation of it; that they would admit references to texts whose relevance, reliability and availability was very variable; and lastly, that the attendant costs for lawyers, government departments and ultimately their clients would be significantly increased, as interpreters would in effect have to equip themselves with these texts and to read them in case they shed some light upon alternative interpretations. Although the 1981 Bill was, because of the amendments to it, more favourably received, this pragmatic objection was still influential in defeating it. See 405 HL Debates cols 276-306 (13 February 1980) and 418 HL Debates cols 64-83 (9 March 1981) and cols 1341-7 (26 March 1981).
36 W Leitch and A Donaldson, 'The Interpretation Act - Ten Years Later' (1965) 16 *Northern Ireland Legal Quarterly* 215, 237.

in common law countries the role of Interpretation Acts has tended to be a limited one, generally confined to such matters as ways of expressing number and gender,[37] or providing certain common form provisions, but generally not attempting to provide a wide-ranging legislative dictionary of uniform stipulative definitions which would be binding on draftsmen and interpreters. This tribute to the flexibility of language and to the dangers of generalisation is characteristic of the traditions of the common law. But it is a largely unexplored question whether this almost total rejection of a legislative dictionary is not itself an example of over-generalisation. The Renton Report concluded that the possibility of enacting some common-form provisions 'could usefully be considered'. This is a task for which the Law Commissions would be admirably suited.[38]

It is a commonplace for the definition sections in the Interpretation Act 1978 to provide that they shall apply 'unless the contrary intention appears', or words to that effect. Whether such an intention exists in any particular case requires the court to consider the legislation as a whole:

> ... the situation when the legislation was enacted; the purpose of the legislation; whether the provision affected is substantive and essential to the functioning of the legislation; whether the provision affected is incapable of being satisfied otherwise than by retaining the original meaning; whether the enacting body would have considered the provision to be so important that they would have refused to enact it in any other form; whether the effect of applying the Interpretation Act rule would be to change the 'character' of the legislation; the effect on private property rights if the rule of interpretation were applied and whether application of the rule of interpretation would result in penal consequences for anyone and, if it would, whether the offence is a heinous one.[39]

Some of these points are illustrated by *R v West London Stipendiary Magistrate, ex p Simeon*.[40] On 30 June 1981 Simeon was arrested for loitering with intent, contrary to section 4 of the Vagrancy Act 1824. In August the Criminal Attempts Act 1981 repealed that offence. Section 8 of the 1981 Act said: 'the provisions of section 4 of the Vagrancy Act 1824 which apply to suspected persons and reputed thieves frequenting or loitering about the places described in that section with the intent there specified shall cease to have effect'. As was noted earlier, section 16 of the Interpretation Act 1978 provides that the legal quality of any action taken or status enjoyed under a repealed Act shall not be affected by the repeal, unless the contrary intention appears.[41] In November 1981 Simeon appeared before a magistrates' court which had to determine whether the proceedings should continue unaffected by section 8 of the 1981 Act, or

---

37 S Petersson, 'Gender Neutral Drafting' (1998) 19 *Statute Law Rev* 93.
38 *Renton*, para 19.10. See above, p 227 and W Leitch, 'Interpretation and the Interpretation Act 1978' [1980] *Statute Law Review* 5; New Zealand Law Commission, *A New Interpretation Act* (1990, Report No 17).
39 H Thornton, 'Contrary Intention' (1994) 16 *Statute Law Review* 182, 190. The text following draws on this article.
40 [1982] 2 All ER 813. Another example is *R v Bristol Magistrates' Court, ex p E* [1998] 3 All ER 798.
41 Above, p 264.

whether there was something in that Act which suggested otherwise. The magistrates did proceed, but the Divisional Court held on appeal that the prosecution should be stopped. As it was the case that other repeals had been effected in the 1981 Act by the simple (and usual) means of a repealing section referring to a Schedule of repeals, the quite deliberate method of repeal adopted in section 8 indicated that Parliament did indeed have an intention contrary to the standard application of section 16. The Court also took into account the well established proposition that, in the interpretation of a statute which imposes penal consequences on an individual's conduct, doubts should be resolved in the individual's favour. The case was taken to the House of Lords which reversed the Divisional Court. It found no contrary intention in the Act. The specific repeal effected by section 8 was simply an example of 'double repeal', a device sometimes used to draw Parliament's attention to particularly important repeals. In this case, the section being repealed was popularly known as the 'sus' law, whose use by the police against ethnic minorities had for many years been a matter of bitter complaint. Its repeal (which had been recommended by a parliamentary select committee) was therefore a matter of political importance. There was, the House of Lords held, nothing in the 1981 Act which indicated an intention to displace the normal operation of section 16 of the 1978 Act.

Apart from the Interpretation Act 1978, support for alternative interpretations may be sought from words or phrases contained or defined in statutes in *pari materia*; that is, statutes which deal with the same classes of persons, things and activities as that in issue. There is, however, 'no authoritative definition of the expression *in pari materia*'.[42] Sometimes successive statutes expressly provide that they are to be construed as one; on other occasions the extent of any similarity will depend on the level of generality that the reader chooses and seeks to rely on. For example, counsel in *Davis v Johnson* placed considerable reliance on provisions in the Matrimonial Homes Act 1967 as amended, and judicial interpretations of that Act, to show that as some of the remedies available to a married woman had been limited where they were in conflict with the husband's property rights, it could not possibly be the case that Parliament had intended just such a conflict to be resolved in her favour in the case of an unmarried woman. The persuasiveness of arguments drawn from similar statutory provisions inevitably depends on the degree of contextual and linguistic similarity between them and the disputed section.

4.2 The judicial interpretation of statutes

(a)   The status of particular interpretations

Firstly, a judicial decision on the words in issue will in many cases constitute an authoritative and final interpretation.[43] Nevertheless, because the statutory words must always take priority in the event of disputed interpretations, a

---

42 Cross, op cit, p 151.
43 '... the section means what a majority of this House declares it means', per Lord Diplock, *Davis v Johnson*, above, p 99.

judicial interpretation cannot be regarded as a direct substitution for them. So, where Parliament re-enacts in the exactly the same terms a provision which has been the subject of judicial interpretation, there is at best a presumption that it intended to endorse that interpretation.[44] This is of particular relevance to consolidation Acts.[45] These are to be interpreted as any other statute. Only where there is some doubt about its meaning should a court look back to the context in which the original sections were enacted and to any judicial interpretation of them.[46] Guidance may also be sought from the judicial interpretation of words or phrases in statutes *in pari materia*, but here, too, the authority of any prior interpretation is no more than persuasive:

> The ratio decidendi of a judgment as to the meaning of a particular word or combination of words used in a particular statutory provision can have no more than a persuasive influence on a court which is called upon to interpret the same word or combination of words appearing in some other statutory provision. It is not determinative of the meaning of that other provision.[47]

(b) Judicial interpretation in general

The judicial interpretation of statutes is a subject which has received a very great deal of attention; more perhaps than it deserves if we recall Cross's observation that 'the vast majority of statutes never come before courts for interpretation'.[48] Those which do are largely concerned with private obligations between natural or legal persons, and with the public obligations which citizens owe to the state, or the state, through the executive branch of government (for example, the police, the Inland Revenue, local authorities, executive agencies, statutory bodies) owes to the citizen. Legislation which is addressed to the internal regulation of government or of public bodies is seldom the object of judicial interpretation.

On the other hand, it is estimated that over fifty per cent of cases in the High Court and over ninety per cent of appeals in the House of Lords involve a question of statutory interpretation, so it is a subject of some importance for the judiciary. It is also of importance for the users of statutes, since a judge's interpretation of a statutory provision is authoritative unless and until changed by subsequent judicial decision or by an amending Act. For the interpreter who wishes to challenge the judicial understanding of a statutory provision, that understanding is a datum that will require an answer. Even where a disputed provision has not been the subject of judicial interpretation, many interpreters will formulate their arguments *as if* it were; in this sense, what

---

44 *Barras v Aberdeen Steam Trawling and Fishing Co* [1933] AC 402; *R v Chard* [1984] AC 279, 294-295, per Lord Scarman; *Lowsley v Forbes* [1998] 3 All ER 897, 905, per Lord Lloyd.

45 Chapter 7 above, pp 256-258.

46 *Farrell v Alexander* [1977] AC 59.

47 Lord Diplock, *Carter v Bradbeer* [1975] 1 WLR 1204, 1206. In *Davis v Johnson*, for example, counsel for Johnson relied on *Tarr v Tarr*, concerning a statute *in pari materia*, and on the Court of Appeal decisions in *B v B* and *Cantliff v Jenkins* which were directly in point. The 'dangers of comparing decisions on different statutes' was noted by Dyson J in *R v Birmingham City Council, ex p Mohammed* [1998] 3 All ER 788, 794.

48 Cross, op cit, p 1; and chapter 4 above, p 172.

judges do about statutory interpretation in general has traditionally been viewed as a model for other interpreters.[49] It is in part for this reason that many writers – and some judges – argue either that there are recognisably 'right' ways for judges to approach the interpretation of statutes or, if not, that there should be.

The nature of the judiciary's role in the interpretation of statutes was stated by Lord Scarman in *Duport Steels Ltd v Sirs* as follows:

> ... in the field of statute law the judge must be obedient to the will of Parliament as expressed in its enactments. In this field Parliament makes and unmakes the law, the judge's duty is to interpret and to apply the law, not to change it to meet the judge's idea of what justice requires. Interpretation does, of course, imply in the interpreter a power of choice where differing constructions are possible. But our law requires the judge to choose the construction which in his judgment best meets the legislative purpose of the enactment.[50]

This is an important constitutional and political point, reflecting the traditional conception of the division of functions between Parliament and the courts. In discharging their function the courts have, over the years, developed a formidably wide range of prescriptions with regard to aspects of the interpretation of statutes. These justify, but do not compel the interpretation reached in a particular case. Academic and practitioner accounts have traditionally stressed the judiciary's failure to develop these prescriptions into a systematic and coherent methodology to match the treatment accorded to areas of substantive law. 'There are', wrote Professor Cross, 'no binding judicial decisions on the subject of statutory interpretation generally as opposed to the interpretation of particular statutes; all that there is is a welter of judicial dicta which vary considerably in weight, age and uniformity.'[51]

There were, for example, 272 decisions reported in the *All England Law Reports* for 1998.[52] Of these, 174 (64%) were made in a statutory context. Many were concerned with the exercise of a power or a discretion by the executive or by a court; many involved a relatively straightforward exercise in determining the scope of the Act; some generated substantial issues of statutory interpretation. These figures, which would no doubt be closely repeated in other years throughout the 1990s, underline firstly the importance for the courts of the task of statutory interpretation; less than a third of the cases reported in 1998 dealt solely with common law rules. Also significant were decisions concerning the application of the rules regulating court procedure, such as those contained in the Rules of the Supreme Court.

Secondly, the sample underlines Cross's point that many of the decisions on statutory interpretation amount to no more than the particular

---

49 When asked their opinion on a statutory provision, barristers, for example, will formulate their advice as if the point were to be argued in court. Law students are, throughout their undergraduate career, expected to discuss disputed points of statutory interpretation in class as if they were appearing before a judge; see above, pp ix-x.
50 [1980] 1 WLR 142, 168.
51 Op cit, p 48.
52 Practice directions have been excluded. As some decisions deal with appeals raising common issues, there is in fact a greater number of individual litigants.

interpretation and application of individual provisions (although this is not to suggest that the task was necessarily easy). Some concern questions about the meaning or scope of statutory words and phrases,[53] some the effect of inter-related statutory provisions,[54] and others the relationship between them and such other authoritative rules as an international treaty,[55] the European Convention on Human Rights or Community law.[56] Almost without exception the arguments relied upon by counsel and judges alike were informed by previous decisions on the same or a similar provision,[57] and most were decided within the precedential and substantive law context of the particular statutory provision.

One of the standard characteristics of the texts written for students and practitioners is that they seek to impose order on Cross's 'welter of judicial dicta', employing the traditional categories of 'presumptions', 'canons of interpretation', and internal and external aids to interpretation.[58] The decisions reported in the 1998 *All England Law Reports* contain many examples of these prescriptions. Some take the form of general principles; others are quite narrow and specific, but every one of them is subject to the overriding proposition that 'everything depends on the context',[59] that is, the particular statute, its purpose, its background, its structure and wording, and the facts of the case:

(a) the absence of an easily drafted defence does not mean that the court should imply one, since if Parliament had intended a defence in this case it would have included one;[60]
(b) the fact that Parliament has included defences to some offences defined by the Act or in another Act creating offences closely connected to those

---

53 For example, the meaning of the word 'causes' in s 85(1) of the Water Resources Act 1991: *Empress Car Co (Abertillery Ltd v National Rivers Authority* [1998] 1 All ER 481 (and compare Lord Hoffmann's observation (at p 487) that answers to questions about causation depend on the purpose for which the question is asked with the extract from Collingwood 'On Causation' in chapter 1, section 11.2); whether, in determining what was 'suitable education' under s 298 of the Education Act 1993, in addition to educational considerations relevant to the child, an education authority was required to take into account the resources relevant to those considerations: *R v East Sussex County Council, ex p Tandy* [1998] 2 All ER 769; and whether, in determining whether to make a disabled facilities grant under s 24(1) of the Housing Grants, Reconstruction and Regeneration Act 1996, a housing authority is obliged or entitled to have regard to its financial resources: *R v Birmingham City Council, ex p Mohammed*, op cit.
54 For example, *R v M* [1998] 2 All ER 939.
55 *Effort Shipping v Linden Management*, op cit; *R v Secretary of State for the Home Department, ex p Johnson* [1998] 4 All ER 635; *R v Bow Street Metropolitan Stipendiary Magistrate, ex p Pinochet Ugarte* [1998] 4 All ER 897 (decision set aside: see *R v Bow Street Metropolitan Stipendiary Magistrate, ex p Pinochet Ugarte (No 2)* [1999] 1 All ER 577. See generally R Gardiner, 'Interpreting Treaties in the United Kingdom' in M Freeman (ed), *Legislation and the Courts* (1997), p 115.
56 See below, section 5.
57 In *R v Tottenham Youth Court, ex p Fawzy* [1998] 1 All ER 365 there was no case law on the point in issue.
58 Written as a Code, an exemplar is Bennion's *Statutory Interpretation*, op cit. See also the guidelines in M Fordham, *Judicial Review Handbook* (2nd edn, 1997). Earlier practitioner works are *Maxwell on the Interpretation of Statutes* (12th edn, 1969) and *Craies on Statute Law* (7th edn, 1971).
59 Per Lord Steyn, *Effort Shipping v Linden Management*, op cit, at 508.
60 *R v Land* [1998] 1 All ER 403; *B v DPP* [1998] 4 All ER 265.

in the disputed Act, but not to the offence in question, indicates that the omission in this case was deliberate;[61]

(c) clear words are required to effect a 'drastic' change in the existing statutory regime;[62]

(d) 'shall' is to be construed as imposing a mandatory requirement, rather than merely a 'statutory nudge' to act;[63]

(e) the proposition that general words in a later statute do not alter specific words in an earlier statute (*generalia specialibus non derogant*) is not a technical rule peculiar to English statutory interpretation, but represents simple common sense and ordinary usage;[64]

(f) a consolidation Act is to be interpreted according to its wording but reference to its antecedents (including any judicial decisions) may be made if its wording is unclear;[65]

(g) a codifying Act is to be interpreted according to its wording but reference to the earlier law may be made where it expressly preserves that law;[66]

(h) the court should be slow to interpret a provision as attaching disqualifying consequences to convictions recorded before the provision was enacted, but such retrospectivity may be justified by reference to the legislature's clear regulatory objective;[67]

(i) there is a general desirability that in construing an international convention the decisions of different jurisdictions should, so far as possible, be kept in line with each other;[68]

(j) in interpreting an international convention the court should adopt a broad rather than a narrow linguistic approach, giving it a meaning which makes sense in the light of the convention as a whole and which gives effect to its purposes: but the starting point must be the language itself;[69]

(k) Parliament could not, in repealing a number of statutes giving constables specific powers of arrest without warrant, have intended to repeal a general power of arrest that they had, while leaving that general power to the citizen; such a result would be absurd;[70]

(l) subordinate legislation may be used to assist the construction of the parent Act, but cannot displace a clear application of the words in the Act;[71]

---

61 Ibid.
62 *Effort Shipping v Linden Management*, op cit, at 512.
63 *R v Dudley Magistrates' Court, ex p Hollis* [1998] 1 All ER 759, 764.
64 *Effort Shipping v Linden Management*, op cit, at 508, 513.
65 *Wellcome Trust v Hamad* [1998] 1 All ER 657, 669.
66 *Eide UK Ltd v Lowndes Lambert Group* [1998] 1 All ER 946, citing the established authority on the interpretation of codifying Acts, *Bank of England v Vagliano Bros* [1891] AC 107.
67 *Antonelli v Secretary of State for Trade and Industry* [1998] 1 All ER 997, 1003-07; compare *Bairstow v Queens Moat Houses* [1998] 1 All ER 343.
68 *R v Immigration Appeal Tribunal, ex p Shah* [1998] 4 All ER 30 (see also *T v Immigration Officer* [1996] AC 742).
69 Per Lord Lloyd, *Adan v Secretary of State for the Home Department* [1998] 2 All ER 453, 458; Lord Steyn, *Re Ismail* [1998] 3 All ER 1007, 1012.
70 *Gapper v Chief Constable of Avon and Somerset Constabulary* [1998] 4 All ER 248.
71 *R v Lord Chancellor, ex p Lightfoot* [1998] 4 All ER 764, applying the leading authority *Hanlon v Law Society* [1981] AC 124.

(m) it is presumed that Parliament does nothing in vain;[72]
(n) where Parliament intends to clarify without altering the meaning it has intended to give to a provision, a formula such as the introductory words 'for the avoidance of doubt' is used;[73]
(o) it is the 'usual presumption that a word should bear the same meaning throughout the same Act';[74] and
(p) it is a principle of legal policy that a person should not be penalised except under clear law.[75]

Catalogues such as these underline a commonly remarked feature of most, but not all, of these prescriptions of interpretation: they are of limited practical assistance in settling doubts about interpretation in particular cases. This is partly due to vagueness, but also because in many cases where one principle appears to support one interpretation there is another prescription, often of equal status, which can be invoked in favour of an interpretation that would lead to a different result: 'support of the very highest authority can be found for general and apparently irreconcilable propositions'.[76] As Popplewell J said in *R v Home Secretary , ex p Naughton*, counsel:

> ... submitted that it is a canon of construction that any ambiguity in a statute affecting the liberty of the subject should be construed in favour of an accused. This is a valid submission, but another equally important canon of construction is to interpret legislation, so far as possible, to equate with common sense. Happily, common sense is still, I believe, part of the English common law. As Lord Goddard said in *Barnes v Jarvis*, '... a certain amount of common sense [must be applied] in construing statutes ...'.[77] Equally, there is always a presumption against construing an Act of Parliament so as to produce an absurd result.[78]

Indeed, the last edition of what was then a standard practitioner text, *Maxwell on the Interpretation of Statutes*, made a positive virtue of this feature.[79] Normative ambiguity may well be valued on occasion, but it is equally unhelpful where clear guidance is sought.[80] The cases *Stubbings v Webb* and *Lowsley v Forbes*

---

72 *Halki Shipping v Sopax Oils* [1998] 2 All ER 23, 43-44.
73 Per Henry LJ, ibid.
74 Per Lord Clyde, *Cutter v Eagle Star Insurance Co*; compare *Allen*, above, p 45.
75 Per Simon Brown LJ, *R v Bristol Magistrates' Court, ex p E*, op cit, at 804.
76 Per Viscount Simonds, *A-G v Prince Ernest Augustus of Hanover* [1957] AC 436, 461.
77 [1953] 1 All ER 1061, 1063.
78 [1997] 1 All ER 426, 438.
79 'Maxwell might well be sub-titled "the practitioner's armoury": it is, I trust, not taking too cynical a view of statutory interpretation in general, and this work in particular, to express the hope that counsel putting forward diverse interpretations of some statutory provision will be able to find in Maxwell dicta and illustrations in support of his case.' *Maxwell on the Interpretation of Statutes*, op cit, Preface.
80 When trying to avoid helping to prepare for a particularly expansive party, there may be some mileage in responding to a request based on the proposition that 'many hands make light work', that 'too many cooks spoil the broth'. On the effect of a 'lack of signposts' in public law, see M Beloff QC, 'Wednesbury, Padfield and All that Jazz: A Public Lawyer's View of Statute Law Reform' (1994) 15 *Statute Law Review* 147.

illustrate these points. Both concerned the interpretation of the Limitation Act 1980. In *Stubbings v Webb*, the question arose whether the newly enacted reduction in section 11(1) from six years to three in the limitation period applicable to actions for 'personal injury' applied to a claim for trespass to the person as well as to negligence.[81] There was a Court of Appeal decision which indicated that where that phrase appeared in the repealed legislation, it did.[82] On the other hand, the report of the Law Reform Committee established in 1977, on which the 1980 reforms were based, was clear that the three-year period should not apply to actions for trespass to the person. In *Lowsley v Forbes*, the question was whether the six-year limitation period specified in section 24 of the Act applied to proceedings by way of the execution of an existing judgment, rather than to a wholly fresh action. In this instance the Report's recommendations coincided with another decision on an equivalent section in earlier legislation.[83] Of these competing arguments, Lord Lloyd observed:

> The question in the end is what Parliament meant by 'action' in s 24(1) of the Act ... In answering that question, the help to be gained from the immediately preceding history is even stronger in this case than it was in *Stubbings v Webb*. For in that case there was a tension between two rules of construction. On the one hand there was the help to be gained from the Law Reform Committee Report. On the other hand there was the presumption that Parliament intended to give statutory effect to the decision of the Court of Appeal in *Letang v Cooper*. ... In the present case, both rules of construction pull in the same direction.[84]

Neither has systematic analysis been encouraged by an uncritical acceptance of the view that literalism, or exegetical interpretation, is generally a bad thing while a purposive approach is a good thing.[85] Little is left to be learnt about the judicial interpretation of statutes by a repetition of the well-worn triumvirate of the literal, golden and mischief rules. A standard formulation of the first of these is to be found in the *Sussex Peerage Case*:

> The only rule for the construction of Acts of Parliament is that they should be construed according to the intent of the Parliament which passed the Act. If the words of the statute are in themselves precise and unambiguous, then no more can be necessary than to expound those words in that natural and ordinary sense. The words themselves alone do, in such a case, best declare the intention of the law giver.[86]

So, for example, the question whether a society offered its members 'facilities and advantages' is one which, for the purpose of section 47(3) of the Value Added Tax Act 1983, is to be answered by giving those words 'their ordinary

---

81 [1993] AC 498.
82 *Letang v Cooper* [1965] 1 QB 232.
83 *W Lamb & Sons v Rider* [1948] 2 KB 331.
84 Op cit, p 906.
85 Chapter 4 above, pp 177-178. This point is relevant also to the interpretation of contracts; see *Summit Investment v British Steel Corpn, 'The Sounion'* [1987] 1 Lloyd's Rep 230.
86 Per Tindal CJ (1844) 11 Cl & Fin 85 at p 143.

everyday meaning'.[87] Where, however, the grammatical and ordinary sense of the statutory words lead to 'some absurdity, or some repugnance or inconsistency with the rest of the instrument', then that sense 'may be modified, so as to avoid the absurdity or inconsistency, but no further'.[88] In their favour it may be said that the literal and the golden 'rules' give expression to the sensible view that words and phrases should be given the meaning they bear in the statutory context in which they appear,[89] unless that yields an outcome which is incompatible with what it is considered that the legislation intended. Beyond that, they add little to the specific resolution of doubts about interpretation in a particular case. Literalism is frequently portrayed as promoting systemic, at the expense of social, values, which are to be discovered and promoted by a purposive approach; but, as we saw earlier, this conception is an oversimplification of what is involved in interpretive tasks.[90] For some interpreters, the method of interpretation is as good as the results it achieves; but one is not necessarily easier than the other.

The mischief rule is famously stated in *Heydon's Case*, quoted in full in chapter 3, but in abbreviated form here:

> That for the sure and true interpretation of all statutes in general (be they penal or beneficial, restrictive or enlarging of the common law) four things are to be discerned and considered: 1st. What was the common law before the making of the Act. 2nd. What was the mischief and defect for which the common law did not provide. 3rd. What remedy the parliament hath resolved and appointed to cure the disease of the commonwealth. And 4th. The true reason of the remedy.[91]

---

87 Per Beldam LJ, *Customs and Excise Comrs v British Field Sports Society* [1998] 2 All ER 1003, 1011. Similarly, the 'educated reader' would have little difficulty in concluding that land on which radioactive material had been dumped, with the consequence that its topsoil had since been classified under the relevant regulations as 'radioactive waste', thus requiring it to be excavated and removed, had by virtue of the reduction in its market value, sustained 'damage' within s 7(1)(a) of the Nuclear Installations Act 1965. Such a reader, Lord Lloyd continued, might be surprised by an interpretation of 'damage' which confined its scope to physical alteration; *Blue Circle Industries v Ministry of Defence* [1998] 3 All ER 385, 389.

88 Per Lord Wensleydale, *Grey v Pearson* (1857) 6 HL Cas 61 at 106. In *R v Home Secretary, ex p Naughton* [1997] 1 All ER 426 the Court of Appeal fully accepted the absurdity of the appellant's interpretation of s 67 of the Criminal Justice Act 1967 which would lead to one prisoner who had been remanded on bail serving out the five-year term of imprisonment to which he had been sentenced for the five offences he had committed (one year for each), while a second prisoner, who had committed exactly the same five offences and been sentenced to exactly the same term, would, because he had spent one year on remand in custody for each offence, walk free. In rejecting this 'complete nonsense' in favour of a more sensible interpretation, and one consistent with the statutory language, the Court made no reference to the 'golden' rule. See chapter 1, section 6.2.

89 See for example, *R v Birmingham City Council, ex p Mohammed*, per Dyson J at 793; *R v Harrow London Borough Council, ex p Fahia* [1998] 4 All ER 137 in which the House of Lords, while expressing sympathy with the appellant's case, was 'unable to extract from the statutory language' sufficient justification to accept it; (per Lord Browne-Wilkinson, p 143); *R v Governor of Glen Parva Young Offender Institution, ex p G* [1998] 2 All ER 295, 298 where the section in question appeared to Simon Brown LJ to be 'plain in its meaning and to mean what it says'.

90 Above, p 153.

91 (1584) 3 Co Rep 7a.

In interpreting older legislation, courts may well continue to employ the language of the mischief rule;[92] likewise, modern legislation may seek to remedy 'mischiefs and defects for which the common law did not provide' or to plug a specific gap in an existing statutory regime.[93] But as the Law Commissions argued in 1965, it is anachronistic to approach the interpretation of legislation dealing with such matters as education, employment, social security, the environment, taxation, and the regulation of companies and financial services as if it were 'only designed to deal with an evil'. Such an approach simply fails to recognise that the bulk of modern legislation, as in the areas mentioned, is enacted 'to further a positive social purpose'.[94] Its interpretation should not therefore be constrained by the limited perspective implied by the mischief rule.

Bennion observes of statutory interpretation:

> ... there is no golden rule. Nor is there a mischief rule, or a literal rule, or any other cure-all rule of thumb. Instead there are a thousand and one interpretative *criteria*. Fortunately they do not all present themselves in any one case; but those that do yield factors that the interpreter must figuratively weigh and balance. That is the nearest we can get to a golden rule, and it is not very near.[95]

For the purposes of the reader who wishes to obtain some foothold on the way in which judges approach interpretation, this perhaps overstates the case. Based on the observations made by a number of Law Lords and other senior members of the judiciary in recent years, judicial interpretation can be briefly analysed as comprising three stages:

(a) Firstly, the judge reads the statute in its legal and factual context so as to acquire an understanding, first, of the legislature's purpose in enacting it and, second, the role of the provision with which he is concerned in giving effect to that purpose. At this stage he may look at any material he chooses.

(b) The next task is to read the particular words in issue in their primary and natural meaning if they are ordinary words, or according to their technical meaning if that is apt; in either case, in the context of the statutory purpose. If the chosen meaning gives effect to the purpose as the judge understands it, the interpretive task is complete.

(c) If the chosen meaning produces an absurd, unintelligible or unworkable result which the legislature cannot reasonably be supposed to have

92 For example, Lord Lloyd in *Effort Shipping v Linden SA*, op cit, at 503; and Lord Goff, *R v Bournewood NHS Trust, ex p L* [1998] 3 All ER 289.
93 For example, *R v Effick* [1995] 1 AC 309, 319, per Lord Oliver, and *Stevenson v Rogers* [1999] 1 All ER 613. In the latter case, the Court of Appeal held that the use of the words 'in the course of a business' in s 14(2) of the Sale of Goods Act 1979 in place of 'a seller who deals in goods of that description' in s 14(2) of the Sale of Goods Act 1893, which the 1979 Act replaced, was a deliberate step designed to rectify the mischief identified by the Final Report of the Committee on Consumer Protection (1962, Cmnd 1781), that, because s 14(2) of the 1893 Act only applied to commercial sales, it offered only limited protection to the consumer in a private sale; see Potter LJ, 619-626.
94 Law Commission, op cit, paras 80-81, n 177.
95 Op cit, p 3.

intended, the judge may rely on an alternative interpretation. This alternative should be one that the statutory words are capable of bearing. In choosing this alternative, the judge may rely on any one or more of the wide range of prescriptions that the courts have approved for this purpose. He may, in addition, rely on a range of extra-statutory material, although there are limits on its use.

This is the kind of analysis which Cross has put forward as constituting the 'rules of English statutory interpretation'.[96] They exemplify how a purposive approach, which, in Lord Griffiths' words in *Pepper v Hart*, seeks 'to give effect to the true purpose of legislation',[97] can be conducted. This approach represents the prevailing mood of the appellate courts to the interpretation of statutes. In 1975 Lord Diplock commented that 'if one looks back over the actual decisions of [the House of Lords] on questions of statutory construction over the last thirty years one cannot fail to be struck by the evidence of a trend away from the purely literal towards the purposive construction of statutory provisions'.[98] By 1997 the trend that began fifty years earlier had, in Lord Steyn's forthright views in *IRC v McGuckian*, become more of an established practice:

> Towards the end of the last century Pollock characterised the approach of judges to statutory interpretation as follows: '... Parliament generally changes the law for the worse, and that the business of the judges is to keep the mischief of its interference within the narrowest possible bounds.'[99] Whatever the merits of this observation may have been when it was made, or even earlier in this century, it is demonstrably no longer true. During the last 30 years there has been a shift away from literalist to purposive methods of construction. Where there is no obvious meaning of a statutory provision the modern emphasis is on a contextual approach designed to identify the purpose of a statute and give effect to it.[1]

Opinions differ on how to present the trends and shifts which have been identified in judicial practice. One view suggests that a sharp distinction

96 Op cit, p 48. Cross relies in particular on the remarks of Lord Simon in *Maunsell v Olins* [1975] AC 373, of Lord Diplock in that case, in *Carter v Bradbeer*, op cit and in *Fothergill v Monarch Airlines* [1981] AC 251.

97 [1993] AC 593, 617. Compare Cockburn CJ in *Allen*, above pp 46-47.

98 *Carter v Bradbeer*, op cit, at 1206.

99 *Essays in Jurisprudence and Ethics* (1882), p 85. More recent echoes of the view that statute law is additional to, rather than an integral part of, the law of the land can be seen in Lord Scarman's observation that the modern English judge, though giving 'unswerving loyalty to the enacted word of Parliament, construes that word strictly, in its statutory context, and always on the premise, usually unspoken, that Parliament legislates against the background of an all-embracing customary law', *English Law – the New Dimension* (1974), p 3. See also above, pp 249-250.

1 [1997] 3 All ER 818, 824. Other examples may be found in *DPP v McKeown* [1997] 1 All ER 737, 743, per Lord Hoffmann; *Harrods Ltd v Remick* [1998] 1 All ER 52 at 58, per Sir Richard Scott VC; *Re M (a minor)* [1994] 3 All ER 298, 309, per Lord Templeman; and in the judgment of Nicholls LJ (now Lord Nicholls) in *Re Marr* [1990] 2 All ER 880 in which his Lordship, rejecting the proposition that where there is an irreconcilable inconsistency between two provisions in the same statute, the later must prevail, said, at 886: 'such a mechanical approach to the construction of statutes is altogether out of step with the modern, purposive approach to the interpretation of statutes and documents'.

between literal and purposive interpretation is misleading. That distinction encourages the view that the judiciary approach the task of interpretation by asking themselves firstly, are the words of the Act plain and unambiguous in their context?, and secondly, if they are not, how can they be interpreted so as to give effect to the intention and purpose of Parliament? Some years ago Glanville Williams argued that a better description of what was then current practice was reflected in the questions: What was the statute trying to do? Will the proposed interpretation give effect to that object? Is the proposed interpretation ruled out by the language of the statute?[2] Freeman's more recent review suggests that these various questions can be reformulated as 'just one "rule" of interpretation, a revamped version of the literal rule which requires the general context and purpose to be taken into consideration before any decision is reached concerning the ordinary (or, where appropriate, the technical) meaning of statutory words'.[3] Likewise Cross speaks of the 'dominance of a single rule of interpretation'.[4] In Freeman's reformulation the traditional 'golden' rule occupies a subservient role, to be relied on whenever the judge determines that the application of the words in their ordinary meaning produces a result which cannot be supposed to have been Parliament's intention. The distinction between interpretation according to the provision's effect and interpretation according to its purpose is used by Cownie and Bradney to suggest that the 'golden' rule and the purposive approach are of equal standing, even if it is the case that recent judicial practice favours the latter.[5] By contrast, Bennion treats purposive interpretation as only one of a range of interpretive presumptions. In his analysis, purposive construction may be linked either with a literal construction, being a case in which the literal meaning of the enactment accords with the legislative purpose, or with a 'strained' construction, being a case where the literal meaning does not, and another meaning is sought in order to give effect to the purpose.[6]

These varying characterisations suggest that care should be taken not to overstate the implications of what Lord Steyn described as the 'modern emphasis' on a contextual approach. As with precedent, the judges have given themselves a good deal of leeway as to what are considered to be legitimate techniques of interpretation. Firstly, the judicial pronouncements, both in and out of court, which are relied upon to support the analysis presented by these various writers, are no more than that, even if they were clearly intended by their authors to be attempts to systematise a range of prescriptions. Other senior judicial voices have expressed reservations 'about the reliability of generalised presumptions and maxims when engaged in the task of finding out what Parliament intended by a particular form of words'. Such generalisations can constrain the judge, since they tend to treat 'all statutes,

---

2   'The Meaning of Literal Interpretation' (1981) 131 *New Law Journal* 1128.
3   M Freeman, 'The Modern English Approach to Statutory Construction' in M Freeman (ed), op cit, p 2.
4   Cross, op cit, p v.
5   F Cownie and A Bradney, *English Legal System in Context* (1996), pp 114-115.
6   Bennion, op cit, pp 731-742.

and all situations to which they apply, as if they were the same'.[7] By contrast, as Lord Reid once said, the 'rules' of statutory interpretation 'are not rules in the ordinary sense of having some binding force. They are our servants not our masters ... in each case we must look at all relevant circumstances and decide as a matter of judgment what weight we attach to any particular rules'.[8]

Secondly, judicial practice does not, for the most part, reflect an explicitly structured procedure. Judges do refer to the 'intention of Parliament' and 'the purpose of the statute' when interpreting a disputed provision, but these references do not routinely require a considered analysis of its legislative background. As the sample of cases from the *All England Law Reports* shows, in most cases judges resolve their doubts by reference primarily to the legal context of which the statute is part – employment law,[9] the law of the family or dealing with children,[10] tax law,[11] – and in particular to any prior decisions. Many judges use sub-headings in their judgments ('the facts', 'the statutory framework', 'the legislative background', 'the state of the argument', 'the question of construction') and some may on occasion adopt a more structured approach which analyses in an increasingly focused sequence, the scheme of the Act, the regime governing the matter in dispute, and the arguments relating to the particular words of the disputed provision. However helpful such methods may be for the reader, none is obligatory, nor are there any conventions governing their use.[12]

Thirdly, one should not be misled into thinking that to adopt a purposive approach necessarily means that there is a single purpose to be found, or that different judges will agree on what the purpose(s) of a disputed provision might be, or how formulated;[13] or, indeed, that judges are agreed on what the adoption of a purposive approach might entail.[14] In short, one should not think that the adoption of a purposive approach will resolve all problems of interpretation.[15] Nor, assuming that a purpose can be identified, should one be misled into thinking that a judge will or can do anything he likes in order

---

7 Lord Mustill, *L'Office Cherifien des Phosphates v Yamashita Steamship Co* [1994] 2 WLR 39, 48.
8 *Maunsell v Olins* [1975] AC 373 at 382. Of the rule of construction that when it re-enacts a word or phrase which has been the subject of a judicial decision, Parliament is presumed to endorse that decision, Lord Lloyd said in *Lowsley v Forbes* at 905, 'the rule, like other rules of construction, is not in any way conclusive. It is an aid: no more'.
9 R Rideout, 'Statutory Interpretation in Labour Law' in M Freeman (ed), op cit, p 17.
10 M Freeman, 'Interpreting Children's Legislation' in M Freeman (ed), op cit, p 65.
11 J Dyson, 'Interpreting Tax Statutes' in M Freeman (ed), op cit, p 45.
12 An examination of judicial interpretation shows that the same judge will sometimes adopt an explicitly structured approach and sometimes not, and that even where the same judge does adopt such an approach, its structure varies from case to case. Compare, for example, Henry LJ's decisions in *R v Crown Court at Stafford, ex p Shipley* [1998] 2 All ER 465 and *DPP v Hynde* [1998]1 All ER 649.
13 See for example the differing views held by the House of Lords in *Brady v Brady* [1989] AC 755 as to the purpose of s 153 of the Companies Act 1985.
14 Per Buxton LJ, *Fletcher Estates v Secretary of State for the Environment* [1998] 4 All ER 838, 844: '"Purposive" construction, whatever exactly it may import, is still nevertheless an exercise in construction, not judicial law-making ..[if the court had construed the Act in a given manner]... that conclusion cannot be displaced ... by appeal to an alternative theory of construction.'
15 Chapter 5, section 3.

to further what he considers the statutory purpose to be. At a general level, it is tempting to see a purposive approach as a modern version of the mischief rule. However, they do differ.[16] The purposive approach is both wider and narrower than the mischief rule. It is wider in that it authorises reliance on extra-statutory sources as a means of elucidating the legislative purpose; the mischief rule confined the judge to what could be discerned about the mischief to be remedied to the Act itself. It is narrower in that the mischief rule supported the proposition that if the statutory words did not 'suppress the mischief, and advance the remedy', then it was apt for the judge 'always to make such construction as shall'. If this is taken to imply that a purposive approach would entitle (or, as the Barons of the Exchequer in *Heydon's Case* put it, oblige) the judge to adopt an interpretation that would give effect to the legislative purpose, but at the expense of the provision's linguistic context, then such an implication would be inappropriate, at least according to current judicial practice.

These points are illustrated in *Cutter v Eagle Star Insurance*.[17] The question arose whether a car park was a 'road' for the purposes of the liability of an insurance company under section 151 of the Road Traffic Act 1988. In reviewing the legislative history of obligatory third-party insurance, Lord Clyde asked whether the purpose was to protect the public from the use of motor vehicles on roads, or more widely, simply from their use? He concluded that it was the latter, and that therefore it was appropriate to construe the word 'road' widely. But, he added, adopting a purposive approach did not mean construing that word so widely that the court was ultimately describing a place which one would not normally think of as a road, especially where the statutory language was otherwise clear. What his Lordship actually said was:

> By giving a purposive construction to the word 'road' what is meant is a strained construction, beyond the literal meaning of the word or what the word would mean in ordinary usage, sufficient to satisfy that expression of the purpose of the legislation.[18]
>
> It may be perfectly proper to adopt even a strained construction to enable the object and purpose of legislation to be fulfilled. But it cannot be taken to the length of applying unnatural meanings to familiar words or of so stretching the language that its former shape is transformed into something which is not only significantly different but has a name of its own. This must particularly be so where the language has no evident ambiguity or uncertainty about it. While I have recognised that there could be some exceptional cases where what can reasonably be described as a car park may also qualify as a road, it is the unusual character of such cases which would justify such a result in the application of the statutory language rather than any distortion of the language itself.[19]

---

16 See Cross, op cit, pp 17-20; Cownie and Bradney, op cit, pp 116-117.
17 Op cit.
18 Compare Bennion's 'purposive-and-strained' construction; op cit, p 740.
19 Op cit, p 425. See also *R v Secretary of State for the Home Department, ex p Gilmore* [1998] 1 All ER 264 in which Pill LJ refused to accept that a purposive construction could be used to extend a specific statutory list of crimes to generic offences; *R v Crown Court at Woolwich, ex p Gilligan* [1998] 2 All ER 1 in which May LJ rejected a purposive interpretation as being unsupported either by the statute in question or the earlier authorities.

Fourthly, and as the judiciary can be quick to reiterate, the judicial interpretation of statutes takes place within the constraints of the division of functions between the legislature and the courts that was described by Lord Scarman.[20] *IRC v McGuckian* was a case concerning tax avoidance. The questions of general interpretive significance to which it gave rise were, first, whether fiscal legislation was to be interpreted literally regardless of the purpose of the disputed section and, secondly, whether the courts were obliged, in dealing with tax avoidance schemes, to adopt a step by step analysis, treating each step as a distinct transaction producing its own tax consequences irrespective of the purpose of their sequence, which was to avoid the payment of tax. It is not necessary here to explore the complexities either of tax avoidance schemes or of the judiciary's response to them during the 1980s and 1990s.[21] For present purposes we need note only that what Lord Steyn described as the 'intellectual breakthrough' on these two fronts came in the House's decision in *Ramsay v IRC*.[22] This case broke with the courts' earlier view that each step did have to be separately analysed,[23] and thus permitted the court to examine the true nature of the composite transaction. How did this *volte face* in statutory interpretation come about?

> The new *Ramsay* principle was not invented on a juristic basis independent of statute. That would have been indefensible since a court has no power to amend a tax statute. The principle was developed as a matter of statutory construction... The new development was not based on a linguistic analysis of the meaning of particular words in a statute. It was founded on a broad purposive interpretation, *giving effect to the intention of Parliament*. The principle enunciated in the *Ramsay* case was therefore based on an orthodox form of statutory interpretation.[24]

In other words, the House was doing no more than it is constitutionally required and entitled to do. It is required to interpret statutes so as to give effect to the intention of Parliament; it is entitled to determine how it will accomplish that task. In this respect, fidelity to the text is no more nor any less important that fidelity to the purpose.[25] Purposive and literalist interpretations may therefore be seen as representing varying emphases on how questions about the construction of individual statutory provisions are to be answered; in particular, on how far a judge is prepared to go in deciding whether a proposed

---

20 Above, p 275.
21 See J Tiley and D Collinson, *Butterworths Tax Guide* (1998), paras 2.01-2.16.
22 [1982] AC 300. Lord Steyn also confirmed that fiscal statutes did not belong to a class requiring special interpretive techniques. See Dyson, op cit.
23 Enshrined in the House of Lords' decision in *IRC v Duke of Westminster* [1936] AC 1. See above, p 249, n 2.
24 Lord Steyn, op cit, p 825 (emphasis added). The orthodoxy was contained in Lord Wilberforce's observation that any tax Act is to be construed in accordance with the principle that the subject is only to be taxed on clear words. 'What are "clear words" is to be ascertained on normal principles; these do not confine the court to literal interpretation. There may, indeed should, be considered the context and scheme of the relevant Act as a whole, and its purpose may, indeed should be regarded'; *Ramsay v IRC* [1982] AC 300, 323.
25 Cross suggests that the purposive approach has given greater emphasis to 'fidelity to the objectives aimed at by Parliament'; op cit, p 20.

interpretation is or is not sustained by the language of the statute. Context, language and purpose are all relevant to this task, but even against the backgound of cases such as *Pepper v Hart* and *IRC v McGuckian*, there are still no settled priority rules for weighing these factors.

4.3   Other extra-statutory material

An obvious source from which arguments about the interpretation of the provisions of an Act may be constructed is its legislative history. At the very least, familiarity with the Act's history can inform the reader about the concerns that the legislature sought to address and the cogency and weight of the alternative constructions then being advanced. It may be that similar or associated arguments now being put forward are supported or undermined by them. Consideration of an Act's legislative history typically means going back to the original statute, to the judicial decisions on its provisions, and to the successive amendments that were made to them, which may well have been made as a consequence of those decisions. Such historical analysis is a regular feature of the judicial interpretation of statutes,[26] and may well include reference to the parliamentary debates as a means of ascertaining the legislative background.[27] There may, indeed, be cases in which, had its attention been drawn to that history, the court would have reached a different decision.[28]

The non-judicial reader too may obtain assistance from Hansard which goes beyond an understanding of the Act's legislative history, for example, as to the meaning or scope of individual words or phrases. Useful as it may be, reliance on this kind of assistance is, if it is to be argued in court, nominally regulated by the statement agreed by the House of Lords in *Pepper v Hart*, discussed below.

Apart from statutory and judicial material, support for alternative interpretations may be found in academic writings, annotations and other commentaries on the Act. Other kinds of material which may be of value are those reports prepared by official bodies upon which the statute was based, the explanatory notes which accompany Bills through Parliament, and the vast range of circulars, pamphlets and leaflets which are prepared by or on behalf of government agencies. The quality and helpfulness of these materials vary considerably. In areas such as health and safety at work, social security, discrimination, taxation and education, departmental directives and guidelines concerning the implementation and interpretation of provisions will, as we have noted, frequently be treated as authoritative by many official interpreters. Sometimes, as in the case of the Codes of Practice made under the Police and Criminal Evidence Act 1984 or the Highway Code, the governing legislation specifies how they may be used by a court.[29] On the other hand, reports of

---

26 See, for example, *Redrow Homes v Bett Bros* [1998] 1 All ER 385; *R v Thames Magistrates' Court, ex p Horgan* [1998] 1 All ER 559; *Wellcome Trust v Hamad*.

27 *R v Dudley Magistrates' Court, ex p Hollis* [1998] 1 All ER 759, 768-769; *R v Secretary of State, ex p Probyn* [1998] 1 All ER 357, 362; *Lowsley v Forbes* [1998] 3 All ER 897.

28 *R v Bournewood NHS Trust, ex p L* [1998] 3 All ER 289 per Lord Goff, p 297.

29 See s 67 of the Police and Criminal Evidence Act 1984 and s 38 of the Road Traffic Act 1988 respectively.

Royal Commissions, the Law Commissions and similar bodies, or the responses given by the Minister to questions posed about the scope of a clause during the parliamentary debates on a Bill, may or may not be helpful. Whether they are depends on such factors as the presence in the report of a draft Bill with accompanying explanations of its legal effects and, if there is, how close it is in substance to the statute as enacted, or the clarity of the response that was given. Sometimes the interpreter may have little to go on which is of much help beyond the text of the statute; in others he may be in danger of being inundated. Sometimes these extra-statutory sources of information raise more doubts than they resolve.

Three questions need to be distinguished: (a) What kinds of explanatory material should be officially provided by the rule-maker and in what form? (b) What kinds of material should be officially recognised as aids to interpretation in formal legal argument? (c) What weight should be given to each kind of aid which is admissible? We propose to identify here the main points relating to each question.[30]

(a) What kinds of explanatory material should be officially provided by the rule-maker and in what form?

This question has for the most part not been extensively discussed in print. Some years ago the Law Commission recommended the use of specially prepared explanatory and illustrative material in appropriate cases,[31] but this recommendation has not been acted upon, at least in legislation. In an early version of its draft Criminal Code, the Law Commission included as an Appendix a series of problem questions and answers designed to elucidate aspects of the Code's interpretation. Moreover, it was intended that this Appendix would have statutory force. This particular proposal was withdrawn in the face of the criticism that it would hinder rather than help the courts in their efforts to interpret the Code as the Commission intended.[32] One might also suspect that the proposal was objectionable precisely because it sought to assume what the judiciary have always regarded as their proper role, namely, determining how to interpret the statute. On the other hand, the publication with a Bill of a 'user-friendly' explanatory memorandum may be seen as a very limited application of the notion that the rule-maker should give some assistance to interpreters.[33]

(b) What kinds of material should be officially recognised as aids to interpretation in formal legal argument?

The question of the admissibility of certain types of material in formal legal argument, on the other hand, has been the subject of considerable judicial and academic attention. On the basis of a number of House of Lords' decisions,

---

30 See Bennion, op cit, p 466ff for a more extended account.
31 Op cit, paras 63-73.
32 Law Commission, *Criminal Law: Codification of the Criminal Law* (1985, Law Com 143).
33 See above, p 238.

the following propositions concerning legislative and pre-legislative policy documents of different kinds may be formulated:[34]

1   the reports of Royal Commissions, the Law Commissions, the Criminal Law Revision Committee, the Law Reform Committee, parliamentary Select Committees and departmental enquiries and working parties may be cited and relied upon to clarify the purpose of the legislation and, in cases where it is ambiguous or obscure, or leads to an absurdity, the meaning of individual words;[35]
2   international treaties and conventions which are incorporated into domestic law (that is, enacted by statute), and the *travaux préparatoires* which preceded them, may be referred to where the words of a section are ambiguous or vague, in order to ascertain their meaning; however the weight to be attached to *travaux préparatoires* will vary from case to case and should only be relied upon where they are accessible and indicate a clear intention on the part of the rule-makers;[36] and
3   the official report of parliamentary proceedings (Hansard) is admissible where the legislation is ambiguous or obscure, or leads to an absurdity, provided that the statements relied on are those of the Bill's sponsor and are clear (*Pepper v Hart*).[37]

The issue in *Pepper v Hart* concerned the tax which ought to be paid by a schoolmaster whose son attended, at a concessionary rate, the independent fee-paying school at which his father taught.[38] For many years school masters at Malvern College had enjoyed this fringe benefit to their employment. The fees they paid (20% of the full fee) more than covered the variable costs incurred by the College in providing for their children (eg food, laundry), while their presence did not increase its fixed costs (eg heating, staff salaries). Nor did the taxpayer's son deprive the College of any full fee-paying pupil. In these respects, the benefit enjoyed by the taxpayer was in general terms similar to that enjoyed by employees, for example, of railway and airline companies,

---

34   *Black-Clawson International v Papierwerke Waldhof-Aschaffenburg* [1975] AC 591; *Fothergill v Monarch Airlines* [1981] AC 251; *James Buchanan v Babco Forwarding and Shipping* [1978] AC 141; *Quazi v Quazi* [1980] AC 744; *Gatoil International Inc. v Arkwright-Boston Manufacturers Mutual Insurance Co* [1985] AC 255; *Davis v Johnson* (chapter 1, section 12.5.3); and *Pepper v Hart* (chapter 1, section 12.6). One of the considerations which motivated the Law Commissions' recommendations was the achievement of a more rational mode of interpretation in which account would be taken of 'the interaction between the form of a communication and the rules by which it is to be interpreted'. Another was clarification of the status of these extrinsic materials in formal legal argument. The latter has been substantially achieved as a result of these cases.
35   *Effort Shipping v Linden SA* (Law Commission Report); *Harrods Ltd v Remick* [1998] 1 All ER 52 (White Paper); *Cutter v Eagle Star* (Departmental Report); *Lowsley v Forbes* (Law Reform Committee).
36   *Effort Shipping v Linden SA; R v Secretary of State for the Home Department, ex p Canbolat* [1998] 1 All ER 161.
37   See chapter 1, section 12.6.
38   See D Miers, 'Taxing Perks and Interpreting Statutes' (1993) 56 *Modern Law Review* 695 for an extended discussion of the issues raised by the case.

who travel free or at a concessionary rate. Such benefits ('perks') are taxable. The basis on which the tax is to be charged is the 'cash equivalent' of the benefit, which is in turn defined as the 'cost of the benefit' to the employer. The point of interpretation in *Pepper v Hart* therefore had implications well beyond its particular facts. The question was whether that cost was the average or the marginal cost per pupil. If it were the former, the schoolmaster would receive a benefit comprising the difference between the average cost and the actual fee he paid; if the latter, he received no benefit (because the fee he paid covered the marginal cost), and was thus not taxable.

The provision in issue was section 154 of the Income and Corporation Taxes Act 1988, a consolidating Act. The original provision was introduced for the purpose of subjecting fringe benefits to a more exacting charge than had been the case. During the debates on this provision, the Financial Secretary to the Treasury was specifically asked about the position of school teachers. As one of the clauses had been drafted, it appeared that they would be treated as receiving a 'cash equivalent' based on the cost to the employer of providing the service to the public (the 'average cost'). The clause was withdrawn, the Minister saying 'now the benefit will be assessed on the cost to the employer, which would be very small indeed in this case'.

The appeal was initially argued in the House of Lords on the basis only of the relevant provisions in the 1988 Act. At this stage a majority of the House agreed with the Revenue's argument, that the cash equivalent was the average cost. Counsel for the taxpayers then drew attention to the parliamentary exchanges, with the result that the appeal was re-heard before seven Law Lords, itself a highly unusual event. By a majority of 6:1, the House agreed to modify the exclusionary rule under which the courts had traditionally refused to consult Hansard for the purpose of resolving doubts about interpretation. 'We profess to give effect to the intention of Parliament when we are construing a statute and yet we refuse to check whether Parliament said what its intention was, what it intended to cover or what a particular word was perhaps intended to mean.'[39] On the basis of the Minister's statements, the House held that Parliament had indeed intended that school teachers should not be taxed on the average cost to the employer of providing the benefit, but on the marginal cost.[40]

The question whether the courts should take account of what was said in debate for the purpose of resolving particular points of interpretation had, over the years, attracted a good deal of academic and, latterly, judicial attention. Aspects of the arguments apply also to the wider class of pre-parliamentary materials. Some of the literature addressed the question whether it is possible

---

39 Lord Griffiths, House of Lords Debates, Vol 405, col 45 (13 February 1980).

40 It may be noted that the Minister said that the benefit will be assessed 'on the cost to the employer'. That, of course, begs the question that was the issue in the case, namely, how is the cost to the employer to be assessed. It is his following comment, that it 'would be very small indeed' which suggests that the Minister had marginal cost in mind. It may be argued that this barely meets the criterion specified in *Pepper v Hart*, that the statement to be relied on by the court is itself clear. See Sir Nicholas Lyell, '*Pepper v Hart*: the Government Perspective' (1994) 15 *Statute Law Rev* 1 and Bennion (1997) op cit, pp 483-487.

to know the intentions of a collegiate body;[41] others doubted the wisdom of attending to them, even where they were capable of being known. As Lord Scarman observed in *Davis v Johnson*, the 'cut and thrust' of parliamentary debate is unlikely to be a reliable guide to the legislators' intentions.[42] The objections to the use of the Official Report of Parliamentary Debates as a source of evidence of legislative intent largely focused on their relevance, reliability and accessibility. Relevance and reliability are also factors affecting the utility of pre-parliamentary materials. There was, too, until 1980, a parliamentary rule of privilege which forbade counsel from citing Hansard in court without prior permission from the relevant House. It was therefore thought inappropriate for judges to cite it.[43]

In essence, two arguments sustained the exclusionary rule. One of these stemmed from the linked constitutional considerations that the statute alone is the uniquely authoritative statement of what the law is and that it is for the judges authoritatively to determine its scope in disputed cases. These points were forcefully expressed by Lord Wilberforce:

> Legislation in England is passed by Parliament and put into the form of written words. The legislation is given effect on subjects by virtue of judicial decision, and it is the function of the courts to say what the application of words used to particular cases or individuals is to be. This power which had been devolved on the judges from the earliest times is an essential part of the constitutional process by which subjects are brought under the rule of law – as distinct from the rule of the King or the rule of Parliament; and it would be a degradation of that process if the court were to be merely a reflecting mirror of what some other interpretation agency might say.[44]

The second argument was pragmatic. As lawyers would routinely have to check Hansard in case there was a relevant Ministerial remark, the costs of obtaining legal advice and of litigation would be increased. For Lord Mackay LC this objection was insuperable: 'practically every question of *statutory* construction that comes before the courts will involve an argument that the case falls under one or more [of the heads agreed to by the majority].'[45] However narrowly those heads are drawn, it would in any case be necessary to discover whether the sponsor had said anything to the point in order to determine whether the *Pepper v Hart* criteria were met. Drawing on the experience in New Zealand and Australia, where costs have not dramatically increased in consequence of the admissibility of parliamentary proceedings, the majority considered these concerns to be exaggerated.[46] Six years on, these costs do not yet appear to be

---

41 Chapter 5, secton 2.1.
42 Chapter 1, section 12.5.3, p 107.
43 See Lord Mackay LC, 'Finishers, Refiners, and Polishers: The Judicial Role in the Interpretation of Statutes' [1989] *Statute Law Rev* 151; Lord Scarman, ibid.
44 *Black-Clawson International v Papierwerke Waldhof-Aschaffenburg*, at 629. In the same case Lord Reid put it shortly: 'the construction of the provisions of an Act is for the court and no-one else' (p 614); and to like effect, Lord Diplock in *Fothergill v Monarch Airlines*, op cit, at 279–280; Lord Browne-Wilkinson in *Pepper v Hart*, op cit, pp 633ff.
45 Op cit, p 614, original emphasis. See also above, p 271, n 35.
46 An important issue is access to Hansard. When the Law Commission and the *Renton Report* objected to its use it was available only on paper. It can now be accessed on the internet (www.parliament.uk), and earlier debates are available on CD-ROM.

substantial. Even if Hansard shows that there was no debate about the disputed interpretation, that finding is itself of value. Like conducting a search for previous decisions, the absence of potentially authoritative lines of argument does not necessarily weaken the interpreter's position: that depends on her standpoint. Had the Financial Secretary to the Treasury given no indication about the position of school teachers, the Inland Revenue's interpretation would have prevailed.

The relaxation of the exclusionary rule in *Pepper v Hart* is both permissive and, nominally at least, restrictive in important respects. Lord Browne-Wilkinson said:

> ... as a matter of law, there are sound reasons for making a limited modification to the existing rule (subject to strict safeguards) unless there are constitutional or practical reasons to outweigh them. In my judgment, subject to the privileges of the House of Commons, reference to Parliamentary materials should be permitted as an aid to the construction of legislation which is ambiguous or obscure or the literal meaning of which leads to an absurdity. Even in such cases references in court to Parliamentary material should only be permitted where such material clearly discloses the mischief aimed at or the legislative intention lying behind the ambiguous or obscure words. In the case of statements made in Parliament, as at present advised I cannot foresee that any statement other than the statement of the minister or other promoter of the Bill is likely to meet those criteria.[47]

It is permissive in that a court is under no obligation to refer to Hansard in order to resolve a disputed point of interpretation. Indeed, subject to the general point that the court is master of its own procedure and may, therefore, resort to Hansard in exceptional cases, it remains the case that a court should not normally use Hansard as an aid to interpretation.[48] The rule is relaxed only in respect of ambiguity, absurdity or obscurity, and these difficulties must appear only as a result of a genuine initial attempt to make sense of the provision in its statutory and linguistic context. 'Genuine' means that the court (or counsel) should not invent such difficulties, certainly not as a result of having read Hansard first.[49] Assuming that these threshold criteria are met, reliance on the sponsor's statements is restricted to instances where they are clear and directed to the matter in issue. The courts have undoubtedly taken these 'stringent tests' seriously.[50] In both *BCCI v Price Waterhouse* and *R v Land*, for example, the court expressly refused to refer to Hansard on the ground that the disputed sections, though giving rise to questions of interpretation, were unambiguous and, in

---

47 Op cit, p 634.
48 See the extended analysis in Bennion, op cit, pp 472-523. Counsel are required to provide copies in advance to the court and to the other side of the extracts upon which they intend to rely; *Practice Note (procedures: reference to Hansard)* [1995] 1 All ER 234.
49 Lord Oliver, op cit, p 620.
50 Per Simon Brown LJ in *R v Crown Court at Stafford, ex p Shipley*, at 483. See also *Melluish v BMI (No 3)* [1995] 4 All ER 453. Marshall suggests that the scope of *Pepper v Hart* can be described in the form of a series of negative propositions arranged in lexical order: it does not apply where there is no ambiguity, etc, nor where the statement is made otherwise than by the Bill's sponsor, nor where the statement is unclear or has been superseded; G Marshall, 'Hansard and the Interpretation of Statutes' in D Oliver and G Drewry (eds), *The Law and Parliament* (1997), pp 139, 146.

the former case, that even if this criterion were met, the Minister's statements did not unequivocally support one interpretation.[51]

Notwithstanding the formal restrictions placed by Lord Browne-Wilkinson on the circumstances under which recourse to Hansard should be permitted,[52] the courts have used the debates to confirm their reading of the disputed section, though none of the threshold criteria was met.[53] This is perhaps not surprising, given that the judiciary have traditionally shown themselves to be unwilling to fetter their discretion in their approach the interpretation of statutes.[54] There are, too, areas of uncertainty. *Pepper v Hart* offers no analysis of the possible varieties of ambiguity with which an interpreter may genuinely be faced. Nor does it offer guidance as to the weight to be accorded to the sponsor's statements when compared either with 'such other Parliamentary material as is necessary to understand them', or with alternative interpretations suggested by other established prescriptions.[55] Whether these or the other formalities and uncertainties contained in *Pepper v Hart* should inhibit interpreters operating outside a judicial context is a different matter. For them, the question is, what materials can I use that best advance my argument? It is only when that argument has to be presented to a judge that these matters become important.

The decision in *Pepper v Hart* also raises wider questions concerning the relationship between the legislature and the judiciary as the authoritative interpreter of its wishes.[56] Lord Browne-Wilkinson observed that courts are frequently criticised for their failure to give effect to the words of Parliament in the sense that they were intended by Parliament to bear. He continued:

> This failure is due not to cussedness but to ignorance of what Parliament intended by the obscure words of the legislation. The courts should not deny themselves the light which parliamentary materials may shed on the meaning of the words Parliament has used and thereby risk subjecting the individual to a law which Parliament never intended to enact.[57]

Put in these terms, a co-operative stance looks both rational and desirable,[58] but as a matter of history, it has not always been an uncontroversial option. It

---

51 [1997] 4 All ER 781, 789-90, and [1998] 1 All ER 403, 407 respectively. See also *IRC v Willoughby.*
52 'Further than this, I would not at present go'; op cit, p 640.
53 For example, *Warwickshire County Council v Johnson* [1993] 1 All ER 299; *Chief Adjudication Officer v Foster* [1993] 1 All ER 705; and *Stubbings v Webb*, in which Lord Griffiths remarked that he would have reached his decision 'even without reference to Hansard'. A more recent example is *Bairstow v Queens Moat Houses.*
54 This was so even in respect of the exclusionary rule concerning Hansard; see for example Lord Denning in *Davis v Johnson*, above, pp 92-94. A useful review of the background to *Pepper v Hart* is contained in an article by Lord Lester QC, '*Pepper v Hart* Revisited' (1994) 15 *Statute Law Review* 10. Lord Lester appeared for the taxpayer in that case.
55 T StJ Bates, 'Parliamentary Material and Statutory Construction: Aspects of the Practical Application of *Pepper v Hart*' (1993) 14 *Statute Law Rev* 46.
56 See Marshall, op cit; Jenkins, '*Pepper v Hart*: A Draftsman's Perspective' (1994) 15 *Statute Law Review* 23.
57 Op cit, pp 637-638, per Lord Browne-Wilkinson.
58 M Freeman, 'Positivism and Statutory Construction: an Essay in the Retrieval of Democracy' in S Guest (ed), *Positivism Today* (1996), p 11.

is one thing to give effect to what Parliament has enacted as law, but quite another to give legal effect to ministerial statements about what the law is. One difficulty is that access to Hansard cuts both ways. *Pepper v Hart* disclosed that civil servants were ignoring representations made by Ministers to Parliament and were seeking to treat citizens more onerously than those Ministers had indicated. No doubt the taxpayer applauded the decision of the House, but would he have done so if the debates had shown that Parliament had intended the cash equivalent to be the average cost? In those circumstances, of course, this would only have confirmed the Revenue's position; but two of the initial five Law Lords who heard the appeal preferred the taxpayer's argument without reference to Hansard. The objection that the government is getting two bites at the cherry – once in the Act and, in the event of ambiguity, etc, once more in the debates – becomes more substantial as one extends the application of *Pepper v Hart* to other areas where the executive exerts power over the citizen, such as police powers, immigration, or planning law. Suppose that what is, on the face of it, an ambiguous section can be shown, by reference to Hansard, to justify the executive's disputed exercise of power over the individual. Might not it be reasonable to object that the court here is failing in one of its principal duties, namely, to protect the citizen against unclear laws? And what of the citizen who has ordered her affairs according to what the law apparently says (absurd, ambiguous, obscure or not): is it just that she should now find herself prejudiced by statements which, when she took legal advice, would not have been judicially acceptable?[59] In the case of domestic legislation the courts have already taken *Pepper v Hart* beyond the confines proposed by the House;[60] it remains to be seen how far they will be prepared to go when faced with powerful countervailing arguments.[61]

(c)   What weight should be given to each kind of aid which is admissible?

The short answer to this question is that it is neither possible nor desirable, in most cases, to be specific. 'Weight' is a metaphor.[62] It is not possible to assign a quantitative value to a particular source or to the arguments drawn from it. The legislature may from time to time specify the degree of persuasiveness. For example, in the Carriage by Air Act 1961, which enacts the Warsaw Convention 1929 as amended by the Hague Protocol of 1955 into domestic law, it is provided that in the event of a conflict between the English and French texts of the Convention, the French shall prevail.[63] By contrast, the Civil

---

59 The Australian Acts Interpretation Act 1901, s 15AB permits judicial access to parliamentary reports. Since its introduction in 1984 the courts have sought to limit reliance on the Minister's words where 'the intention stated by the Minister but unexpressed in the law is restrictive of the liberty of the individual'. Per Mason CJ, *R v Bolton, ex p Beane* (1987) 162 CLR 514, 518.

60 But for the purpose of interpreting European legislation enacted into domestic law, the courts have gone further; see below, p 299.

61 Such as those based on the Human Rights Act 1998; see below, section 5.2.

62 See below, pp 362-363.

63 This was the statute in issue in *Fothergill v Monarch Airlines*. See, for example, s 1 of the Consumer Protection Act 1987 which requires its provisions to be construed in order to give effect to a Community Directive. By contrast, s 122 of the Government of Wales Act provides that the

Jurisdiction and Judgments Act 1982 which, by section 2(1) gave effect to the Convention on Jurisdiction and the Enforcement of Judgments in Civil and Commercial Matters, provides by section 3(3) that the *travaux préparatoires* may be used to ascertain the Convention's meaning and effect, and that the reports are to be given 'such weight as is appropriate in the circumstances'. These circumstances may include the language in which the Articles in the Convention are written. In *Hough v P&O Containers*, the question arose whether the litigation instituted against an English ship owner arising from an accident which occurred while the ship was in a dry dock in Germany, was to take place in London or in Hamburg.[64] The Convention establishes two forms of jurisdiction: special (Article 6) and agreed (Article 17). The question was, which took priority? The court held that because Article 17 used the phrase 'shall have exclusive jurisdiction', while Article 6 used 'may also be sued', the mandatory language took precedence.

Even if it were possible for the courts to develop priority rules for distinguishing between arguments, they would probably not wish to do so, at least as a general proposition. A primary feature of the decision in *Pepper v Hart* is that once the admissibility of the clear ministerial statement has been determined, its weight is for the court to judge. In the absence of any priority rule, the persuasiveness of an argument drawn, for example, from a Law Reform Committee or Select Committee Report, will depend on many factors: the terms and scope of its inquiry, the depth of its research, the nature of its recommendations, the existence of other views on the recommendations, the relationship between them and the Act, and so on. One further consequence of *Pepper v Hart* is that where such a report does contain an unequivocal statement as to what a disputed section was intended to do, a court may rely on that statement both as to its interpretation as well as to its purpose.[65]

The general point can also be made in respect of the persuasiveness of the *travaux préparatoires* that precede the international treaty whose meaning is in doubt. The court may treat them as determinative of the point in issue where they clearly and indisputably point to a definite legal intention, but 'only a bull's eye will do'.[66] Changes in language may reflect a change in policy (that is, in intended meaning) or may be intended to reflect the same meaning but in different words. Such variations in the text of the early drafts of a convention 'are no doubt of interest to historians, but from a lawyer's point of view they are inconclusive'.[67] Moreover, it does not follow that different readers will come to the same conclusion about the implications of what was said in the report: two texts are necessarily better than one. For example, in *Borealis AB v Stagas Ltd*, Sir Brian Neill and Millett LJ reached wholly opposite conclusions

English and Welsh texts of any subordinate legislation shall be treated for all purposes as being of equal standing. In this the Act follows Community law in giving equal validity to all official languages of the European Union.

64 [1998] 2 All ER 978. The facts read 'like a set moot' (per Rix J, at 980). See also *Canada Trust v Stolzenberg (No 2)* [1998] 1 All ER 318, 333 interpreting this Convention.
65 Lord Browne-Wilkinson, *Pepper v Hart*, at 635.
66 Per Lord Steyn, *Effort Shipping v Linden SA*, at 509.
67 Per Lord Lloyd, *Adan v Secretary of State for the Home Department*, at 458.

as to the legal effect of the changes proposed in a Law Commission report, Rights of Suit in Respect of Carriage of Goods by Sea.[68] The question which arose was whether section 3 of the Carriage of Goods by Sea Act 1992, which enacted the draft Bill proposed by the Law Commission, widened or limited the class of persons who are subject to liability under a contract of carriage. It is not necessary here to examine the full legal history of this area of law. Sir Brian Neill's view was that when the Law Commission's proposals were read in the context of that history, the section should be construed as widening the class of persons; Millett LJ (for the majority) was equally firmly of the view that the Commission's Report and the structure of the Act indicated that the intention was not to extend, but to limit liability.

(d) Conclusion

From the point of view of the interpreter, the formal position about the admissibility of these various sources for constructing or supporting arguments about interpretation certain kinds of aid should not be over-emphasised. For almost any purpose it is of paramount importance to understand what the statute is about: for instance, in the area of commercial transactions, she will benefit from some knowledge of commercial dealing in general, the characteristics, problems, customs and usages of the particular trade she is concerned with, the legislator's perception of the situation he was trying to deal with, the strategy and tactics of the particular body of statutory material, and so on. Such background knowledge is almost invariably of great importance in any difficult case. How the interpreter can best acquire it must depend on her experience, opportunities, time and general situation. The only sensible thing to do is to make intelligent use of all available aids to understanding the problem, even if some of them may not be overtly employed in forensic legal reasoning and justification. There are no formal limits on aids to diagnosis and, as we have emphasised in earlier chapters, diagnosis is the first step in a rational approach to interpretation.

5   The European dimension

5.1   Community legislation

In this section we consider briefly the approaches taken respectively by the European Court and by the courts of the United Kingdom to the interpretation of Community law. It is intended only as an introduction; we refer readers to the specialised literature.

---

68 [1998] 4 All ER 521, Law Com No 196 (1991). See also the differing conclusions reached by Laddie J and Lord Jauncey about the legislative history of particular sections in the copyright legislation, *Redrow Homes v Betts Bros*, and Lord Hoffmann's consideration of two pre-parliamentary reports offering different interpretations of the scope of the law: *Newlon Housing Trust v Alsulaimen* [1998] 4 All ER 1.

(a) The Court of Justice of the European Communities

The European Court was established by the Treaty of Rome to be the final authoritative voice on the interpretation of Community law. Unlike the courts here, it has administrative and constitutional functions, and owes its primary allegiance to the Treaties and to their realisation. Its judgments, framed and answered in terms of general propositions of Community law, are delivered after submissions have been made by the parties, the European Commission and the Advocate-General.

By Article 177, national courts may, and in some cases must, refer to the European Court questions raised in litigation which concern the interpretation of a Treaty or the validity or the interpretation of any Community legislation, if the national court 'considers that a decision on the question is necessary to enable it to give judgment'.[69] The Court's decisions are specifically focused upon the questions referred to it by the court of the Member State. It does not however follow that the decision will be determinative of the case at hand, since it too will have to be interpreted by the national court. Although the European Court does not engage in the kind of discursive reasoning typical in this country, English courts do not necessarily find its judgments to be determinative on the questions raised. [70]

It is generally accepted that the predominant interpretive approach adopted by the European Court is teleological; that is to say, one which seeks to advance the purpose for which the particular Treaty provision was enacted. No interpretive exercise is complete without reference to the purpose of the relevant branch of Community law, even where textual analysis is entirely at one with what was apparently intended. It is in this context that the preamble which prefaces Community legislation is of particular relevance. In practice, the interpretive exercise is wider, embracing not only the stated purpose, but also an evaluation of the language of the disputed provision and its role within the legislative scheme:

> The usual practice of the Court of Justice [being] to interpret E.E.C. legislation in the light of its spirit, general scheme and wording as well as the legal context, in particular the system and objectives of the founding treaties and the instrument containing the provision.[71]

---

69 See further *Practice Direction (Supreme Court: References to the Court of Justice of the European Communities) The Times*, 19 January 1999.

70 'The judgment of the European Court [C-145/88: *Torfaen Borough Council v B & Q plc* [1990] 2 QB 19] was intended to be an authoritative interpretation of the Treaty sufficient to enable the domestic court to decide the case. But "every decoding is another encoding" and there have been arguments over what the judgment means', per Hoffmann J, *Stoke on Trent City Council v B & Q plc* [1991] 2 WLR 42, 51.

71 T Millett, 'Rules of Interpretation of EEC Legislation' [1989] *Statute Law Review* 163, 173. See also H Kutscher, 'Methods of Interpretation as seen by a Judge at the Court of Justice', in *Reports of the Judicial and Academic Conference of the Court of Justice of the European Communities* (1976); A Bredimas, *Methods of Interpretation and Community Law* (1978); B Markesinis, *Foreign Law and Comparative Methodology* (1997), ch 7; Bennion, op cit, pp 989ff.

(b)   Courts in the United Kingdom

There are various ways in which the implementation of Community law may come before the courts of the United Kingdom. Where Community legislation is directly applicable, the court is required to interpret the regulation so as to give effect to its objectives. More frequently, the courts are asked to determine the extent to which United Kingdom primary and secondary legislation has given effect to a directive. Directives do not necessarily have direct effect,[72] but even in the case of those that do not, the Court of Justice has ruled that national courts are under the same interpretive obligation:

> In applying national law, whether the provisions in question were adopted before or after the directive, the national court called upon to interpret it is required to do so, as far as possible, in the light of the wording and purpose of the directive in order to achieve the result pursued by the latter and thereby comply with the third paragraph of article 189 of the Treaty.[73]

The court must therefore establish first the purpose of the Community legislation and, secondly, how that purpose can best be achieved in the United Kingdom's substantive and procedural law. The interpretive obligation has been stated by Beldam LJ in unequivocal terms:

> In construing an Act of Parliament passed with the intention of giving effect to a directive of Community law, United Kingdom courts are bound to interpret and apply the legislation so that the provisions of the Act conform with the requirements of Community law unless the words of the Act make such an approach impossible. Thus it is the duty of the court to give a purposive construction to the words used in the Act and not be bound by any strict or literal interpretation. In short, it is to be presumed that Parliament used language which was intended to implement the provisions of the directive.[74]

Sometimes the obligation relates to issues which, to the untutored eye, do not at first sight obviously fall within the scope of Community law. Suppose you are the Chief Constable of a police authority. An aspect of your responsibilities is the policing of the docks in your area. These are being used for the export of livestock to the Netherlands for slaughter and eventual human consumption. Angered by this trade, animal rights activists seek to blockade the port's entrance. You allocate resources to keep the peace and to permit the lorries carrying the veal calves access to the docks. But the activists are very determined; for over a week they attempt to maintain the blockade. There are scuffles and arrests as the lorries arrive. Eventually you decide that you cannot continue

---

72 Above, p 222. *Mighell v Reading* [1999] Lloyd's Rep IR 30.
73 C-106/89: *Marleasing SA v La Comercial Internacional de Alimentacion SA* [1990] ECR I-4135.
74 Per Beldam LJ, *Institute of Chartered Accountants in England and Wales v Customs and Excise Comrs* [1998] 4 All ER 115, 123. Earlier examples of the exercise of this obligation include Lord Diplock's comments in *R v Henn and Darby* [1980] AC 850, 904-905 and *Garland v British Rail Engineering* [1983] 2 AC 751, 771. See also Lord Slynn, 'Looking at European Community Texts' (1993) 14 *Statute Law Review* 12, 23-27; T Rensen, 'British Statutory Interpretation in the Light of Community and Other International Obligations' (1993) 14 *Statute Law Review* 186; MHorspool, 'Statutory Interpretation of European Community Law by British Courts' in Freeman (ed), op cit, p 95.

the current allocation of police officers. You have other policing responsibilities that require a share of your limited resources. At first sight this episode looks like any other public order issue, such as policing a football match, in respect of which you, as Chief Constable, have to determine what resources you can afford to use. You might therefore be surprised when the exporting company argues that your decision to discontinue the previous level of policing contravened Article 34 of the EC Treaty, in that it amounted to a 'measure having an equivalent effect' to a quantitative restriction on exports between Member States. Whether or not it was, you were relieved when the House of Lords held that in any event your decision could be justified under the public policy exception in Article 36.[75]

In ascertaining the purpose of the legislation enacted in response to a directive, the court is at liberty to employ any of the interpretive prescriptions discussed earlier in this chapter. Where it is ambiguous or obscure, the court may rely on clear ministerial statements to resolve such difficulties. But the court will also go beyond the restrictions specified by the House of Lords in *Pepper v Hart*. In *Pickstone v Freemans plc*, a decision that pre-dated *Pepper v Hart*, Lord Keith said that it was 'entirely legitimate for the purpose of ascertaining the intention of Parliament to take into account the terms in which the draft was presented by the responsible minister and which formed the basis of its acceptance'.[76] The Practice Note which requires counsel to serve copies of the Hansard extracts on the other side and the court where she intends to invoke *Pepper v Hart* extends also to *Pickstone v Freemans plc* in the case of Community law. The question, could such extracts be used for the straightforward task of ascertaining the purpose of primary legislation enacted to give effect to a directive was considered in the application heard in *Three Rivers District Council v Governor of the Bank of England (No 2)*.[77] Noting that *Pepper v Hart* concerned the interpretation of primary legislation having no international or European element, Clarke J said:

> ... where the court is seeking to construe a statute purposively and consistently with any European materials, including directives, it is of particular importance to ascertain the true purpose of the statute. In these circumstances I would expect the courts to adopt a more flexible approach than that laid down in *Pepper v Hart* ...[78]

Accordingly, he held that it would be proper to consider ministerial statements as to the purpose of the legislation in question.

Having ascertained its purpose, the interpretive obligation extends so far as the words of the legislation sustain the interpretation sought. As Lord Clyde observed in *Cutter v Eagle Star Insurance Co*, 'even in this [Community law] context, the exercise must still be one of construction and it should not exceed the limits of what is reasonable'.[79] It was, for example, reasonable for the House

---

75 *R v Chief Constable of Sussex, ex p International Trader's Ferry Ltd* [1999] 1 All ER 129.
76 [1989] AC 66, 112.
77 [1996] 2 All ER 363.
78 Ibid, at 366.
79 Op cit, p 426.

of Lords in *Pickstone v Freemans plc* to imply words into the Equal Pay (Amendment) Regulations 1983 'in order to give effect to the manifest broad intention of the maker of the regulations and of Parliament' where the words actually used did not realise that intention.[80] The regulations had been made in response to a decision of the Court of Justice that the United Kingdom's primary legislation did not fully implement the Community's equal pay directive. The House subsequently applied the precedent established by *Pickstone v Freemans plc* to justify interpreting the words 'immediately before the transfer' in the Transfer of Undertakings (Protection of Employment) Regulations 1981 to cover employees who had been dismissed not literally 'immediately' but an hour before the business which had employed them was transferred to another company. These Regulations implemented a directive whose purpose was precisely to protect employees' jobs in circumstances such as these. This justified the adoption of a purposive interpretation, even though it involved some departure from the strict and literal application of the words which the legislature used.[81]

The linguistic context may therefore in some cases limit such departure. As part of his determination of the scope of section 151 of the Road Traffic Act 1988 in *Cutter v Eagle Star Insurance*, Lord Clyde considered the implications of three European Council directives dealing with the approximation of the laws of Member States relating to insurance against civil liability in respect of the use of motor vehicles. The question in this case was whether the word 'road' in section 145 could be construed as including a car park. Reviewing these directives, Lord Clyde held that they did not require such a construction. But he also addressed the question whether it would be appropriate to effect a limited extension of the word for the purpose of the present case (and cases like it), without affecting other parts of the Act. Rejecting this suggestion on the ground that it would be 'going beyond the bounds of legitimate construction' to give a word which is used throughout the Act different meanings in different sections, Lord Clyde said:

> Furthermore, while it may be appropriate to add words by way of modification of the meaning of a statutory expression in order to find a construction consistent with European law, as was done in *Litster v Forth Dry Dock and Engineering Co Ltd*, it would in my view be going beyond the judicial task of construction to add to the word 'road' the words 'or in any public place', in circumstances where Parliament has expressly used that phrase in the context of other particular sections of the Act but has refrained from doing so in s 145.[82]

Nor does the interpretive obligation require the court to invent domestic law. The juridical nature of a directive is to approximate the laws of Member States, not to make them the same. Having ascertained the purpose, the court's duty is to apply domestic substantive and procedural law in order to achieve it. *British Fuels v Baxendale* also concerned the Transfer of Undertakings

---

80 Op cit, p 112, per Lord Keith; Lord Oliver, 125-128. Other examples of the interpretation of the Equal Pay Act 1970 to conform to Community law are *Preston v Wolverhampton Healthcare NHS Trust* [1998] 1 All ER 528 and *Barry v Midland Bank plc* [1998] 1 All ER 805.
81 Lord Oliver, *Litster v Forth Dry Dock and Engineering Co Ltd* [1990] 1 AC 546, 576-577.
82 Op cit, pp 429-430.

(Protection of Employment) Regulations 1981.[83] The question which arose concerned the legal effect of dismissals of employees prior to the transfer of the business to a new employer and the extent of the rights enjoyed by the employees as against the first employer. It is not necessary for our purposes to examine the facts or law closely. The relevant point concerns the variations between the Member States as to the nature of those rights. One right not enjoyed in the United Kingdom but which might be available elsewhere in the Community is specific performance of a contract of employment. 'That', Lord Slynn said, 'I do not find surprising or shocking'. He continued:

> The directive is to 'approximate' the laws of the member states. Its purpose is to 'safeguard' rights on a transfer. The 'rights' of an employee depend on national rules of the law of contract or of legislation. There is no Community law of contract common to member states, nor is there a common system of remedies. The object and purpose of the directive is to ensure in all member states that on a transfer an employee has against the transferee the rights and remedies he would have had against the original employer. ... the [Court of Justice] has clearly recognised that the precise rights to be transferred depend on national law. But neither the directive nor the jurisprudence of the court create a community law right to continue in employment which does not exist in national law.[84]

5.2 The Human Rights Act 1998

An international convention may become part of the law of the United Kingdom in one of two ways: textual incorporation in a statute (direct enactment) or incorporation by reference (indirect enactment). In either case it is the court's duty to interpret the statute so as to give effect to the obligations thereby assumed. Where, in interpreting the Act, the convention also has to be construed, the court should adopt 'a broad rather than a narrow linguistic approach, giving it a meaning which makes sense in the light of the convention as a whole and which gives effect to its purposes'.[85] In the case of a convention to which the United Kingdom is a signatory but which has not been incorporated into domestic law, the court's duty is less extensive. It is to interpret any relevant legislation so as to conform with the convention's obligations, but only so far as the statute's linguistic context permits:

> ... it is already well settled law that, in construing any provision in domestic legislation which is ambiguous in the sense that it is capable of a meaning which either conforms to or conflicts with the convention, the courts will presume that Parliament intended to legislate in conformity with it ...[86]

But, where in the context the statutory language unambiguously points to an outcome at variance with the convention, the court should prefer the statute.

---

83 [1998] 4 All ER 609.
84 Ibid, p 627. Lord Slynn is, by virtue of his earlier role as Advocate-General to the Court of Justice, a particularly authoritative voice on the interpretation of Community law.
85 Per Lord Lloyd, *Adan v Secretary of State for the Home Department*, at 458; Lord Steyn, *Re Ismail* [1998] 3 All ER 1007, 1012. See Gardiner, op cit.
86 Per Lord Bridge, *R v Secretary of State for the Home Department, ex p Brind* [1991] 1 AC 696, 747.

In the case of the European Convention on Human Rights, this preference will, upon the commencement of the Human Rights Act 1998, be reversed. Section 3 imposes a duty on the courts, 'so far as it is possible to do so', to read and give effect to primary and subordinate legislation 'in a way which is compatible with the Convention rights'.[87] For example, in *R v Secretary of State for the Home Department, ex p Brind*, the question arose whether the Home Secretary acted lawfully when he directed the Independent Broadcasting Authority that it should not broadcast words directly spoken by the representatives of proscribed terrorist organisations in Northern Ireland. The authority on which he relied was section 29(3) of the Broadcasting Act 1981, which provided that the Secretary of State could at any time by notice in writing require the Authority 'to refrain from broadcasting any matter or classes of matter contained in the notice'. The Authority argued that the notice was a contravention of Article 10 of the Convention, which confers on everyone the right to freedom of expression. It should be noted that the Article also recognises that signatory states may require broadcasting to be licensed, and that the exercise of the freedom may be subject to restrictions 'in the interests of national security'. The House of Lords held that section 29(3) was unambiguous, and that it would be wrong for the court to approach its interpretation with the express purpose of seeking compatibility with Article 10.

Ambiguous or not, the 1998 Act requires the court to engage in exactly that exercise. This does not mean that if this requirement had applied to the facts in *ex p Brind*, the court would have found for the Authority; it might well have concluded that the section and the Convention right were compatible.[88] What it does mean is that there is no threshold test concerning the statutory words that need to be met before the court must seek their compatibility with any Convention rights. As a result of conducting this exercise, the higher courts may declare that the two sources of law are incompatible. In this case, it is open to the government to rectify that situation either by normal means or, where there are 'compelling reasons' by a 'remedial order'.[89] In determining whether there is any incompatibility, the courts are at liberty to employ any of their recognised interpretive techniques. During the debates on the Act, Lord Cooke commented that the interpretive obligation imposed by section 3 'will require a very different approach to interpretation from that to which the English courts are accustomed. Traditionally, the search has been for the true meaning: now it will be for a possible meaning that would prevent the making of a declaration of incompatibility'.[90] Given the interpretive latitude evident in the cases discussed earlier, and in particular the approach required of the courts in the interpretation of Community law, the qualitative extension in interpretive method required by the Act may not be so radical as this comment suggests.

---

87 The Convention is textually incorporated in Schedule 1 to the Act.
88 As the House of Lords concluded in respect of the relationship between Article 7 of the Convention and s 67(4) of the Criminal Justice Act 1967; *R v Secretary of State for the Home Department, ex p François* [1998] 1 All ER 929.
89 Chapter 7, section 2.2(a).
90 House of Lords Debates, Vol 582, col 1272 (3 November 1997).

For the interpreter of legislation, the Human Rights Act 1998 therefore opens a range of possibilities. The interpretive obligation imposed by section 3 means that arguments constructed from ministerial declarations of compatibility in respect of future legislation will become routine. In *Three Rivers District Council v Bank of England (No 2)*, Clarke J held that the *Pepper v Hart* guidelines should be further relaxed 'where the purpose of the legislation is to introduce into English law the provisions of an international convention'.[91] Community law already offers scope for the recognition of fundamental rights, and has further potential when used in conjunction with Convention rights. And as the White Paper which prefaced the Act indicated, decisions of the European Court of Human Rights in Strasbourg will compete with and may displace decisions of the domestic courts.[92]

---

91 Op cit, p 364.
92 '... the courts will not be bound by previous interpretations. They will be able to build a new body of case law, taking into account Convention rights.' *Rights Brought Home: the Human Rights Bill* (1997, Cm 3782), para 2.8. Section 2 provides that a court or tribunal determining a question which has arisen in connection with a Convention right must 'take into account' any relevant decision of the European Court. On incompatibility see *R v DPP, ex p Kebilene* (1999) Times, 31 March. For exercises on chapter 8, see Appendix I, section F, questions 7-12.

Chapter 9

Reading Cases

1 Reading cases: What? why? how?

In ordinary legal usage the word 'case' is ambiguous. We talk of 'reading cases', 'citing cases', 'bringing cases', 'having a good case', 'winning cases', 'submitting no case to answer' and so on. To bring a case against someone means to institute legal proceedings against him; to ask 'have I a good case?' probably means 'have I a good chance of winning in legal proceedings?' When we talk of looking up, citing or reading a case we are talking about a *kind of document*. Similarly in talking of interpreting cases it is helpful to think in terms of interpreting the rather specialised kind of document typically to be found in the law reports. For our purpose it is useful to adopt, with slight modification, the following definition:

> A case is the written memorandum of a dispute or controversy between persons, telling with varying degrees of completeness and of accuracy, what happened, what each of the parties did about it, what some supposedly impartial judge or other tribunal did in the way of bringing the dispute or controversy to an end, and the avowed reasons of the judge or tribunal for doing what was done.[1]

This definition identifies the principal ingredients with which we are concerned when interpreting cases, viz a written *report*, of a *dispute* between *legal persons*, which came before a *court* (or other tribunal). Such a report should tell us (a) who the parties were, (b) the facts (what allegedly happened), (c) the procedural steps (what each of the parties did about it), leading up to (d) the *decision* and the *order* of the judge or tribunal,[2] and (e) the reasoned justification, usually referred to as the *judgment* in England or the *opinion* in the United States.

---

1 Adapted from N Dowling, E Patterson and R Powell, *Materials for Legal Method* (2nd edn, 1952), pp 34-35.
2 In this context, when we speak of the judge's decision we mean the conclusion at which he arrives having applied the relevant rule(s) to the facts before him. While there may be some doubt as to the precise scope of that conclusion (see below), the decision amounts to a statement of the legal consequences that attach to the facts of the dispute and which create rights, duties, liabilities or immunities in the parties to the dispute. The *order* of the court is the particular implementation of such rights, duties, etc, in concrete form, such as an order to pay so much damages, or granting an injunction, or other form of redress; or an order imposing some penal consequences such as a fine or term of imprisonment. In addition, it should be observed that the word 'decision' is ambiguous. Apart from the meaning attached to it above, it is also used synonymously with 'judgment', to mean the justification for a particular conclusion of law. See J Montrose, 'The Language of, and a Notation for, the Doctrine of Precedent', (1974) 25 *Northern Ireland Legal Quarterly* 246.

The law reports contain written accounts of judicial determinations of certain kinds of law suit. Before considering the nature and functions of these documents, it is useful to set them in a broader context as such accounts are doubly selective: only a small minority of law suits feature in the law reports, and what is reported is typically only an account of one part of the total process.

It is a truism that one important task of law is prevention and termination of disputes.[3] Even on quite a narrow definition of the term only a tiny proportion of all disputes reaches a point where legal proceedings are instituted or seriously threatened. Most disputes are terminated by other means, for example, by negotiation, mediation, arbitration, the abandonment of a claim, or the disappearance, death or absence of one of the parties. The vast majority of civil suits are likewise settled or terminated by one means or another before they reach trial; others are settled during the course of the trial without the need for adjudication by the court. Similarly many crimes go undetected or are not prosecuted and in the vast majority of criminal proceedings that reach the courts the accused pleads guilty, so that no formal determination of guilt by magistrate, judge or jury is required. In such cases the court typically has to decide on sentence, but such decisions are only reported very exceptionally. Of those cases that do involve an adjudicative determination of guilt or liability, far more involve contested questions of fact than disagreements on questions of law. Again only a small proportion of rulings on the latter type of question become the subject of appeal or review in a higher court or tribunal, yet the great majority of cases reported, though by no means all, involve appellate decisions on questions of law. Thus, as every lawyer knows, cases that reach the law reports represent a tiny, atypical minority of all disputes in society or even of litigated cases.

What then are the criteria of selection of cases for inclusion in the law reports? In some jurisdictions and some specialised series in England, all the decisions of particular courts or tribunals are reported. However, this is exceptional. Most English series, including the *Law Reports*, the *Weekly Law Reports* and the *All England Law Reports*, select cases for reporting because they are precedents or potential precedents. In these cases there was a doubt about a point of law and the court resolved the doubt in an authoritative way, not only for that dispute but also for the future.[4] Thus, the main function of law reports is to provide authoritative, reasoned answers to previously doubtful questions of law. They can, in the first instance, be looked on as anthologies of questions, answers and arguments about the scope of the law.

Reports of cases are selected and constructed for quite specific purposes. The most straightforward ways of reading and using them are directly related to those purposes. For example, lawyers of all kinds use them to provide authoritative answers to specific questions of law and as examples of particular applications of general rules. Solicitors use them to predict how a court is likely to determine a legal point in a particular case; barristers use them as raw

3 See above, chapter 1, section 5.2.
4 Whether reported or not, once the decision of the court is final then the matter is closed and cannot be re-litigated – it is *res judicata*. See, for example, *North West Water Ltd v Binnie and Partners* [1990] 3 All ER 547 and *Thrasyvoulou v Secretary of State for the Environment* [1990] 2 AC 273, 289 (Lord Bridge).

material for constructing legal arguments; judges read and use them as sources of both authority and substantive reasons in reaching and justifying their own decisions; academic lawyers use them for a variety of interrelated purposes, including legal exposition, tracing the development of particular doctrines or criticising the decisions or reasonings of the courts. Law students use them as important materials of law study or read them *as if* they were solicitors or barristers or judges or critics performing specific tasks.

All of these readings treat reported cases as authoritative sources of law viewed from different, but closely related standpoints. However, just because the law reports are so extensive, varied, detailed and accessible they invite a wide variety of other readings and uses. For example, they are sometimes treated as historical sources, political texts, examples of different styles of reasoning, specimens of rhetoric, anthologies of stories or even as literature. In legal education they are both over-used, to the neglect of other materials of law study, and neglected in that they tend to be used for an unduly narrow range of purposes.[5]

Because of the wide range of perspectives that can be brought to bear on this kind of text, it is especially important that we should be self-conscious about the What? Why? How? of particular readings. In approaching one or more reported cases it is important to clarify one's standpoint and to ask: what is my purpose in reading this text? What kind of method is suited to this purpose?

Here we shall begin with the most elementary kind of orthodox reading: writing a précis, or case note, of a single case. This can be the starting-point for a number of enterprises. In order to provide a specific context let us assume that a law student starting on the study of bigamy in a course on criminal law is reading *Allen* as his or her first case on the topic.

Writing a case note involves essentially the same techniques and aptitudes as conventional précis writing at school. There are, however, some important differences. Firstly, noting cases is more straightforward in that all modern reports follow a standard format and part of what is involved is a rather mechanical kind of form-filling. Nearly all law reports share a common structure, related to their primary function; they contain reasoned answers to doubtful questions of law that arose out of particular fact situations. The anatomy of a case is a constant: facts, questions(s), answer(s), reasons, outcome or result. Accordingly a standard précis of a case should reflect this structure. Because all of these elements interact with each other, and because it is nearly always artificial to interpret single cases in isolation from other materials, there are considerable practical and theoretical difficulties involved in interpreting and using cases. Hence reading cases is an art requiring skill, experience, judgment and practice. However, this should not obscure the fact that law reports have standard features, and that the most elementary kind of reading can and should proceed according to a regular intellectual procedure. Moreover, with this kind of case-note there are some useful rules of thumb to help resolve some of these difficulties.

The first step in noting any case is routinely to record five items of information: the name of the case; the identity of the parties; the citation

5 See Appendix III, *The Reading Law Cookbook*, section 8, pp 435ff.

(where it is to be found in the law reports); the court; and the outcome (who won at this stage in the proceedings and what the court ordered). These are almost invariably contained in any modern law report.

The second step is to make a preliminary summary of the particular facts of the case. In this context 'the facts' are a given: even if what happened was disputed by the parties or is still a matter of historical doubt, in this context the facts are determined either by a finding of fact by the tribunal or by agreement of the parties or by the case being 'stated' in terms of a hypothetical fact situation, perhaps on the basis of what has been alleged in the pleadings or the indictment. An accurate statement of the facts should be confined to those elements in the situation that are *relevant* to the issues of the case and material to the case as a whole. What precisely is meant by relevance and materiality is problematic. Furthermore, what precisely was in issue in the case depends on how one interprets the facts, but what facts are relevant and material depends on a precise formulation of the issues.

A few rules of thumb can rescue us from this potential impasse: on first reading, our summary of the facts should be provisional, subject to addition, pruning or refinement. Secondly, when in doubt state the facts in chronological order. Thirdly, in this context we are reading the case because it resolves a *general* doubt about the law; in summarising 'the facts' of the particular case, we are only concerned with those elements that are potentially relevant to some *general* issue(s) of law. As a general rule of thumb, much of the colourful background detail – personal details of the parties, addresses, particular times and places – are *prima facie* irrelevant unless there is some reason for thinking that they are relevant.[6] You might ask yourself: what difference would it make if this fact were removed? In deciding what to treat as *prima facie* irrelevant use common sense and such legal knowledge as you have; but when in doubt *include*.

Remember that the case was worth reporting because its facts raised one or more doubtful or disputed questions of law. The art of asking questions is a basic legal skill. Skilful formulation of issues of law in case notes is one specific example of this. As with stating the facts or formulating rules there is often no single correct formulation. There are, however, formulations that are plainly defective because they violate one or more of the following precepts. Firstly, the question must be unambiguously expressed as a *question of law*. So in *Allen* it would be incorrect to pose the question in such terms as 'Did A purport to marry W?' (question of fact) or 'Did A commit bigamy?' (mixed fact and law). The question in the case concerned the scope of the law.

Secondly, the question must be formulated in terms that are general rather than *particular*. Not 'Was Allen guilty of bigamy?', but rather does the crime of bigamy cover this *type* of situation? Often there will be no precisely correct level of generality, because differences about what is the most appropriate level of generality for interpreting or describing a type of situation is often the main point of disagreement in interpretation of the law.

Thirdly, the question should be formulated as precisely and unambiguously as possible in relation to the issue raised by the fact-situation. 'What is the meaning of bigamy?' or 'What kinds of situation are covered by bigamy?' are too vague.

---

6   See the classic discussion of this by K Llewellyn in *The Bramble Bush* (2nd edn, 1951), pp 48-49.

Fourthly, the formulation must encompass all the important issues raised in the case. A common error, especially among beginners, is to assume that a particular case raises only one issue or to overlook some subordinate, but nevertheless, material question. For example, *R v Taylor* raised two quite distinct and important questions, one concerning bigamy, the other relating to precedent in the then Court of Criminal Appeal.[7]

In posing issues, as with stating the facts, there are a number of helpful rules of thumb.

Firstly, it should never be forgotten that reported cases arise out of actual disputes. A dialectical process was involved. The disputed issues in the case represent the points of disagreement between the two sides. In pinpointing what precisely was at issue, it is worth asking: What exactly were they disagreeing about? One important clue lies in looking at the competing answers put forward and analysing how and why they are different.[8]

Secondly, in certain kinds of case the formulation of issues can be made easier by some straightforward expedients. For example, the great majority of reported cases in recent years involves the interpretation of statutes or other rules in fixed verbal form. In such cases, it is useful to express the initial formulation of any issue of statutory interpretation in the following way: 'What is the meaning of ...?' followed by a specific word or words taken *verbatim* from the text in question. This has the great advantage of anchoring the issue in a precise location. So, for example, the main issue in *Allen* can be expressed as 'What is the meaning of "shall marry" in section 57 of the Offences against the Person Act 1861?'[9] However, this is only a first step. While problems of statutory interpretation can almost always be located in a specific part of a text,[10] it may be quite misleading to treat the issue as being solely or even mainly about the meaning of words. For instance, the phrase 'due process of law' in the Fourteenth Amendment to the United States Constitution has been the subject of hundreds of disputed interpretations. What is typically at issue in such cases are choices

---

7 Chapter 1, section 7.3. *Allen* was mainly concerned with a particular issue in bigamy; but, lurking in Lord Cockburn's judgment, and overlooked by the writer of the headnote is a minor, but interesting, question concerning statutory interpretation – viz where a legislative provision has been re-enacted in identical words, but the law changed in a significant respect between the original and the subsequent enactment, in applying the mischief rule of statutory interpretation should the court consider the mischief at the time of the original enactment, or is it open to it to conclude that since the mischief had changed prior to the enactment, the scope of the provision had changed even though there was no change in the wording? In this instance, Cockburn CJ stated that the mischief that the crime of bigamy was designed to prevent was desecration of a solemn ceremony, on an analogy with sacrilege. However, before the passing of the Offences against the Person Act 1861, marriage by civil ceremony had been introduced; it is hardly convincing to suggest that the purpose of the modern law of bigamy is to protect civil as well as religious ceremonies from 'desecration'.

8 See below, pp 345-346.

9 In our experience, novice law students often have difficulty identifying the words in s 57 that were the subject of interpretation in *R v Taylor*, chapter 1, section 7.3.

10 *R v Gould* (see Appendix I, section A5, p 385) is an example of a case involving statutory interpretation where it is somewhat artificial to identify which words were the subject of interpretation, for the issue was whether s 57 should be read subject to a general principle of criminal law. However, the issue can still be 'anchored' on the words 'shall marry' (does the *actus reus* – 'shall marry' – involve criminal intent?).

between competing values or moral principles or lines of authority rather than debates about the meaning of words. It is naive to think that such issues can be satisfactorily resolved by stipulating or agreeing on a precise general definition of the words around which the issues have congregated.

Thirdly, there is sometimes an official formulation of an issue. For example, when the Court of Appeal certifies that a case may go on appeal to the House of Lords on 'an issue of public importance', the precise wording of the issue may be agreed by the parties and approved by the Court. This is a species of the old procedure in which a lower court 'stated a case' for resolution by a higher court. In such instances we have a canonical text that is both authoritative and exact, and which can therefore be relied on for most practical purposes. But again it is naive to think that such texts are themselves sacred and immune from differing interpretations.

In general, there is no standard way of posing issues concerning the scope or meaning of rules not in fixed verbal form, but as with questions concerning statutory rules, judges often explicitly formulate what is in issue in a case. But it is not unknown for the same judge to state and restate the issue more than once using different words and at different levels of generality in the course of a single judgment; we illustrate this point later in the chapter. Where there is more than one judge there may be room for further significant differences in the way in which the issue in a case is formulated.[11] Nevertheless, the language used by the court is usually a good starting point.

Some law reports contain summaries of the arguments of counsel. In an important or a difficult case these may be helpful in identifying and formulating the issues or in reading the judgment(s), as is illustrated by the analysis of the competing interpretations and arguments in *Allen* in Chapter 10.[12]

After these preliminaries we come to the judgment or judgments themselves. Almost all of the theoretical issues discussed in this book apply to the problem of interpreting judgments and the remainder of this chapter is concerned with particular aspects of this kind of interpretation. Interpretation of cases is inherently problematic, but this is not to say that making a précis of a judgment is never straightforward. For most practical purposes, including the writing of a preliminary précis, it is sufficient to ask two questions: what answer(s) did the judge give to the issues of law raised by the facts in this case? What were the main reasons advanced to justify the answers(s)? These are often quite easily summarised, as is illustrated by the model case note of *Allen* on the following page. Problems of interpretation of cases arise either when there is some doubt or disagreement about the use of a past precedent for some particular purpose as a source of authority or of substantive reasons, or when the reader wishes to subject the text to some less orthodox kind of scrutiny or analysis, for example as an example of judicial style or in order to dig out hidden ideological or other assumptions. It is beyond the scope of this book to explore such alternative ways of reading the law reports, but they are touched on in Appendix III.[13] It is relevant, however, to explore what is involved in orthodox legal interpretation. For this purpose we need to look in more detail at what is involved in reading and using reported cases as precedents.

---

11 For example, in *Donoghue v Stevenson*, chapter 1, section 9.
12 Below, pp 347-350.

1.1   Case note on *R v Allen*

R v Allen	Bigamy
CCCR	(1872) LR 1 CCR 357
	Conviction affirmed

Facts   In 1853 A married W1. In 1866 W1 died. In 1867 A married W2. In 1871, while W2 was still alive, A married W3, who was the niece of W1. Indictment for bigamy under section 57 of Offences against the Person Act 1861: 'Whosoever being married shall marry any other person during the life of the former husband or wife ...' A's marriage to W3 was void under existing law (prohibited degrees).

Issue   What is the meaning of 'shall marry' in section 57?

(Alternative formulation: does 'shall marry' include a 'marriage' which would in any case have been void independently of its bigamous character?)

Held   Per *Cockburn LJ.* 'Shall marry' means 'shall go through a form and ceremony of marriage recognised by law'. Mischief rule applied. Purpose of s 57 is protection of *sacred ceremony*. Left open: 'fantastic forms of marriage unknown to the law' – eg *Burt v Burt.*
R v Fanning (Irish case, 7-4 decision) not followed.

Comment
  (a)   does 'being married' have same meaning? (ie void ceremony followed by valid). No – *R v Moscovtich.* Thus same word used in same section in two different senses.
  (b)   rationale of bigamy said to be protection of *sacred ceremony. Sed quaere.* See Glanville Williams, (1950) 13 *Modern Law Review* 417 doubting if bigamy has clear rationale or, indeed, whether there is a need for a separate offence. (See also the use of 'bogus marriages' for immigration purposes).[14]

NB

1. Always include name of case, at least one citation, the result, a précis of the potentially material facts, the issue(s) of law raised in the case, the holding(s).
2. A case note is essentially a précis. The amount of detail that is appropriate depends on the purpose of the particular note and is a matter of judgement.

---

13 Below, pp 426-429.
14 Appendix I, section A5, question 4.

2 Cases as precedents

The use of past decisions to assist in the resolution of present problems is an unexceptional feature of the reasoning techniques we employ in both legal and non-legal contexts. In law, resort to precedent, that is to say the use of prior decisions to assist in the resolution of present disputes, has in general reached a considerable degree of refinement, but it has its roots in common human frailties and needs:

> 'Toward its operation drive all those phases of human make-up which build habit in the individual and institutions in the group: laziness as to the reworking of a problem once solved; the time and energy saved by routine, especially under any pressure of business; the values of routine as a curb on arbitrariness and as a prop of weakness, inexperience and instability; the social values of predictability; the power of whatever exists to produce expectations and the power of expectations to become normative. The force of precedent in the law is heightened by an additional factor: that curious, almost universal, sense of justice which urges that all men are properly to be treated alike in like circumstances. As the social system varies we meet infinite variations as to what men or treatments or circumstances are to be classed as "like"; but the pressure to accept the views of the time and place remains.'[15]

'Precedent' and related notions are not unique to law. People who serve on committees, in administrative agencies and other decision-making bodies may often be faced with a problem which demands a solution but which, for instance, involves issues of conflicting values or competing interests in a borderline case. In the process of reaching a decision in such circumstances, they may, at the same time as they make a decision, express their reluctance to resolve the matter in that particular way in the phrase, 'Let's not create a precedent'. This phrase contains certain assumptions about problem-solving both for the present and the future. It is implicit that future decision-makers have some kind of obligation to come to the same conclusion should a similar case arise; that others who observe or rely upon the decisions of the particular body may expect that similar cases in the future will be similarly decided and thus may base their conduct upon such expectations; that the decision-making process is not constituted simply by the *ad hoc* resolution of particular cases, but involves the rational development of general policies or principles through these cases; and that the individual decisions themselves have status as expressions of policy or principle. Such factors provide a basis for demands that precedents be treated as having force or weight, and should not be ignored upon a whim, but departed from only on the basis of rational argument and justification. These four notions, of obligation, expectation of future behaviour, interstitial growth of policy and principle, and the authority of decisions, form the basis of the common law's treatment of precedent.

---

15 K Llewellyn, *Encyclopedia of Social Sciences* (1931), vol 3, p 449.

3 Two perspectives on precedent

Systems of law may be unique in having developed rules which govern how courts must (not), may (not) and can (not) deal with prior cases. Whatever those rules may prescribe, they are cumulatively and generally known by the expression, 'a doctrine of precedent'. In a sense, nearly all legal systems have a doctrine of precedent, though its requirements may vary from system to system.[16] Even a legal system which explicitly prohibits the citation of prior cases in court can be said to have a doctrine of precedent in that it has a rule which regulates the use of precedent. The doctrine of precedent is seen at its most formalised in the English common law, a system which is unusual both in regard to the fact that it exhibits a high proportion of rules extracted from decided cases, and in its detailed rules which prescribe how the various courts in the judicial hierarchy must, may or can deal with precedent decisions.

A distinction needs to be drawn between accounts of the doctrine of precedent and descriptions of the practice of handling precedent. The doctrine consists of the rules which prescribe how prior cases must, may and can be used; descriptions of practice deal with the techniques which are in fact used by judges and other interpreters in handling the prior cases within the framework of the doctrine.

The distinction between doctrine and practice is not a sharp one. On the one hand, there are tacit conventions, regularly followed by judges in England, which accord greater respect to prior cases than is required by orthodox formulations of the doctrine. For example, the doctrine of precedent prescribes that a Lord Justice of Appeal may overrule, disapprove or not follow a decision of the High Court, or that he may follow it, as a persuasive authority. In practice a Lord Justice of Appeal will feel under some obligation at least to consider a relevant decision of the High Court and to deviate from it only for some good reason. Similarly, the doctrine of precedent does not lay down a formula for extracting rules of law from previous cases, that is, for determining the *ratio decidendi*;[17] indeed English judges have been careful not to make this the subject of a formal rule. Judges in subsequent cases are not bound by the explicit wording used in prior cases; in other words, the *ratio decidendi* is not a rule in fixed verbal form.[18] Nevertheless there is a tacit convention that special attention should be paid to the words used by judges in prior cases and often a passage from a

---

16 See generally N MacCormick and R Summers (eds), *Interpreting Precedents: A Comparative Study* (1997) and in particular within the European Union, J Barcelo, 'Precedent in European Community Law', at pp 407-436; MK Shahabuddeen, *Precedent in the World Court* (1996); and R Schlesinger, *Comparative Law: Cases and Materials* (1960), pp 287-322.

17 See below section 6.

18 Rules may come to be formulated in essentially the same terms, and occasionally one particular formulation may become sanctified. A clear example of this is the celebrated rule in *Rylands v Fletcher* (1866) LR 1 ExCh 265. A second interesting example is s 131 of the Law of Property Act 1925 which abolishes 'the rule of law known as the Rule in Shelley's Case'. By contrast, what was regarded as a canonical statement about the rights of the taxpayer in *IRC v Duke of Westminster* [1936] AC 1, may cease, by later judicial action, to be so; *IRC v McGuckian* [1997] 3 All ER 817, 825.

judgment in the prior case is treated as an adequate formulation of the *ratio*. Sometimes judges and other interpreters lay great stress on the particular words used in such judicial formulations; at other times they ignore them entirely or treat them as too wide or too narrow. We shall consider the problem of the *ratio decidendi* further below; the point to be emphasised here is that orthodox formulations of the doctrine of precedent, tacit conventions or rules of practice which are commonly observed in handling cases, and descriptions of the actual techniques used in practice, are not always easy to distinguish.

Nevertheless the distinction is an important one. Much of the literature on precedent in England has concentrated on the doctrine but says relatively little about how the techniques are in fact used in legal argument. Too great a concern with the niceties of the doctrine may give a distorted impression of the realities of the practice: on the one hand, the range of techniques available and the ways they are in fact used are more varied and subtle than some orthodox accounts suggest; on the other hand, the respect accorded in practice to certain categories of non-binding precedent may be a more important distinguishing feature of the English approach than the alleged strictness of the doctrine.

Accordingly, there are two different perspectives on precedent. On the one hand there is the body of formal rules which provides a general framework for arguing about and using prior cases and which, as we shall see, is generally quite permissive. On the other hand is the wide range of techniques, nearly all of which are permissible, which are available for use by interpreters of different kinds in constructing and presenting arguments involving prior cases.

4 The doctrine of precedent

4.1 Vertical and lateral effect

According to the English doctrine,[19] a previous decision is to be treated as an authority, if it is analogous to a present dispute before a court, if it was decided by a court which, according to the rules of the doctrine, has the status to make decisions which will be deemed to be authoritative, and if the decision has not been abrogated by a statute or a court which has the power to overrule prior decisions.[20] The doctrine of precedent imposes obligations having effect both

19 See R Cross and J Harris, *Precedent in English Law* (4th edn, 1991), chapters III and IV and Bankowski et al, 'Precedent in the United Kingdom' in MacCormick and Summers, op cit, pp 315-353.
20 It is important to differentiate clearly between 'overruling' and 'reversing'. A decision is overruled when a court superior in the judicial hierarchy to (or sometimes at the same level as) the court that made it holds in a subsequent, different, case that its precedent value is nil. This can only occur in respect of courts which themselves had the status to lay down authoritative propositions of law and only in respect of propositions of law. Thus, for example, decisions of magistrates' courts (even if they were reported) cannot be overruled, neither can decisions of fact. Overruling has no effect on the parties; even though the case which decided the law that was applicable to them is no longer authoritative, their respective rights and duties remain *res judicata*, op cit, n 4. A decision is reversed when it is taken on appeal

vertically and laterally, and can be quite simply summarised as follows. When a court is faced with a precedent decision:

(a) if the precedent is a decision of a court superior to it in the judicial hierarchy, then it *must* follow that precedent in the present case (this is normally called 'being bound by' a precedent); or

(b) if the precedent is one of its own previous decisions, then, subject to certain exceptions in which it *may* depart from it, the court *must* follow the precedent; or

(c) if the precedent is a decision of a court inferior to it in the judicial hierarchy, then it is not bound to follow the precedent, but may do so if it chooses; and

(d) precedents decided by superior courts of some other jurisdictions may be treated as persuasive but never as binding.[21]

By comparison with the hierarchical obligation to follow decisions of superior courts,[22] the obligation on a court to follow its own previous decisions or those of a court of co-ordinate jurisdiction has always been more controversial. At times when adherence to precedent has been perceived as stultifying the development of the law, efforts have been made to circumvent or weaken it; at other times the social value of certainty in legal affairs has been accorded priority, even at the expense of what appears just in the case at hand. To the general proposition that it is bound by its own previous decisions, the Appellate Committee of the House of Lords had, for over a century prior to the making of its Practice Statement on Judicial Precedent in 1966, recognised what it spoke of as two exceptions: it would not be bound by a decision given *per incuriam*, nor by one overruled by statute. As a decision given *per incuriam* is

and the appeal court decides that the lower court was wrong as a matter of law, or that it decided a question of fact in a way which was unsustainable on the evidence adduced before it. Clearly this immediately affects the rights and duties of the parties. Any court, save the House of Lords (or any other court which for the litigation in issue is a final court of appeal) is liable to have its decisions reversed on appeal. Rarely, a decision that is procedurally flawed may be set aside, that is, be treated as never having occurred; *R v Bow Street Metropolitan Stipendiary Magistrate, ex p Pinochet Ugarte (No 2)* [1999] 1 All ER 577, HL.

21 For example, decisions of the Court of Session in Scotland, the Irish Supreme Court, the High Court of Australia (see Diplock J in *Gould*, below p 388) or the Supreme Court of Canada. The Judicial Committee of the Privy Council has no appellate function within the legal system of England and Wales, but the advice it gives to the Crown on the disposal of appeals from Commonwealth jurisdictions can be persuasive for courts in this country in cases where the law is similar. This is because the Privy Councillors who give that advice include Lords of Appeal in Ordinary. See for example, Parker LJ, *R v Secretary of State for the Home Department, ex p Khan* [1985] 1 All ER 40, 48.

22 Where a court sits with three or more members, the decision may be unanimous or by a majority. When combined with this obligation, majority decisions can lead to what appears, superficially at least, to be the odd outcome that a litigant may lose his case notwithstanding that there were in total, more judges on his side than on the other. This is not simply a quirky matter of numbers; in close-run appeals; the presence or absence of a particular judge or Law Lord can sway the outcome one way or another. See also Lord Diplock's reference, in *Davis v Johnson*, to the 'arithmetic' of the differing opinions on the interpretation of the 1976 Act; above, p 97.

one in which the previous court failed to take account of a material authority (that is, a yet earlier binding precedent or a statutory provision) that would have led the court to a different conclusion of law, neither this nor the case in which the decision has been overruled by statute can truly be regarded as exceptions. In both instances the earlier decision no longer has any authority, and thus one of the conditions of its being a precedent, viz that it is authoritative, is absent. Accordingly, the decision of the House of Lords in 1966 to allow itself to depart from its own previous decisions was all the more remarkable for not having been prefaced by any earlier declaration of exceptional powers.[23] The House said:

> Their Lordships regard the use of precedent as an indispensable foundation upon which to decide what is the law and its application to individual cases. It provides at least some degree of certainty upon which individuals can rely in the conduct of their affairs, as well as a basis for orderly development of legal rules.
>
> Their Lordships nevertheless recognize that too rigid adherence to precedent may lead to injustice in a particular case and also unduly restrict the proper development of the law. They propose, therefore, to modify their present practice and, while treating former decisions of this House as normally binding, to depart from a previous decision when it appears right to do so.
>
> In this connection they will bear in mind the danger of disturbing retrospectively the basis on which contracts, settlements of property and fiscal arrangements have been entered into and also the especial need for certainty as to the criminal law. This announcement is not intended to affect the use of precedent elsewhere than in this House.[24]

Since then there have been a number of occasions on which the House has been invited to depart from one of its own previous decisions, and a smaller number on which it has done so.[25] These decisions are, of course, important as instances of the exercise of the discretion afforded by the Practice Statement, but they also illustrate one of the prominent and enduring features of the English doctrine, namely, that despite the existence of a clear obligation to follow prior cases, in certain crucial respects the doctrine is permissive and its conditions indeterminate. The Practice Statement specifies some considerations as being relevant to the exercise of the discretion, but otherwise the House is at liberty to formulate its own criteria of 'when it appears right to do so'. As in the interpretation of statutes, the senior judiciary appear content to work with a marked degree of indeterminacy as to the manner of their decision-making, and thus others' efforts to articulate, on the basis of these decisions, the criteria that the House has adopted yield propositions that are themselves substantially indeterminate. Even such apparently basic considerations as the

---

23 Cf *Myers v DPP* [1965] AC 1001.
24 *Practice Statement (Judicial Precedent)* [1966] 1 WLR 1234. Bankowski et al remark on the 'terse' statement of the rationale for observing precedents contained in the Practice Statement, MacCormick and Summers, op cit, p 335.
25 See the potentially limiting refinements proposed by Lord Goff in *Food Corpn of India v Antclizo Shipping* [1988] 2 All ER 513, 516. See further J Harris, 'Towards Principles of Overruling – When Should a Final Court of Appeal Second Guess?', (1990) 10 *Oxford Journal of Legal Studies* 135 and Cross and Harris, op cit, pp 135-143.

significance of the word 'depart', and its difference, if any, from 'overruling', do not appear to be well-settled.[26]

The Appellate Committee of the House of Lords is the supreme judicial authority in our legal system. However, the Court of Appeal is generally acknowledged to be the more significant in terms of the influence of its decisions. This stems from the fact that it hears very many more appeals than does the House of Lords and is, in practice, for financial and other reasons, the court of last resort for most appellate cases.[27] Its position in the legal system has been described as central, and its responsibility for the stability, consistency and predictability of the system frequently emphasised.[28] These considerations are thought by many of the judiciary to militate strongly against a liberty to depart from its own decisions similar to that enjoyed by the House of Lords. Given the Court's centrality, *Young v Bristol Aeroplane Co* is the most important case on the doctrine of precedent. In that case a full Court of Appeal laid down the following proposition and the well-known three exceptions to it:

> The Court of Appeal is bound to follow its own decisions and those of courts of co-ordinate jurisdiction, and the 'full' court is in the same position in this respect as a division of the court consisting of three members. The only exceptions to this rule are: – (1.) The court is entitled and bound to decide which of two conflicting decisions of its own it will follow; (2.) the court is bound to refuse to follow a decision of its own which, though not expressly overruled, cannot, in its opinion, stand with a decision of the House of Lords; (3.) the court is not bound to follow a decision of its own if it is satisfied that the decision was given *per incuriam*, e.g., where a statute or a rule having statutory effect which would have affected the decision was not brought to the attention of the earlier court.[29]

Since this case was decided in 1944, the Court has on occasion reviewed the scope of these three exceptions.[30] In *Limb v Union Jack Removals* it sought to restate aspects of the doctrine in the light of these cases:

(a) Where the court has considered a statute or a rule having the force of a statute its decision stands on the same footing as any other decision on a point of law.

---

26 In *Murphy v Brentwood District Council* [1990] 2 All ER 908, in which the House took the unusual step of convening a Committee of seven Law Lords for the purpose of reconsidering the authority of its earlier decision, *Anns v Merton London Borough Council* [1978] AC 728, four of their Lordships specifically referred to the 1966 Practice Statement. They, like the two who did not, spoke of 'departing' from *Anns v Merton London Borough Council.* The headnote, however, indicates that the decision was overruled (as Lord Mackay LC implied). See generally, R Summers and S Eng, 'Departures from Precedent' in MacCormick and Summers, op cit, pp 519–530.

27 In 1997 the House of Lords heard a total of 83 appeals, of which 40 were civil matters. In the same year the Civil Division of the Court of Appeal heard 1,255 appeals; *Judicial Statistics Annual Report 1997* (Cm 3980, 1998).

28 See, for example, Scarman LJ in *Farrell v Alexander* [1976] 1 QB 345, 371; quoted with approval by Lord Diplock in *Davis v Johnson,* above, pp 102–103.

29 [1944] KB 718. This formulation in the headnote of the case was approved by Lord Diplock in *Davis v Johnson.*

30 It may be questioned whether points (2) and (3) really are exceptions: a decision that was given *per incuriam* or is inconsistent with a subsequent decision of the House of Lords is not authoritative, cannot be binding and requires the exercise of no exceptional power to ignore it; point (1) is less easy, since such a conflict ought, in theory, not to arise if courts are following precedent. See *R v Maginnis* [1987] AC 303.

(b) A decision of a two-judge Court of Appeal on a substantive appeal (as opposed to an application for leave) has the same authority as a decision of a three-judge or a five-judge Court of Appeal.

(c) The doctrine of *per incuriam* applies only where another division of the court has reached a decision in ignorance or forgetfulness of a decision binding on it or of an inconsistent statutory provision, and in either case it must be shown that if the court had had this material in mind it *must* have reached a contrary decision.[31]

(d) The doctrine does not extend to a case where, if different arguments had been placed before the court or if different material had been placed before it, it *might* have reached a different conclusion.[32]

(e) Any departure from a decision of the court is in principle undesirable and should only be considered if the previous decision is manifestly wrong. Even then it will be necessary to take account of whether the decision purports to be one of general application and whether there is any other way of remedying the error, for example by encouraging an appeal to the House of Lords.[33]

Decisions such as *Williams v Fawcett* and *Rickards v Rickards* indicate the shifting content of the doctrine,[34] but these refinements take place in the context of the repetition of the primary proposition laid down in *Young's case*. Lord Donaldson MR, for example, said in *Rickards v Rickards*: 'The importance of the rule of *stare decisis* in relation to the Court of Appeal's own decisions can hardly be overstated'.[35] Likewise, the Court's application in *Circuit Systems v Zuken Redac* of the first of *Young's* exceptions to two of its earlier decisions reveals the same acceptance of *stare decisis* as the foundation for its approach to their precedential value.[36] The weight attached to *stare decisis* explains the emphatic rejection by the House of Lords in *Davis v Johnson* of Lord Denning

---

31 Ignorance of a statutory provision, which, had the court been aware of it, would have compelled it to reach a contrary decision, is a clear example of the *per incuriam* exception: per Stephenson LJ *Bonalumi v Secretary of State for the Home Department* [1985] 1 All ER 797, 802.

32 See Lord Donaldson MR in *Duke v Reliance Systems* [1987] 2 All ER 859, 860 and *Rakhit v Carty* [1990] 2 All ER 202, 208.

33 Per Brooke LJ [1998] 2 All ER 513, 522. In *Kleinwort Benson Ltd v Lincoln City Council* [1998] 4 All ER 513, 547, Lord Lloyd discussed the role of the House of Lords in correcting the common law 'when it has taken a wrong turning'. This justification for the existence of the House as a second tier of appeal is mainly justified, he said, by the fact that the Court of Appeal is bound by its own decisions.

34 In *Williams v Fawcett* [1985] 1 All ER 787 the Court identified as another instance for the application of the *per incuriam* exception, a line of cases which it said had misconstrued the effect of a statutory provision so that individuals were placed in danger of being committed for contempt of court, and in *Rickards v Rickards* [1989] 3 All ER 193 the Court further approved, as a 'rare and exceptional case', that it was justified in not following an earlier decision which it was satisfied had been wrongly decided and where there was no possibility of an appeal to the House of Lords. In *Boys v Chaplin* [1968] 2 QB 1 the Court held that a decision on an interlocutory matter made by a two judge court would not bind a court of three or more.

35 [1989] 3 All ER 193, 198.

36 [1996] 3 All ER 748; per Simon Brown LJ, at 762, 'each ratio is, of course, a binding authority'.

MR's efforts either to liberate the Civil Division of the Court of Appeal from that aspect of the doctrine of precedent, or to create exceptions in addition to those laid down by Lord Greene MR.

The doctrine is more flexible in the Criminal Division of the Court of Appeal which has the same power to depart from earlier decisions of its own (or its predecessors) as does the Civil Division. In addition, as was laid down by *R v Taylor*, it may depart from precedent if it is necessary in the interests of justice to the defendant.[37] This also almost certainly represents the extent of the obligation where the Queen's Bench Division is exercising its appellate or its supervisory jurisdiction. 'The principle of *stare decisis* does not apply in the Divisional Court and we need not follow other decisions of this court when we are "convinced that [they are] wrong".'[38] In the case of the other two divisions of the High Court, it is well settled that in exercising their appellate jurisdiction, the doctrine applies as it is set out in *Young v Bristol Aeroplane Co*.[39] However, High Court judges exercising their original jurisdiction are not bound by previous High Court decisions, but nevertheless should regard them as persuasive and endeavour to reach a similar conclusion.[40]

Three points about the doctrine of precedent stand out. Firstly, it sets rules that are clear but are also permissive. Secondly, the courts have been unwilling to set precise criteria that specify what part of a decision is to be regarded as binding. Thirdly, there is a practice of deference to both persuasive and binding authorities that goes beyond what the stated doctrine requires.[41]

4.2 Doctrinal diversity

The doctrine continues to excite questions of a conceptual kind concerning its nature, rationale and proper formulation.[42] One reason for this is that such questions are intimately related to general theoretical issues about legal interpretation, legal reasoning, the nature of legal rules and the proper role of judges. To some extent different theories of precedent reflect, more or less

---

37 *R v Taylor* [1950] 2 KB 368, chapter 1, section 7.3, as modified by May LJ in *R v Spencer* [1985] 2 WLR 197, 203. See Appendix I, section A5, question 8, p 394. Unlike the Civil Division, the Criminal Division has also employed its powers as a full court of five judges instead of the usual three to overrule its precedents. *B v DPP* [1998] 4 All ER 265 contains a straightforward reaffirmation that decisions of the Court of Criminal Appeal are binding on a divisional court of the Queen's Bench Division sitting in its appellate capacity (per Brooke LJ, p 284). An example of the Criminal Division employing the *per incuriam* exception to overrule one of its own previous decisions is *R v Graham* [1997] Crim LR 358.

38 Simon Brown LJ, *R v Home Secretary, ex p Naughton* [1997] 1 All ER 426, 434, quoting Goff LJ in *R v Greater Manchester Coroner, ex p Tal* [1984] 3 All ER 240, 246. Simon Brown LJ's remarks were quoted with approval by Lord Bingham LCJ in *R v Governor of Brockhill Prison, ex p Evans* [1997] 1 All ER 439, 450-451, 454.

39 Per Lord Goddard CJ, *Younghusband v Luftig* [1949] 2 KB 354, 361.

40 Per Lord Goddard CJ, *Huddersfield Police Authority v Watson* [1947] KB 842, 848.

41 For example, though a *dictum* of a Circuit Judge in the Crown Court can never be binding on a High Court judge sitting in the Divisional Court of Queen's Bench, 'great weight' should be given to it; per Donaldson LJ, *Windsors v Oldfield* [1981] 2 All ER 718, 722.

42 For example the collection of essays in L Goldstein (ed), *Precedent and Law* (1987); Z Bankowski et al, 'Rationales for Precedent' in McCormick and Summers, op cit, pp 481-501.

exactly, general differences within legal theory. The puzzlements that have particularly attracted attention in recent years may be summarised as follows.

One disagreement is about the juridical basis of the doctrine. Some writers have argued that a court cannot, on its own initiative, declare that it shall be bound by its own previous decisions unless there already exists a rule providing that that declaration is itself binding. This logical impossibility, it is argued, extends to a declaration such as the 1966 Practice Statement; for as long as it is operative, there is at least one decision of the House which cannot be departed from, namely the decision embodied in the Statement not to be absolutely bound by past decisions. Connected to this is the question whether the rules of precedent are rules of law or of practice. The thrust of the distinction is that if the rules of precedent are treated as rules of law, then they impose obligations which cannot be modified by the simple device of a Practice Statement, for this does not acknowledge the authority from which such rules emanate. On the other hand, if they are treated as rules of practice only, then they can of course be modified by a Practice Statement in the same way as courts routinely regulate the hearing of cases, the taxation of costs, vacation sittings and so on; but such a Statement could not, it is argued, be effective in a court other than the one which issues it.

Writers disagree on the way in which these questions concerning the doctrine should be resolved. Most accept that the hierarchy of the court structure implies an obligation on inferior courts to follow decisions of superior courts and, apart from the occasional tremor in the Court of Appeal, this obligation is very rarely challenged by judges. There is less agreement on that aspect of the doctrine relating to a court's own precedents. Some regard it as an internal non-binding convention of judicial practice; others treat it as imposing a substantial obligation. Yet others doubt the practical importance of questioning the juridical basis and status of the doctrine: what is clear is that judges do generally follow their own and superior precedents, and seek to give good reasons when they do not. So far as the relationship between the House of Lords and other courts is concerned, the reality is that in *Davis v Johnson* the House unequivocally claimed power to prescribe rules for precedent in the Court of Appeal. This implies that the doctrine of precedent has the status of law for all courts other than the House of Lords, for whom it is only a matter of practice.

Another aspect of traditional discussions of precedent is exemplified by the conflict between a judge who takes the view that adherence to precedent is a value which should take priority over the promotion of some other value in a particular case, and a judge in the same case who takes the opposite view. The values claimed for precedent include predictability, stability, efficiency, the elimination of error and of bias, and general consistency and coherence between decided cases. These can conflict with values present in the social context within which a dispute arises, such as in *Davis v Johnson*.[43] No settled criteria exist for determining which set of values to prefer, and it is in difficult cases such as this that Lord Denning and others have in the past raised the question of the desirability of continued adherence to the doctrine with only

43 Chapter 1, section 12.5.

the limited exceptions of *Young's case*. In his view, the values which the doctrine represents would in most cases be accorded priority, but the removal of the inhibitions which it imposes would avoid the unhappy consequences of rigidity, inflexibility and substantive injustice which may occur.

The doctrine of precedent and its associated reporting arrangements may also be seen as imposing both quality and quantity controls on the number of cases that come before the courts. Like any bureaucracy, the judicial system needs some means by which less important or ill-conceived cases can be filtered out, lest it be swamped with work. One way of accomplishing this is to encourage those responsible for reaching decisions in disputed cases to do so in accordance with precedents. A former Lord Chancellor captured this succinctly: 'By allowing the vast bulk of disputes to be settled in the shadow of the law, a system of precedent prevents the legal apparatus from becoming clogged by a myriad of single instances'.[44] The effectiveness of these precedents will be compromised where they proliferate, since the greater their number, the easier it will be for advisers and advocates to find points of distinction. Accordingly, it is important that only those appealed cases that can be said (by those responsible for their inclusion in any official law reporting series) to add substantively to the law, rather than merely illustrating its application to particular facts, should be included. As improved technology and cheaper publication methods enable more cases to be accessed than in the past, so the perceived need to control the quantity of cases that could be cited in support of a given proposition becomes more urgent.[45]

It may also be argued that apart from any instrumental reasons, the doctrine of precedent performs important symbolic functions, in particular concerning first, the constitutional and political relationship between the courts and the legislature and, secondly, the role of the judge as the maker of authoritative propositions of law.

The claimed consequences of adherence to precedent are that judges decide cases, in particular those involving disputes between citizens and the state, from a position of political neutrality, and that bad law can only be properly changed by Parliament. These tenets of judicial behaviour are, in terms of rhetoric at least, politically significant; but whether they accurately reflect the reality of judicial behaviour is another matter. Notwithstanding that courts are in general not well suited to initiate changes in the law, judges do change law, if only interstitially;[46] judicial decisions

---

44 Lord Mackay, *The Times*, 3 December 1987; quoted in F Cownie and A Bradney, *English Legal System in Context* (1996), p 87.
45 For example, some years ago, Lord Diplock issued on behalf of the House of Lords a practice statement to the effect that unreported decisions retrieved via LEXIS should not be cited in appeals unless they both met the criterion of adding to the law and leave to cite them had been given.
46 Holmes J, *Southern Pacific Co v Jensen* 244 US 205 (1917), 221: 'It is true that the House [of Lords] has a power to develop the law. But it is a limited power. And it can be exercised only in the gaps left by Parliament. It is impermissible for the House to develop the law in a direction which is contrary to the expressed will of Parliament'; per Lord Browne-Wilkinson, *R v Chief Constable of the Royal Ulster Constabulary, ex p Begley* [1997] 4 All ER 833, 838. See further R Dworkin, *Law's Empire* (1986), chapter 7.

make a difference. It is, however, not possible to make a fully reasoned judgment about the supposed neutrality of the doctrine of precedent without also assuming some position on such matters as the methods of training, selection and appointment of judges and their social background;[47] the historic and prevailing conceptions of the relationship between the constituent elements of the state, including the present understanding and reality of the doctrine of the supremacy of Parliament; and the role of the courts as arbiters of disputes.

Nor are generalisations even about the rhetoric of the traditionally conceived role of the appellate courts altogether safe, as the Law Lords at least have a knack of confounding them by the adoption on occasion of diametrically opposite positions as to its role as a final court of appeal and a law maker.[48] For example, within the past few years it has, on the one hand, set its face against altering the common law either in respect of the rebuttable presumption that a child between the ages of 10 and 14 cannot be guilty of a criminal offence or of the defence of self-defence, on the grounds that these are matters pre-eminently for Parliament to decide.[49] By contrast, the House decided, a few years earlier, to regard as 'mere surplusage', the word 'unlawfully' as it appears in section 1 of the Sexual Offences Act 1967, so that it could extend the crime of rape to include 'marital rape', that is, cases in which a husband had had sexual intercourse with his non-consenting wife. Under a rule that was 256 years old, such an act, however objectionable, was not illegal. This change was effected because 'the common law is ... capable of evolving in the light of changing social, economic and cultural developments'.[50]

The doctrine of precedent has, secondly, traditionally been used to support the view that the courts declare, but do not make, the law. The declaratory theory of judicial decisions holds that when judges decide questions of law, they do so on the basis of a body of rules and principles which contain the elements of the answer now given, even if the particular question had never previously been asked. In holding that what is now authoritatively declared was immanent within the rules and principles of the common law system, and thus amenable to discovery and formulation by persons steeped in that system, the declaratory theory distances the judge as an individual from the rules that

---

47 The standard work in Great Britain is J Griffith, *The Politics of the Judiciary* (5th edn, 1997).
48 For a routine statement of the proposition that 'in our constitutional scheme of things it should be for the legislature, not the judiciary, to determine what the policy of the law should be' see Brooke LJ in *B v DPP* [1998] 4 All ER 265, 285. An example of differing conceptions of how this proposition should work in practice is *R v Central Criminal Court, ex p Francis & Francis* [1989] AC 346; see Appendix 1, section F, question 6, pp 401ff.
49 In *C (a Minor) v DPP* [1996] 1 AC 1 the House held (per Lord Lowry at p 40) that the fact that the issue of the age of criminal responsibility was 'not so much a legal as a social problem, with a dash of politics thrown in, emphasises that it should be within the exclusive remit of Parliament'. In *R v Clegg* [1995] 1 AC 482, the House adopted (per Lord Lloyd at p 500) Lord Simon's words in *DPP for Northern Ireland v Lynch* [1975] AC 653, 695, which also raised complex questions of policy in an area of the criminal law, that it was difficult to conceive of any circumstances less suited to a committee of five Law Lords arrogating to themselves 'so momentous a law making initiative'.
50 *R v R* [1991] 4 All ER 481, 489, per Lord Keith. This was (unlike the *doli incapax* presumption and the law governing self-defence) an area of law governed by statute and in respect of which Parliament had in the recent past legislated.

he is articulating. In this way, the doctrine of precedent reflects the political notion that we should be governed not by the rule of men but by rules of law. In reality, however, it is some time since judges, when speaking of their role, have subscribed to this limited vision. In a powerful speech in the case *Kleinwort Benson Ltd v Lincoln City Council,* Lord Goff said:

> When a judge decides a case which comes before him, he does so on the basis of what he understands the law to be. This he discovers from the applicable statutes, if any, and from the precedents drawn from the reports of previous judicial decisions. Nowadays, he derives much assistance from academic writings in interpreting statutes and, more especially, the effect of reported cases; and he has regard, where appropriate, to decisions of judges in other jurisdictions. In the course of deciding the case before him he may, on occasion, develop the common law in the perceived interests of justice, though he does this 'only interstitially', to use the expression of Holmes J in *Southern Pacific Co v Jensen.* This means not only that he must act within the confines of the doctrine of precedent, but that the change must be seen as a development, usually a very modest development, of existing principle and so can take its place as a congruent part of the common law as a whole ...
>
> Occasionally, a judicial development of the law will be of a more radical nature, constituting a departure, even a major departure, from what has previously been considered to be established principle, and leading to a realignment of subsidiary principles within that branch of the law ...
>
> Bearing these matters in mind, the law which the judge states to be applicable to the case before him is the law which, as so developed, is perceived by him as applying not only to the case before him, but to all other comparable cases, as a congruent part of the body of the law. Moreover, when he states the applicable principles of law, the judge is declaring these as constituting the law relevant to his decision ...
>
> It is in this context that we have to reinterpret the declaratory theory of judicial decision. We can see that, in fact, it does not presume the existence of an ideal system of the common law, which the judges from time to time reveal in their decisions. The historical theory of judicial decision, though it may in the past have served its purpose, was indeed a fiction. But it does mean that, when the judges state what the law is, their decisions do, in the sense I have described, have a retrospective effect. That is, I believe, inevitable. It is inevitable in relation to the particular case before the court, in which the events must have occurred some time, perhaps years, before the judge's decision is made. But it is also inevitable in relation to other cases in which the law as so stated will in future fall to be applied. I must confess that I cannot imagine how a common law system, or indeed any legal system, can operate otherwise if the law is to be applied equally and yet be capable of organic change.[51]

This quotation confirms that an important attribute of a judge's decision is that it is retrospective; that is, that it 'does not only state what the law is from the date of the decision, it states what it always has been'.[52] Ordinarily this fiction does not present many difficulties. For the most part, lawyers are able to advise their clients on the basis of the law as it is currently understood, secure in the knowledge that, should it be judicially tested, their understanding

---

51 [1998] 4 All ER 513, 535.
52 Per Lord Woolf MR, *R v Governor of Brockhill Prison, ex p Evans (No 2)* [1998] 4 All ER 993, 996.

will be confirmed. What, of course, typically makes the difference are the factual conclusions that the court reaches, together with its application of the law to those facts.

However, where the court now decides that the law as previously understood was wrong, the declaratory theory means that it has always been wrong and that decisions taken in accordance with it were in error. Again, ordinarily this does not create great difficulties, since in the case of the advice given by their lawyers, clients' legal expectations can be revised according to the corrected law, and in the case of concluded litigation, the principle of *res judicata* means that the litigant in whose favour the law now sits will be barred from re-litigating the issue. It may be small comfort to the disappointed litigant to know that she was right all along, but the implications of a significant change in the law for the legal expectations of many thousands of individuals who have sought to arrange their affairs on what they were advised was settled law (some of which may relate to their expectations of what will happen to their property upon their deaths) are likely to be extensive and costly. Among others, it was for these reasons that, when the House of Lords issued its Practice Statement in 1966, it indicated that it would 'bear in mind the danger of disturbing retrospectively the basis on which contracts, settlements of property and fiscal arrangements have been entered into'.[53]

Retrospective correction of the law can, however, cause some serious difficulty. Suppose you are a prison governor who, in good faith and in accordance with the judicial decisions interpreting the statutory provisions dealing with the length of a custodial sentence, calculate that you should release a particular prisoner on a given day. Then suppose that, as a result of a judicial review of your calculation, a court holds not merely that your calculation was in error, but that the very decisions on which you had based them were in error, and that the prisoner should have been released some time earlier.[54] And further suppose that the prisoner is now suing for false imprisonment. You could be forgiven for thinking that the law is not making your difficult job any the easier, not only in this individual case. From your standpoint, it is surely fair and reasonable to say that, while you accept the principle of retrospection, which applies as much when a court holds that an earlier interpretation of a statutory provision was wrong (and thus that the meaning now attributed to it must be presumed to have been the correct meaning from the date the provision came into force) as it does to a common law rule, you were not acting under any mistake of law, but were simply applying the law as laid down by the courts (even if they are now shown to be wrong), as you were bound to do. But if you adopt the standpoint of the prisoner we are surely faced with what appears to be an unjust outcome. You have been unlawfully (as the Court of Appeal has now confirmed) held in prison. Can it be the case that you are not entitled to some compensation for this? In holding that the principle of retrospectivity did apply and that

---

53 See Lord Denning MR in *Tiverton Estates v Wearwell* [1975] Ch 146, 172-173.
54 *R v Home Secretary, ex p Naughton* [1997] 1 All ER 426; see chapter 1, section 6.2.

you are entitled to some redress, Lord Woolf MR observed: 'the principle can be said to involve a fairytale, but it is a fairytale which is a long established foundation of judicial law making within our common law system and it if is to be undermined or weakened this should be left to the legislature or possibly the House of Lords'.[55]

5 The practice of precedent

One possible explanation for the apparent paradox of a doctrine that is indeterminate, but a practice that is relatively stable, is that judges and practising lawyers use the law reports as a source both of substantive and authority reasons.[56] The doctrine of precedent does not, and probably could not, prevent judges and other interpreters from re-interpreting past cases. In clear cases, that is, ones in which an interpreter entertains no serious doubts, it is generally sufficient to rely simply on authority. But where one or more conditions of doubt are present that create some doubt about what the law authoritatively says, the interpreter is compelled to look at the substance of the matter. One of the great values of Ronald Dworkin's contribution to our understanding of reasoning in law is to show how, even in respect of fit, and especially in respect of justification, prior decisions need to be interpreted in the light of the validity and cogency of the arguments that sustain them.[57] The law reports are not merely a collection of authorities; they are also a massive treasury of substantive arguments. In hard cases judges and counsel typically cite prior cases for the substantive arguments that they contain as well as for their authoritative fiat.[58] The doctrine of precedent does little more than prescribe what weight is to be given to cases as authorities, once they have been interpreted. The practice of precedent is to use prior cases as a source of substantive as well as authoritative reasons.

Precedent techniques are techniques of reasoning about how prior cases should be interpreted. They are typically used in the context of justifying a particular result in a case, or in persuading others to come to a particular conclusion, or in supporting formulations of legal doctrine in the process of exposition or in making certain kinds of predictions. It has long been recognised that a variety of techniques is involved in interpreting cases, but it was Karl Llewellyn who first attempted an extensive examination of this aspect

---

55 *R v Governor of Brockhill Prison, ex p Evans (No 2)* [1998] 4 All ER 993, 1002. In *Kleinwort Benson Ltd v Lincoln City Council*, where the question arose whether the merchant bank could recover money paid to the Council under an agreement later shown to be *ultra vires* the Council, on the basis that the money had been paid under a mistake of law, the majority decision of the House of Lords was based on an interpretation of the law of restitution as affected by the principle of retrospectivity, rather than on any of its wider implications. See Appendix I, section G1, question 6, p 404.
56 Below, pp 359-361.
57 R Dworkin, *Law's Empire* (1986), especially chapter 7. Below, pp 360-361.
58 L Fuller, 'Reason and Fiat in Case Law', (1946) 59 *Harvard Law Review* 376.

of legal reasoning.[59] His somewhat rough and ready list of 64 techniques of following and avoiding precedent decisions suggests that even in England the explicit doctrine and tacit conventions of precedent are not necessarily as restrictive an influence on legal developments as is commonly suggested by formalistic discussions of the subject. Within the armoury of techniques available to courts in dealing with precedents, there are many devices for creating law within the framework of authority.

From the standpoint of the advocate, prior cases are potentially favourable, adverse, or neutral, and it is from this standpoint that we can most easily see the way in which these techniques of reasoning are employed. Where the advocate is faced with an adverse precedent he has a number of choices open to him. He may, for example, argue that the precedent was rightly decided but is distinguishable on its facts or on the issue of law it raised. On the other hand, where the cases are analogous, the advocate may use a number of techniques to argue that the precedent was wrongly decided or is of weak authority by suggesting, for example:

(a) that the precedent involved a faulty interpretation of other prior cases;[60]
(b) that the precedent was a decision given *per incuriam*, that is, in ignorance of a binding statutory or judicial authority;
(c) that the precedent has been subsequently overruled or doubted by other judges;[61]
(d) that the precedent is irreconcilable with prior or subsequent decisions.

These primary techniques are employed quite commonly to avoid prior cases, but in addition there are various secondary techniques for weakening their precedent value, for example, by arguing:

(e) that the deciding court was of low authority;[62]
(f) that the scope of the decision is unclear;[63]
(g) that the reasoning other than from authority is weak;[64]
(h) that the deciding court was particularly influenced by special considerations;[65]
(i) that social conditions have changed;[66]

59 K Llewellyn, *The Common Law Tradition*: Deciding Appeals (1960), pp 75-96.
60 See Lord Buckmaster in *Donoghue v Stevenson* (chapter 1, section 9), where he argues that *George v Skivington* is of weak authority because it misinterprets *Langridge v Levy*. Footnoted references are given here only in respect of examples from *Donoghue v Stevenson*.
61 See Lord Buckmaster in *Donoghue v Stevenson* (chapter 1, section 9), where he discusses subsequent disapproval of *George v Skivington*.
62 See Lord Buckmaster's treatment in *Donoghue v Stevenson* [1932] AC 562, 576 of the American case *Thomas v Winchester* as being of 'no authority'.
63 See Lord Buckmaster (chapter 1, section 9), where he speaks of *Langridge v Levy* as having been 'variously explained'.
64 See Lord Buckmaster, ibid.
65 See Lord Atkin [1932] AC 560, 588, where he treats *Winterbottom v Wright* as a special case because it was decided upon a demurrer.
66 See Lord Atkin (chapter 1, section 9), where this factor is implicit.

(j) that the report of the precedent is unreliable;

(k) that the decision has been criticised by academic writers.

This is by no means a comprehensive list, nor are the techniques of equal weight. A precedent can be favourable either in its result or in its reasoning or both, and there are similarly supplementary ways in which additional weight can be attached to a decision, for example by emphasising the high reputation of the judges in the prior case or the fact of its subsequent approval. The later history of a decision is of importance in assessing its precedent value, but, as with central aspects of the doctrine, there is considerable indeterminacy in the terms that are commonly used to express approval or disapproval of a decision. This can be illustrated by reference to the definitions given in the *English and Empire Digest*. For example, a prior decision is 'doubted' when the later court 'without definitely going to the length of saying that the [earlier] case is wrong, adduces reasons which seem to show that it is not accurate' but is 'explained' when 'the earlier case is not necessarily doubted, but the decision arrived at is justified or accounted for by calling attention to some point of fact or of law which is usually but not necessarily, one not obvious on the face of the report'.[67] We hardly need to underline the difficulties that an advocate, or any other interpreter, could face when applying or relying upon these definitions to determine the impact on an earlier case of, for example, a multi-judgment decision of an appeal court.

Advocates, however, are not the only participants in the legal process who seek to persuade others to accept a particular line of reasoning. Beside their primary task of justifying their decisions, judges too may try to persuade their colleagues (and their wider audiences) that a particular legal solution to a dispute is the one to be adopted. Where a judge is espousing a currently unpopular result, he must rely heavily on his powers of persuasion, and he may employ a number of rhetorical devices to bolster and protect his argument. Some of these devices have been indicated earlier, but we should stress that while some precedent techniques can be isolated, they tend to overlap and fuse into one another and to operate cumulatively, so that their effect can best be appreciated by reading a judgment as a whole.

A good example of the cumulation of techniques in dealing with an adverse authority is to be found in the treatment of *Fanning* in the argument for the prosecution in *Allen's case*.[68] It was possible to argue that (a) *Fanning* was only of persuasive authority (because it was an Irish decision) and (b) it was of weak persuasive authority because there were four dissentient judges and even some of the majority expressed regret in concluding that the appeal should be allowed and (c) that *Fanning* was wrongly decided (for several reasons) and (d) that *Allen* and *Fanning* were distinguishable on the facts. It is pertinent to note that in his judgment Cockburn CJ relied on (a), (b) and (c), but explicitly stated that although it was open to him to distinguish *Fanning*, he was holding it to be wrongly decided. The effect of this was to open the way

---

67 See any volume of the *English and Empire Digest*, 'Meaning of terms used in classifying annotating cases'.

68 See below, pp 348, 361.

for *Allen* to be interpreted relatively broadly, rather than to introduce a fine distinction into the interpretation of 'shall marry'.

Let us now consider the extracts from the speeches of Lords Atkin and Buckmaster in *Donoghue v Stevenson* which are reprinted in chapter 1, section 9. This decision is generally regarded as a landmark in the development of the law of negligence. The potentially relevant precedents at that time were generally considered to stand fairly firmly against the extension of a manufacturer's liability in tort to the ultimate consumer. Nearly all of these precedents were decisions of courts inferior to the House of Lords and so the House was not bound to follow them, but one of the tacit conventions of the doctrine of precedent requires consideration of all relevant precedents irrespective of the place of the deciding court within the hierarchy.[69] Lord Atkin was in favour of allowing the appeal, while Lord Buckmaster supported its dismissal. Yet while they held opposite views as to the outcome of the case, each was able to reconcile his conclusion with the precedents by the use of a number of devices. By looking at this process in respect of their handling of two of the precedents we can see quite vividly a sample of the range and scope of the techniques that operate within the doctrine.

Firstly, let us take the case of *Winterbottom v Wright*. This decision tended to support Lord Buckmaster's position, and thus raised no real difficulties for him, but the case was potentially distinguishable from *Donoghue v Stevenson* and so he sought to emphasise the closeness of the analogy between the two cases:

> The case of *Winterbottom v Wright* is, on the other hand, an authority that is closely applicable. Owing to negligence in the construction of a carriage it broke down, and a stranger to the manufacture and sale sought to recover damages for injuries which he alleged were due to negligence in the work, and it was held that he had no cause of action either in tort or arising out of contract. This case seems to me to show that the manufacturer of any article is not liable to a third party injured by negligent construction, for there is nothing in the character of a coach to place it in a special category. It may be noted, also, that in this case Alderson B said: 'The only safe rule is to confine the right to recover to those who enter into the contract; if we go one step beyond that, there is no reason why we should not go fifty'. [Chapter 1, p 57]

Initially, one should notice Lord Buckmaster's clear statement of his intentions with regard to the precedent value of the case. He asserts that it is 'an authority that is closely applicable'. A closer analogy between the two cases is effected by glossing over their factual differences and stating the facts at a higher level of generality. Observe how 'carriages' and 'ginger beer' are now subsumed in the more abstract category of 'articles'. Lastly, Lord Buckmaster's appeal to the 'floodgates' argument,[70] common to both legal and non-legal contexts, is further reinforcement of his view of the correctness of the case.

---

69 R Cross, 'The House of Lords and the Rules of Precedent', in *Law, Morality and Society* (eds P Hacker and J Raz, 1977), p 145.

70 While appeal to this argument may properly warn a judge or other decision-maker of some problematic consequences of his decision, such as an increased volume of litigation or the creation of difficult problems of continuous variation, it may be of doubtful propriety to use factors such as these to deny the merits of a case outright. See *Attia v British Gas* [1988] QB 304, per Bingham LJ at 320-321, and Chapter 5, section 5.1.

What technique(s), then, might we expect Lord Atkin to adopt in order to undermine the precedent value of *Winterbottom v Wright?* He does not attempt to 'get round' the decision or to overrule it, as he was empowered to do, but chooses the more subtle approach of agreeing with Lord Buckmaster that the case was correctly decided, but arguing that the issue of law raised in *Donoghue v Stevenson* was not an issue in the earlier case.

> It is to be observed that no negligence apart from breach of contract was alleged – in other words, no duty was alleged other than the duty arising out of the contract ... The argument of the defendant was that, on the face of the declaration, the wrong arose merely out of the breach of a contract, and that only a party to the contract could sue ... The actual decision appears to have been manifestly right; no duty to the plaintiff arose out of the contract; and the duty of the defendant under the contract with the Postmaster-General to put the coach in good repair could not have involved such direct relations with the servant of the persons whom the Postmaster-General employed to drive the coach as would give rise to a duty of care owed to such servant. [Chapter 1, p 59]

The main point is that, since the plaintff was not alleging negligence other than in the context of the fulfilment of a contract, then that case can have decided the law only upon that issue, and can have no application to an allegation of negligence as a tort, which is the issue in the present case.[71] By distinguishing the issues in the two cases in this way Lord Atkin is able to dispose of a potentially adverse case while at the same time appearing to respect authority.

George v Skivington, on the other hand, is a decision that appeared to support Lord Atkin's conclusion in *Donoghue v Stevenson*, and in Lord Buckmaster's handling of this case we can see different and more complex techniques. In that case the plaintiff used a shampoo that her husband had bought from the defendant, whose negligent preparation of it caused her hair to fall out. She sued him and won. Lord Buckmaster's main treatment of this case was as follows:

> Of the remaining cases, *George v Skivington* is the one nearest to the present, and without that case, and the statement of Cleasby B in *Francis v Cockrell* and the dicta of Brett MR in *Heaven v Pender*, the appellant would be destitute of authority. *George v Skivington* related to the sale of a noxious hairwash, and a claim made by a person who had not bought it but who had suffered from its use, based on its having been negligently compounded, was allowed. It is remarkable that *Langridge v Levy* was used in support of the claim and influenced the judgment of all the parties to the decision. Both Kelly CB and Pigott B stressed the fact that the article had been purchased to the knowledge of the defendant for the use of the plaintiff, as in *Langridge v Levy* and Cleasby B, who realizing that *Langridge v Levy* was decided on the ground of fraud, said: 'Substitute the word "negligence" for "fraud" and the

---

71 Plaintiffs may plead their case in an area of law which, although it does not seem appropriate to the facts of the case, affords them an additional, or perhaps the only, chance of success. In *De la Bere v Pearson* [1908] 1 KB 280 in which the plaintiff, to his detriment, relied upon the financial advice of a newspaper which had invited readers to seek such advice, the action was in contract. While contractual principles did not clearly cover the facts, this was at that time, the only practical course of action available. On the present law, the best course of action would probably be to plead negligence.

analogy between *Langridge v Levy* and this case is complete'. It is unnecessary to point out too emphatically that such a substitution cannot possibly be made. No action based on fraud can be supported by mere proof of negligence.

I do not propose to follow the fortunes of *George v Skivington*; few cases can have lived so dangerously and lived so long. Lord Sumner, in the case of *Blacker v Lake and Elliot*, closely examines its history and I agree with his analysis. He said that he could not presume to say that it was wrong, but he declined to follow it on the ground, which is I think firm, that it was in conflict with *Winterbottom v Wright.* [Chapter 1, pp 57-58].

Lord Buckmaster here is dealing with an adverse precedent, and the purpose of this passage is to persuade the reader that *George v Skivington* is a decision that has little authority. This is achieved by a combination of the general tone of the language used and an accumulation of various techniques. The passage, when read as a whole, has an overall persuasive effect that *George v Skivington* was a misguided decision, and while some of this effect cannot be analysed precisely in terms of distinctive precedent techniques, a number of separate points can be identified.

Firstly, Lord Buckmaster suggests that the precedent value of the decision must be low because it is an isolated decision, and it is coupled with and relegated to the rank of mere judicial *dicta*, without which the plaintiff would be 'destitute of authority'. This is reinforced towards the end of the passage, where he draws attention to the fact that it has been disapproved in a subsequent decision. He also seeks to undermine the decision by suggesting that it misapplied or misunderstood the earlier decision in *Langridge v Levy*, and is thus of weak authority. Lord Buckmaster also seeks to distinguish *George v Skivington* because in that case the defendant knew who the consumer was to be. This, Lord Buckmaster hints, converts the case into a decision on fraud, which has nothing to do with the tort of negligence. In another part of his speech, he says of this case:

> It is difficult to appreciate what is the importance of the fact that the vendor knew who was the person for whom the article was purchased unless it be that the case was treated as one of fraud, and that without this element of knowledge it could not be brought within the principle of *Langridge v Levy*. Indeed, this is the only view of the matter which adequately explains the references in the judgments in *George v Skivington* to *Langridge v Levy* ... ([1932] AC 562, 571)

In his treatment of *George v Skivington* on this issue of fraud, Lord Buckmaster is employing a technique similar to that used by Lord Atkin when dealing with *Winterbottom v Wright*, though there are other factors at work in Lord Buckmaster's analysis. Thus he treats the case as dubious authority on the tort of fraud; and *in addition*, in the event of its being seen as a case of negligence, as being wrongly decided on the authority of *Winterbottom v Wright.*

The conflict that existed, in Lord Buckmaster's view, between these two cases introduces a new aspect of precedent technique. Here, the case to be avoided is deemed to be inconsistent with an earlier decision on the basis of the judge's interpretation of that earlier decision. Elsewhere in his speech, Lord Buckmaster accumulates other points against *George v Skivington*, finally purporting to overrule it, suggesting in somewhat emotive terms that it should be buried so securely that its perturbed spirit will no longer vex the law.[72]

The task for Lord Atkin in dealing with *George v Skivington* is a more straightforward one. He adopts, though he does not overemphasise, the decision, and seeks to protect its authority by indicating the dissimilarity between the decision in that case and his own interpretation of *Winterbottom v Wright*:

> I find this [possible conflict] very difficult to understand, for *George v Skivington* was based upon a duty in the manufacturer to take care independently of contract, while *Winterbottom v Wright* was decided on … a contractual duty to keep in repair. ([1932] AC 562, 594)

The treatment by these two judges of these two cases should give some idea of the techniques that are in regular use in case law reasoning. Through the use of these techniques, Lords Atkin and Buckmaster were able to come to opposite conclusions as to the effect of the case as a whole: 'without that case the appellant would be destitute of authority' (Lord Buckmaster); 'in my opinion several decided cases support the view that in such a case as the present the manufacturer owes a duty to the consumer to be careful' (Lord Atkin); and as to their effect individually: 'with the exception of *George v Skivington*, no case directly involving the principle has ever succeeded in the courts' (Lord Buckmaster); 'Next in this chain of authority comes *George v Skivington*' (Lord Atkin).

One noteworthy feature of Lord Atkin's speech is that in dealing with adverse precedents he made virtually no use of one of the most common techniques, that of distinguishing on the facts. It is important to understand the reason for this. When two cases are distinguished in this way the facts of each are interpreted relatively narrowly and in detail. This will be reflected in the protasis of a rule for which the case may be made to stand; for the more detailed and specific the interpretation of the material facts of the protasis, the narrower the rule. This would have been incompatible with Lord Atkin's objective, which was to establish the basis for a broad rule concerning the duty of care in negligence.

Donoghue v Stevenson and *Allen* are both good illustrations of the point made earlier in this chapter that even the allegedly strict doctrine of precedent in England and Wales allows a considerable leeway for varying, sometimes conflicting, interpretations of prior cases: in a number of crucial respects it is permissive or vague, or both. Thus many cases treated as relevant by interpreters in the context of legal reasoning are of only persuasive authority; the doctrine permits a wide range of techniques for dealing with such cases, that is to say it allows scope for a variety of types of reason to be taken into account both in determining the interpretation to be put on the case and the weight to be attached to it. It is vague both as to the weight to be attached to such reasons and what classes of reason are valid or legitimate. Even where a judge or interpreter is confronted with a potentially 'binding' precedent, the doctrine lays down no official test for determining what is the binding part of the case. He is permitted to distinguish such cases, but it provides no guidance on the level of generality at which it is to be interpreted, nor what weight to attach to the actual words used in the judgments in the prior case, nor how he is to set

---

72 [1932] AC 562, 576.

about reconciling apparently conflicting 'binding' cases. Indeed, the unhappy interpreter when confronted by a precedent he does not like, may be inhibited from departing from it not so much by the official doctrine of precedent, as by less tangible factors such as his own sense of what is appropriate or the weight of professional opinion.

The room for manoeuvre lies in the nature of legal judgment. Every case is a unique event, and the problem of extending general significance to it involves the identification of elements of that case which are shared by others. This problem is made the more difficult because judges quite often formulate their statements of the facts and of the applicable rule of a particular case several times using different language. Moreover, in many appellate decisions, there will be a multiplicity of judgments, and thus we find that these formulations vary not only within individual judgments but also between them.

To illustrate this fluidity, let us look again at *Donoghue v Stevenson*. Lord Atkin begins his speech by posing the issue in two different ways:

> ... the sole question for determination in this case is legal: Do the averments made by the pursuer in her pleading, if true, disclose a cause of action? I need not restate the particular facts. The question is whether the manufacturer of an article of drink sold by him to a distributor, in circumstances which prevent the distributor or the ultimate purchaser or consumer from discovering by inspection any defect, is under a legal duty to the ultimate purchaser or consumer to take reasonable care that the article is free from defect likely to cause injury to health. (Chapter 1, p 58)

The facts as contained in the pleadings were more specific than Lord Atkin characterises them here, and so we can see that he has implicitly categorised them at more than one level of generality in this one passage alone. Compare now his concluding statement:

> ... if your Lordships accept the view that this pleading discloses a relevant cause of action you will be affirming the proposition that by Scots and English law alike a manufacturer of products, which he sells in such a form as to show that he intends them to reach the ultimate consumer in the form in which they left him with no reasonable possibility of intermediate examination, and with the knowledge that the absence of reasonable care in the preparation or putting up of the products will result in an injury to the consumer's life or property, owes a duty to the consumer to take reasonable care. (Chapter 1, p 59)

Notice here that the agent of harm has changed from 'an article of drink' to 'products', and that the nature of the injury has moved from 'injury to health' to 'injury to the consumer's life or property'. In addition, Lord Atkin has introduced the requirement that the manufacturer sell the product in the form in which he intends it to reach the ultimate consumer, and in this formulation of the proposition of law has dropped the 'ultimate purchaser', who appeared in his formulation of the question to be answered.

Even this does not exhaust Lord Atkin's movement up and down various ladders of abstraction.[73] We will conclude this comparison by looking at Lord Buckmaster's statement of the facts and issue in the case.

---

73 See the questions and other materials on *Donoghue v Stevenson* in chapter 1, section 9. See also W Twining, *Karl Llewellyn and the Realist Movement* (1973), Chapter 10, esp pp 231-245.

... the facts of this case are simple. On 26 August 1928, the appellant drank a bottle of ginger-beer, manufactured by the respondent which a friend had bought from a retailer and given to her. The bottle contained the decomposed remains of a snail which were not, and could not be, detected until the greater part of the contents of the bottle had been consumed. As a result she alleged, and at this stage her allegations must be accepted as true, that she suffered from shock and severe gastro-enteritis. She accordingly instituted the proceedings against the manufacturer which have given rise to this appeal.

The foundation of her case is that the respondent, as the manufacturer of an article intended for consumption and contained in a receptacle which prevented inspection, owed a duty to her as consumer of the article to take care that there was no noxious element in the goods, that he neglected such duty and is consequently liable for any damage caused by such neglect. (Chapter 1, pp 56-57)

The movement between different levels of generality is perhaps more marked here than in the extracts quoted above. Lord Buckmaster states the facts at a low level of generality, including the date on which the injury occurred, but in his formulation of the issue in the case, the bottle has become a 'receptacle' and the decomposed remains of a snail have been abstracted to a 'noxious element'. These extracts illustrate some of the variations that can be encountered within individual judgments and between different judgments.

6 The *ratio decidendi* of a case

When legal advisers, advocates, judges or expositors interpret cases for their particular purposes, they ask such questions as 'for what rule(s) of law is this case an authority?' or 'for what proposition(s) of law can this case be made to stand?' It has been traditional within legal theory to call the rule or the proposition of law which the interpreter asserts is supported by a prior case its *ratio decidendi*. There has also traditionally been considerable disagreement about what is entailed by the use of this term:

> It is a disputed question whether there is any such thing as a or the *ratio* in a given case; it is disputed whether or not there is a *ratio* to be found authoritatively within a given opinion, or whether the so-called *ratio* is simply some proposition of law which a later court or courts find it expedient to ascribe to an earlier decision as the ground of that decision which may then be used to help justify some later decision – perhaps even under the guise of its being that which necessitates the granting of the given later decision. An extreme version of this view would presumably be that the *ratio* of a case is whatever it is any time authoritatively said to be authority for, and thus no one single proposition over time.[74]

Within the 'more or less strict or formalistic to the more or less sceptical' end of the theoretical spectrum, five usages of the term *ratio decidendi* have been dominant in the literature:

---

74 N MacCormick, 'Why Cases Have Rationes and What These Are', in *Precedent and Law*, p 157. See also G Marshall, 'What is Binding in a Precedent' in MacCormick and Summers, pp 503-517.

1. The rule(s) of law explicitly stated by the judge as the basis for the decision, that is, the explicit answer to the question(s) of law in the case.
2. The reason(s) explicitly given by the judge for the decision, that is, the explicit justification for the answer(s) given to the question(s) in the case.
3. The rule(s) of law implicit in the reasoning of the judge in justifying the decision, that is, the implicit answer(s) to the question(s) of law in the case.
4. The reason(s) implicitly given by the judge for the decision, that is, the implicit justification for the answer(s) given to the question(s) in the case.
5. The rule(s) of law for which the case is made to stand or is cited as authority by a subsequent interpeter, that is, the imputed answer(s) to the question(s) of law in the case.

Thus, usages 1 and 3 are exemplified by Cross's definition: 'The *ratio decidendi* of a case is any rule of law expressly or impliedly treated by the judge as a necessary step in reaching his conclusion, having regard to the line of reasoning adopted by him, or a necessary part of his direction to the jury';[75] usage 2 by Walker's: 'a *ratio* is the legal rule justifying a particular legal conclusion in a particular case on the basis of certain ascertained material facts';[76] and usages 1 and 4 by MacCormick's: 'a *ratio decidendi* is a ruling expressly or impliedly given by a judge which is sufficient to settle a point of law put in issue by the parties' arguments in a case, being a point on which a ruling was necessary to his justification (or one of his alternative justifications) of the decision in the case'.[77]

Although usages 3 and 4 offer some scope for differing interpretations of the *ratio* of a given case, all but usage 5 are rooted in the text of the judgment, usages 1 and 2 typically being formulated *verbatim* from the judge's remarks. Allied to these formalistic definitions have been attempts to prescribe methods by which the *ratio* may be ascertained from what the judge has said. Like Walker's reference to material facts, the most celebrated of these is Goodhart's proposition that 'the principle of the case is found by taking account (a) of the facts treated by the judge as material, and (b) his decision as based on them.'[78]

We may characterise these views as the 'buried treasure' argument. In this view it is typically assumed (a) that every case has one predetermined *ratio decidendi* (at least for each question of law), and (b) that the *ratio decidendi* can be found, by reading the case, without referring to other cases, and (c) that the *ratio decidendi* does not, indeed cannot, change over time. These assumptions do not accord with the realities of the practice of handling

---

75 Cross and Harris, p 76. See further A Simpson, 'The *Ratio Decidendi* of a Case', (1957) 20 *Modern Law Review* 413, and (1958) 21 *Modern Law Review* 155.
76 D Walker, 'The Theory of Relevancy', [1963] *Juridical Review* 1, 9.
77 N MacCormick, *Legal Reasoning and Legal Theory* (1978), p 215, amended in 'Why Cases Have Rationes and What These Are', op cit, p 170 (2nd edn now published).
78 A Goodhart, 'Determining the *Ratio Decidendi* of a Case', (1930) 40 *Yale Law Journal* 161, and 'The *Ratio Decidendi* of a Case', (1959) 22 *Modern Law Review* 117. For criticism of this view, see J Stone, 'The Ratio of the *Ratio Decidendi*', (1959) 22 *Modern Law Review* 597.

precedents in our system. Talk of finding the *ratio decidendi* of a case obscures the facts that the process of interpreting cases is not like a hunt for buried treasure, but typically involves an element of choice from a range of possibilities. How unfettered is the choice and how wide the range of possibilities will depend on a variety of factors. One such factor, of crucial importance, relates to (b). In reasoning on a point of law we are typically confronted not with a single isolated precedent, but a collection of potentially relevant precedents. Each case has to be read in the context of all the other potentially relevant cases and this is one factor which limits the range of possible interpretations which can be put on it. Any test for determining the *ratio decidendi*, which suggests, explicitly or implicitly, that a case can be interpreted in isolation, without reference to other cases, is unrealistic and misleading. As the courts lay down new decisions, so the range of plausible interpretations of an earlier case may change over time. As we shall see, it is just not true that an interpreter faced with *Donoghue v Stevenson* and its predecessors in 1933 was in the same position as he would be today. For not only have many subsequent cases intervened, but also some of the factors listed in Chapter 6 have contributed to a different climate of opinion affecting arguments about the scope of the duty of care in negligence.

But usage 5, which is the only usage that allows that the interpretation of prior cases typically involves looking beyond the text to other prior and subsequent events, including other cases, does not mean that the text has no place in such interpretations, nor that they are unconstrained. Even within MacCormick's description of an extreme version of *ratio*-scepticism, the *ratio* is still 'whatever it is any time *authoritatively* said to be authority for' (emphasis added). No formulation of the *ratio* of a case will be accepted which is, for the audience before whom it is presented, insufficiently persuasive in terms of the justifications normally acceptable to them. Those who accept this, yet wish to confine the term *ratio decidendi* to its formalistic usages, perhaps for the purpose of claiming that these have a privileged status in terms of the doctrine of precedent, are led into making a distinction between finding the *ratio* of a case within the four corners of the text but distinguishing this from interpreting the case as an authoritative source of law at the moment of interpretation. This is semantically possible; that it is also unnecessarily confusing and unrealistic can be demonstrated by considering how the formulation of the *ratio* of a case depends upon the interpreter's standpoint.

Most discussions of precedent, in dealing with this issue, assume the standpoint of the judge if they assume any clear standpoint at all. But, as we have seen, judges are not the only interpreters of rules, and in the context of rules derived from precedents many of the issues involved in formulating the *ratio* can be shown to be non-contentious or at least less problematical if we adopt the standpoint of the counsellor and the advocate. This is so because what they are typically trying to do in interpreting a case is more easily understood and clearly defined than what a judge may be attempting. Thus a counsellor may be endeavouring to predict a likely judicial or other official response to a particular rule extracted from a precedent, while the advocate seeks to persuade a particular court to reach a particular result on the basis of reasons which support that result; the cases are part of the raw material from which the advocate's argument is constructed; the roles of the advocate and of the counsellor are relatively clearly defined, and by remarking upon the different formulations of the rule or *ratio* employed from these two perspectives we can see what interpreting cases means in practice.

Let us return to *Donoghue v Stevenson* and examine it, first a few months after the decision in 1932 and then in 1999, from the standpoint of the counsellor advising a client and an advocate arguing his case on a point of law involving negligence. Let us assume that the facts of the present case are that the client had bought a pair of underpants which subsequently turned out to be impregnated with an invisible chemical from which he contracted dermatitis.[79] Because the retailer is bankrupt, the client is contemplating suing the manufacturer, and let us further assume that in 1933 *Donoghue v Stevenson* was the only relevant precedent. The question of law for the counsellor is to predict whether a court would hold that a manufacturer of underwear owed a duty to the ultimate consumer, and so should compensate him if he suffers injury as a result of a defect in the underwear. The answer to this question depends on how widely or narrowly the court is likely to interpret *Donoghue v Stevenson*. At this stage the answer might well be unclear. The case might be interpreted narrowly, applying for instance only to food and drink, or it might be interpreted to include all manufactured goods, or again, to extend the duty of care more widely, along the lines of the 'neighbour' principle. Any of these interpretations stand along with other possibilities as potential formulations of the rule or *ratio* to be extracted from *Donoghue v Stevenson*, and thus the counsellor cannot make a confident prediction. The decision was not unanimous, and if he is cautious, as many solicitors in this position are, he may advise his client that the position is uncertain, and for this reason, among others, that litigation is risky. Thus he might advise writing a solicitor's letter to the manufacturers, but caution retreat if they seem likely to contest an action. Implicit in this advice is a formulation of the *ratio* at a low level of generality.

The cautious counsellor then has interpreted the rule in the precedent as applying only, for example, to articles of food and drink; whereas his more optimistic colleagues would have formulated the rule at a higher level of generality, and would thus advise the client that the risk may be worth taking. The situation would be very different now, when it would be confidently predicted that the client, assuming he can prove his case, has a good cause of action. This is so because since 1932 a number of decisions have, by eliminating a number of possible formulations of the *ratio* of *Donoghue v Stevenson*, reduced the leeways of interpretation, and thus have to some extent clarified the scope of the rule. This is not to say that all doubts about the scope of the rule have been resolved, nor that there is no leeway for choice, but that the number of possible interpretations that might have been imputed to the case in 1933 has been reduced by these subsequent decisions, and thus more confident predictions can be made on the basis of the cumulative effect of these decisions. Thus on this analysis the range of possible interpretations of *Donoghue v Stevenson* is not the same now as it was in 1933; whereas on the buried treasure analogy, the *ratio* is the same.

---

79 *Grant v Australian Knitting Mills* [1936] AC 85.

The advocate's main task is to persuade the court to a accept a particular result, and this will involve her in persuading the court to accept her interpretation of the law and of the precedents. The advocate for the plaintiff in the hypothetical situation, then, must put to the court an argument that explicitly or implicitly incorporates a *ratio* which at the very least is at a sufficiently high level of generality to cover the facts of her client's case. Possibly she would be better advised to advocate a *ratio* at a somewhat higher level, though it would probably have been poor advocacy to maintain that the 'neighbour' principle represented the *ratio decidendi* of *Donoghue v Stevenson*. Conversely, the defendant's advocate would press for as broad an interpretation of the case as is consistent with success on the part of his client. Like the plaintiff's advocate, he too has a number of possible formulations of the rule, though unlike his opponent they will be of a low level of generality, for example:

(a) Scottish manufacturers of ginger-beer in opaque bottles owe a duty of care not to allow dead snails to get into the product;
(b) manufacturers of ginger-beer owe a duty of care not to allow any snails to get into the product; or
(c) manufacturers of articles of food and drink owe a duty of care not to allow any noxious physical foreign body to get into the product.[80]

While each formulation of the *ratio* is consistent with the defendant's success, the advocate would probably have been wise to choose (c), on the ground that the court, either intuitively or by looking for a convincing policy reason for selecting a particular category, would hold that (a) and (b) were too narrow.

This elementary example illustrates the dynamics of interpretation within the adversary process. Typically each side to the action will be pressing an interpretation of relevant precedents that is consistent with the result it is seeking to obtain. Each side may have open to it a number of possible interpretations of a particular precedent that are consistent with the desired result, and good advocacy consists in directing the attention of the court to the most plausible interpretation or perhaps in giving the court a choice of interpretations consistent with that result. Plausibility may be partly a matter of style and intuition, but more importantly it will often be founded on the choice of a way of categorising the protasis that makes sense in terms of some policy or purpose or other reason, whether articulated or not.[81]

If we revert now to the standpoint of a judge we see that it is his primary task to reach a decision in the particular case before him; and where, as in the hypothetical case envisaged above, there is an important recent precedent, to formulate a *ratio* or rule for which that case is taken to stand, and to apply it to the present case. Often, a judge will seek a relatively narrow formulation of the *ratio* that is consistent with a just resolution of the case at hand. The fulfilment of this task is, however, somewhat more complex than in the case of

80 See Stone, op cit, and chapter 1, section 9.
81 See below, pp 340-342.

the counsellor and advocate.[82] Where a judge is in genuine doubt about which of the possible interpretations of a prior case he is to choose, he has a discretion to exercise that is not governed by any rule of the doctrine of precedent. Typically, the competing interpretations differ in respect of one or more elements that can be presented at different levels of generality. There are no categorical rules to direct judges about the selection of appropriate levels of generality; accordingly there are no general rules for determining the *ratio decidendi* of a case, although there are some guidelines. This is not to say, however, that judges could not create rules for such occasions, nor that the absence of rules is necessarily to be lamented.

Despite what we see as a general acceptance of the view that judges (and others) are free to choose what constitutes the *ratio decidendi* of a case, but to choose within a framework of what Llewellyn called 'steadying factors',[83] which in some instances may narrow considerably the range of choice, recurring efforts are made to resurrect its formalistic usage. One such is MacCormick's definition quoted earlier.[84] MacCormick argues that a doctrine of precedent (whatever it may prescribe in terms of the weight to be attached to the *rationes* of prior decisions) presupposes the possibility of identifying and formulating as *rationes*, 'firm and determinate' rulings as to the applicable law. This is so because, since legal disputes are by definition cast in terms of competing claims as to what the law provides in this and cases like it, answers, if they are to have any justificatory force, must likewise be cast in terms of universal propositions of law; that is, that in cases displaying facts of a kind F1, F2 ... Fn, judgment J shall be given.

> A justifiable decision of the dispute, so far as it is a dispute about law, will have to make a ruling on the issues in contention between the parties as to the relevancy of any proposition adduced as a proposition of law by either party or as to the interpretation of such a proposition, or as to the proper classification or evaluation of facts in the light of the descriptive or evaluative concepts or categories involved in the given proposition. A ruling of this kind must be logically universal or at least must be in terms which are reasonably universalisable; and it must be open to ulterior justification in terms of arguments of consistency, coherence, and consequences.[85]

MacCormick is talking about how judges do and should justify their own decisions. We are talking about how future interpreters of past decisions should read and use such decisions in their own arguments. They may defer to clear and crisp rulings and to reasons given in support of them, but in our view they are not bound by such propositions – for the interpretations can change over time. And if they do change, they can only change according to what are then the applicable norms. Judges may well decide cases without satisfactorily resolving or ruling upon points of law, not for reasons associated with rule-scepticism, but because they themselves have reservations about the scope or limits of a rule. As Lord Reid said when arguing the desirability of having more than one speech in the House of Lords when it is dealing with an important question of law:

82 See above, pp 170-172
83 *The Common Law Tradition*, pp 19-61. See also K Llewellyn, *The Case Law System in America* (trs M Ansaldi, 1989).
84 Above, p 334.
85 Op cit, pp 169-70.

My main reason is that experience has shown that those who have to apply the decision and still more those who wish to criticise it seem to find it difficult to avoid treating sentences and phrases in a single speech as if they were provisions in an Act of Parliament. They do not seem to realize that it is not the function of noble and learned Lords or indeed of any judges to frame definitions or to lay down hard and fast rules. It is their function to enunciate principles and much that they say is intended to be illustrative or explanatory and not to be definitive. When there are two or more speeches they must be read together and then it is generally much easier to see what are the principles involved and what are merely illustrations of it.[86]

When formulating theories of the *ratio decidendi* of a case, the following aspects of contemporary English discourse and practice in interpreting cases should be borne in mind:[87]

(a) The great majority of reported cases nowadays relate to the interpretation of statutes or other rules in fixed verbal form. This operates as a constraint on subsequent interpretation because the statutory or other text provides a more clearly identifiable 'anchorage' for interpretation and argument than do the texts of judicial opinions.

(b) Common law rules are not rules in fixed verbal form. Even judges of inferior courts do not always consider themselves to be strictly bound by the actual words used in explicit formulations of rules in binding precedents. They may, of course, and often do, give such explicit formulations very considerable weight, but they also sometimes reformulate the rules more widely or narrowly in their own words. The situation might conceivably be different if English judges abandoned the discursive style of legal justification that is a striking characteristic of the common law tradition and restricted themselves to carefully drafted rule-statements as the basis for their decisions;[88] but it is almost inconceivable that they will change their practice in this way.

(c) Explicit formulations of propositions of law, and propositions implicit in the reasoning in prior cases, are regularly invoked by lawyers and judges in later cases as part of their arguments. In respect of binding precedents such propositions are often presented as if they are the binding part of the case, but such assertions are open to challenge, both in terms of the proposition in question, and in terms of the theory of what is the binding aspect of a precedent.[89]

(d) Neither Parliament nor the courts have sought to lay down either an authoritative definition of the term *ratio decidendi* or clear criteria for

---

86 *Broome v Cassell Ltd*, op cit, p 1085. See further Denning LJ in *Candler v Crane, Christmas & Co* [1951] 2 KB 164, discussed in W Twining, *Rethinking Evidence* (1990), pp 232-235.

87 These points are elaborated in W Twining, 'Demystifying Precedent in English Law', in G Visintini (ed), *La giuris prudenzia per massime e il valore del precedente* (1988).

88 Compare the style of judgments given by the Court of Justice of the European Communities; above, p 297.

89 See the remarks of May LJ in *Ashville Investments v Elmer Contracters* [1988] 2 All ER 577, 582. See also *Re State of Norway's Application (No 2)* [1989] 1 All ER 745 and *Re Hetherington* [1989] 2 All ER 129. See generally, A Peczenick, 'The Binding Force of Precedent' in MacCormick and Summers, op cit, pp 461-479.

determining the *ratio decidendi* of a past case. Whatever the reasons for this, it has the effect of providing for a certain amount of leeway in the interpretation of precedents. Whether this is an example of mystification, acuity, or pragmatism is open to debate.

(e) There is no theoretical consensus about the correct way of extracting authoritative propositions of law implicit in judicial reasoning. Disagreements in this regard relate mainly to the precise scope of such propositions (including the level of generality at which each element should be formulated) rather than to their 'core', which is often relatively uncontroversial.

(f) 'It is a truism that dicta are of varying degrees of persuasiveness.' Cross wrote this of *obiter dicta*;[90] it applies equally to other explicit rule-formulations in judicial opinions.

(g) It is common in legal reasoning to interpret a series or a group of precedents rather than isolated cases. This is an incontrovertible fact whose implications are not always recognised or accepted. In our view, this supports the contention that the texts of precedents are and should be interpreted and reinterpreted in the context of other factors, including other precedents, and that such other factors serve to constrain the range of plausible or colourable interpretations in a context. According to this view, interpretations of precedents can and do change over time, but this does not involve commitment to some version of radical indeterminacy in interpretation.

7 X = X = X

The idea of precedent as a source of law is an especially clear illustration of the interaction between the general and the particular.[91] Because precedents are especially important in the common law, there has been much theorising and controversy about the relationship. However, on several relevant points there is widespread agreement: 'the facts' of a case are particular; the facts, at least in a hard case, give rise to a question of law; such questions of law should be expressed in general terms: not 'is the defendant guilty/liable?'; in deciding the particular case the court gives an authoritative answer to the question(s) of law. That answer may be explicit or implicit.[92]

The relationship between the facts, the issue(s), and the answer can be formally restated as follows:

- the facts: X happened
- the issue: if X happens, then what? (legal consequence(s))
- the answer: whenever X happens, then Y (proposition of law).

---

90 Cross and Harris, p 77. *Obiter dicta*: things said 'by the way'.

91 For a more detailed discussion, see W Twining, 'Narrative and Generalisations in Argumentation about Questions of Fact' (1999) *S Texas Law Review* (forthcoming).

92 One area of controversy is what weight to give to the actual words by a judge in this context. Few consider that courts are formally bound by the precise wording, but in practice great weight is quite often given to such formulations.

In this formulation X is a constant despite the transition from the particular to the general. This transition from particular situation to general question and general answer involves a shift from 'this was the situation' to 'in situations of this type, the law prescribes …'. The crucial point in this context is that X is a constant; in short X=X=X.

One of the main problems of interpreting cases is that the level of generality of X is indeterminate. The same applies to the 'moral' of parables and morality tales. But if the facts are known, and if X=X=X, how can X be clear at the particular level, but unclear at the general level? The answer is, of course, that how exactly the facts are to be categorised is also indeterminate. X represents a particular situation seen as a type. How precisely that situation should be interpreted, what elements are material, what is the best or an appropriate description of the situation is a matter of interpretation. And, since X=X=X, the problem of interpreting X is almost constant.[93]

Descriptions of situations are typically expressed in language. The choice of language is not significant solely because of the more or less obvious rhetorical potential of emotive or value-laden terms. For example, a categorisation may be judged to be appropriate because it reflects the way that a significant reference group thinks or talks (for instance, using the concepts of a particular trade to describe the situation in a commercial case) or because it corresponds with or fits, explicitly or implicitly, some general principle or policy (for example describing a situation in a way that brings out that a non-expert was relying on the judgment of an expert in a reasonably proximate relationship).[94] This idea of choosing appropriate categories to describe particular fact-situations is at the core of Karl Llewellyn's important, but elusive, idea of 'situation sense'.[95]

In some respects precedents are like parables or morality tales. There is, as every lawyer knows, an intimate relationship between general rules and particular cases. Similarly, as every theologian and moralist should know, there is an intimate relationship between parables (and other morality tales) and their significance: that significance can be expressed in such terms as the point, or the moral, or some other general lesson or idea that it illustrates. Stories appeal strongly to the imagination. Part of that appeal lies in their concreteness, their particularity. That power can be undermined if the moral or point is spelled out or otherwise made explicit. Perhaps the most obvious common element is indeterminacy: indeterminacy as to what exactly is being argued or what is the general significance of the particular example; for example, what precisely is the moral of the parable of the prodigal son? Indeterminacy is

93 As we have seen (above, p 308) as a practical matter there are some differences: for example, we advise beginning law students, in learning how to write a précis or note of a case, to adopt as a rule of thumb: 'In respect of the facts, when in doubt include'. The reason for this is that it is easier to edit out unnecessary detail than to add extra facts at a later stage. So a student's preliminary note of a case contains not a definitive statement of 'the facts', but a provisional formulation of potentially material facts.
94 See Lord Denning's famous 'persuasive' categorization of the facts in the case of *Candler v Crane, Christmas & Co*, below, p 368.
95 K Llewellyn, *The Common Law Tradition: Deciding Appeals*, op cit, discussed in W Twining, *Rethinking Evidence* (1994) at 230-242.

generally presented as a weakness in an argument. But, as John Wisdom pointed out, one of the attractions of case by case argument is that one is not forced to define the boundaries of X in advance.[96] It can be valid and sensible to say 'this is a clear case of X' without *defining* X. That is part of the key to understanding the attraction of precedent at common law. It is a form of argument by analogy which does not commit the arguer to a position beyond what is needed for the case at hand. This may be why in theology, moral education and precedent at common law, emphasis on particular stories often treats indeterminacy as a virtue.[97]

---

96 J Wisdom, *Other Minds* (1956); Renford Bamborough (ed), *Wisdom: Twelve Essays* (1974).
97 For exercises on chapter 9, see Appendix I, section G, pp 404ff.

Chapter 10

Rules, Reasoning and Interpretation

1   Introduction

The sub-title of this book is 'a primer of interpretation'. We have now reached a stage where a puzzled interpreter, if he has learned the lessons of earlier chapters, should be in a position to diagnose the source(s) of his doubt and to identify how potentially sound arguments for resolving them may be constructed, at least in any reasonably straightforward case. The purpose of this concluding chapter is to take the puzzled interpreter a stage further; to consider in greater detail the nature of reasoning in law and of its relationship with interpretation.   The final section addresses the question whether it is possible to develop a general theory of legal interpretation.

2   From diagnosis to argument

Diagnosing problems and tackling them are not identical operations. Sometimes, once the nature of a problem has been settled, the solution is straightforward or even self-evident. Sometimes a solution may be arrived at without much understanding on the part of the person(s) involved. Sometimes a problem, once understood, is seen to be insoluble. But more often a solution can be achieved only after a good deal of hard graft.

All these possibilities occur in the context of interpretation. Some problems of interpretation, once diagnosed, need no elaborate apparatus of analysis and reasoning for their resolution. It is small comfort to an official who has to administer a silly rule to recognize clearly that he has been presented with an acute dilemma because someone earlier in the process has made an error or because of some feature of the system that he is not in a position to alter or avoid; the dilemma remains and may not be easily resolved. Perhaps all that he can hope to do is make the best of a bad job. Similarly the cautious solicitor may feel that an interpretation favourable to her client is so unlikely or so risky that she must advise him not to pursue his chosen course of action (or to plead guilty or to settle), however unhappy the client will be about the result. In particular contexts the factors affecting interpretation and application may point clearly in a single direction.

Even where there is some prospect of establishing a clear or a favourable interpretation, it is a foolish interpreter who expects the problem to resolve itself. A reasoned response to a problem of interpretation typically requires analysis, research, more analysis and the construction of arguments, backed at each stage by that elusive quality, good judgement. In the last four chapters we have emphasised the factors which give rise to difficulties in interpretation. Identifying the main conditions of doubt lays the foundation for the next steps, viz identifying the range of possible or plausible interpretations of the relevant rule or rules, or parts thereof, and constructing arguments in favour of and against each of the main candidates. Whatever the context, a rational approach to interpretation involves constructing and weighing arguments; the process is usefully seen as *dialectical*, in the sense that arguments for and against a proposition, and arguments for and against those arguments, are set against each other, as in a contest. The medieval *disputatio* and arguments on a point of law in adversarial proceedings provide an excellent model for dialectical processes, not least because the role of the main protagonists is clear: it is to construct and put forward the strongest arguments on one side and to reveal the weaknesses on the other. It is important to note that reasoning in interpretation is dialectical whether or not the actual process in which the interpreter is involved approximates more closely to an adversarial proceeding, such as a school debate, a law school moot, or arguing in court, or to an inquisitorial or investigative enquiry, such as a theologian struggling with an obscure text, a legal scholar trying to resolve a doubtful point or a judge deliberating about a disputed question of law that requires a ruling. Whenever a serious doubt is involved, perhaps the most important part of the equipment of the skilled interpreter is skill in reasoning, which is part of, but not co-extensive with, skill in persuasion.[1]

Well-developed powers of reasoning, like a good command of language, are an important 'lawyer-like' quality. The two are interdependent aspects of a general ability to think clearly. The purpose of this chapter is to provide a starting point for approaching those aspects of reasoning that are particularly important in interpretation. Just as the differences between problems of interpretation in legal and non-legal contexts can easily be exaggerated, so there may also have been a tendency in juristic literature to dwell too much on the allegedly unique or unusual features of 'legal reasoning'.[2] In our view,

---

1   Compare this with the roles of the Advocate-General of the Court of Justice of the European Communities, whose duty is, 'with complete impartiality and independence, to make, in open court, reasoned submissions on cases brought before the Court of Justice .... '(Article 166 of the Treaty of Rome) or of an *amicus curiae*, B Markesenis, *Foreign Law; Comparative Methodology* (1997), chapter 15.

2   'Legal reasoning' is used here in a narrow sense to cover those kinds of reasoning that are appropriate to recommending or justifying a conclusion on a question of law in a particular legal system. Lawyers' reasonings, a term borrowed from Julius Stone, is used to cover the whole range of types of reasoning appropriate for the various kinds of intellectual tasks typically undertaken by lawyers in their professional capacity. See W Twining, *Law In Context: Enlarging a Discipline* (1997), pp 248-250. It is part of the thesis of this chapter that even specialized kinds of legal reasoning share many features of practical reasoning in non-legal contexts. Although it is conceded that there may be some unique or unusual features of common law legal reasoning, as contrasted with civil law reasoning on the one hand and non-legal practical reasoning of various kinds on the other, the terms 'legal reasoning' and 'lawyers' reasonings' are not here confined to such features, but cover all the modes of reasoning relevant to the task at hand. No attempt is made here to deal with possible differences between legal reasoning in the common law and in other legal systems.

an understanding of what is involved in reasoning in general is a more appropriate basis from which to approach the more specialised or peculiar aspects that may be features of reasoning within a particular legal system. And this is the case when approaching reasoning in the broader context of interpretation of rules in general. But carefully selected legal examples can be useful for this purpose, for a number of reasons. Firstly, judicial decisions are among the most elaborately reasoned and public forms of decision-making; the law reports are a rich treasure-house of examples of practical reasoning of more than one kind. Secondly, examples of legal reasoning are useful indicators of what aspects of the subject of reasoning, that is, logic in a broad sense,[3] are especially relevant to problems of interpretation; and thirdly, as every law teacher should know, the adversarial process serves as an excellent pedagogical device for developing ability in reasoning and analysis.

We propose to analyse in detail the structure of some possible arguments for each side in the case of *Allen* as a preliminary to making a number of basic general points about the nature of reasoning in interpretation, with particular reference to the standpoint of the advocate. In a later section we shall consider how these matters may appear from the standpoints of some other kinds of interpreter. Although nearly all the examples will be legal, most of the points also apply to interpretation in other contexts. We return to *Allen* precisely because it brings together many of the strands that have been identified in the two preceding chapters: its primary concern is with the interpretation of a disputed statutory phrase, while there are also precedents both from within and without the jurisdiction whose interpretation is a matter of doubt. Readers may find it helpful to refresh their memories, either from chapter 1, section 7.2, or the case note in chapter 9, section 1.

3 The structure of argument in *R v Allen*

The facts in *Allen* can be briefly restated as follows:

In 1853 Allen married W1.
In 1866 W1 died.
In 1867 Allen married W2.
In 1871, still being married to W2, Allen purported to marry W3.
W3 was the niece of W1.
Under the law at that time, marriage to a niece by marriage was void. Accordingly, independently of his marriage to W2, Allen's marriage to W3 would have been void.

The facts are not in dispute. But they were considered to raise a difficult question of law, sufficient to justify reserving the case for consideration by the full Court for Crown Cases Reserved, the predecessor of the Court of Criminal

---

3 'Logic', in the broad sense, refers to the study of reasoning of all kinds, not just deductive or closed-system reasoning (see below, pp 350ff).

346 Rules, Reasoning and Interpretation

Appeal. It can be inferred from the report, as well as from the judgments in the Irish case of *R v Fanning*,[4] that the instinctive feeling of the judges was that this kind of fact-situation ought to fall within the scope of the offence of bigamy and, judging by opinions expressed by several classes of first-year law students, this would be in line with lay opinion even today. How then did the doubt arise? We suggest that there were two primary and two secondary conditions of doubt in the case. Firstly, the words 'shall marry' were ambiguous: had the words been 'shall go through a form and ceremony of marriage' the problem would never have arisen. Secondly, the authorities were in conflict; in particular, the Court of Criminal Appeal in Ireland had recently decided, by a majority of 7-4, that the equivalent Irish provision did not cover this kind of case. The Irish court was at that time of high persuasive authority, but a feature of *Fanning* was that the majority judges went out of their way to express regrets at feeling compelled to come to this conclusion. A subsidiary source of difficulty is that there was a doubt about the precise nature of the mischief that the crime of bigamy is designed to prevent. The question, 'Why is bigamy considered to be wrong?' is not as straightforward as it might seem.

This third source of doubt was closely connected with a fourth condition, viz that a change had taken place in the general situation since the time the original provision was drafted. In 1603, when the exact wording of the statutory provision was first introduced, making bigamy a capital felony,[5] the Church had sole jurisdiction to celebrate valid marriages. Originally bigamy had been considered analogous to blasphemy and sacrilege as being essentially the desecration of a solemn religious ceremony. However, when in 1836 provision was made for celebration of marriages in a secular form,[6] the original rationale for bigamy lost some of its force. For it seems strange to treat the deception involved in going through a 'second' marriage ceremony in a register office as analogous to blasphemy. Yet other reasons might be advanced for retaining an offence of bigamy in some form or other: in the words of Cockburn CJ, it can be the means of 'a most cruel and wicked deception'; in the case of civil ceremonies there is still an element of deception, including falsification of the register; in the case of religious ceremonies, an offence against religion is still involved, although it is a matter of controversy whether this is an appropriate sphere for criminal regulation; also the law of bigamy is commonly seen in more general terms as an important penal instrument for furthering a general policy of supporting the institution of monogamy. But, as Glanville Williams brilliantly argued,[7] these policies are not identical, and each could be said to be adequately catered for by other provisions, even if the offence of bigamy was abolished. The answer to the question 'What's wrong with bigamy?' is not self-evident.[8]

4   *R v Fanning* (1866) 10 Cox CC 411 is an Irish case decided six years before *Allen* and discussed in detail in the latter case. For citations to all the other cases discussed in *Allen*, see chapter 1, section 7.2.
5   Jac 1, c 11. Section 57 of the Offences against the Person Act 1861 re-enacted with minor modifications s 22 of the Offences against the Person Act 1828.
6   Marriage Act 1836; see now Marriage Act 1949.
7   'Bigamy and the Third Marriage' (1950) 13 *Modern Law Review* 417.
8   In *Whiston v Whiston* [1998] 1 All ER 423, the question arose whether, having entered into a bigamous marriage, the 'wife' could subsequently claim ancillary relief following the grant of a decree of nullity. While agreeing that the crime of bigamy 'is treated less seriously today than it

Against this background, let us look at *Allen* from the standpoint of counsel on each side preparing their respective arguments.[9] The situation is defined for each of them in almost identical terms: the facts are given; there is a single question of law which can be expressed in neutral terms as follows: 'What is the meaning of "shall marry" in section 57 of the Offences against the Person Act 1861?' Their respective roles within the adversarial process are also relatively clearly defined.

The structure of the argument in this kind of case is quite simple: counsel for each side will advance competing interpretations of the words 'shall marry' and reasons in support of his interpretation and against that of his opponent. On the face of it, there are three main meanings that could be attached to the critical words:

(A) 'shall marry' means 'shall validly marry'; or
(B) 'shall marry' means 'shall go through a form and ceremony of marriage recognised by law'; or
(C) 'shall marry' means 'shall purportedly enter into a marriage that would have been valid, but for its bigamous character'.

If either *A* or *C* were accepted, Allen would not be guilty of bigamy; if *B* were accepted, then the result would be different. Counsel for Allen has a tactical choice to make: whether to argue for interpretations *A* and *C* in the alternative, or whether to concentrate on one of them. On close examination *A* has very little chance of success. The main arguments relating to it might be stated as follows:

Conclusion A: 'shall marry' means 'shall validly marry'.

Pro	*Contra*
The same word should be construed in the same way in the same statute (*Courtauld v Legh* (1869) LR 4 ExCh 126 130 per Cleasby B). In the very same section the words 'being married' mean 'being validly married' (*Catherwood v Caslon* (1844) 13 M & W 261): therefore 'shall marry' should be interpreted to mean 'shall validly marry'.	This interpretation would lead to an absurdity. For, if the accused is already validly married, the second marriage cannot be valid (*Bayard v Morphew* (1815) 2 Phillim 321). Accordingly no one would ever be guilty of bigamy. It was clearly the intention of the legislature to create some offence. (An application of the maxim *ut res magis valeat quam pereat*; Bennion, *Statutory Interpretation* (3rd edn, p 432).

was', Ward LJ insisted that it remains an offence which 'strikes at the heart of marriage. Where the criminal act undermines our fundamental notions of monogamous marriage I would be slow to allow a bigamist then to assert a claim, an entitlement at which she only arrives by reason of her offending'; (pp 427 and 429). See Appendix 1, section A5, questions 1-4.

9 The arguments set out below are a reconstruction of possible arguments, derived from a number of sources. The actual arguments of counsel as reported in the various reports of *Allen* concentrated almost exclusively on the case law. See especially 12 Cox CC 193, pp 194-195

The absurdity argument is clearly a very strong one. But one effect of accepting it is that section 57 then provides a striking example of the same word being used in two quite different senses within the space of four words in a single statutory provision. However, counsel for Allen would probably be wise to drop any attempts to argue for interpretation A. He is accordingly left with alternative C; some of the possible arguments for and against this conclusion can be tabulated as follows:

Conclusion C: 'shall marry' means 'shall purportedly enter into a marriage that would have been valid, but for its bigamous character'.

Pro

(a) There is strong authority in the case of *Fanning* (for citations see Chapter 1, section 7) for the proposition that, where the second marriage would have been void independently of its bigamous character, no offence was committed. So much for some possible arguments for and against *C*. Now let us look at some arguments for and against interpretation *B*, which is supported by the prosecution.

(b) (i) The case of *Burt v Burt* (for citations see Chapter 1, section 7) supports the proposition. (ii) This case was approved in *Fanning*.

(c) (i) In *R v Millis* (for citations see Chapter 1, section 7) Tindal CJ said that the second marriage to constitute bigamy must mean a marriage of the same kind and obligation as the first. (ii) This *dictum* was approved in *Fanning*.

(d) (i) 'shall marry' is ambiguous. This interpretation is a possible one.

Contra

(a) (i) *Fanning* is an Irish case and so is only of persuasive authority. (ii) *Fanning* is a weak authority because the judges were divided 7-4 and even the majority were reluctant to allow the appeal. (iii) *Fanning* was wrongly decided. The situation in *Fanning* involved deception of both the priest and the woman and so fell within the mischief of bigamy; *Fanning* was based on a misinterpretation of the earlier cases. *Fanning* is also inconsistent with *Brawn's case* (for citations see Chapter 1, section 7). (iv) The cases are distinguishable on the facts: *Fanning* concerned a defect in the ceremony; *Allen* concerned a defect in the capacity of one of the parties.

(b) *Burt v Burt* is distinguishable on the facts: the *ceremony* in that case was not proved to be capable of producing a valid marriage; the ceremony in this case was capable of producing a valid marriage.

(c) *Millis* was concerned with the validity of the *first* marriage. The statement by Tindal CJ was merely a *dictum*, based on his own reasoning, and it is not binding.

(d) (i) This interpretation defeats the intention of the legislature by

(ii) This interpretation is the closest to interpretation A (ie that 'shall marry' means 'shall validly marry'), which in turn is in accordance with the principle that where possible the same meaning shall be given to the same words in the same Act of Parliament (*Re National Savings Bank* (1866) 1 Ch App 547). (iii) Penal statutes must be construed strictly in favour of the accused (for authorities see Bennion, op cit, pp 271ff).

(e) *Brawn* was disapproved in the more recent case of *Fanning*.

leaving part of the mischief unprovided for. (ii) Interpretation C is not the same as interpretation A. Also, the presumption concerning the same words in the same statute may be displaced by evidence showing an intention to use the words differently in different parts of the Act (see Bennion, op cit, pp 900, 942) (iii) This interpretation is forced and strains the natural meaning of the words.

(e) This interpretation is inconsistent with *Brawn*, which has not been questioned since by an English court.

So much for some possible arguments for and against *C*. Now let us look at some arguments for and against interpretation *B*, which is supported by the prosecution.

Conclusion B: 'shall marry' means 'shall go through a form and ceremony of marriage recognised by law'.

Pro

(a) *Brawn* supports this interpretation (see further above).

(b) *R v Penson* (for citations see Chapter 1, section 7) supports this interpretation.

(c) (i) This interpretation would make the scope of the rule co-extensive with the mischief (*Heydon's case* (1584) 3 Co Rep 7a, discussed above, pp 153-154). (ii) The *original mischief* was a desecration of a solemn *religious ceremony*; section 57 of the Offences against the Person Act 1861 merely re-enacted the exact words of the earlier statute. (iii) The mischief rule applies to the time of the original enactment, ie 1603. (See Bennion, op cit, pp 707-723.)

(d) Bigamy always involves an act in fraud of the law to give the colour and

Contra

(a) See above.

(b) *Penson* is distinguishable on the facts.

(c) (i) *Heydon's case* does not apply to penal statutes (*A-G v Sillem* (1864) 2 H & C 431, 509 per Pollock CB). (ii) The scope of the mischief is unclear. By 1861 marriage by civil ceremony had been introduced. Accordingly the rationale of bigamy must have changed. (iii) The relevant date for determining the mischief is 1861.

(d) (i) This argument is obscure. (ii) In any case the argument does not

pretence of marriage where the reality does not exist. This case involved an act in fraud of the law.

apply to *Allen,* since marriage to a deceased wife's niece cannot exist anyway and W3 would be presumed to know this.

(e) Bigamy often involves a villainous fraud ... a cruel and wicked deception.

(e) This is not necessarily the case. See, for example, *Penson,* where the woman was apparently a party to the proceeding.

(f) The words 'shall marry' are fully capable of being construed in this way without being forced or strained.

(f) There is at least one other equally natural interpretation.

(g) This interpretation is restricted to a form and ceremony recognized by law. In *Allen* the ceremony was of this kind. The wider issue is not before the court.

(g) This interpretation opens the door to convicting people of bigamy who have gone through all sorts of fantastic ceremonies (see *Burt v Burt*).

These will suffice for present purposes. Judged by standards of good advocacy, some of the points are much stronger than others, though much depends on the specific context in which the argument is to be made. Not all of them were used in argument by counsel in the actual case; on the other hand, not all the points made by Cockburn CJ in his judgment have been included. But this analysis provides a basis for illustrating some basic general propositions about the nature of modes of reasoning typically employed in interpretation of rules.

4 Reasoning, rules and law

The following points are intended as a simple general statement of certain cardinal features of the kinds of reasoning used in arriving at or justifying conclusions on points involving the interpretation and application of rules. Like Hart's summary statement about certain cardinal features of language, this is intended merely as a jumping-off point from which to approach some of the literature on reasoning in general and on common law reasoning in particular.

(i)   People are engaged in reasoning when they take certain propositions as the basis for making one or more other propositions; or, in other words, when they take one or more propositions, called the premises of an argument, and use these to infer another proposition, called the conclusion of the argument.[10] *In the present context, reasons are premises in the process of reasoning in which propositions containing one common factor (premises) are synthesised to produce or support other propositions (conclusions).*

We have neither the space nor the expertise to give an adequate account of the nature of reasoning in general. There is no substitute for studying one or

10 Adapted from J Hospers, *An Introduction to Philosophical Analysis* (2nd edn, 1973), p 128.

more of the introductory works listed in the suggestions for reading, before moving on to specialised works on legal reasoning. In this respect, one general warning needs to be given about elementary texts on logic and critical thinking.[11] Most of the examples used in such works are examples of reasoning towards *conclusions of fact*, whereas, in the context of interpreting rules, typically the main conclusions are *normative*, that is to say, they take the form of ought-propositions. For example, in *Allen* the main arguments of counsel and of the court were concerned not with the discovery of truth or with explaining facts, but with judgments about what meaning *ought* to be attributed to the disputed words 'shall marry' and whether Allen *ought* to be convicted. Much of what is said in elementary discussions of deduction, induction and reasoning by analogy in relation to conclusions of fact can be translated into the context of normative reasoning. But in this kind of reasoning there are specialised features that need to be taken into account.[12]

The following quotation is a fairly typical example of an elementary introduction to reasoning in general:

> *In logic,* Reasoning is the process of inference; it is the process of passing from certain propositions already known or assumed to be true, to another truth distinct from them but following from them; it is a discourse or argument which infers one proposition from another, or from a group of others having some common elements between them. The inference is necessary in the case of deductive reasoning; and contingent, probable or wrong, in the case of inductive, presumptive or deceptive reasoning respectively. There are various types of reasoning, and proper methods for each type. The definition, discussion, development and evaluation of these types and methods form an important branch of logic and its sub-divisions. The details of the application of reasoning to the various sciences, form the subject of methodology. All these types are reducible to one or the other of the two fundamental processes of reasoning, namely deduction and induction. It must be added that the logical study of reasoning is normative: logic does not analyse it simply in its natural development, but with a view to guide it towards coherence, validity or truth.[13]

Two points are worth making about this passage. Firstly, in normative reasoning, some of the premises and nearly all the main conclusions are normative, and so are not true or false, in the sense of being empirically verifiable or falsifiable. To take a very simple example, the last step in the reasoning of the court in *Allen* could be re-stated in the form of a simple syllogism as follows:

Major premiss:	Whosoever being married shall go through a form and ceremony of marriage recognised by law, ought to be convicted of the offence of bigamy.
Minor premiss:	Allen, being married, went through a form and ceremony of marriage recognised by law.
Conclusion:	Allen ought to be convicted of the offence of bigamy.

11 See further Appendix IV, p 441.
12 See G Von Wright, *Norm and Action* (1963), preface.
13 T Greenwood in D Runes (ed), *The Dictionary of Philosophy* (1942), pp 264-265; see also P Edwards (ed), *The Encyclopedia of Philosophy* (1967), passim, especially 'induction'.

Expressed thus, the major premiss and the conclusion are normative; the minor premiss is a proposition of fact. Thus for the formulation quoted above to be applicable to the context of interpreting rules, the word 'truth' has to be interpreted to be wider than empirical or factual truth.[14]

Secondly, the quotation states that all types of reasoning are reducible to one of two fundamental types, deduction and induction. It is often said that there are at least three types of reasoning to be found in the contexts of arguments on points of law: induction, deduction and reasoning by analogy. There is no necessary contradiction here, for many logicians maintain that reasoning by analogy is one kind of inductive reasoning.[15] It may be useful, at this stage, to consider each of these types specifically in relation to interpretation and application of rules.

Deduction. This is typically from general to particular, as in the above example of syllogistic reasoning in *Allen.*[16] In deduction the conclusion must follow from the premisses as a matter of logical necessity; if you accept the premisses, you must also accept the conclusion, as it is logically compelling or *conclusive.* Deduction has a part to play in reasoning in interpretation, but it is important to remember that there is more than one kind of reasoning. A common error is to equate words like 'logical' and 'reasoning' with deductive reasoning and to treat all other modes of reasoning as 'illogical' or 'fallacious'. For our purpose, the important distinction is between *conclusive* and *inconclusive.* Reasoning is conclusive where the conclusion follows necessarily from the premisses; this is sometimes referred to as 'closed system reasoning'; it is inconclusive where the premisses *support* but do not *compel* the conclusion; this is sometimes referred to as 'open system' reasoning.[17]

The place of formal logic in legal reasoning is one of the most problematic topics in jurisprudence. We propose to attempt no more than to warn the beginner against some elementary pitfalls.

Firstly, it is important to realise that the term 'logic' is used, even by philosophers, in a number of different senses. It is sometimes used as a synonym for reasoning, as in the phrase 'the logic of justification'. It is sometimes used

---

14 On the meanings of 'truth' and the distinction between truth and validity see, for example, Hospers, op cit, chapter 2; Max Black, *Critical Thinking* (1952), pp 39-43. In the present context, even if the major premiss is expressed in terms of 'shall be guilty' or the conclusion in terms of 'is guilty' or 'is liable', it is appropriate to treat them as normative.

15 There are other types of reasoning. Another type, regularly resorted to by Sherlock Holmes and emphasized by CS Peirce, and of considerable significance in 'fact-finding' processes in legal contexts, is 'abduction' or 'retroduction', that is to say an inference yielding an explanatory *hypothesis*, rather than supporting a factual generalization (as in induction) or in establishing a particular result (as in deduction). For example, '(1) The surprising fact, C, is observed; (2) but if A were true, C would be a matter of course; (3) hence, there is reason to suspect that A is true.' WB Gallie, *Peirce and Pragmatism* (1952), pp 94-99. See also D Schum, *Evidential Foundations of Probabalistic Reasoning* (1994), pp 461ff.

16 Syllogistic reasoning is only one species of deductive reasoning. There are valid deductive arguments which proceed from general to general, or from particular to particular, or from particular to general. Inductive arguments can proceed from general to particular or from general to general. S Mellone, *Elements of Modern Logic* (2nd edn 1948, 1958), pp 172ff.

17 See, for example, ER Emmet, *The Use of Reason* (1960), chapters 4 and 10; *Learning to Think* (1966), chapter 2; PF Strawson, *Introduction To Logical Theory* (1985) chapter 8 and D Walton, *Informal Logic: A Handbook Of Critical Argumentation* (1989).

more narrowly to refer to particular kinds of reasoning, notably deductive or closed system reasoning. Terms like 'formal logic', 'symbolic logic', 'mathematical logic' refer to specialised and continually developing fields of study. In everyday discourse words like 'logical' and 'illogical' are often used very loosely to refer to arguments which the speaker considers to be strong or weak, valid or invalid. The first warning to the beginner is to take care how he, and others, use terms like 'logic', 'logical' and 'illogical'.

Secondly, even where 'logic' is confined to reasoning leading to necessary conclusions, very general questions of the kind 'what is the role of logic in legal reasoning?' are ambiguous and misleadingly simple. For example, this question has been variously interpreted to mean: 'To what extent do judges and advocates explicitly resort to deduction in justifying their decisions?'; 'To what extent can judgments and other examples of argument towards conclusions of law be *reconstructed* in terms of formal logic?; 'To what extent is it feasible to resort to deductive-type arguments in legal reasoning?'; or 'To what extent is it *desirable* to do so?'; or even: 'What illumination can be gained by applying the techniques of formal logic to examples of legal reasoning?' All these questions are different, although they are related to each other. They are complex questions; beware of glib answers to them.

Thirdly, there is an unfortunate tendency in juristic controversy to present answers to some of these questions as disagreements between extremists. For instance, it is not uncommon to contrast a view that a legal system is a closed and complete system of rules from which all conclusions on points of law in particular cases can be deducted as a matter of logical necessity (sometimes referred to as 'the slot-machine model') with the dictum of Holmes J that '(T)he life of the law has not been logic, it has been experience',[18] which can be interpreted to mean that deductive logic plays no role at all in legal reasoning. Stated in this extreme form, both views are patently absurd. It is encouraging to find that few jurists who have been accused of adopting the slot-machine model have been guilty of any such crudities and that even a cursory reading of Holmes reveals that he was concerned to show that logic is only one of a number of factors in 'determining the rules by which men should be governed' rather than to deny that it had, or should have, any influence in this respect. There are, of course, real differences of opinion, as well as emphasis, among jurists (and between legal traditions) on questions of the kind mentioned above. But the differences are not of an all-or-nothing kind. Indeed, there is probably a higher degree of consensus on some of these matters than might at first sight seem to be the case. For example, within the common law tradition the following conclusion by Guest would probably be widely accepted as relatively uncontroversial:

> Arguments need not be cast in a strictly syllogistic form, provided that they exhibit a logical structure. In the dialectic of the law, logic has an important part to play at a stage when a suggested rule has to be tested in order to discover whether or not its adoption will involve the contradiction of already established legal principles. When a rule is tentatively asserted as an explanation of existing cases, it is not

18 OW Holmes Jr, *The Common Law* (1881), p 1.

always possible to attend immediately to the logical consequences involved in its enunciation. In *Mersey Docks & Transport Co Ltd v Rea, Ltd*, Scrutton LJ expressed the opinion that the House of Lords' case of *Elder Dempster & Co Ltd v Paterson, Zochonis & Co Ltd* had established a principle of 'vicarious immunity' of an agent in English law. An agent, he said, while carrying out a contract, is entitled to any immunity which may be possessed by his principal. In subsequent cases, however, decisions were reached without reference to this principle, and it came to be realized that this rule could not be applied deductively to the facts of these later cases without producing an inconsistent result. Eventually the rule was discarded. In this type of situation logic may be used to detect contradictions and to iron out inconsistencies, to test hypotheses and to discover similarities.[19]

It is worth commenting briefly on one point raised by the last sentence of this quotation: what may be termed arguments about inconsistency. One kind of argument commonly found in reasoning in interpretation is a claim that if a particular interpretation is accepted this will be inconsistent with some other rule. Such arguments need to be treated with caution for a number of reasons. Firstly, it is quite common for some kinds of rules to 'hunt in pairs'.[20] Typically this happens with prescriptions which are both general and vague, such as the maxims of Equity, some rules of statutory construction or those prescriptions which are designated as 'principles' by Dworkin and as 'guiding standards' by Eckhoff.[21] Such rules indicate reasons which must or may be taken into account in particular cases, but do not dictate any particular result. They are too vague to be contradictories or logically inconsistent with each other, but they may point in different directions. Appeals to such prescriptions should not be treated as examples of arguments about inconsistency.

Secondly, arguments about 'inconsistency' and 'contradiction' may often be more appropriately expressed as arguments about what constitutes an appropriate level of generality for a rule or a concept in a particular context. For example, traditionally a great deal of effort was expended by analytical jurists in trying to elucidate concepts such as 'personality', 'possession' and 'ownership' in terms of consistent principles which transcended particular branches of law. Thus attempts were made to 'reconcile' cases dealing with possession in larceny, trespass, land law, bailment, etc. In English law such quests have often ended in failure because English judges have not attempted to use these concepts consistently at this level of generality. They were more responsive to considerations of policy in particular contexts, than to arguments about consistency at a high level of abstraction. A single example from the law of bigamy illustrates the point. In *R v Sarwan Singh* the question arose whether a potentially polygamous marriage is a valid first marriage ('whosoever being *married*') for the purposes of section 57 of the Offences against the Person Act 1861.[22] It was argued for the Crown that since such marriages had been

---

19 AG Guest, *Oxford Essays in Jurisprudence* (1961), pp 195-196.
20 G Paton, *Jurisprudence* (4th edn, DP Derham, 1972), p 252; see above, p 278.
21 R Dworkin, 'The Model of Rules' (1967) 35 *U Chicago Law Review* 14, reprinted in *Taking Rights Seriously* (1977); and T Eckhoff, 'Guiding Standards in Legal Reasoning' (1976) 29 *Current Legal Problems* 205. See also chapter 1, section 10.1 above.
22 [1962] 3 All ER 612 (Quarter Sessions), overruled by *R v Sagoo* [1975] 2 All ER 926, CA; see Appendix I, section A5, p 390.

recognised for some purposes (eg in nullity proceedings) they should be recognised as valid for the purpose of a prosecution for bigamy. The Court rejected this argument. The decision is not an example of logical inconsistency; rather it is an example of the particularistic tendencies of the common law – because polygamous marriages are recognised for some purposes in English law it does not follow that they should be recognised for all purposes. Similarly one aspect of the allegedly more 'logical' approach of civilians is perhaps better expressed in terms of their greater concern to develop consistent bodies of principles and concepts at a higher level of abstraction than has been traditional in the common law.

Induction is inconclusive. Typically, inductive reasoning is from particular to general, but the term may be used in a broader sense to encompass all kinds of reasoning in which the premisses support, but do not compel, the conclusion. The following is a simple example of induction.

In case 1 elements a, b, c, d, and e were present and the plaintiff succeeded.
In case 2 elements a, b, c, d, and e were present and the plaintiff succeeded.
In case 3 elements a, b, c, d, and e were present and the plaintiff succeeded.
Conclusion: in all cases in which elements a, b, c, d, and e are present, the
     plaintiff should succeed.

The cases support the general conclusion, but they do not compel it; one reason why this is so is because there is always a possibility that a new case may turn up and undermine the conclusion. In the world of fact, inductive reasoning is concerned with probabilities; in normative contexts it is more accurate to talk of the relative *strength* or *cogency* of (inconclusive) reasons. Thus to have three cases in support of a proposition is stronger than to have one case in support of it, if they are all decisions of the same court. But one decision of the House of Lords would on its own be stronger than three decisions of the High Court.

Reasoning by Analogy (sometimes called reasoning by example) is typically reasoning from particular to particular. Hospers puts the matter as follows:

> An analogy is simply a comparison, and an argument from analogy is an argument from comparison. An argument from analogy begins with a comparison between two things, x and y. It then proceeds to argue that these two things are alike in certain respects, A, B, C, and concludes that therefore they are also alike in another respect, D, in which they have not been observed to resemble one another. ... It will be apparent at once that an argument from analogy is never conclusive.[23]

A great deal of attention has been paid to reasoning by analogy in Anglo-American juristic literature because it is widely held that this is the characteristic mode of common law reasoning. A classic statement is by Edward Levi:

> The basic pattern of legal reasoning is reasoning by example. It is reasoning from case to case. It is a three-step process described by the doctrine of precedent in which a proposition descriptive of the first case is made into a rule of law and then applied to a next similar situation. The steps are these: similarity is seen between

---

23 Hospers, op cit, p 476.

cases; next the rule of law inherent in the first case is announced; then the rule of law is made applicable to the second case.... The finding of similarity or difference is the key step in the legal process.[24]

Later we shall suggest that this view is, in some respects, an oversimplification and exaggerates the part played by reasoning by analogy (or example) in legal reasoning. But this kind of reasoning is important in interpretation, and Levi's account of it is well worth reading, especially for its vivid account of the way in which common law concepts and doctrines quietly adapt to new situations and changing needs in the process of application: 'the rules change as the rules are applied'.[25]

A simple example of reasoning from case to case would take the following form:

In case 1 factors a, b and c were present and the result was judgment for the plaintiff.
In case 2 (the present case) factors a, b and c are present; therefore judgment should be for the plaintiff.

In other words, similarities between the *facts* are advanced as reasons for recommending or justifying the same *results* (particular conclusion).

In case law it is not uncommon for precedents to be cited by opposing sides in the form of *competing analogies*:

In case 1 a, b and c were present and the result was judgment for the plaintiff.
In case 2 a, b and d were present and the result was judgment for the defendant.
In case 3 (the present case) a, b, c and d are present.
Counsel for plaintiff: 'Case 3 is more like case 1 than case 2, because of factor c, therefore judgment for plaintiff.'
Counsel for defendant: 'Case 3 is more like case 2 than case 1 because of factor d, therefore judgment for defendant.'

In such cases the result turns on the relative importance or weight to be attributed to particular elements of similarity or difference, in this example factors c and d.

What is the relationship between reasoning by analogy and induction in the context of reasoning from case to case? The process described by Levi involves three steps. Firstly, a similarity between the present case and a prior case is seen. Secondly, a rule is formulated for which the prior case is said to stand.[26] The relevant point here is that this stage involves reasoning from particular (a case) to general (a rule) and thus resembles induction; a generalised statement of the material facts of the case becomes the protasis of

24 E Levi, *An Introduction to Legal Reasoning* (1948), p 1.
25 Ibid, p 3.
26 In the context of the doctrine of precedent this is the step of determining a *ratio decidendi* of a case, which is discussed in chapter 9, section 6.

the rule. As we shall see later, there is often considerable leeway for choice concerning the level of generality at which the protasis is to be formulated.

The third step, according to Levi, is to apply the rule to the present case. This is reasoning from general to particular and so resembles deduction. Sometimes, indeed, this stage can be re-stated in the form of a syllogism.[27] But often reasoning from case to case explicitly involves one less step:

Case 1 resembles case 2 in respect of a, b and c.
Therefore case 1 should be treated like case 2.

The explicit reasoning is from particular to particular without a general rule being articulated at any point. Some interpretation of the rule is *implied*, but in an indeterminate way, in that any one of an indeterminate number of rule-formulations of differing levels of generality could be selected.[28]

Reasoning by analogy is typically associated with rules derived from cases and other rules not in fixed verbal form. But much the same kind of process can take place even though a statutory provision is involved, because in a particular case interpretation is often confined to elucidating only such aspects of the meaning(s) of doubtful words as are immediately relevant to the case; thus in treating *Burt v Burt* as distinguishable (ie different) from *Allen*, Cockburn CJ left open the question whether in order to establish bigamy the form and ceremony must be one recognised as valid in England, or by local law wherever it happened to have been celebrated, or by some local laws but not others:

> In thus holding, it is not at all necessary to say that forms of marriage unknown to the law, as was the case in *Burt v Burt*, would suffice to bring a case within the operation of the statute. We must not be understood to mean that every fantastic form of marriage to which parties might think proper to resort, or that a marriage ceremony performed by an authorized person in an unauthorized place, would be marrying within Sect 57. of 24 and 25 Vict. c. 101.[29]

Thus the court's interpretation did not purport to be a complete exposition (if such were possible) of 'shall marry'; it was sufficient to remove the doubt in *Allen*, but some doubts were left unresolved for the future about the scope of the rule for which *Burt v Burt* was an authority. In a future case, *Allen* and *Burt v Burt* might provide a basis for an argument about competing analogies. For example, would *Allen* cover a case in which A, being validly married, went through an Islamic ceremony of marriage to B in England or Wales in 1998?[30]

---

27 A good example is contained in the judgment of Pearson LJ in *Hardy v Motor Insurers' Bureau* [1964] 2 QB 745, 763-764.
28 All or any of factors a, b and c could be crucial or relatively unimportant, and each factor could be categorized at one of an indeterminate number of levels of generality, as for example the facts in *Donoghue v Stevenson* were re-stated in a number of differing ways in chapter 1, section 9. Thus reasoning by analogy is closely related to induction, but where the formulation of the general rule is left implicit, there is an extra element of indeterminacy over and above the points that (a) reasons of this kind are inconclusive and (b) the formulations of rules derived from precedent by judges and others are not frozen; ie they are not examples of statements of rules in fixed verbal form.
29 See chapter 1, section 7.2.
30 See Appendix I, section A5, question 2(d).

(ii)   Reasoning in interpretation is a species of practical reasoning. The distinction between theoretical and practical reasoning is a subject of controversy among philosophers, but for present purposes it is sufficient to say that practical reasoning is concerned with giving and evaluating reasons for and against acting or deciding in a certain way.

Reasoning in interpretation shares many of the features of modes of reasoning commonly employed in various kinds of decision-making. In particular, as we have seen, practical reasoning is typically normative; that is, it deals with conclusions about how people *ought* to act or decide as contrasted with, for example, descriptions or explanations in the world of fact. Secondly, in the context of interpretation most or even all of the reasons in an argument may be logically inconclusive, in that they do not support their conclusions as a matter of *logical necessity*. None of the reasons that might have been advanced in *Allen* logically compels the choice by the court of one of the conflicting interpretations of 'shall marry'. Some of the reasons are stronger than others, but none requires a particular conclusion. Similarly, the *cumulative effect* of all the arguments on one side may be very much stronger than the cumulative effect of the opposing arguments, but may nevertheless not be logically compelling. Thirdly, reasoning in interpretation encompasses a variety of kinds of reasons and types of reasoning. Thus in the analysis of possible arguments of counsel in *Allen* are to be found: arguments appealing to authority (precedents); arguments appealing to considerations of policy; arguments appealing to logical consistency; and arguments appealing to the natural or ordinary meanings of words.

Similarly, as there are different types of reasoning, induction, deduction and analogy, the relationship between the *reasons* advanced in *Allen* may vary also according to the type of *reasoning* employed. Often, in legal interpretation, the three types may be woven together within a single argument in a complex series of intermediate as well as ultimate conclusions; and it is misleading to make statements of the kind 'the basic pattern of legal reasoning is reasoning by example' or 'case law reasoning is inductive and the application of statutes is deductive'.[31] These contain a core of truth, but they are misleading in that they oversimplify.

(iii)   A number of independent reasons may be advanced for or against a conclusion respecting a question of interpretation or application. Some of these reasons may be of differing kinds.

Three attempts to systematise the kinds of reasons which are appropriate in legal contexts may be briefly mentioned. In *Legal Reasoning and Legal Theory*, Neil MacCormick develops an account of judicial reasoning which starts from the premiss that judges are under a duty 'to give only such decisions as can be justified by a good justificatory argument'.[32] The first kind of argument, which should be used in the simplest cases where a clear rule is agreed to be applicable, is by deduction. Where difficulties arise about the rule or its applicability, a judge should resort to 'second-order justification', which is consequentialist in nature. However, it is not sufficient that a proposed

31 See Levi, op cit, esp pp 1-5, 19ff.
32 DN MacCormick, *Legal Reasoning and Legal Theory* (1978), p 250.

justification 'makes sense in the world', that is, is likely to produce beneficial results, it must also 'make sense in the system', a requirement which has two facets. It must be consistent with the system, that is, it may not contradict any of its valid and binding rules; and the justification must cohere with the recognised principles and analogies which may be derived from the system. It is not possible to do justice to MacCormick's thesis in a short space; but we may observe that it is concerned with reasoning by judges rather than argumentation as a whole, which may involve appeals to sympathy, special pleading, prejudice and other non-rational arguments.

Robert Summers's typology includes 'all basic types of good reasons found in common law cases'.[33] While he identifies five types – substantive, authority, factual, interpretational and critical – Summers concentrates on substantive reasons. These are divided into three subtypes: goal reasons which derive their justificatory force from their predicted beneficial results; rightness reasons which derive their justificatory force from the existence of some norm guiding conduct; and institutional reasons which are goal or rightness reasons tied to specific institutional roles or processes.

An example may help to distinguish them. Suppose a consumer sues a retailer for breach of contract for supplying him with completely defective goods, but the retailer refers the court to a contract which the consumer signed before the goods were delivered which contains a clause purporting to divest the consumer of any claim for compensation should the goods turn out to be faulty. Leaving aside any statutory authority, a court could strike out the exemption clause by an appeal to some notion of fairness in bargaining – the retailer being in a stronger position than the consumer, and there being effectively little choice between the terms offered by all retailers, it would be unfair to allow the practice of excluding all liability (a rightness reason) – and to the consequences of such clauses being held valid parts of a contract: consumers would suffer financially, safety and production standards might drop, citizens would lose respect for the law (goal reasons). On the other hand, rightness and goal reasons could be invoked to uphold the exemption clause: parties to contracts are entitled to expect courts to enforce their terms when they have been freely entered into, and were courts to strike down terms in contracts *ex post facto*, commercial enterprise would be rendered unpredictable. In addition, a court might argue that if such exemption clauses are regarded as unfair or leading to undesirable consequences, it is for Parliament to change the law, not the courts (an institutional reason).

There are obvious analogies between Summers's goal reasons and MacCormick's consequentialist arguments,[34] but for the purposes of justifying decisions, Summers gives priority to substantive over authority (precedential) reasons, even in simple cases where MacCormick would argue in favour of reasoning from agreed principles of law.

---

33 RS Summers, 'Two Types of Substantive Reasons: The Core of a Theory of Common-Law Justification' (1978) 63 *Cornell Law Review* 707, 716; *Essays on the Nature of Law and Legal Reasoning* (1992). See Appendix I, section H, question 15.

34 As there are between these and Dworkin's policies; see p 125 above. Dworkin, however, excludes the possibility of appeals to policy as a legitimate ground for deciding cases in adjudication. A close analogy also exists between Summers's rightness reasons and Dworkin's principles. See also the discussion of consequentialist and moralist argument, pp 130-131 above.

Ronald Dworkin's account of legal reasoning is widely regarded to be the most important and most controversial modern theory.[35] It claims both to prescribe how valid and cogent arguments about questions of law should be constructed and to describe the actual argumentative practices of able advocates and judges, while accepting that there are some deviants. It describes 'good practice'. In simplified form, Dworkin's model of legal reasoning is embodied in the approach of his ideal judge, Hercules, who owes allegiance to his legal system and who accepts the interpretive ideal of the integrity of that system.[36] Hercules proceeds in two stages, in reasoning about what is the best interpretation of the law.[37] Firstly, he considers which of two or more competing interpretations best fits the system in terms of past legislative and judicial decisions and institutional practices. This threshold test of 'fit' may eliminate some *prima facie* attractive interpretations and places a brake on Hercules' personal preferences. However, in many cases 'fit' is not determinative, either because more than one interpretation may satisfy the test, or because, when Hercules digs deeper, 'the brute facts of legal history' may themselves be subject to reinterpretation in the light of the fundamental principles of political morality which are embedded in the system and constitute its integrity.[38] Where 'fit' is not dispositive, Hercules is confronted with a 'hard case' and proceeds to the stage of justification. Dworkin summarises this stage as follows:

> Hard cases arise, for any judge, when his threshold test does not discriminate between two or more interpretations of some statute or line of cases. Then he must choose between eligible interpretations by asking which shows the community's structure of institutions and decisions – its public standards as a whole – in a better light from the standpoint of political morality. His own moral and political convictions are directly engaged. But the political judgment he must make is itself complex and will sometimes set one department of his political morality against another: his decision will reflect not only his opinions about justice and fairness but his higher-order convictions about how these ideals should be compromised when they compete. Questions of fit arise at this stage of interpretation as well, because even when an interpretation survives the threshold requirement, any infelicities of fit will count against it ... in the general balance of political virtues. Different judges will disagree about each of these issues and will accordingly take different views of what the law of their community, properly understood, really is.[39]

Three points about Dworkin's model of legal reasoning are directly relevant in this context. Firstly, his thesis rejects any version of positivism which denies that moral reasoning is an integral part of legal reasoning or which asserts that morality is irrelevant to the identification of law. Secondly, Dworkin's strong version of integrity and his exclusion of policy reasons from judicial reasoning implies acceptance of a narrower range of types of reasons as valid and a more definite hierarchy of the weight or cogency of reasons than the more open-ended schemes of MacCormick and Summers. Thirdly, like Summers's

---

35 R Dworkin, *Law's Empire* (1986), and 'Hard Cases' (1975) 87 *Harvard Law Review* 1057. See S Guest, *Ronald Dworkin* (2nd edn, 1997) chapters 7 and 8.
36 See above, pp 138ff.
37 See especially, *Law's Empire*, op cit, pp 238ff.
38 Ibid, p 255.
39 Ibid, pp 255-256.

substantive reasons, Dworkinian principles not only purport to resolve issues not determined by 'fit' or authority; they can also be used to reinterpret past authorities and the system as a whole. This potentially weakens the weight of authority reasons, especially those advanced as simple 'fiats' of the kind, 'this is the law because Parliament (or the House of Lords) has said so'.

It may be noted that all three accounts are of value in illuminating the range of reasons to which judges refer when deciding cases, but their concern with judicial reasoning should not encourage the view that they should be equated with all types of legal reasoning, nor that reasons necessarily make up the entirety of legal argumentation. It may also be noted that all three – MacCormick, Summers and Dworkin – claim to be descriptive, but they disagree on what the reality is. Likewise, although each claims to be prescribing how judges ought to decide cases, their prescriptions vary considerably. Whereas Summers accords priority to substantive reasons, which include goal reasons, Dworkin has argued that decisions should be based on principles, not on policies which prescribe goals. MacCormick, as we have seen, treats consequentialism as the basis of 'second-order justification'.

From the argument for the defence in *Allen*, let us select four of the reasons in favour of the conclusion that 'shall marry' means 'shall purportedly enter into a marriage which would have been valid but for its bigamous character':

(a) *Fanning* supports the proposition;
(b) *Burt v Burt* supports the proposition;
(c) penal statutes must be construed strictly in favour of the accused;
(d) this interpretation is the one most in harmony with the interpretation given to the words 'being married'.

Some of these reasons were of different kinds and were independent of each other: (a) and (b) were reasons based on precedents – a kind of invocation of authority; (c) was a direct appeal to a general principle of statutory construction; and (d) was an ingenious, and probably weaker argument, based indirectly on the presumption that the same word should be construed in the same sense in the same Act. One of the main arguments for the other side was of a different kind again: it was a direct appeal to the policy of the statute. These are only a few examples of the wide range of different kinds of reason which are commonly adduced in support of conclusions in interpretation.

The reasons listed above were independent of each other; that is to say, if any one of them was removed the others still stood. In a famous passage the philosopher John Wisdom put the matter as follows:

> In such cases we notice that the process of argument is not a *chain* of demonstrative reasoning. It is a presenting and re-presenting of those features of the case which *severally co-operate* in favour of the conclusion, in favour of saying what the reasoner wishes said, in favour of calling the situation by the name which he wishes to call it. *The reasons are like the legs of a chair, not the links of a chain.*[40]

---

40 J Wisdom, 'Gods', in *Proceedings of the Aristotelian Society* (1944), pp 185, 194; reprinted in A Flew (ed), *Logic and Language* (First Series, 1951), pp 187, 1995 (italics added).

The reasons for the competing interpretations in *Allen* do not constitute the whole of the argument for each side. For reasons against each conclusion are also involved. For example, where *Allen* was arguing for conclusion *C* (that 'shall marry' means 'shall purportedly enter into a marriage which would have been valid, but for its bigamous character'), one support for this argument was the Irish case *Fanning*. Part of the argument for the prosecution consists of reasons why the court should not follow this case. Here again, more than one independent reason could be advanced against following *Fanning*:

(i)   as an Irish case, it is only of persuasive authority;
(ii) it is a weak precedent because the court was divided;
(iii) the facts in *Allen* and *Fanning* are distinguishable;
(iv) *Fanning* was wrongly decided.

This is another example of what Wisdom, later in the same passage, calls '*the cumulative effect of severally inconclusive premisses*'.

Thus Wisdom's striking metaphor of the legs of a chair needs to be modified, especially if arguments of both sides are taken into account.

Whereas counsel for *Allen* was erecting legs (arguments (a), (b), (c), (d) and (e)) in support of his main conclusion (conclusion *C*), counsel for the other side was concerned to destroy or, at least weaken, their supportive effect. For example, in respect of argument (a), this relationship may be depicted thus:

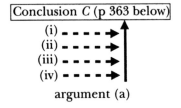

argument (a)

This model will require modification later, but it adequately depicts in simplified form the basic structure of this kind of argument.

Talk of legs of chairs and links in chains in relation to reasoning is, of course, metaphorical. Another metaphor commonly resorted to in this context is that of weighing or balancing. This is the metaphor adopted by the Norwegian jurist, Torstein Eckhoff, in a paper which, despite differences in terminology, is very close to the spirit of the analysis presented here. Distinguishing between legal rules, which state relationships between operative facts and legal consequences, and 'guiding standards' which guide reasoning in interpreting rules, Eckhoff writes:

> To know the relevant reasons is not the same as having reached a solution. The weighing of reasons still remains. This weighing is, of course, very easy when all relevant reasons pull in the same direction. But still it is a different process from that of subsuming a set of facts under a rule. And a weighing of reasons which pull in different directions can give rise to considerable doubt and scruples. ...
>   Take, for instance, principles of sentencing which I conceive of as typical examples of guiding standards. They supply answers to the question of what must

be taken into account when deciding whether an offender should be sentenced and what the sentence should be. They tell us, for instance, that the gravity of the offence and the age and record of the offender must beconsidered. But they do not determine whether a particular offender should be discharged or imprisoned, or what the length of his prison sentence should be. These questions are left to the judge who has to base his decision on a weighing of the relevant factors.

In dealing with the relations between guiding standards and judicial discretion, Eckhoff continues:

> I am inclined to believe that judges, within certain limits, are free to decide which reasons they will take into account when making evaluations. I do not say that this necessarily must be so, but I hold it to be a quite normal situation in the legal systems with which I am familiar. To be sure, there are guiding standards to the effect that certain reasons *must* be considered. But in addition to these obligatory reasons there are also arguments which are considered acceptable but not obligatory. There are, in other words, arguments to which a judge *may*, but not must, pay attention.
>
> Secondly, even in cases where only such reasons as the judge must take into account are at stake, will the weighing of pros and cons give some leeway for judicial discretion. Most guiding standards do not say anything about the weight of different reasons. And if anything is said it is, as a rule, only an approximate indication. The normal situation is, in other words, that the weight is not fixed beforehand but is determined by the decision-maker in light of the circumstances of the individual case.[41]

These guiding standards are thus similar to Dworkin's principles, except that Eckhoff does not accept the notion that there is a single right answer.

(iv)   The relations between reasons in an argument supporting a conclusion in interpretation can be very complex.

In the last diagram the 'leg' supporting conclusion *C* in *Allen* was depicted as a simple straight arrow. But this is a simplification. A more accurate depiction of the reasoning in respect of the first leg of the arguments of counsel in regard to this conclusion would be something like this:

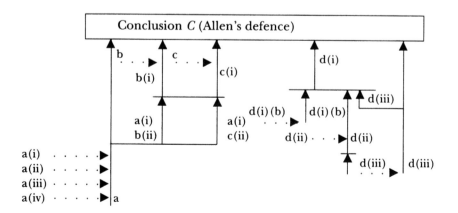

41 Eckhoff, op cit, pp 208, 217-218; see further Chapter 9, section 5.

However, even this picture simplifies. For if we were to try to make explicit every proposition and every step in reasoning in counsel's argument, the number of propositions would be greatly increased; indeed such a process of reconstruction is potentially endless. For it is characteristic of this kind of reasoning that not every step is meticulously and laboriously spelled out in practice. Legal argument, and everyday practical discourse, can often benefit in a number of ways from an economy of style that leaves a large number of inferences implicit rather than articulated. But it is an endemic weakness of the theoretical literature on legal reasoning that it regularly presents an oversimplified picture of what is an extremely intricate process. A few important steps tend to be selected and presented as the whole. Consider the number of explicit propositions and the number of implicit inferences that could be reconstructed from the judgment of Cockburn CJ in *Allen* or of Lord Buckmaster in *Donoghue v Stevenson* and ask yourself whether their reasoning is more like a chain, a chair, an intricately woven piece of cloth, a seamless web, a balancing or weighing process, or is best seen, in non-metaphorical terms, as a complex argument.

MacCormick has criticised the use of such metaphors as giving the misleading impression that legal arguments are judged by 'the exact and objective measurements of the honest butcher's scales'.[42] It is an everyday experience in law, as in other contexts such as morals or aesthetics, that preferences can and are expected to be made even though both the kinds of arguments which are or may be appropriate in the context, and the criteria upon which their relevance, cogency and acceptability are to be judged, are in various respects indeterminate. In the dialectical process which typifies legal argumentation, preferences are expressed in terms of one argument being more or less convincing, or stronger, than another; and such preferences are defensible notwithstanding that no exact and objective measurement of them is possible, so long as some criteria exist which are recognised by the disputants. The process of making and expressing choices may be conveniently described as one of balancing or weighing arguments; but we should also recognise the limits of such metaphors and remember that what we are concerned with is complex arguments.

(v)   What constitutes a valid or invalid, a good or bad, a cogent or weak, reason in an argument about interpretation varies from context to context. There are certain special features of reasoning in the context of legal interpretation that are either unique or are given more emphasis than in non-legal contexts; but there are also features that are found in both legal and non-legal contexts.

The story is told that before delivering judgment in *Donoghue v Stevenson* Lord Atkin consulted his children, telling them the facts and asking them what they thought the result should be and whom they thought their 'neighbour' was.[43] If Lord Atkin in his speech had said 'I am in favour of allowing the appeal because my daughter thinks that it is clearly just that the pursuer [plaintiff]

42 *Legal Reasoning and Legal Theory*, op cit, p 112 (2nd edn now published). See further, T Anderson and W Twining, *Analysis of Evidence* (1991), chapter 6, Section B.

should recover', or if he had quoted his children's opinion as authority for the neighbour principle, these would have been two clear examples of reasons that would not have been considered valid within this context. Similarly, if a judge says 'I find the plaintiff irresistibly attractive and accordingly cannot help but decide in her favour' or 'I find for the plaintiff, as he has offered me £100, if I do so', these would generally be considered to be *bad* reasons for his decision.

At the very end of his speech in *Donoghue v Stevenson*, Lord Atkin supports a somewhat narrower formulation of the governing principle, in the following words: 'It is a proposition that I venture to say no one in Scotland or England who was not a lawyer would for one moment doubt. It will be an advantage to make it clear that the law in this matter, as in most others, is in accordance with sound common sense.' Such appeals to common sense are not uncommon in appellate judgments. History does not relate how many people's views Lord Atkin canvassed in order to test out public opinion on the matter, but it is not impossible that his children (and his own feelings) represented most of his sample. It would probably be generally accepted that this particular reason as formulated in the speech was valid (in the sense of permissible), inconclusive, but of some persuasive force, although of a lower status in the hierarchy of legal reasoning than an argument from authority. Lord Atkin based his statement of the neighbour principle largely on an interpretation of two cases, *Heaven v Pender* and *Le Lievre v Gould*.[44] His reasons in support of this proposition are generally accepted to be permissible, inconclusive and not very cogent.

This example usefully illustrates a number of points about judicial reasoning and its relationship to reasoning in non-legal contexts.

Firstly, 'valid' in this context means permissible, but not necessarily conclusive. This applies equally in legal and non-legal contexts relating to interpretation of rules where, as we have seen, reasoning is typically of the open-system type. 'Valid' is commonly used differently in the context of closed-system reasoning, when it is normally confined to reasons that form part of a chain of arguments leading necessarily to a conclusion.

Secondly, in English law there are certain rules that determine a hierarchy of types of reason in legal contexts. Examples of such rules that we have earlier encountered include the doctrine of precedent and the rule that a provision in an Act of Parliament takes precedence over an inconsistent provision in a statutory instrument or a judicial decision. Thus in legal contexts certain kinds of reasons are conclusive, if clearly applicable, and some are more strongly persuasive than others (for instance, the House of Lords should give more weight to a decision of the Court of Appeal than to a decision of a court of first instance or a decision from another jurisdiction). Thus a distinctive feature of legal reasoning is that there are special rules concerning the validity and weight of certain types of reasons; whereas in other contexts involving interpretation of rules there are few principles or rules beyond the general principles of logic and clear thinking dealing with the validity, cogency or relative priority of different kinds of reasons.

43 E Cockburn Millar (née Atkin), 'Some Memories of Lord Atkin' (1957) 23 *Glim*, 13, 15.
44 (1883) 11 QBD 503; [1893] 1 QB 491. See [1932] AC 563, 582, chapter 1, section 9.

We have seen in previous chapters that some of these legal rules, such as the doctrine of precedent and the rules of statutory interpretation, are less determinate than might at first sight appear. Because of this indeterminacy many of the factors affecting reasoning in interpretation apply in much the same way in legal and non-legal contexts.

Thirdly, there are certain conventions of style that may vary from context to context. Thus the difference between saying 'Common sense supports this conclusion' and 'My daughter, who is a very sensible girl, supports this conclusion' may not be very different analytically, but clearly one is stylistically appropriate to the context, and the other is not. Conversely, in an ordinary domestic situation an ingenious and cogent lawyer-like argument by a child to his parents might backfire precisely because it is lawyer-like and hence inappropriate – for Father might respond: 'We don't want any barrack-room lawyers *here*.'

(vi)   Advocacy, in both legal and non-legal contexts, typically involves a combination of rational and non-rational means of persuasion.

So far in this chapter we have been concerned with analysis of typical modes of *reasoning* in interpretation; but not all argument in this kind of context is purely rational in the sense that it is based solely on appeals to reason, as contrasted with appeals to emotion, to the will, to intuition, to common sense and so on. For example, the task of the advocate is to persuade people to decide or to act in certain ways: and reasoning is only one of a whole range of methods of persuasion. A realistic approach to processes of interpretation needs to give due weight to this fact and to recognise that, from a psychological point of view, it is artificial to draw sharp distinctions between rational and non-rational factors in persuasion and decision-making. The good advocate needs not only to be skilful in rational argument; she also needs some psychological insight.

Appellate judicial processes place more emphasis on procedures designed to maximise rationality than almost any other kind of decision-making: questions of fact are normally separated from questions of law and are treated as settled; the issues are carefully identified and framed in advance; there are fairly elaborate rules defining the validity and force of different types of argument; the ethics of advocacy and the tradition of elaborate, public, reasoned justification for decision are among the factors that are thought to uphold honesty and rationality in argument and decision.[45]

Yet in cases involving a doubt on a question of law, argument by both advocates and judges may consist of a combination of rational and non-rational factors. It is beyond the scope of this work to explore the pyschology of decision-making or to enter into the controversy about the degree of rationality that is to be found in judicial processes. But the general point can be illustrated quite simply by a few examples.

---

45 See generally S Toulmin, *The Uses of Argument* (1958); K Llewellyn, *The Common Law Tradition* (1960); and JAC Brown, *Techniques of Persuasion* (1963).

As regards advocacy, consider three rules of thumb which almost invariably appear in discussions of the art of appellate advocacy: (a) study the particular court; (b) 'always go for the jugular vein' (alias, the principle of concentration of fire); (c) 'the statement of facts is the heart'.[46]

Each of these standard pieces of advice is based on psychological assumptions about the nature of persuasion. The first is obvious: individuals, including judges, will be more susceptible to persuasion by some arguments than others. The advocate addressing an unfamiliar court or a varied bench of judges is likely to be at a disadvantage compared with one who is addressing a single judge whom he has encountered often before, for he is in a better position to predict likely reactions to particular lines of argument.

A famous American advocate, John W Davis, put the second point as follows:

> More often than not there is in every case a cardinal point around which lesser points revolve like planets around the sun, or even as dead moons around a planet; a central fortress which is strongly held will make the loss of all the outworks immaterial. The temptation is always present 'to let no guilty point escape' in the hope that if one hook breaks another may hold.[47]

The psychology of this is also fairly obvious: it is better not to distract attention from your best point; a cumulative argument tends to be more persuasive than a series of disconnected points; and a succinct, forceful argument is likely to be more effective than a long-winded one that includes weak as well as strong points. The importance of this advice will vary according to the context: it is more directly applicable in the United States, where appellate argument is based to a large extent on written briefs, supplemented by oral presentation, than in most other common law jurisdictions where argument is for the most part presented orally in court.

The third rule of thumb is the most interesting, not least because it illustrates the artificiality of rigidly separating fact and value in the context of persuasion. The gist of the advice is that the manner in which the facts are presented can have more persuasive force than any abstract argument. Lord Atkin's daughter acknowledges this rather charmingly when she says of her father: 'When he gave us the facts of a case and asked us what we thought about it, his way of presenting the problem was such that there was never any suggestion in our minds that the other side could have a leg to stand on.'[48]

John W Davis put the matter this way: '[I]t cannot be too often emphasised that in an appellate court the statement of the facts is not merely a part of the argument, it is more often than not the argument itself'.[49]

The judgments of, for example, Lord Atkin and Lord Denning provide ample illustrations of this point, which helps to explain the phenomenon of

---

46 On the art of advocacy, see Appendix I, section H, question 17, pp 410-411, and Appendix IV, pp 441-442. See also W Twining, *Rethinking Evidence* (1994), chapter 7.

47 J Davis, 'The Argument of an Appeal' (1940), reprinted in *Jurisprudence in Action* (Association of the Bar of the City of New York, 1953), p 183.

48 Op cit, p 15.

49 Op cit, p 181.

common law judges stating the facts more than once during the course of a single judgment. Consider the persuasive force of this famous example:

> Did the accountants owe a duty of care to the plaintiff? … They were professional accountants who prepared and put before him these accounts, knowing that he was going to be guided by them in making an investment in the company. On the faith of these accounts he did make the investment whereas if the accounts had been carefully prepared, he would not have made the investment at all. The result is that he has lost his money.[50]

In our experience most law students find this virtually irresistible. It is misleading to suggest that telling a story in a persuasive manner involves a simple appeal to emotion rather than to reason. For it is not difficult to articulate reasons, in the form of implicit principles, why this is an appealing characterisation of the situation. But, it is also an error to suggest that appellate advocates and judges never resort to direct appeals to emotion: read through the speeches of Lord Buckmaster and Lord Atkin in *Donoghue v Stevenson* and identify the emotive words and phrases used in them.

One final point: we have seen that it is possible to point to clear cases of valid and invalid reasons, reasons that are stronger than others, and of styles of argument that are inappropriate to a particular context; but even in the relatively formal context of legal interpretation in the courtroom, the criteria of validity, of cogency and of appropriateness are vague - this is in an area where the penumbra covers more territory than the core. For this reason advocates, judges and other interpreters are called on to exercise 'good judgment' in choosing which reasons to emphasise and which to play down or drop entirely. Those who seek an easy recipe for this are recommended to turn to *Poor Richard's Almanack*: 'At twenty years of age the will reigns, at thirty, the wit; and at forty, the judgment'.[51]

5 Lawyers' reasonings

So far in discussing reasoning and interpretation we have focused almost exclusively on the standpoints of the appellate advocate and the judge in legal proceedings. What of other interpreters? If we look at the events and legal arguments in *Allen* from a number of other standpoints, it may help to see how fairly highly structured legal argument relates to the kinds of reasoning that are appropriate at other points in the process.

Firstly, the standpoint of the legislator or other rule-maker: questions about the nature of the mischief and whether there is any need for a separate offence of bigamy have already been touched on. *Allen* revealed a fault in drafting, in the shape of an unnecessary ambiguity, but it also had the effect of eliminating the ambiguity for the future. Part of the reasoning in *Allen* related to what the

---

50 *Candler v Crane, Christmas & Co* [1951] 2 KB 164, 176, per Denning LJ (dissenting); and see Appendix I, section H, question 14, p 409.
51 B Franklin, *Poor Richard's Almanack* (1741).

law *ought to be*, strictly speaking, the kind of reasoning appropriate to this kind of question should be the same, irrespective of the person who is advancing the argument.[52] But in practice the appropriateness of a particular line of argument will be judged in part by contextual factors: arguments concerning what the law ought to be tend to be inhibited by a number of factors in forensic and analogous contexts, such as considerations of relevancy to the issues in the present case, the patience of the court and the constraints of arguing within the framework of existing well-settled doctrine; whereas arguments in a more general legislative context tend to be more free-ranging. Thus one aspect of the arguments in *Allen* overlaps with the kind of reasoning appropriate for deciding what the law of bigamy should be for the future.

Secondly, the standpoint of the prosecutor at the time of the decision on whether or not to prosecute: clearly interpretation of the relevant rule(s) is only one of a number of factors to be taken into account in deciding whether or not to prosecute a suspected bigamist and, more generally, in deciding on a policy respecting when to prosecute in bigamy cases. We do not know on what grounds the decision to prosecute Allen was taken: that there was a doubt about the law may have come as a surprise to the prosecution; it may have provided a welcome opportunity to seek clarification of the law (a test case, as it were), or the prosecution may have been brought in spite of the doubt. The relevant point here is that legal reasoning in the narrow sense is relevant to, but is only one aspect of, the reasoning appropriate to decisions to prosecute.

Another interesting standpoint for present purposes is that of Allen himself and his advisers. Consider the position of a friend of Allen, who has some practical legal knowledge, and who is called on to advise him as a friend, without any of the ethical or other professional inhibitions that might affect the approach of a practising lawyer in this situation. Let us first take the decision whether or not to go through the ceremony with Harriet Crouch (W3). The crucial question for Allen at this moment is that of the Bad Man: 'if I go through this ceremony, what will happen to me?' The law reports do not tell us whether Harriet knew of Allen's subsisting marriage, why Allen wanted to marry her (or if he really did) and whether either party in fact realised that their marriage would be void anyway (although they were presumed to know the law). Nor do we have enough information from the report to make confident predictions about the likelihood of detection, or of a decision to prosecute, or of the prosecution being able to adduce sufficient evidence to secure a conviction, or about the kind of sentence to be expected in the kind of case (in 1872) if Allen were to be convicted. Yet all these factors are relevant considerations for advising Allen about the decision whether to go through the ceremony with Harriet; if his decision is reasoned, the appropriate kinds of reasoning will by no means be confined to the factors that potentially formed part of the legal argument.

---

52 Dworkin would argue that the question is not what the law *ought* to be, but what it is: the duty of courts is to confirm existing rights. Secondly he would argue that where there is doubt as to what those rights are; the only legitimate arguments are those based upon principles; see above pp 360-361.

As to the specifically legal issues, Allen is presumed to know the law. What does this imply? Firstly, that he can confidently predict that his 'marriage' to Harriet would be held to be void. Secondly, that the law is unclear as to whether going through the ceremony with her would amount to bigamy in law. Suppose that Allen had in fact heard of *Fanning* from friends and, relying on it, had decided to go through the ceremony (after all, he was presumed to know *Fanning*). Does that make the court's decision unjust? Could such a consideration be plausibly woven into counsel's argument on his behalf at an appropriate stage?[53]

Now, let us move to a later point in time: he has been arrested and charged and is due to appear before Baron Martin at the Hampshire Assizes. Perhaps the main questions for Allen (and his legal advisers) are: should he plead guilty or not guilty? If not guilty, what strategy should he adopt? These appear to be questions on which Allen could reasonably expect advice from his professional legal advisers. What kinds of factors should be taken into account in framing advice on these questions? Or, to put the matter differently, what kinds of reason and reasoning would it be appropriate for lawyers to adopt in this context? Clearly it is not identical with the reasoning appropriate to answering the narrow and specific issue of law reserved by Baron Martin. But by this stage in the process the issues have been narrowed and defined more closely, and there is more overlap between arguments of counsel and the reasonings of his advisers.

Thus 'legal reasoning' in the narrow sense of reasoning on a doubtful question of law in the courtroom is only one part of lawyers' reasonings; it occurs in relatively pure forms in certain artificially defined contexts: appellate argument, counsel's opinion on a point of law, law examinations and so on. But it also has a role to play in other contexts as part of other kinds of practical decision-making, such as Allen's decision about whether to go through the ceremony, or whether or not to plead guilty and also, possibly, at the sentencing stage. There is a certain artificiality in isolating reasoning on questions of law in their purest form: not only does this give a false sense of how such reasoning operates in practice, but also there is a real danger that such a separation may also direct attention away from other aspects of lawyers' reasonings, such as reasoning towards conclusions of fact, reasoning about sanctions or reasoning in the process of bargaining; and these may be at least as important in practice and at least as interesting from a theoretical point of view.[54]

6 Epilogue: towards a theory of legal interpretation?

In a brilliant article entitled 'How to Read the Civil Rights Act,' Ronald Dworkin argues that in dealing with problems of interpreting statutes in hard cases, judges need a 'theory of legislation', that is, 'a theory of how to determine

---

53 On the retrospective effect of a judicial decision generally and in respect of statutory provisions of uncertain penal effect, see above, pp 264 and 323ff.
54 For exercises on chapter 10, see Appendix 1, section H.

what legal rights and duties [the legislature] has established when it enacts a particular set of sentences'.[55] Anglo-American writers who have advocated literal or liberal approaches to interpretation could be said to be advancing prescriptive theories of legislative interpretation. Sir Rupert Cross, in his attempt to combine the literal and liberal approaches in a single principle, was not merely expounding rules of interpretation; he also claimed that this is the correct way for judges and others to approach the task.[56] Similarly, though sometimes on a grander scale, civilian writers tend to conceive the primary function of the legal scientist in this area as being the development of prescriptive theories of interpretation. The same might also be said of some writers on international law and on the law of the European Union.[57]

Recently, increasing attention has also been paid to legislation from a sociological perspective and there have been calls for the development of sociological theories of legislation, dealing with how legislative rules are made, with their implementation, impact and other aspects of how they operate in practice, and with interpretation of legislation seen as a form of behaviour.[58] There has been a substantial number of detailed studies on the creation and emergence of norms in general and of particular statutes; there is a developed, though controversial, body of 'impact studies', but there have been relatively few detailed sociological studies of interpretation. It is probably also true to say that general sociological theories of legislation are still in their infancy.

The purpose of this book has been to provide a broader approach to the art of interpreting rules than traditional works on 'legal method', first, by viewing the handling of rules as a basic human art and, secondly, by emphasising the importance of understanding the nature and context of interpretation as a foundation for developing the relevant general skills. We have examined rules as responses to problems, the nature of rules in general, how and why problems of interpretation arise, what is involved in reasoning about competing interpretations in legal and other contexts, and the special factors that have to be taken into account in interpreting cases and statutes in common law jurisdictions, especially England and Wales. Three general themes have been given special emphasis: that the main conditions that give rise to problems of

---

55 R Dworkin, 'How to Read the Civil Rights Act', *New York Review of Books*, 20 December 1979, p 37.

56 J Bell and G Engle, *Cross on Statutory Interpretation*, op cit, pp 1-2, 46-47. Similarly, Bennion's impressive *Statutory Interpretation*, op cit, is both descriptive and prescriptive.

57 On international law, see, for example, M McDougal, H Lasswell and J Miller, *The Interpretation of Agreements and World Public Order* (1967). On the law of the European Union, see, for example, H Kutscher, 'Methods of Interpretation as seen by a Judge at the Court of Justice' in *Reports of the Judicial and Academic Conference of the Court of Justice of the European Communities* (1976), and A Bredimas, *Methods of Interpretation and Community Law* (1978). Continental writers such as Jhering and Geny have argued elaborate, though conflicting, prescriptive theories for the interpretation of codes of law. See Lenhof, 'On Interpretative Theories: A Comparative Study on Legislation' (1949) 27 *Texas Law Review* 312. A major comparative study of statutory interpretation is DN MacCormick and R Summers (eds), *Interpreting Statutes: A Comparative Study* (1991). See further Appendix IV.

58 See R Tomasic, 'The Sociology of Legislation', in R Tomasic (ed), *Legislation and Society in Australia* (1980), p 19 and 'Towards a Theory of Legislation: Some Conceptual Obstacles', [1985] *Statute Law Review* 84. See further Appendix IV.

interpretation in legal contexts also arise in many non-legal contexts; that what constitutes an appropriate interpretation is relative to the situation, role and objectives of the particular interpreter; and that in order to understand and interpret any rule it needs to be looked at in the context of the situation and problems which led to its creation and of the processes in which it operates in practice. This emphasis on the situation of interpreters and the background of rules to be interpreted, together with a greater emphasis on problems than on rules, justifies calling our general approach 'contextual'. This leaves open the questions whether we have advanced a theory of interpretation, if so what kind, and if not, why not? It may be appropriate to conclude by addressing these questions.

It should be clear that no attempt has been made here to present an empirical theory of legislation of the kind advocated by Tomasic and others. The focus has been on the art of interpretation rather than on describing and explaining the behaviour of rule-makers and interpreters. Nevertheless, we have drawn, directly and indirectly, on the work of Alfred Schutz, RG Collingwood and Karl Llewellyn, as well as on recent sociological and other writings on law. Some of the ingredients of the context of interpretation as we have depicted it will be familiar to sociologists of law: the pervasiveness and variety of rules; the relativity of social problems and their definitions; the significance of process, standpoint, role and purpose in interpretation; the uses and limitations of naive instrumentalism and of simple rationalistic models; the notions that rules come into existence in a variety of ways; that they are often instruments of power, but yet they can be the products of negotiation, compromise or incremental growth rather than conscious rational creation; that their significance may be expressive, symbolic, instrumental or aspirational, or a combination of these; that rules are not self-enforcing, and do not necessarily or even often have direct impact on behaviour or attitudes in a simple relation of cause and effect; that the creation and interpretation of rules may take place in a context where conflict or consensus or something in between predominates; that individuals and groups are often subject to multiple systems of rules, but that to talk of 'systems' often involves fiction or hyperbole; that it is difficult to avoid talking of rules as if they were things, yet such 'reifying' talk often serves to obscure an underlying indeterminacy and complexity in the real world. Some of these ideas are familiar and are elaborated with great sophistication in the literature; others await further development. Thus this book has not attempted to develop a general theory of legislation, but it has drawn on relevant literature in a variety of disciplines and we hope that, in turn, it may provide one possible jumping-off point for further exploration of that literature.

What of a prescriptive theory of interpretation? If by this is meant a recommended set of rules or procedures which it is claimed will yield right or correct answers in particular cases, then no such theory is advanced here. We do not believe that there is one right answer in hard cases or that problems of interpretation can be solved primarily by rules. However, some general advice has been offered to interpreters: clarify your standpoint and objectives; consider the nature and characteristics of the material to be interpreted; diagnose the conditions that have given rise to the puzzlement or problem; identify the range of plausible or possible interpretations in this context, and consider what arguments might be advanced for and against each alternative; differentiate problems of interpretation from problems of locating or identifying potentially applicable rules and, in particular, do not conflate puzzlements about rules and about roles.

We have also suggested a general intellectual procedure for approaching statutes, subordinate legislation, and similar instruments. This can be succinctly restated as follows: after clarifying your standpoint and objectives and assembling a 'package' of relevant material, find your way round the instrument as a whole (if necessary with the aid of an algorithm); then anchor the problem of interpretation precisely in a specific word or words in the text; consider the word(s) in the context of the clause, the section and the instrument as a whole, including the general design that can be extracted from within its four corners; articulate the competing meanings of the words to be interpreted and consider these in the context of the instrument itself, of evidence of its general background and its purposes, of general principles and of analogous or otherwise relevant rules. Eliminate possible interpretations that would produce absurd results at a general level (eg that 'shall marry' means 'shall validly marry') and, perhaps, in this particular case. Then diagnose carefully the condition(s) giving rise to the present doubt, and from these proceed to construct arguments for and against each of the competing interpretations. Following such advice should often narrow the range of possibilities, sometimes to a point where there is only one serious alternative. This procedure points in a general direction, but it does not amount to a fully developed theory either of interpretation in general or of judicial interpretation in particular.

Why have we not gone further? This question needs to be answered at a number of different, though related, levels. One reason is simply a matter of the objectives of this book: it is intended as an introduction to its subject; to echo IA Richards, the main aim has been to help to understand some of the difficulties in the way of interpreting rules rather than to provide a recipe, if such were possible. This in part represents a reaction against over-generalised recipes – facile prescriptions based on too little diagnosis; but it also stems from a concern to bring out the pervasiveness of problems of interpretation in the everyday world of affairs in contrast with the tendency to emphasise the unique features of legal interpretation. Our concern has been to emphasise the generality of problems and the particularity of appropriate solutions.

Nearly all of the theories mentioned in the opening paragraph of this section are narrowly focused theories of *legal* interpretation, whereas our concern has been broader in that we have tried to explore at least some connections between interpreting rules in legal and non-legal contexts, without claiming to deal with all types of interpretation. The contrast is even greater because most standard legal theories are either explicitly or implicitly theories of *judicial* interpretation, whereas we have been concerned to emphasise the problems of a wide range of different participants in legal and other processes. Thus, although this is intended as an introduction, it is rather more broadly focused than most jurisprudential treatments of the subject. But, it might be objected, surely judicial interpretation is the central case of legal interpretation and, as such, ought to be the primary concern of lawyers and law students? It is undoubtedly true that judicial interpretation has special claims to our attention, not only because of the authority and finality of judicial decisions, but also because how judges have interpreted or will interpret particular legal rules has a direct bearing on the concerns of other actors, including the good citizen, the Bad Man, the expositor, the cautious solicitor, the advocate, the administrator, and the agent of enforcement - whether official or otherwise. Actual and potential judicial interpretations cast a long shadow even on those legal questions which rarely, if ever, come before the courts. Also, judicial decisions represent the paradigm case of correct, authoritative interpretation. Nevertheless the centrality of judges has been greatly exaggerated in the past, with the result that other factors have been overlooked or neglected. Judicial rulings and reasonings are only part of a variety of relevant factors, the relative importance of which depends on the particular context of interpretation.

There is another reason for not concentrating exclusively on judicial interpretation. Questions of role and objectives are intimately related to the activity of interpreting, but it is important for clarity of thought to differentiate between puzzlements about the former (Who am I? What am I trying to do?) and genuine puzzlements about interpretation, attributable to one or more conditions of doubt, such as ambiguity of wording, indeterminacy of purpose, or changes in circumstances since the creation of the rule. It happens that 'the proper role of the judge' is one of the most intractable issues of jurisprudence; accordingly for purposes of exposition some difficulties of interpretation are more easily understood if one adopts a less problematic standpoint, such as that of the advocate or the Bad Man. This point was stressed in relation to the *ratio decidendi* because much of the traditional debate, in our view, has its roots in puzzlements about the proper role of judges rather than in what is involved in reading cases intelligently. The same considerations apply to other aspects of legal interpretation, because interpretation is typically part of some broader activity.

It follows from the above that a rounded prescriptive theory of judicial interpretation involves a theory of adjudication or, at the very least, a clear conception of judicial role. Here we agree with Dworkin, as we do on the point that in difficult cases the resolution of doubts in interpretation (and particular justifications for such resolutions) often, if not always, presupposes some theory of political morality. We would suggest that a theory of legislative interpretation also requires an adequate way of classifying types of statutes (and other documents), at least to the extent that the very different kinds of attitudes, techniques and other interpretive baggage that, for instance, are associated with written constitutions, commercial codes, taxing statutes and international conventions – what we have referred to as the specialist subcultures – are adequately differentiated. We have not attempted to develop a theory of adjudication, a theory of political morality or a taxonomy of legislation in this book; accordingly a rounded theory of judicial interpretation is beyond its scope.

7 Literary analogies, radical indeterminacy and noble dreams

In recent years jurisprudence has witnessed an explosion of interest in interpretation from a variety of perspectives and disciplines.[59] Here we shall only touch briefly on three related strands that bear directly on themes of this book in order to indicate our general position in relation to each.

Firstly, as part of a more general 'Law and Literature Movement', analogies between legal and literary interpretation have been extensively canvassed and debated. The central question from our standpoint is: what are the similarities and the differences between interpreting literary and artistic texts, such as novels, poems, plays or musical scores, and interpreting authoritative legal texts such as cases and statutes?[60]

Most commentators would concede some obvious differences. For example, cases, statutes and constitutions contain authoritative prescriptions, whereas works of literature and art generally do not. Furthermore, interpretation by judges and other officials is an integral part of the exercise of power by people whose decisions typically have direct practical consequences on the lives of others. The consequences of the interpretive choices of, for example, producers of plays, conductors of orchestras, scholarly commentators or readers, tend to be qualitatively different. The enterprises of legal and literary interpretation normally take place in dissimilar contexts. Thus, generally speaking, literary (or artistic) and legal interpretation involve activities in which the setting, the nature of the texts, the point of the enterprise and its consequences are all significantly different.

At first sight, then, the analogy seems unpromising. However, one needs to beware of the dangers of over-generalisation (note, for example, the number of qualifiers in the preceding paragraph). Legal interpretation involves a variety of actors (and others) pursuing different purposes in many contexts. The same is true of artistic and literary interpretation. There are clear differences between Brendel interpreting a Beethoven sonata in a public concert and the Lord Chief Justice of England and Wales interpreting the Offences against the Person Act 1861 in *Allen* or *Taylor*. There seems to be a rather closer analogy between a review of a recent novel in the *New York Review of Books* and a critical article by Ronald Dworkin in the same journal commenting on a recent decision of the United States Supreme Court. But to what extent are these comparable in respect of their underlying conceptions of interpretation?

Even in respect of paradigm cases of judicial and literary interpretation there are important similarities. Often, but not always, both are concerned to elicit meaning from canonical texts. It is striking, but not entirely surprising, that legal and literary theories of interpretation tend to cluster around three 'ideal types': those that emphasise the text itself; those that emphasise the historical context of the text, including the author's concerns and the broader

---

59 See Appendix IV, pp 438-442.
60 See D Miers, 'Legal Theory and the Interpretation of Statutes' in W Twining (ed), *Legal Theory and the Common Law* (1986), chapter 7.

historical setting; and those that emphasise the active role and relative freedom of the interpreter to attribute meaning to the text or even to 'construct' it. In literary theory (and theology) extensive, sometimes acrimonious, debates have surrounded the relative priorities that should be given to the text, the historical context, and the situation and creative role of interpreters. As we have seen in respect of statutory interpretation, both judges and jurists have differed about the weight to be attached to the actual language used in a text, to the historical background and reasons for its creation, and to the role of a subsequent interpreter in making sense of the text at a different time and in a different context.

In practice, in both law and literature, few theories of interpretation fit one ideal type to the exclusion of the others. Disagreements appear to be mainly about priorities and emphasis. However, deeper differences lie beneath the surface. For example, a 'strict constructionist', by attaching special importance to the words actually used, may be making dubious or wrong assumptions about the nature of language, for example about the extent to which words have single, precise, settled meanings that can be established by 'literal' interpretation. The motives for such postures may be political: a judge may adopt a strict construction as a way of limiting, or seeming to limit, the extent of his or her discretion and may seek to justify this in terms of some conception of democracy.[61]

Similarly, those who emphasise context may be taking a lot for granted about the existence of a clear historical intention or purpose,[62] about the feasibility of discovering what it was, or about its relevance to determining the meaning of the text. They too may have political or other ulterior motives for rooting interpretation in the past. Those who favour 'constructive', 'liberal' or 'free' interpretation in legal contexts are not only emphasising that interpreting is an activity involving choice, but are also making judgments about the desirability of using the past (text or context) to constrain or guide such matters in law, literature and theology, but these seductive analogies need to be treated with great caution. In particular, we are sceptical about the value of wholesale importation into legal contexts of concepts and arguments developed for different purposes in quite different settings. Often they obscure more than they illuminate.

Next, there is the question of indeterminacy. Critical legal scholars, drawing in part on 'deconstructionist' techniques associated with French intellectuals such as Derrida and Barthes, have revived some old issues in fresh ways; in particular, to what extent are judges and other interpreters free to interpret and apply legal texts as they please?[63] It is doubtful whether many critical legal theorists subscribe unreservedly to extreme forms of 'radical indeterminacy', such as the view that there are no constraints on interpretation in most standard legal contexts. However, they have usefully posed some sharp questions about the nature and extent of textual and contextual constraints on 'free interpretation'.

---

61 For example, R Bork, 'Neutral Principles and First Amendment Problems' (1971) 47 *Indiana Law Journal* 1; R Dworkin, *Law's Empire* (1986), pp 450-451.
62 See chapter 5, section 2.
63 See Appendix IV, p 442.

Again, we suggest that strong versions of indeterminacy or free interpretation deserve to be treated with caution. We accept that interpretation is an activity involving choice, that there are many conditions that can give rise to puzzlement or doubts in interpretation, and that in guiding, evaluating or arguing for a particular interpretation it is important to take account of the situation, role and purpose of the interpreter. However, it does not follow that there cannot or should not be important constraints on freedom to choose or construct interpretations, nor that there are no clear cases. In our view, the extent and nature of the leeways and constraints facing a particular interpreter are largely dependent on context, and this too is subject to interpretation. Focusing on the situation of any particular interpreter is the beginning but not the end of wisdom.

Thirdly, Ronald Dworkin has contributed to some of these debates, but he has also gone further in advancing the thesis that law is itself an 'interpretive concept';[64] that is, that law and legal practice are generally best understood by adopting an interpretive point of view that is rooted in political morality. In short, one can understand what the law is only by looking at what it ought to be from the perspective of a normative political theory.

We have already touched on some of Dworkin's ideas. Here, we shall only briefly consider one further aspect of his work: the idea that interpretation aims at understanding a phenomenon in 'the best possible light' or making the text 'the best it can be'.[65] It is possible to treat this particular thesis as being so abstract as to be merely banal, for example, by adding the words, 'from the point of view of the interpreter'. We prefer to treat it as making a more substantial and provocative claim. Dworkin's argument draws directly on an analogy with literature. Imagine a disagreement about whether *Hamlet* is better interpreted as being 'about' delay or incest or death or politics or baseball.[66] What is the nature of the disagreement and how might it be resolved? Dworkin's answer is that the best interpretation is one that both fits the text (at least to the extent of maintaining the identity of the play) and makes it the best it can be according to some general aesthetic theory. Thus it might be hard to argue that it was about baseball, because of fit, but there would be scope for reasoned discussion of the merits of the other interpretations. After mature consideration agreement might be reached, for example, that the most aesthetically pleasing or profound interpretation centred on death or on a combination of two or three themes. Similarly, the best interpretation by a judge of a statute or precedent is the one that both fits the text and all the relevant authoritative sources in this legal system and has the strongest justification in the principles of political morality underpinning that system. Dworkin's main point seems to be that a disagreement about *Hamlet* or a legal

---

64 *Law's Empire*, op cit.
65 Ibid, chapter 2. See also R Dworkin, 'Law as Interpretation' (1982) 60 *Texas Law Review* 527; Miers, op cit.
66 Dworkin, ibid. This is a liberal and charitable reading of Dworkin's use of Hamlet. The example of baseball illustrates Dworkin's point about 'identity': a production which presented Hamlet as a moody pitcher and Polonius as a coach might be difficult to construct unless it bore the same relationship to Shakespeare as *West Side Story* to *Romeo and Juliet*, that is, a work of art inspired by, but having a separate identity from, the original.

text is thus susceptible to rational argument in terms of appeals to its fit with relevant material and to its justification in terms of the most appropriate normative theory.

This is one possible view of what is involved in interpreting and arguing about the merits of different interpretations in both law and literature. Dworkin's theory has been the subject of extensive criticism and debate, which cannot be pursued here.[67] We shall confine ourselves to a single point. A general thesis of this book is that interpretation is relative to standpoint and context. In our view Dworkin's conception of interpretation fits some contexts better than others.

Let us revert briefly to literary analogies. Dworkin's notion of the best interpretation of *Hamlet* fits one kind of literary criticism, which one might find, for example, in an extra-mural class or in the context of planning an amateur production of the play. The text is taken on its own terms and the best interpretation of it is constructed in terms of some implicit or explicit aesthetic theory. There is even some scope for criticism within this narrow framework by suggesting, for example, that the text could have been even better than its best interpretation if the ending had been different.

This is clearly one possible way of interpreting *Hamlet* (or some legal texts) for certain purposes. It only captures one small part of Shakespeare scholarship, much of which is concerned with interpretation in other senses. And it assumes an essentially sympathetic and largely uncritical relationship with the text.

This is surely only one kind of literary interpretation. Take, for example, a work entitled *How to Read Donald Duck* by Dorfman and Mittelart.[68] This is a hostile critique of some Walt Disney publications from a Marxist perspective. It argues, *inter alia*, that the texts in question are full of racist, sexist and bourgeois stereotypes and prejudices; that they both assume and promote imperialist, capitalist and fascistic values; and that they are full of internal 'contradictions'. Whether or not this reading is close to the texts and is in any sense charitable, it would be strange to say that it is not an interpretation. One doubts whether Dworkin would take that view. But it is also strange to suggest that the authors are making Disney's texts 'the best they can be'. One does not need to be a Marxist to find this illuminating. By asking questions about the portrayal of female characters, power relations and implicit values, the authors may change our perceptions of Disney productions or give us a basis for rationalising what was previously an instinctive dislike.

Asking questions about the values and assumptions underlying a text or an institution or a practice or about other features which make us see the object in a new light is one form of interpretation. This is an activity concerned with exploring the nature, meaning and significance of texts and other objects in a critical way. This too is only one kind of interpretation, but it is an important one and it is difficult to reconcile with Dworkin's approach. His conception of interpretation asks us to look at law and legal practices from an aspirational, participatory point of view. This may well fit some standpoints admirably; but

---

67 See Appendix IV, p 442.
68 A Dorfman and A Mittelart, *How to Read Donald Duck: Imperialist Ideology and the Disney Comic* (trs D Kunzle, 1975).

on its own it is not adequate, for example, for the Bad Man or a tax consultant or a relatively detached foreign observer, let alone for a radical critic who rejects the basic values of a given system.[69] Washing the law in cynical acid, casting a cold eye on how people in fact exercise power or manipulate rules, satirising or parodying or lambasting certain practices, or seeking to give an account of a given legal system or particular legal phenomena in a relatively detached way in order to describe or understand, all require a variety of lenses in addition to rose-tinted ones. Constructive interpretation may indeed be a noble dream for some, and radical indeterminacy a nightmare,[70] but these are only two of the visions of law and of interpretation to be found in our existing stock of theories, let alone in possible other ones.

Have we advanced a theory of legal interpretation? Is such a theory either feasible or desirable? We began this book with a quotation from IA Richards, which might be taken as suggesting scepticism about feasibility: 'Neither this book *nor any other* ... can give a recipe for discovering what the page *really* says.' Is this scepticism of one right answer or of more than that? Here analogies with literature are illuminating, at least up to a point. Debates as to whether there is a correct or best way of interpreting a novel or a poem (or the Bible or a musical score) may throw some light on the question: is there a correct way of interpreting legal rules? This is a perennially controversial area: there are rigorists and liberals in theology and literature as well as law; recent conflicts between structuralists, historicists and others may serve to remind us that pluralism in literature is a widely subscribed option, but one that has not gone unchallenged. There is, too, a view with a respectable ancestry that accepts no single theory of literary interpretation as paramount, yet implies that this does not necessarily involve commitment to the extreme relativist position that there are no standards of criticism. Our view of legal interpretation is rather like that. It might be termed moderate relativism: we are sceptical of the claim that there is one right answer to every problem of interpretation, but that does not imply that there are never clear cases or better answers; we are sceptical of the notion that legal interpretation can best be studied through the doctrine of precedent and the rules of interpretation, rather than through analysis of problems set in the context of relevant processes, roles, standpoints and techniques, and of the nature of the materials and texts to be interpreted. Finally, we are sceptical of the idea that it is either feasible or desirable to develop a prescriptive theory of interpretation that will be *determinative* of all or even a significant number of seriously contested questions; but that is not to say that nothing can be done to elucidate the nature of some of the more common problems nor to give some general guidance as to how to set about tackling them. In that limited sense this book has tried to lay a foundation for such a theory.

69 W Twining, 'Other People's Power' (1997) 63 *Brooklyn Law Review* 189.
70 HLA Hart, 'American Jurisprudence through English Eyes: the Nightmare and the Noble Dream' in *Essays in Jurisprudence and Philosophy* (1983), chapter 4.

Appendix I

Supplementary Material and Exercises

Note. The material in this Appendix is designed to bring out and develop points dealt with in the text and to give practice in using some basic skills in rule-handling. Some require only a few minutes to complete, others will take much longer; a few involve use of a law library. We have devised a substantial number of questions in order to give teachers, students and other readers an element of choice.

Note to teachers. Some of the exercises are based on material readily available in either a paper or an electronic law library. We have therefore not included all of the lengthy extracts that were in the third edition.

Section A   Chapter 1

Section A1   Mapping law: an exercise

1. Draw a map of the main legal orders in the world in 1999.
2. Draw an historical chart of the rise (and fall) of the main legal cultures in the world.
3. What is the basis for 1 and 2 and what is the relationship between them?

Section A2   Pluralism: Newspaper exercise (a variant)

Buy a weekday edition of a leading broadsheet newspaper, such as *The Times, The Independent, The Guardian, Financial Times* or *The Daily Telegraph.* Read the *whole* paper and mark any item that involves Global (G, including space), Transnational (T), International (I), Regional (R), non-state local (L), or Foreign domestic (F) relations that might have legal implications involving some legal order(s) other than United Kingdom law. Before starting define what you mean by 'legal order' for the purpose of this exercise.

Section A3   Prison rules

Immediately following the Rules concerning visitors and letters (chapter 1, section 4.3.4), the Prison Rules make provision for prisoners' access to legal advice:

37 Legal advisers
(1)   The legal adviser of a prisoner in any legal proceedings, civil or criminal, to which the prisoner is a party shall be afforded reasonable facilities for interviewing him in connection with those proceedings, and may do so out of hearing but in the sight of an officer.
(2)   A prisoner's legal adviser may, with the leave of the Secretary of State, interview the prisoner in connection with any other legal business in the sight and hearing of an officer.

37A Further facilities in connection with legal proceedings
(1) A prisoner who is a party to any legal proceedings may correspond with his legal adviser in connection with the proceedings and unless the Governor has reason to suppose that any such correspondence contains matter not relating to the proceedings it shall not be read or stopped under Rule 33(3) of these Rules.
(2) A prisoner shall on request be provided with any writing materials necessary for the purposes of paragraph (1) of this Rule.
(3) Subject to any directions given in the particular case by the Secretary of State, a registered medical practitioner selected by or on behalf of such a prisoner as aforesaid shall be afforded reasonable facilities for examining him in connection with the proceedings, and may do so out of hearing but in the sight of an officer.
(4) Subject to any directions of the Secretary of State, a prisoner may correspond with a solicitor for the purpose of obtaining legal advice concerning any cause of action in relation to which the prisoner may become a party to civil proceedings or for the purpose of instructing the solicitor to issue such proceedings.

During the 1970s and 1980s a number of prisoners who had been refused access to legal advice successfully sought to show that refusal constituted a violation by the United Kingdom government of rights contained in the European Convention on Human Rights. At the same time, the courts became increasingly prepared to subject the decisions of the prison authorities to judicial review. An important judgment was that of the House of Lords in *Raymond v Honey* [1983] 1 AC 1. Read Lord Wilberforce's speech in that case and answer the questions that follow.

QUESTIONS

1. Lord Wilberforce refers to a number of rules of varying authority. Place the rules to which he refers in order of ascendancy.
2. Lord Wilberforce discusses the European Convention for the Protection of Human Rights and Fundamental Freedoms and the decision of the European Court of Human Rights in *Golder v United Kingdom*. What authority did this Convention and the decision of the Court of Human Rights have in the law of the United Kingdom at the time of the decision in *Raymond v Honey*?
3. In 1998 Parliament enacted the Human Rights Act 1998. What would be the effect of that Act had the facts in *Raymond v Honey* arisen after the Act came into force?
4. Lord Wilberforce observes that the Divisional Court accepted the argument that the application by the prisoner was not a 'communication' within the Prison Rules governing letters, and thus the governor could not stop it by an exercise of the discretion given him by Rule 33(3). If the application was not a communication, what was it? What do you understand by a 'communication'?

5. For what reasons might a prisoner's letter be 'objectionable' (Rule 33(3))? (chapter 1, section 4.3.4).

6. Suppose that a prisoner has a friend outside the prison who happens to be a journalist. Is a prison governor acting *ultra vires* Rule 33 when he requires the friend to give an undertaking that he will not use any communications from the prisoner for professional purposes. Is such a requirement in breach of Article 8 of the European Convention on Human Rights? See *R v Secretary of State for the Home Department, ex p Simms* [1998] 2 All ER 491.

Section A4   Complex rules

A4.1   Powers of entry and search under sections 8 to 14 of and Schedule 1 to the Police and Criminal Evidence Act 1984

These sections of the Police and Criminal Evidence Act 1984 permit the police to obtain a warrant to search for evidential material relevant to the investigation of an offence. They allow the police access to such material not only on premises occupied by a person suspected of the offence, but also on those occupied by someone who is not under suspicion. For this reason it was considered desirable that as the material became more sensitive to the holder, so the preconditions to the issue of a search warrant should become more onerous for the police. Read these sections and the Schedule and then answer the following questions.

QUESTIONS

Determining the inter-relationships between the various categories of material specified in these sections, and identifying the correct set of access conditions as set down by Schedule 1, is not a simple task. What conditions apply to the following items of relevant evidential material:
(a) the patient records of a registered medical practitioner;
(b) the client records of a faith healer;
(c) the pupil records of a school;
(d) the client records of the probation service;
(e) the client records held by an accountant;
(f) the video tape held by a journalist recording his interviews with members of an animal liberation group suspected of acts of arson;
(g) a piece of blood-stained clothing sent anonymously to a journalist by someone alleging that it belongs to a man suspected of rape;
(h) pieces of glass held by a doctor who has been struck off the medical register, taken from the body of a man suspected of being involved in the rape of a young girl;
(i) pieces of human skin held by the same person as in (h), taken from under the fingernails of a man suspected of being involved in the rape of a young girl;
(j) the same two items as in (h) and (i) held by the man's solicitor?

One way of easing the burden is to recast the principles in the form of an algorithm to allow the reader to eliminate more quickly alternatives that do not apply.

Simplified algorithm designed to show the inter-relationship of sections 8–14 of and Schedule 1 to the Police and Criminal Evidence Act 1984

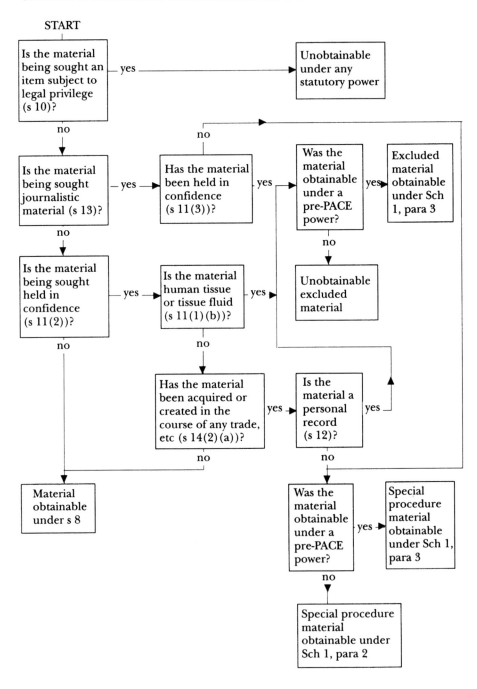

A4.2 Section 67 of the Criminal Justice Act 1967

Read the cases *R v Home Secretary, ex p Naughton* [1997] 1 All ER 426 and in *R v Governor of Brockhill Prison, ex p Evans* [1997] 1 All ER 439 (chapter 1, section 6.2) and write a case note on each one. Then read and write a case note on *R v Secretary of State for the Home Department, ex p Probyn* [1998] 1 All ER 357.

When you have written the case notes, write an annotation of s 67 of the Criminal Justice Act 1967 and its associated statutory provisions, to show:

(a) how the legislation has been interpreted; and
(b) how the legislation could be more helpfully presented.

Section A5   Bigamy

Read the judgments in *R v Gould* [1968] 2 QB 65 and *R v Sarwan Singh* [1962] 3 All ER 612 set out below and answer the questions that follow.

R V GOULD

DIPLOCK LJ read the following judgment of the court.

On 22 March 1967, the defendant was arraigned at Inner London Sessions on a charge of bigamy, and in the absence of his counsel, who was late in arriving at the court, he pleaded guilty to that offence. His counsel, when he arrived, sought leave of the deputy chairman to withdraw that plea, because he wished to advance the defence that at the time of his second marriage the defendant held honestly and reasonably the mistaken belief that a decree absolute dissolving his previous marriage had been granted. The deputy chairman, taking the view that even if that were established it would not amount to a defence, refused to allow the plea of guilty to be withdrawn and, accordingly, the defendant was convicted and sentenced to a conditional discharge.

The question of law in this appeal is whether, on a charge of bigamy under section 57 of the Offences against the Person Act, 1861, a defendant's honest belief upon reasonable grounds that at the time of his second marriage his former marriage had been dissolved in a good defence to the charge. In *Rex v. Wheat* [1921] 2 K.B. 119 the Court of Criminal Appeal decided that it was not. The deputy chairman rightly regarded himself as bound by that decision. But we are not.

In its criminal jurisdiction, which it has inherited from the Court of Criminal Appeal, the Court of Appeal does not apply the doctrine of *stare decisis* with the same rigidity as in its civil jurisdiction. If upon due consideration we were to be of opinion that the law had been either misapplied or misunderstood in an earlier decision of this court or its predecessor, the Court of Criminal Appeal, we should be entitled to depart from the view as to the law expressed in the earlier decision notwithstanding that the case could not be brought within any of the exceptions laid down in *Young v. British Aeroplane Co. Ltd.* [1944] K.B. 718 as justifying the Court of Appeal in refusing to follow one of its own decisions in a civil case (*Rex v. Taylor* [1950] 2 K.B. 368). *A fortiori*, we are bound to give effect to the law as we think it is if the previous decision to the contrary effect is one of which the *ratio decidendi* conflicts with that of other decisions of this court or its predecessors of co-ordinate jurisdiction.

The offence of bigamy is a statutory offence. Our task is therefore to construe the relevant section of the statute which is in the following terms:

His Lordship then quoted s 57 in full (see chapter 1, section 7.1) and continued:

> The enacting words, which are absolute in their terms, set out the three elements in the offence: (a) a married person; (b) going through the form or ceremony of marriage with another person; (c) during the life of his or her spouse.
>
> The circumstances referred to in the first two parts of the proviso relate to element (b) and element (c) respectively and are true exceptions, that is to say, but for the proviso they would fall within the enacting words which precede it, but the second two parts which refer to cases where the former marriage has been dissolved or declared void at the time of the second marriage are not exceptions. They subtract nothing from and add nothing to the enacting words, for a person whose former marriage has been dissolved or avoided is no longer a married person and element (a) in the offence is absent. As a matter of legislative history they are survivals from somewhat similar provisions in the original Act of James I (2 Jac. 1, C. 11), which first made bigamy a felony. What is now the third part of the proviso applied then to divorce *a mensa et thoro* and was a true exception, for that kind of divorce pronounced by the Ecclesiastical Court did not dissolve a marriage; but what is now the fourth even at that date was not an exception from the enacting words, for a person whose former marriage had been declared absolutely void by the Ecclesiastical Courts was no longer married. But in 1603, when the jurisdiction of the Ecclesiastical Courts was still in the realm of political controversy and statutory draftsmanship was in its infancy, it may well have been prudent to state expressly what the consequences of decrees of the Ecclesiastical Courts should be as respects the newly created felony. In 1861, which was four years after the transfer to the Court for Matrimonial Causes of the former matrimonial jurisdiction of the Ecclesiastical Courts and the grant to that court of what was then a novel jurisdiction to grant divorce *a vinculo*, the draftsman of the Offences against the Person Act may have thought it prudent to include in the proviso provisions corresponding to those in the Act of James I and its successor, 9 Geo. 4, c. 31, s. 22, lest their omission might give rise to the suggestion that the words 'being married' in the enacting part had been dissolved or declared void by a decree of the Court for Matrimonial Causes. At any rate, we cannot find any other plausible reason for the inclusion of these two provisions in the proviso.
>
> The present case, however, does not fall within the proviso. The defendant's former marriage had not been dissolved or declared void at the time of the ceremony of his second marriage. The only relevance of the proviso is the light (if any) which it throws upon the preceding enacting words. They are, as we have already pointed out, absolute in their terms. If they are to be construed literally, a mistaken but honest and reasonable belief, by the defendant in a fact which would make his act of going through the second form or ceremony of marriage lawful and innocent, would be no defence.
>
> The question, therefore, is: Are they to be construed literally or as subject to the presumption which is usually applied to statutes creating new criminal offences that a crime is not committed if the mind of the person doing the act in question is innocent?
>
> This question came before a court of 14 judges of the Queen's Bench Division as a Crown Case Reserved in 1889: *Reg. v. Tolson* (1889) 23 Q.B.D. 168). By a majority of nine to five they held that the presumption did apply, that the offence created by the enacting words was not an absolute offence, but that *mens rea* was an essential ingredient. In *Reg. v. Tolson* the fact which the defendant believed, which, had it been true would have made her second marriage lawful and innocent, was that her husband by the former marriage was dead although seven years had not elapsed

since last she saw him. She could not bring herself within the first exception of the proviso. She relied upon a mistaken though honest and reasonable belief that element (c) in the enacting words - viz., the continuing life of the first spouse - was absent. It is significant, in view of what was said about this decision in *Rex* v. *Wheat*, that the majority reached their decision in spite of and not because of the first exception in the proviso, and the minority were largely influenced in their dissent by its presence there. It is made very clear by Lord Coleridge C.J., (pp. 201-2) who was at first inclined to dissent, that their decision was based squarely upon the enacting words themselves and was that these, *despite the proviso*, were to be construed as subject to the general rule applicable to statutes creating serious criminal offences that *mens rea* is a necessary ingredient in the offence.

In *Rex* v. *Wheat* the defendant's mistaken belief related to element (a). He claimed to have had at the time of his second marriage ceremony an honest and reasonable belief that his former marriage had been dissolved. The Court of Criminal Appeal, consisting of five judges, held that this belief, had it been proved, would have been no defence. They sought to distinguish *Reg.* v. *Tolson* upon the ground that that decision turned upon the presence of the exception relating to seven years' absence as indicating that an honest belief in the death of the former spouse before the seven years had elapsed was a defence, which, but for the exception, it would not have been. But this is almost exactly the converse of the reasoning of the judges in *Reg.* v. *Tolson.* The court in *Rex* v. *Wheat* also accepted the argument of Sir Gordon Hewart A.-G. (p. 125) that

> 'this exception creates or involves a presumption of death, which, unless rebutted by the prosecution, entitles the accused to an acquittal; in other words the person accused is presumed to believe under such circumstances that the former wife or husband is dead at the time of the second marriage, and therefore has no intention of doing the act forbidden by the statute - namely, marrying during the life of the former husband or wife.'

But this reasoning, with great respect, does not bear analysis. The defendant has no need to rely upon any presumption of death; it is for the prosecution to prove in every case of bigamy that the former spouse was alive at the time of the second marriage. Nor does the proviso depend upon the defendant's belief in the death of the former spouse but upon his lack of knowledge that the former spouse was alive. In the case of a young and healthy spouse who goes abroad there may be no reason whatever for believing that he or she is dead. An honest defendant may freely admit that he believed his former spouse to be alive at the time of the second marriage as long as he did not *know* her to be so at any time within the previous seven years. That was pointed out in terms by Cave J. in *Reg.* v. *Tolson* (p. 183) and was the very reasoning which persuaded Lord Coleridge C.J. that the first exception did not qualify the application to the enacting words of the general presumption that *mens rea* is a necessary ingredient in the offence.

Upon this reasoning which, with great respect, not only misinterprets the judgments in *Reg.* v. *Tolson* but is in itself fallacious, the court in *Rex* v. *Wheat* (p. 125) expressed their opinion that 'this decision is not in conflict with the decision of the majority of the judges in *Reg.* v. *Tolson*, but is in accord with the principle of the judgment in *Reg.* v. *Prince*' (1875) L.R. 2 C.C.R. 154. We, however, agree with Latham C.J. in the Australian case which we are about to cite that these two English decisions of courts of co-ordinate jurisdiction are in conflict. *Reg.* v. *Tolson* decides that *mens rea* is a necessary ingredient of the felony described in the enacting words despite their absolute terms. *Rex* v. *Wheat* decides the contrary. *Reg.* v. *Prince*, which was discussed at length in *Reg.* v. *Tolson* was decided upon another statute which the court held was intended to punish abduction of a girl without her father's consent

– an act which the court regarded as *malum in se*, whereas the legislature in 1861 cannot be thought to have regarded the act of marrying for a second time as *malum in se* after a previous marriage had ceased to subsist.

In 1937 the matter came before a High Court of Australia which included Latham C.J. and Dixon J., who has earned a world-wide reputation as a common lawyer which is outstanding in the 20th century. The decisions of the High Court of Australia even when so constituted may be persuasive only - but how persuasive they are. In *Thomas v. The King* (1937) 59 C.L.R. 279 the defendant's mistake of fact related to element (a). His former marriage was to a woman who had herself been previously married. At the time of his second marriage he believed honestly and upon reasonable grounds that his first wife's *decree nisi* had not been made absolute at the date when he married her. Had his belief been correct, his first marriage would have been void *ab initio*, not merely voidable; but what is important is that his mistake of fact was as to whether or not the court had made a decree dissolving the previous marriage of his first wife. All members of the High Court regarded the case as indistinguishable in principle from *Rex v. Wheat*. The majority (Latham C.J. and Dixon J. with whom Rich J. agreed) considered *Rex v. Wheat* to be inconsistent with *Reg. v. Tolson*. Latham C.J. said so in terms (p. 292). Dixon J. after discussing two suggested grounds of distinction says (p. 309):

> 'The truth appears to be that a reluctance on the part of courts has repeatedly appeared to allow a prisoner to avail himself of a defence depending simply on his own state of knowledge and belief. The reluctance is due in great measure, if not entirely, to a mistrust of the tribunal of fact - the jury. Through a feeling that, if the law allows such a defence to be submitted to the jury, prisoners may too readily escape by deposing to conditions of mind and describing sources of information, matters upon which their evidence cannot be adequately tested and contradicted, judges have been misled into a failure steadily to adhere to principle. It is not difficult to understand such tendencies, but a lack of confidence in the ability of a tribunal correctly to estimate evidence of states of mind and the like can never be sufficient ground for excluding from inquiry the most fundamental element in a rational and humane criminal code.'

Starke J. dissented on the ground that he ought to follow *Wheat's* case and that a mistake as to whether a marriage has been dissolved is a mistake of law and not of fact. This formed no part of the *ratio decidendi* in *Wheat's* case and was disposed of, as we think unanswerably, by Dixon J. (p. 306). Evatt J. also dissented, but on the broader ground that public policy required that a person who married again during the lifetime of another person who had been his wife did so at his own risk. He did not seek to support this by consideration of the wording of the Victorian Act which was in similar terms to the English one. No member of the court suggested that there was any relevant distinction between a mistaken belief in a fact which, if true, would have the legal consequence of making the former marriage void *ab initio*, and one which would have the legal consequence of avoiding a voidable marriage or of dissolving a valid one. The decision of the majority was that a mistaken belief, held honestly and upon reasonable grounds, is a fact which if true would have had the legal consequence that the defendant was not married at the time of the second marriage ceremony (i.e. that element (a) in the offence was lacking) was a good defence.

In *Reg. v. King* [1964] 1 Q.B. 285 the Court of Criminal Appeal in England followed the decision of the High Court of Australia. The mistake of fact there was that at the time of his former marriage the defendant's own previous marriage to another person had not been dissolved. Had this been so the former marriage would have been void *ab initio* and his second marriage in respect of which he was charged with bigamy would not have been bigamous. In this respect the case was on all fours with *Thomas* v. *The King*. The Court of Criminal Appeal, however, expressed the view (p. 292) not only that their own decision did not conflict with the decision in *Wheat's* case, but that the Australian High Court themselves felt that *Thomas* v. *The King* was clearly distinguishable from *Wheat's* case. With great respect, this later view must have been formed *per incuriam*. We have already referred to the passages in the judgments of Latham C.J. and Dixon J. which show the contrary.

If there is a distinction in principle between *Wheat's* case and *King's* case wherein does that distinction lie and how is it to be extracted from the wording of the section? In *King's* case the court approved and followed the direction of the Common Serjeant, Mr Bosanquet, in *Thomson's* case (1905) 70 J.P. 6 of which Avory J. had said in *Wheat's* case: 'We doubt if it can be supported consistently with our present decision.' This, as the court pointed out in *King's* case was *obiter*, but where does the distinction lie? The mistake in both cases was of the same kind: whether or not a court of competent jurisdiction had made a decree dissolving a marriage. No one apart from Starke J. has ever suggested that this is not a mistake of fact. In both cases the fact mistakenly believed to have been true would, if true, have had the legal consequence that at the relevant time for seeing whether element (b) of the offence existed, i.e., the date of the second marriage ceremony, element (a) was absent – i.e., the defendant was not married. The legal consequences differ in one respect only, that in *King's* case the defendant would never have been married to his former reputed wife, whereas in *Wheat's* case he would at some time previous to the relevant time have been married to his former wife.

But what construction could be placed upon the words of the section which would result in this distinction between the legal consequences of the supposed fact being relevant to the guilt or innocence of the honest and reasonable believer of the fact? There might perhaps be a plausible argument, based on the second part of the proviso, that the expression 'being married' in the enacting words should be construed as 'having been married'. This would have the effect of making the provisions of the proviso relating to dissolution and declarations of nullity of the previous marriage true exceptions to the enacting words instead of surplusage as they are if 'being married' is construed in the present tense, in which grammatically it is. We doubt if in any event it would be permissible to let the tail in the proviso wag the dog in the enacting words. But even if it were, the only effect would be that the fact mistakenly believed to have been true in *King's* case would, if true, have made the second marriage innocent because the defendant did not come within the expression 'having been married' in the enacting words, whereas the corresponding fact in *Wheat's* case would, if true, have made the second marriage innocent because the defendant did come within the exception in the proviso as being a 'person who, at the time of such second marriage, shall have been divorced from the bond of the first marriage'.

Once it is accepted, as it has been in *King's* case, that the offence is not an absolute one and that honest and reasonable belief in a fact affecting the matrimonial status of the defendant which, if true, would make his second marriage lawful and innocent can constitute a defence, there can in our view be no possible ground in justice or in reason for drawing a distinction between facts the result of which would be that he was innocent because he did not come within the enacting words at all, and facts the result of which would be that he was excluded from the enacting words by the proviso.

Given that the belief is formed honestly and upon reasonable grounds, there can be no difference on grounds of moral blameworthiness or of public policy between a mistaken belief that a decree absolute has been granted as in *Wheat's* case and one that it has not as in *King's* case. Indeed, it needs little ingenuity to postulate circumstances in which the existence of a decree absolute would make the defendant's first purported marriage void *ab initio* as the absence of a decree absolute would have done in *King's* case and *Thomas* v. *The King*.

To draw such fine distinctions would we think, in the words of Dixon J. (p. 311) 'lead to consequences which would not only be contrary to principle but which would be discreditable to our system of criminal law.'

We think that *Wheat's* case was wrongly decided. We agree with the High Court of Australia that it conflicts with *Tolson's* case. In this respect we respectfully differ from the opinion expressed by the Court of Criminal Appeal in *King's* case, but our decision is in conformity with the result arrived at in *King's* case and those parts of the reasoning which led to that result.

The prosecution accept that the defendant at the time of the second marriage did honestly believe that his former marriage had been dissolved and that he had reasonable grounds for that belief. This appeal is, accordingly, allowed and the conviction quashed.

R v SARWAN SINGH

TR FITZWALTER BUTLER: This must be almost, if not actually, the first case of bigamy that has come before quarter sessions. Quarter sessions have obtained jurisdiction to deal with cases of bigamy only by virtue of a very recent Act (the Criminal Justice Administration Act 1962, s. 12(1)), the material section of which has only just come into force. It is, perhaps, somewhat strange that the first or almost the first case should raise what is obviously a very difficult question of law, and I am very much indebted to both learned counsel in this case for their extremely eloquent arguments from which I have derived great assistance. I think that counsel for the Crown is right when he says that there is certainly no criminal case which has dealt with the point now before me, and that the matter is open for my decision. Under s. 57 of the Offences against the Person Act, 1861, the crime of bigamy is defined as follows:

> 'Whosoever, being married, shall marry any other person during the life of the former husband or wife, whether the second marriage shall have taken place in England or Ireland or elsewhere, shall be guilty of felony ...'

The issue in this case is whether a marriage which took place according to Sikh law in India a considerable number of years ago is a valid marriage for the purpose of constituting a marriage within the words 'being married' which occur in the first portion of s. 57. The evidence with regard to this matter is really not in dispute. The marriage took place somewhere about the year 1944, at a time when Jullundur was part of British India and persons who were living there were citizens of British India. It took place many years before the coming into force of the Hindu Marriage Act, 1955. Under that Act, I am satisfied from the evidence, a person marrying according to Sikh law can lawfully marry only one wife. Prior to 1955, and at the time when this marriage took place, the position was entirely different, because, according to the evidence, a Sikh then could have more than one wife. He could have as many wives as he chose, though apparently it is clear that the first marriage always had to take place in the presence of a priest and the Holy Book, and the position in regard to the subsequent marriages appears on the balance of the evidence to have been the same. It is quite clear, therefore, that what is alleged to constitute the first marriage in this case was a potentially polygamous marriage, and, therefore, the issue which I have to decide is whether a potentially polygamous marriage can constitute a valid first marriage for the purpose of a prosecution for bigamy.

Many cases have been cited before me, and several learned authors. None of the cases is directly in point, though from several of them I have derived considerable assistance. The only criminal case in which the matter is touched on is *R.* v. *Naguib* [1917] 1 K.B. 359, where the Court of Criminal Appeal, as is pointed out by both learned counsel, expressly refrained from deciding the point now at issue. The learned judge at first instance, AVORY, J., did express an opinion (p. 360) that was merely in the nature of an *obiter dictum* that a first marriage that was either polygamous or potentially polygamous, could not be a marriage for the purpose of a prosecution for bigamy. That is the only case, so far as the researches of both learned counsel have been able to discover, where the matter has been directly adumbrated in a criminal case – I do not say adjudicated on, because the opinion was only *obiter*. A number of other cases has been cited: cases in the Court of Appeal, the Divorce Court and other courts, and I have had the advantage of considering the opinions of a number of learned judges.

The argument addressed to me by counsel for the defendant can be summarised very shortly. He says that the marriage relied on by the prosecution as constituting the valid first marriage was a potentially polygamous union and that such a marriage, any kind of polygamous union or potentially polygamous union, cannot be recognized as a marriage by this criminal statute, which he says must be construed strictly. Counsel for the Crown, on the other hand, says that it is the question of status that has to be considered. Several of the cases which have been quoted, in particular *Hyde* v. *Hyde and Woodmansee* (1866) L.R. 1 P.&D. 130 and *Sowa* v. *Sowa* [1960] P. 70, were not concerned with the status of the parties but were cases which adjudicated on relief which was being sought between the parties. He says that in those cases, though the persons were married, what the court held was that the marriage was of such a nature that it was unsuitable that it should be brought within the matrimonial jurisdiction of English courts. I have carefully considered those cases. I think that counsel for the Crown is right in saying that the headnote in *Hyde* v. *Hyde* does go rather beyond what the court decided, particularly having regard to the last paragraph of the judgment which says (p. 138):

'This court does not profess to decide upon the rights of succession or legitimacy which it might be proper to accord to the issue of the polygamous unions, nor upon the rights or obligations in relation to third persons which people living under the sanction of such unions may have created for themselves. All that is intended to be here decided is that as between each other they are not entitled to the remedies, the adjudication, or the relief of the matrimonial law of England.'

That case was cited with approval in *Sowa* v. *Sowa* where, although the court did not deal expressly or even by inference with the issues which I have to decide, there are certain passages which, I think, help me in coming to the conclusion which I have reached. The headnote in that case says that a polygamous marriage does not come within the word 'marriage', nor do the parties to it come within the words 'wife', 'married woman' or 'husband' for the purposes of the Matrimonial Causes Acts or the Summary Jurisdiction Acts relating to matrimonial matters; and that for the purpose of enabling relief to be granted no distinction can be drawn between (a) the High Court jurisdiction and summary jurisdiction, or (b) polygamous marriages and those which, though potentially polygamous, are de facto monogamous. Towards the end of the judgment of HOLROYD PEARCE, L.J., this passage occurs (p. 85):

'Counsel for the appellant [the wife] sought to obtain some help from *Baindail* (*orse. Lawson*) v. *Baindail* [1946] P. 122, but that case does not affect the present. It was there held that a party to a previous potentially polygamous marriage could not validly contract a subsequent Christian monogamous marriage, and that our Divorce Court would recognize the existence of the potentially polygamous marriage for the purpose of pronouncing a decree of nullity in respect of a subsequent Christian marriage. That decision does not touch this point. The recognition of the fact of the previous polygamous marriage is no recognition of it as a marriage suited to and within the matrimonial procedure and jurisdiction of our courts. It is merely the recognition of a fact disabling a party from entering into a later Christian marriage which as such was a proper subject for consideration and decree by the courts.'

Counsel for the Crown has called my attention to two later cases, first, to *Baindail (orse. Lawson)* v. *Baindail,* which was referred to in that case, and then to *Srini Vasan (orse. Clayton)* v. *Srini Vasan* [1946] P.67. I have no doubt, having considered those cases, that, for some purposes, a polygamous marriage, or a potentially polygamous marriage, is recognized by the courts of this country. Counsel for the Crown urges me to say that it would be inconsistent with those decisions to hold that such a marriage was not a valid marriage for the purpose of a prosecution for bigamy. I have also had brought to my attention *Brinkley* v. *A.-G.* (1890) 15 P.D. 76 and I have no doubt from that decision that any monogamous marriage, even if it was a marriage in a non-Christian country, could be a valid marriage for the purpose of a prosecution for bigamy. I think, however, that the distinction that has to be drawn is not really between what is sometimes called Christian and non-Christian marriage; the true distinction is between monogamous and polygamous marriage.

Finally, counsel for the defendant addressed to me what I think was a very powerful argument. If, for the purpose of a prosecution for bigamy, a potentially polygamous marriage were recognized, then, in view of the fact that the offence of bigamy can be committed wherever the second marriage takes place, whether in England or any other part of the world, a man who married under a ceremony of polygamy a second wife might in some circumstances be liable for prosecution for bigamy; and I cannot believe that the criminal law and those who framed the statute under which the offence of bigamy was constituted ever contemplated that such a position could properly arise.

Having given my careful consideration to this matter, and recognizing as I do that there is no express authority which directs me to any conclusion, I have formed the clear view that the marriage which is to be the foundation for a prosecution for bigamy must be a monogamous marriage, and that any polygamous marriage, or any potentially polygamous marriage, cannot afford a foundation for the prosecution. Therefore, having given the matter my earnest and careful consideration, I have come to the conclusion that the marriage to which the evidence in this case relates, being on the undisputed evidence a potentially polygamous marriage at the time it took place, cannot form a valid first marriage for the purpose of this prosecution. I should only add that I should have liked time further to consider this important matter, but, in view of the fact that the liberty of the subject is involved, and in view of the fact that I have in my view formed a clear mind with regard to this point, greatly assisted as I have been by the arguments of both learned counsel, I have thought it right to give my decision without further consideration.

[No evidence being offered by the prosecution, the jury formally returned a verdict of 'not guilty.']

Sarwan Singh was overruled by *R v Sagoo* [1975] 2 All ER 926.

QUESTIONS

1. D, a married man, goes through a form and ceremony of marriage with his girlfriend P, who believes him to be single. Unknown to D, his wife (W) is killed in a car accident as he and P are exchanging their marriage vows. Does D commit bigamy? Would your answer be different if:
(a) unknown to D, when he and W married 10 years ago, W lied about her age, and was in fact $15\frac{1}{2}$ years old; or
(b) the marriage between D and W was potentially polygamous, as they had been married in a country where polygamy is lawful and D had a wife by a former marriage; or
(c) unknown to P, the whole ceremony through which she was going was a hoax arranged between D and a friend of his who is a defrocked priest; or
(d) D had not seen W for seven years, mainly because for the last six years he has been prospecting in the Australian outback?
2. (a) D married W1 in a potentially polygamous marriage. D married W2 in the same jurisdiction. Following the death of W1, D moved to England where he went through a form and ceremony of marriage with P. Did D commit bigamy?
(b) D, a British subject, married W1 in London in 1992. In 1993 D travelled to Pakistan, where he converted to Islam. In 1994, while W1 was still alive, he went through a Muslim ceremony of marriage with W2. Is D guilty of bigamy under English law?
(c) The facts are as in (b), except that W1 accompanied D to Pakistan and also converted to Islam. W1 agreed to the marriage to W2.
(d) The facts are as in (b), except that the second marriage took place in London.
3. 'MY, aged 39, posed as a man to marry a girl, it was alleged at St Albans Crown Court yesterday. She was said to be already married and to have convinced the "bride" and friends and relatives that she was a man. She even showed a photograph of a baby that she said was her son from a former relationship. Y pleaded guilty to signing a false declaration to obtain a marriage, and bigamy.

Mr Gordon Ward, for the prosecution, said: "Y was born and brought up as a girl and married as a woman in 1967. She lived with her husband as man and wife but started posing as a man, wearing men's clothes and using a man's name, usually Paul Jennings. In 1975 she met CG, aged 19, through a dating agency and they went out together. She was trying to convince the girl that she would make a suitable husband." Later she went to Hertford Register Office and gave her age as 23 and a marriage was arranged. They lived together for two and a half months after their honeymoon but then Y suddenly left. She reappeared three days later and explained that she "could not live the lie any longer". Mr Ward said Y was having hormone treatment before the offence, and it was still continuing.

Y, a former private in the WRAC, appeared in the dock wearing a grey check suit, collar and tie with short dark hair and a beard.

She was freed by Judge Anwyl-Davies QC, and given a two-year conditional discharge and ordered to pay £250 costs. The judge told Y: "This is possibly a unique example of the cruelty of nature. You had to live with this burden for all these years and nothing but compassion and sympathy must go out for your predicament, which, for all I know, will continue for many years to come. You were forced to lead a life of deception, but I have to bear in mind the bitter deception on G. Her hopes of happiness were bitterly dashed by your disclosure."

Mr Frank Stock, for the defence, said Y was an emotional wreck. She was trying to get a divorce and a sex change operation. "She was born a girl but throughout her life she has had none of the emotions, instincts or desires of a woman.""

Explain how this case relates to s 57 of the Offences against the Person Act 1861 and to *Allen*. See further *S-T (formerly J) v J* [1998] 1 All ER 431.

4. *The Times* of 5 December 1998 reported the following case under the headline: 'Five jailed for bigamy case face deportation'. 'Four men and a woman involved in a bigamy scheme were jailed and recommended for deportation yesterday. Three of the men married the lap dancer, S... C... within 18 months of each other; the man and the woman were also married in the illegal scheme which resulted in ten bogus weddings. The five each paid up to £2,500 for marriages of convenience in an attempt to escape civil unrest in Sierre Leone, Harrow Crown Court was told .... Three of C's husbands have never been found. B...J..., who has pleaded guilty to conspiracy to defraud the Home Office, failed to turn up in court. Sentencing [five defendants] to prison, Judge Robert Sich said: "Offences of this sort strike at the whole foundation of the immigration system. I am afraid that I have come to the conclusion that I have to put sympathy to one side and pass custodial sentence on these defendants. I have come to the conclusion that a deterrent element is necessary. Immigration is a very sensitive subject, which has all sorts of ramifications. It must be ensured that everybody plays by the same rules. As soon as one category is seen as securing an unfair advantage, that will give rise to resentment and grievance".'

(a) Assuming that the three men who married SC were bachelors who knew of the other ceremonies and were informed of the 'illegal scheme', were they guilty of bigamy?

(b) Assuming that the only charge was bigamy, were their actions part of the mischief of bigamy?

(c) Should 'bogus marriages' in the context of immigration be treated as a good reason for retaining s 57 of the Offences against the Person Act 1861 in its present form?

(d) Is the offence of bigamy, as defined in *Allen*, over-inclusive or under-inclusive in this context?

5. In the light of the cases you have read, redraft s 57 of the Offences against the Person Act 1861 to reflect the present law.

6. What is the function of the law of bigamy, and how is it used?

7. What information would you find (a) necessary and (b) useful if you were conducting an enquiry which has been asked to look at, and consider possible changes in, the law of bigamy?

8. The cases *R v Taylor* (chapter 1, section 7.3), *R v Gould* (Appendix I, section A5) and *R v Newsome* [1970] 2 QB 711 discuss the application of the doctrine of precedent in the Criminal Division of the Court of Appeal. Formulate a series of propositions summarising what these cases say about this matter.

Section B   Chapters 2 and 3

1. Reread the materials on standpoint and role in chapter 1, section 11. Construct a replacement for the Johnny exercise set in some context other than that of the home and designed to illustrate the main factors to be considered when diagnosing a problem of interpretation from the standpoint of the final adjudicator. Provide a commentary in note form, explaining all the points raised by the exercise. What difference(s) are attributable to the change of context?

2. Some years ago the government became concerned about the increasing number of injuries (and fatalities) caused by 'glue-sniffing'. Suppose that you were the Minister whose department has been charged with the responsibility for preparing a report on the subject, together with proposals for some kind of legislative control. What kind of information would you require to prepare your report and how would you set about discovering it? What groups and individuals would be likely to be instrumental in the formulation of policy objectives? What considerations would you take into account when determining whether to introduce legislation or not? Assuming you did decide to use legislation, what possible strategies are available to you to control the incidence of 'glue-sniffing' and what legal techniques would be most appropriate for implementing them? What general conclusions would you draw concerning the proper steps to be taken in inquiries of this sort?

3. Identify and write down ten examples each of rules in fixed verbal form and rules not in fixed verbal form. In what ways does the absence of a fixed verbal form affect the formulation of a rule?

4. Give one or more examples of: (a) an entirely purposeless rule; (b) a rule the main purpose of which was to uphold a moral principle regardless of the consequences; (c) a rule with several partly competing or conflicting purposes; (d) a rule which outlived its original purposes, but which none the less continued to serve a useful function.

5. Analyse the following rules in terms of their protasis and apodosis:
(a) rules 1-4 and 9 of the school rules in chapter 1, section 4.3.1;
(b) s 57 of the Offences against the Person Act 1861 (chapter 1, section 7.1);
(c) s 11(1) of the Wildlife and Countryside Act 1981 (chapter 1, section 6.1.1); and
(d) Article 12 of the Habitats Directive and regulation 39 of SI 1994/2716 (chapter 1, sections 6.1.2 and 6.1.3).

6. Distinguish between a prescriptive and a descriptive proposition. Which of the following propositions are descriptive and which prescriptive?
(a) rule 3 of the school rules in chapter 1, section 4.3.1;
(b) 'I think the judge will decide in our favour';
(c) 'If you move your pawn there, you will be checkmated'; and
(d) a textbook statement of the law of bigamy.

7. Distinguish between an exception to and an exemption from a rule. Are the following examples of exceptions or exemptions:
(a) rules 7-9 of the school rules in chapter 1, section 4.3.1; and

(b) a general amnesty on illegally held firearms, so that their owners can give them up to the police without fear of prosecution?

8. List as many synonyms or near-synonyms for the word 'rule' as you can; for example, principles, conventions.

9. List as many species of the genus 'rule' as you can; for example, moral rules. Sporting rules would be a species, but rules of football would count as a sub-species for this purpose.

10. Aeroplane-hijacking has been a problem in recent years.

(a) Assume that only one of the law's five basic techniques (chapter 3, pp 150-152) is to be used to deal with this problem. Which of the five do you think would be most likely to be most effective and why?

(b) Assume that any of the other five may also be used, in addition to the one chosen under (a) above. Which ones would you use, and explain how and why.

Your answers should reflect careful thought about the main features of the law's five basic techniques and about how these features determine the utility and limits of each technique.

11. Study the existing law dealing with the consumption of alcohol or of gambling. Explain how each of the five basic techniques in Summers's theory comes into play in the operation of the present overall regime.

12. Distinguish between the function(s), and the use(s), of a rule.

13. What is the function of the rules of inheritance in Arusha society, and how are they used? (see chapter 1, section 5.1).

14. Assemble and diagnose five examples of legalisms, using the diagnosis of the *Case of the Legalistic Child* (chapter 1, section 3.5) as a model. How do your examples help to elucidate the concepts of 'legalism' and 'formalism'? What difference, if any, is there between a 'lawyer like' and a 'legalistic' argument?

15. In the Paula Jones case, the then President of the United States, Bill Clinton, claimed never to have had sexual relations with Monica Lewinsky, notwithstanding that she had performed *fellatio* on him. Most people would say that a man and a woman who have engaged in oral sex have indeed enjoyed 'sexual relations'. That he was able to make this denial was founded on the definition of 'sexual relations' stipulated in his deposition in the Paula Jones case. This provided that 'a person engages in "sexual relations" when the person knowingly engages in or causes ...(1) contact with the genitalia, anus, groin, breast, inner thigh, or buttocks of any person with an intent to arouse or gratify the sexual desire of any person...". Thus Monica Lewinsky did have sexual relations with Bill Clinton when she fellated him, but, so long as he did not touch any of the specified parts of her anatomy, he did not have sexual relations with her. What arguments might be advanced for and against this interpretation? Might this be carrying legalism too far?

Section C Chapter 4

1. Distinguish between a question of fact, a question of law, and a question of mixed law and fact. Are the following questions to do with *Allen* (chapter 1, section 7.2) questions of fact or questions of law:

(a) whether Allen went through a second ceremony of marriage;

(b) whether Allen, in his second 'marriage', 'married' a person who was within the prohibited degree of consanguinity; and

(c) whether Allen, being married, married?

2. List 20 transitive verbs which can be used with the word 'rule', and divide them into sub-categories.

3. What is the relationship of the following activities to that of interpretation:

(a) deciphering the Rosetta Stone;

(b) reading a play by Shakespeare;

(c) complaining about shoddy service in a restaurant;

(d) disciplining a student for an alleged breach of university regulations;

(e) marking examination scripts; and

(f) drafting a statute?

4. What is meant by the application, and the interpretation, of a rule? What are the differences between them?

5. Does application of a rule necessarily presuppose that some interpretation has been put on it?

6. Identify some of those who might be required, or wish, to interpret the following rules:

(a) the school rules in chapter 1, section 4.3.1;.

(b) the Prison Rules in chapter 1, section 4.3.4;.

(c) the rule in *Buckoke v Greater London Council* (chapter 1, section 8);

(d) the rule in *Donoghue v Stevenson* (chapter 1, section 9); and

(e) s 57 of the Offences against the Person Act 1861 (chapter 1, section 7.1).

Would all those you have identified necessarily be likely to interpret the rule in a spirit of co-operation with the rule-maker? If not, how might that affect their interpretation of it?

Section D   Chapter 5

1. Study in outline the law relating to obscenity in this country.

(a) Identify as many reasons as you can think of for having rules about obscenity.

(b) Identify as many problems as you can discover that have arisen in respect of the administration of these laws, and diagnose why these problems have arisen.

(c) One of the conditions of doubt about the law relating to indecent displays is that what constitutes an indecent display depends upon each individual's response, which is neither easily measurable nor consistent. Would it be an improvement to identify in the relevant legislation, for example, (i) various parts of the body that it shall be deemed indecent to display, or (ii) those circumstances under which it would be indecent to display any particular part of the body? Can you think of any other devices for deciding what is 'indecent' or 'obscene'?

(d)   Suppose that a country with a much stricter attitude to the public display of the body than is the case in Britain, were to legislate, *inter alia*, that it would be indecent 'to leave the leg uncovered in public at any point above a line drawn two inches from above the kneecap'. What difficulties might arise in the administration of this rule? In particular, how would you advise the country's rule-makers to deal with the following cases: (i) doctors' examinations of patients at road accidents and the like; (ii) marathon-runners; and (iii) people sunbathing in swimming trunks in their back gardens which are overlooked by an office block?

2. Fill in the 'game' chart opposite very approximately, making provisos in footnotes if you wish. Answer in terms of standard cases. The five categories of answer to be used on the chart are:

√ nearly always, or always
a to a greater extent
b to a lesser extent
x never, or only exceptionally
½ about half and half

A. Duplicate bridge	F. Boxing
B. Patience	G. Advocacy
C. Mountaineering	H. Bargaining or negotiating
D. Roulette	I. War
E. Professional football	J. 'Scorer's discretion' (see Hart, *The Concept of Law*, 2nd edn, 1994, pp 141-147)

Section E   Chapter 6

1. Using the diagnostic model for conditions of doubt set out on pp 208-214, identify the doubts which arose in the following problems contained in chapter 1:
(a) chapter 1, section 3.2;
(b) chapter 1, section 3.5, question 3;
(c) chapter 1, section 4.3.2, question 2;
(d) chapter 1, section 4.4.1, questions 1-4;
(e) chapter 1, section 8, question 1; and
(f) chapter 1, section 10.3, question 4.

2. Read Professor L Fuller's allegory, 'The Case of the Speluncean Explorers', (1948-49) 62 *Harvard Law Review* 616 and diagnose the conditions of doubt which arose according to each of the judges in the Supreme Court of Newgarth.

3. The best way to use and to test the value of the diagnostic model for conditions of doubt is to take any random series of cases involving one or more disputed points of legislative interpretation and to diagnose the conditions of doubt involved in each case. We recommend the following cases as illustrating a broad variety of the conditions of doubt listed in Chapter 6: *Fisher v Bell* [1961] 1 QB 394; *Knuller v DPP* [1973] AC 435; *R v Collins* [1973] QB 100; *R v Arrowsmith* [1975] 1 All ER 463; *Dockers' Labour Club v Race Relations Board* [1976] AC 285; *Miliangos v George Frank* [1976] AC 443; *Farrell v Alexander*

	A	B	C	D	E	F	G	H	I	J
Equipment eg ball	√									
Teams or sides	√									
Governed by established rules	√									
Scoring (points, goals, etc)	√									
Physical exertion	x									
A large element of chance	b									
A large element of skill or strength	a									
Purpose: enjoyment by participants	√									
Purpose: enjoyment by spectators	b									
Referee, umpire or judge	√									
Special clothing	x									
Do you usually think of it as a game?	yes									

[1977] AC 59; *Royal College of Nursing v Department of Health and Social Security* [1981] 1 All ER 545; *Mandla v Dowell Lee* [1983] 1 All ER 1062; *Coltman v Bibby Tankers* [1988] AC 276; *R v Kearley* [1992] 2 AC 228; *Mallinson v Secretary of State for Social Security* [1994] 2 All ER 295; *R v Governor of Brockhill Prison, ex p Evans* [1997] 1 All ER 439; *Cutter v Eagle Star* [1998] 4 All ER 417; *B v DPP* [1998] 4 All ER 265.

4. Take any ten cases from a recent volume of the *Law Reports* and analyse their conditions of doubt.

5. A club for bearded men was set up in 1960 in a small town at a time when sporting a beard was interpreted symbolically as a reflection of certain social values. For some years there were no precise criteria of membership. Now two things have occurred: first, beards have lost much of their symbolic force in the town and many more people have beards; second, membership of the club carries with it certain privileges with regard to the purchase of cheap tickets on charter flights abroad. There has been a sudden rise in applications for membership and there is a feeling that criteria for membership should be made much more precise. You have been asked to draft rules embodying such criteria.

(a) What are the difficulties in devising fair and workable criteria?

(b) What other facts are relevant to you as draftsman?

(c) Draft the rules and give reasons for your choices.

Section F   Chapters 7 and 8

1. Choose (i) a government Bill, and (ii) a private Member's Bill, and follow their progress through Parliament. Using the parliamentary debates, and any other material you can discover, try to answer the following questions:

(a) for what reasons was the Bill introduced;

(b) were any particular individuals or groups influential in pressing for the Bill to be enacted;

(c) what differentiates a Bill's parliamentary stages;

(d) what obstacles lay in the path of the private Member's Bill;

(e) how many amendments were moved by the Opposition and by government backbenchers during its stages, and how many were finally accepted by the government;

(f) what were the primary objectives of the Bill;

(g) for what reasons (if any) was the Bill opposed;

(h) how effective was the Opposition (if any); and

(i) what factors do you think will affect the impact of the Bill should it become law?

2. Compare the drafting of clause 1 of the private Member's Domestic Violence Bill with that of the 1976 Act (chapter 1, sections 12.3 and 12.4). Do you think that the problems in *B v B, Cantliff v Jenkins* and *Davis v Johnson* would have arisen if the private Member's Bill had been enacted verbatim?

3. Choose any recent Act of Parliament and examine it with the following matters in mind (not all Acts will contain instances of every matter mentioned

below, but, for example, the Wildlife and Countryside Act 1981 and the Wildlife and Countryside (Amendment) Act 1985, as well as the Police and Criminal Evidence Act 1984 contain many of them):

(a) from the definition section, find examples of an exhaustive and a non-exhaustive definition, connotative and denotative definitions, a definition imported from an earlier Act of Parliament, and a technical definition;

(b) find examples of the following powers: to make subordinate legislation, to arrest without warrant, to enter premises, and to seize property;

(c) if the Act amends earlier legislation, does it do so textually or non-textually?;

(d) to what parts of the United Kingdom does the Act apply?;

(e) when does the Act come into force?;

(f) can you identify any instances of poor drafting, as exemplified as condition 13 in the diagnostic model (p 211)?

4. Part of the government's response to the problem of 'glue-sniffing' (Appendix I, section B, question 2) was the Intoxicating Substances (Supply) Act 1985. Read this statute and identify any difficulties with its implementation that occur to you. What impact do you think this Act may have had? How would you find out?

5. Set out on p 402 is the Gobbledygook Test devised by the Plain English Campaign. Note that this is only a rough and ready way of rating the difficulty an untutored reader might experience when trying to comprehend a text. Applying the test to an example in chapter 1, section 6.2, the Zebra crossing regulations rated 81 and their explanation in the Highway Code scored 23. Section 14 of the Police and Criminal Evidence Act 1984 (Appendix I, section A4.1) rated 53. Apply the test to: the Prison Rules on letters (chapter 1, section 4.3.4), s 57 of the Offences against the Person Act 1861 (chapter 1, section 7.1), and s 1 of the Domestic Violence and Matrimonial Proceedings Act 1976 (chapter 1, section 12.4).

6. We referred in Appendix I, section A4.1 to ss 8 to 14 of and Schedule 1 to the Police and Criminal Evidence Act 1984 in order to underline points made in chapters 1 and 7 concerning the complexity of legislation. Consider s 10(2), which says: 'Items held with the intention of furthering a criminal purpose are not items subject to legal privilege'. Suppose you are a solicitor. Over the past few years you have been giving advice to a client concerning the purchase and sale of some houses. Some of the client's funds have been supplied to her by one of her relatives. It now appears that, wholly unknown to your client, the funds were the proceeds of a series of frauds committed by the relative and some accomplices, who have been looking for ways in which to invest their gains in order to hide them from the police, known as money laundering. Because the police have been conducting their enquiries in secret and do not wish to alert the suspects, whom they believe are engaged in another crime, they successfully applied for a production order under para 12 of Schedule 1 to compel you to disclose to them all the documents concerning your client's property transactions. Do you think that these documents are 'items subject to legal privilege'?

When you have given this some thought, read the speeches of Lord Bridge and Lord Goff in *R v Central Criminal Court, ex p Francis & Francis (a firm)*

This test measures the approximate level of difficulty of a piece of writing. It is a rough measure because it deals only with word length and sentence length: many other variables, like sentence structure and size of print, help to make reading easy or difficult. Never write just to please the test: a low score does not guarantee simplicity or clarity.

Follow the instructions to work out the level of difficulty of the text, remembering that:

- Numbers and symbols are counted as short words
- Hyphenated words are counted as two words
- A syllable, for the purpose of the test, is a vowel sound. So *advised* is two syllables, *applying* is three.

Instructions	Sample A	Sample B	Sample C
1 Count a 100-word sample.			
2 Count the number of complete sentences in the sample and note the answer in the Sample A column.			2
3 Count the total number of words in all the complete sentences and note it in the Sample A column.			3
4 Find the average sentence length by dividing the answer for instruction 3 by the answer for instruction 2.			4
5 Count the number of words of three or more syllables in the full 100 words. This gives the percentage of long words in the sample.			5
6 Add the answers for instructions 4 and 5. This gives the test score for the sample.			
7 Repeat with two more samples, B and C.			
8 Add the three test scores.	Test scores A + B + C =		
9 Divide by three to get a final average score.	Average of A, B & C =		
10 Compare your score with the results below. (The lower the score, the more comprehensible the material is likely to be.)			

Woman magazine 25
Sun 26
Tit Bits 28
Daily Mirror 28
Daily Express 29
Daily Mail 31
Standard letter, BF 405, (Dept of Health and Social Security) 33
Morning Star 34
Daily Telegraph 34
The Times 36
The Guardian 39
'Cars' (Office of Fair Trading leaflet) 40

Notes to British Visitor's Passport Application Form 45
Standard letter (Dept of Employment) 49
'Conditions of Use' (Application for an ACCESS credit card) 49
(The calculations on newspapers were made on 14 July 1980.)

* Adapted from R Gunning's FOG (frequency of gobbledygook) formula. The formula is considered the best for testing material for adult readers.

(The Gobbledygook Test is reprinted with the permission of the Plain Language Campaign, PO Box 3, New Mills, High Peak, Derbyshire, SK22 4QP.)

[1989] AC 346. This case illustrates firstly the difficulties that complexity in legislation – in particular the use of the passive voice – can generate, and secondly, two of the most common arguments that courts (and other interpreters) use when interpreting rules, especially statutory rules: arguments concerning the language of the rule, and arguments concerning its purpose. Now answer the following questions.

(a) What would be the scope of s 10(2) if it had been drafted: 'Items made with the intention of furthering a criminal purpose are not items subject to legal privilege'?

(b) Re-draft s 10(2) so that it more clearly indicates:
   (i) what the majority concluded that it meant; and
   (ii) what the minority concluded that it meant.

(c) Do you think that Lord Bridge's distinction between positive and negative absurdity is one that properly differentiates legitimate from illegitimate interpretation by a court?

(d) When rejecting Lord Goff's argument that because it would be absurd if legal privilege were to extend to an item once the holder had effected his criminal purpose, the words must be interpreted as including anyone holding the items so long as someone once had a criminal purpose, Lord Bridge does not regard the temporal implication ('entertained ... at any time') as illegitimate, but does regard the implication that this can be held by anyone as being so. Is he being consistent when he accepts one implication and rejects another?

(e) In what ways does Lord Goff differ from Lord Bridge in his analysis of the relationship between s 10(2) and the case *R v Cox and Railton*?

(f) Can you see any danger to civil liberties in the majority's view that the police's efforts to investigate crime will be hampered if legal privilege should extend to items in respect of which the client has a criminal purpose, but where the solicitor is innocent?

(g) Analyse the speeches of Lords Bridge and Goff in terms of Summers's distinctions between authority, substantive and institutional reasons for decisions.

7. In dismissing the appeal by a majority of 3:2, their Lordships' speeches in *ex p Francis & Francis* also illustrate a second perennial debate concerning the proper role of the judiciary when interpreting legislation whose language does not meet the task for which it was apparently intended; as Lord Oliver (who was in the minority with Lord Bridge) put it (at p 390 of the Law Report), the question whether the courts should fill a lacuna 'involves stepping outside the judicial role and assuming, without the benefit of public discussion or debate, that mantle which is properly reserved to the legislature alone'.

What assumptions about the role of the courts in a democracy does this remark make?

8. In an extra-judicial comment on *ex p Francis & Francis*, Lord Oliver disclosed that, following the decision, he had checked Hansard to see whether the interpretation reached by the majority was the one that the government had intended. He concluded that the Minister's replies to questions about s 10(2) were 'consistent only with its having been inserted to cover the case of a holder who himself was a party to the criminal purpose. So the draftsman clearly did

exactly what he was instructed to do ...'. ('A Judicial View of Modern Legislation' 14 *Statute Law Rev* (1993) 1, 7); in other words, that the minority's understanding of the section's purpose and scope was right. Suppose that this information had been before the House (it heard *ex p Francis & Francis* before the decision in *Pepper v Hart*): would the majority, if it wished to pursue its interpretation of s 10(2), have been bound to adopt the Minister's replies?

9. Suppose (i) that an Act authorises the deportation of persons described as being of class A; (ii) that during the debates on the scope of persons within class A, the Minister was specifically asked whether persons in sub-class A1 were included, to which she said, yes; (iii) that in its enacted form, there is some ambiguity in the formulation of A, so that it does not, on a straightforward interpretation, extend to persons in sub-class A1; (iv) that the immigration authorities are seeking to deport a person within that class; and (v) that you are representing A1's interest in not being deported. In a judicial review application, the immigration authorities cite the Minister's words in support of their proposed deportation of your client. What arguments can you put forward as to the limits to be placed on *Pepper v Hart?*

10. To what extent are interpreting poems, novels, legal texts and the Bible analogous activities?

11. The following principle, modelled on existing equivalent provisions in Australia (s 15AA of the Acts Interpretation Act 1901, as amended) and New Zealand (s 5j of the Acts Interpretation Act 1924) was included in the Interpretation of Legislation Bill 1981: that in the event of ambiguity in its application in a given case, 'a construction which would promote the general legislative purpose of the provision is to be preferred to a construction which would not'. Consider critically the desirability of adopting such a provision into the law of England and Wales.

12. In *R v Governor of Brockhill Prison, ex p Evans (No 2)* [1998] 4 All ER 993, reference was made to Article 5 of the European Convention on Human Rights (see chapter 1, section 10.3.3). The Court of Appeal declined to establish any qualification that would affect the application of that Article while the Human Rights Bill was before Parliament. What effect does the enactment of the Human Rights Act 1998 have upon the reasoning in that case?

Section G   Chapter 9

Section G1   Reading cases

1. Examine any ten cases reported in the past five years in which there have been dissenting judgments and examine the techniques used in each case by any two judges who disagreed with each other in arriving at divergent interpretation of the same precedents.

2. In chapter 9 we analysed the way in which Lord Buckmaster and Lord Atkin handled the two precedents, *Winterbottom v Wright* and *George v Skivington*. Now read the whole of their speeches in the law reports and, using this analysis as a model, compare their handling of *Langridge v Levy*, *McPherson v Buick*, and *Francis v Cockrell*.

3. Consider the following facts: Over a period of two years John Doe invested heavily in the Rio Bravo Nickel Co, which subsequently went bankrupt. He was encouraged to invest on the strength of optimistic reports prepared by the company's accountants, which were described by an independent expert witness as 'defective and deficient' and as presenting the position of the company at that time as 'wholly contrary to the actual position'. John is thinking of taking action against the accountants. Assuming that the year is 1934 and that *Donoghue v Stevenson* is the only relevant precedent, construct an argument from the standpoint of:

(a) a cautious solicitor acting for John;

(b) an optimistic solicitor acting for John;

(c) the accountant's barrister;

(d) John's barrister;

(e) a judge in the mould of Lord Buckmaster; and

(f) a judge in the mould of Lord Atkin.

Would your argument be any different today?

4. In March 1996 a father quarrelled with his two daughters and executed a will cutting them out of his estate. After a reconciliation, on 17 July 1996 his solicitors received a letter from the father giving instructions to prepare a new will to include substantial gifts to each of his daughters. On 16 August the managing clerk asked the firm's probate department to draw up a will or codicil effecting the changes. The managing clerk then went on holiday. After his return, he made an appointment to see the testator on 17 September. However, the testator died on 14 September before the new dispositions to the daughters had been effected. The daughters sued the solicitors for negligence.

(a) What arguments might have been made at the time for and against the existence of a duty of care in this case? Might the result be different if the beneficiaries of the intended gifts were not yet born at the time the testator gave instructions to include gifts for all his grandchildren? See *White v Jones* [1995] 1 All ER 691.

(b) Suppose that in addition to any remedy that a disappointed beneficiary might have, the testator's estate had a remedy against the negligent solicitor, albeit that that remedy did not assist the disappointed beneficiary in any way. Would it be just in those circumstances to place the solicitor at risk of two separate claims for the same error? See *Carr-Glyn v Frearsons* [1998] 4 All ER 225.

5. A fire engine driver is answering an emergency call. As Lord Denning put the matter in *Buckoke v Greater London Council* (chapter 1, section 8, p 53): 'He ... approaches the traffic lights. He sees 200 yards down the road a blazing house with a man at an upstairs window in extreme peril. The road is clear in all directions. At that moment the lights turn red. Is the driver to wait for 60 seconds, or more, for the lights to turn green? If the driver waits for that time, the man's life will be lost.' Being legalistic, the driver does indeed wait for the 60 seconds, and the man in the burning house dies. His widow sues the fire authority in negligence. Will she succeed? See *Capital and Counties plc v Hampshire County Council* [1996] 4 All ER 336; *Munroe (John) Acrylics Ltd v London Fire and Civic Authority* [1996] 4 All ER 318; and *Church of Jesus Christ of Latter-*

Day Saints (Great Britain) v Yorkshire Fire and Civil Defence Authority [1997] 2 All ER 865 (consolidated appeals).

6. Suppose that litigation concerning the application of a common law rule is current in the High Court (A v B) at the same time as another case (C v D), which deals with the same point of law is on appeal to the House of Lords. Under the common law rule, which is stated in an old Court of Appeal case (E v F), judgment ought to be given for the defendant. Suppose further that E v F is now widely regarded as bad law. Although it has not been the direct subject of litigation for many years (solicitors have managed to give advice that avoids its implications), the Law Commission has criticised it, judges have taken side-swipes at it whenever they can, and a private Member's Bill to overrule it did reach its Second Reading before it was talked out. Before C v D is decided by the House of Lords, the High Court decides A v B in favour of the defendant (complying, though very reluctantly, with its obligation to follow decisions of the Court of Appeal). A few days later, the House decides in C v D that the law should be changed so that it now favours the plaintiff in such cases, and overrules E v F. Assuming that the unsuccessful plaintiff in A v B can action within the time available an appeal, would he (assuming full comparability of fact and law with C v D) be successful in his appeal?

Would it make any difference if instead of the House of Lords decision in C v D, the law were changed by a statute coming into force after the facts giving rise to the litigation in A v B had occurred?

G2 Exercises on 'the *ratio decidendi* of a case'

1. Identify the range of meanings of the following expressions: *ratio decidendi*; *obiter dictum*; a binding decision; decision; reason for deciding; material to the decision; the facts of a case.
2. Can a case have more than one *ratio decidendi*?
3. Must every case have at least one *ratio decidendi*?
4. Was the 'neighbour principle' a necessary part of Lord Atkin's decision in *Donoghue v Stevenson*?
5. Is the 'neighbour principle' an *obiter dictum*? Are there any examples of *obiter dicta* in the extracts from Lord Buckmaster's speech?
6. What facts did Lord Atkin treat as material in *Donoghue v Stevenson* (a) expressly (b) impliedly?
7. Can the *ratio decidendi* of a case be changed by subsequent cases?
8. Can there be (a) a *ratio decidendi*, (b) a reason, which is not a rule?

Section G3 Exercises on *Donoghue v Stevenson*

(You should read the whole case before attempting these exercises.)

Procedure

1. From reading the report, what do you understand to have happened in the action before the case reached the House of Lords?

2. Which was settled first in this case – the issues of fact or the issues of law?
3. The appeal was allowed. Was this the end of the matter? If not, what further possible steps might have followed?
4. The issues of fact had not been finally settled before the case reached the House of Lords. How did Lord Buckmaster and Lord Atkin know what the facts were?

Rules

5. State the rule or rules of law which Lord Buckmaster thought applied to this case. Were they (or was it) in fixed verbal form? How do you know?
6. What do you think that Lord Atkin meant by a general principle? Is it different from a rule?
7 Can you analyse the neighbour principle in terms of its protasis and apodosis? If not, why not?
8. The case 'was a clear instance of the court's taking account of the new conditions of mass production and complex marketing of goods wherein there are many intermediaries between manufacturer and consumer, and by a conscious work of judicial legislation, imposing on manufacturers certain minimum standards of care in favour of the consumer' (Street).
(a) What evidence is to be found in the speeches of Lords Atkin and Buckmaster that they took into account 'new conditions of mass production', etc?
(b) Which of the cases discussed in the speeches involved problems arising out of the advent of mass production?
(c) How new were these 'new conditions'?
(d) Why should mass production create a need to change the legal rules governing the relations between manufacturer and consumer?

Reasoning

9. Is it fair to say of Lord Atkin's speech in *Donoghue v Stevenson*: 'He came to the conclusion early on that the plaintiff should win and thereafter all his efforts were directed to manipulating the authorities so that they fitted in with the conclusion'?
(a) If this is fair comment, does it involve a serious criticism of Lord Atkin's behaviour?
(b) How free was Lord Atkin to manipulate the authorities?
10. What is a 'source' of law? What 'sources' were considered binding on them by Lord Atkin and Lord Buckmaster?
11. Comment on the passage at [1932] AC 567 beginning 'Now the Common Law must be sought ... the appellant's case'.
12. Comment on the paragraph at [1932] AC 576, 'One further case mentioned ... on this view the case does not advance the matter'. Are American decisions a 'source' of law in English courts? What does Lord Buckmaster mean by 'authority' and by 'the source of the law'? Does Lord Atkin's attitude to American cases as possible 'sources' of law differ from Lord Buckmaster's?
13. At [1932] AC 573 Lord Buckmaster says that Brett MR laid down 'unnecessarily the larger principle which he entertained'. What does this mean?

Do you consider Lord Atkin's 'neighbour' generalization (ibid, p 580) was 'unnecessary'? If so, is Lord Atkin being hypocritical in the passage commencing 'I venture to say ... unduly restricted' (ibid, pp 583-4)?

14. Why does Lord Buckmaster say that the *dicta* of Brett MR 'are rightly relied on'? ([1932] AC 571). What does this mean?

15. 'In my view, therefore, the authorities are against the appellant's contention, and apart from authority it is difficult to see how any common law proposition can be formulated to support her claim' ([1932] AC 577). Comment.

16. Alderson B: 'The only safe rule is to confine the right to recover to those who enter into the contract; if we go one step beyond that, there is no reason why we should not go fifty' (*Winterbottom v Wright* (1842) 10 M & W 109, 115). Do you agree?

17. What does Cardozo J mean when he says in *MacPherson v Buick* 217 NY 382 (1916): 'Precedents drawn from the days of travel by stagecoach do not fit the conditions of travel today'? What implications might this have for the doctrine of precedent?

18. 'The majority [in *Donoghue v Stevenson*] did appeal to social convenience and policy as one of the justifications for their decision: "the categories of negligence are never closed". This is an argument which has always been somewhat suspect in England.' Heuston, (1957) 20 *Modern Law Review* 1, 4-5. Comment.

19. 'Even if [the neighbour principle] is regarded as dictum, the carefully considered and often approved utterances of a Law Lord are in no way to be equated to the (perhaps ill-reported) remarks of a puisne judge made at *nisi prius*. There are *dicta* and *dicta*.' Heuston, ibid, p 8. Comment.

20. Is the *ratio decidendi* of *Donoghue v Stevenson* the same today as it was in 1933?

Section H   Chapter 10

1. Which do you think were (a) the strongest, and (b) the weakest, arguments advanced by each side in *Allen*?

2. Using the approach adopted at pp 347-350 analyse the main arguments which might have been advanced for each side in (a) *Buckoke v Greater London Council* (chapter 1, section 8); (b) *R v Taylor* (chapter 1, section 7.3); (c) *R v Gould* (Appendix A, section A5).

3. Give an example of a conclusion which is valid, but not true, and of a conclusion which is true, but not valid.

4. Distinguish (a) 'open' and 'closed' systems of thinking; (b) predictability from logical necessity; (c) descriptive and normative statements.

5. Distinguish, giving legal examples, deduction, induction and reasoning by analogy.

6. 'In fact the fallacy of "Argument by Analogy" is that it is never possible to argue by analogy' (Emmet). Does this mean that one of the most important forms of legal reasoning is fallacious?

7. 'The reasoning may take this form: A falls more appropriately in B than in C. It does so because A is more like D which is of B than it is like E which is of C. Since A is in B and B is in G (legal concept), then A is in G. But perhaps C is in G also. If so, then B is in a decisively different segment of G, because B is like H which is in G and has a different result than C' (Levi). Is it possible to fit either Lord Atkin's or Lord Buckmaster's reasoning in *Donoghue v Stevenson* into this form?

8. Read pp 56-57 of J Stone, *Legal System and Lawyers' Reasonings* (1964) and find five examples from case law of competing analogies.

9. 'Does this mean that in all those numerous instances of doubt and uncertainty which arise in the application of legal rules, courts really have a completely free choice in the matter and arrive at merely arbitrary decisions? Anyone who studies the elaborately reasoned judgments of English courts must be surprised if not shocked to hear these carefully considered conclusions stigmatized as arbitrary. These are certainly no more, and indeed usually a good deal less, arbitrary than the decisions which we take in other non-legal affairs of daily life.'

Give an example of an arbitrary and a non-arbitrary decision in (a) a legal, and (b) a non-legal, context. What exactly is meant by 'arbitrary' in these contexts?

10. 'Scientific thought concerns itself with analysing and classifying the elements of given fact-situations and determining their relations to one another for the purpose of acquiring ability to predict the relations between these elements if recurring in a future situation. This procedure involves the same basic thought processes which are involved in the procedure of judicial thinking – the isolation of identities, their formulation in general propositions, and the application of these propositions to specific situations. Here, however, the resemblance ends.'

(a) In what ways do scientific and judicial thinking differ?

(b) Is there only one mode of reasoning characteristic of each type of thinking?

11. Restate in your own words, as persuasively as you can:

(a) the case for Johnny in the broom episode (chapter 1, section 3.5); and

(b) the case for the prosecution in *Allen* (chapter 1, section 7.2).

Identify the propositions which make up the argument in each instance.

12. Give examples of (a) clearly good reasons; (b) clearly bad reasons; (c) reasons about which there might reasonably be disagreement as to whether they were good or bad, valid or invalid, cogent or weak, in relation to a particular result in (i) the case of Johnny and (ii) *Allen* (chapter 1, sections 3.5 and 7.2 respectively).

13. State the facts (a) in *Donoghue v Stevenson* (chapter 1, section 9), (b) in some extra-legal dispute with which you are familiar, in a manner which illustrates the axiom: 'the statement of facts is the heart'.

14. Read Lord Denning's judgments in the following cases: *Hinz v Berry* [1970] 1 All ER 1074; *Dutton v Bognor Regis UDC* [1972] 1 QB 373; *Miller v Jackson* [1977] QB 966 and *Lim Poh Choo v Camden and Islington Area Health Authority* [1979] 1 All ER 332. Do you agree that these contain 'persuasive' statements of the facts of each case? To what technique(s) does Lord Denning resort in order to make his judgments persuasive?

15. Read Professor Summers's article concerning legal reasoning which was referred to in chapter 10, p 359, n 33. Now read the decisions of the Court of Appeal and of the House of Lords in *Farrell v Alexander* [1976] QB 345; revsd [1977] AC 59; *White v Jones* [1995] 1 All ER 691 and *R v Bow Street Metropolitan Stipendiary Magistrate, ex p Pinochet Ugarte* [1998] 4 All ER 897, and
(a) analyse the reasons given in the judgments in terms of Summers's five types;
(b) are there any other arguments used by the judges which do not readily fall within Summers's typology?
16. Carry out the same exercise as in question 15 using the judgments of Lords Denning, Diplock and Scarman in *Davis v Johnson* set out in chapter 1, sections 12.5.2 and 12.5.3.
17. In *The Common Law Tradition*, Karl Llewellyn reiterated what he regarded as the 'Seven ABCs of Appellate Argument':

> *First*, and negatively, *the Insufficiency of Technical Law: it is plainly not enough to bring in a technically perfect case on 'the law'* under the authorities and some of the accepted correct techniques for their use and interpretation of 'development'. Unless the judgment you are appealing from is incompetent, there is an equally perfect technical case to be made on the other side, and if your opponent is any good, he will make it ...
>
> *Second, the Trickiness of Classification* :a 'technically' perfect case is of itself equally unreliable in regard to the interpretation or classification of the facts. For rarely indeed do the raw facts of even a commercial transaction fit cleanly into any legal pattern; or even the 'trial facts' as they emerge from conflicting testimony. No matter what the state of the law may be, if the essential pattern of the facts is not seen by the court as fitting cleanly under the rule you contend for, your case is still in jeopardy. This is of course the reason for the commercial counsellor's concern with 'freezing' the transaction by a well drawn document which does fit cleanly into known and highly certain legal rules ...
>
> Per contra, and *third*, the *Necessity of a Sound Case 'in Law': Without a technically perfect case on the law*, under the relevant authorities and some one or more of the thoroughly correct procedures of their use and interpretation, *you have no business to expect to win* your case. Occasionally a court may under the utter need for getting a decent result go into deliberate large-scale creative effort; but few courts like to ...
>
> *Fourth, the Twofold Sense and Reason*: the real and vital central job is to satisfy the court that sense and decency and justice require (a) the rule which you contend for in this *type* of situation; and (b) the result that you contend for, as between these parties. *You* must make your whole case, on law and facts, make *sense*, appeal as being *obvious* sense, inescapable sense, sense in simple terms of life and justice. If that is done, the technically sound case on the law then gets rid of all further difficulty: it shows the court that its duty to the Law not only does not conflict with its duty to Justice but urges to decision along the exact same line.
>
> It is a question of making the facts talk. For of course it is the facts, not the advocate's expressed opinions, which must do the talking. The court is interested not in listening to any lawyer rant, but in seeing, or better, in discovering, from and in the facts, where sense and justice lie.
>
> This leads to interesting corollaries:
>
> *Fifth, the Statement of Facts is the Heart*: It is trite that it is in the statement of the facts that the advocate has his first, best, and most precious access to the court's attention. The court does not know the facts, and it wants to. It is trite, among good advocates, that the statement of the facts can, and should, in the very process

of statement, frame the legal issue, and can, and should, simultaneously produce the conviction that there is only one sound outcome.

Sixth, Simplicity: It is as yet less generally perceived as a conscious matter that the *pattern of the facts* as stated must be a *simple* pattern, with its lines of simplicity never lost under detail; else attention wanders, or (which is as bad) the effect is drowned in the court's effort to follow the presentation or to organize the material for itself ...

Seventh, the Principle of Concentration of Fire: Even three points, or two, can prove troublesome as dividers of attention unless a way can be found to make them sub-points of a single simple line of attack which gains reinforcement and cumulative power from each sub-point as the latter is developed ...

To which Llewellyn added two further points:

The function of the oral presentation is, if that be do-able, to catch and rivet attention, to focus the issue into a single challenging question, to make the facts create ineluctable conviction as to where right lies, and to fit that conviction into a persuasive, even compelling legal frame. The brief can develop the frame; but the oral argument must get the case set into the desired frame, and for keeps....

If a brief has made the case for what is right, and has made clear the reason of the rightness, and has found and tailored and displayed the garment of law to clothe the right decision fittingly, then it is not only unwise but indecent not to furnish also in that brief a page or two of text which gathers this all together, which cleans up its relation to the law to date, which puts into clean words the soundly guiding rule to serve the future, and which shows that rule's happy application to the case in hand. What is wanted is a passage which can be quoted verbatim by the court, a passage which so clearly and rightly states and crystallizes the background and the result that it is *recognized* on sight as doing the needed work and as practically demanding to be lifted into the opinion.

(*The Common Law Tradition* (1960), pp 237–246.)

(a) To what extent did counsel in (i) *Allen* and (ii) *Davis v Johnson* observe these precepts?

(b) Choose a variety of cases from different areas of law and analyse counsel's arguments in terms of Llewellyn's advice.

(c) To what extent is this advice to advocates applicable to arguments about questions of fact, of policy, and of what the law ought to be? Compare the advice given to students wishing to become barristers and solicitors: Appendix IV, suggestions for further reading.

Appendix II

Algorithms and the Structure of Complex Rules

Many rules, especially legal rules, are very complicated, often involving exceptions, qualifications, provisos and double negatives. In these cases, the reader may be in doubt as to the relationship between the various parts of the rule, and it may help to rewrite the rule in diagrammatic form. Section 67(1) of the Criminal Justice Act 1967 reads (see chapter 1, section 6.2):

> The length of any sentence of imprisonment imposed on an offender by a court shall be treated as reduced by any relevant period, but where he was previously sentenced to a probation order, a community service order, an order for conditional discharge or a suspended sentence in respect of that offence, any such period falling before the order was made or suspended sentence passed shall be disregarded for the purposes of this section.

At first sight, this may seem a little confusing because of its multiple use of subordinate clauses, because it contains two propositions, the second of which has a variety of sub-options, and because it is an unbroken narrative. We can rewrite the section in a schematic form:

1. The length of any sentence of imprisonment imposed on an offender by a court shall be treated as reduced by any relevant period,
2. but where he was previously sentenced to:
    (a) a probation order,
    (b) a community service order,
    (c) an order for conditional discharge; or
    (d) a suspended sentence in respect of that offence,
any such period falling before the
    (a) order was made; or
    (b) suspended sentence passed
shall be disregarded for the purposes of this section.

The advantage of this type of presentation over conventional prose style is that it is clearer to the reader. The text should therefore be more easily understood. The layout also provides a simple checklist of the conditions under which the provision operates. To assist our understanding of the structure of complex rules we can employ another type of presentation, the algorithm. An algorithm is a precise set of instructions for solving a well-defined problem.[1]

---

1   This is adopted from B Lewis and P Woolfenden, *Algorithms and Logical Trees* (1969). See also DM Wheatley and AW Unwin, *Algorithm Writer's Guide* (Longmans, 1972); I Horabin and B Lewis (D Langdon (ed)), *Algorithms* (Educational Technology Publications, New Jersey, 1978); and T Cormen, *Introduction to Algorithms* (MIT Press, 1990).

It takes the form of a structured series of questions with answers providing instructions for total or partial (when more questions need to be answered) resolution of the problem. Here is the rule in the example above stated in algorithmic form:

Algorithm designed to instruct a court of the limitation on its power to reduce a sentence of imprisonment where the offender has served a 'relevant period'

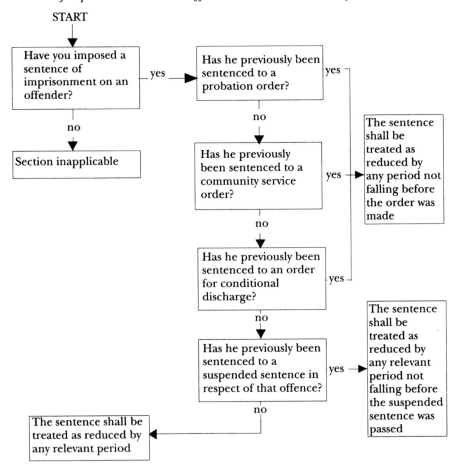

An algorithm comprises a sequence of questions to which the answer is either 'yes' or 'no', each answer automatically taking the reader to the next question relevant to her case. Either of these answers may take the reader outside the ambit of the rule, or provide a solution to her specific case, in which event there is no need to proceed further. Indeed, in such a case, if the algorithm has been constructed properly it should be impossible to proceed further. This last statement indicates a fundamental attribute of the algorithm: it eliminates choice for the reader of a rule. Provided she can answer the questions, the reader of a rule in algorithmic form should always reach the conclusion appropriate in her case. It follows from this also that the reader may not need to read the whole rule, which might otherwise be a source of confusion for her, for the process of questions and answers should mean that she reads only those parts that are applicable to her case. These attributes of the algorithm follow from the fact that in the algorithm the rule is broken down into a series of questions to which the reader can only answer 'yes' or 'no'. This allows us to state one basic rule for algorithm construction.

(a) To each question there can only be one 'yes' and one 'no'. Each 'yes' or 'no' takes the reader automatically to the next relevant question, but this also means that only one question can follow on each answer. In other words, following each answer, the reader has no choice as to the next question. This leads to a second basic rule:
(b) There can be only one question following each answer. The rule above is subject to variation where an answer leads to a conclusion (usually called an 'outcome'). In that event, of course, that part of the algorithm is complete, and no more questions need or can be asked.

The function of an algorithm is to present rules in a visually more comprehensible form than conventional prose.[2] An algorithm will not resolve doubts that may arise as to the scope of a rule. In the example used above, if the reader does not know what is meant by 'any sentence of imprisonment', converting the rule into algorithmic form will not help him to resolve his doubt, though in some cases the conversion may help him to identify more closely the *locus* of his doubt. An algorithm only affects the arrangement of the parts of a rule,[3] and because it cannot resolve doubts arising as to the interpretation of words employed in the rule, or as to the rule's policy, it is defined as a precise set of instructions for resolving a well-defined problem. Converting complex rules into algorithmic form is a useful preliminary to interpretation.

Algorithms can be used both by those who wish to discover the effect of a rule in a particular case and by those teaching and learning about the interpretation of rules. Income tax and VAT returns, house purchase, claims for social security benefits and the like bring the layman into contact with complex rules of law, and here the clarity of the algorithm can help him to establish quickly whether the provisions of a particular rule apply to his case, while its structure may eliminate possible error by saving him the trouble of having to understand the whole provision when only a part of it is applicable.[4]

---

2 Other visualisations are possible; see ER Tufte, *Envisioning Information* (1990), *Visual Explanations* (1997); I Goldrein, 'Multipliers and lump sum payments' (1998) 148 *New Law Journal* 1149, 1237; R Fox, 'Algorithms can take Flow Charts to Next Step for Complex Situations' (1996) 3 *The Law Teacher* 2.
3 It is therefore a precise tool for identifying syntactic ambiguity; see D Miers, 'Barking up the Wrong Tree: Determining the Intention of Parliament' (1992) 13 *Statute Law Rev* 50.
4 See the algorithm in chapter 1, section 6.4. By reason of their structure algorithms are readily usable in electronic form; see, for example, Ferret *Information Services, Welfare Benefits Advice and Assessment System* (1998), and *Legal Aid PC* (1998).

As in the case of sections 157 and 158 of the Radiocommunications Act 1992 (Australia), the draftsmen may construct the algorithm for the reader. Algorithms may also help lawyers to familiarize themselves with the effect of recently published legislative rules; although by virtue of their professional expertise in rule-handling, as a class, they perhaps have less need of assistance.[5]

Algorithms can be a useful educational technique for imparting and acquiring an understanding of the inter-relationship of the parts of a rule. They are adaptable, so that it is possible to move from simple to more difficult exercises. They can also be used to organize into manageable form large quantities of data or other material,[6] for example, the primary, secondary and other authoritative rules in. such areas as company or family law, civil and criminal procedure. They can also be used to show the individual elements of rules not in fixed verbal form, such as, in the example on p 418, the requisites of the tort of defamation. This simplified statement would of course require supplementation from a standard textbook or practitioner's work.

We do not wish to exaggerate the claims made for algorithms in the context of rule-handling. Their more obvious limitations are that they become cumbersome when applied to lengthy rules, that they can take a long time to construct, and that their utility wanes as one becomes familiar with particular rules. Algorithms are a tool for promoting skill in the handling of complex rules and, as such, may be dispensed with at times. In addition, the legal examples given in this Appendix to illustrate what use may be made of algorithms and how they are constructed have primarily been isolated sections from statutes. It goes without saying that this is an artificial way of reading statutory rules, which are normally part of a much wider range of provisions, and which need to be read in the light of them. Thus, the algorithms are to varying degrees incomplete, in that they do not explicitly take account of other relevant rules, and an interpreter who is seeking to present a comprehensive statement of a rule would have to account for them, either by including their text in his algorithm, or by referring to them in some other way.

The process of reasoning in algorithms is not unlike a commonsense approach to problem-solving, in that one seeks to eliminate possibilities by adopting some coherent plan; but perhaps the most important aspect of the acquisition of proficiency in reducing a rule from prose to algorithmic form is

---

5   See, for example, above, p 384 on ss 8-14 of the Police and Criminal Evidence Act 1984; S Wilton, 'Remanding Unruly Juveniles' (1989) 139 *New Law Journal* 718-719 and 'Structured Decision Making in the Fine Default Court' (1988) 138 *New Law Journal* 167; and A Mennie, 'Enforcement of Judgments Flowchart' (1988) 138 *New Law Journal* 254-5, 'Choice of law in contract flowchart' (1998) 148 *New Law Journal* 590.

6   Compare JH Wigmore's technique for analysing masses of evidence: *Science of Judicial Proof* (1937); T Anderson and W Twining, *Analysis of Evidence* (1991). A Wigmore chart is used to give a comprehensive picture of the relations between propositions in an inferential argument about a question of fact based or complex evidence. It is more like the picture of the structure of argument in *Allen* (pp 347ff) than an algorithm or a flow chart, in that relations between the nodes 'tend to support' or 'tend to negate'. Wigmore charts are technically a form of 'directed acyclic graphs whose nodes indicate propositions and whose arcs represent probabilistic linkages among nodes': D Schum, *Evidential Foundations of Probabilistic Reasoning* (1994), pp 169-70. A chart is like an algorithm in that it is binary and is a pictorial device that can be used to structure material, but the two devices should not be confused.

the intellectual discipline that is involved. Before you can present a rule in this way you must be in a position to understand the inter-relationship of the different parts of the rule, and we conclude this brief discussion with the algorithm (on p 419) designed to assist algorithm-writers to evaluate their algorithms, and some exercises in constructing an algorithm.

Exercises

1. Set out below is section 17 of the Juries Act 1974 which provides for majority verdicts in jury trials. Construct an algorithm designed to tell a trial judge when a majority verdict will be acceptable.

> (1) Subject to subsections (3) and (4) below, the verdict of a jury in proceedings in the Crown Court or the High Court need not be unanimous if-
> (a) in a case where there are not less than eleven jurors, ten of them agree on the verdict; and
> (b) in a case where there are ten jurors, nine of them agree on the verdict.
> (2) Subject to subsection (4) below, the verdict of a jury (that is to say a complete jury of eight) in proceedings in a county court need not be unanimous if seven of them agree on the verdict.
> (3) The Crown Court shall not accept a verdict of guilty by virtue of subsection (1) above unless the foreman of the jury has stated in open court the number of jurors who respectively agreed to and dissented from the verdict.
> (4) No court shall accept a verdict by virtue of subsection (1) or (2) above unless it appears to the court that the jury have had such period of time for deliberation as the court thinks reasonable having regard to the nature and complexity of the case; and the Crown Court shall in any event not accept such a verdict unless it appears to the court that the jury have had at least two hours for deliberation.
> (5) This section is without prejudice to any practice in civil proceedings by which a court may accept a majority verdict with the consent of the parties, or by which the parties may agree to proceed in any case with an incomplete jury.

2. Construct an algorithm designed to help a law student understand the structure of section 57 of the Offences against the Person Act 1861 (chapter 1, section 7.1). Would this have been helpful to you before you read *Allen* and *Taylor* (chapter 1, sections 7.2 and 7.3)? Could an algorithm have helped the judges to interpret section 57 in those two cases?

3. Construct an algorithm designed to tell a prisoner what restrictions if any exist upon his sending and receiving letters while in prison (chapter 1, section 4.3.4).

4. Construct algorithms designed to show (a) under what circumstances a person commits an offence of killing, injuring or taking a wild animal, and (b) the prohibited means by which a wild animal may be taken or killed (chapter 1, section 6.1).

5. Construct one or more algorithms designed to show how the provisions in section 67 of the Criminal Justice Act 1967 applied in the cases *R v Home Secretary, ex p Naughton* [1997] 1 All ER 426 and in *R v Governor of Brockhill Prison, ex p Evans* [1997] 1 All ER 439 (chapter 1, section 6.2).

Algorithm designed to show the main requisites for liability in defamation

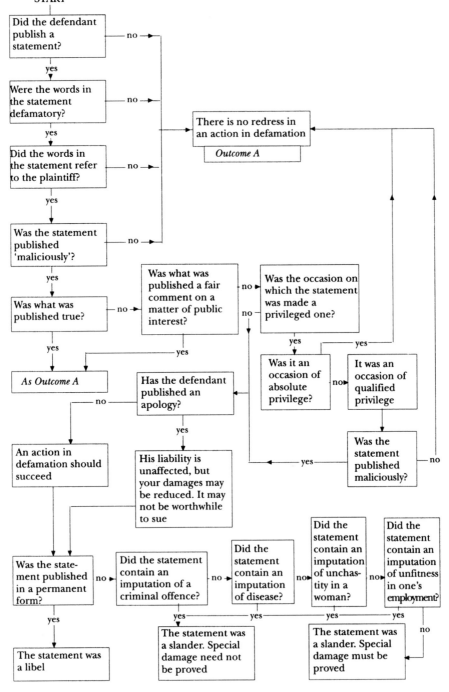

Algorithm designed to help algorithm-writers evaluate their algorithms

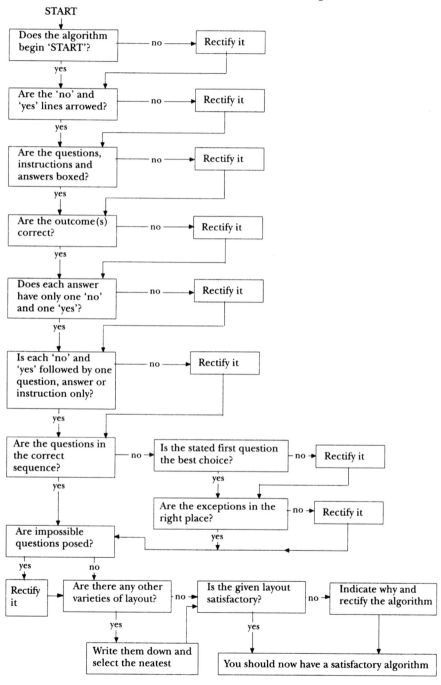

Appendix III

The Reading Law Cookbook[1]

A primer of self-education about law

Abbreviations

BT	W Twining	*Blackstone's Tower* (1994)
CLT	K Llewellyn	*The Common Law Tradition: Deciding Appeals* (1960)
FD	J Farrar and A Dugdale	*Introduction to Legal Method* (3rd edn, 1990)
KLRM	W Twining	*Karl Llewellyn and The Realist Movement* (1973)
LIC	W Twining	*Law in Context: Enlarging a Discipline* (1997)
LLR	J Holland and J Webb	*Learning Legal Rules* (2nd edn, 1993)
MP	D Miers and A Page	*Legislation* (2nd edn, 1990)
TCAL	S Mentschikoff and I Stotzky	*The Theory and Craft of American Law* (1981)

For other citations and abbreviations, see any standard work on how to use a law library.

> I keep six honest serving-men;
> (They taught me all I know)
> Their names are What and Where and
> When
> And How and Why and Who.
> I send them over land and sea,
> I send them east and west;
> But after they have worked for me,
> I give them all a rest.
>
> I let them rest from nine till five,
> For I am busy then,

---

[1] Adapted from W Twining (1989) 24 *Valparaiso University Law Review* 1, reprinted in *Law in Context: Enlarging a Discipline* (1997), chapter 12.

As well as breakfast, lunch, and tea,
For they are hungry men.
But different folk have different views;
I know a person small –
She keeps ten million serving-men,
Who get no rest at all!
She sends 'em abroad on her own
affairs,
From the second she opens her eyes –
One million Hows, two million
Wheres,
And seven million Whys!

Rudyard Kipling

1   Clarification of standpoint

Who am I?
At what stage in what process am I?
What am I trying to do?
Above, 67ff, 116ff, 169ff.

2   Reading any text: Why? What? How?

For what purpose(s) am I reading this?
What are the salient characteristics of this kind of text?
What technique(s) of reading are appropriate for my purpose(s) in reading *this* text?

3   Legal literature in general

(a)   Two useful distinctions

(i)   Within legal discourse: law talk and talk about law. For example: any proposition of law (eg the rule in *Hadley v Baxendale* (1854) 9 Exch 341) is law talk; any historical, sociological or critical statement about legal rules or phenomena falls under 'talk about law'. Legal discourse is often a mixture of law talk and talk about law, with the latter predominating.
(ii)   Within legal literature a corresponding distinction between law books and books about law.[2] 'Law books' include primary sources (eg law reports,

2   RL Abel, 'Law Books and Books about Law' (1973) 26 *Stanford Law Review* 175.

legislation, and secondary accounts of legal doctrine such as treatises, restatements, reference works); 'books about law' is a much wider and more varied category, including historical, philosophical and critical works by legal scholars and many kinds of writings by non-lawyers. These distinctions are, of course, not clear-cut and often break down.

(b)   A total picture of legal literature

Walk around the law library identifying the main types of books, distinguishing between law books and books about law. Then explore the rest of the library and ask: how many law books are there here? How many sections do not contain a significant number of books about law? (BT, ch 5)

4   Newspapers

4A   Introductory: the Newspaper Exercise (see chapter 1, section 1)

WHY?   (a) Affective: law as a subject of study is interesting, relevant to everyday life, personal relationships and public affairs; and it changes daily.
           (b) Consciousness-raising about:
              (i)   the pervasiveness of law in society;
              (ii) the relevance of legal perspectives in interpreting current events;
              (iii) the relevance of international, transnational, European, foreign, Islamic, African, Jewish law in an interdependent world (non-parochialism);
              (iv) the amount of law that students have already experienced before law school;
              (v) the problematic nature of the concepts of 'law' and 'legally relevant'.
WHAT?   Today's newspaper.
HOW?   (a) Reading a whole newspaper per instructions.
           (b) Systematic content analysis.

4B   Media treatment of law (and order)

WHY?   (a) To explore various aspects of the relationship between law and public opinion and opinion-formation – eg 'moral panics'.
           (b) To analyse or deconstruct media treatments of legal issues and events.
WHAT?   News as socially constructed forms of 'knowledge'.
HOW?   (a) Case studies of media treatments of particular issues or events.
           (b) Deconstruction (see below).

REFERENCES

Steve Chibnall, *Law and Order News* (1977); S Cohen, *Folk Devils and Moral Panics* (1972); A Chase, 'Lawyers and Popular Culture' (1986) *ABF Res Journal* 281; J Gaines, *Contested Culture* (1992); S Redhead, *Unpopular Cultures* (1995); Symposium (1989) 98 *Yale Law Journal* 1545.

4C Routine up-date

WHY?	Keeping up to date (a) generally, (b) on specific issues.
WHAT?	This week's or today's news (newspaper, Law-Tel, Lexis, New Law Journal, specialized services).
HOW?	Skim, mark, digest, file.

5 Policy documents

WHAT?	Reports of official committees, private organizations, etc and other documents dealing with issues of public policy or law reform or perceived 'problems' to which law might contribute, eg Royal Commissions; Reports and Working Papers of Law Commissions and law reform bodies; JUSTICE Reports; First Report of Select Committee on Violence in Marriage (above, pp 79-86).
WHY?	Eg diagnosis and analysis of a problem to the solution of which it is thought that law might contribute. (cf 'There oughta be a law.') Part of legislative history of a particular statute.
HOW?	*Quick*

Why? When? Who? To do what? How? What conclusions and recommendations? Then what? So what?

Slow

Why? The historical context of the enquiry leading to the report. *Why then?* Motives for giving task to this committee (whitewash; delay; public demand; to stimulate or dampen public debate; to remove an issue from party politics; social engineering).

When? Main dates in sequence of events from initial triggering event to 'end' of story (eg enactment, shelving or rejection of recommendations).

Who? Membership of committee. Who chose them how? (Spread of interests; orthodox 'great and good'; loaded; significant absentees.)

To do what? Precise terms of reference. How were these interpreted by the committee?

How? Procedures followed. Oral 'evidence'? Specially sponsored research? Public meetings? Discussion documents ('Green papers') etc.

What? Conclusions and recommendations. Perception and diagnosis of the problem. History, context, date. What were perceived to be the main controversial issues. What options considered, rejected. Overt/covert disagreements within the committee.

Then what? Post-report events.

So what? Historical, analytical, theoretical significance of the report and its story for this reader.

Some variants

1. Other kinds of report (eg 'fact-finding' enquiries); other kinds of policy document.
2. Some official reports provide exceptionally useful syntheses and statements of existing law, historical background, public debates and social data. They are accordingly useful as materials of law study for a variety of purposes.

Note: Reports of Royal Commissions, official committees and the like have probably been more *politically* significant in UK than in USA. Nevertheless it is fair to say that they number among neglected materials of law study in both countries.

REFERENCES

Above ch 2; symposium (1980) 48 *Modern Law Review* 558; MP, chs 11 and 12; M Komarovsky, *Sociology and Public Policy: The Case of Presidential Commissions* (1975); RA Chapman, *The Role of Commissions in Policy-Making* (1973); AM Platt (ed), *The Politics of Riot Commissions* (1971); S Cretney, 'The Politics of Law Reform' (1985) 48 *Modern Law Review* 505.

6   Legislation

Quick

WHY? Eg (a) To learn about the structure and content of the instrument as a whole.

(b) To find and interpret the exact words in the text applicable to a particular point of law.

(c) To use as raw material for a legal argument.

(d) Other.

HOW? For (a), chart the design of the statute (above, pp 413-419; FD, chs 7-8); thereafter depends on exact purpose. For (b) and (c), clarify standpoint; identify relevant statutory materials; where appropriate, locate exact words in text giving rise to doubt; consider immediate textual context: adjoining words; this section; statute as a whole; collect relevant non-statutory materials; state competing interpretations; specify the conditions of doubt; construct argument.

REFERENCES

Above, ch 7; KLRM, pp 239-245; MP, chs 11-12; J Bell and G Engle QC, *Cross on Statutory Interpretation* (3rd edn, 1995); F Bennion, *Statutory Interpretation* (3rd edn, 1997); D MacCormick and R Summers (eds), *Interpreting Statutes: A Comparative Survey* (1991); G Calabresi, *A Common Law for the Age of Statutes* (1982).

Slow
No cookbook can make you skilful at handling statutes.

7 Law Reports I: Orthodox reading

7A The single case

1 Précis ('briefing a case')

Quick
WHY?   A necessary foundation for most purposes for which cases are read.
WHAT?   'A case is the *written memorandum of a dispute or controversy* between *persons,* telling with varying degrees of completeness and of accuracy, *what happened, what each of the parties did about it,* what some supposedly impartial *judge or other tribunal* did in the way of bringing the dispute or controversy to an *end,* and the avowed *reasons* of the judge or tribunal for doing what was done.' (Dowling et al. See above, pp 305ff.)
HOW?   A standard form of précis covering:
            (a) Title; citation; court; topic(s); outcome (who won?); order.
            (b) Facts; question(s) of law; competing answers to questions; holding (court's answer to question); reasons for decision. Comment. Eg case note of *R v Allen,* above, p 311.
Slow   (c) Additional details, eg on procedure, arguments of counsel, treatment of prior authorities; reasoning of individual judges; historical background to this case (see below, 8B and 10).

2 Attacking an adverse precedent

WHY?   To weaken authority and persuasive force of a precedent.
WHAT?   A potentially adverse precedent.
HOW?   Precedent techniques – ie cumulation of *reasons* for not following or applying prior case to the case at hand.
            Eg Treatment of *Fanning* in *Allen* (above, pp 361-362). This was an *Irish* case; four judges dissented; *Fanning* based on misinterpretation of prior cases; *Fanning* inconsistent with prior cases.
            NB: Cockburn CJ could have distinguished *Fanning,* but chose not to do so. Why not?
            Above, pp 325ff; CLT, pp 77-92.

3 Boosting the precedent value of a favourable precedent

Eg this case is indistinguishable from the present case; it is a judgment of Dixon (a former Chief Justice of Australia; see Diplock LJ in *Gould,* above p 388) (or some other respected judge); the reasoning was impeccably based on principle and authority; it has been followed in subsequent cases; it makes sense.

7B   Groups of cases

1 Synthesizing all relevant precedents on a single question of law

WHY?   Eg to resolve a doubt about the law; constructing a legal argument; exposition of a legal topic.
WHAT?   A collection of authoritative decisions and arguments about the issue in question.
HOW?   Grand style synthesis of potentially conflicting precedents.

2 Studying a sequence of cases on a topic

WHY?   TCAL, pp 297-298
WHAT?   A temporal sequence of precedents in a single jurisdiction.
HOW?   FD, ch 8; TCAL, pp 297-298; E Levi, *Introduction to Legal Reasoning* (1949) on Negligence/Product Liability and the Mann Act; C Manchester et al, *Exploring the Law* (1996), part 3.

8   Law Reports II: Less orthodox readings

The law reports tend to be over-emphasized in legal education in respect of orthodox reading, at the expense of other materials of law study. On the other hand, they are also an under-exploited resource in terms of other purposes and methods of analysis. The following is a sample of alternative modes of reading and using law reports.

8A   Reconstructing the arguments in a single case

Eg charting the structure of the arguments in *Allen,* above, pp 347ff.

8B   Analyzing the conditions of doubt giving rise to disagreement or doubt about the law

Objective: to diagnose in depth *why* there was a doubt or dispute about the law in a past case.
WHAT?   The reported opinion(s) (and, if available, summary of arguments of counsel and/or the briefs).
WHY?   (a) as a preliminary to reconstructing the arguments in the case; or
            (b) to analyze the case in depth as raw material for constructing an argument on a point of law; or
            (c) for some other purpose.

HOW?

Quick   What conditions gave rise to the doubt(s) in this case?

Which of these conditions relate to

(a) events preceding the creation of the rule or doctrine relevant to the case?

(b) incompleteness, indeterminacy or imperfection of applicable doctrine at the time;

(c) events after the original creation of the rule or doctrine;

(d) special features of this case?

Slow   (a) Which of the check-list of 36 conditions of doubt (above, ch 6) apply to this case?

(b) Are there any others?

(c) Which of these conditions formed the basis, on its own or in combination, for a colourable argument for one side?

(d) Was this an appellate case worth appealing or was it foredoomed? (CLT, pp 25n, 27; KLRM, pp 248-249.)

(e) Was this a 'hard case' in Dworkin's sense? Did any of the issues relate to matters that are 'essentially contested'?

8C Analysis of styles of reasoning of judicial opinions

Objective: to analyze a single opinion or a collection of opinions in terms of the style employed.

WHAT?   Judicial opinions.

WHY?   (a) to determine whether an individual judge or a particular court conformed to a given style of reasoning at a given moment of time or during a given period; or

(b) as an aid to predicting how a known judge or court is likely to respond to a particular point or line of argument; or

(c) to compare and contrast predominant styles of individual judges, courts or legal traditions in different times or places. Eg to compare the judgments of Lord Mansfield and Lord Eldon; the opinions of the US Supreme Court or speeches in the House of Lords in 1900, 1950 and 1990; appellate cases in different common law and civil law jurisdictions; the styles of the Court of Justice of the European Communities and the European Court of Human Rights.

HOW?

Quick   To what extent does the material fit into Llewellyn's ideal types of Grand Style and Formal Style reasoning?

Slow   See Gillis Wetter, *The Styles of Appellate Judicial Opinions* (1960), discussed in CLT, pp 465 ff and KLRM, pp 265-266, 455.

8D   Critical analysis of the corpus of opinions of a single judge

Eg J Jowell and JPWB McAuslan (eds), *Lord Denning: The Judge and the Law* (1984).

8E   Critical analysis of alleged political biases of one or more courts, by considering treatment of cases involving women, ethnic minorities, students, labour unions, etc

Eg JAG Griffith, *The Politics of the Judiciary* (5th edn, 1997).

8F   Deconstruction of judicial opinions

Eg Murphy and Rawlings, 'After the Ancient Regime' (1981) 44 *Modern Law Review* 617; C Husson, 'Expanding the Legal Vocabulary: The Challenge Posed by the Deconstruction and Defense of Law' (1986) 95 *Yale Law Journal* 969; D Balkin, 'Deconstructive Practice and Legal Theory' (1987) 96 *Yale Law Journal* 743; M Freeman, *Lloyd's Introduction to Jurisprudence* (6th edn, 1994), ch 12 (critical legal studies) and ch 13 (feminist jurisprudence).

8G   Quantitative analysis of judicial opinions

Eg Glendon Schubert, *Judicial Behaviour* (1964).

8H   Economic analysis of legal doctrine

R Posner, *Economic Analysis of Law* (5th edn, 1998).

8I   Narrative

W Twining, 'Lawyers' Stories', in *Rethinking Evidence* (1994), ch 7; B Jackson, *Law, Fact and Narrative Coherence* (1988); W Wagenaar, P van Koppen and H Crombag, *Anchored Narratives* (1993).

8J   Participant perspectives

The experience and consequences of being involved in litigation from the standpoint of the parties or other participants (eg witnesses; legal worms).
C Knapp: '... no study of law is adequate if it loses sight of the fact that law operates first and last *for, upon* and *through* individual human beings'; John T Noonan, *Persons and Masks of the Law* (1976); Charles Dickens, *Bleak House;* Jonathon Harr, *A Civil Action* (1996). See further below at 10 (Contextual studies.)

9 Trial records

One of the most neglected kinds of materials of law study.

9A Analysis of evidence in cases involving disputed questions of fact

WHY?	(a) Organizing a mixed mass of evidence in order to structure an argument about a disputed question of fact.
	(b) Microscopic analysis, construction and evaluation of arguments from evidence.
WHAT?	Eg trial records and secondary accounts of trials involving disputed questions of fact. National trial competition problems.
HOW?	Wigmore's Chart Method.

REFERENCES

JH Wigmore, 'The Problem of Proof' (1913) 8 *Illinois Law Review* 77; T Anderson and W Twining, *Analysis of Evidence* (1991); W Twining, *Theories of Evidence: Bentham and Wigmore* (1985), ch 3 and appendix; J Kadane and D Schum, *The Sacco-Vanzetti Case: A Probabilistic Analysis* (1996).

9B Miscarriages of Justice

WHY?	Analyze what factors contributed to acknowledged or alleged failures in the criminal justice system.
WHAT?	Trial records or secondary accounts of *causes célèbres* (eg Sacco-Vanzetti; Alger Hiss; Bywaters and Thompson; Luke Dougherty in the Devlin Report).
HOW?	Various methods. See eg Landsman (1986) 85 *Michigan Law Review* 1095; Twining, *Rethinking Evidence* (1994), ch 8; Ludovic Kennedy, *The Airman and the Carpenter* (Hauptman) (1985); Paul Foot, *Who Killed Hanratty?* (1971); Bob Woffinden, *Miscarriages of Justice* (1987); J Kadane and D Schum, op cit; annual reports of the Criminal Cases Review Commission.

9C Models

Eg famous cross-examinations. F Wellman, *The Art of Cross-Examination* (various editions).

10 Contextual studies of leading cases

WHY?	In-depth study of a leading case in its historical context.
WHAT?	Contextual studies of particular cases.
HOW?	Problematic. See W Twining, 'Cannibalism and Legal Literature' (1986) 6 *Oxford Journal of Legal Studies* 423.

Examples: *Hadley v Baxendale, Carlill v Carbolic Smoke Ball*, and *Rylands v Fletcher*: these and other examples of leading cases are discussed in AWB Simpson, *Leading Cases in the Common Law* (1995). See also his *Cannibalism and the Common Law* (1984, Penguin 1986) discussing the case *R v Dudley and Stephens. Brown v Board of Education*, R Kluger, *Simple Justice* (1975); *Palsgraf v Long Island*, John T Noonan, Jr, *Persons and Masks of the Law* (1976), pp 111-151.

11 Reading a juristic or other secondary text: the historical, the analytical and the applied

Assuming the purpose is to enter into a dialogue with the text on issues on which it is potentially significant.

11A Historical

Quick   What were the author's central concerns in writing this text? What was biting her?

Slow   Who was the author?

When was the text written, published?

What was the immediate (practical, intellectual, personal, cultural) context of its creation?

Where does it fit in the author's total opus/intellectual development?

Whence? Sources, 'influences' etc.

What were the author's main concerns?

11B Analytical

1 Exposition

Quick   What questions does the text address?

What answers does it give to those questions?

What are the reasons (evidence, premisses, arguments) advanced in support of the answers?

Slow   Detailed textual analysis and interpretation.

2 Dialogue

Quick   Do I agree with the questions?

Do I agree with the answers?

Do I agree with the reasons?

Slow   Critical analysis of multiple interpretations.

Which is the least vulnerable interpretation of the question(s), answer(s), reason(s) etc?

11C Applied

Implications and Applications

Quick	So what?
	What are the logical implications of the answers?
	What is the historical significance of the text?
	What is the contemporary significance of the text?
Slow	Detailed study of implications, consequences and other 'significance'.

Quentin Skinner, *Machiavelli* (1981); *The Bramble Bush*; KLRM, pp 140-152; on 'The Path of the Law', see (1983) 58 *Cornell Law Review* 275; Symposium (1997) 83 *Brooklyn Law Review*, W Twining, 'Talk about Realism'(1985) 60 *New York University Law Review* 333-338; 'Reading Bentham'(1989) LXXV *Procs of the British Academy* 97.

12 Case-books

See: B Currie, 'The Materials of Law Study'(1951) 3 *Journal of Legal Education* 331, and (1955) 8 *Journal of Legal Education* 1; KLRM, pp 128-140. For a feminist perspective see Frug (1985) 34 *American University Law Review* 1065.

13 Textbooks

W Twining, 'Is your Textbook Really Necessary?' (1970) 11 *Journal of Society of Public Teachers of Law* (NS) 81; cf (1973) 12 *Legal Studies* 267 (1973); D Sugarman, 'Legal Theory, The Common Law Mind and the Making of the Textbook Tradition', in W Twining (ed), *Common Law and Legal Theory* (1986), ch 3.

14 Law Reviews

Symposium (1985) 36 *Journal of Legal Education* 1; F Rodell, 'Goodbye to Law Reviews' (1936-37) 23 *Virginia Law Review* 38 and (1962) 48 *Virginia Law Review* 279.

15 Cookbooks (nutshells, swots, outlines, etc)

standpoint:	law student	law teacher
	why?	*why not?*
	To save effort.	It saves effort.
	It provides structure.	It reveals the ball.
	It succinctly summarizes information.	It substitutes for skill and understanding.
	It is useful for professional exams.	This is not a cram course.
what?	Well-organized, concise summary.	Superficial nutshell of facts.
how?	Memorize.	Don't!

16 Not dealt with

Reference works, treatises, restatements, treaty series, legal history, constitutions etc, etc (BT, pp 112-18).

17 Reading about law

See: Main library.
Why? What? How? – That is another story.
JJ Marke (ed), *Deans' List of Recommended Reading for Pre-Law and Law Students* (1984); E Gemmette, 'Law and Literature: An unnecessarily suspect class in the Liberal Arts Component of Law School Curriculum' (1989) 23 *Valparaiso University Law Review* 267; R Posner, *Law and Literature: A Misunderstood Relation* (1988); A Welch, *Strong Representations: Narrative and Circumstantial Evidence in English Law* (1992); Martha Nussbaum, *Poetic Justice: The Literary Imagination and Public Life* (1995). See further, Appendix IV, p 442 and William Twining on 'Horizontal Reading' in *Law In Context*, at 234-236.

Appendix IV

Suggestions for Further Reading

The following is a selective bibliography of writings which provide possible starting points for exploring in more detail some of the more general themes and particular topics touched on in the text. See also William Twining, *Law in Context: Enlarging a Discipline* (Oxford, 1998), pp 234-236.

General

We know of no single work which covers exactly the same ground as the present one, but the following have points of contact in a number of places. Max Black, *Critical Thinking* (Prentice-Hall, 1952); Douglas Walton, *Informal Logic* (Cambridge University Press, 1989); ER Emmet, *The Use of Reason* (Longman, 1960) and *Learning to Philosophise* (Longman, 1960; Pelican, 1968) are useful general introductions to the more analytical aspects of the study of rules and their interpretation. Mary Douglas (ed), *Rules and Meanings* (Penguin, 1973) and the entertaining D Fraser, *Cricket and the Law: the Man in White is Always Right* (Sydney University Law School, 1993) provide useful insights into sociological and anthropological literature. James B White, *The Legal Imagination* (Little, Brown, 1973) contains a great deal of material, non-legal and legal, which could be used to illustrate and expand many of the themes in this book.

For readers with no prior legal background useful starting points are Brian Simpson, *Invitation to Law* (Basil Blackwell, 1988); Jeremy Waldron, *The Law* (Routledge, 1990); John Adams and Roger Brownsword, *Understanding Law* (Fontana, 1992); Wade Mansell, Belinda Meteyard and Alan Thomson, *A Critical Introduction to Law* (Cavendish, 1995); A Bottomley (ed), *Feminist Perspectives on the Foundational Subjects of Law* (Cavendish, 1996); Phil Harris, *Introduction to Law* (Butterworths, 5th edn, 1997); and Fiona Cowney and Anthony Bradney, *English Legal System in Context* (Butterworths, 1995). A number of books have been published in recent years which deal with legal method and legal skills: John Farrar and Tony Dugdale, *Introduction to Legal Method* (Sweet and Maxwell, 3rd edn, 1990); Iain McLeod, *Legal Method* (Macmillan, 1993); Simon Lee, Marie Fox and Christine Bell, *Learning Legal Skills* (Blackstone, 1996); J Holland and J Webb, *Learning Legal Rules* (Blackstone, 3rd edn, 1996) and David Carson, *Learning Critical Skills* (Blackstone, 1998). Karl Llewellyn's *The Bramble Bush* (Oceana, 2nd edn, 1951) is very different in conception and style, but was also directed to beginning law students in the United States. Our own approach has been influenced by Llewellyn (even the legalistic child grew out of one of his examples). Chapters 1–5 of *The Bramble Bush* are directly relevant.

Most standard introductions to jurisprudence either concentrate on the ideas of leading jurists or so-called schools of jurisprudence, or else approach the subject through standard issues in political theory. The approach adopted in this book is designed to stimulate students to think about theoretical issues actively ('to do jurisprudence') before proceeding to the detailed study of what others have said about these theories ('reading about jurisprudence'). We therefore hope that this book can be used as a preliminary to reading HLA Hart's *The Concept of Law* (Clarendon Press, 2nd edn, 1994); Ronald Dworkin's *Law's Empire* (Fontana, 1986); writings by Karl Llewellyn or Critical Legal Studies writers. Among general works on jurisprudence that can be recommended are: George Fletcher, *Basic Concepts of Legal Thought* (Oxford University Press, New York, 1996); J Harris, *Legal Philosophies* (Butterworths, 2nd edn, 1997); R Cotterrell, *The Politics of Jurisprudence* (Butterworths, 1989); MDA Freeman, *Lloyd's Introduction to Jurisprudence* (Stevens, 6th edn, 1994); N Simmonds, *Central Issues in Jurisprudence* (Sweet and Maxwell, 1986). See also Richard Susskind, *The Future of Law* (Oxford University Press, rev edn, 1998); P Washburn, *Philosophical Dilemmas* (Oxford University Press, 1997); and G Samuel, *Epistemology and Method in Law* (Ashgate, 1999).

Chapters 1–2

On problems, see John Dewey's *How We Think* (Harrap, 1909) and *Logic: The Theory of Enquiry* (Holt, Rinehart and Winston, reprinted 1966); Clarence Morris, *How Lawyers Think* (A Swallow, 1937, 1962); M Constanzo, *Problem Solving* (Cavendish, 1994), ch 2; S Nathanson, *What Lawyers DO: A Problem-solving Approach to Legal Practice* (Sweet and Maxwell, 1997); G Polya, *How to Solve It* (Princeton University Press, 2nd edn, 1957); and John R Hayes, *The Complete Problem Solver* (Lawrence Erlbaum, 2nd edn, 1989). On 'social problems' see A Giddens, *Sociology* (3rd edn, 1997) and the literature cited there. On domestic violence see Lorna Smith, *Domestic Violence* (HMSO, Home Office Research Study 107, 1989) and S Edwards, *Policing Domestic Violence* (Sage, 1989). On 'moral panics' see Stuart Hall, *Policing the Crisis* (Macmillan, 1978) which deals with official and press responses to an alleged increase in the incidence of mugging. On the contrast between the way lawyers and their clients perceive and define 'problems', see Z Bankowski and G Mungham, *Images of Law* (Routledge, 1976), pp 32ff. For a useful account of the constraints on rational policy-making as a response to problems, see JJ Richardson and AG Jordan, *Governing Under Pressure* (Basil Blackwell, 2nd edn, 1985), and on alternative methods of dispute resolution see S Goldberg, E Green and F Sander, *Dispute Resolution* (Little, Brown, 1985) and M Palmer and S Roberts, *Dispute Processes: ADR and the Primary Forms of Decision-Making* (Butterworths, 1998).

Chapter 3

The philosophical and sociological literature is vast and rapidly expanding. The following is a selection of standard theoretical writings. Helpful general discussions of the nature of rules are to be found in Max Black, *Models and Metaphors* (Cornell University Press, 1962); Newton Garver, 'Rules' in P Edwards (ed), *Encyclopedia of Philosophy* (Macmillan, 2nd edn, 1967); D Schwayder, *The Stratification of Behaviour* (Routledge, 1965); K Baier, *The Moral Point of View* (Cornell University Press, 1955; Random House, 1965); P Collett (ed), *Social Rules and Social Behaviour* (Basil Blackwell, 1977); and F Schauer, *Playing by the Rules* (Oxford University Press, 1991). Also worth consulting are D Emmett, *Rules, Roles and Relations* (Macmillan, 1966); RS Downie, *Roles and Values* (Methuen, 1961); Peter Brooks and Paul Gewirtz (eds), *Law's Stories* (Yale University Press, 1996), chs 4–6 and references in the *Reading Law Cookbook* (Appendix III above); and R Epstein, *Simple Rules for a Complex World* (Harvard University Press, 1995). Rather more advanced are G von Wright, *Norm and Action* (Allen and Unwin, 1968); D Lewis, *Convention* (Harvard University Press, 1969); G Gottlieb, *The Logic of Choice* (Allen and Unwin, 1968); Edna Ullman-Margalit, *The Emergence of Norms* (Oxford University Press, 1977); A Ross, *Directives and Norms* (Routledge, 1968); and F Waismann, *The Principles of Linguistic Philosophy* (Macmillan, 1965), especially chs 1, 2 and 7. See also Judith Shklar, *Legalism* (Harvard University Press, 1964).

On the distinction between rules, habits, commands and predictions, see especially Hart, *The Concept of Law* (op cit), passim, and the defence and refinement of Hart's views in DN MacCormick, *HLA Hart* (Arnold, 1981). On rules and principles see R Dworkin, *Taking Rights Seriously* (Duckworth, 1977) and *A Matter of Principle* (Harvard University Press, 1985). On analysis of duty, right, etc, see W Hohfeld, *Fundamental Legal Conceptions* (Yale University Press, 1964) and RWM Dias, *Jurisprudence* (Butterworths, 5th edn, 1985), ch 8. On 'systems' see C Sampford, *The Disorder of Law* (Basil Blackwell, 1989). On attitudes to rules see, for example, Jean Piaget, *The Moral Judgment of the Child* (Routledge and Kegan Paul, 1932) and JL Tapp and FJ Levine, 'Legal Socialisation: Strategies for an Ethical Legality', (1972) 27 *Stanford Law Review* and works cited there. On justified departures from legal rules, see M Kadish and S Kadish, *Discretion to Disobey* (Stanford University Press, 1973); KC Davis, *Discretionary Justice* (University of Illinois, 1971); HW Arthurs, *Without the Law: Adminstrative Justice and Legal Pluralism in Nineteenth Century England* (University of Toronto Press, 1985); D Galligan, *Discretionary Powers* (Oxford University Press, 1986); R Baldwin, *Rules and Government* (Oxford University Press, 1995); and K Hawkins, *The Uses of Discretion* (Clarendon Press, 1992).

On the functions of rules and the law jobs theory, see K Llewellyn, *Jurisprudence* (Chicago University Press, 1962), ch 14; K Llewellyn, 'The Normative, the Legal and Law Jobs', (1940) 49 *Yale Law Journal* 1355; and KN Llewellyn and EA Hoebel, *The Cheyenne Way* (University of Oklahoma Press, 1941), especially chs 10 and 11. In considering the law-jobs theory it is useful to take account of R Merton, *On Theoretical Sociology* (Free Press, 1967); Alan Hunt, *The Sociological Movement in Law* (Macmillan, 1978) and R Cotterrell, *The Sociology of Law: An Introduction*

(Butterworths, 2nd edn, 1992). See further William Twining, *Karl Llewellyn and the Realist Movement* (Weidenfeld and Nicolson, 1973), ch 9 and Appendices B and C. On regulation see Keith Hawkins, *Environment and Enforcement* (Clarendon Press, 1984); R Baldwin and JC McCrudden, *Regulation and Public Law* (Weidenfeld and Nicolson, 1987); A Ogus, *Regulation: Legal Form and Economic Theory* (Oxford University Press, 1994); Julia Black, *Rules and Regulators* (Oxford University Press, 1997); and R Baldwin, C Scott and C Hood (eds), *A Reader on Regulation* (Oxford University Press, 1998).

On interpreting 'reality' see Douglas, *Rules and Meanings* (op cit); Peter Berger and Thomas Luckman, *The Social Construction of Reality* (Allen Lane, 1967); and William Twining, *Rethinking Evidence* (Northwestern University Press, 1994).

Chapters 4–6

On the interpretation of the world about us, see Z Bauman, *Legislators and Interpreters* (Polity Press, 1987). On theories concerning the interpretation of legal and literary texts, see Dworkin, *Law's Empire* (op cit) and *A Matter of Principle* (op cit), ch 7; P Goodrich, *Reading the Law* (Basil Blackwell, 1986); R Posner, *Law and Literature* (University of Chicago Press, 1989), especially ch 5; James B White, *Heracles' Bow* (Unversity of Wisconsin Press, 1985); S Fish, *Is There a Text in the Class?* (Harvard University Press, 1980) and *Doing What Comes Naturally* (Clarendon Press, 1989); T Eagleton, *Literary Theory: An Introduction* (Basil Blackwell, 1983); and M Kelman, *A Guide to Critical Legal Studies* (Harvard University Press, 1987). See also references in the *Reading Law Cookbook* (Appendix III above).

On the relationship between rule-makers and interpreters see L Fuller, 'The Case of the Speluncean Explorers', (1949) 62 *Harvard Law Review* 616 and L Jaffe, *English and American Judges as Law-Makers* (Clarendon Press, 1969). R Megarry's *Miscellany at Law* (Stevens, 1955) and *A Second Miscellany at Law* (Stevens, 1973) are rich treasuries of concrete, often amusing, examples of many of the points made in Chapters 4–6.

The main themes in Chapter 5 take Hart's *The Concept of Law* (op cit) as their starting point. For a contrasting approach see particularly L Fuller, *The Morality of Law* (Yale University Press, 1969). Two works offering additional perspectives are P Bobbit, *Constitutional Interpretation* (Blackwell, 1991) and A Marmor, *Interpretation and Legal Theory* (Clarendon Press, 1992). On language and the law see Jim Evans, *Statutory Interpretation* (Butterworths, 1989), especially ch 2, and B Bix, *Law, Language and Legal Determinacy* (Oxford University Press, 1995). In addition to the works by Black and Emmet cited under the heading 'General', the following introductions to semantics and clear thinking are recommended: R Thouless, *Straight and Crooked Thinking* (Pan, 1974); Susan Stebbing, *Thinking to Some Purpose* (Penguin, 1939); S Ullman, *Words and Their Uses* (Muller, 1961); Stewart Chase, *The Tyranny of Words* (Methuen, 6th edn, 1947); J Wilson, *Thinking With Concepts* (Cambridge University Press, 1971); and Anthony Flew, *Thinking About Thinking* (Fontana, 1975). At some stage during their education, all law students should read JL Austin, *How to Do Things with Words* (Oxford University Press, 1962).

On the 'intention' of the legislature see RWM Dias, *Bibliography of Jurisprudence* (Butterworths, 3rd edn, 1979); R Bork, 'Neutral Principles and First Amendment Problems', (1979) 47 *Indiana Law Journal* 1; A Scalia, *A Matter of Interpretation: Federal Courts and the Law* (Princeton UP, 1997) and Dworkin, *Law's Empire* (op cit). For discussion of Dworkin's ideas, see Marmor, op cit, and S Guest, *Ronald Dworkin* (Edinburgh University Press, 2nd edn, 1997). On the development of rules in response to novel or exceptional circumstances, see L Fuller, 'Reason and Fiat in Case Law', (1946) 59 *Harvard Law Review* 376 and 'Human Purpose and Natural Law', (1958) 3 *Natural Law Forum* 68, and Ian McNeil, 'The Many Futures of Contracts', (1974) 47 *Southern California Law Review* 691.

Chapters 7 and 8

For a systematic description of the preparation, enactment, interpretation and impact of legislation, see D Miers and A Page, *Legislation* (Sweet and Maxwell, 2nd edn, 1990). The *Statute Law Review* (Oxford University Press) is a valuable periodical which also deals with the teaching of legislation.

The Government and Politics of Britain by J Mackintosh (Hutchinson, 5th edn, 1982) and *The Legislative Process in Great Britain* by SA Walkland (Allen and Unwin, 1968) are standard works. On law, government and politics, see further Richardson and Jordan, *Governing Under Pressure* (op cit), the Cabinet Office's *Better Regulation Guide* (1998); D Butler, A Adonis and T Travers, *Failure in British Government: the Politics of the Poll Tax* (Oxford University Press, 1994); and C Harlow and R Rawlings, *Law and Administration* (Butterworths, 2nd edn, 1997). On parliamentary matters see *Parliament* by J Griffith and M Ryle (Sweet and Maxwell, 1989) and D Oliver and G Drewry, *The Law and Parliament* (Butterworths, 1998). *Parliamentary Scrutiny of Government Bills* (Allen and Unwin, 1974) by J Griffith is a classic study of the impact of parliamentary debate on legislative proposals.

On devolution, see R Hazell (ed), *Constitutional Futures: A History of the Next Ten Years* (Oxford University Press, 1999); and V Bogdanor, *Devolution* (Oxford University Press, 1979). On Community law see J Usher, *EC Institutions and Legislation* (Longmans, 1998) and *General Principles of EC Law* (Longmans, 1998); P Craig and G de Burca, *EU Law: Text and Materials* (Oxford University Press, 2nd edn, 1998) and I Ward, *A Critical Introduction to European Law* (Butterworths, 1996); E Ellis and T Tridimas, *Public Law of the European Community* (Sweet and Maxwell, 1995); P Giddings and G Drewry (eds), *Westminster and Europe* (Macmillan, 1995).

On the European Convention and the Human Rights Act 1998 see J Wadham and H Mountfield, *Blackstone's Guide to the Human Rights Act 1998* (Blackstone Press, 1998); F Jacobs and R White, *The European Convention on Human Rights* (Clarendon Press, 1996); and Luke Clements, *European Human Rights: Taking a Case Under the Convention* (Sweet and Maxwell, 2nd edn, 1999).

A specifically legal account of the preparation of legislation is F Bennion, *Statute Law* (Longman, 3rd edn, 1990); specialized accounts of drafting include E Driedger, *The Composition of Legislation and Legislative Forms and Precedents* (Department of Justice, Ottawa, 2nd edn, 1976), R Dickerson, *Fundamentals of Legal Drafting* (Little, Brown, 1965); G Thornton, *Legislative Drafting* (Butterworths, 3rd edn, 1987); and V Crabbe, *Legislative Drafting* (Cavendish, 1994). Introductory works include V Crabbe, *Understanding Statutes* (Cavendish, 1995) and D Gifford and J Salter, *How to Understand an Act of Parliament* (Cavendish, 1996). *In on the Act* by Sir H Kent (Macmillan, 1979) is the memoirs of a former Parliamentary Counsel, and provides a rare and valuable, if a little dated, account of the Parliamentary Counsel Office. A different perspective is provided by the plain English movement: see M Cutts, *Lucid Law* (Plain Language Commission, 1994).

There have been many publications critical of the arrangements for the preparation and enactment of Bills. Among these is the now classic report of the Renton Committee, *The Preparation of Legislation* (Cmnd 6053, 1975); see further Sir R Andrew, *Review of Government Legal Services* (1989, Cabinet Office), and 'Making the Law', the Report of the Hansard Society Commission on the Legislative Process (1992; Chairman, Lord Howe). There have been a number of reports prepared by the Procedure Committees of each of the House of Commons and the House of Lords. In the late 1990s the Commons' Modernisation Committee published a number of proposals; these are discussed in D Miers, 'Legislation and the Legislative Process' (1998) 29 *The Law Librarian* 87.

The literature on interpretation falls broadly into two groups. On the one hand are texts that aim to give a technical account of the courts' approach; prime amongst these is F Bennion's magisterial *Statutory Interpretation* (Butterworths, 3rd edn, 1997); see also his *Pepper v Hart in its Context* (Oxford University Press, 1995). Rather different are texts designed for the student and wider jurisprudential interests. These include J Bell and G Engle, *Cross on Statutory Interpretation* (Butterworths, 3rd edn, 1995); M Freeman (ed) *Legislation and the Courts* (Ashgate, 1997); Jim Evans, *Statutory Interpretation* (op cit); N MacCormick and R Summers, *Interpreting Statutes: A Comparative Study* (Dartmouth, 1991); and W Eskridge, *Dynamic Statutory Interpretation* (Harvard University Press, 1994). Though dated, a critical account is the Law Commission's excellent *The Interpretation of Statutes* (Law Com No 21, HC paper 256). More recent assessments of the nature of statutory interpretation derive their inspiration from theoretical writing on language: general introductions are Goodrich, *Reading The Law* (op cit) and B Jackson, *Semiotics and Legal Theory* (Routledge and Kegan Paul, 1985).

Chapter 9

In the British literature on the interpretation of cases, discussion has centred very largely on the rules of precedent; see in particular, R Cross, *Precedent in English Law* (Clarendon Press, 4th edn, J Harris, 1991). Theoretical treatments are R Wasserstrom, *The Judicial Decision* (Stanford University Press, 1961) and L Goldstein (ed), *Precedent in Law* (Clarendon Press, 1987). N MacCormick and R Summers, *Interpreting Precedents* (Dartmouth, 1997) provides a valuable comparative account.

As should be clear from the text, we are more in sympathy with the analysis adopted by KN Llewellyn in *The Common Law Tradition* (Little, Brown, 1960) and *The Case Law System in America* (trs M Ansaldi, ed P Gewirtz, University of Chicago Press, 1989). Other classic works by American writers such as B Cardozo, *The Nature of the Judicial Process* (Yale University Press, 1921); J Frank, *Courts on Trial* (Atheneum, 1949) and OW Holmes, 'The Path of the Law', (1897) 10 *Harvard Law Review* 457 are recommended. Useful accounts of how judges approach their tasks are Lord Devlin, *The Judge* (Oxford University Press, 1961); B Laskin, *The Institutional Character of the Judge* (Hebrew University of Jerusalem, 1972); RB Stevens, *Law and Politics* (Weidenfeld and Nicolson, 1979); A Paterson, *The Law Lords* (Macmillan, 1982); JAG Griffith, *The Politics of the Judiciary* (Fontana, 5th edn, 1997); and M Detmold, *Courts and Administrators* (Weidenfeld and Nicolson, 1989). On South Africa see D Dyzenaus, *Judging the Judges and Ourselves* (Hart, 1998).

Chapter 10

Useful introductions to reasoning in general include the works by Black, Emmet and Flew cited under Chapters 4–6 and R Hospers, *Introduction to Philosophical Analysis* (Routledge, 2nd edn, 1969). See also Peter Alexander, *An Introduction to Logic* (Allen and Unwin, 1969); S Mellone, *Elements of Modern Logic* (Tutorial Press, 2nd edn, 1958); M Cohen and E Nagel, *An Introduction to Logic* (Routledge, 1963) and N Rescher, *Dialectics* (State University of New York, 1977).

On practical reasoning see S Toulmin, *The Uses of Argument* (Cambridge University Press, 1964) and D Gauthier, *Practical Reasoning* (Oxford University Press, 1963). Especially relevant for lawyers is the work of Chaim Perelman. The *locus classicus* is C Perelman and L Olbrechts-Tyteca, *The New Rhetoric: A Treatise of Argumentation* (University of Notre Dame Press, 1969). Some readers may find it easier to start with Perelman's *The Idea of Justice and the Problem of Argument* (Routledge, 1963). J Raz (ed.), *Practical Reasoning* (Oxford University Press, 1978) contains useful essays whose themes are explored in his more difficult *Practical Reason and Norms* (Hutchinson, 1975).

On legal reasoning see J Stone, *Legal System and Lawyers' Reasonings* (Stevens, 1964); S Burton, *An Introduction to Law and Legal Reasoning* (Boston, 1985); DN MacCormick, *Legal Reasoning and Legal Theory* (Clarendon Press, 2nd edn, 1994); R Summers, 'Two Types of Substantive Reasons', (1978) 63 *Cornell Law Review* 707 and *Essays on the Nature of Law and Legal Reasoning* (Berlin, Duncker and Humbolt, 1992); Dworkin, *Law's Empire* (op cit); R Alexei, *A Theory of Legal Argumentation* (Clarendon Press, 1989); P Atiyah and R Summers, *Form and Substance in Anglo-American Law* (Oxford University Press, 1987); M Detmold, 'Law as Practical Reason', [1989] *Cambridge Law Journal* 436; and C Sunstein, *Legal Reasoning and Political Conflict* (Oxford University Press, 1996).

On advocacy see D Napley, *The Technique of Persuasion* (Sweet and Maxwell, 4th edn, 1991); R du Cann, *The Art of the Advocate* (Penguin, 1964); EA Parry, *The Seven Lamps of Advocacy* (Allen and Unwin, 1923); K Evans, *Advocacy at the Bar* (Blackstone Press, 2nd edn, 1995); A Boon, *Advocacy* (1993), M Stone, *Cross-Examination in Criminal Trials* (Butterworths, 2nd edn, 1995), Inns of Court School of Law, *Advocacy* (Blackstone Press, 1998).

On advocacy and story-telling, see William Twining, *Rethinking Evidence* (1994, Northwestern University Press), ch 7. Books on mooting are useful sources for exercises in and guidance about advocacy: Tim Kaye and Lynne Townley, *The Book of Moots* (1995); Paul Dobson and Barry Fitzpatrick (eds), *The Observer Book of Moots* (Sweet and Maxwell, 1986); J Snape and G Watt, *Cavendish Guide to Mooting* (Cavendish, 1997).

On the relationships between literary and legal interpretation discussed in the Epilogue, see the references given under Chapters 4–6, in particular writings by Dworkin, Fish, White and Posner. See also K Abraham, 'Statutory Interpretation and Legal Theory: Some Common Concerns of an Unlikely Pair', [1979] *Rutgers Law Review* 676 and D Miers, 'Legal Theory and the Interpretation of Statutes', in W Twining (ed), *Common Law and Legal Theory* (Basil Blackwell, 1986), ch 7. On the Critical Legal Studies movement see the special issues of the *Stanford Law Review* (1984), 36, 1-674 and the *Southern California Law Review* (1985), 58, 1-725 and Kelman, *A Guide to Critical Legal Studies* (op cit). An accessible summary of the main arguments is C Norris, 'Law, Deconstruction, and the Resistance to Theory', (1988) 15 *Journal of Law and Society* 166. See also P Nerhot, *Law, Interpretation and Reality* (Kluwer, 1990). On the interpretation of theological texts see H Marshall, *New Testament Interpretation: Essays on Principles and Methods* (Paternoster Press, 1979) and R Grant with D Tracy, *A Short History of Interpretation of the Bible* (SCM Press, 2nd edn, 1984).

Index

abduction, 352
Abinger, Lord, 59
absurdity, *see* statutory interpretation
abstractions, 198, *see also* generality
abstraction, ladder of, 56, 60, 328, 331-3
Acts of Parliament, *see* legislation
adherence to rules, 29, 155-6, 174
administrative-regulatory rules, *see* regulatory techniques
adversarial process, 337, 344-7
advocates, advocacy, 172-3, 344, 366-8, 410-11
    role and standpoint, 326-7, 335-7, 347
aesthetic theory, 377-8
Alderson, B, 202, 308
algorithms, 32, 40-2, 263, 373, 384, 413-19
All England Law Reports, 275-6, 284
alternative dispute resolution, 23-30, 306
ambiguity, 197, 199, 211, 216
    normative ambiguity, 278-9, 354
    syntactic ambiguity, 200
amendment, methods of, *see* legislation
analogy, *see* reasoning
analytical jurisprudence, 198
apodosis, 132-5, 249, 340-2, 395, 407
application of rules, 157-80, 213-4, 219
Arden, J, 257
argument
    analysis and structure, 345-50, 361-3
    construction, 268-96,
    styles of, 366-8, 428
Arusha, 24-5, 170
ascription, 183-7
Atiyah, P S
    Accidents, Compensation and the Law , 26-7
    Pragmatism and Theory in English Law, 141
Atkin, Lord, 58-60, 177, 326-33, 364-51, 367-8, 404-8
attitudes to rules, 152-5, *see also* legalism
Austin, John 129
autopoiesis, 139

'Bad Man, The', *see* Holmes, O. W.
baffled medic, the, 117, 194
Baier, K, *The Moral Point of View*, 135-6
Baker, P and Langan, P, *Snell's Principles of Equity*, 61-2

Baker, Sir George, 83-4, 103
Bankowski, Z and MacCormick, D N,
    'Statutory Interpretation in the United Kingdom', 218, 269
Bankowski, Z and Mungham, G, *Images of Law*, 156
Barthes, Roland, 376
Beck, R., and D. Wood, *Home Rules*, 15-16
Beldam, LJ, 280, 298
benefit-conferring laws, *see* regulatory techniques
Bennion, F
    Statute Law, 214, 263
    Statutory Interpretation, 185, 252, 276, 281, 283, 285, 347-50, 371
Bentham, J, *Works*, 4, 28
"better legislation", *see* legislation
bigamy, 42-50, 129, 135, 144-5, 151, 182, 196, 216, 307-11, 327-8, 345-51, 354-5, 357-8, 361-4, 368-70, 385-95
Bills, *see* legislation
Binchy, W, 66
borderlines, 124, 179, 181, 312 *see also* continuous variation
Boudin, K, *et al.*, *The Bust Book: What To Do Till The Lawyer Comes*, 76, 156
Brearly, M and Hutchfield, E, *A Teacher's Guide to Reading Piaget*, 17
Broom, Herbert, *A Selection of Legal Maxims*, 61
Browne-Wilkinson, Lord, 108-9, 292-3, 321
Buckmaster, Lord, 56-8, 326-33, 364, 404-8

Calvino, I, 75-6
Cane, P, 26-7
"case", 305 *see also* law reports, precedent
case notes, 307-12,
case stated, 308, 310
cessante ratione, cessat ipsa lex, 61, 153-4, 190-4
civil law drafting, *see* legislation
civil servants, 70-2
Clarke, J, 288, 303
class words, 181, 198, 203
Clinch, P, 256
closed system reasoning, *see* reasoning
Clyde, Lord, 285, 299-300

ratio legis, 183
rationalism,
Rawls, J, 'Two Concepts of Rules', 69-70, 77
Raz, J, *Practical Reason and Norms*, 14-15, 124
reading,
  routine, 207-8
  problematic, 208-220
  skills, 421-33
  see also materials of law study
reasoning, 343-70, 408-11
  by analogy , 326-32, 341-2, 351-8
  closed system, 352-5, 358, 365
  deductive, 351-5
  inconclusive, 355-8, 365
  inductive, 351-8
  and interpretation, 343-70
  lawyers', 368-70
  legal, 368-70
  normative, 358
  practical, 344-5, 358-63, 368-70
  questions of fact, 416, 430 *see also* fact
  syllogistic, *see* deduction
  see also advocacy, algorithms; argument,
    logic, consequentialist argument,
    validity
reasons, 185-6, 192-4
  authority, 325
  instititutonal, 359
  rightness, 359
  substantive, 325, 359
reconciliation of rules, *see* consistency
regulations, 22-3, 300
regulatory techniques, 29-31,
  administrative-regulatory rules, 150-2
  benefit-conferring laws, 151-2
  remedies,
    grievance-remedial rules, 150
Reid, Lord, 284, 338-9
reification, 143-6, 372
remedies, *see* regulatory techniques
Renton Committee, *The Preparation of
  Legislation*, 227, 245, 250-2, 271-2
repeal, 272-3
res judicata, see precedent
retributionists, 69-70
retroactive effect, *see* legislation,
retrospective effect, *see* legislation ,
retroduction, *see* abduction
Richards, I A, 314, 373, 379
Riddell, P, 236
roles, 169-75
  see also interpreters, standpoint
Ross, H L, *Settled Out of Court*, 25-6
rule-handling, 166-8
rule-maker, 175-6, 183-90
  indeterminate and collegiate, 187-90
  and interpreter, 212
  see also co-operation, legislation,
    standpoint

rules
  character, 133
  complex, 31-42, 245-53, 383-5, 413-19
    see also algorithms, structure of
      rules
  co-extensive with policy, 118, 191, 209-10
  concept of, 123-7
  definition, 123-4
  density, 142-3, 241-2
  form and structure, 131-4, *see also*
    apodosis, protasis,
  functions of, 147-50
  as guides, 147, 354, 362-3
  norms, 1235
  primary, 138
  purposes, 23-30, 152-6, 183-90, *see also*
    mischief rule, reasons
  and relationships, 14-23
  and results, 23-31
  "rules of thumb", 14-15, 124-5, 154
  secondary, 138
  as techniques of social management, 150-2
  tacit and unwritten, 131, 136-7, 144, 146,
    313-14
  variety of rules, 136-8, 203
  see also adherence to rules; application of
    rules, attitudes to rules; doubt,
    conditions of; drafting; functions
    of rules; interpreters; language;
    policy; reasons; structure of rules;
    system; validity
Ryan, W *et al, The Increasing Use of Logical
  Trees in the Civil Service*, 41
Ryle, M, 243-4

Sampford, C, *The Disorder of Law*, 140-1
sanctions, 133-4
Scarman, Lord, 105-8, 267-8, 271, 275, 286,
  Law Reform: The New Pattern, 153
Sceptic, 188-9
Schauer, F, 154, 124
school rules, 16-18
Schutz, Alfred, 372
Scottish Law Commission, 256-7
secondary rule, 138
Select Committees, 78-86, 121-2, 243
settlement, 25-7, 306
separation of powers, 275, 286, 291, 321,
  376
Shah, I, *Tales of the Dervishes*, 9
Shakespeare, W
  Hamlet, 377-8
  The Merchant of Venice, 9-10, 173-4, 175
Silk, P, 242
situation sense, 308-9, 410-11
Slynn, Lord, 301
social control and management, 24-5, 147-50
social problems, 114-5, 121-2, 151-2
standards, guiding, 354, 362-3

Printed in the United Kingdom by
Lightning Source UK Ltd., Milton Keynes
140933UK00001B/22/P